SACRAMENTO PUBLIC LIBRARY
828 "I" STREET
SACRAMENTO, CA 95814

3/2010

D1042109

CIRCLE *of* GREED

CIRCLE *of* GREED

< • < • • < • <

The Spectacular Rise and Fall of the Lawyer
Who Brought Corporate America to Its Knees

> • > • > • > • >

PATRICK DILLON
AND CARL M. CANNON

Broadway Books

NEW YORK

Copyright © 2010 by Carl Cannon and Patrick Dillon

All rights reserved.
Published in the United States by Broadway Books, an imprint
of the Crown Publishing Group, a division of Random House,
Inc., New York.
www.crownpublishing.com

BROADWAY BOOKS and the Broadway Books colophon are
trademarks of Random House, Inc.

Library of Congress Cataloging-in-Publication Data

Dillon, Patrick, 1945–
    Circle of greed: the spectacular rise and fall of the lawyer
who brought corporate America to its knees / By Patrick
Dillon and Carl M. Cannon.
    p. cm.
1. Lerach, William S. 2. Lawyers—United States—Biography.
I. Cannon, Carl M. II. Title.

KF373.L46D55 2010
340.092–dc22
[B]

                    2009024787

ISBN 978-0-7679-2994-3

Printed in the United States of America

10 9 8 7 6 5 4 3 2 1

First Edition

Contents

Acknowledgments

Before we begin tipping our hats to those who made our work possible, a word of explanation about how this book came to be written. Carl Cannon first came across William Lerach in 1977 while covering courts for the *San Diego Union*, a newspaper where Patrick Dillon often edited stories dispatched from the courthouse, a beat he had once covered himself. It didn't take Cannon long to interest Dillon and other editors in the emerging saga of Bill Lerach, a flashy newcomer to the San Diego legal scene. In time, Carl and Pat became friends as well as colleagues, keeping a running conversation about life and current events going for three decades even as Carl left his native California and made a career as a political writer in Washington, and Pat moved to the San Francisco Bay Area, where he held a number of editorial positions.

Cannon kept track of Lerach's legal activities over the years, weighing in occasionally with an article about Lerach's effect on the nation's legal, business, and political landscape. Meanwhile, as an editor and columnist, Pat found himself writing and commissioning articles about the long shadow Lerach cast over Silicon Valley and the high-rolling founders of the New Economy. At one point, Pat and Bill intended to write a book together entitled "Plundering America," about Lerach's war of attrition against corporate fraud in America. Those plans were put on hold for reasons now revealed in our book, produced a decade after "Plundering America" was scratched. After it became apparent that the Justice Department was in the process of terminating Lerach's legal career, Dillon called Lerach to inform him that there was still a book to be done, but it would be *about* Lerach, not coauthored *by* him.

Pat subsequently called Carl and invited him to be his coauthor. Carl, who had just days before finished a book with his father, Lou Cannon, comparing the presidencies of George W. Bush and Ronald Reagan, gave his friend a succinct initial response: "No." Obviously, that answer was not the last word. Pat subsequently informed Bill Lerach that he and Carl had signed a contract to write a book about Lerach's life and career. Lerach's response was, "Well, I guess if someone is going to do it, I'm glad it's going to be you two. I may not love some of it but you guys will be fair."

When friends and acquaintances learned of this project, they would invariably ask if Lerach was cooperating. Informed that he was indeed, most people would ask why he was doing so. This is a question we asked ourselves over the course of reporting and writing this book. And make no mistake, Bill Lerach's level of cooperation was extraordinary. He literally opened his house to the authors on separate reporting trips to San Diego throughout the winter and spring of 2008. He opened the files of old cases. He directed his longtime secretary, Kathy Lichnovsky, to provide documents, phone numbers, or source material. Bill met Carl in Pittsburgh on a nostalgic trip to see his old haunts—and his family—before heading to prison. Once in prison, he met with Pat on three separate occasions. Still, the question of "why?" remains, especially considering that Lerach never asked for—nor was he offered—any approval over the manuscript. He never saw a word of it prior to publication, and did not try to shape this book in either its conception or execution. So what was in it for him?

The authors believe that Lerach cooperated for two reasons. First, the rationale he cited himself: He knew our work and trusted it, even though he knew we did not necessarily share his political views or his mostly dark vision of publicly held corporations. Secondly, and we think this is more significant: Lerach was and is convinced he has a compelling story to tell. Not necessarily about the particulars of the government's criminal case against him, but a larger story—the one about the defects and failures of entrepreneurial capitalism, and Lerach's attempts, however flawed his methods may have been, to hold corporate executives to account. We think that Bill Lerach believed he'd get a fair shake on that theme. We will leave it to the reader to decide if we delivered on that score.

> • >

OF COURSE, MANY OTHERS helped us as well. Even though she was following her boss's wishes, Kathy Lichnovsky's assistance and forbearance was above and beyond the call of duty. Bill Lerach's brother Richard and his cousin Jim Kerr were open-hearted and generous with their time. So was Bill's wife, Michelle, who, if she had any misgivings about this book, kept them to herself. Star Soltan, Bill's third wife, patiently answered queries as well.

Bill's boyhood chums, as well as his high school and college friends, many of whom are quoted in Chapters 2 and 3, answered all our queries cheerfully and in a timely way. One sad note, however: Gene Carney, a faithful friend of Bill's who played sandlot baseball and football with him when they were grammar school age—and who came to his sixtieth birthday party in San Diego—died last summer as this book was being edited. Gene was a gentleman who had developed into a fine baseball writer as his second career. His help was greatly appreciated, and he was a national treasure.

Former FBI special agent Virginia Curry, who lost her husband at age thirty-nine to melanoma, yet who remained dedicated to her job, was instrumental in helping the authors piece together the art-theft case that tripped up Lerach confederate Steven Cooperman and subsequently Lerach himself. Likewise, we owe a great debt to Richard Robinson, the diligent federal prosecutor who stayed with this investigation for eight long years—and who was still willing to revisit the case in order to assist our efforts at re-creating the events inside the U.S. Attorney's Office in Los Angeles. We are equally grateful to his colleagues, Douglas Axel and Robert McGahan, tenacious government lawyers who shared valuable details and insights—and to John Keker, the irrepressible and incomparable defense lawyer who represented Bill Lerach in his long battle with the government.

Two of Lerach's friends and allies, lawyers Jonathan W. Cuneo and Patrick Coughlin, also provided essential assistance. Pat Coughlin, Lerach's principal partner in the San Diego law firm that bore both men's names, helped Pat Dillon negotiate the thicket of the Enron litigation and the tobacco wars, as well as intra-firm politics and history. Meanwhile, Jon Cuneo helped Carl Cannon re-create the political backstory behind the "Get Lerach Act" in mid-1995 in Congress, and its counterpart referendums in California the following year. Sean Coffey, whom the authors came to see as heir-apparent to Lerach in securities class action law—albeit an Eagle-scout version of Lerach—helped the authors to understand the epic WorldCom litigation, as well as the rivalries within the plaintiffs' bar created by Lerach's omnipresence. And former U.S. solicitor general Paul G. Clement, provided expert guidance through the actions of the Bush administration as it prepared for a landmark Supreme Court decision on class action lawsuits. We thank him for his generous gift of time.

San Diego lawyers Colin W. Wied and James J. Granby assisted the authors—as they had assisted Lerach three decades ago—in the details of the Pacific Homes case, Lerach's breakthrough trial. So did an advocate on the other side in that long-ago litigation, a gracious Chicago attorney named Samuel W. Witwer, Jr. Speaking of Chicago lawyers, while Lerach nemesis Daniel R. Fischel declined to speak to us, his attorney Alan Salpeter was accessible, and the help he provided was simply indispensable. We would also like to thank retired federal judge Lawrence Irving, in whose courtroom Bill Lerach experienced a crushing defeat and who also offered numerous insights on subsequent cases, including Lincoln Savings and Enron, that resulted in some of Lerach's greatest victories. Thanks, too, to Helen Hodges, Lerach's colleague who furnished the blueprints of the Enron case, as well as Paul Howes, another Enron litigator and Lerach colleague, who furnished the intricate detail so valuable to our story. Thanks also to Richard Borow, a civil-defense lawyer who opposed Lerach in court and ultimately became his friend.

We attempted to interview everyone who figured prominently in this narrative and, thankfully, most reciprocated. Gerald Parsky, despite being active in Republican Party politics, wouldn't return calls for some reason. Mel Weiss, Lerach's mentor, after weighing his options, regrettably decided not to cooperate. For those who participated in these events but didn't consent to assist us, we hope we got it right anyway.

In cases in which court transcripts or other official records existed, we used them. If such records were not available, the dialogue quoted is dependent on the memory of the participants—and source-noted accordingly. We relied on Lerach's recollections for some of his ex-parte conversations, as well as conversations with his friends and adversaries. Where possible, we checked his quotations with other participants. Often, and gratifyingly for the authors' peace of mind, his recall closely matched that of others, including Howard B. Turrentine, a retired San Diego judge in his nineties, who recalls his old cases with great clarity and was happy to share his memories of two litigators he never forgot, Bill Lerach and Mel Weiss.

The authors also owe a debt of gratitude to the superb efforts of business reporters who have written about Lerach previously, most especially Peter Elkind, a senior writer for *Fortune* magazine, whose insightful and groundbreaking coverage foreshadowed much of what was to come. The list of other journalists whose work informed our own also includes Jeffrey Toobin of *The New Yorker*, whose profile of Lerach left an indelible impression on friends and foes alike; Stephen Pizzo, Mary Fricker, and Paul Muolo, whose 1989 groundbreaking book, *Inside Job*, remains the clearest view of the savings and loan crisis, the antecedent to our recent financial meltdown; *Fortune* writer Bethany McLean, who along with Elkind, authored the captivating book *The Smartest Guys in the Room*, about the Enron debacle; and to Kurt Eichenwald, for showing us the way with his impeccably reported *Conspiracy of Fools*. Finally, to legions of reporters from *The Wall Street Journal* and *New York Times* and others whose bylines appeared in *Forbes, Business Week*, the *Financial Times*, and numerous local newspapers, journals, white papers, and websites.

Andrew Stuart, our agent, believed in the book from the moment Pat Dillon suggested it to him. We also thank Phyllis Grann, who, after decades of stardom in the New York publishing galaxy, remains undimmed, demonstrating her formidable powers of persuasion to get us to trim some 70,000 extraneous words from the manuscript. Random House lawyer Matthew Martin, who politely challenged our authority by patiently combing the source notes with us; Broadway Books assistant editor Annie Chagnot cheerfully attended to the tedious details preparing the book for publication; and our meticulous copy editor Janet Biehl comprised a highly professional team.

This book was shaped concurrently in a house on Lombard Street in San Francisco, and another located across the country in Arlington, Virginia. We thank Anne Dowie and Sharon Cannon, our wives, for patiently indulging our obsession and for accepting the conversion of their dining rooms into document and record repositories. Much of the first half of the book was also written in Bozeman, Montana, where we were hosted by our good friend Tom Mickel and generously ministered to by Sue Doss and Dudley Lutton. We polished the second half of the manuscript in adjacent offices at the Hoover Institution at Stanford University, courtesy of Professor David Brady and Mandy MacCalla, his able assistant.

Writing a book is both a solitary pursuit and a collaborative effort. This one couldn't have been written without the assistance of all we've named. And to those we haven't, you are not lost in our memories. You have the authors' gratitude, and although it goes without saying, we'll say it anyway: Any mistakes, omissions, or misinterpretations are the fault of the authors, not those who lent their help.

PROLOGUE

At 7:25 A.M. on October 29, 2007, Frank Cucinotta, a fifty-year-old third-generation Italian-American, eased a jumbo white SUV passenger limousine out of the cobbled parking court of the Beverly Wilshire Hotel, a venerable fourteen-story Italianate property with a tradition of pampering Hollywood stars, players, movers-and-shakers, and anybody else who could afford to see and be seen. When the stoplight turned in Cucinotta's favor, he guided the vehicle onto Wilshire Boulevard; turned right, away from the Rodeo Drive shopping mecca; and joined the traffic already bunching east toward downtown Los Angeles, a ten-mile route he knew would require no less than an hour.

On this day, on the way to a nine A.M. appointment at the federal courthouse, riding in the rear seat—and rifling and tearing pages from the *Los Angeles Times*, the *Financial Times*, the *New York Times*, and *The Wall Street Journal*—was attorney William S. Lerach, his exclusive employer for more than eight years. Now sixty-one, Lerach was known as the kneecapper of corporate America. For three decades, as Americans created the greatest gain of wealth in the history of the world, the vengeful, fearless, abrasive, tactically brilliant Lerach had shaken down the "who's who" of the Fortune

500 list. No one had been immune—not Disney, not Drexel Burnham, not Citibank, Goldman Sachs, Bank of America, Merrill Lynch, Credit Suisse First Boston, Global Crossing, AT&T, Hewlett-Packard, Apple Computer, Exxon, Time Warner, R.J. Reynolds, Arthur Andersen, WorldCom, Enron. Not Michael Milken or T. Boone Pickens. Not Charles Keating, Ivan Boesky, Al Dunlap, Michael Ovitz, Ron Perelman, Bernard Ebbers. Not Kenneth Lay or even Dick Cheney. During those thirty years Bill Lerach, and the firm Milberg, Weiss, Bershad, Hynes & Lerach—for whom he had been the shrewdest and most aggressive legal strategist, its boldest negotiator, its star litigator—returned more than $45 billion in fraud judgments and settlements to millions of shareholders, small and large, and institutional investors—minus his own cut, which was not inconsiderable.

Acting outside the regulatory agencies that he routinely mocked as weak and politically beholden, this self-appointed legal Robin Hood peered at life roguishly through his signature oversize glasses, which his enemies and the newspaper and magazine illustrators parodied almost as often as his grayish blond Brillo hair. His sandpaper-textured, profane-laced megaphone voice also came in for notice. It wasn't really the voice that offended; rather, it was the invective that hurtled from it. "I'll own your fucking house in Maui and the diamonds on your wife's fingers," he'd tell an outwardly defiant but secretly quaking corporate captain. Or he'd snarl at opposing counsel: "This case is going to bring an ignominious end to your mediocre career!" Anyone who stood in his way was, in his mind, fair game; hence Lerach was a staple for *Fortune, Forbes,* and *Business Week* covers and for the pages of the *New York Times,* the *Financial Times,* and *The Wall Street Journal.*

The reason he generated such fear, and attention, was not merely his tactics—it was his results. To hear both his admirers and detractors tell it, Lerach had evolved into a fourth force in American capitalism, adding the *Lerach factor* to supply and demand and competition. He did it by building a 180-attorney colossus and employing dozens of private investigators, including former FBI agents and assistant U.S. attorneys, who prowled for vulnerable companies by monitoring their volatile stock and financial performances through his law firm's technically advanced software systems.

When he spotted a precipitous drop in earnings followed by a sharp drop in the stock price, he and his colleagues would search the database for the company's prior public statements talking up its financial performance, usually on what turned out to be bogus revenue recognition. If these optimistic statements were soon followed by a pattern of insider selling—"footprints in the snow," he called it—just before the stock crashed, Lerach and his team would outpace other law firms to find plaintiffs and file court complaints, anointing his firm and himself as lead counsel, while determining which other firms, if any, would be allowed to join the action and share the spoils, ranging as high as 30 percent of a judgment or settlement. Initiating, managing, attacking, counterattacking, bullying, bluffing, and even inventing new avenues for shareholder lawsuits; allowing investors, no matter how small, to take on corporate giants and the titans who guided and managed them, Lerach and his colleagues would litigate hundreds of cases, more than all other securities law firms combined. His tactics even helped corporate insurers, who were able to up their premiums for "Lerach protection." His opponents, including competing law firms and prominent politicians of both parties, compared him to a Mafia don. He secretly liked that, and he didn't even mind letting anyone know that his two favorite movies were *The Godfather* ("One lawyer with a briefcase can cause more damage than a thousand men with guns") and *Godfather II*. In his telling, Lerach was feared for a reason and in furtherance of a good cause. If he made himself rich in the process—and estimates of Lerach's own fortune ran upward of $700 million—that was the reward for exposing corporate fraud, incompetence, and greed. The greed was epitomized by the astronomical executive compensation packages he railed against—*by-products*, he told wide-eyed judges, mediators, and congressional panels, of the fraud he continuously targeted and exposed. He often compared his firm to an enforcement arm of the Securities and Exchange Commission, with three essential differences: his firm was more perspicacious ("Watch next for bad loans from banks," he told an interviewer in 2002); it was more aggressive; and it was more efficient, because it put its own resources at risk by asking only for contingent fees, meaning it had to win the case to win the fees.

What's more, he delighted in rubbing himself in Corporate America's face. Once when he was appearing before a hostile but morbidly curious crowd of business executives, Lerach swaggered to the podium and declared: "What enforcement do you really want at work regulating your marketplace? You want government bureaucrats, not subject to the economic discipline of the marketplace? Or do you want guys like me? I may be rancid butter, but you know I'm on your side of the bread."

Naturally, he had made enemies—in competing law firms, on Capitol Hill, and especially in boardrooms from Silicon Valley to Wall Street, where he existed in a parallel corporate subconscious as a modern Vandal or Visigoth. Buttoned-down and otherwise sober executives would vehemently denounce Lerach as a "bloodsucking scumbag," or an "economic pirate." (One Silicon Valley executive went so far as to publicly wish him out of human existence.) A verb had even been given his name. In boardrooms, to be "Lerached" meant being threatened with having to surrender more than a million documents and risk testimony from CEOs on down to the lowliest document clerks in order to fend off a $100 million lawsuit. More often than not, CEOs and the boards they served would decide against fighting these Lerachian wars of attrition and would enter out-of-court settlements. They were expensive but not as costly as litigation—especially a lost trial. The circumspect executives would chalk it up to the cost of doing business and turn to their insurance carriers to bail them out, but they came to believe that what Lerach was doing was nothing less than legalized extortion. They weren't alone in this assessment. When Lerach came to Washington, D.C., in 1995 to lobby unsuccessfully against a Newt Gingrich–driven tort reform intended to put him out of business, California congressman Christopher Cox likened him to Al Capone. Silicon Valley venture capitalist L. John Doerr, who helped raise more than $40 million in a 1996 statewide "Get Lerach Initiative" aimed at clipping his wings in California courts, referred to him as "a cunning economic terrorist." When George W. Bush talked in two presidential campaigns about "frivolous lawsuits," he was referring in large part to the class-action securities litigation that Lerach and his colleagues brought against businesses Bush had championed, including those of his longtime friends.

Among them was Enron chairman Kenneth Lay, who oversaw the

nation's seventh-largest company, with 22,000 employees and vast, complex holdings ranging from broadband trading to energy and commodities to risk management. *Fortune* had called it "America's most innovative company" for six straight years until, in 2001, its tangled financial web collapsed and it was forced to declare itself bankrupt. When it did, Lerach pounced. Before orchestrating a $7.3 billion settlement, the largest in history with the banks that suppported it, Lerach had successfully portrayed Enron as the very symbol of the corporate scandals that had rocked Wall Street throughout the decade. With thespian-worthy performances that began, prior to the beginning of the trial, by displaying boxes of shredded Enron documents before the press outside the Houston federal courthouse, Lerach not only skillfully picked over the bleaching bones of Ken Lay's company; he shook down Wall Street and embarrassed the president of the United States. After declaring victory, Lerach issued a public warning that would have repercussions.

"With this judgment we got Kenny boy and his friends," he announced. Later, he added, "Now we're going after Dick Cheney." Lerach had turned his sights on Halliburton and its former CEO, the vice president of the United States. In Lerach's lawsuit against Halliburton, his thinly veiled assertion was that Cheney had fled the company just ahead of the stock collapse, finding refuge in the White House. The attorney had maneuvered himself into a position to subpoena and demand public testimony from the vice president, and he doubted that Cheney would be able to successfully hide behind a claim of executive privilege. Lerach was itching for the confrontation.

Instead, on this late October day, William S. Lerach was traveling down Wilshire Boulevard, through Los Angeles's corporate canyon, flanked by tall, glass-encased office towers—"Fraud Lane," he called it—recalling lawsuits he had filed against its inhabitants and neighbors. There were so many, he had almost lost track. Each had contributed, though, through its own missteps, to Lerach's means to own vacation homes in Steamboat Springs, Colorado, and in Hawaii, as well as a 10,000-square-foot villa in Rancho Santa Fe, just outside San Diego, a manse complete with a 2,970-gallon saltwater aquarium—not quite large enough for a shark, as he liked to joke but large enough to host a menacing moray eel that was fond of him, especially at feeding time. His latest residence was a 16,000-square-foot Tuscan-style mansion filled like a museum with catalogued African art and other precious statues and relics on five and a half acres overlooking the Pacific Ocean on San Diego County's "Gold Coast." When he bought the place, Lerach had planned to entertain governors, senators, and presidents there. And he would have, too, except for this legal business that was taking him to the federal courthouse in Los Angeles this morning.

As the ride progressed toward downtown, past venerable and leafy Hancock Park (once an oilfield, now home to the elite families of Los Angeles), Lerach seemed oblivious that his ride-along Chihuahua, Tommy, was climbing his chest to lick his face; he did not even bother to flick the dog hairs from his $3,000 Brioni suit, its muted gray blue nearly matching the sky over Los Angeles, which had been clouded by smoke from the property-destroying wildfires that had been burning more than half a million acres in the hills for days.

Lerach's attention was turned to three newspaper articles. The first was a *New York Times* piece speculating on what the Federal Reserve would do when it met the next day to set interest rates. The article suggested that the Fed would note that, except for the housing market, the economy appeared to be showing surprising strength. And yet, it cautioned, a serious downturn could still be imminent, especially when the housing slump interacted with possible problems in the credit markets. "Act sooner than later," Lerach said derisively under his breath, as if speaking directly to Fed chairman Ben Bernanke, who had succeeded Alan Greenspan, the person who had given Charles Keating and Ken Lay his benediction even when their giant scams were imploding.

The second article drew greater focus. Another *Times* piece, this one signaled that E. Stanley O'Neal was expected to end his six-year reign at Merrill Lynch as early as that day. The article retraced O'Neal's rise and ignominious fall after an $8.4 billion write-down, noting that the chairman and chief executive of the world's biggest brokerage firm could receive as much as $159 million as a termination package. Lerach swore loudly, startling his tiny dog: "Goddamn loser CEOs, raking it in!" Those words, minus the expletive, would be the headline in an op-ed piece that Lerach would pen and that the *Washington Post* would publish on a Sunday, less than two weeks later. As an aftermath to the collapse of Enron and the huge recovery already obtained, Lerach's firm still represented investors seeking more than $30 billion from Merrill Lynch, along with Credit Suisse First Boston and Barclays Bank PLC. His firm was arguing that the financial firms had colluded with the energy giant to hide its losses. This so-called "scheming case" was headed to the Supreme Court. At stake for Lerach personally were fees of more than $100 million before taxes.

Bill Lerach gazed out the window, his mind suddenly distant, as the limousine passed slowly by MacArthur Park, the patch-worn subject of a rhapsodic 1968 song; its amphitheater shell once hosted jazz, big band, and folk music concerts. Cucinotta pointed through the windshield at the downtown skyline approaching. Lerach seemed not to notice, musing aloud about an event four years in the past, when he had stood at a podium at the 2003 commencement at the University of Pittsburgh Law School, from which he had graduated thirty-three years earlier. He said softly that of all his public appearances—before judges, business executives, television commentators, legal and congressional panels—that moment had meant the most to him.

He had recited landmark cases—*Brown v. Board of Education, Gideon v. Wainwright, Griswold v. Connecticut*—in which individuals, aided by crusading lawyers, had obtained access to the courts, which overturned repressive state laws and vindicated individual rights. He traced the ascending arc of consumer protection laws and suits against tobacco companies, which he had called "the oligopoly of death." He cited more legal high-water marks. Then he turned somber, recounting the assault on trial lawyers such as himself, during the current decade, by corporate and Wall Street interests, various would-be populists, and politicians of various stripes, particularly conservatives in and out of the Bush administration who, in the name of "tort reform," were making it more and more difficult for attorneys to seek redress in the name of shareholders. "But remember, no good deed goes unpunished," he had warned the future lawyers in Pittsburgh, not aware that his speech contained an element foreshadowing his own life.

Cucinotta turned the limo off Wilshire toward the stodgy-looking federal district courthouse, a Depression-era Works Progress Administration project finished in 1940. Lerach had appeared in its courtrooms hundreds of times. Finally, a right turn to their destination, 255 East Temple Street, the address of the twenty-one-story modern office tower sheathed in red granite named the Edward R. Roybal Federal Building.

Because of the size and scope of the Los Angeles federal court jurisdiction—it services nearly eighteen million residents and processes nearly 12,000 criminal and civil cases yearly—two buildings, the old courthouse and the Roybal Building, handle the load. Lerach had an appointment in each. First he would appear before a U.S. magistrate, who would administer Lerach's criminal arraignment, following a hard-earned agreement he made with government prosecutors a month earlier. According to the agreement, he would plead guilty to a single federal conspiracy charge of obstructing justice—a felony that could mean one to two years in prison and the almost certain forfeiture of his license to practice law. The government had been investigating him and several colleagues in his San Diego office and in New York, headquarters of the founder of his firm Melvyn Weiss, for more than seven years.

The investigation had been hanging over Lerach even as he tried and negotiated the Enron settlement the same year. Every time he and his legal team ratcheted up the pressure against the officers and managers of the energy giant and its banks, word that a government investigation was progressing would reach him.

"We'd fire a shot, they'd fire a shot," he would later say.

In his mind, he had been involved in a war of attrition with the federal government, the same kind of war he had so successfully waged against Corporate America. Reflecting on his own guilt and feeling his own fear, he had called John Keker.

At sixty-six, John W. Keker was to the defense bar as Bill Lerach was to tort law. After Princeton and Yale Law, he had clerked for Chief Justice Earl Warren, then became assistant federal public defender for the Northern District of California. Specializing in criminal defense and business litigation, he had twice defended investment banker Frank Quattrone, had represented George Lucas, defended Google in a trade secret case against

Microsoft, acted as an independent chief prosecutor in the federal case against Oliver North, and managed to get a reduced sentence for Andrew Fastow, who had been Enron's CFO and at the center of the very scheme Bill Lerach had unraveled to the tune of $7.3 billion and counting.

For all Keker's bona fides, the one that stood out was his crippled left arm. His elbow had been shattered by an enemy gunner while Keker was leading a Marine platoon in Vietnam in 1965. The arm, hanging limp in his suit coat, as he held his glasses in his right hand or struggled to move an exhibit with his good arm and twisting body, served his reputation for toughness and determination.

Standing erect, his jaw set and his crew cut still trimmed at Marine Corps length, clad in a double-vented blue suit, Keker was waiting when Lerach cleared security in the lobby of the federal building. The two men mounted the wide marble stairs to the airy indoor atrium in order to take another stairway to the third-floor arraignment room. As they strode across the wide, sunlit, well-appointed space, Lerach noticed a large portrait hanging on an opposite wall. He changed stride, leading Keker and their team of attorneys to the portrait and stood before it, appraising it, letting the irony of the encounter sink in. Looking down on them from ten feet above was Vice President Cheney.

Lerach muttered something unintelligible and shook his head. Then he turned toward the elevators to keep the appointment for his arraignment— a short but arresting formality, because greeting him behind a Plexiglas window sat more than a dozen hardcore federal inmates who were also being arraigned that morning, on charges ranging from interstate drug trafficking to gang violence, federal bank robbery, and worse. They wore jail jumpsuits with shortened sleeves that revealed arms stenciled in tattoos. Most were shorn, the overhead lights accentuating their hardened, menacing faces. The theatrical contrast between those kept behind glass awaiting their hearings and those on the other side clad in business suits awaiting theirs gave defendants standing outside the glass window their first glimpse of the social inferno they might soon enter.

With Keker at his side, Lerach stood stoically, listening to the magistrate read the particulars that government lawyers had filed against him.

His posture was attentive and deferential. This was something he knew he would have to endure, to get behind him, to earn relief, if just for the moment. Half an hour later he and his legal entourage crossed the great plaza separating the two federal buildings. Lerach and Keker, the two towering figures in their own fields of law, mounted a single stairwell and entered the courtroom of U.S. District Judge John F. Walter. There they were greeted by four assistant U.S. attorneys who had worked for the better part of six years to achieve this moment for the government. The opposing attorneys bantered solicitously, obliging the courtroom protocol informed by their experience, awaiting the judge.

Judge Walter entered and immediately got down to business. He read the charge, asked if the defendant understood it, and then asked if he understood its magnitude, reading each implication, one by one.

"Do you understand that by pleading guilty to this charge you face a serious prison sentence?"

Lerach had been steeling himself to answer firmly: "I do."

"Do you understand that by pleading guilty to this charge you will no longer be able to vote?"

"I do," said Lerach.

"Do you understand that by pleading to this charge you will no longer be able to run for public office?"

Again, "I do, your honor."

And finally, "Do you understand that by pleading to this charge you will no longer have the right to bear firearms?"

Lerach reacted with a mild shrug noticed only by a few family members, including his daughter Shannon and wife, Michelle, seated in the benches behind him. "I do, your honor."

Having accepted the plea, the judge set the date for sentencing two months hence—January 2008—allowing each side to prepare arguments that would help guide him in determining the length of the sentence. The process lasted less than thirty minutes, and in its aftermath Lerach looked and sounded fatigued; so did his wife. But he was still not without fight.

As he and his family and attorneys plodded back down the stairs and started for the exit, Lerach again noticed two portraits hanging on the wall near the stairwell. On the left was President George W. Bush. On the right was Vice President Richard Cheney, the man he had been looking forward to suing. Now he wouldn't even have a law license. Lerach strode to the portraits, standing below Cheney's. Looking up, he pumped his fist and said, "I can't vote. I can't run for office. I can't bear firearms. It should have been you up there in that courtroom, not me."

> • > • • > •

DRAGON SLAYER

William S. Lerach first heralded himself to the elite circles in America's legal community in 1977, from the sterile downtown county courthouse on Front Street, a few blocks from the old waterfront in San Diego. The setting was Superior Court Judge James L. Focht's nondescript courtroom; the case, *Barr v. United Methodist Church*. By the time it ended, class action litigation (a single legal action on behalf of many plaintiffs against common defendants) would never be the same in California. And ultimately the victorious lawyer would see to it that no corporate entity within the United States would be invulnerable to outside scrutiny.

No U.S. church denomination had ever been the subject of a successful class action lawsuit. The unfolding case owed its drama not only to the legal precedents at stake, or to the conflicted feelings among the litigants themselves (pious Methodists and retired ministers who found themselves suing their own denomination) but also to the intensely personal competition between the rival attorneys.

The Methodists' lead lawyer was Samuel W. Witwer, Sr., a barrel-chested eminence whose regal presence and mane of silver hair all but announced his wealth of experience. The son of a steelworker, Witwer was born in 1908, the year William Jennings Bryan ran for president the third and last time. Like Bryan, Witwer came out of the Midwest, his reputation proceeding him like a billowy cloud: Harvard Law, class of 1933; lay leader in the Methodist Church; and then lawyer, who after five decades of futile efforts by others succeeded in reforming Illinois's antiquated constitution. The "Father of the Illinois Constitution," they called him. Adlai Stevenson remarked that Witwer was "a man who never quits." In 1960 the Illinois Republican Party chose Witwer to be its standard-bearer for a U.S. Senate seat. Dwight D. Eisenhower approved of this nomination and, in a memo to Richard Nixon, referred to Sam Witwer as "a very smart man."

Nearly two decades later Witwer strode into San Diego with the air of a man accustomed to deference. He brought with him a mellifluous, authoritative-sounding *basso profundo* voice, the distinctive diction of a practiced orator, and an abundance of self-confidence.* "He was the only man I ever saw," Bill Lerach said, "who could strut while sitting down."

Witwer harbored reciprocal feelings about Lerach. The first time he ever laid eyes on the younger man, Witwer and his attorney son Samuel W. Witwer, Jr., were checking into the Westgate Plaza Hotel, San Diego's newest and finest, only to hear loud, whiskey-fueled cross-talk emanating from the lobby between Lerach and another lawyer they presumed to be Mel Weiss. "We're going to take down the Methodist Church!" Lerach boasted. Public woofing was not typical behavior of the shining lights of the San Diego bar, but Lerach was not from that town.

Born and raised in Pittsburgh, Bill Lerach was new to the West Coast; he liked California, had come to stay, and *loved* being in court on this case. He was thirty-one but appeared younger with his long blond curly hair, Sundance Kid mustache, round wire-rimmed glasses, and a suit that— although tailored—looked too large on his slender frame. He was easy to

---

* One of the authors, Carl Cannon, was assigned to the legal affairs beat for the *San Diego Union-Tribune* at the time. Cannon covered much of the Pacific Homes litigation and witnessed first-hand—and wrote about—the tense interplay between Bill Lerach and Sam Witwer. Coauthor Patrick Dillon, an editor for the paper then, edited some of those articles.

underestimate. As the Pacific Homes battle played out, Samuel Witwer and the rest of the nation's corporate establishment came to see what they were up against. By dint of temperament and talent, William Shannon Lerach constituted a perfect instrument of destruction in an emerging hybrid of the legal profession: the superlawyers of the plaintiffs' bar who viewed themselves as avenging angels for the little people cast on the slag heap of free enterprise. This theme would emerge more clearly in the years ahead; meanwhile the realization that in the process of attempting to reform American capitalism they could become quite rich did nothing to diminish their adversarial zeal. Quite the opposite, actually.

> • >

THE SAN DIEGO CASE concerned a string of retirement facilities called Pacific Homes, established as a nonprofit corporation in 1929 for retired Methodist ministers and lay leaders. In the late 1970s the corporation was in financial trouble, a victim of the residents' increasing life spans, the overgenerous impulses of its founders, a flawed business plan, runaway inflation, and bad management—with some graft thrown in. The Methodist hierarchy bailed the homes out at first, but as the losses mounted, Pacific Homes' officials resorted to acquiring more buildings and attracting new residents with "life-care contracts," even as they spent the money paid up front by new retirees to keep the existing retirement facilities afloat. However well intentioned the Methodist elders had been originally, they eventually found themselves running an elaborate Ponzi scheme.

The legal case began in 1977, when a Pacific Homes retiree named Frank Barr placed a call to a San Diego law firm, Wied & Granby, to which he had been referred by his estate planning attorney. Barr told the Wied & Granby attorneys his story: months after he had paid more than $300,000 for a "life-care contract," Pacific Homes officials had announced that all residents would have to pay several hundred dollars more each month to keep the place afloat. The homes were near bankruptcy, it seemed to Barr, and the officials clearly had known this was the case even while soliciting the contracts. Barr told the attorneys, Colin W. Wied and James J. Granby, that some of the residents simply didn't have additional income at their disposal and were worried about losing their homes.

He had called the right lawyers. Wied and Granby were close friends who took the law, and their obligations under it, seriously. They were well situated, too, former U.S. Navy guys in a U.S. Navy town, with good educations and solid reputations in the city's legal circles. Both would serve as president of the San Diego Bar Association, and Wied would later be named state bar president. Their only drawback was the size of their firm. Wied & Granby consisted essentially of Wied and Granby, along with a young associate, David J. Yardley. Nonetheless, intrigued by the case and indignant at the way their clients had been treated, they filed a lawsuit on behalf of the disgruntled Pacific Homes residents. Yet they soon realized—both because of the complexity of the case and because of the caliber of white-shoe law firms from Los Angeles, Chicago, and Philadelphia arrayed against them—that they needed a big gun of their own.

Granby asked an attorney friend if he knew of anyone in Southern California with experience in class action litigation in which auditors had been negligent. "The firm that specializes in that kind of work is Milberg Weiss—and it has an office in San Diego," the friend said. "They are the best in the country."

Granby placed a call to the San Diego office of Milberg, Weiss, Bershad & Specthrie, which was run by Bill Lerach. The two partners took an immediate liking to Lerach, who listened intently as they spelled out the facts of the Pacific Homes case. Lerach liked them well enough too; mainly he liked the looks of their case,* so a plan was made for all of them to go to New York to secure the blessing of Lerach's boss, Milberg Weiss's cofounder and senior partner, Melvyn I. Weiss.

Weiss was initially dubious about a case that presented public relations challenges for a payoff that might not be that large. "Have you lost your

---

* "I remember meeting with these guys and thinking that they have hearts of gold, but that they weren't ready for what they were facing," Lerach told the authors in 2008. "I guess they knew that, which is why they'd come to us. I was immediately enchanted with the case. It took about two minutes."

mind?" Lerach remembers Weiss telling him. "We're a bunch of Jews, and you've got us suing a Christian church! Keep doing your securities cases in federal court."

Lerach, who was not himself Jewish, was undeterred. Weiss often talked this way to his young partners as a way of making them defend their prospective cases so he could see how committed they were to the litigation. In truth, Mel Weiss was intrigued by Pacific Homes, and he encouraged Lerach to bring these California lawyers to New York so he could take their measure—and size up their case. Milberg Weiss's New York offices were located at One Penn Plaza, atop Penn Station. When the lawyers gathered for lunch in the building's lower level, the Californians were struck by how the tables shook and the plates rattled as the trains passed by below—and by how nothing seemed to rattle Mel Weiss.

The next day they went over the case again. This time Weiss listened intently, saying little. Finally the senior partner said, "What do you want to do?"

"Well," Wied asked, "is it a good case or not?"

After a ten-second pause, Weiss's face broke into a slow smile. "It's a dynamite case," he replied.

At that point the two law firms hashed out an agreement on the terms of their split, which they confirmed with a handshake: two-thirds of any contingency fee awarded the plaintiff's lawyers would go to Milberg Weiss, one-third to Wied & Granby. The only thing left at that point was for this bicoastal legal team to take on the venerable United Methodist Church—and win.

> • >

ON FEBRUARY 18, 1977, Pacific Homes sought to buy time by filing for Chapter 11 protection in federal bankruptcy court, while attorneys for the various Methodist entities responsible for the homes tried to restructure the residents' contracts. The deal the church offered the residents was essentially this: the terms of the life-care contracts would be altered so that each resident would pay $350 per month for room and board—and $800 per month when they crossed the threshold into needing convalescent care. For its part, the church's General Council on Finance and Administration would pony up $1 million a year for the next nine years. "The Annual Conference said the residents should pay a bit more because the life-care contracts were signed when there was no inflation," Samuel Witwer explained to the press. "They [the Conference] offered the $9 million as a matter of Christian charity."

To make this bailout plan work, church lawyers told a federal bankruptcy judge, 93 percent of Pacific Homes residents would have to sign on to the deal. As 1977 wore on, 90 percent of the residents agreed, but church officials could not get that last 3 percent. They might have, had Lerach not intervened. As emotions among the residents boiled over, two warring factions emerged. The first were Wied and Granby's "rebels," who had become radicalized and who were quite willing to sue. The second and much larger faction, whom Lerach dubbèd the "Tories," remained devoted to the Methodist Church. Among the "Tory" loyalists, a pious and opinionated ringleader emerged. He was seventy-six years old and well-spoken, as befit his previous profession as a member of the U.S. Congress. His name was Jerry Voorhis.

"There's this old bird out there who's causing us all kinds of problems," junior attorney David Yardley told Lerach. "We've got to get him calmed down."

Lerach, recognizing Voorhis's name, appointed himself to the task. A lifelong liberal Democrat, Voorhis would have been dismayed to hear himself labeled a Tory. A five-term member of the California delegation in the House of Representatives, Voorhis had been ousted from Congress by Richard Nixon in an acrimonious 1946 campaign in which the future vice president and president portrayed the Democratic incumbent as being under the thumb of Communist-controlled labor unions. Voorhis had indeed accepted campaign contributions from such unions, but he was a diligent public official who had once been named "the hardest working man in Congress." Many years later political journalist Christopher Caldwell described him as an "upright Christian socialist" who was also "a sanctimonious know-it-all [who was] well to the left of his constituents." Bill Lerach had no quarrel with Voorhis's left-leaning politics—by then Lerach had become a Democrat himself—but he also found the former congressman hard-headed and haughty.

"He was a know-it-all," Lerach remembered. But he was also threatening to derail the Pacific Homes suit before it got off the ground and as such could not be ignored. "He'd had these run-ins with Yardley, but I sort of tried to charm him. I talked to him about what a bastard Nixon was. I just gave him a world-class ass-kiss."

Meanwhile the church's lawyers persuaded the bankruptcy judge to move their status to Chapter X, a designation designed to further shield them; the move was granted, but it came too late. "The fat was really in the fire," noted Methodist bishop Jack M. Tuell.

"I wouldn't ever want to see this come out in a courtroom, but we didn't start to have these problems two years ago," John Kirkman, church treasurer, told members of the Annual Conference who met in 1978 in Arizona. "We started to have them when someone said you can replace capital losses by borrowing and paying it back later. I don't know of any financial enterprise that can operate that way but a chain letter."

It was a lesson the financial world would learn again and again over the next three decades—and as recently as March 2009, with the jailing of an extravagant thief with a Dickensian name, Bernard Madoff. In the case of Pacific Homes, Kirkman's observations did indeed show up in court, because one Methodist who was not enamored with his church's leadership sneaked a tape recorder into the Arizona meeting. Not that it was necessary. The Methodists and their lawyers were about to run into the buzz saw named Lerach. Before this case was over, he would present so much compelling evidence that the Methodists would sue for peace before they could even put on their first witness.

> • >

THE CASE WAS ASSIGNED to Judge Ross G. Tharp, a folksy Ronald Reagan appointee with a handlebar mustache and a resemblance to the comedic actor Dabney Coleman. Tharp's unease with the case was almost physical, and he did nothing to hide his discomfort at presiding over the lawsuit against a venerated Protestant denomination. The Methodists' legal defense consisted of three lines of argument: the first was procedural, the second constitutional, and the third an assertion that was more a public policy position than a legal theory.

Witwer and the defense team maintained that no matter what had transpired regarding the retirement facilities, the church wasn't liable because it neither owned nor controlled Pacific Homes Corporation. The United Methodist Church, argued Allan Reniche, another member of the defense team, "is not the alter ego of Pacific Homes Corp. or anything or anyone else." William "Beau" Miller III, another attorney representing the Methodists, asserted that Pacific Homes' board, although composed of former Methodist pastors and officials, was "fiercely independent" of the mother church.

The Methodists' second line of defense flowed out of the first but went further. Legally speaking, their lawyers said, no liable body called the United Methodist Church existed. It wasn't organized as a corporation in California or anywhere else and as such was not a judicial entity that could be sued. Methodism, according to its own internal ecclesiastic bylaws, was a spiritual "confederation" of like-minded parishioners; for that reason, taking money from one arm of Methodism to pay for the alleged misdeeds of another was not only grotesquely unfair but an unconstitutional assault on the freedom of religion. A contrary ruling "would substantially change the face of religion in America," Witwer maintained. "It would violate every possible aspect of First Amendment rights of churches to conduct their business without harassment in civil court."

In one form or another, the church's stated desire to go about its business without the "harassment" of plaintiffs' lawyers or the courts was an argument that Bill Lerach would hear repeatedly from defendants—albeit usually large for-profit corporations—during the next three decades in his career as a litigator. Invariably, his answer would be to point, as he did in the Pacific Homes case, to the huge assets owned or controlled by the defendants—especially compared to the paltry resources of his little-guy clients. The United Methodist Church, Lerach emphasized, controlled some

$7.5 billion in assets at the time when it was trying to abrogate the contracts of Pacific Homes' retirees on fixed incomes.

"Those $7.5 billion are the assets of 43,000 individual churches," Witwer responded. "Each university, hospital, home is a separate institution that owns its own property. There is not property of fund, as such, that belongs to the UMC. You can't structure an entity out of a confederation."

This reasoning led to Witwer's last line of defense, a rationale that was more a public relations strategy than a legal philosophy: if the church were held liable for the financial collapse of Pacific Homes, money would be siphoned from other, even more worthy enterprises in the church's mission, including clothing and feeding the poor. Moreover, church officials insisted, holding ecclesiastical groups liable for badly run businesses in their far-flung empires would have the effect of prompting faith-based organizations to abandon their work of helping society's less fortunate.

Tormented by this prospect, Tharp quietly urged the parties to settle the case. Although the judge didn't like Lerach personally—he found the young lawyer arrogant, and his heart was more with the Methodists—he was impressed with Lerach's pretrial preparation, and he thought the church's lawyers were underestimating the effect the debonair young attorney might have on a jury.

Tharp believed that if the case went to trial, the Methodists would be dunned for a huge verdict. And he feared that Witwer might be right about the effects of such an outcome. In other words, he worried that a precedent-setting case emanating from his California courtroom might cripple the ability of Methodism, or any other religious entity, to undertake its good works. To forestall such a result, Tharp pushed hard for a settlement—too hard, as it happened.

On March 20, 1978, the judge issued a four-paragraph opinion removing the United Methodist Church as a defendant, while keeping the General Council on Finance and Administration (the Methodists' finance body) in the lawsuit. Accepting Witwer's assertion that the United Methodist Church was "a connectional structure maintained through a chain and series of conferences," Tharp said that because it had never been legally incorporated, it could not be sued in a California court. "Methodism has continued for more than two centuries to proclaim a freedom of spirit as opposed to the bondage of an organization," the judge wrote. He was quoting, he noted, from "a respected, unbiased source, *The Encyclopedia Britannica.*"

"A contrary ruling," he added, "would effectively destroy Methodism in this country, and would have a chilling effect on all churches and religious movements by inhibiting the free associations of persons of similar religious beliefs. If all members of a particular faith were to be held personally liable for the transgressions of their fellow churchmen, church pews would soon be empty and the pulpits of America silent."

Apprehensive that the appeals courts might disagree with his interpretation of the law as well as his apocalyptic vision, Tharp took the highly unorthodox step of attaching to the ruling a personal letter to the attorneys on each side. In this missive he said he believed that the suing residents had a strong claim and that the plaintiffs were likely to win "enormous" damages if the case went to trial. This gambit did not succeed. In seeking the middle ground, Tharp managed to alienate both sets of lawyers as well as the bankruptcy trustee representing Pacific Homes. Yet Tharp's ruling made many of the residents jumpy—and some of the "rebels" urged their neighbors to take their chances with the Methodist authorities rather than the judicial system. Lerach was nervous, too, which explained his filing of a nearly identical suit in federal court in San Diego.

Lerach needn't have worried. His victories over the Methodists were only beginning.

> • >

ONE YEAR LATER, on March 8, 1979, California's Fourth Circuit Court of Appeal overturned Tharp's order in a thorough reversal that left Lerach and his clients holding all the aces. A three-judge panel, in a decision written by a respected justice named Howard B. Wiener, concluded unanimously that the United Methodist Church's legal claims to immunity were specious or, at the least, outdated. "To hold otherwise," the justice wrote, "would permit an unincorporated association to escape liability by this simple technique of requiring express consent from all units of the association."

In their written opinion, the appellate justices expressed both disdain for Tharp's decision to consult the encyclopedia and skepticism toward his assertion that an adverse decision would spell the end of Methodism in this country. They repudiated the trial judge, who was removed from the case, rejected the arguments of the church's lawyers, and utterly embraced the legal premises advanced by Lerach.

"The trend of case law has been the rejection of legal niceties to assure full recognition of the unincorporated association as a separate legal entity," the court wrote.

The appeals court didn't stop there, although it could have. Delving into the United Methodist Church's own organizational texts—helpfully supplied in its legal briefs by plaintiffs' counsel—the court also refuted the Methodists' contention that the church was a loose confederation of like-minded souls and agencies. "In summary, UMC is a highly organized religious body working through specific agencies to accomplish laudable goals."

That left one issue: what if this lawsuit would undermine such "laudable" social goals? That trepidation had undone Ross Tharp. The appellate court, while not minimizing the potential ramifications, did not shy from it. "This concern, legitimate as it may be, is properly placed with the religious body to consider before becoming involved in commercial affairs and [cannot] be considered in our resolution of the issue before us," Justice Wiener wrote. "A religious organization should not be relieved of its lawful obligations arising out of secular activities because the satisfaction of those obligations may, in some tangential fashion, discourage religious activities."

This unanimous ruling left the Methodists aghast. In desperation they sought refuge in the U.S. Supreme Court, even knowing relief was improbable. The first stop in the federal litigation was in the courtroom of respected U.S. District Court Judge Edward J. Schwartz.* Lerach had rushed

---

* The term *respected* for a judge can be a cliché, but in Schwartz's case it is an understatement: upon his retirement, the federal courthouse in San Diego was named in his honor.

this case into court, largely to avoid Tharp, and his haste showed: in a hearing to determine whether the plaintiffs' complaint could be certified as a class action, the weakness of the case became apparent—the main flaw being that Lerach's plaintiffs were elderly people with faulty memories and mixed feelings about their own lawsuit. Church lawyers had exposed these vulnerabilities during their depositions—made "mincemeat" of his clients, Lerach would say. After about an hour Judge Schwartz called a recess.

"We're getting killed here," Lerach whispered to his cocounsel, David Yardley. "They are beating our brains out."

Schwartz had a different reaction. After the break, the judge told the lawyers that they might have a strong case for class action status, but that he wasn't going to certify the class with elderly witnesses who were plainly confused. There is no transcript of his remarks, but Lerach remembers hearing Schwartz say: *You find plaintiffs who can represent the class, and I'll certify the claim.*

A federal judge known for his fairness and prudence is unlikely to have phrased his thoughts precisely this way. What is true, however, is that the federal judges Lerach faced in court over the course of his high-impact legal career—right up until the last jurist, the one who would sentence him to prison—tended to be more sympathetic to him than to his fellow lawyers, the media, or even the public. If you asked some of these judges why, they would answer that Lerach earned their respect by the comprehensive preparation he put into each case, and because he knew the law and was quick on his feet in the courtroom—and was clearly dedicated to his clients. Something else might have been at work as well, and not just in the Pacific Homes case. Lawyers are trained to be advocates, while judges must remain impartial. But all judges were lawyers first, and some of them seemed to live vicariously through the swashbuckling Lerach, who, whatever anyone else could say about him, was an impassioned and articulate advocate.

Whatever Schwartz actually said, Lerach regained his swagger when it came to the Pacific Homes case. "He saved me, and he saved the case," Lerach recalled later. "And boy, did we find plaintiffs!"

The trial that would finally decide the fate of the Pacific Homes residents took place in state, not federal, court—even though Schwartz did affirm the class, and the U.S. Ninth Circuit Court of Appeals upheld his ruling without comment. Witwer and his legal team knew that getting relief from the Supreme Court was a long shot, but by then (this was mid-1979) they were frantic. So they tried the high court too. "To defend the lawsuit would require a restructuring of the . . . denomination to create a monolithic unit, able to speak with one voice and act in a unified manner," the Methodist lawyers wrote in their petition seeking emergency relief from the nation's highest court. "To default would threaten each local church, conference and board with judgment against whatever is later deemed 'association' property in its control."

The Methodists had an ally: the National Council of Churches, the umbrella organization of all mainstream Protestant churches, filed an amicus curiae (a "friend of the court" brief) warning that the California rulings, if allowed to stand, "would unconstitutionally abridge the free exercise of religion, for it would necessarily force all religious denominations to reexamine and reorganize their internal church policies in light of the unprecedented potential for civil liabilities." The Supreme Court was unmoved. As in 1978, the high court declined to hear the case. The church's fate—and William Lerach's first landmark case—would now be in the hands of a San Diego jury.

Before that happened, Lerach and his team, heeding Judge Schwartz's admonition, decided to choreograph a narrative so evocative in its human drama that it would simply overwhelm the Methodists' defenses. At a meeting of several dozen of his most active plaintiffs, all of whom were potential witnesses, Lerach had an inspiration.

"A trial is like putting on a play or making a movie," he told them. "We tell a story. It's our story. We write it. It has to be the truth, but we weave our best information together and use it to tell your stories. You are going to be actresses and actors in this movie we're going to make. How many of you were in high school plays when you were young?"

As numerous wrinkled hands shot in the air, and the faces of the retired Pacific Homes rebels broke into well-worn smiles, Lerach continued:

"Here's what we're going to do," he said. "We are going to have auditions."

> • >

IN THE TWO-YEAR PERIOD between the instigation of this litigation and the trial, Lerach was able to assemble a massive amount of paperwork from Pacific Homes. These documents, although not as vivid as the witnesses who would testify at trial, told their own story and set the predicate for the dramatic production Lerach would direct. His exhibits included newspaper articles dating back to 1958, business cards of Pacific Homes employees, advertisements and brochures aimed at soliciting new residents, marketing plans, official stationery, conference newsletters, press releases and other public relations efforts, tax records, internal church correspondence that discussed the Homes' tax-exempt status, letters to the IRS, public statements of clergymen and UMC officials, minutes of conference meetings and other church memos, public speeches of church officials, phone directories, letters between UMC officials, nursing home certification documents, Methodist yearbooks dating back to 1927, retirement homes industry awards, balance sheets, and the transcript of that smuggled tape recording warning that only a "chain letter" could keep Pacific Homes afloat.

It was a mountain of physical evidence, and each page was gathered—then offered to the court—to bolster at least one of the two great pillars of Lerach's case. The first was that Pacific Homes had always presented itself publicly, and functioned privately, as an official arm of the Methodist Church. "The United Methodist Church owned, controlled, sponsored, and endorsed Pacific Homes," he would tell the jurors in the case. "This was truly a United Methodist Church retirement home and these defendants are responsible for its financial collapse." His second contention was that the retired ministers running the homes—Pacific Homes' board of directors was appointed by Methodist leaders—had known for a long time that their business model was failing. But instead of facing reality, they kept signing up new residents, using their lump-sum payments on operating costs instead of investing that money for the future. This was essentially fraud, although Lerach was careful not to use that word.

"The money was misused," he told the jurors. "The money was gone by 1976. It should have had over twenty million dollars in life-care reserves. It was all gone."

The trial began on August 13, 1980, in the courtroom of Judge Focht, an amiable jurist chosen as Ross Tharp's replacement. Focht had learned, as the two sides wrangled over pretrial motions all summer, that the litigation would be testy, and that the rival teams of lawyers genuinely disliked each other. Thirty years later Samuel Witwer, Jr., still remembered with distaste finding out that the Supreme Court had denied the church's motion—in a taunting phone call from Lerach.

In front of the jury, however, Lerach employed charm instead of ridicule. "I rise to speak for 1,730 elderly persons," he said in an opening argument, in which he painstakingly explained to the jury of eight women and four men what a class action was—how his 168 plaintiffs represented all the homes' residents. Lerach, who had taken pains to crop his wild blond Afro before jury selection began, was careful not to alienate churchgoing jurors. He made a point of mentioning the many good works of the Methodists, even acknowledging their noble intentions when launching the retirement homes. One question raised by the case, Lerach told the jurors, was "How could something that should have been so good end up so bad?"

During a trial spanning nearly four months, Lerach sought to furnish the answer to that question himself. Incompetence and cowardice—with a dose of fraud—were the answers he implanted in the jury's mind. Humanizing this harsh judgment were the eminently sympathetic elderly residents who'd cast their lot with Lerach.

The lead-off actress in his theatrical production was a frail eighty-one-year-old widow named Josephine Owen. Taking the stand at ten A.M. on August 19, 1980, she began under Lerach's gentle prodding to relate how she became interested in Pacific Homes. "After my husband died, I was alone and my children felt I shouldn't live alone," she testified. "Being a Methodist, I was naturally interested."

It was a deft beginning for Maestro Lerach, who in the trial's opening scene had introduced the concept of his clients' vulnerability, their piety, and an unshakable faith that Pacific Homes and the United Methodist Church were one and the same. Mrs. Owen's observation, in fact, brought no fewer than four defendants' attorneys to their feet in objection. Judge Focht, already weary of the ill will between the legal teams on the first day of testimony, heard them out, annoyance showing on his face.

It didn't matter. The trial's dynamics were set in the first few days—and never significantly varied. In their own opening statements, the defendants' attorneys made the same argument to the jury that they had to the California appeals court. Samuel Witwer, Sr., had handed off the lead role to Allan Reniche, who offered the jury an alternative to Lerach's view of Methodism: "The only glue is volunteerism," he said. "The only thing that really holds Methodists together is love."

It was a sweet sentiment, and the church lawyers pushed their hardest, but they didn't have much material to work with—and Lerach had an arsenal.

"What do you need in a trial?" Lerach rhetorically asked the young lawyers assisting him. "You need victims!" And he kept producing them. His second elderly witness was Eric J. Ettles, a retired seventy-two-year-old engineer who told the jury that he had been attracted to a Pacific Homes facility called Casa de Mañana because of ads he'd seen stating that it was backed by the Methodist Church. "This gave us full protection with all these guarantees we needed, backed by a religious organization," he said. "We couldn't see how we could go wrong."

Judge Focht allowed Lerach to read the deposition to the jury of a former Pacific Homes publicity director named Abbie Sargent. She had died a month before the trial began, but Lerach had taken her deposition in 1979. Sargent had testified that from 1963 to 1968 the main thrust of Pacific Homes' promotion plan was to recruit new residents by playing up its ties to the Methodist Church. "It was our strongest point," she said.

For three months the trial went this way. When Lerach rested his case in the first week of December, the Methodist lawyers didn't bother to put on a defense. Methodist church negotiators had already approached Lerach with the idea of a settlement. Coopers & Lybrand, one of the world's "Big Eight" accounting firms, which had signed off on the books, had seen the handwriting on the wall a year earlier, immediately after the California appellate court decision. Within a week of that ruling, in fact, Coopers & Lybrand had settled with Lerach, opting out of the litigation for $1 million. It turned out to be a bargain for the accounting firm. The settlement agreement forged during the first week of December cost the United Methodist Church $21 million.

And so, on December 10, 1980, plaintiffs' lawyers William S. Lerach, Melvyn Weiss, and Gregg A. Johnson, and assistant Kathy Strozza, assembled in the San Diego courtroom of presiding Superior Court Judge Edward T. Butler. Joining them were ten lawyers representing the church and its affiliated agencies, among them Samuel Witwer's son, along with two other bankruptcy lawyers representing Pacific Homes itself. "An unlikely looking jury," Butler quipped while looking at the attorneys arrayed in his courtroom's jury box. The presiding judge then read the terms of the agreement:

- The Annual Conference agreed to pay $21 million in cash, $15 million of it up front, the rest in increments of $1 million per year through 1986.
- Approximately $5 million of that amount was designated to the members of the *Barr* class action suit—the residents themselves.
- The balance of the money, less lawyers' fees and expenses, was to be used to reorganize Pacific Homes and to provide supplemental medical and convalescent care for those residents in need of it.
- The monthly fee schedule paid by Pacific Homes residents was to be restored to the lower amount stipulated in their life-care contracts.
- The conference would establish a "resident assistance fund" that would ensure that no *Barr* class member would ever be forced to leave Pacific Homes for lack of funds.
- The residents would have representation on Pacific Homes' board of directors, to ensure that their interests were protected.

- If Pacific Homes ever found itself with excess cash flow, the money would be used to repay current residents for any payments they had previously made in excess of their contracts.

"I would like to think perhaps that finally the spirit of Christmas settled over this courtroom today," Butler said. "Finally an atmosphere of cooperation and a willingness to adjust and to settle very substantial differences between very sincere and dedicated groups of litigants."

In the nine months since the lawyers had wrangled over jury selection, much had happened; the American people had rejected the incumbent U.S. president, Jimmy Carter, and installed Ronald Reagan in the Oval Office. And while the Pacific Homes jurors had been cloistered in trial, hearing about the foibles of a do-gooder group that had bitten off more than it could chew, the United States entered an era of go-go capitalism that would make a star—and a pariah—out of the lead plaintiffs' attorney. Former government regulators such as Kenneth L. Lay would see that big money could be made in a deregulated environment that began under Carter and accelerated under Reagan. In the spring of 1981 Lay headed to Houston to run a Houston energy company that would morph into Enron. That year John McCain would meet Charles H. Keating, Jr., at a dinner of the Navy League in Arizona that would provide entrée to a scandalous alliance. Bernard J. Ebbers and a host of market manipulators were beginning to see the possibilities open to them if government regulators turned a blind eye. In 1980, at the time of the Pacific Homes trial, CEO pay was forty-two times the pay of the average worker in the United States. Twenty years later CEOs would make 531 times the amount of their workers.

In 1980, at least in San Diego, the business of American business wasn't yet epitomized by high-profile takeover artists, corporate raiders, and privatizing buccaneers dedicated to amassing more wealth than they could ever have spent in three lifetimes, at the cost of breaking companies apart, laying off workers, and moving jobs offshore. Nor was the profession of the law yet exemplified by rapacious trial attorneys whose monumental judgments and staggering legal fees amounted to a redistribution of wealth in its own right.

Judge Butler, speaking as the traditionalist he was, gave voice to the ethos of a sun that was setting. "This settlement is not to be taken, as I see it, by anybody as being a victory for anybody but the community of San Diego, the residents of the homes, and the various church and other entities that are involved here."

It was an appealing sentiment, but in the aftermath of the Pacific Homes case, almost no one viewed the result that way, starting with the retired mostly Methodist residents themselves—and their legal team. Photographs taken after the settlement show a beaming Lerach standing amid a sea of elderly clients, mostly women, who looked upon the young lawyer as their personal champion. This heroic theme was also present in a pair of sketches done by one of the two sons of Kathy Lichnovsky, a San Diego legal secretary who helped Lerach during the case by typing up motions at night and who went on to become his able and longtime administrative assistant. The drawings show a mounted Saint George, an early Christian paragon who is invariably depicted on horseback, killing a dragon with his lance. The dragon is labeled the Methodist Church, a bitter pill for the Methodist officials who went through this crucible of a case. The more significant feature of the drawings, however, is that the face of the third-century saint is that of Bill Lerach.

Another metaphor invoked in those halcyon days—this one by the journalists covering the case—was the 1925 Scopes Monkey Trial, which had tackled the issue of teaching evolution in the public schools. In this analogy Lerach was Clarence Darrow, with the Methodist lawyers, particularly Samuel Witwer, Sr., cast as the foil, as William Jennings Bryan.

These historical comparisons were imprecise, however, and ultimately unhelpful to Lerach because they encouraged his prideful instincts. To this day, what most Americans know of the Scopes trial comes from the play *Inherit the Wind*. It was written in the mid-1950s as a metaphorical warning, not against religious extremism but against McCarthyism.* In the play

---

* As Lerach faced off with federal prosecutors in 2007 and 2008, *Inherit the Wind* enjoyed a revival on college campuses before young audiences who saw it as a warning against the kind of blind obedience that had led the United States into the Iraq War.

Bryan (Matthew Harrison Brady) comes off as a backwoods blowhard, a kind of ultrareligious ignoramus. This is unfair to the memory of Bryan, who was a windbag but was also a prairie Populist with a deeply developed social conscience. Bryan's true concern about Darwinism was rooted neither in science nor in the Bible; like many Populists of his day, he worried that the embrace of Charles Darwin's theories would evolve into a doctrine of "Social Darwinism," in which society turned its back on those less fortunate. In other words, William Jennings Bryan's fears about the likely effects of unfettered capitalism on working people were not dissimilar to those harbored by William Shannon Lerach.

Be that as it may, Lerach's performance in the Pacific Homes case earned him rave reviews from allies and adversaries alike. Three decades later Sam Witwer, Jr., remembered Lerach as "nasty and belligerent" in his interactions with the Methodist attorneys and their clients—but also as a committed lawyer who had a firm grasp of the case law, a deftness with the media, and impressive powers of persuasion with a jury; and as a tireless advocate who would work in court all day and then adjourn to his law office at night and spin off insightful and effective motions and legal responses.

"His work ethic was so prodigious that it was difficult to fathom," Witwer recalls. And when the case ended, on his last day in San Diego, Sam Witwer, Jr., had to stop by Milberg Weiss's high-rise office to deliver a document. Lerach spotted him and waved him into his office, crammed with bankers' boxes of papers from the Pacific Homes case. Lerach looked worn out to Witwer, a human side of him emerging as the two men made small talk over coffee, discussing their families and hometowns. Lerach told Witwer that the trial had been a draining experience, adding that he wanted him to know that the process was "nothing personal." Witwer found this unpretentious version of the fierce courtroom litigator disarming, even likable, and left San Diego wondering if he had judged the Methodists' nemesis too harshly.

Colin Wied, the lawyer who had first called on Lerach for his help with the case, also had conflicting feelings about his one-time colleague but no doubts at all about his legal prowess. "Bill was an absolutely brilliant lawyer in every respect," Wied recalled later. "He could write briefs like nobody I've ever seen, and he handled all kinds of delaying tactics by the church's lawyers. He was a tremendous tactician, cogent and compelling on his feet. He even dressed immaculately. He delivered the goods. He told the jury what was going to happen in that case, and it did. He could really tell a story."

Lerach had first come to San Diego to practice law in a support role representing Mellon Bank in its suit against U.S. Financial. After Pacific Homes he would never be a bit player again. "Yeah, he'd been here on the U.S. Financial case," Wied said. "But this lawsuit, Pacific Homes, was the case that launched him."

The case foreshowed his success, and his fall. Many of the themes, good and bad, present in this case would weave through Lerach's career: the easy relationship with the trial judge, his ability to outwit other lawyers during the day and outwork them at night, the meticulous legal preparation, the suing of secondary defendants such as Coopers & Lybrand, and the ability to ferret out fraud and to instill in his clients and his staff the sense that he was an avenging crusader who was indeed slaying dragons like the mythical knights of yore. All that would continue to the next case, and the case after that, until the day came when Bill Lerach's net worth was often greater than the corporate titans he was suing. Which is a reminder that while the Pacific Homes lawsuit was about justice, it was also about money. And if the love of money is truly the root of all evil, it is worth noting that dark strands were also present back in the Pacific Homes case. Along with the good works were the other things: the hubris, the taunting, the acrimony with the opposing side, the hyperpartisanship born of a Manichean worldview.

In San Diego Lerach put down roots and made his legal mark. He had challenged an entity held in high repute and had tarnished that reputation. Lerach had also taken on the cream of the Chicago legal establishment. A decade later he'd do so again, although that time it wouldn't end well. As 1980 came to a close, he earned a paycheck of $150,000. "I thought it was all the money in the world," he recalled. "We took a case against a popular religious organization, faced big-time lawyers from Los Angeles and Chicago and Philadelphia, fought in two judicial systems for nearly four years—and got a fantastic settlement. If we could do that, we could do anything."

There is a postscript to this story, however, and it comes from Colin Wied. Three decades later Wied and Granby were among those asked by Lerach's defense lawyer to write character references for the federal judge who was preparing to sentence Lerach to prison. Granby complied, as did 150 others, but Wied did not. Asked why, Wied didn't answer directly. He told this brief story instead: in a conversation long after their joint case had ended—when Lerach's caseload mushroomed—Wied once asked Lerach casually, "How do you guys get all your cases?"

"Bill quickly volunteered that it was illegal to pay prospective clients," Wied recalled. "That wasn't what I was implying, and I didn't know what to say. It kind of ended our conversation."

2

> • > • > • > • >

THE YOUNG MAN
FROM PITTSBURGH

In later years, when Bill Lerach emerged as one of the most renowned trial lawyers in America, a legend would grow up about the Lerachs of Pittsburgh, one woven by Bill himself and peddled to a fawning media. In this telling, Lerach's father was a broken man who had been sacrificed on the shoals of free enterprise—specifically the stock market crash of 1929. Typical of the news coverage, repeated time and again, is this 1999 excerpt in the *San Francisco Chronicle*:

SON OF THE GREAT CRASH, 1946

William Shannon Lerach—the attorney despised most by corporate America—was born a victim of the stock market.

In September 1929, after receiving a substantial inheritance, Lerach's father, Richard, went to work as a stockbroker. He invested everything he owned in the market. The next month, the market crashed, and the elder Lerach was ruined.

In 1933 and 1934, President Roosevelt signed landmark securities legislation to prevent the kind of speculation, manipulation and outright fraud that triggered the crash and caused millions of Americans to lose their savings and jobs.

The legislation came too late for Richard Lerach, who was relegated to selling metal parts for the rest of his days. But for his youngest son, William, it would provide the means for a career of wealth and notoriety.

Bill Lerach could be dramatic in his telling of this stark parable, often at his father's expense. He would never overcome a deep antipathy for "corporate America" after watching his father work "for almost nothing," the *Chronicle* said in the same article. "They treated him like they treat pencils," Lerach told the San Francisco reporters, "shaving him down until there was nothing left but a nub."

Bill related this account so often, he believed it himself. At times there were subtler versions. "I think what influenced me . . . was that the financial catastrophe that befell my father defeated him, and resulted in his becoming a little man," he told the *Pitt*, his university's alumni magazine, in 2002. "And I don't mean that in a demeaning way. My father was a great guy, and he was very good to us, and I loved him very much . . . but he was a cog in a wheel."

This was the narrative that Lerach constructed for the jury of public opinion—and he kept relating it until the day he went to prison. The press never challenged it, which poses an interesting question: is it accurate? The answer seems to be that, although there is some truth in it, the story takes such liberty with the facts that it's as much myth as reality. The full story is much more nuanced—and more interesting.

> • >

ON MARCH 14, 1946, the day of William Lerach's birth, Harry Truman held a press conference to explain his unsuccessful attempts at presidential mediation while trying to avert a national steel strike. The strike, when it came, rippled out from Pittsburgh, crimping the rest of the economy, as Truman had feared. Truman's gambit did not help him in Pennsylvania, a state he would lose to Thomas Dewey in 1948, and it certainly did not help him in the Lerach household. Bill's father, Richard Emil Lerach, worked for many years as a salesman and in middle management for an outfit called Williams & Co., a Pittsburgh metal-supply operation that purchased steel tubing and other products from the mills and sold them to firms too small to do business directly with behemoths such as U.S. Steel. Richard Lerach was a middleman. He was pro-business by nature and staunchly conservative at a time when that term had nothing to do with social issues such as abortion or gay rights, or even necessarily the Republican Party. But Richard E. Lerach was definitely a Republican. He not only didn't vote for Harry Truman—he would proudly tell friends that he'd voted against Franklin D. Roosevelt every time FDR ran for president.

Richard and his wife, Evelyn, possessed a personal conservatism born of experience. They were born and raised in Pittsburgh, first-generation Americans of parents who had come to the United States as infants. They met in the mid-1930s in a Pittsburgh neighborhood called Northside, where both had grown up, and they married in 1938 when he was twenty-nine years old and she was twenty-six. Richard's father had died when he was ten years old, after which he was raised by his mother and his mother's sister in a house on Kennedy Avenue. That street traverses a distressed African-American area today, but it was then at the heart of a bustling community whose residents were in the middle of the middle class. Richard and Evelyn had a son, Richard F. Lerach, born in 1940, whom the family called Dick. Six years later came a second boy, named William Shannon, his middle name deriving from his paternal grandmother, Anna Shannon, who came from County Armagh in Ireland. Richard Emil Lerach was uncommonly devoted to his mother. Except for one year at nearby Allegheny College, he never lived farther than one hundred yards from her.

Bill and his older brother grew up in that Kennedy Avenue house and attended public elementary schools. With the neighborhood boys they played baseball, basketball, football, hockey, and indoor games including pool, cards, and a nearly addictive board game called APBA Baseball. They attended Perry High School a few blocks from their home, where Dick, but not Bill, was a celebrated athlete, starring on the football team and playing tennis and golf as well.

Growing up, Bill spent the most time with two other Kennedy Avenue kids, Gene Carney and Jim Kerr. Their favorite playground was an abandoned clay tennis court at the end of Kennedy Avenue and surrounded on three sides by woods, where, after school or on weekends—or all summer long—the Kennedy Avenue crew would play sandlot baseball. The field held hazards, including a metal bolt that stuck from a pole near third base. Bill Lerach received his emergency room baptism when he ran into that bolt, puncturing the top of his head and producing, Carney noted later, "the bloodiest mess I'd ever seen."

Jim Kerr, Bill's first cousin (their mothers are sisters), still calls his old playmate "Billy" when he reminisces about their boyhood days—just as Lerach still calls him "Jimmy." He was a year and half older than Bill, and some of Kerr's fondest memories involve playing wintertime hockey in the Lerach family basement when the boys were elementary school age. Bill was an undistinguished scholar at Perry High and didn't play on the school's varsity athletic teams, although he was sports editor of the high school newspaper and worked on the yearbook. Other than dating girls—his first serious girlfriend was Peggy Hayes, a cheerleader who attended Carnegie Mellon on a music scholarship—the extracurricular activity that most inspired him was acting. In 1963 he landed the coveted male lead in the senior play, *Ask Any Girl*.

The girl who starred opposite him was Tricia Sutton, also a cheerleader, who was popular and active in school activities. Sutton liked Lerach then and likes him now. In an e-mail exchange with the authors after Lerach went to prison, she described her long-ago costar as "a great guy" and "BFF," instant-message-speak for "best friends forever."* In her memory

---

* Sutton described herself, tongue-in-cheek, as Bill's former "cousin"—an in-joke in their neighborhood, because she was married briefly to one of Lerach's cousins. But her loyalty to her high school friend is no laughing matter: in one exchange with the authors, Sutton referred to Lerach as "a political prisoner."

Bill Lerach was charming; a "fast talker" and "a wheeler dealer" whose busy schedule required that he cut a corner now and then. "One day, however, his 'slickness' caught up with him when he placed his own foot firmly in his own mouth," she recalled, not unfondly.

The two were students in an Advanced Placement class assigned to read *The Fall of the House of Usher* by Edgar Allan Poe. "As we were discussing the book in class, our teacher, knowing what a rascal he was and trying to catch him on a point, asked him to relate the exciting end of the tale," she recalled. "Bill had never read the book, but had seen the *movie* and figured he could ease through the oral exam. Bill was on a roll of recitation and was getting more and more excited about the gruesome story and when he was just about to tell the climax of the story said, 'And then Vincent Price . . .'

"Everyone, including the teacher, burst out laughing."

In truth, Bill Lerach developed an appreciation for reading while at Perry High, especially nonfiction. His intellectual curiosity was unlocked by "Miss Roberts," the tenth-grade history teacher. Ethel Roberts appeared to her students as an unprepossessing spinster with bunched white hair and long black dresses, but her love of history infected an entire generation of kids on Pittsburgh's Northside. Later, a scholarship was endowed in her name at West Virginia University, Miss Roberts's alma mater.

Dick graduated in 1958, five years earlier than Bill, and enrolled at the University of Pittsburgh, where he eventually attended law school. In later years Bill would talk of a childhood of "used cars and hand-me-down clothes," but that description owes more to his parents' conservative attitudes about money—and in particular, to their mother's idiosyncratic frugality— than to circumstances of actual want. The Lerach boys had after-school and summer jobs, Bill's being less strenuous than his brother's. Bill worked in a pool hall, and a funeral home, and one summer in a plant nursery, while his older sibling held down a more lucrative, and physically demanding, job digging and tending graves at Uniondale Cemetery.

Money was valued but not scarce. When Dick went to see the dean of the law school, he was asked a single question: "Can you pay the tuition?" When the older Lerach son answered affirmatively, he was admitted. As Bill entered his last week of high school, preparing to enroll at Pitt himself, his brother completed his first year of law school. Then their close-knit little family was struck by tragedy.

> • >

RICHARD EMIL LERACH was only twenty years old on the day of the 1929 stock market crash, an event that occurred a full seventeen years before Bill was born. Apparently it's accurate that his father had taken a job in a stock brokerage, and evidently he did invest a small inheritance, as well as some of his mother's money, in the market. Richard E. Lerach lost his family's investments, as did many Americans, and became risk averse. There is scant evidence that this was the seminal event in Richard Lerach's life, however. The man worked, saved, married, and bought a house, grew berries in the backyard, voted Republican, and took up golf. He and his wife raised their sons to believe in the rewards of steady employment, a paycheck, and a pension. Certainly there had been internal tension in the household, which Lerach would allude to later in life, perhaps without realizing it: his own father was very close to *his* mother—Bill's grandmother—but staying close to home was not something Bill really respected. "He never got out of the starting blocks," he told the authors in reference to his father. "His big move to freedom was that he moved fifteen houses away from his mother. Went to visit his mother every single day of his life, I swear to God, on his way home from work. She made him pies and ice tea. He never separated from that, never got a degree of independence."

Sitting in the lobby of Pittsburgh's William Penn Hotel in January 2008, during a nostalgic visit to his hometown prior to his sentencing in a California courtroom, Bill Lerach petted his beloved dog Tommy and reminisced about his father's instinctive prudence. During his last year in high school, as Sputnik and the ensuing space race suddenly conveyed new status to scientists, Bill's father had gently nudged him to think about a career in engineering. Engineers made $1,000 a month, the man told his younger son, and could usually find work for big companies that offered nice retirement benefits. Although he said little in response, his father's notion was a nonstarter to young Bill, who had trouble mastering high school math, let alone the advanced calculus required of engineers. Nor was the teenage boy impressed by his dad's conventional aspirations for his sons, and his fixation on a profession that offered job security. It seemed, well, so provincial.

At least, that's one way of looking at it. There are others.

One is that Richard Lerach's own imagination had been fired by the "space race," and the new frontier that President Kennedy had challenged a nation to explore—a mission to the moon. But in 1960 Bill's father took him to see *Inherit the Wind*, an experience that was so galvanizing that Bill told both Gene Carney and Jim Kerr afterward that the movie had changed his life. His natural bent for acting, his concern for social issues, his competitiveness—all of that could be harnessed into a career in the law.

Perhaps Richard E. Lerach's real failure, at least in the psyche of his second son, was not his fault at all—was nobody's fault. The event that left his younger son feeling abandoned, and eventually estranged from the memory of his dad, came on June 16, 1963. It was Father's Day, three days before Bill was to graduate from high school. Richard Emil Lerach had taken Bill golfing that day, driven them both home, eaten a sandwich, said goodnight, and gone to bed, where he lay down and died in his sleep. He was fifty-four years old. Bill awoke that night to the sound of his mother screaming.

Frantic, Evelyn called her sister's house down the street—and Jim Kerr's father came racing over to try to revive him. The next thing Bill knew, an ambulance arrived at the house, as did his big brother. Nothing could be done. Richard E. Lerach was a victim of a little-known condition called chronic myocarditis. Unknown to anyone, his heart had been compromised by a strep infection that his body had not completely purged. It lay dormant in the lining of his heart, an invidious time bomb that suddenly detonated that fateful June night.

At this point in their lives the uncertainty, hardship, and heartbreak that Bill Lerach would later attribute to the stock market crash of 1929 did indeed descend. Dick was able to remain at Pitt law school, but Evelyn and seventeen-year-old Bill moved from the Kennedy Avenue house to an apartment in a neighborhood known as Oakland, near Pitt's campus. Evelyn went to work at the Western Pennsylvania School for the Blind; Bill cobbled together enough scholarship money to enroll at Pitt. Mother and younger son became inseparable, and she became his confidante.

To his friends, living with his mother seemed a productive arrangement. Peter A. Morgan, a member of Bill's 1963 freshman pledge class of the Delta Tau Delta fraternity, believed that his friend enjoyed "the best of both worlds" by living with his mother while fully immersing himself in university life: "She encouraged him to make the most of his intelligence and talents, and the fraternity friends helped him grow in self-esteem and social confidence." Morgan also remembers Lerach as a young man who often dominated any political discussion he happened to be engaged in—on the basis of "facts and forceful argument."

By his senior year Lerach was living with three Delta Tau Delta fraternity brothers in an apartment on Shady Avenue. One of them, Erl G. "Puck" Purnell, who went off to the navy and is now an Episcopal rector in Connecticut, recalls that by then the roommates had drifted away from the fraternity scene, though he and Lerach remained active Republicans. Soon both men would break with the GOP as well.

The way Bill Lerach would rationalize his closeness to his own mother is twofold. First, he identified with Evelyn Lerach—saw in her the traits he hoped to possess. "It is a shame my mother didn't get a chance in the modern era, she would have been a CEO—she could have been anything," he said. "She was smart, sassy, combative, manipulative, all the assets to succeed, much more of a role model than my father." The other way was that he differed from his father—and from most of those in the Lerach clan—by harboring dreams of leaving Pittsburgh.

After his father died, Bill Lerach would tell his mother that he didn't want to be ordinary. After graduating from Pitt law school, Dick Lerach would take a job with the kind of big company his father had in mind for his sons, first for three years in New York and then in Pittsburgh, where he joined the legal office of U.S. Steel. There he rose through the ranks to eventually become general counsel of the corporation. When her younger son described visions of something much bigger, Evelyn Lerach would invariably reply that she wanted great things for him, too. But what?

Perhaps it was the classic movie about the Scopes trial that simmered inside him, or maybe it was a simple lack of imagination. But he decided to follow his brother's path and apply to Pitt's law school. Evelyn typed his one-page essay. It passed muster, and Bill entered the law school in 1967. It was a good match from the opening day of classes. His first year in law school, despite receiving a C in a popular class in criminal law, Bill was ecstatic. "I finally found something I can do," he'd tell family and friends. "It's what I was meant to do."

3

> • > • • > • >

THE YOUNG LAWYER
FROM PITTSBURGH

At Pitt, Lerach was active in politics, holding positions in the Young Republicans and in student government. He had a knack for leadership, and
although he and others in his circle, such as his roommate Peter Morgan,
would change political parties and become committed liberals, a populist,
working-class, chip-on-the-shoulder streak ran through Lerach's political
sensibilities then and now. In 1965, as demonstrations against the Vietnam
War were breaking out on other campuses, Lerach and Morgan organized a
campus rally in support of the troops. "Our take on the antiwar protests
[taking place] on other campuses was that they did not show any respect for
the soldiers who were fighting the war," Morgan recalled. "We both had
friends fighting in the war, who had not had the benefits of a college defer-
ment."

In law school Lerach's then-conservative politics initially informed his
legal philosophy rather than the other way around. In 1972 he coauthored
an article for the *University of Pittsburgh Law Review* asserting that federal
judges should exercise more control over "strike suits"—class action securi-

ties lawsuits—which were characterized in the article as "procedural monstrosities" that abuse the class action process. The article argued that the real purpose of strike suits is often extortive: "The plaintiff in such an action frequently hopes to use the class allegations as a bargaining weapon to be disposed of when an appropriate premium has been extracted from the defendant." If anything, Lerach was ahead of his time. Melvyn Weiss, his future mentor, was still four years away from molding his "fraud on the market" theory into federal jurisprudence, and the Republican Party hadn't yet declared war on trial lawyers.

By the time those battle formations were drawn along firmly partisan lines, Lerach would be on the other side. Nonetheless, those close to him understood that Bill Lerach had indeed found his calling. He would never get another middling grade and ended up graduating second in the Pitt law school class of 1970. His only worry was money. In June 1968, after his first year of law school, he had married his college sweetheart, Jaylyn Barnard, whom he'd met when both were active in Republican politics at Pitt. Between family expenses and tuition, he was feeling pinched, and he mentioned one day to another friend that he might have to drop out of law school. It was a fortuitous conversation. That friend, Dennis Unkovic, was the son of Alexander Unkovic, one of Pittsburgh's most respected and beloved attorneys. Dennis told his father about a friend who was this "brilliant" law student but might be unable to finish school. So Bill was hired as a law clerk at Meyer, Unkovic & Scott during his second year in law school—and he remained there until he graduated.

The partners hoped Bill would join their firm, but by then he had been noticed by Pittsburgh's top law firm—the venerable Reed, Smith, Shaw & McClay. The white-shoe firm was offering a starting salary of $13,500, while Meyer Unkovic paid its first-year associates something closer to $7,200. Lerach went to the famous firm, engendering no hard feelings from Unkovic as he left. That was apparently typical of the philosophical older man. Young lawyers in Meyer Unkovic's offices would do what corporate defense lawyers often do when their corporate clients are sued; they vent and fume, ingratiating themselves with the client by taking out their ire on the plaintiff's attorney. One day Alexander Unkovic pulled young Bill aside and told him with a playful smile: "You know what I think of plaintiffs' attorneys? I think: 'God bless the man who sues my client!'"

> • >

REED SMITH WAS FOUNDED in 1877 with the express purpose of representing the business interests of Pittsburgh's wealthiest and most eminent families. The firm's list of clients reads like a roster of the names on buildings and parks throughout western Pennsylvania: Carnegie, Frick, Mellon, Heinz, Westinghouse. More than 200 attorneys and 350 support staff occupied its Pittsburgh headquarters in the ornate, cathedral-like Flemish-Gothic building. Among them decorum and respectability were de rigueur. But Reed Smith played hardball, and Bill Lerach received, along with a starting salary of $13,500, a continuing education in the law. The firm specialized in defending its well-heeled corporate clients from civil lawsuits. Here Lerach learned how defense lawyers thought, and it wasn't always pretty. He learned to obfuscate, and to create the veneer of compliance while holding back potentially damaging information, all toward the end of bleeding the plaintiffs of time, money, and energy. These were the tricks of the defense trade, and in his three years at Reed Smith, Bill Lerach learned them. By implication, he also acquired the aggressive tactics he would employ as a plaintiffs' attorney to counteract them.

At Reed Smith these lessons started with one maxim: "Almost nothing bad will happen if you have the evidence under control." At the outset of a lawsuit, the defense knows the facts and the plaintiff does not. So the job of the defense is to keep the plaintiffs from getting the facts in order to prove the case. At Reed Smith this was called "persistent resistance." Practicing it effectively required an almost passive-aggressive personality. A defense lawyer will look at a subpoena and immediately divine reasons not to produce the sought-after documents: counsel might say that complying with the request would give away the client's trade secrets or was privileged information for one reason or another. Such tactics didn't always work, but what did the firm being sued have to lose? At worst, they'd ultimately be compelled to produce documents and witnesses they didn't want to produce. At best, the plaintiff would lose interest or, even better, become so flummoxed by the delaying tactics that his lawyers missed a filing deadline—and the case would be thrown out on technical grounds. Stalling was more profitable for defense firms than cooperating: it also meant more billable hours. The inside joke at the firm was that Reed, Smith, Shaw & McClay really stood for "Bleed, Shit, Stall, & Delay."

Lerach could do it with the best of them. In one 1975 case Reed Smith represented MSA, the world's leading manufacturer of industrial safety equipment. The plaintiff was a worker who had been injured so severely while using an MSA protective device that it left him brain-damaged and unemployable. The worker had a wife and children and, more to the point, a savvy and persistent lawyer. As the young associate helping to defend the case, Lerach handled the production of documents demanded by the plaintiff. Poring through hundreds of documents, he came across one from a lower-level MSA employee to a senior executive warning that the product at issue had failed on three or four occasions—and might injure or kill someone who was using it. The employee's recommendation: issue a warning or withdraw it from the market. Lerach took his finding to a partner on the case, handing him the entire file.

"There is a very bad document here and you'd better take a look at it," Lerach said gravely.

The partner looked at the two-page document marked by a paper clip and read it slowly, Lerach later recalled. Showing no emotion, he casually tore the two pages out, crumpled them, and threw them in his wastepaper basket. "No sense making their job any easier for them," he explained. "And always remember," he added as he trimmed away the tiny shards from where he'd torn the document away, "to remove the little pieces of paper left behind." The veteran litigator looked up at his young associate. "Did you see any other problems?"

"No," Lerach replied.

"Good job, then," the partner replied.

In the intervening years when he related this account, Lerach would always be careful to say that the plaintiff eventually received a healthy settlement. He'd also concede that his own reaction then had been not shock but approbation for the job he was charging billable hours to do.

Yet he was not a perfect fit at Reed Smith, which Lerach attributed to his lack of an Ivy League law degree. There was a culture clash between Lerach and Reed Smith, all right, but it had little to do with diplomas. Temperamentally he was suited for something else. The idea of sitting around hoping a lawsuit would resolve itself because your opponent missed a deadline was anathema to him. He had a restless mind and a confrontational nature—and a gut-level appetite for legal combat. He liked to force the action, not forestall it.

He would soon get his chance, as part of a big-time lawsuit at Reed Smith. It would also be his last case there—and it would launch him toward the West and into the rarified air he'd told his mother he dreamed of breathing. It would happen more quickly than his bosses expected, but Bill Lerach was a young man in a hurry. This too was a residue from his boyhood family life. His father had died suddenly at fifty-four; his father's father had died in his fifties too, during the great influenza epidemic of 1919. Three of his four maternal uncles had died before they reached sixty—and the one who lived into his sixties, Lerach's namesake, "Uncle Bill," struggled with heart disease. "I saw myself destined for a relatively short performance on Earth," he told the authors in early 2008, as he prepared himself mentally for the ordeal of a prison sentence. "I think it instilled a sense of urgency, a little recklessness, and maybe behavior that was oblivious to the consequences."

> • >

LERACH'S OPPORTUNITY WOULD ARRIVE courtesy of Reed Smith's richest client, Mellon Bank, which by 1974 had acquired dozens of other banks and undergone several reorganizations resulting in a holding company, Mellon National Corporation. Among the thousands of investments it made along the way was $7 million that one of its trusts had invested in a San Diego institution known as U.S. Financial. As with Pacific Homes, the press releases put out by U.S. Financial painted a picture of a thriving and profitable conglomerate. In reality, the firm was little more than a shell that created phony earnings and used the inflated stock to acquire other properties. Robert H. Walter the U.S. Financial chief executive, pleaded no contest in federal court to charges of conspiracy and filing false reports with the Securities and Exchange Commission. He was sentenced to three years in federal prison, which may have pleased the investors but did not get their money back.

Although Mellon Bank was traditionally a reluctant litigant, trust money was involved, and it had little choice. Mellon's officers instructed its law firm, Reed Smith, to go after its $7 million. Lerach, who had just turned twenty-nine and was recently separated from his wife, was eager for the assignment. He was paired with J. Tomlinson Fort IV, a Harvard man and buttoned-down Reed Smith partner who was as tradition-bound as Lerach was rebellious.

Their contrasting styles and personalities engendered tense relations. Tom Fort found Lerach impetuous. Lerach considered the older man a stuffed shirt and called him "Tom Tom Fart-Fart" behind his back to other young Reed Smith lawyers. For his part, Fort was frustrated that the younger man seemed impervious to constructive criticism. Actually, the problem went deeper. It wasn't that Lerach didn't want guidance; it's just that early in the U.S. Financial litigation, he decided he wanted it from someone else.

Because the U.S. Financial meltdown stemmed from numerous multi-state operations, the lawsuit was under federal jurisdiction. Dozens of claimants, including Mellon Bank, had filed suit. To avoid confusion and to try to achieve some sort of efficiency (which the court had signaled it would prefer), an attorney representing one of the other claimants had already sought and received classification by the court as the lead plaintiff. The attorney was Melvyn I. Weiss. A federal judicial panel that would assign jurisdiction for the case was scheduled to meet in Colorado, so Weiss called for a strategy meeting of the plaintiffs' counsels in Denver the night before.*

---

* Lerach has told the story of meeting Mel Weiss in Denver several times (although Weiss himself once told the *New York Times* that he believed they first met in San Diego).

When Bill Lerach stepped off the United Airlines flight from Pittsburgh to Denver's Stapleton Airport, it was his first time west of the Mississippi River. Even in late spring snow still hugged the peaks of the Rockies thirty miles to the west, which he spied through the haze. He and Fort collected their luggage and hailed a taxi downtown to Denver's venerable Brown Palace Hotel. Instead of going to their rooms, they strode straight through the ornate wood-paneled lobby to the elevators, riding to the eighth floor, where they found room 825, the Eisenhower Presidential Suite. They joined a gaggle of lawyers around a rectangular, mahogany table.

One of the lawyers, a gruff-looking, intense man with a dark, trim beard and unmistakable New York accent, was calling the shots. This attorney was explaining antifraud provisions of the federal securities acts under Section 10b of the Securities Exchange Act of 1934 and Rule 10b-5 of the Securities Act of 1933. Most of the attorneys, including Fort and Lerach, were familiar with these rules, but no one dared interrupt, so intense, so articulate, and so intimidating was the speaker. His name was Melvyn Weiss.

Weiss was already earning a reputation as an expert in the arcane legal subspecialty of unraveling auditors' hieroglyphics and was on his way to becoming an outspoken critic of the big corporate-sponsored accounting firms—one of the earliest voices warning that something had gone terribly wrong with the system.

"For over 30 years, ever since accountants were required by law to certify the financial statements of publicly held firms, there has been very little questioning of the accountant's role and of his performance," Weiss explained publicly. "As a result, an unhealthy reliance developed between the auditor and the company paying his fee, leading to a situation where the accountant started to forget his real clients—the ones who rely on the financial statements."*

---

* The account here is drawn from four separate interviews the authors had with Lerach in mid-January 2008, as well as an account in the *Times* Lerach gave to Timothy L. O'Brien in 2004, and another he gave to Joseph C. Goulden in his 2005 book, *The Money Lawyers.* The versions are similar, although each contains details the others do not.

He had a working knowledge of the field he was critiquing. Before attending law school, Weiss had been an accounting student himself, albeit an uninspired one, at Baruch College in New York. He would reach the campus on the number five subway line that he'd board daily from his home in the Bronx. He was a city kid, a Yankee worshiper, a street stickballer, a verbal brawler. His father was an auditor, a green-eyeshade persona specializing in small businesses in the wholesale meat district. As a teen, Mel helped his father run through the figures posted in multiple columns on butcher paper "biff sheets." Thousands of digits, in difficult-to-decipher handwriting, particular to the pen or pencil of the butcher who had done the tallying, would have to be tediously reconciled. Although it gave Mel an aversion to his father's vocation, he retained a head for numbers.

He went to law school at night, and after graduating, clerking in a venerable Manhattan law firm, and doing a stint in the army, Weiss worked for small offices handling personal injury cases, often before juries, and delved into real estate law and derivatives cases in which he represented shareholders who thought the companies they held stock in were not being run with their intentions in mind. By the time he met Lawrence Milberg in 1965, Weiss was confidently equipped and dexterous with the tools of his trade, including an aptitude for dissecting financial sheets prepared by corporate accountants. He would describe his role as "taking a knife and slicing into the belly of the corporation to find out what had gone on."

That's what he had done with the U.S. Financial case, dissecting it as a self-contained real estate company that "left nothing to chance." Now Weiss began issuing instructions, directing each of his fellow attorneys like a quarterback playing street football in the Bronx: "You go long to the hydrant; you button hook at the Buick . . ." as to their role before the federal panel the following day.

Lerach remembered the thespian command in Weiss's soft voice, the assurance with which he issued his orders, the clarity of his game plan, and the brute force of his intellect. Weiss took a breath, ready to hit the sweet spot that would be delivered before a judge and jury if it came to it. The fraud, he said, resided in the fact that "this company entered into transactions with its affiliates on the last day of every reporting period, thereby creating virtually all of the profit for the entire reporting period." In other words, he pointed out, "U.S. Financial was advancing the money to buyers to make their down payments." It was nothing but a churn of money with no economic substance, he concluded, except for thousands of investors who had millions drained from their pockets. Perhaps even more important, Weiss reminded the other attorneys, U.S. Financial's accountants and banks were in on this scam. In fact, since U.S. Financial had all but scorched its own earth, the more fertile ground might well lay with the accountants Touche Ross, investment banking house Goldman Sachs, and its major commercial banker, Union Bank of California.

"We must go after them equally aggressively," Weiss said firmly, looking around the table and then cracking a smile. "They'll make it seem as if we are committing an unpardonable sin by suing them."

Lerach was smitten. Mel Weiss could frame a complex fraud case completely—and yet compactly—with a skill Lerach had never before encountered. Weiss was field general and salesman at the same time. Each of the attorneys represented individual claimants, Weiss acknowledged: each appeared to qualify under the rules governing the period of time their class of plaintiffs suffered the losses. Yet they should be gratified that as lead plaintiffs' counsel, his firm, Milberg Weiss, had the most experience and most success in class action matters. He already had damage experts to calculate how much the stock had been fraudulently inflated during the class period. He looked around the table at each of the lawyers and repeated to them the losses their clients claimed they'd suffered. As lead counsel, he would strive to return to each of them more than they had lost. He would have to control the case, perhaps with some assistance from one or two of those gathered in the room. But he would be in charge.

No one argued.

The next day the attorneys appeared before the panel of federal judges who would decide the venue; several made their cases as to why they should be included in the class action and why it should be tried in New York and not San Diego. One of them, a young attorney from the venerable New York firm of Sullivan & Cromwell, representing Goldman Sachs, told the panel, "There is not a judge anywhere in San Diego sufficiently sophisticated enough to try this complex financial matter." This reasoning did not win the day. The judges voted to send the case where the defendant company resided—San Diego. The day before, Mel Weiss had all but predicted that outcome, even while arguing for a change of venue to New York. In fact, everything that Weiss had foretold unfolded just as he had said it would. This fact was not lost on Lerach, who by the time he returned to Pittsburgh had a new idol and soon-to-be mentor.

"I thought to myself, 'Okay, now you've found the guy who's going to show you what to do in life,'" Lerach recalled.

Weiss also had his eye on the young attorney from Pittsburgh. The decision to try the U.S. Financial case in San Diego was the antecedent to creating a powerful East Coast—West Coast axis, eventually to be known as Milberg Weiss Lerach, that would become corporate America's most feared, most hated, and by many accounts meanest law firm.

> • >

PREDICTABLY, TOM FORT HAD a different reaction to Mel Weiss. Days later, back in Pittsburgh, Lerach was feeling almost giddy when he got off the elevator and strode toward his office at Reed Smith. On the way he passed Fort's secretary, Jean Stiver, a secret Lerach confederate. She stopped Lerach, saying she had something to show him. It was a memo Fort had dictated for the partners following the Brown Palace meeting. It described the case and notified the other partners that Milberg Weiss would be the lead counsel against U.S. Financial and that the case would be tried in San Diego.

Lerach's eyes locked on the final passage, searing in its derision: "As for Melvyn Weiss, whom I can only describe as conducting himself as a 1930s Hollywood movie star . . ."

Lerach chuckled and handed the memo back. "Doesn't everybody want to be a movie star?" he said. "I'm going to California."

4

> • > • • > • >

GOLDEN STATE

The palm trees came into view first, and then, from the right side of the first-class cabin, Bill Lerach noticed the Spanish-Moor motif of Balboa Park's museums and exhibition halls, its world-famous zoo, and its renowned botanical gardens, as the airliner descended into San Diego. An aspiring gardener, he made a mental note to visit. But that was a secondary consideration on this trip, his first ever, from Pittsburgh to the West Coast. At twenty-eight years old, on track to become the youngest partner at venerable Reed Smith, he would be working on the biggest case of his career.

A minute later, on its final approach toward its landing at the downtown airport, Lindbergh Field, the plane seemed to be gliding just over the city itself, over a smattering of low-rise buildings with a newer, upstart high-rise here and there. Just beyond and drawing nearer, the long, narrow harbor stretched out, shimmering in the still-bright December afternoon light. Berthed and anchored throughout the harbor were dozens of large gray naval vessels—tankers, destroyers, minesweepers, tenders, submarines, aircraft carriers—announcing to even the most uninformed visitor that San Diego was a company town, and the company was the U.S. Navy.

By New Year's Day 1975 the city's innocence had receded into the past, not only because of disillusionment in military communities over the outcome of the Vietnam War, but also because of the shocking plunge from grace of a man who literally answered to the name "Mr. San Diego." That was the name of a civic award given out each year, and C. Arnholt Smith had won it twice. A local newspaper opined that Smith was really "Mr. San Diego of the Century."

A high school dropout, Smith literally presided over the city's economy. He owned the largest bank; he owned the largest hotel; he owned the San Diego Padres baseball team; he owned the state's premier commuter airline; he owned a tuna fleet; he owned a shipbuilding business; he owned Yellow Cab operations in thirteen California cities; he owned the biggest shopping center in Southern California; he owned a diversified manufacturing organization; and he owned a lot of land. From his Westgate-California offices above San Diego, Smith could turn in any direction and look down on something he owned.

Among the other beneficiaries of Smith's influence was his friend and business colleague Robert H. Walter, the head of U.S. Financial Corp., whose developments were sometimes conjoined with Smith's landholdings. Smith's U.S. National Bank (USNB) was also one of Walter's banks of choice. In 1973 USNB collapsed under the weight of $400 million in outstanding debt—mostly loans to companies he controlled—making it the biggest bank failure in U.S. history. Even earlier, the Justice Department and the Securities and Exchange Commission had turned their attention to Smith's suspected self-dealings through his Westgate-California Corporation, which used his USNB as its moneylender and launderer. *Forbes* magazine's description of C. Arnholt Smith as "perhaps the swindler of the century" turned out to be wishful thinking. Greater frauds, and greater scam artists, were in America's future—and Mel Weiss and Bill Lerach would sue most of them.

When Lerach landed in San Diego in December 1974, ready to do battle with lawyers representing banks and accounting firms that had aided U.S. Financial's fraudulent empire, Smith was facing an indictment by a federal grand jury for embezzlement and fraudulently commingling funds in an arrangement that comptroller of the currency James E. Smith had termed "total fraud . . . self dealing run riot."

This irony delighted Lerach, who appreciated the nuances of greed, except for one fact. Smith and Westgate would have been as ripe for a private securities lawsuit as Walter, except that Smith's bank was insolvent and so was his fraudulent corporation. "The bastard left nothing for the rest of us," Lerach quipped.

> • >

CLASS ACTION WAS A legal doctrine that crossed the Atlantic Ocean with the Pilgrims and was codified into federal jurisprudence as early as 1820; it was spelled out specifically by the U.S. Supreme Court as Rule 48 in 1842. The advent of the Great Depression unleashed a torrent of lawsuits against corporations, and in 1937 the high court codified that old rule into a new one, Federal Civil Rule 23.

The stock market collapse and onset of the Depression had led to the near-crumpling of the nation's banking system. A frightening 1,456 banks failed in 1932, and after Franklin Roosevelt's landslide election that year, the pace only picked up. In Washington a consensus quickly developed that new legislation was needed, and fast, to rein in an unregulated banking system that Senator William Gibbs McAdoo of California said colorfully "does credit to a collection of imbeciles." Congressional hearings were held hurriedly—and in Roosevelt's First Hundred Days, Congress passed a sweeping measure called the Banking Act of 1933, popularly known then and forever more as Glass-Steagall, after its authors, Senator Carter Glass of Virginia and Congressman Henry B. Steagall of Alabama. Steagall's passion was federal deposit insurance; Glass was obsessed with forbidding financial institutions from engaging in both commercial and investment banking. The compromise bill that bore their names accomplished both aims.

Revelations unearthed during the 1932 congressional hearings into the banks' relationship with Wall Street led to further reforms. The Truth in Securities Act of 1933, as it was initially called, required new securities to be registered in advance with the Federal Trade Commission and to be accompanied by detailed filings disclosing "every important essential element" of the stock being issued twenty days prior to the stock going up for sale. It also held underwriters and corporate officers responsible for the truthfulness of those representations—a provision that would lead to much litigation in the next half century. The following year the Securities Exchange Act of 1934 extended those provisions to all stocks sold publicly, not just new ones; required financial disclosure from officers of publicly held corporations; gave the Federal Reserve the power of regulating how much purchasers of new securities could rely on bank credit—thus setting the margin rate; and established the Securities and Exchange Commission (SEC) to oversee all this new regulation.

From the start, the SEC was outgunned. Moreover, there were methods to beat the system that had gone unanticipated by Congress. One of them came to light the following decade. In 1942 reports came flooding into SEC headquarters* that companies were defrauding investors by withholding *good* news instead of bad news. Milton Victor Freeman, assistant solicitor for the commission, was informed by SEC regulators in the Boston regional office of a problem in a Holyoke, Massachusetts, firm called American Tissue Mills. Company executives spread rumors that American Tissue was in poor shape—it was actually going gangbusters—then bought up the stock when worried investors began to divest themselves of their shares. Meanwhile an SEC attorney named Mayer U. Newfield had noticed reports of similar activity in other regional offices. In May 1942 Newfield went to Freeman, and the two lawyers hashed over the problem.

Freeman informed Newfield that a section of the 1934 Act, Section 10b, covered fraud in the purchase as well as the sale of securities—and authorized the commission to adopt rules and regulations prohibiting such behavior.

---

* As Washington geared up for war in 1942, the SEC was moved temporarily from the capital to Philadelphia, which is where these events occurred.

"Why don't we just take Section Seventeen under the '33 Act, and insert the word 'purchase,'" Freeman suggested.

"Great," replied Newfield. "That clearly covers the manipulations we are talking about."

And so they did. On May 16, 1942, in a session that took less than ten minutes, the change was made. Four of the five commissioners were present at the meeting, none of whom objected.

"Well, gentlemen," remarked Sumner T. Pike, one of two Republicans on the commission, "we are all against fraud, aren't we?"* In a 1996 letter to Freeman—at the height of the passions in Congress running against Bill Lerach and Mel Weiss over their aggressive methods—Newfield offered his view that the "sole purpose" in adopting the rule was to give the staff of the SEC clear lines of authority and a new enforcement tool for rooting out fraud with regard to the purchase of securities. "No one dreamed at that time of the avalanche of fraud litigation which followed," he said.

Perhaps that was true within the confines of the SEC. But in passing the 1933 Securities Act, Congress clearly had private litigation in mind as a way of reining in crooked corporate executives. No less a legal thinker than Yale law professor and future Supreme Court justice William O. Douglas noted this legislative intent in a 1933 piece he coauthored for Yale's law review.

"The civil liabilities imposed by the Act are not only compensatory in nature, but also *in terrorem* (to frighten)," wrote Douglas and Harvard Business School professor George E. Bates. "They have been set high to guarantee that the risk of their invocation will be effective in assuring that the 'truth about securities' will be told."

Four decades later Mel Weiss persuaded his older partner and mentor Larry Milberg that the updating of Rule 23 in 1966—a step taken to open the courts to victims of racial discrimination—had also increased access to legal redress for disenfranchised investors, including those with claims too

---

* Freeman, in a 1993 foreword to a *Fordham Law Review* article discussing the fiftieth anniversary of Rule 10b-5, recalled the quote in nearly identical language: "Well, we're against fraud, aren't we?"

small or too costly to pursue individually. By coalescing hundreds, even thousands, of such claims by victims with common grievances and representing them all with just a few named claimants, they could initiate class action lawsuits the way civil rights attorneys had fought for the rights of multitudinous victims. What they were doing, and doing consciously, was emulating a famous case that had changed the law and American society. That case was *Brown v. Board of Education.* The case of record ended up as the one involving the school board in Topeka, Kansas, but NAACP lawyers had conjoined separate school desegregation cases from five states into one.

What's more, under a new theory called "fraud on the market" that had been given birth by legal academics—and quickly embraced, applied to Rule 10b-5, and put into practice in class action securities lawsuits by Mel Weiss—these plaintiffs need not have actually seen or relied on misleading statements to bring the lawsuits. If the plaintiffs' attorney could prove that they relied on the public assumption that the market price of a stock reflected the market's response to all the available public information about a company, when, in fact, a fraud had been perpetrated by cooking the books or releasing information that was untrue, a serious securities fraud case would exist. In addition, Weiss postulated that if other parties contributed to this fraud either by endorsing it in their accounting analyses or by helping concoct complex business deals that aided the fraud, those companies—the accountants, investment banks, vendors, even lawyers—could be equally culpable.

There were hurdles. The first was conjuring up the clients to begin with; a second was informing others in the prospective class about a legal action on their behalf. This took time and money, both of which would have to come from those filing the claim. Weiss saw a pathway through the obstacle course. By taking cases on contingency (meaning deriving their fee from only the settlement or judgment, and even fronting the court costs), their firm, Milberg Weiss, would relieve their clients of financial pressure and help convince them to become plaintiffs.

Their first big case, the test case of Weiss's entrepreneurial legal theories, was a lawsuit on behalf of shareholders against Dolly Madison Industries. This suit accused the multistate conglomerate of fraudulently leveraging shareholder money to acquire more than thirty companies in an eighteen-month period. It accused the company of hyping these acquisitions and concealing the financial impact on shareholders in order to inflate the stock price. In short order, the company began writing down its assets and the stock price tanked, but not before insiders in the company unloaded their shares. Further, the company's auditing firm, Touche Ross, one of the renowned Big Eight, had signed off on the books. They too were defendants, under Weiss's "fraud on the market" theory.* The big accounting firm was defended by Louis J. Goffman, one of the lions of the Pennsylvania bar, but by the end of an arduous trial in the summer of 1973, Touche Ross settled for $2 million.

Although paltry in comparison to settlements they would negotiate in the decades ahead, $2 million was a huge amount to recover in 1973. Its impact was even greater: not only could a class action for fraud be waged against the main defendant, it could be successfully deployed against third parties, whom Weiss famously called "schemers."

Free enterprise was about to enter American civil jurisprudence. It was no longer about the law but the business of the law. On both personal and professional levels, Mel Weiss was onto something big with these new strategies. In his mind, he could do good work, gain respect, and make money. In one of the first class action lawsuits against a major accounting firm, the defrauded investors would get some recompense for their losses at Dolly Madison. For making it happen, the law firm of Milberg Weiss earned $500,000.

Milberg Weiss's ascendancy to the top of the plaintiffs' bar would be meteoric. Weiss was already prosecuting another lawsuit in California—in Silicon Valley, although few people called it that yet—against officers of a high-tech company called Ampex. Weiss would employ the "fraud on the

---

* Weiss's legal theory on Dolly Madison was revealed in a subsequent paper: "Why Auditors Have Failed to Fulfill Their Necessary Professional Responsibilities—What to Do About It," Abraham J. Briloff Lecture Series on Accounting and Society, School of Management, State University of New York at Binghamton, 1992.

market" strategy in that case too and have his legal theory affirmed by a federal appellate court.

> • >

WEISS'S SECRETARY HAD RESERVED suites for the U.S. Financial plaintiffs' legal team at the private oceanfront La Jolla Beach and Tennis Club, a luxurious haven within a wealthy enclave, the town of La Jolla, about a twenty-minute drive north of San Diego proper. Lerach and Tom Fort wondered why, if they would be spending most of their time in meetings or in court in downtown San Diego, Weiss had insisted they decamp so far away in the midst of a resort they would not have much chance to enjoy. Their doubts evaporated as soon as they were shown to their rooms overlooking the unblemished, honey-colored sand beach stretching for nearly a mile both north and south. Lerach opened the sliding glass door to his veranda and stood transfixed, listening to the boom and crash of the surf, watching the walkers and joggers, casually enjoying spectacular scenery and perfect weather on a winter's day. He had been on the ground for only an hour, but the moment delivered a couple of epiphanies. First, if this was the style in which Mel Weiss preferred his entourage to travel, Lerach was all for it. The second was the realization that this was where he wanted to live forever.

The next morning they trekked to the federal courthouse in downtown San Diego. A decrepit three-story building, a blend of classicism and Spanish colonial revival designed to recognize San Diego's Hispanic heritage, it had been constructed in 1913 to house the U.S. Post Office, federal offices, and courtrooms. The difference between "quaint" and "deferred maintenance" was obvious to the attorneys as they mounted the steps to the designated courtroom. Lerach flung open the embossed leather door to a room that looked like a throwback to the set from *Inherit the Wind*. It was tiny and packed with lawyers as well as the onlookers anxious to watch them try the biggest civil case in San Diego history.

As he was about to take his seat in the crowd, Lerach noticed the door to the judge's chambers opening slightly and closing and then opening again. From the opening he saw a pair of eyes anxiously regarding the crowd as a performer might from behind a curtain on opening night.

Then the bailiff announced: "All rise." The Honorable U.S. District Court Judge Howard B. Turrentine strode through the door and to the bench.

An elfin man in his early sixties, Turrentine was a native Southern Californian, graduating from San Diego State College and earning his law degree from the University of Southern California. He had served as a Navy lieutenant commander in World War II, then returned to San Diego, where he set up a private practice until being appointed to the county Superior Court bench by Governor Ronald Reagan. A Republican and a friend of C. Arnholt Smith, Turrentine subsequently received an appointment to the federal bench by President Nixon in 1970. Still relatively new, Turrentine was the type of jurist one of the defense lawyers had had in mind in Denver when complaining that no judge in San Diego was sophisticated enough to try a complex financial case.

As the judge took his seat, he scanned the courtroom. Lerach recognized the same eyes that had been peering through the crack in the door.

"Good morning," said the judge. "I have a few matters of housekeeping. First, I wonder if the attorney who suggested that there is insufficient experience among the judges in this city to try a case as financially complex as this one is in the courtroom."

A hard silence ensued, followed by the sounds of people shifting in their seats, making themselves smaller. From the rear of the room a hand went up.

"Would you come up here where I can see you?" ordered the judge.

William R. Norfolk, a young hotshot out of Duke Law School working for Sullivan & Cromwell, one of the world's prestige law firms, and representing Goldman Sachs, climbed sheepishly out of his seat and shuffled toward the bench with the body language, Turrentine thought, of a schoolboy being sent to the principal's office.

"Young man," said the judge, taking the measure of the New York attorney, "before this case is over, I think I'm going to prove you wrong."

Indeed, Turrentine did prove his mettle during the ensuing months, mediating while attorneys for the plaintiffs and defendants battled over interpretations of *borrowing* and *lending* versus *investing*, translating financial statements and auditors' and analysts' reports, challenging each other's expert witnesses, and haggling over the meaning of thousands of documents, posters, graphs, and charts. Neither side was willing to give ground on even the most minor points unless Turrentine moved them along. Eventually the crowd, dulled by the deluge of numbing facts and arcane presentations, began to recede. At the end of each day the withered and frustrated plaintiffs' lawyers would retire to their side of the downstairs bar in the Westgate Plaza Hotel while the defendants' attorneys convened in another corner. Occasionally, if something mutually entertaining had occurred in court that day, the two teams would join each other for rounds of drinks. Earlier, on one such day, the plaintiffs' lawyers were baffled by a batch of documents the defense had turned over. They seemed to lead nowhere, until Weiss weighed in.

"Is this what you are looking for?" Weiss asked the team, reaching into a pile of documents and pulling out a few and explaining their implications as if performing a card trick.

It was blind luck, but Weiss's colleagues were in awe. His theatrical streak was often on display after hours as well. As he contemplated what had brought him to California on this case, Weiss would survey the opulence of the hotel bar, verbally noting the fate of its creator, C. Arnholt Smith, and feel compelled, even in the company of the defense lawyers, to raise his glass and remark, to reassure all present, especially his underlings: "Thank God for greed. Here's hoping it's a growth industry."

> • >

WITH WEISS AND SENIOR COLLEAGUES from the other New York firms taking the lead in trying to prove that their clients' losses were directly attributable to Goldman Sachs, Union Bank, and Touche Ross's scheme to help U.S. Financial commit fraud, Lerach found himself taking depositions with defendants and negotiating with their attorneys behind the scenes. And he also found enjoyment in punching and counterpunching, especially if his side was drawing the most blood.

The case dragged on. Judge Turrentine, determining that the litigation was indeed complex, concluded that he ought to hear it himself on the grounds it might be beyond the comprehension of a jury. By this time Lerach, Fort, Weiss's colleague Irving Morris, and other attorneys had lined up key witnesses—real live victims—who would testify that they had been harmed by U.S. Financial's fraud and by Touche Ross—and they wanted a jury to see them. Weiss challenged the judge's ruling, and Turrentine submitted it to the federal Ninth Circuit Court of Appeals. While it languished there, Lerach continued to negotiate with the defense lawyers for a settlement.

> • >

THE EVENING OF MARCH 29, 1976, Weiss invited Lerach to join him for dinner at the Beverly Hills Hotel in Los Angeles. It was Oscar night. They took their seats indoors at the Polo Lounge and ordered cocktails. Weiss wasted little time getting to the point.

"You've done a good job in steering the settlement effort," he assured Lerach. "This case is still going on for a long time, but I'm confident that we're going to get a huge, big score." Then he told Lerach that he had to return to New York and needed someone on the ground in charge in San Diego.

"We had come to like each other," Lerach recalled. "We were kindred spirits."

Weiss invited Lerach to join his firm. "He wanted me to conclude the case in California and then move to New York . . . I said: 'I don't know. I don't want to do that. I'm going to make partner at Reed Smith this year. I'd like to see if I can stay out here. I'd really like to move to California.'"

Weiss seemed surprised. "I don't know whether there will be any more work going forward out here," he said, adding that nevertheless he'd mull over the idea of a California office and talk it over with his partners in New York.

Lerach had another demand too. He wouldn't join Milberg Weiss unless he was made a partner going in.

Weiss was taken aback for a second time but quickly recovered when the drinks arrived. The two men dined and ordered more drinks, and then, at Weiss's urging, they walked out of the dining room to the front entrance of the hotel. A red carpet had been laid out, and people were collecting on either side. Within minutes a limousine pulled up. Out stepped Richard Burton and Elizabeth Taylor. Lerach thought it was as if the whole scene had been staged by Mel to win him over.

Ultimately, a settlement in the U.S. Financial case would indeed be negotiated—for $62.5 million, the largest settlement for this type of case in history—but that would not happen until early 1978, when the Ninth Circuit reversed Judge Turrentine and ruled that the case could go before a jury, which was a presumptive death knell for the defendants. Turrentine would later award the plaintiffs' lawyers 25 percent of the settlement fee, which pleased Reed Smith, Lerach's old firm, and Milberg Weiss, his prospective employer, which received $5 million of the bounty.

In 1976, long before the settlement, Lerach traveled to New York, meeting and passing muster with Weiss's partners. Lerach joined the Milberg Weiss firm, receiving a $40,000 salary with the designation of partner and a small percent of the overall fees. With the same negotiating panache that he was developing with legal adversaries, Lerach persuaded Weiss to allow him to remain in San Diego, at least as long as he could stay in business. A big dreamer, even he could not have foreseen the cases and the fortune that would come his way.

> • >

BILL LERACH'S MOVE WEST must have been a blow for Evelyn Lerach, who by now was affectionately known as "The Commander" in the Lerach clan, but she kept her tacit agreement with her ambitious younger son and did not try and talk him out of leaving. In fact, she agreed to drive to California with him. So in March 1976 Bill and Evelyn Lerach climbed into Bill's white and blue Pontiac LeMans, stuck his fat dachshund named Gus between them on the bench seat, and set out for a weeklong road trip across the United States. If Evelyn never remonstrated with her younger boy for leaving her behind, she did give him a bit of grief over one aspect of his makeover—and that was his decision to alter the pronunciation of the family name.

In the Ohio River Valley the name "Lerach" is pronounced "Lyric," like the words to a song, which is how his brother, Dick, and most of their kinsmen pronounce it to this day. Bill, explaining that he was tired of correcting people, changed its sound to "Leer-ack," with the emphasis on the first syllable. Bill may have had another reason for changing it, a reason so idiosyncratic that few would have believed it: to his ear, it sounded less Germanic that way.

This, among many other bits of family lore, arose one day in late January 2008 as the two Lerach bothers, Bill "Leer-ack" and Dick "Lyric," took their own road trip through the bleak western Pennsylvania landscape to Morgantown, West Virginia. Although the purpose of the excursion was grim—they were going to visit John Torkelsen, Bill's onetime chief expert witness, now serving time in federal prison—the conversation in the car was tender, entertaining, and at times humorous.

When the subject of their father came up, Bill blurted out a one-word description: "Cheap!"

"Conservative," countered Dick.

"Cheap," Bill repeated.

"Frugal," Dick offered.

"Aggressively and dedicatedly cheap," Bill said, and his older brother started laughing.

On the matter of how to pronounce the family name, however, and where the name comes from, it was Dick who was the more persuasive.

"Our father pronounced it 'Lyric,'" said Dick.

"Changing it was the only thing mother ever criticized me for her entire life," replied Bill.

"It's a German name," said Dick.

"They were French Huguenots who ended up in Austria," replied Bill. "I just don't want to be German!"

Dick was ready for this: "In the spring of 1867, our great-grandfather emigrated to a part of the Austro-Hungarian Empire known as German-Bohemia," he said. "They were ethnic Germans living outside of Germany. Today it's part of the Czech Republic."

"So, not from Germany . . . ," interjected Bill.

"There are seventy Lerachs in the world, they all live in Germany, and one is even named Adolf," Dick continued, a smile playing at the corners of his mouth. "I met one of them, and he said, 'Isn't it a shame we lost the Fatherland . . . but at least some of our people made it to Argentina.'"

Bill couldn't help but smile at this unwanted information, which was delivered deadpan by a brother he loves deeply. But remaking yourself into something that you believe is better—longing to be something noble—is not a habit easily discarded. "It could be that they were really French Huguenots who ended up in Alsace Lorraine," Bill mused aloud, apropos of no known facts. "And Huguenots, as you know, are good people . . ."

> • > • > • > • >

A HOUSE ON THE HILL

Occasionally, while still ensconced at the La Jolla Beach and Tennis Club during the U.S. Financial case, Lerach would allow himself the luxury of strolling to the water's edge and taking in the oceanfront view. When he gazed north past the pier (which serviced the University of California's Scripps Institution of Oceanography), he would scan the caramel-color cliffs, focusing on a single spot. Atop an arrowhead-shaped bluff, the most prominent formation, high above the beach, and overlooking the Pacific perched an enormous mansion. Lerach regarded the copper roof with its green patina and imagined what art treasures lay inside or what beauty its gardens held for an exploring guest or its owner, whom he envied. Once he imagined out loud who might live in such a colossus. An eavesdropper, who shared Lerach's admiration for the clifftop mansion, said breathlessly: "That's the Gagosian mansion." No elaboration was offered. None was needed.

Earl Gagosian, the son of an Armenian immigrant, had started in the hotel business at twenty-three, as a construction supervisor with TraveLodge. He advanced to vice president, then left to launch Royal Inns of America, serving as president and chairman for seven years and building seventy new hotels. Before going bankrupt in the mid-1970s, Gagosian managed to build the 17,000-square-foot mansion on nearly six acres overlooking the ocean high above La Jolla. Its succession of owners included an Iranian coffee baron, a federally protected witness (rumor had it), an acquisition-minded entrepreneur by the name of Edward L. Burns, and billionaire financier Ron Burkle.

Within two years of sighting the mansion, Lerach would bring suit against three companies—Inns of America, Nucorp, and Occidental Petroleum—that had been owned or overseen by three of the mansion's title-holders, Gagosian and Burns and Burkle. Although Lerach didn't do it because he coveted the house, it wasn't quite a coincidence, either. As the 1970s gave way to the 1980s, if you owned a mansion and a company in California, you were increasingly likely to eventually be sued by William S. Lerach. One of his big early lawsuits, and one of his first memorable encounters, would involve a friend of Gagosian's. His name was Kirk Kerkorian.

An eighth-grade dropout and, like Gagosian, the son of an Armenian immigrant, Kerkorian had come a long way since his father was picking fruit in California's Central Valley. After flying in the Royal Air Force during World War II—he couldn't wait for the United States to join the war—Kerkorian flew mail and passengers between Los Angeles and Las Vegas. In 1947 he purchased a small charter airline for ferrying groups to Vegas. It brought in a small fortune, which Kerkorian parlayed into a series of real estate deals, which among other treasures landed him title to the Flamingo and the land under Caesar's Palace, the new jewel of the Las Vegas strip. But he soon ran afoul of the Securities and Exchange Commission and his lenders. Under pressure from Bank of America, Kerkorian sold most of his Las Vegas holdings, including his private plane. But as he folded camp in Nevada, Kerkorian reminded friends and colleagues to always "keep a back door open." For him that door was Hollywood.

Starting in 1969 he had been buying stock in the once-mighty MGM studios. At the beginning of 1970 Kerkorian, by securing more loans from Bank of America, attained working control of the ailing studio, which announced soon after Kerkorian assumed the helm that it would "embark on a significant and far-reaching diversification into the leisure field." The first big splash would be the MGM Grand Hotel in Las Vegas. Kerkorian would be returning to Vegas as its king. Groundbreaking took place in 1972, with a legion of stars, champagne, and networking entertainment executives.

The twenty-six-story MGM Grand opened on December 5, 1973, featuring 2,084 rooms, a 1,200-seat showroom, a cavernous shopping arcade, a movie theater, and a jai alai court. The cost to build the world's largest hotel was $107 million, a price tag that led Bill Lerach to visit Kerkorian's Beverly Hills office one day in 1977. Lerach was representing shareholders who maintained that the King of Vegas had diluted the value in his own company to save himself from financial ruin.

The case had been initiated by a New York attorney, Ron Litowitz, a partner at Bernstein, Litowitz, Berger & Grossman, and it was to be heard in the Delaware Chancery Court. That firm would handle the Delaware part of the case, but it needed a West Coast representative, and Lerach had been asked to participate. It was a "derivatives" case, meaning that the alleged cause of action was that corporate executives were breaching their fiduciary responsibility by not operating the company in a way that benefited the majority of shareholders. It was a new area of law to Lerach, and a tricky one. These cases were normally centered in Delaware, a state where the civil courts were considered unfriendly to plaintiffs' lawsuits.

"The field was not level," Lerach recalled. "So plaintiffs did what plaintiffs normally do in that environment, they pestered and pecked and settled their cases cheaply and made their living." What he was describing was a practice that he would perfect in time—peck and pester until the defendant caved. Others—industry CEOs, members of Congress, even Supreme Court justices—would have a different regard for this practice. They would call such lawsuits "frivolous."

Lerach began by demanding MGM's financials. After poring through these documents, he gleefully described them to Mel Weiss as a "factual goldmine." The financial statements, loan and sales documents, memoranda of understanding, and demands for repayment on loans provided a map of what Lerach called "a road to hell being pursued with abandon." Gradually he would put together a picture of Kerkorian that was far different from the cool-hand Las Vegas financial impresario whom the public had known and admired. Kerkorian was running out of money. A gas shortage, the first in modern American history, meant that Americans were neither flying nor driving as much. His two Las Vegas enterprises, his charter airline company, and his hotels were losing money.

Kerkorian had turned his attention to Hollywood and MGM not because he was enamored with the film industry but because of MGM's real estate—specifically, its lots in Culver City. He closed the studio's sales and distribution arm. He sold forty valuable acres. Yet he still owed money to Bank of America, and as construction on the MGM Grand ran late and over budget, Kerkorian had sold off MGM's props, furnishings, and memorabilia, including the red slippers Judy Garland had worn in *The Wizard of Oz*. "He's in hock up to his eyeballs," Lerach recalled. "Right as these events are reaching thermonuclear crisis, MGM, which hasn't made a nickel or paid a dividend in years, announces it's paying a special dividend. Of course the biggest beneficiary is Kerkorian, who owns fifty-one percent of the company."

It was an audacious declaration from someone in such desperate straits. The records Lerach and his colleagues were reviewing yielded revealing insights into just how desperate and daring Kerkorian, who emerged a multibillionaire, had been with his gamble. The initial loans to secure the Las Vegas property had been unsecured with Bank of America. Lerach ultimately concluded that the loans to Kerkorian were so tenuous that they threatened Bank of America itself. "They were loaning him money for the interest so they could avoid having to write down the loan," Lerach said. Over the next ten years Lerach would repeatedly encounter this tactic, which contributed to the demise of Drexel Burnham, Continental Bank, Lincoln Savings and Loan, and other financial institutions of their ilk. He would make his reputation ferreting out such fraud—and suing its perpetrators. "Your interest gets paid and it looks like the loan is current. Bank examiners look for loans that are not keeping current," Lerach recalled. "The bank was trying to avoid exposure. Kerkorian knew it."

With Lerach on his tail, Bank of America chairman A. W. "Tom" Clausen called a meeting with Kerkorian and his attorneys. Bank of America demanded its interest payments. Kerkorian balked, pointing out the delicate situation that both he and Clausen were in, at least until the MGM Grand was up and running. Clausen would not yield: enough was enough. He granted Kerkorian a small amount of time to gather the money, and the two parted civilly. Kerkorian and his attorneys worked every financial network at their disposal. Finally they arranged for a $9 million short-term loan from a bank in Düsseldorf, Germany. When that bridge loan came due, the Germans wouldn't budge on extending it, despite a personal visit to Germany by Kerkorian. He managed to avoid disaster by selling the studio's one remaining precious asset—the MGM film library, containing immortal movies such as *Gone with the Wind, West Side Story,* and *The Wizard of Oz.* The buyer was Ted Turner, who proved himself as shrewd as Kerkorian. Not only did Turner purchase the multimillion-dollar assets for less than $9 million, he later converted the film library into television content through his Turner Network Television, earning billions in the process.

For his part, Kerkorian not only dodged a bullet but went on to repurchase MGM and own half the hotel rooms on the Las Vegas Strip, becoming even richer than Turner. But not before, as Lerach liked to recall, "I was right up Kerkorian's ass."

"He had virtually given away the film library," Lerach said. "He had wasted the corporate asset in a crisis to save his own ass rather than auctioning it off to the highest bidder or taking steps to sell in a way as to maximize its value."

This was the basis of the shareholder lawsuit against Kerkorian. After reviewing company documents and those from the Bank of America, and deposing dozens of witnesses including Clausen, Lerach believed he had Kerkorian cornered. As he and Ron Litowitz rode the elevators to the offices of Wyman, Bautzer, Rothman & Kuchel (atop one of the towers in Century City in West Los Angeles) to take Kerkorian's deposition, the two attorneys discussed using a good cop/bad cop routine. Litowitz would be the diplomat; Lerach would be the bad cop. He could hardly wait.

They were ushered into a small conference room with a round table. Seated were Frank Rothman, Kerkorian's attorney, one of his associates, and a clerk. As if on cue, once everyone was in place, Kerkorian sauntered in, glistening with confidence. He wore a lush dark brown suede jacket and brilliant white shirt that contrasted with his lined and tanned face and jet-black hair.

Lerach unfolded a large file and began his questions, going slowly, plodding over details. Within minutes Rothman sensed that this session was going to be painstaking. After letting a few more questions and answers go by, the attorney interrupted, reminding Kerkorian that he was due for his lunch at the Beverly Hills Hotel in forty-five minutes. Lerach kept his head down and questioned his prey, who, it was clear, had been prepped to provide indefinite, but not untruthful, recollections.

"Do you remember negotiating loans from the Bank of America?"

Kerkorian was vaguely aware of them.

"Do you remember pledging your yacht?"

Kerkorian couldn't remember.

"Your house?"

Same answer.

Rothman was growing even more impatient. "When are you going to ask something relevant?" he snapped.

Lerach shuffled his files and flipped open documents like a card dealer. "Do you remember meeting with executives of a German bank?"

"I may have. I just don't remember," came Kerkorian's reply.

No fool, Rothman saw where the line of questioning was heading. Kerkorian had been doing what he was told to do, answer vaguely, avoid direct responses, and volunteer no facts. But now Lerach had him outright lying.

"Do you remember meeting with German bank officials in New York?"

Kerkorian had been to New York often—he just couldn't remember if he had met German bankers there. He was being slowly bled by adhering to Lerach's script. Rothman could see things falling apart.

"Are you familiar with Mr. Clausen?" Lerach asked.

Kerkorian allowed that he was.

"Do you have any reason to doubt Mr. Clausen's integrity?"

Kerkorian saw no reason not to sing the praises of the Bank of America chairman, and he did so, although he did not identify Clausen as his personal loan manager. More documents were produced along with more questions about when the Bank of America loans were due and why Kerkorian had sought financial assistance from the Germans. Lerach could feel heat rising from Rothman, who was beginning to rise from his chair.

Quickly, Lerach pulled the trump card: "Do you recall the Germans threatening to drag you into bankruptcy unless you paid back your loan?"

The question had barely left Lerach's mouth when Rothman was on his feet, towering over the table. "How dare you demean this man! He is a great American. I will not tolerate this kind of impudence."

Lerach felt a flush of fear as Kerkorian, who as a young man had boxed under the moniker "Rifle Right Kerkorian," rose out of his chair as well. But the former prizefighter grabbed Rothman and spun him around and out the door.

In the elevator Litowitz, somewhat shaken, recovered enough to say: "I think we got their goat." It was a phrase Lerach would himself utter happily thousands of times over the next thirty years. And he would be speaking of some of the most powerful business chiefs in America.

Within a week Lerach received a telephone call from his New York colleague. Frank Rothman had called. They wanted no more depositions, no more questions. They wanted to settle. The amount would be well into seven figures.

For a shareholder derivative settlement, this was huge. Still, Mel Weiss and Bill Lerach (who had not been the counsel of record) believed they had missed an opportunity: Bank of America had not been named a defendant. That was where the deep pockets were. They would not make such an oversight again. In the hundreds of lawsuits they would file in the future, and after the billions they would collect in settlements and awards, neither man could recall ever overlooking another wealthy culpable defendant. For now, however, Mel Weiss was pleased.

Not long after the Kerkorian settlement, Lerach received a phone call from Weiss. The U.S. Financial settlement was in the works; the settlement with Kerkorian had been more than anyone expected. Weiss had been looking at the *New York Times* real estate section.

"There are a couple of nice-looking houses near you," he told his young partner. "You ought to take a look."

Lerach, who had just installed a swimming pool and Jacuzzi in the house he was sharing with his wife, Kelly, on a lovely cul-de-sac in San Diego, demurred. "I don't read the *New York Times* real estate section," he replied.

"No attorney of my firm is going to be living where you live in a house like that," Weiss inveighed. "There's this place up in Del Mar for around $750,000—"

Lerach gasped, saying he couldn't imagine paying that much for a house. "Listen to me," Weiss retorted. "You can afford it. Believe me. You're going to make lots of money."

Twenty-five years later that prophecy would be manifested in full. In 2005 Lerach would move into a La Jolla blufftop mansion nestled into its own peninsula overlooking the sea. The house was the largest single-family oceanfront property in San Diego County. It featured imported limestone, eighteen-foot-tall cypresses, a home theater accessed by an elevator, numerous patios, a pool and tennis court, servants' quarters, antique fountains from Italy and France, and the breathtaking sobriquet "Jewel in the crown of La Jolla" from the local press.

The house had been built in 1990, replacing its razed predecessor, the mansion Bill Lerach had first glimpsed from below, the estate once known as the Gagosian mansion.

> • > • > • > • >

OGRE OF THE VALLEY

In his office forty-nine floors above Penn Station in midtown Manhattan, Lerach's partner and mentor got struck by gold—or maybe it was gold lust.

"Seymour Lazar," the voice at the other end of the telephone told Mel Weiss. "You remember me? I'm the guy you once sued. The Armour lawsuit? You lost."

Weiss remembered. In 1973 he'd brought a securities class action lawsuit on behalf of Armour & Co. shareholders, after the Securities and Exchange Commission had accused a group of rogue shareholders (among them Lazar, then a high-profile attorney) of trying to manipulate the price of Armour stock in order to acquire the giant food company. "You do remember me, then?" Lazar continued, in that fateful 1976 phone call. "I'm also the Howard Hughes guy. You've heard about that, right?"

Who hadn't?

Earlier that year Lazar had generated sensational headlines along with Los Angeles "palimony" attorney Marvin M. Mitchelson for promoting a sketchy document as the handwritten will of the late billionaire Howard Hughes. It was determined to be a fake, but Mitchelson and Lazar generated buckets of publicity championing the claims of their client, a service station owner named Melvin Earl Dummar. It was only the latest in a litany of legal dustups in which Seymour Lazar had made—or lost—millions of dollars. He was a hard man to keep down, however, and he would again make a fortune while helping Mel Weiss and Bill Lerach reap a windfall of their own. He was trouble, no question, but like all talented con men, he could make outsize greed sound as normal as spring rain.

Born in 1928, Lazar grew up in the San Fernando Valley and graduated from University of Southern California's School of Law in 1951, intending to be an entertainment attorney and impresario. He was diminutive, with unlimited chutzpah. His client base included comedian Lenny Bruce, jazz trumpeter Miles Davis, Broadway producer David Merrick, and Johnny Rivers, who told *The Wall Street Journal* that Lazar helped him negotiate his first recording contract shortly before he generated a string of hits, including "Secret Agent Man." Lazar's array of friends encompassed beat poet Allen Ginsberg, criminal defense lawyer Melvin Belli, LSD guru Timothy Leary, and corporate raider Meshulam Riklis. Still another was a young Hollywood cabaret singer from the 1950s. "I was very shapely and nice to look at, but Seymour saw more than that," recalled Maya Angelou, the singer-turned-poet-laureate. "He knew I was always writing and encouraged me to be more than a cocktail singer." The two dated and remained longtime friends.

Lazar, driving a Rolls-Royce and living in Beverly Hills, was ever the boulevardier (he said Pierre Cardin made him a leather suit) when he grew bored with being a lawyer. He had sued his own father, who had disinherited him. But Lazar's real talent, he soon found, was in predicting mergers and acquisitions and trading on the parties' stocks. Lazar's broker, B. Gerald Cantor, founder of the then-small Beverly Hills retail firm Cantor Fitzgerald & Co., introduced him to Riklis, who complained to Lazar about being a frequent target of shareholder lawsuits and about the damned attorneys who earned their livings suing corporations and the executives and boards who ran them. Lazar remembered thinking it sounded like an easy way to make money.

Lazar moved to Palm Springs, where he invested in land that no one had yet envisioned for development, and bought into oil wells. Sitting on the bougainvillea-bedecked patio of his Palm Springs villa, he studied the financial press. Mel Weiss, he saw, had tapped into a growing pattern of corporate misdeeds. That led to his 1976 telephone call to Weiss. "If I read *The Wall Street Journal*," he boasted to Weiss, "I can come up with a class action a day."

Then he cited the Ampex case, *Blackie v. Barrack*, a pioneering victory that Mel Weiss had achieved in federal district court less than a year earlier. Prior to *Blackie*, lawyers could sue for securities fraud only if they could prove that individual plaintiffs had actually read and relied on misleading statements or were kept in the dark by purposeful omissions. The new ruling determined that members of a class did not have to have personally been misled by omissions—or even to have read the statements—in order to collect damages. Accepting the logic of academic theories presented by Weiss and the other plaintiffs' attorneys, the court ruled that investors could properly rely on the information available to anyone—how the market was responding. An efficient market would reflect all the necessary information about a company; thus the price was an aggregate score of how the stock market reacted to a company's statements. The market itself was the de facto reader. Of course, the market could be fooled. That was the point. That was why Lazar was calling Mel Weiss. Indeed, this decision would help Lazar change his life. He was offering to help change Weiss's life too.

"You are too busy being lawyers," Lazar told Weiss. What the firm really needed, in order to be competitive, was a professional stalking horse—to hunt for securities class action cases. Lazar was offering to *sell*, not lend, his name as the lead plaintiff.

Weiss was impressed. He wanted to lock in a plaintiff he could count on. His mind moving quickly, he also realized the drawbacks. His practice was based on contingency fees. If he were to advance Lazar for his time and effort, the firm would have to front the money. The only way to pay him would be contingent on the results, just as the firm was paid its fees based on the awards in their cases. Overriding that consideration was another, larger one. In class actions, in order to avoid conflicts with the rest of the class of plaintiffs, it was illegal to pay individual plaintiffs. On the other hand, lawyers referred cases to other lawyers all the time. For this they received referral fees, which *were* legal. If Lazar would accept deferred compensation, and if he would receive it as an attorney bringing litigation "ideas" to Milberg Weiss for a referral fee, a percentage of the award, then maybe they could do business.

Lazar was way ahead of him. He already worked with a Riverside, California, law firm, Best, Best & Krieger. Why not designate one of the partners in the firm—Paul Selzer, Lazar's real estate attorney—to receive the referral fees?

Weiss said he would confer with David Bershad, his managing partner, who controlled the accounts payable. Bershad, then thirty-seven, was the polar opposite of Mel Weiss. A philosophy major at Cornell, class of 1961, he graduated from Columbia Law School in 1964, where he'd been a star in the school's moot court competition. Bershad was reticent, especially when it came to opening the firm's safe, which was literally locked in a credenza in his office. He would approve the relationship with Lazar only if it flowed through the Riverside law firm and only if the firm filled out a 1099 federal tax form for its referral fee. Weiss then telephoned Lazar, offering him up to 10 percent of the firm's fee, should they win—and nothing if they lost. Like the firm itself, everyone connected to it had to put themselves at risk. Lazar, who had made courting risk his profession, accepted.

First into the Milberg Weiss stable, Lazar would continue his business relationship with the firm for the next twenty-five years, picking off targets such as Bear Stearns, Lockheed, Pacific Gas & Electric, United Airlines, Standard Oil, Genentech, Denny's Restaurants, W. R. Grace, New Image, Xerox, Prudential Insurance, Occidental Health, and Standard Oil/British Petroleum in more than seventy lawsuits that returned $44 million to the firm.

> • >

IN SAN DIEGO, Bill Lerach was reading the financial sections himself. One day he noticed that the Walt Disney Company had announced what seemed a routine real estate transaction. Lerach's mind was conditioned to think of the possible grift first, the innocent explanation second. When

Walt Disney erected his famous theme park in Orange County, California, he had built a train that ran around the perimeter of Disneyland. The narrow-gauge line had cost $240,000 in 1955. Walt Disney owned it himself, and now his heirs were planning to sell the railroad to the company—in exchange for stock. "Wait a minute!" Lerach said to himself. "Why would the Disney family want more stock in Disney?" A possible answer hit him quickly: "A takeover is coming. They know it's coming. They know the stock will pop—and they are getting themselves into position to take advantage of this knowledge before their shareholders."

Lerach has never revealed how he found a willing client to act as a plaintiff—it was not Lazar—but he was the first to file a complaint in Los Angeles Superior Court. Lerach requested the court's help in speeding up the discovery process of evidence that would enable him to ask for an injunction to stop the sale. The Disney lawyers knew where Lerach was going and wanted to head him off. A hearing was convened.

The small courtroom was made to seem even smaller by the galaxy of Disney lawyers assembled to rebuke Lerach's intervention. Their body language revealed their disdain. Not only was this upstart from San Diego besmirching an icon; he was insinuating himself into the business affairs of one of the most profitable and respectable businesses in America. There, for the defense, was Leonard S. Janofsky, a partner of one of the foremost firms in Los Angeles and former president of both the California Bar Association and the American Bar Association. Joining the defense team was former head of the American Bar Foundation Seth Hufstedler, whose wife, Shirley, also an attorney, was serving as secretary of education in the Carter administration; Robert Warren, the managing partner of Gibson Dunn and Crutcher, one of the nation's most distinguished law firms; and half a dozen other legal luminaries. Together they shared hundreds of years of experience in corporate legal matters.

Janofsky scorned Lerach's action as a predatory "strike suit" aimed at Walt Disney's beloved widow, Lillian, and other members of the Disney family, but the trial judge reminded Janofsky of the court's obligation to render justice fairly and treat counsel for both sides with respect. Without fanfare the court granted Lerach's motion to expedite the discovery process.

Before he could file for an injunction to stop the railroad transaction, Lerach received a phone call from a conciliatory Bob Warren, representing the defense. Warren proposed a settlement in return for dropping the case. Lerach agreed.

Within weeks of the settlement Lerach heard the news he had been expecting: the Disney company was indeed the target of a hostile takeover attempt. The man trying to get it was Saul P. Steinberg, a notorious corporate raider, whose Disney foray popularized the term *greenmail*—the act of taking money midway through a takeover bid just to go away. Helping Steinberg finance the assault on Disney was Drexel Burnham Lambert, along with a rogues' gallery of other operators, some with their own agendas: Ivan F. Boesky, Sid Richardson Bass, Irwin "Irv the Liquidator" Jacobs—and Lerach's previous foil, Kirk Kerkorian.

"We sued them again," Lerach said, referring to a second suit against both Disney and Steinberg for their greenmail deal. The defendants offered to settle for $5 million. The plaintiffs' attorneys, Lerach and J. Michael Hennigan, a partner at the Los Angeles firm of Hennigan & Mercer, demanded $45 million. The case went to trial in June 1989, five years after it was filed. Michael H. Diamond, a partner at the Los Angeles office of Skadden, Arps, Slate, Meagher & Flom, led the Disney defense team. Diamond would always remember Lerach as being "extremely aggressive and extremely well prepared."

One of the first to suffer Lerach's lashes was former Disney CEO Ronald W. Miller, Walt Disney's son-in-law. Although Miller was a large and physically rugged man—he'd played tight end on the football team at Southern Cal and, for a year, with the Los Angeles Rams—he had been devastated when he was ousted as chairman five years earlier, sobbing at his desk when he received the news.

Now he was to relive some of that grief.

The case was tried in state court, before Los Angeles County Superior Court Judge Abby Soven. This was a case "of blackmail euphemistically called greenmail," Lerach told the judge passionately. "The raider was enriched [while] the directors were entrenched." The defendants, he added, "worked together for their own selfish ends."

When Lerach got Miller on the stand, he asked Miller about his children's sale of Disney stock one month before the 1984 greenmail payment to Steinberg—after which the stock dropped nearly $15 in two days. Miller expressed resentment at Lerach's implication. Those who witnessed the exchange saw what would become a characteristic Lerach response: dancing eyes, puckering lips, and an explicit putdown. Lerach asked Disney's ex-CEO what he did the day after Steinberg launched his takeover bid, reminding the witness that it occurred on a Friday afternoon.

"Did you go to the office?" Lerach asked.

"No. I didn't go to the office because the conversations were taking place in New York . . ."

"You went and played golf?"

"Yes."

"Did the same thing on Sunday?"

"Yes."

After three weeks of such testimony—before the defense even put on its case—Steinberg and Disney's directors settled for what Lerach had originally proposed: $45 million. The settlement put corporate executives on notice: they could be sued coming or going. As for the particular lead counsel in this case, it was clear that once Bill Lerach got his teeth into a case, he would keep chewing.

Lerach settled into a venue that allowed him to continue honing his skills. By picking and choosing his cases, he was able to bide his time and to choose his prey shrewdly. It would soon be said of him that, like the greenmail artists, he was really demanding payment from those he sued merely to go away; but his technique worked only because he prepared each case as if it were going to a jury trial. After the Pacific Homes case, the Southern California legal community was all too aware that Bill Lerach was confident of his chances with a jury and quite willing to go to trial. This was a fate most corporate defendants and their counsel (and many plaintiffs' attorneys) dreaded. Jury trials take time, energy, and revenue. Preparation is difficult, and the cost of a trial, with attorneys' fees and expert witnesses factored in, could run upward of $50,000 per day. Worse, outcomes were unpredictable, a lesson that Lerach himself was to learn later, when he became a defendant in a large civil suit. In these years as a plaintiffs' lawyer, however, Lerach was perfecting his skill at laying out compelling narratives in court complaints—instruments of torture, he called the documents. In the right-hand corner of every cover of every complaint, Lerach consistently inserted the words: *Plaintiffs Demand a Trial by Jury.* Attorneys who opposed him, some bitterly, invariably expressed admiration for the thorough level of pretrial preparations undertaken by the senior partner in the West Coast offices of Milberg Weiss.

Another Lerach trait, however, drew fierce contempt from corporate defense lawyers and in boardrooms from Silicon Valley to Wall Street: Lerach simply presumed that deceit and market manipulation were more likely to cause large profits than, say, a particular executive's business acumen. Lerach fancied that he possessed such a keen sense for corruption that he could practically sniff out the fraudulent deals. What was undeniably true—he demonstrated this time after time—was that Lerach had a knack for boring in on witnesses and defendants during depositions, negotiations, or trials, exposing their vulnerabilities and helping his own case. Whether this was due to the ubiquitousness of frauds, to Lerach's nose for vice, or simply to his interrogating skill wasn't really the point. The end result was usually the same: a large settlement and occasionally a large judgment in his favor.

> • >

IN 1981 MILBERG WEISS filed suit against an American icon, Mattel Inc. It wasn't the first time the much-beloved (by kids) company had been sued in a class action securities case—and it wouldn't be the last. Mattel was launched in 1945 out of a garage workshop in Southern California by Ruth and Elliott Handler. In 1955 the fledgling company rolled the dice by borrowing all it could to advertise its toys on *The Mickey Mouse Club.* Sales took off. "Barbie," and then "Ken," soon followed. By 1963 the Hawthorne, California–headquartered firm went public, and its marketing slogan—"If it's Mattel, it's swell"—had become virtually a national anthem. Attempting to grow too big too fast, however, Mattel acquired six firms, four of which flopped; and it decentralized its operations, which increased its overhead. To cover up its mistakes, Mattel played loose with the books. When it came to honest accounting, Mattel was anything but swell.

Mattel signed a consent decree with the SEC agreeing to establish an "audit committee" and purged its executive ranks, but the damage had been done—shareholders lost millions of dollars. Then pioneering securities class action lawyer David B. Gold of San Francisco, Bill Lerach, and a flock of other plaintiffs' lawyers entered the picture. Five class action securities suits were filed against Mattel; the company would settle them for some $30 million. Even that wasn't the end of the litigation. Further frauds were detected, and Milberg Weiss would file two more class action lawsuits against the company on behalf of shareholders hurt by Mattel's mismanagement. (Two decades later, under different management of what had become a huge conglomerate, disastrous executive decisions led to a meltdown of Mattel's stock price. Bill Lerach would lead litigation that garnered a $122 million settlement for shareholders.)

All that was in the future. On a winter's day in late 1981 Lerach and Sherrie R. Savett, a young associate at the Philadelphia firm of Berger & Montague, were suing Mattel in a smaller case. Arrayed against them was a formidable Southern California law firm named Irell & Manella and one of its best litigators, Richard H. Borow. Their attorneys, Lerach believed, were thwarting his attempts to ferret out information from witnesses and company officers who might have committed fraud. Dick Borrow challenged the two plaintiffs' lawyers on issue after issue until Lerach concluded that stalling was part of his strategy—under the theory that the defense team had time on its side because it was being paid by the hour, as opposed to investing its own money in hopes of winning a contingency fee.

Borow's characterization at the time—and it remains so nearly thirty years later—was that he never forestalled any legitimate discovery requests from the plaintiffs, and that the pretrial tactics used by his firm were zealous but completely appropriate. Either way the strategy inexorably slowed the pace of litigation, for Lerach and Savett were indeed feeling the squeeze of time and money.

The case was being heard in federal court in Los Angeles, where Borow and his colleagues were old hands. They had drawn Judge Manuel L. Real, an owlish-looking but imposing and controversial judge whom Lyndon Johnson had appointed to the federal bench in 1966. Real was controversial as much for the way he handled his courtroom as for his legal decisions. ("This isn't Burger King," he would tell lawyers in his courtroom. "We don't do it your way here!") He earned the dubious distinction of being the most reversed federal judge by the Ninth Circuit Court of Appeals. Mercurial, tempestuous, and a stickler for detail, Real insisted on a strict schedule— he thought no civil suit should take longer than 120 days to come to trial.

As the Mattel case neared, Lerach and Savett worked eighteen- and nineteen-hour days to prepare. Richard Borow worked hard, too. "Every document we asked for was fought over," Lerach recalled. "Dick Borow would challenge me every step of the way." One day, during depositions, Borow instructed one of his clients not to answer a Lerach question.

Lerach thought defense counsel had gone too far. "I'm not taking this crap any longer," he announced. "I'm going to call Judge Real."

Calling a judge was not part of the federal court protocol. As Lerach later remembered it, defense lawyers scoffed, advising the young litigator to take two aspirin until the feeling passed. Instead, Lerach picked up the phone. The attorneys were still mocking him. He reached Judge Real's secretary. He complained to her. He wanted the judge to straighten out the opponents. Suddenly Lerach found himself talking to the judge.

"Is there a speaker phone there?" the judge asked.

Lerach answered affirmatively.

"Are defense counsel there?"

Again Lerach said yes.

"Tell me what is going on," Real said.

One by one the defense attorneys, all known to the judge, explained that the depositions were taking a little longer than usual, nothing out of the ordinary, the judge could certainly understand . . .

A moment of silence on the other end of the line was followed by a firm, crisp instruction: "I have a calendar opening at four-thirty this afternoon. At that time we will have a conference call and I will want both sides to present their positions."

Later that afternoon, the two sides presented their arguments. Borow and his team offered examples of questions that they had deemed improper. Lerach and Savett barraged the judge with examples of questions they had been unable to secure answers for, explaining why the queries were essential to the case moving forward. Lerach and Savett made a point of implying that they were trying to follow the judge's instructions to be ready for trial by the date he had set.

Finally the judge's voice boomed through the speaker phone: "I want these depositions to go forward. I expect these questions to be answered. As for you Mr. Lerach, if you have any more problems, feel free to call my chambers at the end of any day."

The fight in the Mattel case became so intense and, Lerach thought, so personal that he vowed that after it was over he would never speak to Dick Borow again. Borow was having different thoughts. He wasn't taking things as personally. He respected Lerach's pit-bull style, and although he was using every stratagem he knew, he sensed that the plaintiffs' attorneys were making inroads.

As is customary in civil litigation of this type, the defense attorneys sought a summary judgment—a motion to dismiss the case for lack of evidence. Lerach would always recall opening the hearing on the motion to dismiss on the wrong note: he had the wrong title on a piece of paper, which was the kind of error that typically set Real off. The judge didn't miss the opportunity to caustically correct the young plaintiffs' lawyer, but in the end he denied the defense motion and ordered that the trial go forward.

With the case on track for trial, Lerach soon received a call from his nemesis. Dick Borow wanted to know if there was a settlement demand, a call that often signals the beginning of a negotiation to avoid a trial. And so it was in this case. Eventually the parties agreed on a figure of $3.9 million, a healthy amount at the time. More cases, and much bigger payoffs, were coming. In some of those cases, opposing counsel would be Richard H. Borow. Unexpectedly, a mutual respect spilled into a friendship.

> • >

"I HAVE THE GREATEST law practice in the world. I have no clients." It became the quote heard round the boardrooms, used against Lerach by his detractors and self-described blood enemies as proof of his cynicism, his arrogance, his boastfulness, his worthiness of being regarded as "less than pond scum."

He had been describing to a *Forbes* reporter the business model of Milberg *West*, as it was now called, especially by Lerach's colleagues at Milberg *East*. Actually, Lerach's early business model was no model at all—it was essentially a race to the courthouse, with the goal being to be the first to file. Lerach had no previous experience drumming up cases and was new to California, so initially his cases came from eastern referrals, most of them from his own firm, which was now officially named Milberg, Weiss, Bershad, Schulman & Lerach.

And though Seymour Lazar's gambit to Mel Weiss was particularly brazen, it seemed—to Milberg Weiss's partners, at least—the next logical step in an emerging legal specialty: class action security lawsuits. Law firms pursuing such cases were nurturing a pool of people willing to purchase small shares of stock in hundreds of companies listed on the New York Stock Exchange. By so doing they became potential clients. In a way, class action lawsuits on contingencies were more like attorney-client investments. Success in such cases bred more success, and the word circulated in the plaintiffs' bar: there were two sizzling-hot trial lawyers to call on behalf of their clients. The first was San Francisco's David Gold, the dean of the West Coast class action lawyers; the second "it" barrister was none other than Bill Lerach, the upstart who was beginning to carve up big companies and carve out large fees. Both were viewed as highly competent and tough. And they got results, sometimes in tandem. Lerach and Gold combined on several high-profile cases. One was against Memorex, one of the first suits against a Silicon Valley company, which returned $25 million. Another was a suit against Washington Public Power, or WPPS (pronounced "Whoops"), the largest municipal bond default in history ($2.5 billion), which, after Milberg Weiss took the case to trial, yielded a series of settlements that recovered $750 million for shareholders, the largest ever reached at the time.

With these settlements came renown among the plaintiffs' bar—and other lawyers came knocking on Lerach's door. That meant he set the rules of the game. A partner of another firm, preferably but not always Milberg East, would bring Lerach plaintiffs in class action lawsuits, presumably with big potential payouts. Lerach started to draw the line at a minimum $5 million potential fee, which meant targeting at least $50 million for a judgment or settlement. He would file the suit on the West Coast, and he would control the case, either as lead or as cocounsel, while the referring law firm was responsible for its client.

"These suits were not clientless, but obviously clients had minimal impact because they lack the sophistication to control them [the lawsuits]," he said in a magazine interview. "They are just shareholders. I don't consult with them on tactics, although I keep them posted. Client involvement would restrict my ability to litigate with budgetary considerations."

By the late 1970s the flow of clients from east to west became so great that Lerach had no need to generate his own. Seymour Lazar became a regular after receiving his first payback of approximately $40,000 on April 19, 1984, for acting as a plaintiff in a civil case in San Mateo County, California. Lerach was enjoying a litigator's dream. He was being bankrolled by Milberg East, which took care of all administrative concerns, and he had a steady stream of plaintiffs. "All I had to do was bring the cases," he said.

Lerach's workload increased exponentially. Soon he perfected a kind of modern assembly line that would have done the industrial barons of turn-of-the-century Pittsburgh proud. It didn't produce machines, or steel beams, or any product. It produced lawsuits. By the late 1980s Milberg West was filing—and settling—securities class action lawsuits so fast, and for so much money, that Lerach designated a firm partner named Keith Park to see the paperwork through on the settlements. Park was known for being meticulous, not showy. He was the first lawyer Lerach hired in Milberg Weiss's California office, and he lacked the stomach for the pressurized, high-wire litigation that made the firm notorious. Likewise, Lerach lacked enthusiasm for the tedious follow-through required on his cases. Yet Park's paperwork was hardly unimportant. As the firm's fee on many of these settlements was worth millions—or tens of millions—dotting the *i*'s and crossing the *t*'s on the negotiated paperwork was an essential task.

In time, the fees became so large that just a few days' delay in being paid could mean the loss of a significant sum of money. For this reason Lerach instituted a new policy with the companies, lawyers, and insurers who sought to avoid a trial by paying a settlement: interest on the agreed-upon amount—generally about 8 percent—began on the day of the handshake cementing the deal. Many of the lawyers opposing Lerach would rather have knifed him in the gut than shake his hand. But shake his hand they did, and the money rolled into Milberg Weiss's coffers.

His firm so dominated the field of class action securities lawsuits that "if other firms did not come to us with California cases, they very much risked being excluded altogether from these cases," Lerach wrote in an article, recounting the history of Milberg Weiss. This was another line that would come back to haunt him. He would later be characterized as a "Godfather, or Mafia-like character," who either blackmailed other firms into referring their cases and clients or was capable of muscling out the competition. He would not argue with at least some part of that assessment.

Meanwhile machinations in Washington helped cement Lerach's position.

In March 1980, with deregulation all the rage in politics, Congress passed the Depository Institutions Deregulation and Monetary Control Act. The new law, hailed as the first sweeping reform of U.S. banking laws since the Great Depression, had a number of provisions, among them lowering the level of funds that banks and savings and loans (known as "thrifts") had to keep in reserve; letting state-chartered banks charge the same interest rates as federal banks; and allowing thrifts to offer trust accounts and to make consumer loans up to 20 percent of their total assets. This act was signed into law by President Carter, who in his last State of the Union address singled it out as one of his signature achievements.

The following year a Democratic House and a Republican Senate passed an even more sweeping law called the Depository Institutions Act, which largely unfettered savings and loans from their historic function of providing home loans. Signed enthusiastically by Ronald Reagan on October 15, 1982, this measure raised the ceiling of consumer lending to 30 percent of assets, authorized thrifts to make commercial, corporate, and agricultural loans of up to 10 percent of their assets, and raised the ceiling on the thrifts' direct investment in nonresidential real estate to 40 percent of their assets. The new law, President Reagan assured the nation while signing the bill, "will make the thrift industry a stronger, more effective force in financing housing for millions of Americans in the years to come."

The optimism of Carter and Reagan would not prove to be well founded. Such deregulation unleashed a class of unscrupulous savings and loan executives on an unsuspecting public—and sowed fertile fields in which Lerach could litigate. In the meantime new technologies being developed in California were making it ever so much easier to commit fraud, to manipulate financial markets, and to filch on a massive scale. Lerach and his partners would be waiting for these bandits too, using the same technologies against them.

> • >

FOR BILL LERACH AS for the rest of the country, the Computer Age was ushered in with the faint *beep, beep, beep* sound of the Soviet satellite Sputnik that circled the globe in 1957 to general amazement and not a small amount of panic. Lerach's father initially thought it a communist hoax, but he and his wife and sons joined the other families on Kennedy Avenue, including Gene Carney's, to peer into the October sky looking for the thing.

In Washington, the space race was more than a diversion. Suddenly money was available for aerospace firms to build rockets and for paving companies to build the interstate highways, envisioned as a necessary component of civil defense in the event of nuclear war. Bill and Gene Carney— then eleven years old—were so inspired by Sputnik that they dabbled with their own rudimentary rockets. Plastic rockets, powered by water pressure, worked best for them, although they never solved the problem of reentry.

Their little devices seemed to prefer to land on the roofs of houses in the neighborhood.* The boys made parachutes out of old handkerchiefs, tying them with string to rocks and small toys, and threw them as high as they could into the air. As a grown man, Bill Lerach and his firm would file class action lawsuits against the major companies that produced America's rockets: Lockheed Martin, Boeing, Rockwell International, Northrop. He would also file class actions against the great semiconductor firms that invented and sold the integrated circuits that made the rockets fly: Intel, Advanced Micro Devices, Cypress Semiconductor, IBM, LSI Logic, and National Semiconductor.

In the late 1970s and early 1980s Lerach was the skunk—albeit a bespectacled skunk in an expensive suit—in Silicon Valley's garden party. Garden orgy was more like it. The celebrated high-tech companies that did so much to increase American productivity and remake the U.S. economy were experiencing their first great market run, capturing venture capital, going public, securing more money, and publicly promoting CEOs as the visionaries who would produce a galaxy of life-changing products. *Time* magazine featured a group of new IPO zillionaires in a cover story "Golden Geeks," dubbing them "Instantaires." This was not an isolated example. As vainglorious pronouncements were spouting daily from Silicon Valley, a kind of unreflective euphoria emanated from California, sweeping the country. America, it seemed, was pandering to wealth. The unleashing of venture capital and the harvesting of it—raising more than $50 billion annually to launch five hundred public companies a year—was encouraged by successive occupants of the White House, cheered by a pliant Congress, and protected by an undermanned SEC. Lerach publicly made note of the market volatility of these highly capitalized start-ups, as well as the pressure on corporate officers to lure investors. It was a recipe for fraud, he often

---

* South of Pittsburgh, in a West Virginia hamlet called Coalwood, future NASA engineer Homer "Sonny" Hickam, Jr., author of *Rocket Boys*, was similarly inspired, as were thousands of American boys. No Sonny Hickams, the Kennedy Avenue boys soon wearied of the challenges of rocketry and returned to sports. "Fortunately," Gene Carney told the authors, "the U.S. space program did not depend on us."

warned, adding ominously that the flight from San Diego to San Jose, the gateway to Silicon Valley, would take just over one hour.

In Palo Alto, the heart of Silicon Valley, a small law firm, McCloskey, Wilson & Mosher, was launched in 1961 by three partners. Paul N. "Pete" McCloskey, Jr., a Marine Corps Korean War hero, would later enter Congress as a maverick Republican, come out in early opposition to the war in Vietnam, and be the first House member to publicly broach the idea of impeaching Richard Nixon.* Prior to all that drama, however, McCloskey and his partners had quietly discovered a recipe for rapid growth: help build the companies you represent. It required entrepreneurship, capital, and infrastructure; its prime practitioner would be Larry W. Sonsini, a former high school quarterback who, despite his slender physique, played on the freshman rugby team at the University of California. He attended law school at Berkeley, too, and was hired directly out of Boalt Hall by McCloskey, Wilson & Mosher in 1966. Sonsini had been told by a law school mentor: "There's something going on down in The Valley. There are a lot of young businesses starting, and they're companies that are going to have to go public." What his mentor was suggesting was that well-positioned business lawyers could pretty much print their own money.

Sonsini quickly found himself at the crossroads of venture capital and invention. He networked, signing on as counsel to nascent semiconductor companies such as LSI Logic, Cypress Semiconductor, and National Semiconductor. Soon he would add hardware and software firms that would help give the U.S. economy and stock markets an unprecedented rocket ride.

The strategy was to represent start-up companies, help them grow through all stages of development, and not only retain them as clients but also maintain an equity role. Wilson Sonsini represented Apple Computer,

---

* On a trip home to his congressional district in 1971, McCloskey told a group at Stanford University that it was time to start "a dialogue to discuss impeachment." This was before Watergate—McCloskey was trying to end the Vietnam War—and when he failed to enlist even liberal House Democrats in the effort, he decided to challenge President Nixon in the 1972 Republican primaries. His quixotic campaign garnered but a single delegate to the GOP convention in Miami.

a start-up they also helped stake. In 1980, when Apple went public—the largest offering since Ford Motor's IPO in 1950—Sonsini and his partners in the eight-lawyer firm earned a fortune. During the next five years, seventeen more lawyers were added to the firm's litigation arm alone. By 1988 the firm had grown by more than 100 percent, and its profits per partner averaged $430,000, almost $100,000 more than the partners at big San Francisco firms were earning. Naturally, those partners took notice.

By 1989 more than forty major national law firms had opened up offices in Silicon Valley. "That was a period of raw greed," Wilson Sonsini partner Boris Feldman recalled in a magazine interview. "Greed was always an important component in the Valley, but it was sort of restrained greed: the sense that if you build a good company, you'll be rewarded for it. But during that time framework, what people forgot was the element of building value. It was much more like a gold rush. The values in the Valley were, if not corrupted, then certainly strained."

As Mel Weiss had predicted, greed had become a growth industry. Another set of beneficiaries were the directors and officers of companies that underwrote liability insurance. Beginning in the 1930s, Lloyd's of London introduced coverage for company board members and officers who had previously not qualified for indemnification policies. With the rewriting of the rules of civil procedure in 1966, making it easier to launch lawsuits against corporations, and with Mel Weiss's fraud on the market strategy putting ancillary participants in play, directors and officers found themselves at greater risk regardless of whether they were affiliated with a primary or a secondary defendant corporation. By the mid-1980s, insurance records showed that 31 percent of all publicly held companies and 42 percent of all banks had experienced at least one securities claim against them. Consequently, nearly 95 percent of Fortune 500 companies took out such insurance, called D&O policies, protecting their directors and officers from being personally liable.

One important caveat played into the hands of plaintiffs' attorneys: the "dishonesty exclusion." A carrier would be exempt from paying a claim if the company making the claim had committed fraud or willfully violated securities law. On the other hand, by settling without admitting to any dishonesty, a company could collect on its D&O claim. Thus, the incentive was to settle, even a spurious claim. By the end of the 1980s the average settlement was $8 million.

From this specter emerged an unlikely poster boy. Not that he needed the speaking fees by then, but Bill Lerach became one of the insurance industry's most sought-after speakers. "I'd go in and scare the shit out of their clients," he later recalled mischievously. "And after I'd leave, the insurance company would raise its policy rates."

Within the growing competitive reality of securities litigation, another trend began attracting notice: the number of repeat plaintiffs, especially in cases filed by Milberg Weiss, East and West. One such plaintiff, William Weinberger, a retired accountant from Pompano Beach, Florida, was party to ninety such securities fraud cases. In one lawsuit, defense lawyers asked Weinberger about it. The serial plaintiff, then eighty-eight years old, testified that he had subscribed to a newsletter called *New Issues*, a tout sheet on new companies going public during the first big wave of public offerings. Weinberger said he'd bought about one hundred shares of nearly every new company the newsletter ballyhooed, saying: "As long as I paid for the service, I used the service."

Many of those investments turned into instruments for filing lawsuits. At the outset, at least, Weinberger was not in league with Milberg Weiss; he just bought these stocks knowing that, sooner or later, there was a good chance Lerach would sue the companies, and he'd get an added dividend. He was not even the most litigious of the plaintiffs, called "pets." Attorney Tower Snow, a frequent Lerach opponent, observed sarcastically: "I mean, Mr. William Weinberger [was] the most defrauded man on Earth. He'd been individually defrauded by 120 public companies."* For his part, Lerach played it straight. "There are hundreds of investors willing to step forward and sue and vindicate their rights if they know the opportunity is there," he responded.

---

* Snow's point was on target, but his implication wasn't literally correct. A 1995 congressional report identified a retired lawyer named Harry Lewis as the plaintiff in more than *three hundred* cases against publicly held companies.

The opportunity was there all right, and Lerach started getting referrals from all over the country: from attorney Alfred G. Yates, Jr., an old pal from Pittsburgh; from Philadelphia lawyers Leonard Barrack, Richard Greenfield (whose limousine license plate read: Rule 23), and Richard S. Schiffrin; from Steven J. Toll, a respected Washington, D.C.–area securities attorney; and from various partners in an array of New York firms that often competed with Milberg East. Lerach's phone would ring in California, and it would be one of his own partners on the line complaining about Lerach's temporary alliance with one of these lawyers on a security case.

"Why are you doing business with *that* son of a bitch?" a Milberg Weiss attorney would ask Lerach. "He screwed me in Delaware."

"Well, we're gonna give them a chance to make good in California," Lerach would reply. "And it still goes to our bottom line."

So intense was the competition to be first to the courthouse, Lerach would often receive telephone calls at five A.M. Pacific Coast time. Most people receiving a call at that hour worry about a loved one. Lerach worried about how fast he could get dressed. The phone would ring at some ungodly hour of the morning, and Lerach would turn over in bed and say to Kelly: "New business."

He was simply rolling in cases. He didn't need more plaintiffs. What he needed was a reliable expert witness with a bent toward plaintiffs' lawsuits. Mel Weiss, always there when Lerach needed him, was about to provide this too.

> • >

JOHN TORKELSEN WAS A Princeton graduate, class of '67, a mannerly and politically connected investment banker thriving in the start-up arena, sometimes relying on subsidies from a federal small business assistance program. His two companies, Princeton Venture Research and Equity Valuation Advisors, specialized in valuing and appraising public and private companies, primarily start-up technology companies. Torkelsen oversaw forty-seven employees, many of them MBAs, and he frequently entertained bankers, investors, innovators, and politicians at his 6,000-square-foot Victorian on

Library Place, just a few blocks northwest of old Nassau Street and the Princeton campus.

Torkelsen had parlayed his credibility as an investor with a critical eye on risk assessment, an attribute that played well before judges and juries trying to determine the amount of losses suffered by shareholders in class action lawsuits. In Torkelsen, Lerach and Mel Weiss had acquired another legal entrepreneur. He was willing to work on contingency, claiming nothing if a case in which he testified was lost. On the other hand, if the firm won and if his testimony helped determine the outcome, he would command a premium. Over the next two decades, as Milberg Weiss ascended to the peak of securities shareholder lawsuits, Torkelsen and the firm would fit like hand and glove, or so it seemed.

Another acquisition was Paul L. Tullman a fifty-year-old Milberg Weiss partner and Mel Weiss's Long Island neighbor. Tullman had been talking for some time of leaving the firm and renewing his career as a stockbroker. It didn't take long for Weiss, Bershad, and their partners Steven Schulman and Robert Sugarman (also a Long Island neighbor) to conceive of a plan whereby Tullman would become more valuable as a broker and plaintiff referrer than as an attorney. Because he was still a member of the New York State Bar, he would receive attorney's "referral fees," even though his work had nothing to do with the law. Tullman had a big Rolodex filled with clients, friends, and clients of other brokers who would soon become named plaintiffs for the firm. For this new partnership with the firm, he would earn nearly $9 million.

In landing these three accomplices, Milberg Weiss scored the kind of trifecta that thrilled Mel Weiss when he hit them at the racetrack: Lazar, an eager plaintiff willing to sit for hours in depositions delivering coached answers; Torkelsen, whose stage presence as an expert witness was worthy of an Oscar; and Tullman, who was in a perfect position to spot cases and the plaintiffs who would bring them in.

Flush with a growing number of settlements in New York and on the West Coast, Mel Weiss was already anointing his coast-to-coast operation as "the Rolls Royce of securities litigation." The firm was ready to try big, headline-making cases, he told his top partners, and he would become the recognized dean of all securities class action attorneys. Noting that Lerach had grown out of his shared office space, Weiss directed his young protégé to plant the firm flag on the finest, most prominently located, and tallest building in San Diego. That wasn't hard. The sleek twenty-story glass building known as One America Plaza had just been completed, and space at the top was available. Every office had a high view of the city. From Lerach's corner, he could literally duplicate the waterscape view of C. Arnholt Smith, San Diego's biggest bank bandit. He could see the harbor, the yachts, the powerboats, the naval flotilla, and the Pacific Ocean horizon beyond.

Of course, he couldn't see 475 miles north to Silicon Valley, not literally, but he could see in his mind's eye where his caseload would come from. For the next two decades no other law firm and no other lawyer would sue so many Fortune 500 firms. High-tech giants—firms such as Apple Computer, Lucent Technologies, Hewlett-Packard, Oracle, IBM, Intel, 3Com, Tyco, Raytheon—were Lerach's specialty. But he also went after venerable American corporations, ranging from AT&T and Honeywell to ExxonMobil and The Gap. He sued accountant firms such as Touche Ross and Arthur Andersen; he sued financial institutions Citibank, Merrill Lynch, and Drexel Burnham; he sued telecommunications companies as well as multi-complex behemoths such as Enron and Halliburton. And he relished the animosity he engendered doing it.

Lerach also evolved into a prominent Democratic Party donor. In time the (mostly) liberal practitioners of the New Economy, both in and out of Silicon Valley, would express surprise that Lerach didn't cut them any slack for their politics, their record of job creation, or the innovations they produced that made life better for so many Americans. This was a misreading of Lerach's worldview, even though he expressed admiration for capitalism, just not unbridled capitalism. These entrepreneurs were essentially libertarian Democrats who wanted the government out of their bedrooms and their boardrooms—just as they wanted Wall Street out of their labs. This wasn't Bill Lerach's philosophy. He'd gone from being a Goldwater Republican to a Great Society Democrat, and he saw his role as being supplemental to government—not at odds with it—precisely because business executives were forever figuring out ways to circumvent regulators and manipulate the market to their own benefit.

For Lerach, it wasn't really about national politics, at least not when he started out: in his first big case with political overtones, four of the so-called Keating Five were Democratic senators. Bill Lerach didn't care about the next so-called "killer app" in Silicon Valley, or that the New Economy's proprietors were creating jobs and increasing human productivity and connectivity in this place the romantics once called the Valley of the Heart's Delight due to its abundance of fruit orchards. Milberg Weiss had taken him on as partner, allowing him to reside in San Diego if he could drum up cases. And so Bill Lerach needed cases. He hated fraud; he liked suing and litigating. It wasn't that complicated.

He was happy to become the ogre in the Valley of the Heart's Delight or any other valley—and a scourge of Wall Street as well.

> • > • > • > • >

THE BIG CON

Down the street from Lerach's shiny San Diego high-rise office was a venerable lending institution known as San Diego Federal Savings & Loan, a company that began in 1885 with origins not dissimilar to those of George Bailey's mythical "building and loan," in *It's a Wonderful Life*.

In the early 1980s, as Lerach was making a name for himself in the law, the public face of San Diego Federal was Edwin J. Gray, a senior vice president and director of public affairs. Despite the proximity of their offices, Ed Gray and Bill Lerach didn't travel in the same social circles—their mutually exclusive political views saw to that. As Lerach evolved into a big-government liberal, Gray remained a steadfastly small-government conservative (he'd been president of the San Diego Taxpayers' Association) who had joined the Reagan Revolution while Lerach was still in law school, later following his muse to Sacramento and eventually to Washington.

In the nation's capital, however, their paths would cross, and Edwin Gray would emerge as an unlikely and staunch ally of Lerach and his clients, a vast array of mostly elderly investors who had been fleeced in one of the great robberies in the history of American financial chicanery. Nobody saw the collaboration coming, not Lerach, not Gray, and certainly not

Ronald Reagan, the man who put Ed Gray on a collision course with his own political party. On May 1, 1983, Gray raised his right hand and took the oath of office as the seventeenth chairman of the Federal Home Loan Bank Board (FHLBB), the regulatory agency charged with overseeing the nation's savings and loan institutions. Then forty-six years old, Gray had been press secretary to Governor Reagan in Sacramento and had served briefly in the Reagan White House as director of Office of Policy and Development. Attorney General Edwin Meese III, an original Reaganite and a fellow San Diegan, administered the swearing-in, anointing Gray to head the regulatory agency overseeing federally chartered savings and loans. In that post as chief of the FHLBB, Gray would have authority for the Federal Savings and Loan Insurance Corporation, known by its acronym, FSLIC, which insured deposits at nearly all thrifts in the United States.

Seven months earlier Reagan had signed the legislation making it easier for federally insured financial institutions, regardless of their size, portfolios, or economic expertise, to compete in the increasingly sophisticated financial markets. The Depository Institutions Act* was "the most important legislation for financial institutions in fifty years," the president proclaimed in an October 15, 1982, Rose Garden ceremony. Promising that it would open the doors to more jobs, more housing, and faster growth for the economy, the president added, "All in all, I think we hit the jackpot."

Instead, and despite Ed Gray's efforts, the Federal Home Loan Bank board would become a cog in the circle of greed that helped define the 1980s; Reagan's so-called "jackpot" would be claimed by an astonishing array of schemers and swindlers. These con men, in turn, would provide an unprecedented pot of gold for the lawyers who pursued them—foremost among them Bill Lerach. The government agency that Gray headed was born out of the calamitous 1929 stock market crash that signaled the onset of the Great Depression—and that wiped out Richard E. Lerach's meager

---

* This 1982 law is often referred to as the Garn–St. Germain Act, after its chief sponsors, Senator Jake Garn, a Utah Republican, and Fernand St. Germain, a Rhode Island Democrat, who served for many years as chairman of the House Banking Committee.

family savings, planting the seeds of myth, and of class resentment, that would motivate his younger son.

In the aftermath of World War II, S&Ls helped fuel the explosion of middle-class home ownership that changed the face of the nation. Insiders had a name for this formula—they called it "three-six-three," meaning that S&L executives borrowed from their depositors at 3 percent, loaned money at 6 percent, and were on the golf course by three P.M.

These mom-and-pop S&Ls were idealized in Frank Capra's 1946 classic *It's a Wonderful Life*, in which Jimmy Stewart plays George Bailey, the scrupulous and civic-minded proprietor of Bailey Brothers Building and Loan, who stays home to help the town while his brother Harry goes off to the war. Capra cast Stewart in his morality play as a quiet hero who didn't qualify for military service because of a boyhood injury, but who nonetheless saves the mythical town of Bedford Falls—and his own soul—by standing up to the rapacious banker, Mr. Potter, played by the legendary Lionel Barrymore. The movie premiered the year Bill Lerach was born, and he watched it many times. As he grew older, Lerach tended to view corporate executives as modern-day versions of the loathsome Mr. Potter. Lerach fancied himself as an angel arrayed against such greedy executives—but not the lovable and bumbling angel "Clarence" of Frank Capra's conception. Bill Lerach would become ruthlessly unsentimental at rooting out the fraudsters. In his mind, he would become a different kind of angel. The avenging kind.

> • >

FOR DECADES THIS COMMUNITY banking network, along with its benign stereotype, hummed along—until housing costs started climbing faster than the old recipe could handle. To ease the inflationary pressure on new home buyers, Congress put a cap on the interest rates that thrifts could pay on deposits; the theory was that by paying out less for deposits, S&Ls would shrink interest on home loans as well. But this initiative did not anticipate how high inflation would climb. By 1979, Jimmy Carter's third year as president, inflation was over 13 percent, yet federal regulations allowed the thrifts to pay only 5.5 percent on deposits. New unregulated financial institutions—money market funds—came into being that were allowed to pay higher interest rates and thus began attracting depositors at the expense of the thrifts. What's more, owing to a new agility made possible by innovations in information technology, depositors could easily shop for the highest interest rates anywhere in the nation—and instantly park their money in those institutions. S&Ls, the "thrifts" that owed their ethic to Benjamin Franklin and their image to Jimmy Stewart, were suddenly obsolete, even without the machinations of Mr. Potter and his ilk.

In 1980, as Jimmy Stewart's friend Ronald Reagan campaigned against President Carter in an election that turned on the nation's mounting financial problems, nearly 85 percent of the nation's 3,800 S&Ls were losing money. In March Carter signed legislation phasing out the interest-rate limits on S&Ls. Congress also raised the FSLIC insurance coverage on deposits from $40,000 to $100,000. This was advertised as a way to protect Americans' savings, but the average thrift account had only $6,000 in it, and the origins of the legislation raised the question of who it was really supposed to benefit. As a practical matter, thrifts could now attract large amounts of money with less risk to their depositors or themselves.

The new law invited the participation of shady operators who were just as unsentimental as, and far more imaginative than, Hollywood's idea of a cold-blooded banker. Debt became a medium of exchange. Corporations loaded up their leverage to pay for deals they otherwise could not have afforded; profits went to defraying interest on multimillion-dollar loans; and ownership of venerable corporations changed hands through arrangements and takeover schemes so byzantine that regulators could hardly keep pace.*

"If you were in real estate, a savings and loan was the perfect cash cow,"

---

* Several authoritative books were written detailing the S&L scandal of the 1980s, the most thorough probably being *Inside Job: The Looting of America's Savings and Loans* by Stephen Pizzo, Mary Fricker, and Paul Muolo (New York: HarperCollins, 1991). Given what happened to the U.S. economy in 2008 and 2009, however, the single most distressing line about the S&L crisis may have come from Martin Mayer, author of *The Greatest-Ever Bank Robbery: The Collapse of the Savings and Loan Industry* (New York: Collier, 1992). "Deposit insurance," Mayer wrote, "proved to be the crack cocaine of American finance."

federal bank examiner William Black explained. "It was the perfect vehicle for someone who was greedy."

One of these thrifts would soon become a symbol for what plagued the industry. Lincoln Savings and Loan Association was based in Irvine, California. Federal regulators in the San Francisco branch of the FHLBB informed Gray that deeply troubling activities were occurring at this institution. Bad judgment alone wasn't the issue, the examiners suggested. The price of the stock appeared to have been artificially inflated. Elderly people living in retirement communities near the thrift's twenty-three branches were purchasing shares in $1,000 lots from people who were not certified to sell securities. Tellers had made it easy for them by showing them glossy promotional material and offering forms they could use to transfer insured funds from other banks and thrifts. These purchases, the customers were told, were just like banks' certificates of deposit—only better. There was no downside, would-be customers were assured. There was only upside: they offered higher returns than CDs. They were federally insured because Lincoln was federally insured. Therefore Lincoln would be able to stand by its commitments. This was all false. Customers who purchased Lincoln securities were buying stock in the thrift, nothing less, nothing more. They were definitely not depositing money in a federally insured savings account.

Those primarily at risk were Lincoln's own clients, many of them elderly, susceptible depositors. Horrified by what he was hearing, Gray asked for daily reports from his field examiners. He instructed them to be prepared to take drastic action. That might be a problem, he was told, and it had to do with the identity of the blustery, politically connected man in charge at Lincoln. His name was Charles H. Keating, Jr. It was a name destined to be linked to scandal and shame—and to one of Bill Lerach's greatest legal triumphs.

> • >

CHARLES KEATING WAS DOING everything in his power not to cooperate with federal bank examiners. In fact, he was resisting Gray's attempts at reform—enlisting an A-list of financial heavyweights to portray Ed Gray as Chicken Little. Keating even ginned up Alan Greenspan, then an esteemed private economist, who argued that deregulation was working. Greenspan gave his stamp of approval to some twenty innovative thrifts, including Lincoln Savings, which he singled out in writing as being a soundly run institution with record profits that "poses no foreseeable risk to FSLIC." When he wrote this letter, Greenspan, the future chairman of the Federal Reserve Board, was a paid consultant working for Charles Keating. Within two years, nineteen of the twenty institutions on Greenspan's list had failed.

Lerach would use such dubious assessments to his advantage as he battled in court to recover the looted billions siphoned out of Lincoln Savings and Loan. By this time—the mid-1980s—he had completed the metamorphosis from Rustbelt Republican to West Coast Democrat. It was opposite of the ideological journey that Ronald Reagan had traveled, as both men shed the skins they were born into and reinvented themselves as their more natural political beings in the tolerant sunshine of California.

The Lincoln Savings and Loan case would be a crucial way station in Lerach's philosophical evolution. The sins—and sinners—of market capitalism would soon reveal themselves in a virtual roll call of names and companies, starting with Drexel Burnham and moving on to Enron, WorldCom, Martha Stewart, Conrad Black, Ken Lay, Bernard Ebbers, even Dick Cheney's Halliburton. Each time one of those names made headlines, Lerach would tell anyone who would listen, "I told you so." Lerach had been radicalized—and no corporation, and no man, had more to do with it than Lincoln Savings and Loan and Charles Keating.

> • >

AT THE TIME HE purchased Lincoln Savings, Charlie Keating pledged to retain Lincoln's experienced executives and continue its primary business of making home loans. He did not keep this promise. Within months all company officers were replaced by staffers from American Continental, and its home loan programs were gutted. Next, Keating—through Lincoln—purchased $2.7 billion in high-risk junk bonds, mostly from Michael Milken's

Drexel Burnham. These were far riskier waters than Lincoln had ever navigated, and the men at the helm had little experience in such ventures. Meanwhile, not liking the noise Ed Gray was making in Washington, Keating began doling out contributions to key congressional members—nearly half a million dollars in all. This money went to members of the House and Senate who hailed from states where either American Continental or Lincoln Savings was doing business, and to members on relevant congressional committees who were in positions to influence legislation. The largest amounts went to five U.S. senators, four of them Democrats: John Glenn of Ohio ($200,000), Alan Cranston of California ($90,000), Donald W. Riegle, Jr., of Michigan ($76,100), and Dennis DeConcini of Arizona ($55,000). Those were only the direct federal contributions: Keating had other ways of funneling political money, including a stunningly large $850,000 gift to voter registration groups run by Cranston's son Kim.

The Republican benefiting most from Keating's largesse was John McCain, the junior senator from Arizona. Earlier, when he served in the House of Representatives, McCain had used Keating's vacation home on Cat Cay in the Bahamas, making nine trips on American Continental's private jet, sometimes with his wife, daughter, and babysitter. One photo obtained by *The Arizona Republic*, a Phoenix newspaper, showed McCain on vacation in the islands. He was seated on a bandstand wearing a straw party hat. Next to him, swigging from a bottle, sat Keating's son, Charles Keating III.

As McCain and the four Democrats would learn to their eternal embarrassment, these contributions and financial arrangements came with strings attached. As far as Keating was concerned, the quid pro quo was specific: Keating wanted Ed Gray and his people off Lincoln Savings's back. In fact, he wanted Gray removed from his job. On March 24, 1987, Keating flew to Washington and met the next morning with DeConcini, who had once floated Keating's name as a possible ambassador to the Bahamas. Keating wanted DeConcini and McCain to accompany him to San Francisco to persuade the head of the regional FHLBB to call off the dogs. DeConcini indicated his willingness but told Keating that McCain was reluctant to do such a thing.

"McCain's a wimp," Keating replied. "We'll go talk to him."

The meeting with McCain was set for 1:30 P.M. By that time McCain had been apprised by a DeConcini staffer of the "wimp" comment—and didn't appreciate it. Keating handed McCain a list of demands that he wanted the legislator to make to the regulators. McCain flatly refused to fly to San Francisco and said blandly that he'd look into whether Lincoln was getting a fair shake. An agitated Keating questioned McCain's courage and loyalty. McCain responded heatedly that he hadn't spent five and a half years in the Hanoi Hilton to be called a coward. Keating stormed out, but he had more cards to play, he wanted McCain to know. Almost immediately word spread around Washington that Ed Gray was planning to resign.

On April 2, 1987, Gray received a call from Dennis DeConcini asking him to come, alone, to DeConcini's Senate office. Immediately Gray knew he'd walked into an ambush. Waiting were Senators McCain, Glenn, and Cranston. Gray shook hands stiffly and was directed to his chair. The agenda was clear: why was Gray putting so much pressure on Lincoln Savings?

Gray told the senators that if they were concerned about a single thrift, they should direct their inquiry to the district office. He gave them the name of James Cirona, president of the eleventh-district FHLBB in San Francisco. A week later, on April 9, Cirona, accompanied by his second in command, Michael Patriarca, and Richard Sanchez, the examiner in charge of the Lincoln Savings investigation, flew to Washington. They were joined by William Black, a government lawyer, who was about to be transferred to San Francisco, where he would become general counsel to the district FHLBB. There were no surprises this time. Gray had briefed Cirona, who was well prepared for the confrontation with the Keating-friendly senators and resolved to have the last word.

DeConcini, the host, led off. "We wanted to meet with you because we have determined that potential actions of yours could injure a constituent," he told the FHLBB contingent. The constituent, of course, was Keating. McCain weighed in, trying to leaven the attack. "I don't want any part of our conversation to be improper," he said, adding words that may well have salvaged his political career: "I wouldn't want any special favors for them."

Leaning toward Cirona, Glenn, who was still struggling to pay off a $3 million debt from his ill-fated run for the 1984 Democratic presidential nomination, said: "To be blunt, you should charge them or get off their backs."

Sanchez began the government's presentation. He cited a 1984 examination of Lincoln showing loan deficiencies that Keating promised to fix and did not. Lincoln had underwriting problems with all its investments, equity securities, debt securities, land loans, and direct real estate investments. For all fifty-two of the real estate loans that Lincoln had made between 1984 and 1986, the files contained no credit reports. Examiners found $47 million in loans to clients who had inadequate credit.

"This is a ticking time bomb," Cirona interjected.

Patriarca sensed it was time to quit circling. "I've never seen any bank or S&L that's anything like this," he said. "They violate the law and regulations and common sense." He paused, letting this observation sink in with the senators then detonated the bomb. "We're sending criminal referral to the Department of Justice. This is an extraordinarily serious matter. It involves a whole range of imprudent actions. I can't tell you strongly enough how serious this is."

DeConcini would not fold, pointing out that Lincoln's accountants had also complained at the rigor and length of the regulators' examinations. "Why would Arthur Young say these things?" DeConcini asked. "They have to guard their credibility, too. They put the firm's neck out with this letter."

At that point Patriarca decided to school the senators on what was becoming an epidemic, a phenomenon that Mel Weiss and Bill Lerach had invented nearly a decade before—the presumption of scheme liability.

"They have a client," Patriarca said, implying that the mathematics of pure accounting was only one part of the relationship between a company and the firm it paid to consult on constructing its books—and then sign off on them.

"You believe they'd prostitute themselves for a client?" DeConcini asked.

"Absolutely," replied Patriarca. "It happens all the time."

Ed Gray formally left his job in May. As he was packing up, ready to leave his office, Gray was asked what it might take to clean up the S&L mess. He hesitated. The number $40 billion was suggested. He shrugged, saying, "Nowhere near enough." He was right.

> • >

LESS THAN A YEAR earlier, on May 18, 1986, about a thousand students, along with their parents and friends, gathered for a ceremony conferring master's degrees at the Haas School of Business at the University of California, Berkeley, to hear the guest speaker whom the students had voted to address them. Ivan Boesky, then forty-eight, tanned, and exuding flinty self-confidence, strode to the podium.

The son of a Russian-Jewish family from Detroit whose father had owned a trio of topless bars, Boesky had become the prince of Wall Street, amassing a fortune by betting on stock price fluctuations in corporate takeovers that he had predicted. His purchases were audacious and massive, sometimes occurring just days before a corporation announced it had been acquired or was acquiring. The day he appeared at Berkeley, his portfolio was reported to be worth nearly $2 billion, and he was speaking to an audience eager for his insights. "We are riding a wave of takeovers," he told his audience. This was truly a time of survival of the fittest, he suggested, warming to the sound of his own convictions. That year alone Wall Street could expect more than three thousand mergers and buyouts, many of them hostile, with a total worth approaching $130 billion. Huge profits were being made. Acumen, even avarice, was the coin of the realm.

"Greed is all right by the way," he said, pausing for effect. "I want you to know that. I think greed is healthy. You can be greedy and still feel good about yourself."

The audience erupted in laughter, applause, and cheers.

Six months later, on November 14, 1986, the SEC made an announcement that shook the financial world. Ivan Boesky had been caught in an insider-trading investigation that had cracked open a classic circle of greed.

"Ivan the Terrible," as Boesky was dubbed for his take-no-prisoners style, cut a deal, agreeing to pay $100 million in fines, return profits, and accept life banishment from stock trading. Facing up to five years in prison, he also let regulators eavesdrop on his telephone conversations. The resulting subpoenas would ensnare other princes of Wall Street, among them junk bond magnate Michael Milken. At his zenith, in 1986, Milken awarded himself $550 million in bonuses, more than the yearly profit for Drexel Burnham Lambert, the 10,000-person company that employed him. Milken's operation was handling 250,000 transactions a month and controlling as much as $10 billion in funds through junk bonds issued by nearly one thousand companies. Through this market rose a new breed of risk takers—corporate raiders Henry Kravis, Carl Icahn, Ron Perelman, Saul Steinberg, and T. Boone Pickens; Rupert Murdoch, the global media baron; William McGowan, who made MCI one of the nation's premier phone systems; Ted Turner, who created twenty-four-hour cable news; Frank Lorenzo, the airline takeover king—and, of course, Charlie Keating.

Bill Lerach would sue them all, starting with Keating.

> • >

BILL LERACH AND HIS partners Len Simon and John Stoia could hardly believe it. The more they delved into the facts of their case against Charles Keating and American Continental Corporation, the longer the list of defendants grew. It started with Milken and Boesky and just kept going; it was astonishing how many individuals and institutions aided in Keating's scheme. All told, they would end up suing more than fifty individuals, ten banks, four accounting firms, half a dozen law firms, and just as many companies. Nearly one hundred named defendants would appear on the class action certification document when it was filed in December 1989, making the lawsuit against Keating et al the most sweeping deployment of the concept of scheme liability ever filed.

Lerach and his firm were not only going after Keating and Lincoln Savings; they were pursuing his relatives; they were pursuing Arthur Young, Ernst & Young, Arthur Andersen, and Touche Ross and Deloitte, the accounting firms; they were pursuing Bankers Trust, Credit Suisse First Boston,

Saudi Investment Bank Corp., Saudi European Bank, Lambert Brussels Associated Limited Partnership, and many others. "We just drained the sink," Lerach would say.

Drained the swamp was more like it. The Social Darwinism that William Jennings Bryan had feared was now a fact of American life. Ronald Reagan's critics would label the 1980s the "decade of greed," but the problem was more fundamental. Four decades after Frank Capra had inspired a weary nation with *It's a Wonderful Life*, America's finest universities were turning out pampered, materialistic graduates who cheered wildly for the Mr. Potters in their midst instead of the George Baileys. With the help of the nation's politicians, American capitalism was producing a lot of Mr. Potters. Jimmy Stewart had also starred in a prewar classic called *Mr. Smith Goes to Washington* in which an accidental senator single-handedly stands up to political graft. In real life the ethics of mid-1980s Washington was summed up by the crass question that Dennis DeConcini posed to the Senate Ethics Committee: "What is wrong with intervention for someone who sends you a check for your campaign?" he asked. "That's what has made me the senator I am."

The system's failure seemed complete. Free market capitalism couldn't handle being unshackled from government regulation; and despite the efforts of the federal bureaucracy, the Republican executive branch wasn't terribly interested in performing the government's necessary oversight role. Meanwhile members of the Democratic-controlled Congress worried more about the campaign contributions that kept them in power than about defending the interests of everyday Americans. That war heroes and national icons of both parties—John Glenn and John McCain—succumbed to this temptation demonstrated the system's corrupting power. McCain compared assisting Charles Keating to helping "the little lady who didn't get her Social Security." Actually, the little old ladies involved in this case bought bogus securities from a schemer, who then turned to powerful political figures to whom he had given money for protection.

The third branch of government had yet to be heard from, however, and in that forum Keating would answer for his crimes. The little old ladies would not only get their day in court, courtesy of Lerach, they would also get their day in the Senate offices of the Keating Five on Capitol Hill. This additional branch was the court system, among whose practitioners were crusading prosecutors and hard-eyed plaintiffs' lawyers offended by the chicanery, collusion, and obscene excess all around them. At the vanguard, waving their banner and charging into legal battle, were Mel Weiss, Bill Lerach, and an army of like-minded trial lawyers.

A reckoning was coming.

8

> • > • > • > • >

INTO THE BREACH

Following Ed Gray's departure from the Federal Home Loan Bank Board, the tide seemed to turn in Charles Keating's favor. On the heels of the government audit describing Lincoln as careening out of control, a new chairman was installed. M. Danny Wall, a former staff director of the Senate Banking Committee, shelved the audit and ordered jurisdiction of the Lincoln investigation transferred from San Francisco to the Washington, D.C., office.

Wall did what Keating had wanted the group of senators—ultimately and ignominiously to be known as the Keating Five—to do, which was get the examiners off his back. In Phoenix, at American Continental's headquarters, a celebration was in full swing. It was quite a party. One reveler hurled a computer from a second-floor balcony. Keating puffed out his chest, struck a Superman pose, and ripped open his shirt to exhibit a faux tattoo displaying a skull and crossbones over the letters FHLBB. A secretary stepped onto a desk to take photos. Robert Kielty, the company's senior vice president and general counsel, joined her. Keating grabbed a roll of adhesive tape and wrapped it around the two, lashing their legs together. Potted plants and displays were sent crashing. Kielty popped a champagne bottle and emptied the contents down another secretary's blouse. "Get this champagne colder!" Keating shouted.

The reprieve gave Lincoln Savings and Loan a green light to expand its tentacles, and within the next two years its reported assets grew on paper by nearly 40 percent, to $5.46 billion. The growth was driven by risky bets in raw landholdings, unsecured construction loans, and major increases in holdings of Michael Milken's junk bonds. By then, the media were on to American Continental. The *New York Times* noted, "Lincoln, with assets of $4.9 billion and 25 branches in Southern California, has been a concern to regulators of the thrift industry because of its untraditional investment activities." All the while, its dicey debentures were being hawked to customers such as Ramona Jacobs, the conservator for her paralyzed daughter. Jacobs was destined for disappointment—and to be one of Bill Lerach's most effective clients. The same was true for Rae Luft, a Russian immigrant in failing health, and Leah Kane, another elderly woman who purchased $15,000 of American Continental stock. Thousands more unsuspecting people did the same—solicited, according to an internal Lincoln memo to its bond sales force, precisely because they were vulnerable and unlearned. "Always remember," the memo stated, "the weak, meek and ignorant are always good targets." This memo would be unearthed in the relentless discovery process overseen by Bill Lerach and a platoon of allied plaintiffs' lawyers.

Now the chickens were coming home to roost, as Lerach was fond of saying.

American Continental's death spiral took only a year to complete. Wall could not sit on the Lincoln audit any longer. Under pressure, he sent a memorandum to the Justice Department recommending a criminal investigation, just as the agency's senior examiners had done under Ed Gray two years earlier. On April 13, 1989, American Continental filed for protection under Chapter 11 of the Federal Bankruptcy Code. Immediately, it stopped making payments of interest and principal to its 23,000 investors, including Leah Kane, who'd put her life savings in it only three months before. In a statement Keating admitted that the company had foreseen no way its investors would ever see their money—estimated at more than $285 million. The following day the FHLBB seized Lincoln Savings and Loan. Leah Kane wondered if she needed a lawyer. She didn't know it, but Bill Lerach was already representing her.

> • >

HIGH ATOP SAN DIEGO, the expanding offices of Milberg, Weiss, Specthrie, Bershad & Lerach palpitated in a furious frenzy, emulating the atmosphere at so many Silicon Valley start-ups that Lerach and his colleagues would earn their fortunes suing. Printers whirred in continuous motion, telephones and teleconference speakers chorused voices, while lawyers and their assistants hurried through the hallways carrying documents from one office to another. The firm was now filing an average of twelve lawsuits a month. Even with the increased workload, an influx of new attorneys, and impending prospects for more revenue and even greater rewards, Lerach was customarily the first in every morning, often arriving before seven thirty A.M. His loyal assistant Kathy Lichnovsky would follow, bearing an egg, bacon, and cheese breakfast croissant she'd picked up at a downtown Jack in the Box. Lunch arrived at his desk between 11:30 and 11:45 A.M., and usually the fare was the same—ham and Swiss on rye ordered from the Westgate Hotel across the street, with Best Foods mayonnaise that he'd slather on himself from a large jar stocked in a refrigerator nearby. When he'd vary, the choice would be Braunschweiger on rye, always accompanied with this favorite brand of mayo. Unless they wanted to see the boss's Captain Queeg imitation, his staff knew not to substitute another brand—or let the mayonnaise jar get empty. The sandwich was to be served with a can of Lipton tea, and a red Dixie cup filled with ice. Lerach was a man of habits. They weren't all good habits: the Dixie cup would also accompany him on the drive home, this time filled with a small amount of ice and a large amount of Scotch—Johnnie Walker Blue Label. The whiskey became an inside joke at the firm. Eventually, fearful that their private joke would backfire on them publicly, Lerach's partners created a new position, "director of transportation," hiring veteran limousine driver Frank Cucinotta to ensure that their meal ticket arrived at his destinations promptly and safely. If Lerach did go out for lunch, he normally walked two blocks to a steakhouse named

Rainwater's, where he ordered the three-cheese meatloaf with mashed pota-
toes. He was back at his desk in forty minutes. The primacy of work never
varied.

The pace became so feverish that Lerach rewrote the office lease so that
the temperature never rose above sixty-five degrees Fahrenheit—to keep
everyone alert. In the huge corner office with its view to eternity were a
marble-topped bar and group photos of Lerach, his wife, two daughters
Gretchen and Shannon from separate marriages, and various colleagues on
exotic outings—playing steel drums on a Caribbean beach, fly-fishing in
Alaska, hoisting umbrella-covered drinks under Hawaiian palms—along
with those sketches, painted by Kathy's son, depicting Lerach as Saint
George. Lerach's cases were literally stacked, as bulging legal folders vied for
space on table tops, his desk, and his floor.

Each bore the name of a company that he was suing or preparing to
sue. Behind his desk, on side-by-side credenzas, clear acrylic squares, six
inches tall and two inches thick, were arranged in rows bearing his legal trophies as if preserved in amber. Each held a diminutive reproduction of a
verdict, judgment, or settlement, the name of the company, date of the
award, and the amount—beginning with the first, the $50 million U.S. Fi-
nancial award in 1978, followed by the painstakingly won 1980 United
Methodist Church settlement of $21 million, an amount that was growing
to more than $40 million because the terms of the settlement called for fu-
ture profits to go to the residents and their heirs. Lerach hadn't kept any fee
for this follow-up service, although he was entitled to it. He could afford to
be magnanimous. The work had been so good, he had earned $2.3 million
the previous year, just $300,000 less than his mentor Mel Weiss. In the San
Diego office the number of plastic trophies was multiplying by four or five
each year, attesting to the firm's success and the upward arc of class action
lawsuits throughout America. *Forbes* magazine would soon estimate that
plaintiffs' lawyers would earn in excess of $10 billion in complex litigation
in a single twelve-month period; Milberg Weiss, mainly due to Lerach's activities, captured nearly 60 percent of the yield.

One Lerach trophy, a relatively small payout for $6.75 million in 1985,
was particularly noteworthy. The company, Priam Corp., a Silicon Valley

manufacturer of computer disk drives, was one of about two hundred similar firms to suffer downturns in an industry shakeout in the mid-1980s. Lerach sued, arguing that the company had not adequately warned investors about the riskiness of its venture into the sector. He had taken measure of the company's vulnerability and guessed correctly that it lacked the resolve and resources to defend itself in court. Relying on public records and statements, he produced what would become his trademark, a chart tracing the company's stock price over time, with colored boxes drawing attention to key junctures, especially when a company's stock dropped toward the executives' stock options "exercise" price or when company officials unloaded stock before a sharp decline. In a perfect Lerach world, this event would be preceded by positive remarks from company officials, driving the price up, followed by a sell-off before another decline. Priam adhered to this very pattern, and he let its lawyers know in gory detail what a protracted trial would look like. Financial ruin. Humiliation. Disgrace. The board of directors decided to capitulate, settling for about 20 percent of what Lerach claimed as their total exposure.

Fighting a lawsuit with Lerach to its conclusion is "so non-productive," observed Paul M. Wythes, a Silicon Valley venture capitalist and a Priam director. "These companies are trying to compete in a world market." He was pointing out what so many other U.S. executives were learning. Insurance industry studies found that in 1987 the costs of tort litigation were running at about 2.6 percent of the United States' total gross national product, compared with less than 0.4 percent in Japan and West Germany. Three years later Priam declared bankruptcy.

That wasn't Lerach's concern—in his mind, they all deserved their fates. Meanwhile his legal tactics had become clear. Young tech companies in volatile markets were easy prey. During the next two decades they would provide the bulk of hundreds of lawsuits and recoveries, most settled out of court. Already at the close of 1988 the Lucite trophies were challenging the amount of available space. For one particular prize, however, there would always be room, and Lerach would point it out to visitors with irreverent glee. It commemorated a multimillion-dollar settlement in 1984 that got Silicon Valley's goat to start bleating. It began on December 7, 1984, Pearl

Harbor Day, when Lerach's legal team served a securities fraud complaint against Seagate Technology and its flamboyant CEO Alan F. Shugart, an entrepreneurial engineer who helped invent the floppy disk and was considered in Silicon Valley not just a pioneer but an example of all that the New Economy made possible, technologically and personally.

Born with a clubfoot in 1930 in Los Angeles and raised by a single mother, Shugart majored in engineering physics at the University of Redlands and took a job at IBM in 1951. He rose through the ranks, becoming director of engineering in 1969. Later that year he left the staid "Big Blue" for Memorex (which would be sued by David B. Gold in a landmark case four years later). By then Shugart and some Memorex confederates had launched Shugart Associates, a company that was supposed to build a complete business operating system to compete with IBM, but it ran out of money in two years. Shugart's venture capitalists eased him out of the company that bore his name. Shugart licked his wounds by opening a bar in Santa Cruz, where he liked to surf. He bought a salmon fishing boat and became its captain. But as he later told *Business Week*, "I had a tough time meeting my Porsche payments." In 1979 a former Memorex colleague, Finis Conner, had an epiphany: the new personal computer market badly needed a cheap hard drive. This had always been Shugart's engineering forte, and Conner called him. Together they restarted Shugart Technologies, naming it Seagate.

Seagate's first product was a breakthrough, a 5¼-inch disk drive with five megabytes of memory that retailed for $1,500. Both the PC industry and Al Shugart were on their way. The colorful Shugart once described the key to success this way: "Find a parade and get in front of it." It was a description containing hints of both self-deprecation and truth. It could also have been used to describe the working philosophy of one William S. Lerach, who thought Shugart's parade needed a little rain on it.

In 1984 Seagate's stock price suffered a precipitous decline—a phenomenon not uncommon in the fledgling disk drive sector. Lerach never viewed such drops as vagaries of the volatile high-tech market, and his inevitable lawsuit accused Shugart and his managers of "reckless" misrepresentation and a "scheme" to conceal company problems while pocketing huge payoffs—$15 million, in Shugart's case, from insider sales. Shugart, taking Lerach's boilerplate legal language personally, launched a counterattack in the press, likening Lerach "and his kind" to vultures, an epithet that was to be chorused in various iterations by hundreds of CEOs, who loudly complained that Lerach was actually interfering in the work their shareholders expected of them.

Lerach pressed on, presenting Shugart with the specter of a trial, even estimating for him how many hours they would log putting up a defense and how much he and his company would likely shell out for legal expenses. The numbers were staggering. Shugart was apoplectic, telling friends that he felt Lerach was mocking him and the entire tech industry. "Al Shugart hated lawyers so much he kept a lawyer doll (named Bill) on his desk so he could periodically snap its head off," one plaintiffs' attorney recalled. Spitting mad, Shugart settled for $9 million. Lerach collected $3.1 million in fees and another $1.26 million in expenses. In the process, he made a lifelong enemy. Shugart vowed that he would dedicate a considerable amount of his "mind share" to trying to put Lerach out of business.

"Enough is Enough," blared the full-page 1990 magazine ad paid for by Shugart and aimed at Lerach. "Are securities lawyers holding your company ransom?" In the ad Shugart urged other executives to send him their business cards, if they wanted to join his campaign against plaintiffs' lawyers. It only encouraged Lerach, who believed Shugart was helping him get business by making his name even better known. Not long after the advertising blasts, Shugart received an envelope from Lerach. Inside was the lawyer's business card with a note that said: "Dear Al: There's more coming."

Lerach was about to make good on his promise. One of the cases ready to file, *Froman v. Seagate*, accused Shugart of just the opposite of what Lerach normally alleged. In this lawsuit Lerach represented a plaintiff who complained that he'd sold stock when Seagate reported a loss, but that Shugart had failed to notify shareholders when the company experienced a subsequent upturn and instead purchased company stock himself, while concealing critical positive information. The suit was brought, that is, because the company's stock had gone *up*. Shugart was infuriated, but there was nothing intrinsically nefarious about seeking relief for shareholders with this cause of action. This was precisely the kind of activity, brought to the attention of the Boston office of the Securities and Exchange Commission in the early 1940s, that had led to the expansion of Rule 10b-5 in the first place. Nonetheless, Lerach would later chortle to friends that he wished he could have seen Shugart's face when, even after showing a profit, he still received a legal complaint accusing him of insider selling and then insider buying—all within a three-week period. The suit, noting that three weeks was a short time for a $2 billion company to reverse its fortune, was filed on September 22, 1989, in federal district court. "I have his picture on my wall right in front of me—I hate him," Shugart told a business journalist. "He and the people like him are a drag on society."

Shugart would be sued by Lerach three times.

> • >

ANOTHER TROPHY BEARING THE name of Ronald O. Perelman, one of America's richest profiteers, would soon be added. For more than two decades the cigar-chomping Perelman reaped his fortune buying and selling beleaguered corporations. One of these entities—SCI Television—he purchased for $120 million and the assumption of $750 million in debt. He would consolidate this holding with several others in a package that paved the way for Fox Television. Finally he would sell his holdings to Rupert Murdoch for $3 billion. Along the way the purchase and consolidation of SCI had shareholders howling that not enough consideration had been given to their ownership interests.

Lerach had plaintiffs lined up, ready to take on the famously combative, highly litigious, and heavily lawyered Perelman. Working on the case in Los Angeles was Jeff Westerman, a 1980 graduate of Lerach's alma mater, the University of Pittsburgh Law School. Westerman, a diligent attorney, had uncovered promising facts, but he possessed a deferential nature. Lerach decided he needed someone with a blood instinct. He went outside the firm, hiring a friend, Patrick Frega, a high-profile personal injury lawyer from the San Diego area. Frega grew up poor in a tough New Jersey town; his father was run over one night walking home from a bar. Frega played football in college as a diversion from his anger. It didn't work. "I probably would have become a mob hit man," he would later say. Instead he joined the U.S. Marine Corps, training as a sharpshooter. He was deployed to Vietnam and then to "classified" areas, presumably in Laos and Cambodia, where his job was to target and eliminate "key" opponents.

"In no other profession could I have done this legally and gotten paid for it," Frega observed. His career as a military hit man ended when he suffered a near-fatal leg wound. After recovering, through the grace of the GI Bill, he attended a small law school in Florida. Later Frega moved to San Diego and set up private practice. Lerach had seen him perform and considered him not just a fearless but a "terrifying" litigator. Lerach vowed to one day turn him loose in one of his own cases. The Perelman case seemed made to order. Frega wasn't a securities lawyer, but he learned fast, working all night, night after night, firing off memos to Lerach about how to pursue the case. "There's no stopping him," Lerach told friends.

"He took Ron Perelman's deposition. If I was civil and above board," Lerach later said, in reference to the critics who complained of his own meanness, "then Frega was an assassin. He ripped Perelman's throat out. He got up in his face and got him so *fertummelt*, so flummoxed . . . 'So, you were lying?' Perelman yells back, 'Yeah, I was!' He was pissed and confused.

"Westerman, my timid little antelope, was in the deposition and couldn't believe it," Lerach continued. "He came to me with a memo saying Frega's behavior was over the line. Somehow Patrick saw a copy. He got Westerman aside and said to him: 'You little fuck, if you ever complain to Lerach about me again, you're going home to mama in a body bag with a toe tag on.' Westerman never spoke another word the rest of the case."

The lawsuit was settled for nearly $30 million. Frega received a check for more than $1 million. That was before his life took an indelible turn. "He was aggressive and insecure, and somehow felt he had to ingratiate himself with judges," Lerach recalled, lowering his voice. "And he did things he should not have done."

A twenty-one-count indictment listing Frega as a defendant claimed that from 1983 to 1992 he and San Diego Superior Court Judges James A.

Malkus and G. Dennis Adams engaged in more than 163 overt acts of racketeering conspiracy and mail fraud. Presiding Judge Bruce Greer was also implicated in the scheme, in which Frega stood accused of giving more than $100,000 in gifts to the three judges in return for favorable rulings netting him hefty fees. Greer resigned from the bench and became a prosecution witness. Frega, Malkus, and Adams went to federal prison. Before he began serving a forty-two-month sentence, Frega (whose wife sued for divorce) was also forced to declare bankruptcy. With his friend and legal colleague in prison, Lerach paid for Frega's four children to continue their schooling, also contributing monthly allowances to each.

That Lerach was willing to help at all held some irony, because Frega nearly dragged him down with himself and the others. Lerach was suing on behalf of shareholders who claimed that executives of Henley Corp., in the aftermath of a merger with Allied Signal, instituted a program called the Henley Executive Stock Purchase Plan, whereby they were able to give themselves nonrecourse loans from the company to purchase stock. Shareholders wanted an injunction, putting an end to the plan and redistributing money to themselves. Lerach drew a difficult judge and was combative in return. The judge transferred the case to Judge Greer, who, Lerach would eventually learn, had been scheming with Frega. Within weeks the plaintiffs prevailed, winning an award of more than $35 million. Lerach's fee was estimated to be $10 million.

After some delays a hearing was finally set before the judge to finalize the number. The night before, Lerach received a call from Frega. "Don't worry, I talked to Judge Greer, you're going to get your fee," Lerach heard his friend say.

Lerach nearly panicked. "You what?"

Frega sounded taken aback; he thought he had done his friend a favor. "Don't worry about it," he told Lerach. Lerach did receive the fee, and later, after Judge Greer flipped, the plaintiffs' lawyer, now a public figure for pulling corporate America's chain, received attention from law enforcement. Judge Greer told criminal investigators that Frega had talked to him about Lerach's fee. The implications were obvious to the authorities, as they were to Lerach. What they could not prove, and what Lerach swore did not happen, was a quid pro quo for Frega. "Thank God I hadn't given Pat one penny," Lerach said long after the fact.

In retrospect, it is fascinating to contemplate what might have happened if Lerach had been caught up in the web woven by Frega and the judges. At the least Lerach would have lost his license to practice law. Corporate America would certainly have dodged many multimillion-dollar bullets fired repeatedly over the next twenty years. The U.S. Department of Justice would have had one less high-profile attorney to pursue in a bicoastal investigation that took seven years and cost many millions of dollars.

> • > • > • > • >

MAKING A CASE

Prominent in Bill Lerach's trophy collection was a settlement with Nucorp Energy, a San Diego–based oilfield equipment supplier and energy explorer that had sold to unsuspecting investors some $150 million worth of securities late in 1981, less than a year before declaring bankruptcy. As a metaphor, the trophy resembled a glass half empty because Lerach had sought $250 million in his lawsuit on behalf of shareholders and settled for $41 million. For the firm Milberg Weiss and for Bill Lerach, it would also come to resemble a glass whose bottom had dropped out.

Requiring five years of discovery prior to a seven-month jury trial that would produce more than 13,000 pages of trial transcripts along with some fifty witnesses and thousands of articles of evidence, Nucorp would stretch the firm's resources, costing more than $5 million and tying up its star litigator.

Lerach and his team secured hundreds of documents—memos and notes—from the defendants and interviewed dozens of witnesses, including Nucorp officers and managers. The ex-Nucorp executives conceded their part in the questionable revenues, creative accounting methods, and dubious claims of oil reserves that had continued to lure investors. After learning that

Lerach had said: "I'll be living in his house"—literally the cliffside mansion that Lerach had been coveting in La Jolla—Nucorp president Richard Burns instructed his attorneys to settle.

Lerach next turned his attention to others he deemed responsible for the fraud: the company's underwriter, Wall Street's Donaldson, Lufkin & Jenrette; its auditor, Arthur Andersen; its lender, Continental Illinois Bank and Trust of Chicago; and finally a major Nucorp investor, Circle K Corp., a Phoenix-based convenience-store chain that was the first to install gas pumps. These were Nucorp's enablers, Lerach believed, and they were liable for damages as well. More to the point, they had deep pockets.

The remaining defendants, particularly Circle K, were determined not to cave, as Nucorp had done. For his part, Lerach welcomed a courtroom duel, especially with that big $41 million settlement behind him. Here was a golden chance to present the scheme liability concept to a jury, showing an out-of-control company could go only as far as its auditors and under-writers let it. The only negative, he thought, were the plaintiffs.

"They're institutional investors, not widows and orphans," he worried aloud to San Francisco attorney David Gold, who put this lone misgiving aside and signed on as cocounsel, adding more firepower to Lerach's arsenal.

The trial began in federal court in San Diego on Tuesday, October 20, 1987, one day after "Black Monday," the worst one-day percentage decline in stock market history, before U.S. District Court Judge J. Lawrence Irving. A fifty-two-year-old former trial attorney appointed to the bench by President Reagan, Irving had a reputation for being cordial and impartial.*

The issues in the giant jigsaw puzzle that Lerach would construct before the jury involved the complicated responsibility that each of the defendants might or might not bear, individually or together, in Nucorp's transgressions. Throughout the trial more than a dozen defense lawyers representing the four defendants would vigorously argue that their clients bore no responsibility for the various schemes Lerach was alleging. In fact, they

---

* As it turned out, Irving served a relatively brief period on the federal bench. In September 1990, objecting to the 1987 mandatory federal sentencing law, he became the first federal jurist in the nation to resign in protest over "mandatory minimums."

would argue, they were equally and unwittingly victims of Nucorp's activities themselves.

"What if it turns out that Continental lost money, what if Continental is a victim?" asked Bill Tucker, an attorney defending Continental Bank.

To win the $200 million jury award he sought, Lerach would first have to demonstrate Nucorp's transgressions—which he'd already done in securing the previous settlement with the company, but not before a jury—and then tie each of the defendants, individually and collectively, to those schemes. Essentially he was trying five cases in one, something the jury would have to sort through in order to assess culpability of one, two, three, or all four defendants—or none at all.

This was a tall order, particularly in front of a jury consisting of a retired navy electrician, a housewife married to a retired army noncommissioned officer, a retired telephone company manager, a twice-divorced housewife, a retired San Diego County public works employee, and a former schoolteacher whose expertise was in home economics. Only one, the schoolteacher, had a college degree. And only one, the navy electrician, had more than six figures invested in the stock market. The problem, both sides knew, would be keeping their evidence and their questions coherent, their witnesses' answers relatively understandable, and the jury attentive.

As he had in the Pacific Homes case seven years earlier, Lerach opened by ingratiating himself with the jurors, reminding them that all participants would be spending considerable time together, while "evidence of a true life story" unfolded. "Unfortunately, it is a story in which there are no heroes, and it has not a happy ending," he continued. "You are going to learn about a story of dishonesty and professional negligence."

Warming to his task, Lerach told the jury that Nucorp was nothing more than "a deception, an illusion." Exhibits proving as much would come in the form of charts, graphs, internal memos, and press releases linking each of the four defendants to Nucorp's dealings and downfall—and its investors' losses. To assist them in sorting out culpability, Lerach told the jurors that his expert witness, a man named John Torkelsen, would explain the amount of damages investors suffered because of the defendants' collusion with Nucorp.

Forming a rapport with a jury, as Lerach had done in the Pacific Homes case, required a deft touch. Initially, at least, he struck the right notes. During his cross-examination of Nucorp chief Richard Burns, Lerach skillfully got the man he'd already sued and settled with to essentially explain in his own words how he had had a conflict of interest regarding the rosy scenarios he was putting out.

"I was surely impressed with that curly-haired fella," juror Russell Colson recalled of Lerach more than twenty years later. "He was very smooth, very articulate. There was just this manner about him. His body language was just so great."

But in the seven years since he had tried the Pacific Homes case, Lerach had become a bit hardened. In the Nucorp case, even his sense of humor had an edge to it. In an introductory phase of the trial, Tucker, the Continental Bank attorney, laid out a detailed history of the bank's relationship with Burns. "Let me give you some names—you will be hearing of people associated with the Continental Bank—so that when their names come up in the evidence you won't be hearing them for the first time. Mr. O'Keane, [James O'Keane, a Continental energy specialist, who handled the Nucorp credit account] we have already told you about. He is the banker with heart . . ."

Lerach couldn't resist. "I have to tell the court that I once had a friend who needed a heart transplant," he said by way of rejoinder. "While consulting with the surgeon he said, 'I only have one request. I would prefer that my transplanted heart be that of a banker.' When the surgeon asked 'why?' he said, 'Because it's never been used.' "

The jury cracked up. Even the defense joined in the laughter. Judge Irving, too, obviously delighted in the rejoinder. Later in the trial, however, while cross-examining O'Keane, Lerach's wit turned harsh:

"And one of the places you wanted to force them to raise cash [to pay back a loan] was in the sale of the notes to the insurance companies?"

"I didn't really care where they raised the cash," O'Keane answered.

"As long as they raised it and paid you?"

"Sure," O'Keane answered, his demeanor signaling he thought the question to be misinformed. Banks were in business to make money on their loans.

"Good solid loan-sharking stuff, right?" Lerach asked, grinning. Likewise, when it came time to question Burns, Lerach could not conceal his disdain. It was subtle, but this demeanor toward Burns put Lerach's own personality on the jury's screen as well.

> • >

BEFORE HE PUT TORKELSEN on the stand, Lerach wanted to follow up on a significant discovery. Among the hundreds of documents his research team planned to introduce into evidence was the deposition of a member of Donaldson, Lufkin & Jenrette's Los Angeles office who had helped underwrite Nucorp's public offerings. The witness, Steven Lebow, then a twenty-four-year-old MBA from the Wharton School of Business, had originally been scheduled to testify on behalf of the defense. But when Steven F. Goldstone, an attorney with the New York firm of Davis, Polk & Wardwell, learned that Lerach's team had uncovered inconsistencies in Lebow's deposition, he withdrew Lebow's name from the defense witness list. Lerach requested, and Judge Irving granted, a court order compelling Goldstone to produce his client within ten days. Goldstone objected, trying to explain that Lebow was too junior to explain the DLJ underwriting decisions he had witnessed. Both Lerach and Judge Irving scoffed at Goldstone's recalcitrance, reminding him that it was he who had scheduled the witness in the first place.

On December 9, after greeting the jury, Irving asked Goldstone if the witness was in the courtroom. "No, your honor, we are unable to produce Mr. Lebow," Goldstone answered, begging the judge for more time. In fact, Goldstone had asked a federal appeals judge for a ruling that would block Lebow's testimony. Still, the Davis Polk partner assured the judge he would try to have the witness available the next day. Judge Irving could not disguise his anger. Lerach was enjoying the drama.

Clearly peeved, the judge gave Goldstone a hard deadline. Either produce the witness the next morning or face the consequences. That evening, in his hotel, Goldstone received the news he expected to hear: the appeals court turned down his petition. A tense courtroom reopened for business on December 10. Bill Lerach and David Gold scanned the audience, trying to spot Lebow. At the defense table Goldstone tensely reviewed his notes, not looking up. Judge Irving entered briskly, greeted those in attendance, and sped through some housekeeping matters. Then he turned his attention to Goldstone, who was already standing. "Mr. Goldstone, is Mr. Lerach's witness with us?"

"With the greatest respect, your honor: No, your honor, I have advised my client not to produce Mr. Lebow because of the 'tactical disadvantages' it will present." He also announced he had appealed Judge Irving's court order but had been turned down the previous evening. He asked the judge for more time to file another appeal.

Judge Irving's patience was at an end. Either produce the witness after the noon recess, he said, or face a default judgment. Those in the know gasped. Goldstone was risking losing the case before it had been tried. Lerach felt his face flush and his head lighten, and he clutched the table in front of him for fear of fainting. At the defense table, James Goldman, helping in the representation of Arthur Andersen, was equally shocked.

After the lunch break Judge Irving looked hard at Goldstone, repeating his earlier question. Goldstone gave the same answer. Irving erupted. "In twenty years of practice and five years as a judge, I have never seen anything so incredible," he said. "A total refusal to cooperate with opposing counsel, playing games, tactical or otherwise with the court and counsel, about 'I will produce, I won't produce,' a court order, then 'I won't produce,' then 'I will produce, but only on conditions.'"

The judge announced for all to hear: "I find defendant Donaldson Lufkin Jenrette in default," adding that they had lost this case for willfully violating his order. "You are excused Mr. Goldstone," the judge said flatly. With that, Goldstone hightailed it out of the courtroom.

After appeals had been exhausted, his client Donaldson, Lufkin & Jenrette would be made to forfeit $20 million paid by the company's insurers. As for Goldstone, there *are* second acts in American life. He would continue to practice law on Wall Street before joining RJR Nabisco in 1995 as its chairman and CEO. There Goldstone helped undo the ill-considered merger between R.J. Reynolds and Nabisco and helped broker a historic settlement between the giant tobacco company and forty state attorney generals, led by New York's Eliot Spitzer, who by then had become a symbiotic ally of Bill Lerach not only in tobacco litigation but in major fraud cases as well.

> • >

ON DECEMBER 28, 1987, following a Christmas break, John Torkelsen appeared as an expert witness. Lerach led him through his biography. A Princeton National Merit Scholar with a degree in chemical engineering and an MBA from Harvard, Torkelsen identified his current business as Princeton Venture Research, explaining that the New Jersey firm performed financial analysis, investment banking, and management consulting for professional investors, banks, insurance companies, university endowments, and pension funds—advising them on investment decisions. The company also assisted start-ups, helping them with their documentation in order to raise capital.

Essentially, Torkelsen was a venture capitalist who sat on the boards of two companies, one doing computer work for the National Institutes of Health, and the other working for the National Security Agency. Harvard had been a client, and so had MIT, as had Fidelity, John Hancock Insurance, Chase Manhattan Bank, and Bankers Trust. His consultancy had developed proprietary computer software for analyzing economic data. One sector that benefited from the programs was the oil and chemical industries.

Lerach glanced at the jury. His witness clearly was making an impression. What the jury and the judge did not know was that Torkelsen was incentivized to make such an impression. Specifically, he had a unique and secret agreement with the Milberg Weiss firm: he would be paid on a contingency basis, just like the law firm that hired him. If the firm won, Torkelsen won—as much as ten percent of the fee awarded to the firm. In a case such as this with the plaintiffs asking for $200 million, whereby plaintiffs' attorneys would share around $40 million in fees, Torkelsen's performance over nearly three days on the stand could be worth as much as $4 million to him.

After a few preliminary questions, which Lerach and Torkelsen had rehearsed, Lerach segued into asking Torkelsen if he had reviewed and analyzed evidence—including SEC documents and Nucorp's securities trading—and whether he had read transcripts of prior trial testimony. Yes, he had. He had even prepared his own graphs and charts tracing the issuing of Nucorp's debentures and price fluctuations during the class action period. Lerach entered two charts into evidence. Both were similar to exhibits that Lerach and his own team of lawyers had prepared in previous cases showing the rise and precipitous decline of Nucorp stock along with the issuing of debentures.

Torkelsen was asked to tell the jury how many shareholders were holding Nucorp stock during the months of the decline. Basing his answer on trading records, Lerach's superwitness estimated that by the end of 1981 more than nine thousand individuals held common stock, when he factored in debenture holders. Lerach then asked about favorable auditors' reports, buoyant press releases, and equally optimistic financial reports—including prospectuses released by Donaldson, Lufkin & Jenrette—that used such phrases as "record levels of sales," while Torkelsen traced the announcements along the graph showing the sharp upward trajectory of Nucorp stock prices. Clearly, he offered, the company news was highly material to the stock price. Torkelsen also told the jury that Nucorp was suffering from a lack of financial control as it expanded by acquiring new companies, leaving it with excessive inventories and forcing it to drastically cut prices for drilling equipment. Under law, those problems should have been disclosed.

At four thirty P.M., noting that Lerach and Torkelsen had put the jury through a rigorous day, Judge Irving called a recess. "Have a nice evening," he concluded. Lerach approached Torkelsen, his eyes twinkling, and said under his breath: "I don't think the defense is going to have a very nice evening."

The defense's cross-examination of Torkelsen began the next day with a sustained barrage from James Goldman, one of the attorneys representing Arthur Andersen. First, he attacked Torkelsen's expertise in virtually every facet—from accounting and auditing to petroleum engineering, to geology, to heavy oil, to oil machinery—compelling the expert witness to concede that he was not an expert in any of those fields. Then after a series of jabbing questions, he got Torkelsen to acknowledge that Nucorp was a speculative player in a volatile industry. He asked Torkelsen whether, if his own client Arthur Andersen had not contributed material misstatements on behalf of Nucorp, the jury would even need to consider Torkelsen's testimony. Finally Lerach stepped in, and the judge sustained his objection. But Goldman had sprung a trap: "You're not offering expert testimony that Arthur Andersen is responsible for any of the particular misstatements that are involved in this case—isn't that right?"

Torkelsen, sensing he was cornered, answered: "That's correct."

Ever so slightly, Goldman had pried his client away from the other defendants. With new footing, he launched an attack on Torkelsen's damage analysis, the very heart of the witness's expertise, in an attempt to show that even someone who purchased a stock at an inflated price could have sold that same stock at an even more inflated price.

"It's complicated," Torkelsen acknowledged. Reading the looks on the faces of the jurors in the courtroom that day, observers could conclude that they agreed with Torkelsen. It *was* getting complicated. The questions and answers lasted throughout the morning in a courtroom that was overheated due to an incorrect thermostat setting somewhere in the building. Judge Irving apologized to the jury for their discomfort. The jurors were also challenged by the mind-numbing calculations that Goldman called upon Torkelsen to make on market forecasts of heavy oil reserves, probable reserves, and proven reserves—as well as how each affected Nucorp's ultimate market capitalization. Further he attacked, taking Torkelsen deep into the weeds, in an effort to have the witness trip himself up. This was a calculated gamble because the defense lawyer could lose the jury's attention—and sympathy.

Late in the session Goldman asked the witness whether Wall Street had placed too much value on Nucorp's unproven heavy oil reserves. Torkelsen fought him off, deflecting attention from Wall Street to the accountants who signed off on Nucorp's rosy scenarios.

"The accountants used those heavy oil reserves to create an accounting function that increased the earnings of other oil, Torkelsen replied. "Not in the context of you were going to pull that heavy oil out of the ground right now and make a profit today. It was because it was an accounting treatment that the auditors applied that goosed—excuse me, that increased the earnings from the—"

Judge Irving broke in: "Is that a Wall Street term?"

"We use it quite frequently, your honor."

"Financial analysts use that?" the judge asked.

"Actually we do," Torkelsen told him. "It's a term for cooking the books."

More sparring followed. Goldman struck a blow by questioning Torkelsen about inconsistencies between his estimation of damages in earlier depositions and his current testimony on the stand. The judge, taking note that a college football game, the Holiday Bowl, was taking place in San Diego later that evening and that the New Year recess was almost upon them, told the jury he intended to release them early.

Lerach was not ready to quit for the year—or even the evening. He needed to redress Goldman's attack on his expert. "Now, was that a proceeding where there was submitted to the court for its approval a partial settlement of this litigation with certain other defendants?"

"Yes," Torkelsen answered.

Raising his voice to be certain to be heard, Lerach then asked: "And your testimony was taken in that regard to overcome the objections of Arthur Andersen and these other defendants who tried to scuttle the settlement, isn't that right?"

In unison, the defense lawyers leaped to their feet, raising a chorus of objections. The jury also tensed.

"The objection is sustained to that question," Judge Irving said quickly.

Red-faced, Lerach spun and stormed back toward the plaintiffs' table, hurling his notes to the floor as he sat, uttering, "Let's go to the football game."

> • >

COURT RESUMED AT NINE FIFTY A.M. on January 5, 1988. Without the jury present, Stuart L. Kadison—a World War II veteran, Stanford law graduate, venerated trial lawyer, and the lead attorney representing Arthur Andersen—approached the bench. "Even if it should not please the court," he began, "on behalf of my client, Arthur Andersen and Company, I move for a mistrial by reason of deliberate misconduct of counsel [Lerach] for the class plaintiffs in the presence of the jury, shortly before the close of proceedings on Wednesday, December 30, 1987."

Lerach's question of Torkelsen "assumed a falsehood," Kadison maintained—namely, that Arthur Andersen had attempted to derail the previous Nucorp settlement. Moreover, the assertion could have had no other purpose than to bias the jury. "The jury reacted, both visibly and audibly," Kadison noted. "It was probably the most dramatic moment of the trial. After the court sustained the objection . . . the jury observed Mr. Lerach storm back to the counsel table, throw his notes on the floor, and subside . . . Mr. Lerach's misconduct was conscious, it was deliberate, and it was calculated to inflame and prejudice the jury against the defendants, and our client in particular."

Kadison wasn't asking the judge to rein in Lerach—he was asking him to throw out the case or at least reprimand Lerach in front of the jury.

"At some point there has to be a limit to amateurish and infantile behavior in the presence of the jury," Kadison continued. "I think the damages done in terms of prejudice to our client are beyond repair and certainly was in no way our fault."

Even if the judge disagreed, Kadison added, he should read a cautionary statement to the jury unbinding the defendants to the previous settlement. The judge affirmed this point and informed the defense lawyers that he was inclined to rule against the motion. However, he added: "I do intend on saying something to the jury."

Lerach did not object.

Following that the judge called a recess. In the elevator Lerach pushed his way into a crowd that included Kadison. He addressed his opponent, senior to him by nearly three decades, for all to hear: "Kadison, this case is going to bring an ignominious end to your mediocre career!" He knew immediately that the remark would eventually cost him—just not how much.

When court resumed at 10:35 A.M. on January 5, Judge Irving bade the jurors a happy New Year, and the plaintiffs called a new witness. His name was Fred Hervey, then seventy-nine years old. The jury learned that he was from El Paso, Texas, where he had twice been mayor. During the Depression, Hervey—who had dropped out of high school to support his family—and his brother opened a drive-in root beer stand and also sold tamales, beans, pies, and other food cooked by their mother. In 1936 he opened a second store. After serving in the U.S. Navy during World War II, Hervey returned home and opened three more restaurants, a supermarket, and a radio station. In 1951 he ran for Congress but lost. Nonetheless, *Fortune* magazine recognized him in a list of young men who had proved that America was still a land of unlimited opportunities. Six years later he expanded his restaurants and supermarket into what would eventually become the nation's second-largest convenience store chain—Circle K Corp.—with fifteen hundred outlets in fifteen states. In September 1980 Circle K purchased one million shares of Nucorp stock for $23.5 million, borrowing the whole amount to invest in Nucorp's oil-drilling efforts. Further questions, which Lerach had to repeat because of Hervey's hearing difficulties, showed that Circle K reflected on its books as assets a 10 percent interest in a Nucorp heavy oil–drilling project that Lerach and Torkelsen had already derided, in South Texas's sand tar pits. At the same time Hervey was elected to serve on Nucorp's board of directors. Hervey then recounted joining Nucorp's CEO Richard Burns in a hotel room for a meeting with the president of Mercantile Bank, which, along with defendant Continental Bank, held Nucorp's line of credit. According to his testimony, Hervey was still considering investing in Nucorp; Burns suggested to the Mercantile president that he loan Hervey the money to make the deal.

"And it was a surprise when the president of the bank said: 'We would be glad to loan Fred Hervey all the money'?" Lerach asked.

"That's right. And I said: 'Well, don't you think maybe I'll put up six million and you'll only put up seventeen million?' And he said, 'No, you're going great places with Dick Burns,'" Hervey continued in his nasal, West

Texas twang: " 'You just take all of that money because you are going to need it, and you're going to put it to real good use. You and Dick Burns are going to make history.' "

With Circle K's attorney Charles "Chuck" Dick listening intently, Lerach then walked Hervey back through the company's financial quarterly reports for the year leading up to the purchase, showing him charts plotting a steady decline in Circle K's earnings until the final quarter of 1981, when the company factored its investment in Nucorp and the energy company's stated record earnings into its own earnings report, showing improved results. On December 15 of the same year—1981—Circle K sold 1.25 million shares to the public at between $11.62 and $14.50 per share, raising some $15 million. Lerach also elicited an admission from Hervey that Circle K had dumped its previous auditors and hired Arthur Andersen—on Richard Burns's recommendation.

Hervey explained that, to his thinking, there was logic to this move. He had been told that Arthur Andersen had more expertise in gas and oil accounting. And since Circle K would be backing Nucorp's drilling ventures, it made sense to share accountants anyway. This observation inspired a response from Lerach: "Mr. Hervey, isn't it a fact that in order for Circle K to pick up a part of Nucorp's earnings and include them in Circle K's earnings via the equity method, that Circle K had to, in fact, demonstrate that it had significant influence over Nucorp's operating and financial policies?"

"Well, I don't know what you mean by 'demonstrate,' " Hervey replied. "They just merely had to do what the auditors said, 'You have to do it this way.' " At the defense table, Chuck Dick, the Circle K attorney, took notes but did not object.

Lerach wanted this to be indelible with the jury: "And, in fact, and in truth, Circle K *did* have significant influence over Nucorp's operating policies and financial policies—and that's why it could use the equity method."

Hervey thought about it and answered: "We just had—we had—we just carried out what the auditors said, 'Here's what you have to do.' "

Digging deeper, Lerach cited a 1981 Arthur Andersen internal document and asked Hervey to vouch for a memo that said: "Circle K could demonstrate 'significant influence' over Nucorp's operating and financial policies because Fred [Hervey] would go on the Nucorp board of directors and executive committee. With his election to the executive committee, he would represent one vote out of four on that committee."

Even more potentially damaging was Hervey's admission that he had been warned of Richard Burns's insider selling before his previous company plunged into bankruptcy and that he had not done a credit check on his new business partner. With a growing inventory of expensive oil-recovery equipment pressing the company's bottom line, Hervey also conceded attending a meeting when the board discussed canceling or deferring taking delivery of the equipment "to fight for time," because "there is no question we had an inventory problem." Yet, Hervey acknowledged, this problem was not disclosed on the company's September 1981 prospectus.

"Now, isn't it a fact that shortly after that information came to your attention, that you learned that management at Nucorp Supply had been cooking the books?" Lerach asked.

"No," Hervey answered hesitantly. "The 'cooking the books' statement was heard by me in the hallway of the offices of Nucorp by David Tenwick, a codirector of Nucorp, and an outside director of Circle K, and I asked David—Mr. Tenwick, I said, 'What do you mean by cooking the books?' And he said to me: 'We found that some of the sales of one month were put over into the sales of a succeeding month, which distorted the picture somewhat.' It was at that point that I said to him, 'Well, now, that's not—that is inconsequential. Why would you . . .' He said: 'Well, as far as I'm concerned, it was inconsequential, but I think we had to put a stop, to make sure that the sales went into the right month.' And I said, 'Well, you have solved—you have corrected the problem?' He said, 'I have.'"

Lerach moved into Circle K's investment in Nucorp's oil exploration and steered Hervey into telling the jury that the lack of drilling performance became a concern—at one point returning about $145,000 on a $5 million investment.

The Circle K chairman conceded that he tried to get out of the drilling investment because it was "too big a risk, too big a gamble." He conceded that Nucorp agreed to refund the investment with commensurate shares of stock valued at $20 per share provided that Circle K purchased 150,000 shares of Nucorp stock at that price. Lerach then produced documents that Hervey recognized showing that the Nucorp shares Circle K agreed to purchase would have traded before the public offering just a month later.

However, according to Circle K documents and Hervey's testimony, Circle K dropped out of the stock purchase because the price of Nucorp stock was already starting to drop. Instead it announced it would purchase three million shares of Nucorp stock on the open market—as prices had fallen below $20 a share. The move was twofold: Circle K was hedging its bets, but by making a purchase in the open market, Circle K, Nucorp's largest investor, was sending a message to prospective investors that it still had confidence in Nucorp.

"Now if Nucorp stock continued to go down and down, it was going to have the impact of requiring Circle K to write off that investment on its books, wasn't it?" Lerach asked.

Hervey was quick to answer: "Well, yes. If you've got stock in a company and it goes broke, you're going to lose—you're going to lose your investment."

Circle K's qualms about the drilling operation, and Nucorp's repurchase of Circle K's share of that operation did go through, but were not disclosed on the public offering prospectus. This, Lerach was trying to demonstrate, constituted fraud on the part of Nucorp and Circle K, with help from the other defendants—a fraud that was perpetrated on uninformed investors.

"We should not have invested—we shouldn't have gotten mixed up with Nucorp anyway," Hervey said, "and whenever we got mixed up with Nucorp, I'll guarantee you we had to pay and pay through—pay through the nose."

This concession was a major point for the plaintiffs, or so it seemed. But (and this wasn't clear until later) something was happening in the jury box. Maybe it dated to Lerach's exhibition before the New Year's break. Maybe it was Hervey's life story or his age, or simply his candor. Yet somewhere along the line Lerach had succeeded in turning Hervey into a sympathetic figure.

One onlooker picked up on the subtle turning of the tide. His name was Patrick Coughlin. He was a thirty-two-year-old assistant U.S. Attorney in San Diego, who specialized in criminal prosecutions of white-collar crimes. He was solidly built, with curly hair and a slightly lopsided mouth that turned down from right to left, giving him a tough-guy appearance more resembling the football player he'd been at Santa Clara University. After graduating from law school at the relatively obscure Golden Gate University, he joined the U.S. Attorney's office in Washington, D.C. There he prosecuted felony crimes, including one of the largest RICO cases in U.S. history, as well as an infamous oil fraud that had, as part of its complexities, a murder-for-hire element. In the nation's capital Coughlin earned a reputation for being a fearless and dogged prosecutor, and after four years he was transferred to San Diego. At the time of the Nucorp trial Coughlin had found himself between cases. He was tiring of government prosecution work, and starting to dream of making more than his $45,000 government salary. He had mentioned his interest in private practice to a friend who recommended he do some diligence on Milberg Weiss Lerach, a firm where his fierceness and penchant for hard work might be a good match. So he made himself at home in Judge Irving's courtroom, paying particular attention to his prospective boss Bill Lerach.

"I was impressed with his preparation, particularly in a complex trial such as this," he remembered two decades later—just after his name replaced Lerach's on the door announcing him as head of the firm Lerach had once ruled. "I was also struck that he did not play well to the jury. He played well to the judge, to his opponents, to the witnesses, although he could be heavy-handed in front of the jury. But I noticed he never looked at the jurors. If they think you are ignoring them, they can turn on you."

> • >

ON MONDAY MORNING, MARCH 15, 1988, the fifty-ninth day of the trial, Jim Goldman, the Arthur Andersen defense attorney, called as a witness Daniel R. Fischel, a thirty-eight-year-old professor of law and business at the University of Chicago, who specialized in teaching corporate finance and economic analysis of the law. At Goldman's urging, Fischel, a slight, intense-looking man with wavy hair and wearing what appeared to be a fixed grin, told the court that he was a principal in the corporate finance and securities area of a company called Lexecon, a ten-year-old Chicago-based consulting firm specializing in the application of economics to an array of legal and business problems. Its clients included Ford, General Motors, General Electric, and Sears Roebuck. Among the more than sixty employees, Fischel added, were two Nobel Prize winners in economics.

Following Goldman's guidance, Fischel explained that he had studied at the University of Chicago Law School under Richard A. Posner, a brilliant, prolific, and controversial legal thinker and writer credited with being one of the early proponents of a doctrine called the "economic analysis of law." Adherents to the "law and economics movement," as it is also known, apply economic theories as a way of ascertaining which legal rules and precedents are economically efficient—and likely to survive. It's a pragmatist school of thought, which taken to its ultimate logical conclusion holds that in certain cases willingly breaching contracts makes more economic sense than honoring them.

Bill Lerach was unimpressed with Posner and had even a lower opinion of Fischel. As far as he was concerned, both men hid behind esoteric theories to defend the likes of Michael Milken and Charles Keating at a time when those men were doing real damage—not theoretical harm—to working Americans who were looking for an honest return on their investments. Lerach's contempt for these Chicago professors was on display as he rose to his feet from the plaintiffs' table, objecting to the very mention of Posner's name by Fischel. It was irrelevant, Lerach said. As events would unfold, both Fischel and Posner became very relevant—to Lerach's detriment. Judge Irving overruled the objection, and Fischel continued, telling the jury he had graduated first in his class and later clerked for Justice Potter Stewart of the U.S. Supreme Court. Lerach was not physically violent by nature, but as he listened to Fischel rattle off his bona fides, he thought to himself—and later said aloud to David Gold—"Someday I'm going to wipe that grin right off that little shit's face."

Over Lerach's objection, Fischel also told the court that Milberg Weiss had filed a Supreme Court brief listing several of his published articles, including the "fraud on the market" theory that Lerach's firm had developed, in a table of authorities, citing his expertise in the functioning of securities markets. Further, Fischel recounted being invited to consult for the Securities and Exchange Commission and the New York Stock Exchange, and being asked by William Proxmire, chairman of the Senate Banking Committee, to testify before Congress on issues related to shareholder rights.

As Lerach had done with John Torkelsen, Goldman urged his own expert witness to expound on the extent of his preparation for the Nucorp case, including the review of SEC filings, quarterly and annual reports, press releases, analysts' reports, and trading information, as well as materials on the oil and gas industry. He mentioned that he had read the transcripts of the previous witnesses, including Torkelsen's testimony on behalf of the plaintiffs.

"As a result of your review of those documents and other documents, have you come to some opinions?" Goldman asked.

"Yes, I have," Fischel answered.

Sensing impending objections, Judge Irving called a recess. Outside of the jury's presence he asked Goldman to outline what Fischel was prepared to say. "He is here to testify about, among other things, the nature of risks associated with investing in stocks and other securities, and in particular Nucorp's securities, and how those risks explain movements of stocks in general and movements in Nucorp's securities in particular," Goldman told the judge. "The plaintiffs have tried to prove that the alleged fraud explains all or substantially all of the movement in the price of Nucorp's securities. We feel we're entitled to prove that that isn't correct."

Judge Irving was skeptical. "Frankly, Mr. Goldman, I have some difficulty understanding how, whether this stock was speculative or not, it has any relevance to any issue in this case," he said. "But let me hear further from Mr. Lerach."

"He admits the man is going to testify about the riskiness of investing generally," Lerach told the judge. "That can't have anything to do with this case . . . If this witness gets into this and they try to imply to the jury that somehow they [plaintiffs] are a bunch of plungers who ought to suffer, they are without recompense, you're going to have to deal with that very dramatically and sternly."

Irving took heed and instructed Goldman to allow his witness to summarize his opinions out of earshot of the jury. If the judge considered the opinions relevant to the case against the defendants, he would then rule on the admissibility.

Fischel would be put back on the stand the following morning, albeit with constraints. When they concluded the day, to prepare for the next, both sides were girding for what they knew would be a long and bloody slugfest in front of the jury, not only as to the witness's overall credibility and effectiveness but over nearly every question, every answer, every one of more than fifty exhibits.

Bill Lerach and Dan Fischel had now entered a phase when no ground could be given. Mountain climbers have a name for a similar circumstance as they near the summits of the world's tallest peaks, when the oxygen grows thin and no misstep is without consequence. They call it "the death zone."

> • > • > • > • >

MAKING ENEMIES

The next morning, March 16, 1988, the battle resumed. Goldman led off by asking the Chicago law professor to explain what the term *risk* meant to him with regard to Nucorp. Fischel delivered a haymaker, saying that Nucorp's collapse mirrored a large and precipitous depression in the oil industry.

Sitting at the plaintiffs' table, Lerach comforted himself with the thought that this explanation was transparently self-serving. Goldman's client, auditing giant Arthur Andersen, was the most culpable defendant. As Torkelsen, his expert witness, had tried to explain, after Nucorp's malfeasance, the auditors were the next most culpable in perpetrating the fraud in this tight little circle of greed. Everything false flowed from their financial sign-offs. Still, he wondered whether the jury was buying it. A glance at the jurors was not reassuring. Goldman and Fischel seemed to have their full attention.

Fischel was maintaining that Nucorp had "put all its eggs in this one basket," in the energy market of the early 1980s after legislation signed by President Reagan had decontrolled the price of oil. Immediately, prices shot up, Fischel noted, adding: "Nucorp's entire business strategy was premised on a strong market for its products." Fischel then described what happened when demand turned downward and the industry experienced oversupplies of goods it once needed—products that Nucorp was selling. It was this phenomenon, as natural to capitalism as water flowing downhill, that Fischel attributed to Nucorp's demise. It was delivered with such simplicity that no jury member, no matter his or her education or experience in the market, could fail to understand.

The jurors seemed attentive to Fischel's observation, elicited in deft questioning from Goldman, that during the class period, as Nucorp's stock began to tank, its officers and directors, including Circle K founder and major Nucorp creditor Fred Hervey, continued to raise money and invest in the company, while declining to sell their stock—a signal they were trying to right the ship rather than abandon it.

Furthermore, Fischel cited several reports from analysts besides DLJ, each of them giving qualified recommendations for *purchasing* Nucorp stock at this time; he noted one particular prediction that "large capital gains" were to be made if market conditions created, as expected, increased energy demands.

Under Goldman's questioning, Fischel rebutted John Torkelsen point by point as to why Nucorp went bankrupt. "None of the statements identified by Mr. Torkelsen as causing an increase in the price of Nucorp relative to the industry . . . had any significant effect on stock prices," he testified. Several jurors leaned forward. One, the former schoolteacher, seated in the lower right-hand corner of the jury box, looked accusingly at Lerach, or so he thought. She'd been doing it for most of the trial, he reminded himself. Finally, when Fischel's presentation neared its conclusion, the judge declared his intention to send the jury home for the day. Turning to Lerach, Irving asked if he was prepared to cross-examine Fischel.

"I'm ready to go. I feel confident I can finish him tomorrow." It was a revealing choice of words but not an accurate prediction, because the two would battle each other for more than a decade to come.

> • >

THE NEXT DAY, March 17, 1988, would come the cross-examination. This would be Lerach's stage. On it he would not only defend his best witness, he would attempt to undercut Fischel and impeach the credibility of the defense's entire case. Their exchange of words over the next two days covered more than 230 pages of trial transcripts. But mere words, transcribed by a court reporter on one-dimensional pages of paper, do not convey the fury embedded in their intellect, or their sarcasm, or their disdain for each other, as evidenced by the flash in the eyes, the sneers on the lips, the upturn of the brows, the prolonged stares, even the screeches in their voices. As Judge Irving later observed: "These two really went at it."

Lerach began with a nuanced tactic, referring to Fischel as "Mr. Fischel," whereas the defense attorneys consistently addressed their august expert as "Professor Fischel." Certainly it was a mere pinprick meant to deflate Fischel's standing with the jury, but after a thousand such pinpricks, who could predict how much blood Lerach might be able to draw?

"You have never gone to a graduate school of business?" Lerach asked, beginning right away to unmask the witness.

"Not as a student, although I teach at a graduate school of business," Fischel demurred.

"Sir," Lerach began, using another of the subtle disparagements both would invoke, "would you please just answer my questions if you can? You never went to a graduate school of business as a student; is that correct?"

"Correct," Fischel answered.

"You never studied accounting?"

"That's correct."

"You never majored in corporate finance?" Lerach continued.

"That's correct."

After continuing to dilute Fischel's experience, Lerach then asked a question that would come back to haunt him. Citing sworn testimony Fischel had given in a deposition two months earlier, he wanted to know how much Fischel had billed the defendants for his services as an expert witness up to that point—asking him if he remembered that the sum was "several hundred thousand dollars." Fischel replied, "I do."

"How *many* hundreds of thousands of dollars was it?"

"I don't know exactly," Fischel responded. "I could perhaps estimate . . ."

"Well, when you meant—when you said several hundred thousand dollars, what did you have in mind?" Lerach asked. "Five hundred, six hundred, seven?"

Fischel appeared to ponder the implications of the question. Was Lerach trying to expose him as a hired gun?

"No," he answered. "Over time a significantly lower sum. But I don't send out bills, we have a bookkeeping department."

Lerach moved on to something else. In this phase he intended to expose Fischel further as a pretender. The line of questioning centered on Fischel's self-congratulations over Milberg Weiss citing one of his published articles in a Supreme Court brief. In that testimony Fischel had left something out.

Lerach exhibited the article in question, "The Use of Modern Finance Theory in Securities Fraud Cases Involving Actively-Traded Securities," reminding Fischel it was the same one "you mentioned so frequently in your testimony that the Supreme Court cited recently." Fischel, not knowing where Lerach was headed, sounded pleased.

"And you're very proud of the article and the fact that it's been cited by the Supreme Court . . . ?"

"I'm very proud of the article," Fischel replied.

"And you remember, you sort of made a point of the fact that my law firm had filed a brief in that Supreme Court case where we cited your article?"

"I was very proud of that, too," Fischel said.

"Now the underlying theory that was accepted by the Supreme Court in this new case is known as 'fraud on the market' theory—correct?"

Fischel agreed.

Lerach moved parallel to Fischel and looked back toward the jury before asking the next question. "Are you the father of the 'fraud on the market' theory?"

Seemingly unsure of where this was all going, Fischel said, "I don't know how to answer that question, Mr. Lerach."

"Did you originate the theory?" the plaintiffs' lawyer asked, still gazing out at the courtroom audience. "Were you instrumental in getting the courts to first accept that theory?"

Fischel was now happy to answer, explaining that while he understood that the courts had been debating the theory prior to the publication of his article, he nonetheless "could take credit for providing the economic rationale for the controversial theory that was viewed as a 'pro-plaintiff theory.'"

Lerach too felt pleased with the answer. He directed Fischel to page nine of the article, where a subhead said: "The Fraud on the Market Theory and the Market Model of Investment Decision." He asked Fischel if he could find a federal case cited in the article, *Blackie v. Barrack*. After Fischel indicated he had found it, Lerach said: "That was a landmark decision on the 'fraud on the market' theory, wasn't it?"

"That's why it is cited first," Fischel replied self-assuredly.

"I wonder, do you recognize the father of the 'fraud on the market' theory as being present in this courtroom?" Lerach asked. He was waiting for the answer as a hunter might await his prey at a watering hole. "Who was the lead counsel in *Blackie v. Barrack* that won the landmark victory for the plaintiffs and established the 'fraud on the market' theory?" Lerach asked, as if he were a schoolteacher addressing a recalcitrant pupil.

"I don't know," Fischel said simply.

"It was my law firm, wasn't it, sir?" Lerach, said, modulating his megaphone voice for all in the courtroom to hear.

"I don't know. I have no reason to disbelieve you," Fischel answered.

By now Lerach was playing center stage of his own opera. "Don't you know that my partner, Mel Weiss, argued that case to the Ninth Circuit?"

Fischel said he did not but added, "I would be happy to acknowledge your prominence in this area."

"I'm not asking for an acknowledgment of prominence. I'm asking whether you're aware that *Blackie v. Barrack* was argued by Melvyn I. Weiss of Milberg Weiss," Lerach said, raising his voice even higher. From his chair at the defense table, Chuck Dick, the attorney for Circle K, stared at Lerach, thinking to himself that the plaintiffs' lawyer had wound himself up like a cheap wristwatch that was about to explode.

Lerach stood in the well of the court, silent, arms crossed. The silence continued, tensely. Then he asked the defendants' expert witness: "So when the Supreme Court cited your article, sir, they were citing an article which relied upon a decision that our firms were instrumental in getting decided; isn't that true?"

A commotion broke out at the defense table. "Objection, relevance, no foundation," chimed in Chuck Dick.

Although intrigued by the line of questioning himself, Judge Irving had no recourse but to sustain the defense.

But Lerach was just getting started. For the better part of the day he and Fischel sparred over allegations that Nucorp insiders and Continental Bank and Circle K Corp. schemed to manipulate the price of Nucorp stock. At the heart of Lerach's argument was that Circle K had purchased Nucorp stock with funds from Continental to rebuild market confidence and invigorate Nucorp's falling stock prices. The security for the loan from Continental was the purchased Nucorp stock—in other words, a classic daisy chain.

Answering Lerach's question as to whether this was or was not improper, Fischel responded with his own question: "If Burns knew in October 1981 that Nucorp was insolvent, as the plaintiffs have alleged, would he have ever agreed to give the bank the right to seize every asset that he owned as a result of changing the form of collateral to be tied to the market value of the stock if he knew the stock was really worth nothing?"

"I don't know," Lerach shot back. "I've never participated in a fraud of the magnitude of the one Mr. Burns orchestrated. But would you—"

Objections interrupted him. The judge agreed that Lerach's comment should be stricken, and the jury was admonished to disregard it. Lawyers for each side had reason to believe they were getting their points across. Lerach had implanted the concept of a giant fraud; the defense had introduced the idea that Lerach was a hothead. Actually, both sides may have been underestimating their audience: in the jury box, foreman Richard Bunch thought to himself that Fischel's answers sounded like common sense.

Lerach wanted to get back to the market-manipulation argument. He asked Fischel if he was familiar with a tradition in which, a company's stock was listed on the New York Stock Exchange, the president of the company would frequently be the buyer of the first hundred shares to pass over the tape?"

Fischel stared at him blankly and then said: "It sounds like a nice tradition."

Then Lerach got to the point. "Have you ever gone fishing in the ocean?"

"As a matter of fact, my father used to take me, Mr. Lerach," Fischel responded.

"Well then, you know what it is to chum, don't you?" Lerach asked.

Fischel said he was not familiar with the term.

"Well, chumming is when you throw a little bait in the water so the fish will come up and you can catch them," Lerach told him.

"I'm sure you're an expert on fishing," Fischel retorted.

Lerach snapped off his next question: "You know, Mr. Burns was a high roller. In fact, you've seen in a deposition he's referred to as an oil/gas wheeler-dealer? Have you seen that?"

Fischel did recall seeing a reference in *Business Week*.

"Now, doesn't it sort of strike you that Mr. Burns purchasing $45,000 [of Nucorp stock] at the time he was trying to bring about that public offering is analogous to doing a little chumming or flipping a chip to the croupier at the table?" asked Lerach.

"No, because if I understand your description of chumming, all you're losing is the bait that you're throwing into the water. That doesn't sound like it's worth very much money," Fischel countered. "However, when you pay real dollars to purchase securities that aren't worth what you're purchasing them for, you're deliberately inflicting losses on yourself, which doesn't sound very chummy to me."

This quip prompted laughter among the audience and within the jury box.

Lerach didn't join in. Chumming, he said, was really something more serious. "Now sir, as a supposed expert in stock market behavior, you are aware that it is a very serious violation of the securities laws for insiders of a public company to engage in what are known as 'induced stock purchases' at or about the time of a public offering of the company's securities?"

> • >

AFTERWARD, AS HE WALKED OUT of the courtroom with Gold, Lerach felt a hard-earned exhilaration. Even with Fischel in the way, the case against Nucorp had finally been made for the jury. What he failed to consider, at least for the moment, was the fact that the trial was now nearly six months long and that the case against the defendants, Arthur Andersen, Circle K, and Continental Bank, was still in midair.

Trial resumed shortly after eight thirty A.M. on March 18, a Friday. Lerach reminded Fischel and the jury of his testimony the previous afternoon addressing the hypothetical question of whether the price of Nucorp stock would be boosted by phony earnings reports. Immediately he showed Fischel previous testimony from Burns stating that poor earnings during the summer of 1981 would be withheld from the company's quarterly statement that was to precede its offering of $150 million in common stock.

"Would you agree with me that the insiders believed they needed those July profits for the September securities offering?" he asked.

"Without knowing more, I would not accept that statement, no sir."

Here we go again, Lerach thought to himself.

They argued for the next half hour over the value of earnings reports, with Lerach implying through previous testimony that these statements provided gravity for perspective investors while Fischel described them as only a part of an equation. Even though he'd grown used to such equivocation, Lerach appeared incredulous.

"Sir," he said sternly, "isn't it a fact that earnings computed in accordance with generally accepted accounting principles as reported to the investment community in accordance with the regulations of the Securities and Exchange Commission are an important determinant of stock prices?"

Fischel could not be budged. "In some cases they are, in other cases they are not, depending on the situation."

Again, Lerach felt his face turning red like the mercury in a thermometer, revealing his barely controlled anger. "And in a case of a company like Nucorp, which trumpeted every one of its releases on earnings as reporting record earnings and forecasting continued record earnings, you would say that that is an instance where it's likely that the earnings had an impact on the stock, correct?"

The witness stood firm. "No, sir. In fact, I've tried to analyze that question by looking at exactly how Nucorp's stock price performed in relation to various earnings releases, and, for example, when Nucorp announced the heavy oil as proved and therefore reported increased earnings, it stated very clearly in its earnings release that it was reporting increased earnings because of its accounting change in the way earnings were reported."

An exasperated Lerach felt as if he were wrestling a greased pig. He finally asked Fischel what then were the most important factors investors should consider. This prompted the answer that Fischel had been dying to deliver: "I believe that the well-accepted finance literature is that cash flows and the riskiness of cash flows are the primary, if not the exclusive determinant of securities values," he said.

Lerach pounced on the answer. "Well, sir, you can be exactly sure that Nucorp's investment banker, as well as Nucorp, was telling the public during 1981 that the company had a strong cash flow already and was projecting dramatic increases in cash flow. Correct?" He stared hard at Fischel who offered no response.

"Isn't that true, sir?" Lerach persisted.

"Appears to be true, yes, sir," Fischel answered.

Sensing the wind at his back once again, Lerach continued. "And if you go back and look at Mr. Burns's press release on July 28, 1981, it said that Nucorp had recorded record earnings, record revenues and record cash flow for the six months ended June 30. The only thing he didn't say, it was record negative cash flow . . ."

Triumphant, Lerach turned to Fischel's contention that the flagging energy industry had more to do with Nucorp's bankruptcy than the allegations of wrongdoing. He began by attacking the witness's graphic representations of an industry in decline. He challenged the scale of one graph showing the number of oil rigs in operation and accused Fischel, its author, of distorting the figures to give the impression that the depression of the industry, beginning in 1982, was greater than it really was. This tactic led to a flurry of further attacks; Lerach offered his own graphs and recomputed scales and literally wrote over Fischel's exhibits by superimposing numbers of his own.

On the bench Judge Irving glanced at the jury box. He sensed restlessness as the citizen jurors, none trained in finance, tried to follow the plaintiffs' attorney's attack on the defense witnesses' exhibits. Sensing the jury's flagging attention, he allowed a few more testy skirmishes before calling a morning recess. After the jurors had exited the courtroom, the judge said: "In addition to the usual reasons we're taking the break, I'm also taking it for purposes of hopefully the blood pressures of both the questioner and the witness would be hopefully depressed a bit during the recess. Please, Mr. Lerach, keep in mind the admonition of this court throughout this trial not to editorialize in the presence of the jury. Professor Fischel, remember your role here is as a witness, and not an advocate."

Then it was the defense's turn once again. James Goldman, the Arthur Andersen attorney, elicited an opinion from his witness that industry analysts had been so optimistic about the drilling activity in 1981 that they helped create a demand for Nucorp products. In turn, when expectations were not met, rather than get caught in oversupply themselves, oil-drilling firms had slammed on the brakes. As a result, Nucorp was stuck with its own inventory as well as materials and components it had already ordered and in some cases paid for. When word got out, its stock price began suffering.

Juror Russell Colson took note, thinking to himself: *That's a pretty logical explanation.*

Goldman also tried to demonstrate how Lerach, using different trajectories for different columns on his graphs and Fischel's, was able to manipulate the appearance of the downward trajectory of drilling activity to make it appear to be flatter than it was—in order to refute Fischel's contention that the drop-off had been close to catastrophic.

Then came Goldman's finale: "Professor Fischel, did anything that you saw or heard during the course of your cross-examination by Mr. Lerach cause you to change your basic opinion to the effect that it was the depression in the oil industry that caused most of the decline of Nucorp's securities?"

"No," came the answer.

The jury was excused and told they would be recalled the following week, after the attorneys and the judge had conferred about presenting their closing arguments. In the end, the defense was disarmingly simple, and although presented by individual attorneys for their individual clients, it coalesced into a single narrative: *Hindsight is perfect. As it turned out, there were wrongdoers. But the wrongdoers were at Nucorp and they already settled. As for everybody else, the plaintiffs and even the defendants—two of whom, Continental Bank and Circle K—lost money too by betting in a volatile market. The plaintiffs were overreaching.*

This was all too simplistic, Lerach thought. In his head, he was already beginning to summarize his closing arguments. *Just because you lost money is not a defense and doesn't mean securities laws weren't violated,* he would tell the jury. That argument and others would be nuanced according to each and all of the defendants' and the witnesses' testimony, but they would also be constructed around his own epistemology:

In an era when small investors—with the federal government's encouragement—are all but required to put their life's savings in the stock market, free market capitalism cannot be a rigged dice game. It cannot be a crooked enterprise in which company executives, with the help of other company executives, disseminate fanciful information about their corporation's profits and prospects, knowing that picture to be a false one based on bogus numbers, in order to attract money from investors; and then, after that money comes in, and the stock prices fall to their natural level—in other words, the level they'd have reached in a transparent world, with honest information—then turn around and shrug and say, "Oh, well, you knew the risks." It is particularly egregious when those self-same executives who put out the bogus information dump their own stock, at inflated prices, before anyone knows what's going on. "Securities fraud" is one jargon phrase for this. So is "insider trading," but what it really is . . . is stealing, and it is despicable.

That was the gist of Bill Lerach's argument in Nucorp. Actually, it was the gist of all his cases. It's why criticism of his methods and persona didn't faze him. It's why he slept well at night. He was right, of course, although to use his own logic, just because his motivation was to address fraud didn't mean he never overreached in any of his lawsuits—or that he and his partners were immune from the temptation of taking ethical shortcuts themselves.

In this particular case, in his self-righteousness, Lerach had overlooked something—the rectitude of his opponents, particularly Chuck Dick, the attorney for Circle K, and his client Fred Hervey. Then forty-two, Dick had just been named managing partner of the San Diego office of Baker & McKenzie, one of the largest law firms in the world.

Dick was born in Manhattan, Kansas, and earned undergraduate and law degrees at Iowa State. During his undergraduate years he had considered entering a seminary and becoming an Episcopal priest. Deferring that decision, he decided to have a go at law school and soon found its rigors appealing.

After graduating, he joined the navy reserve, serving as an attorney in the judge advocate branch in the late 1960s. His assignment brought him to San Diego about the same time Lerach settled there. Aside from his legal work for the United States Navy, Dick was smitten by the climate, the beaches, and the sunny, low-key disposition of the city—an indelible alternative to where he had grown up—just as Bill Lerach had been. One reflection of his midwestern upbringing did stick with him, however. Those who knew him had never heard him utter an unkind word about another human being, raise his voice in anger, or invoke an expletive stronger than "darn." He presented a stark contrast to Bill Lerach's profane bluster.

So did Fred Hervey, the elderly, hard of hearing high school dropout, World War II veteran, and self-made business icon. Hervey, Chuck Dick would argue in his closing arguments, was not a perpetrator of fraud but a victim of it himself. In Hervey, Dick held the very card Bill Leach had played in the Pacific Homes case.

"You need victims," the plaintiffs' lawyer who had won on behalf of aggrieved retirees had said. This time Chuck Dick, the defense lawyer, had an elderly victim. His victim, Fred Hervey, deserved the jury's sympathy. He would see to it that he got it.

At eleven thirty A.M. on April 5, 1988, Dick, wearing his customary bow tie and disarming smile, began his plea on Circle K's behalf. "Accused of being a cheat, branded for deceitful conduct, charged with high offenses and fraud, the people at Circle K come to you, ladies and gentlemen, for protection."

Then he laid down his trump card: "Fred Hervey is in the evening of his life, as the shadows grow longer, humbled to receive the summons as one of his last official acts . . . as one of the people at Circle K, to come into this courtroom and, at a time when he should be basking in a sense of accomplishment that comes with all that he has achieved and built and constructed and shaped and molded in his life. He comes into this courtroom charged as a cheat and as a man who, in utter and reckless disregard for the rights of others, conspires to defraud." For two hours, Dick would affirm various defense witnesses while directly attacking the plaintiffs' interpretation of the facts, their witnesses' testimony, and their allegations that Circle K aided and abetted Nucorp's fraud. All through his mesmerizing presentation, one primary message rang out: "Fred Hervey may not have been clairvoyant," his lawyer said. "But he was an honest man."

"Protect the people at Circle K," Chuck Dick beseeched the jury in his final sentences. "Preserve their honor. Tell them that whatever may have been the facts we have unearthed in our autopsy of Nucorp, that the words with which they stand charged and branded are inapplicable."

Judge Irving asked Lerach if he was ready to proceed with closing arguments of his own. The attorney, his voice off-key and husky, answered: "Your honor, in light of the hour, if we're going into a recess for ten minutes, that would be five to four P.M. The jury is obviously tired, if you look at them. Mr. Dick made quite an argument. I mean to compliment him that it was, it was a very powerful argument . . . Does your honor have an inclination of perhaps starting tomorrow, even starting a little bit early?"

The following morning, Bill Lerach reiterated the plaintiffs' case against each defendant, starting with Arthur Andersen and ending with Circle K, point by point, from prebilling, to literally putting stock in difficult-to-drill heavy oil, to Nucorp's "fraud on the market," to disputing much of Professor Fischel's expertise and opinions. Had he been trying the case against

Nucorp, there would have been no doubt that the energy company was guilty of fraud. What remained in the jurors' minds at the end of the two-hour oration, however, was a basic question: had Nucorp defrauded not only its investors but also its own lenders, its analysts, and its underwriters?

Judge Irving spent the afternoon instructing the jury. Even though the case involved numerous defendants, the mathematical possibilities were not problematic. Weigh guilt or innocence for each of the defendants based on the evidence presented for each defendant. Try to be as straightforward as possible.

On Thursday morning, April 7, the jury filed into an austere room adjacent to Department 8, Judge Irving's courtroom. Richard Bunch, the foreman, directed them to take their places around a rectangular table. Off to one side on a desktop sat a coffeepot. By way of other creature comforts, nothing else was offered for the occasion. Bunch, a deliberate man, laid out a wide strip of paper so he and his colleagues—two men and three women—could construct a timeline and retrace inflection points in a kind of taxonomic scheme. Essentially it came down to identifying causes and weighing their effects. But something else pervaded the deliberations, something customary in jury rooms: the personalities of the attorneys and witnesses. "Lerach treated us like school kids," Bunch would eventually say, passing on his recollection of how he and at least two other jurors had responded to the plaintiffs' lawyer. "On the other hand, that Circle K guy, the lawyer, was the best-prepared and put on a good case for his client."

At three P.M. on Tuesday afternoon, April 12, 1988, four business days after they had begun deliberations, Judge Irving's clerk telephoned each of the attorneys, asking them to appear in court. Expecting that a verdict might be at hand, everyone assembled within twenty minutes. No verdict, as it turned out, but the judge had received a note, which he read aloud: "Judge Irving, may we have a calculator for use in the jury room?"

The judge asked the lawyers in the courtroom: "Does anyone have any objection, first of all, to the court taking in a calculator?" Lerach was elated by the question, which implied calculations for monetary damages.

The jury also wanted to hear a tape that Lerach had introduced into evidence. It had been recorded during a Nucorp board meeting that Hervey had attended. The meeting had been contentious because Nucorp had been forced to reveal some accounting sleights-of-hand to its board. The contents of that discussion cut both ways. Hervey had not been pleased with the revelations. Yet he could also be heard acquiescing in some instances for Nucorp's sake and the sake of his own bottom line. Abby Silverman, filling in that afternoon for Chuck Dick, had asked the judge to direct the jury to listen to the whole tape, so as not to take Hervey's quotes out of context.

Once he received the calculator, Bunch, the jury foreman, put it to use, while another juror wrote some figures on the sheaf of paper laid before them on the table. Instead of calculating damages, the jury was trying to determine how significantly Nucorp's reported bottom line had been inflated by its prebilling practices. They had also recounted the battle of the graphs, an epic war that had become nearly physical between Lerach and Fischel, in which Lerach literally wrote over Fischel's numbers, even turning some charts around. The jurors had become confused over these tactics—and the plaintiffs had not been the beneficiaries. Finally, as Lerach feared, Chuck Dick's closing arguments had rung an emotional bell. The passionate defense lawyer had planted the seed firmly in each juror's mind: was Circle K a villain or victim?

The deliberations continued into the next day. Lerach was growing nervous, even while assuring Mel Weiss over the telephone of his confidence. He reminded his mentor that this was an unsophisticated jury trying a sophisticated case—but remember, they had asked for a calculator. Trying to assess damages from three separate deep-pocket entities was no easy task among lawyers, let alone laypeople. Two more days of deliberation produced no news, nor notice from the jury room. At noon the judge sent the jury home for the weekend.

Judge Irving called the attorneys together on Thursday, April 21, to inform them that he would be leaving town on Friday and would not be back until the following Tuesday, April 26. Judge John Rhoades, the presiding federal judge, would fill in. The following Monday Rhoades received a note from the jury room. They had a verdict. His clerk called Judge Irving, who said he could be back by 1:30 P.M. Then Judge Rhoades called the jurors in and sat them in the jury box, telling them that Judge Irving would hear their verdict. At the same time Rhoades's clerk called the attorneys and told them a verdict had been reached and the time of its delivery—1:45 P.M.

Hearing this news, Lerach dialed a Manhattan number. When the phone rang in Mel Weiss's office atop Penn Station, Lerach received no answer. Thinking his mentor must be at lunch, Lerach left a message: "The jury's coming in at one forty-five."

At one thirty P.M. Pacific Time, Judge Irving rushed up the rear steps of the federal court building, entered his chambers by a back door, and hastily donned his black robe. His clerk had notified him that all counsel were present. He asked them to state their names for the record, and as they did, a palpable tension filled the room.

The bailiff opened the door to the jury room, and the lawyers stood as the panel filed in, led by Richard Bunch, and took their seats. A socially circumscribed ritual attends to this moment too, this passing in review, in which the eyes of jurors and those judged seldom meet, adding to the tension. Once the jurors were in their places, all in the courtroom took their seats.

The judge turned to Bunch: "Has the jury reached a unanimous verdict?"

"Yes, sir," he said.

The judge directed him to hand the verdicts to his court clerk, who then read them aloud, beginning with Executive Life Insurance Company, a separate plaintiff from Lerach's class action plaintiffs, which had bought Nucorp notes through Drexel Burnham: "We the jury, in the above-entitled cause unanimously find as follows: In Nucorp Energy Securities Litigation on claims brought by Executive Life Insurance Company—we find against Executive Life Insurance Company." Four more counts remained, and to each the jury assigned the same unfavorable judgment. Finally, Bunch said: "We assess the amount of damages to be zero."

Judge Irving peered down at the plaintiffs' table, his eyes meeting Lerach's. Both knew what the first verdict meant, even though Lerach's plaintiffs were not involved. From the jury box Russell Colson glanced up, catching sight of Lerach, who had begun a downward slide in his chair. In turn, for each and every charge against each and every defendant, the jury had drawn the same conclusion, and as each was repeated, the sound became a knell of defeat for Lerach and his plaintiffs: "We find against the plaintiffs. We assess the amount of damages to be zero."

In Lerach's corner office with the view of San Diego Harbor and beyond, the telephone rang. It was Mel Weiss calling back. He had gotten Lerach's message—one-forty-five—and gotten it wrong. "One hundred forty-five million!" he virtually shouted triumphantly into the voice mailbox receiver.

"We had a miscommunication," Lerach would say later, long after the jurors—Bunch, a retired county surveyor; Clara Crocker, a housewife; Russell Colson, a retired salesman; Helen Saylor, a retired schoolteacher; Howard Dillman, a retired telephone company superintendent; and Marianne Fox, a construction crane operator—had been polled, and long after he and his entourage had trooped out of the courthouse and straight to the Westgate Plaza Hotel, where Bill Lerach returned Mel Weiss's phone call before joining his colleagues at the bar.

While dulling their distress with round after round of Scotch whiskey, Lerach and his team of lawyers assessed the causes of their defeat. It wasn't an easy process, because it was difficult to demonize Fred Hervey or even dislike Chuck Dick. It was far easier to focus their disappointment, frustration, and rage at one man—Daniel Fischel, the contrarian from Chicago. Obsessing on Fischel would prove an even costlier mistake than trying the Nucorp case all over again.

> • > • > • > • >

THE WITNESS FROM HELL

Normally the drive northward from downtown San Diego to Del Mar, the halcyon seaside town where he'd settled with Kelly and their seven-year-old daughter Shannon, required less than twenty-five minutes. But this was not a normal night—and Lerach was not going home. He was in the backseat of a limo heading to Los Angeles, where he was due in court in nine hours. Still stinging from his courtroom defeat that afternoon, preoccupied by how he would account for the thrashing to the New York office, and numbed by alcohol, Lerach settled in for the two-hour trip.

"On to the next battle," he announced to himself and his driver, cavalierly attempting to hide his budding self-doubt with a show of bravado. Then he reverted to the curses heard round the table at the bar where he and his team had retreated in defeat. He cursed the drive ahead of him, he cursed the attorneys who'd ganged up to undo him, and cursed the "stupid" jurors who hadn't understood his slam-dunk case.

He pulled a recorder and dictated some thoughts, more or less along the lines of his verbal diatribe, but with a slight enamel of circumspection— "The theory that heavyset jurors tend to be good plaintiffs' jurors because they are happy-go-lucky types appears to be incorrect . . . Women are much more opinionated than men, less susceptible to reason, less likely to change their minds based upon the arguments of others." As the town car cruised northward to Los Angeles, he fell asleep. His intention was to put these thoughts to paper, to be distributed to his colleagues as soon as he found time and distance from his defeat to craft a memo that wouldn't taste of sour grapes.

The media, specifically *Barron's* and *The Wall Street Journal,* altered Lerach's plans. On May 2, 1988, both publications lauded Fischel's testimony for turning the tide for Nucorp in the eyes of the jury. Lerach could not contain himself. He scrawled fifteen "takeaway" points over nearly five pages. To anyone who read the memo later—and many would eventually do so, including his enemies—Lerach's written venting would lend itself to various interpretations. His friends assumed he had been frustrated, exhausted, embarrassed—and obviously inebriated. His adversaries concluded that the mean-spirited memo perfectly captured Bill Lerach's character. These opponents had been on the other side of Lerachian rants, and they had complained to each other about his coarse and bullying nature. And here it was, a gift that they came by mysteriously: Lerach's inchoate rage on paper, in a document revealing his crass side and his reflexive penchant for vituperative, even immature, clichés. His vanity, insecurity, impatience, arrogance, and overconfidence, and his bent for recrimination, were all there, along with a disquieting contempt for the everyday Americans whom Lerach made it a point of pride to champion. Schoolteachers, working-class men, overweight people, and—most disturbingly—women. Within days of his penning the confidential internal memo, it was being circulated in law firms and in court chambers throughout the United States.

Mel Weiss was hardly thick-skinned when it came to being embarrassed. What troubled him more than Lerach's intemperate, unguarded musings about a jury that had turned on him was an addendum to Lerach's memo. In it he suggested that the firm assign several associates, supervised by partner Leonard Simon, to build a dossier on Daniel Fischel. To his later regret, Weiss did not act on his misgivings. Perhaps it was because he too considered the expert defense witness a pernicious force. In the partisan politics in which both Lerach and Weiss dabbled, Lerach was proposing opposition research. What Simon and his team would unearth first appeared to be a bonanza. Then it turned into fools' gold; then it turned into a tort.

Weiss was also taken aback to learn of still another conclusion that Lerach had reached in the wake of the Nucorp debacle. From now on the firm's star lawyer would stick to identifying and drawing up cases, getting them certified, and launching them toward positive outcomes. He would not try a case before a jury—ever again. The fearsome litigator who had rocked Southern California's legal establishment with his virtuoso performance in the Pacific Homes case had had his own confidence upended. Within months Lerach tendered an offer to Patrick Coughlin, the assistant U.S. attorney, who had watched his flawed courtroom performance in the Nucorp trial. After passing muster with Weiss, Bershad, and others in the New York office, Coughlin would join Milberg, Weiss, Bershad, Hynes & Lerach— or Milberg West—as a partner in the litigation division and a trial specialist. His starting salary would be $72,000, nearly doubling what the government had been paying him. For the firm, it was a bargain.

In bestowing trial responsibilities on Pat Coughlin, Lerach was making a huge professional and emotional transfer. Somewhere along the way, and not solely due to his humiliating defeat in Judge Irving's courtroom, Lerach had started to lose his romance with the law. "I began to get cynical. I began thinking the system wasn't working," he would say later. And he set about beating not only his opponents but also the judicial system itself.

Nonetheless, even with the turmoil and costly trial setback, there was solace—$41 million from the Nucorp directors and officers, plus another $9 million from the default judgment against Donaldson, Lufkin & Jenrette. These consolation prizes were not insignificant. In fact, they were part of a growing pattern.

By the late 1980s, companies, particularly those with assets greater than $1 billion, faced a 63 percent chance of being sued by shareholders. The average settlement in 1988 was $6 million, with the average cost of putting up a defense in excess of $1 million. That was the average of more than 300 separate claims filed against about 250 companies. Big claims against deep-pockets companies averaged more than $40 million in court settlements, slightly less in mediated settlements, which the courts were then required to approve. This proved to be a bonanza, with huge insurers such as AIG and Fireman's Fund getting into a market where premiums could run as high as $30 million depending on the size of a company and the history of claims against it.

And of course, the fraud exclusion built into D&O insurance policies played directly into Lerach's hands. For a CEO caught in Lerach's sights, the allegation of fraud had a hideous and frightening ring to it. Rather than fight the charge and risk losing indemnification, the overwhelming percentage of the companies that he and his colleagues sued chose to settle without ever going to court.

This, in turn, created a new line of opportunities for lawyers who, although not involved in the initial litigation, stepped in to help negotiate the settlements. For attorneys such as Los Angeles lawyer Robert F. Lewis, a partner in the firm of Lewis, Brisbois, Bisgaard & Smith, riding the wake of a Lerach lawsuit made for a good living. A 1961 graduate of UCLA Law School, Lewis saw a new wave of business liability sweeping the nation. He decided to specialize in insurance coverage, and for over two decades he helped clean up more than one hundred securities cases in which Lerach had won settlements. Gradually the two lawyers came to respect each other. One negotiation in particular cemented their relationship. Both lawyers recalled a contentious battle to arrive at a settlement in a securities case, followed by an even more contentious battle between Lerach and the insurance carrier represented by Lewis.

Ultimately the two lawyers seemed stalemated, about $10 million apart in their negotiations. Late one evening, as they were entering what seemed the thousandth hour of dickering, Lewis pushed himself away from the conference table and said to Lerach: "You like Scotch, I hear. Let's go over to my office and have a drink. At least we can make ourselves comfortable while we argue."

Lewis's office was on South Figueroa Street, an easy walk from the federal courthouse in the heart of Los Angeles's reemerging downtown business district. Once there Lewis opened a credenza and brought out an expensive single malt. With the first drink they resolved to finish their settlement negotiation before the night was through. By the second, their resolve to do battle was softening. By the third, they were toasting each other. "By the sixth," Lerach quipped, "we were best friends." Somewhere along the line, they struck a deal, toasting each other one last time and promising to finalize their agreement in the morning.

Lerach navigated his way back to his hotel, the Bonaventure, a modern landmark structure of cylindrical glass towers a short walk up the hill from Lewis's office. He leaned forward as if into a headwind, feeling the warm flush of the liquor, the giddiness following a settlement, and the goodwill toward his opponent and newfound friend—and the agreement they had managed to strike. He remembered riding the outdoor bubble elevator and feasting on the sight of the vast neon city as he soared above it. He remembered entering his hotel room and exhaling. That was all he remembered.

The next morning, after the wake-up call, Lerach still had a good feeling about the evening with Lewis, the kind of experience that was becoming rarer as he and his firm became pariahs in the legal profession. Except for one thing: he couldn't remember the amount he and Lewis had settled upon. Embarrassed, he fished Lewis's business card out of his pocket and found that the attorney had written his home phone number on the back. Reluctantly he dialed the number, hoping the settlement amount would arrive in his mind before the call was answered on the other end. A vague-sounding Lewis picked up. At first Lerach tried subterfuge, thanking him for the drinks and congratulating him on the settlement the two had achieved. Lewis was equally congratulatory. Lerach suggested Lewis fax the amount over to his firm's Los Angeles office where his assistants would draw up the formal agreement. Lewis hesitated. Lerach asked him if something was wrong. Lewis did not answer.

Lerach realized he was not alone in his embarrassment. "Bob, can you remember what we settled for?" he asked sheepishly. "Because I can't."

Lewis laughed—he couldn't remember either. And so, with the playing field thoroughly leveled, the two chastened adversaries proposed a late breakfast, at which they would take up where they left off.

"We settled for around $24 million," Lerach said nearly two decades later. "I'm sure it was close to what we had agreed on the previous night."

> • >

BY APRIL 1990 the complaint against Charles Keating and his companies, American Continental and Lincoln Savings, had grown to 235 pages and was in its fifth version. New plaintiffs and amended causes of action were added to include the litany of Keating's nefarious and never-ending efforts to persuade lawmakers to intervene on his behalf. The lawsuit detailed the manipulations by Keating and other agents and individuals in his employ—accountants, bankers, attorneys, and politicians—that ended up harming 23,000 plaintiffs who had lost more than $288 million. The suit demanded compensatory damages, including interest—and triple the amount of the initial loss in punitive damages. The Lincoln lawsuit had grown into the largest commercial litigation of its time.

It was only one of many high-profile cases on the agenda of Milberg Weiss. In the Washington Public Power Supply System case, for example, Milberg Weiss was a co-litigant that sued the giant utility after it defaulted on its bonds, losing $2.3 billion of investor money. Three quarters of a billion dollars was on the table, which could mean as much as $180 million in fees to the firm. That was a lot of money—but the firm was into the case for the equivalent of 36,000 billable hours, amounting to nearly $10 million in expenses. The stakes were sufficiently high to inspire Mel Weiss to help try the case.

Not by coincidence, Weiss found himself crossing paths with Dan Fischel, the emerging perennial adversary, who had been hired by the defense as an expert witness. Prior to a hearing one day, Fischel approached the now-legendary Weiss, extending his hand and introducing himself.

"I know who you are," Weiss sneered. "And I will destroy you."

Even as their wins and fees were growing, Lerach noticed that their parallel costs kept mounting, including referral fees for other lawyers outside the firm as well as their growing stable of stalking horses—now known as "professional plaintiffs." Lerach would also hear regularly from Dave Bershad, demanding that he chip in to the "referral fund." It was a tidy cover, but the method of raising the recompense was complicated. Bershad and Weiss devised the scheme. Those who were part of it, the inner circle of very

senior partners (and Lerach was one of them), would award themselves an-
nual bonuses. The bonuses would more or less match the amount the firm
spent on referrals and indirectly reward the serial plaintiffs in their stable.
In a zero-sum game then, the money still came from the firm as a whole.
And it meant that in order to pay for plaintiffs, all the attorneys at Milberg
Weiss would contribute, directly or indirectly, whether they knew it or not.

While prominent and precedent-setting cases bolstered their firm's reputation, Mel Weiss and Bill Lerach both realized that their ability to compete for big prizes was made possible only by a stream of smaller, more
efficient cases to be won or settled quickly. To land those cases, they relied
on a stable of scouts such as Paul Tullman and reliable plaintiffs such as Seymour Lazar.

Already Lazar had paid off, helping the firm file first in a 1987 case,
making it the lead counsel representing plaintiffs who maintained that the
$7.4 billion merger of Standard Oil and British Petroleum had short-
changed shareholders. For Lazar's efforts, Dave Bershad directed that two
separate $50,000 checks (one dated June 29, 1987, the other August 17,
1989) be sent to Lazar's Palm Springs attorney, Paul Selzer, for "furtherance
of arrangements" and "your share of fees." Both payments appeared on the
surface to be legitimate referral fees between lawyers. What was not legal
was the "credit" Lazar received from his attorney for private legal work. In
other words, the reward was passed through an intermediary to a plaintiff
who had signed a mandatory court document pledging that he expected
only normal recompense and no more than any other member of the
class suing the petroleum giants. This was only one of seventy such lawsuits
in which Lazar would participate as a Milberg Weiss plaintiff. In all, he
would receive the equivalent of $2.4 million in payments over twenty-three
years.

By his own admission, Bill Lerach was not good at finding plaintiffs.
With help from the likes of Lazar, however, the cases were good at finding
him. By 1988 his stable of stalking horses was growing. One particular litigant would have the biggest impact on Lerach's growing prominence—and
eventually on his downfall. His name was Steven G. Cooperman.

Like his soon-to-be running mate Seymour Lazar, Cooperman, then forty-six years old, led a colorful life. The son of Russian immigrants who had run a dry goods store in Norwalk, Connecticut, he had been a Beverly Hills ophthalmologist and Brentwood socialite. He advertised his medical services on television, sent limousines for his patients, and retained Red Skelton as his celebrity spokesman. He also amassed an array of impressionist and modern art, collected signed letters from the likes of Napoleon and Tchaikovsky, and bought luxury automobiles, including a 1931 Packard, to go along with his two homes in Brentwood, a home on the Gold Coast of Connecticut, and a property in Palm Springs. Although his medical practice was lucrative, his professional passion was playing financial markets, both as a stock investor and as a minor arbitrageur. Friends joked that he performed eye operations while wearing headphones so he could listen to financial broadcasts.

In 1983 Cooperman married his third wife, the former Nancy Graef, an airline flight attendant, after meeting her at a Brentwood party and romancing her on an anything-goes spree to Europe. "Everything was totally, totally, totally ultra-luxurious, first class," she would later testify at the couple's divorce trial in 2004.

With his medical practice at its peak, Cooperman earned more than $2 million a year. Later, he received an annual income of $500,000 from disability insurance, due to a heart condition. Nevertheless, by late 1988 his financial state was in decline, due to prodigious spending habits and a variety of self-inflicted wounds. An accusation lodged with the state Board of Medical Quality Assurance by California's attorney general charged Cooperman with "unprofessional conduct," and having committed "gross negligence and incompetence" in three instances in 1980, 1984, and 1987. He stood accused of performing unnecessary surgery on three patients and fabricating medical records to justify it. Cooperman surrendered his license to practice medicine. On the other hand, he surrendered nothing else, least of all his own extravagance. Nancy could see what was happening and at one point asked him to curtail his spending. Cooperman griped back: "You are like a cold, wet blanket spoiling my fun."

Cooperman was also addicted to gambling with other people's money. Turning his attention to playing financial markets, he sought backers to take arbitrage positions in takeover-vulnerable companies, teaming with entrepreneur Jonathan Rosenthal to try to purchase enough stock to acquire IPM Technology, a Los Angeles–based company that refueled, maintained, and unloaded cargo from aircraft in the Southwest. Although the company posted $54 million in sales in 1988, its stock never climbed above $9 a share. Cooperman and Rosenthal, saying they had backers who could buy IPM "with their pocket money," asked for a look at the company's books in order to prepare their offer. Seymour Kahn, the company president, blocked them. Within days of receiving their request, Kahn purchased 34.3 percent of the company's stock from his nephew Saul Steinberg for $3.9 million, which amounted to $4.50 a share. The purchase gave Kahn a majority of stock—58 percent—but he said he would offer the remainder for the same $4.50 a share. Cooperman and his partners were not mollified. He complained that by arranging to purchase a majority stake in the company for a price lower than what Cooperman and Rosenthal were willing to pay, Kahn had violated its fiduciary duty to the company's shareholders. The San Diego office of Milberg, Weiss got the call.

Lerach was reluctant to take the case simply because the potential fee fell short of his fee threshold. On the other hand, Cooperman was a player. Earlier he and Uri Sheinbaum had formed a partnership to try to buy Del Webb Corp., the builder of the Flamingo, one of the early Las Vegas grand hotels, whose partial owner had been mobster Bugsy Siegel. At one time the company was among the largest residential developers in America. But after the severe stock market downturn of 1987, the company was moving to reduce debt by liquidating assets. Cooperman and Sheinbaum had assembled a group they said was willing to pay $156.4 million for the whole company, which was resisting—arguably to the detriment of shareholders. This case was more to the Milberg Weiss scale. Naturally Lerach took charge of drawing up the complaint. He also agreed to represent Cooperman in his suit against IPM Technology.

As he began constructing the complaint, Lerach encountered something unusual in Cooperman: he would call at least once a day asking for progress reports. That was understandable, given the man's obvious taste for financial intrigue. But Cooperman also began pointing Lerach to other potential cases he'd been scouting out. During one daily telephone conversation Cooperman asked Lerach when he would next be in Los Angeles and invited him to dinner. When they agreed on a date, Cooperman gave Lerach an address on Santa Monica Boulevard close to Cooperman's Brentwood home, saying it was one of his favorite West L.A. steakhouses. Lerach couldn't have missed it when he arrived at the appointed hour. Even among the eclectic shops and restaurants along the 3100 block of Santa Monica Boulevard, Marquis West singled itself out with its long, low rococo exterior, framed by light granite stones and a white balustrade running the length of the roofline. It was a place Steve Cooperman adored because it matched his flamboyance. A short, pudgy, fast-talking man, wearing overly large tortoiseshell glasses, a well-groomed mustache, and plenty of gold adorning his wrists and exposed chest, Cooperman projected a celebrity presence. Danny DeVito could have played him in a movie—except that Cooperman saw himself as a classic leading man. Arriving by town car, Lerach entered the restaurant and found himself instantly pleased with its interior, a cross between a retro New York chop house and a gentlemen's club.

Cooperman, already at the bar, greeted Lerach warmly and introduced Dr. Ronald Fischman, his friend and business colleague. Lerach ordered a Scotch, drank it quickly, ordered another. Fischman signaled the maître d', who escorted them into their booth against a wall in the middle of the dining room. Cooperman dispensed with the menu when the waiter arrived, suggesting they order chopped salads and New York strip steaks. From the wine list he selected a first-growth Bordeaux. Cooperman then reaffirmed his regard for Lerach, his firm, and the firm's track record and reminded him of his own financial escapades and the "scoundrels" he found himself bumping into. Something about the word "scoundrel" struck Lerach as particularly fitting.

"I want to do business," Cooperman said, lowering his voice conspiratorially and leaning across the table toward Lerach.

"We already are," Lerach rejoined.

"No. I want to be your plaintiff. You know . . . there are plenty of cases out there, and there can be plenty more."

Lerach sat back as if surveying his poker cards. He chose to hear not danger but opportunity. "Okay, it could be a good fit," he replied. "You be the plaintiff, and I'll bring the cases."

Cooperman leaned in even closer. "What's in it for me?" he asked. "Listen, I've checked this plaintiff thing out. I want twenty percent of the fee."

Lerach recoiled, obviously taken aback, not only by the boldness of the proposal but by the self-certainty with which Cooperman offered it. He countered quickly.

"You will be working with one of the most successful, if not the most successful plaintiffs' advocates in America. If you are going to do business with us it will be on our terms . . . We pay ten percent." He said it quickly and with equal self-assurance. Later, he would wish he hadn't said it at all.

Even then he hedged. "Look, nobody's paying you any money," Lerach said, glancing at Fischman for approbation. "Do you have a relative who's a lawyer, or even better, a lawyer to whom we can pay referral fees? We must have an intermediary. So get yourself a lawyer."

Sitting back, Cooperman looked pleased. "That won't be a problem," he said.

From that moment a relationship was forged that Lerach would come to liken to holding a wolf by the ears. "You don't want to hang on," he later noted ruefully, "and you certainly can't afford to let go." At the time, however, the association with Cooperman presented just the opportunity he'd been looking for. With his own stable of plaintiffs he could operate even more independently from New York.

Within weeks Cooperman made good on his offer, pointing Lerach toward a case involving the giant Newhall Land and Farming Company. By snatching up Mexican land grants, Newhall had once owned California land stretching from Monterey to Los Angeles. Over time and generations the company had morphed into an agricultural behemoth, oil extractor, and real estate developer. Cooperman owned shares in the conglomerate before meeting Lerach, and from time to time he exercised his ownership rights to disrupt Newhall deals by filing lawsuits seeking injunctive relief and then negotiating settlements in order to cease the litigation. Now Cooperman had stumbled onto another injunctive opportunity and urged Lerach to file on behalf of him and other shareholders in Los Angeles Superior Court.

The case would require nimble litigation work, Lerach quickly determined. He also knew that in this type of case, if he worked fast, the rewards could be reaped quickly. It certainly happened that way now. The company capitulated, settling for about $5 million. Milberg Weiss's fee came to $1.75 million. According to their agreement, Cooperman was due $175,000.

The scheme hatched by Cooperman and acquiesced to by Lerach at the Marquis West paid off instantly. Lerach saw only one disconcerting wrinkle: in the aftermath Cooperman asserted that he had an immediate need for cash, explaining that some market bets had not paid off. He also had not yet been able to nail down his attorney, who was out of town. So Cooperman suggested a solution: could he arrange for a bridge payment? Lerach was astonished. This did not coincide with Lerach's image of Cooperman. Maybe his capital was tied up, Lerach thought. After all, the man was a gambler. Despite his misgivings, Lerach called Mel Weiss to relay Cooperman's conundrum, reminding his mentor that Cooperman had helped them bank a quick $1.75 million. He added, not quite as an afterthought, that like Weiss, Cooperman was an art collector. That addendum shed light on an alternative.

Weiss flew to Los Angeles, where Cooperman met him and drove him to his Brentwood home, a relatively unimposing, two-story Cape Cod style, with a large porch, white picket fence, and tidy garden. Inside Cooperman showed off his collection of Monets and Picassos. The notoriously poker-faced Weiss could barely restrain himself as he admired what he saw on Cooperman's walls, especially Picasso's *Nude Before a Mirror*. "Henry Ford once owned this piece," Cooperman boasted. Weiss, who fancied himself the Henry Ford of the plaintiffs' bar and owned a sizable collection of his own Picassos, was duly impressed.

To fulfill the terms of their agreement, Weiss took an option to purchase a Cooperman art piece, to be exercised within nine months. The option price they agreed on was $175,000, not coincidentally the exact amount of Cooperman's claim on the Newhall settlement. Although Weiss went through the motions of calling an art appraiser in San Francisco to determine a legitimate market price for the selected piece, no actual art purchase transpired. What did change hands was $175,000, in the form of a check, along with the paperwork noting the option. Cooperman would cash the check and store the paperwork, the first of a flurry of Milberg Weiss documents that would fill up boxes that he would store like a pack rat. Cooperman's obsession with hanging on to all documents would eventually prove to be a bonanza to prosecutors while contributing to his own partial salvation.

Although he stayed out of the art deal between Cooperman and Weiss, Lerach did contribute his own quid pro quo. At Lerach's urging, on January 30, 1989, Cooperman purchased one thousand shares of Charles Keating's ACC stock for $4.50 a share, two months before the company declared the bankruptcy Lerach had seen coming.*

> • >

AS THEY PUT THE finishing touches on their case against Lincoln Savings and Keating and the fifty individuals or entities accused of contributing to their giant fraud, one last name was added as a defendant. It was Lerach's old nemesis, the Chicago-based economic consulting and expert witness litigation support firm called Lexecon.

In the run-up to the ACC/Lincoln lawsuit Len Simon, John Stoia, Kevin Roddy, and the team of young Milberg West lawyers sifting evidence believed they had found a prize among the hundreds of thousands of pages of documents they had reviewed. In a memo dated March 21, 1990, Simon laid out the case against Lexecon. The Milberg Weiss lawyers discovered numerous billing logs showing that Lexecon had done extensive work for Lincoln while collecting more than a million dollars in fees from the now-bankrupt thrift. Adding substance to the discovery were two Lexecon reports, commissioned by Keating, vouching for Lincoln's solvency, that were

* For a mere $4,500 investment and adding his name as a plaintiff to the lawsuit, Cooperman would ultimately collect $1,013,000 from Milberg Weiss over and above what other plaintiffs were awarded by the court. Another plaintiff was Cooperman's friend Fischman, who had joined the eye doctor and Lerach at dinner a few months earlier. He bought one hundred shares on January 23, a week before Cooperman.

used by Keating to help stave off federal banking regulators. Lerach's lawsuit cited the fact that more than 23,000 members of the plaintiffs' class had lost their savings during the government delay in shutting down Lincoln Savings, meaning that anyone who helped delay the day of reckoning for Keating's companies was culpable for their losses. Lerach couldn't sue the U.S. Senate, or the Office of Thrift Supervision, but he figured he certainly could sue Daniel Fischel.

Fischel, of course, was one of Lexecon's founders and chief executives. The professional expert witness, Milberg Weiss attorneys had learned, was already scheduled to appear on behalf of auditors Arthur Young, named as defendants in the Lincoln case. Fischel was also scheduled to testify as an expert witness on behalf of defendants in two other big cases Milberg Weiss was trying—one against E. F. Hutton, the other against Apple Computer. As in the Nucorp case, Fischel could be standing in the way of hundreds of millions of dollars in plaintiffs' recovery and lawyers' fees. By landing on the list of defendants in this landmark lawsuit, Fischel could instead be linked with Keating as a coconspirator under the civil arm of RICO, the federal Racketeer Influenced and Corrupt Organizations Act, the same legislation that had allowed federal law enforcement to pursue criminal cases against the Hell's Angels, organized crime figures, and international drug rings.

That was Lerach's hope, anyway. In addition, a judgment in a RICO case carried the possibility of tripling the award asked for by the plaintiffs. Fischel and Lexecon were now on notice: they were not only on the hook for $400 million, but Fischel himself might be permanently tainted as a prospective expert witness in future cases. This little legal addendum wasn't strictly about liability; it was also about payback.

> • > • > • >

A GIFT HORSE NAMED KEATING

On Tuesday morning, April 3, 1990, two men exited the elevator on the twentieth floor of the Central Savings Building in downtown San Diego. One was tall and handsomely angular and exuded a confident, civil bearing. The other was shorter and appeared diffident. The former was Stephen C. Neal, a partner in the Chicago office of Kirkland & Ellis, a global firm that boasted a thousand lawyers. Neal was a trial attorney specializing in complex litigation usually involving white-collar defendants. He had graduated from Stanford Law School in 1973, after earning an undergraduate degree from Harvard in 1970. His colleague—and his client—was Daniel Fischel.

Bill Lerach made no attempt at politeness as Fischel and his lawyer were ushered into a large glass conference room. Accompanying Lerach was Len Simon, who had authored the memo essentially accusing Lexecon, the Chicago-based consulting firm, and Fischel, its principal partner, of conspiring to prop up Charles Keating and Lincoln Savings. Fischel and Neal had arrived with a singular mission: to persuade Lerach and his team to undo their filing of civil racketeering charges against Lexecon and Fischel in Los Angeles federal district court.

Fischel opened by disclosing what Lerach already knew, that another defendant, Arthur Young, had hired him as an expert witness in the auditors' defense. Before Fischel could state the obvious, he heard Lerach declare: "Well, you're not going to be able to testify as an expert witness because you're tainted by the complaint we're filing against you."

Neal reacted by issuing a soft challenge, suggesting that the plaintiffs had little compelling evidence against his client. The words had barely left Neal's mouth when Lerach interrupted, discharging his words as bullets, one shot at a time: "This trial is going to be a circus," he said. "As for the merits? Your client is going to be trampled in the stampede."

Lerach turned on a wincing Fischel, ready to deliver another fusillade. Neal counterattacked, reaching into his briefcase and pulling out a document from which he read: "Conservative sixty-year-old Republicans are probably so devoted to the system and so wedded to the idea that each person is responsible for what happens to him in his own life that this bias cannot be overcome . . ." He was quoting the toxic memo Lerach had authored post-Nucorp. Although Neal's maneuver caught Lerach off guard, it did nothing to diminish his abiding fury toward Fischel.

"We will not be blackmailed," Lerach hissed.

The meeting was over.

> • >

BEFORE THE YEAR WAS OUT, Keating would be charged by state prosecutors with forty-two felony counts; a federal indictment would follow, as would convictions in both state and federal court. These were fortuitous developments for Bill Lerach and his firm. The federal government particularly was becoming a de facto partner in the plaintiffs' litigation. With each revelation, the government passed along the results of its own discovery. And with each admission of guilt that the government extracted from one of the Lincoln/ACC principals and perpetrators, the securities case that Milberg Weiss lawyers were assembling drew ever tighter.

Now the Milberg Weiss lawyers could concentrate on the accountants, underwriters, and even lawyers whom Keating had engaged to help him commit his massive fraud. Even with the government's help, litigating against close to one hundred defendants was a tricky endeavor. Milberg Weiss would need assistance. Private law firms throughout the nation were jockeying for their share of the spoils. Still, by virtue of filing first, Lerach had put his firm in position to be lead counsel, making him the grand patron of the case. In this capacity he could reward his confederates: Alfred G. Yates, his friend from Pittsburgh; Leonard Barrack and Richard D. Greenfield in Philadelphia; Max Berger of New York; Leonard M. Ring of Chicago; David B. Gold of San Francisco; Steve Toll of Washington; and Ronald Russ from up the road in Orange County, California.

All had furnished plaintiffs for Lerach lawsuits over the years, assisted on cases, and shared in what Lerach liked to call the "whack-up"—the divvying-up of the legal fees. Judging from the legal complaint and from what each attorney had been learning through the press, the potential whack-up in this case would be astronomical.

The potential bonanza was not limited to the plaintiffs' bar. Having glimpsed preliminary complaints filed in federal district court in Los Angeles on behalf of the plaintiffs, prominent defense lawyers, envisioning their own multimillion-dollar fees, began aligning with the deep-pocket clients popping up among the growing list of defendants. Those joining the fray included Stuart Kadison and James Goldman, Lerach's opponents in the Nucorp case, once again representing auditors Arthur Andersen; James J. Brosnahan, one of the most respected attorneys in California; Arthur Liman, who had headed up the Rockefeller Commission investigation of the Attica Prison riot, defended fugitive financier Robert Vesco, and most recently served as chief counsel to the Senate Select Committee investigating Iran-contra; Griffin Bell, former U.S. Attorney General; and Abbe D. Lowell, one of the best-known criminal defense lawyers in Washington, D.C., who would later serve as the Senate minority counsel opposing the impeachment of Bill Clinton.

The final roster of defendants was listed in a 230-page complaint that had grown from Lerach's forty-five-page first draft. Kevin Roddy was assigned to polish the latest version. He worked feverishly throughout the day and night on Friday, April 6. It was three days after Neal and Fischel had met with the Milberg attorneys in their gambit to have Fischel's name deleted from the list of defendants. Although new to the Milberg firm, Roddy knew the request by Fischel and his lawyer for mercy was a nonstarter. "We had them right in our gunsights," he recalled years later. Roddy circulated the draft to Milberg Weiss lawyers and to the federal court clerk for further circulation. Within days no fewer than one hundred lawyers received the complaint.

In his high-rise office overlooking Lake Michigan, Daniel Fischel took a phone call from M. Laurence Popofsky, a senior partner at Heller Ehrman, one of San Francisco's oldest, most distinguished law firms. Among its clients was accounting giant Ernst & Young, newly merged with Arthur Young, which had been one of Charles Keating's mainstays. Ernst & Young found itself pulled into the undertow of the Lincoln litigation, but that wasn't why Popofsky was calling. He had just read the Milberg Weiss complaint being circulated by the federal court clerk. What he told Fischel was fulfilling Lerach's prophecy: "They're trying to taint you as a witness." After hanging up, Fischel dialed Neal, his attorney, who was sitting in his office in an eighty-six-story Chicago tower a few blocks away. In this phone call Fischel learned something even more alarming.

"I just received a call from Charlie Keating," Neal told Fischel. "He wants me to represent him."

Fischel was thunderstruck.

"What do you want me to do?" Neal asked him.

Without delay, Fischel answered: "I think Charlie needs you more than I do."

Now it was Neal's turn to be astounded. In seventeen years as an attorney, he had acted as lead counsel in criminal and civil white-collar cases representing, among others, General Motors in its lawsuit to buy out Ross Perot. He had defended Navy Admiral Elmo Zumwalt against charges that he was responsible for the deaths and illnesses of thousands of victims of Agent Orange, the defoliant deployed during the Vietnam War. But defending Charlie Keating, the trenchant financier who was becoming the very personification of greed and corruption, represented the challenge of a career. It was that challenge, he would recall nearly twenty years later, while remaining Keating's attorney, that compelled him to tell Fischel: "Okay Dan, I'll help you get another attorney."

In California another pivotal telephone conversation was under way between two attorneys. "I'm not interested in trying this case; not interested in getting in the middle of the trial," Bill Lerach was saying. "But I can furnish a great backup team—blockers, running backs, tight ends, wide receivers. With a good result, we'll make a lot of money. I need a quarterback."

Joseph W. Cotchett listened intently. He liked the football analogy. At six feet four inches tall, with the physique and swagger of an offensive tackle, Cotchett had represented both the National Football League and several of its teams over the years. After graduating from Hastings School of Law in San Francisco in 1964, he joined the U.S. Army, serving first in an intelligence unit, then as a Special Forces paratrooper. He was still serving as a reserve colonel in the Judge Advocate Corps reserves when Lerach invited him to serve as the lead trial attorney in the Lincoln case. Cotchett was an imposing presence known for literally taking over a courtroom—and not only because of his size and bearing. His mother had been a Ziegfeld Follies showgirl, and while growing up in New York, young Joe had been impressed with the results performance art could produce. "Joe is magnificent, dominant, and a much better trial lawyer than I could ever be," Lerach told his colleagues, reminding them that Cotchett had won the biggest jury trial in Silicon Valley—a $200 million verdict against Technical Equities.

"We've got the government out front, and they're getting documents within forty-eight hours, where it might take us a year," Lerach continued in his pitch to Cotchett. "We've got the media in a feeding frenzy because they can tell this is a world-class fraud, and they're feasting on every leak we send them. This is a showcase for legal theater."

Yes, but Keating had filed for bankruptcy, Cotchett pointed out. When it came to getting money, there'd be no one home. Not only that, because he was named in a RICO complaint, Keating would not be covered by D&O insurance. Short of hiring legions of private investigators to discover where offshore the tycoon had parked his ill-gotten gains, as they assumed he had, what was the recourse?

"Nearly fifty deep-pockets defendants who aided in the scheme," replied Lerach. In what he hoped was an added inducement, he told Cotchett that through slick legal maneuverings, the case had been transferred from a problematic federal judge in Los Angeles intent on a quick start to the trial—thus foreshortening the plaintiffs' discovery, in a complicated, multidefendant case that Lerach had likened to a stew simmering slowly— to a court in Tucson, Arizona, that Lerach believed would prove much friendlier terrain.

Federal District Judge Richard Mansfield Bilby of Tucson had been keenly following the massive fraud case being assembled by the government and lawyers for shareholders against the most prominent businessman in Arizona—and he let this interest be known. In the spring of 1990 the federal Judicial Review Commission did transfer the class action lawsuit against Charles Keating and his codefendants to Arizona. And after reaching out to receive it, Judge Bilby was assigned the case.

When he received the news of the transfer, California's most feared litigator let out a loud whoop, raced into the common area outside his office, and with staff and lawyers looking on, crouched and performed a lopsided somersault. As Bill Lerach splattered himself on the floor, he did it with such glee and such force that he threw out his back and had to be helped back into his chair, grinning and grimacing at once.

> • >

POWERFUL WINDS WERE FAVORING the plaintiffs. Their attorneys, along with federal prosecutors, government ethics panels, and Resolution Trust lawyers, were amassing like a vast and well-organized posse against Charles Keating and his fellow defendants—and even against the U.S. senators and government regulators who had enabled Keating's behavior. From his office tower in San Diego, Lerach watched events unfold in ways that he believed would not only produce a big payday but also firmly establish him as the unrivaled King of Torts.

On October 8, 1989, *The Arizona Republic* broke the story that Arizona senator John McCain's wife and her father had invested $359,000 in a Keating-owned shopping center in Phoenix; that the McCains had traveled on Keating's corporate jet, including vacations to Keating's plush vacation villa at exclusive Cat Cay in the Bahamas; and that McCain had quietly reimbursed Keating to the tune of $13,433 but had not recused himself from Lincoln Savings–related matters before Congress. Five days later Common Cause asked the Justice Department and the Senate Ethics Committee to look into the activities of the "Keating Five"—McCain and the four Democrats who'd tried to help him stave off federal regulators. And the Justice Department was boring in on Keating. Soon, in a packed hearing room on the House side of the Capitol, Danny Wall, who had succeeded Ed Gray at the FHLBB, and Charles Keating would make dramatic appearances before a subcommittee chaired by a Texas Democrat named Henry B. Gonzalez in hearings that would greatly assist Lerach's case.

Gonzalez had a reputation for being erratic, stubborn, bellicose—and highly principled. He had a hair-trigger temper and a propensity to grandstand. Many congressional Democrats considered Gonzalez an embarrassment, and even those who admired him were worried when he took over the chairmanship of the House Banking, Finance, and Urban Affairs Committee in December 1988. But what could anyone say? The previous chairman, Rhode Island Democratic representative Fernand J. St. Germain, had coauthored the legislation that allowed operators such as Keating to get their claws on the nation's thrifts in the first place. Gonzalez, who voted against deregulation, began holding hearings early that year, and reporters covering the burgeoning S&L crisis in general, and the "Keating Five" scandal in particular, had learned that the House Banking Committee was unearthing damning morsels of information—including the whopping amounts of money that Charlie Keating had funneled to the five senators.

At Gonzalez's fifth hearing, held on November 14, 1989, he called out of the audience some of the investors bilked by American Continental—whose testimony would put a human face on the Lincoln Savings debacle.

"It gives a whole new meaning to bank robbery, don't you think?" said Shirley Lampel, a near-blind fifty-eight-year-old widow from Tustin, California, who lost her nest egg of $30,000 when American Continental went belly-up. "Up against the likes of Charles Keating and the influence he was able to buy from elected officials, we didn't have a chance—we had been targeted by Keating—with help from the Keating Five."

Ramona Miller Jacobs, another Lerach client, choked back tears as she told the committee that she had bought $11,000 worth of American Continental corporate debentures in hopes of earning enough return to buy a van to transport her paralyzed daughter Michelle. "Mr. Keating and his coconspirators had other plans for our money," she testified. In words that were music to Bill Lerach's ears—after all, he helped put them there—Jacobs added, "Mr. Keating did not do this by himself. There are a whole lot of people."

These heart-wrenching accounts left banking committee members of both parties itching to take their wrath out on someone. That opportunity came just a week later, on November 21, 1989, at a theatrical session in a packed hearing room. For six and a half hours Danny Wall and his top deputies tried to convince banking committee members that the Office of Thrift Supervision (as the FHLBB had been renamed earlier that year) had not been derelict in its duty.

Then, at four thirty P.M., in a highly choreographed bit of theater that Chairman Gonzalez believed quite correctly would make good film for the six P.M. network news broadcasts, Charles Keating swept into the room flanked by five lawyers and flunkies. At six foot five, towering over his entourage, the former Olympic swimmer did not appear to be sixty-six years old. Red-faced and fidgety, Keating first requested through his attorneys that all television cameras in the hearing room be turned off. Keating had never been camera shy, but then again, he had never been so vulnerable.

"Are you ready to answer questions?" asked Gonzalez.

"No, sir," replied Keating. "I have no testimony to give today."

"May I ask why?" Gonzalez said, raising his eyebrows in feigned surprise.

"On the advice of counsel, I respectfully exercise my Constitutional prerogative and privilege and authority and decline to answer questions here today," Keating replied. With that he made his way through the throng, out into the hall, and into his waiting black Cadillac. One of Keating's subalterns left behind a three-page press release ostensibly issued by American Continental that blamed regulators, and not himself, for the demise of Lincoln Savings.

By then the buccaneer act had gone stale. A reckoning was coming—and everyone knew it. The first head to roll was Wall's. On December 4,

1989, Wall wrote a four-page letter of resignation, asserting his belief that he had been made a "scapegoat" for the savings and loan crisis. President Bush accepted it immediately.

He was hardly the last person in Washington who would pay a price for the sins of Charles Keating. In April Keating had held a press conference— at which he took no actual questions from the media but still managed to make news. Near the conclusion Keating told reporters: "One question, among the many raised in recent weeks, had to do with whether my financial support in any way influenced several political figures to take up my cause. I want to say in the most forceful way I can: I certainly hope so."

It was a quote that Bill Lerach would put to good use.

> • >

LERACH HAD WATCHED IN AWE as Gonzalez conducted the hearings. He'd given millions of dollars to Democratic officeholders, candidates, and causes during his career but never a nickel to the banking committee chairman from Texas. Actually, it was the other way around: Gonzalez had given Lerach something—an idea for a publicity stunt that would rattle his opponents and be an amusing caper at the same time.

Lerach instructed John Stoia to round up his most compelling plaintiffs. Stoia knew that wouldn't be difficult—he'd already done so for Gonzalez's staffers. "We're going to get them back on television," Lerach said, grinning mischievously.

L'affaire Keating was largely a scandal of Democrats, but a lawsuit was a lawsuit, and Lerach used his Democratic Party connections to help smooth the path for what he had in mind. Stoia and Len Simon were tasked with scheduling their most compelling clients to testify on Capitol Hill. Lerach himself put in a call to well-connected Washington lawyer Jonathan W. Cuneo. Under his instructions, Cuneo wrote letters to the administrative assistants of each of the Keating Five, asking for an audience with the California women who were scheduled to testify.

Within two days Ramona Jacobs also received a call. John Stoia was on the line: "How would you like to go back to Washington?" She was game, but she had a severely handicapped daughter she was caring for. Stoia assured her that the firm would pay for assistance for her daughter, Michelle. As for Rea Luft, she couldn't believe it. She was going to be picked up and flown to the capital of the United States of America. Important people in the government wanted to hear from her. She told Stoia she thought she must be dreaming, and upon hanging up the phone, she broke into tears.

The four-hour-fifty-minute transcontinental plane trip from Los Angeles to Washington's Dulles International Airport was made much more accommodating for Ramona Jacobs, Leah Kane, and Rea Luft in the first-class cabin, courtesy of Bill Lerach and John Stoia. Luft in particular was the most grateful. At ninety-two she was legally blind, nearly deaf, and mostly confined to a wheelchair. As the plane descended through the clouds into Dulles in the early evening of January 30, 1990, the Keating Five were preparing to attend President Bush's State of the Union address. A van took the women to the Willard Hotel, near the White House on Pennsylvania Avenue, where they would be treated to $400-a-night rooms, accommodations only slightly less lavish than those that Charlie Keating enjoyed at this, his favorite hotel when he was in town.* Lerach loved the taste of irony, especially when he was the one arranging it.

As they cruised east along the Dulles access road, Lerach laid out their itinerary. There would be some sightseeing. He hoped that they could testify Wednesday on Capitol Hill to the Senate Judiciary Committee, which was taking up legislation relating to Lincoln Savings. This was not assured: DeConcini was chairing the committee, and he was understandably cool to Lerach. Still, it would be like appearing in a movie, Lerach told his clients, recalling his instructions to his elderly witnesses nearly two decades earlier in the Pacific Homes case. Then, he explained, he had another Capitol Hill trip planned for them. They were going to visit four of the five Senate offices of the Keating senators. Cuneo had managed the arrangements. Only

---

* At the Willard, Keating was known as "C-Note Charlie," because he handed out $100 bills like candy to the staff, most of whom wore "We Love Charlie" buttons sent in advance by Keating's staff.

DeConcini refused. Lerach was undeterred. *We'll see about that,* he thought to himself.

Once in his room, Lerach called Cuneo to go over the next day's agenda. Had he contacted the media? "Yes, they're in play," Cuneo said. Lerach, noting that he'd made sure the van was equipped with a large (comparatively crude) mobile phone, joked that it was shaping up as more of a guerrilla incursion than a visit.

Then it was time for the trip to the Hill. After making certain Rea Luft was comfortable, they proceeded past the Capitol to the Russell Senate Office Building. There they were met by television camera crews and reporters, tipped off by the irrepressible Cuneo. Entourage in tow, Lerach cleared the security gate and headed for the elevator that would transport the group for their unannounced but hoped-for meeting with members of the Keating Five.

The little band of women and attorneys charged through the hallways with the media following. Dennis DeConcini wouldn't see them? Well, Lerach decided—that would be their first stop. They first headed down a short corridor to the sparkling new Hart Building, toward DeConcini's office. As expected, the door to the office was shut and the senator was unavailable, reported a DeConcini aide who had been dispatched from an interior room. Lerach made certain the television lights illuminated the face of the embarrassed underling. Reporters also dutifully wrote down the reaction of the three Keating victims. "The man is a coward," Ramona Jacobs said of DeConcini. "He doesn't have the guts to stand up to three women."

Next in the line of fire was Alan Cranston, whose offices were two floors down. At seventy-five, Cranston was as old as some of Lerach's victims. In November he had been publicly excoriated during the House Banking Committee hearings. Having taken his lumps that day, and sensing himself on the downward slide toward the end of a long and full political career, Cranston decided to play this differently from DeConcini. Cranston did not invite the Lincoln Savings survivors inside his inner sanctum, but he did acknowledge their grievances and said that if he could do anything for them while they were in Washington, to let his office know.

Lerach's expedition wound its way down the halls and into and out of elevators, more a demonstration than a finding of satisfaction. Finally they came to 241 Russell, the office of John McCain. The senator, dressed in dark blue suit and red tie, bade them join him inside his private office. Chairs had been set in a semicircle facing McCain's desk. Through the window to the southwest, they could see the Lincoln Memorial.

Instead of repairing to his desk, McCain stood in the middle of the semicircle patiently listening while Lerach introduced each of his clients and informed the senator of their histories with Lincoln Savings and of their losses. McCain looked pained. Then dropping down—Lerach swears it was on bended knee—the senator from Arizona, the former navy aviator, the brave prisoner of war, the heroic American icon, bowed his head and said solemnly and so quietly that someone had to remind him that Rea Luft could barely hear: "I have betrayed my family. I have betrayed my constituency. I am very sorry that I have hurt you and your families." Ramona Jacobs and Leah Kane would never forget that electric moment. It remained indelible twenty years later, even as McCain waged a spirited campaign to occupy the great white house down Pennsylvania Avenue. "He looked very embarrassed and very disturbed," they both recalled, in nearly identical words.

The scene would remain always with Lerach, too, as partisan as he was, even after his own career had suffered worse setbacks than any of the Keating Five's (although not worse than Charlie Keating's), and even after his conviction and disbarment, even after he'd been denied an opportunity to vote for Barack Obama.

John McCain couldn't undo anything in his past or in Charlie Keating's—but on a January day in 1990 the senator validated the pain and feelings of three hurting women. As penance, McCain embraced campaign finance reform with a vengeance, bucking the powers that be in his own party along the way. Twelve years later Congress finally passed the legislation that the Arizona Republican and Senator Russell Feingold, a Wisconsin Democrat, had ardently championed. Its formal title was the Bipartisan Campaign Reform Act of 2002, but everyone knew it simply as "McCain-Feingold." It was the most sweeping attempt at limiting the influence of fat-cat donors since the aftermath of Watergate.

> • > • > .• > • >

A TROJAN HORSE NAMED KEATING

Within months Senator McCain would prove to be a trophy witness in the civil lawsuit on behalf of 23,000 class action plaintiffs against Charles Keating and the confederate banks and auditors. McCain would lament publicly his poor judgment for attending the two meetings with the federal banking regulators. He would bemoan taking money from Keating and express regret for writing letters to regulators on Keating's behalf. And while McCain, the only senator who testified before Judge Bilby and the jury in the Keating trial, was forthright in his testimony and appeared to despair at his predicament on the witness stand, his embarrassment served mainly as a reminder to Lerach of the real axes he was grinding.

During a 1990 Christmas party Kevin Roddy mentioned to Lerach that he would be leaving the next morning for Phoenix to depose Senator McCain. Roddy remembered saying something to the effect of "I guess we're going to ruin his Christmas vacation." To which Lerach, drink in hand, drew close and hissed: "I don't really give a rat's ass about McCain. I want us to bury that little fucker Fischel under the courthouse steps."

> • >

FOUR MONTHS LATER in a federal courtroom in San Jose, California, Milberg Weiss's newest partner, Patrick Coughlin, found himself in a pretrial hearing in the chambers of U.S. District Court Judge James Ware, in a shareholder lawsuit he was about to try before a jury against a Silicon Valley darling named Apple Computer. In the suit the plaintiffs' lawyers claimed their clients had been deceived in a press release by Apple executives who had exaggerated the capabilities of a new disk drive, thus creating false expectations among purchasers, who drove up the price of Apple stock in anticipation of greater computing performance and a competitive advantage over its rivals. The drive, which had taken four years and $50 million to develop, had been code-named "Twiggy" and would power a new computer named "Lisa" (Local Integrated Software Architecture), coincidentally sharing the name of Steve Jobs's oldest daughter.

It was rolled out in the spring of 1983, with Apple targeting business customers wanting more advanced performance and willing to pay nearly $10,000 per machine for a more sophisticated operating system. Within a week Apple stock soared to $70 a share, an all-time high. Five months after the rollout Apple had sold more than 100,000 Lisas. Throughout those five months complaints flooded Apple offices in Cupertino, California. The Lisa was not as fast as advertised. In fact, it was downright slow and clumsy. It wasn't an Apple—it was a lemon. The company itself seemed to be in trouble.

Apple's chief defense attorney, Laurence Popofsky, devised a trial strategy that had worked in the Nucorp case in San Diego: he would argue that since Apple had lost money on its own product, it was therefore inconceivable that the company had not deliberately released a faulty product on the market. As far as shareholders were concerned, they had taken a risk on a potentially volatile high-tech stock in an efficient market. Of course the chief proponent on this "efficient market" rationale was Daniel Fischel.

It was during the pretrial hearing, as the plaintiffs' attorneys and attorneys for the defense were outlining their cases, previewing their evidence, and listing potential witnesses that Fischel's name arose. Popofsky was prepared to argue that any mention of his inclusion as a defendant in the Lincoln case be prohibited by Judge Ware.

Thanks to Coughlin, Popofsky got his chance. "He's named as a defendant in a RICO case we've got going in the Lincoln case," Coughlin told the judge in chambers, while the judge's court reporter recorded his statements. "We actually think he is a crook . . . who helped Lincoln carry out one of the largest frauds in the country."

Popofsky was apoplectic, strenuously arguing that since Fischel hadn't been convicted of anything, Coughlin's remarks were outrageous and unprofessional. Coughlin was taken aback, but the words he had unleashed could not be retrieved. Later Fischel approached Coughlin in the courtroom. "I heard you called me a crook," he spluttered.

Coughlin, normally an imposing man, recoiled but managed to stammer, "I'm sorry. I apologize." He offered to strike his statement from the record. "I shouldn't have said that."

Fischel refused his offer, saying only "No. I might want to use it later."

Coughlin had little time to be nonplussed. He had to focus on persuading the jury to turn on Apple chief A.C. "Mike" Markkula, Jr., a Silicon Valley legend who had parlayed his own business expertise, $91,000 of his own money, and a $250,000 bank line of credit to become a one-third owner of Apple. Although Fischel did indeed deliver his opinion that Apple shareholders had been hurt only by putting themselves at risk in a risky market, Coughlin clung to his argument that, sitting before the jury, was a tangible instrument of deceit.

In his closing arguments, he circled the Lisa displayed in the middle of the courtroom, and asked the jury: "Ladies and gentlemen, do you wonder why my opponents and their experts never bothered to turn this device on? Why they never offered a demonstration?" Then, patting the computer, he rose on his toes and declared, "Because it doesn't work!"

The jury took little time in deliberating. The panel found Markkula and John Vennard, an Apple president in charge of disk drives, liable for $100 million in damages.* Gasps were heard from the audience, from the defendants, and even from their attorneys. The verdict generated page-

---

* On September 7, 1991, Judge Ware overturned the jury verdict as excessive. He also found that the two Apple executives had not violated securities laws. But he also ordered

one headlines across the nation and incited riotous meetings and conference calls in boardrooms from Silicon Valley to Wall Street. At Wilson, Sonsini, Goodrich & Rosati in Palo Alto, the law firm that had helped Apple launch its original IPO, senior partners conferred with nervous clients. A $100 million jury verdict was a warning. A new, hostile sentiment might be brewing against volatile high-tech companies and the executives who comprised the firm's client list. A new word was entering their business vocabulary and it was as fearsome a word as *attacked* or *mugged.* The word was *Lerached.*

Two nights after the audacious verdict Milberg Weiss West held a riotous victory party at the luxurious Omni Hotel, near the waterfront in downtown San Diego. The music was loud, backslaps abounded, and booze flowed. It was a big, open event, or so it seemed, with guests of guests not even affiliated with the firm joining the celebration. Amid the congratulations on this great victory, the future prizes were in view—as were the obstacles to winning them. Before long, the pending case against Keating, Lincoln Savings, and the other big-name defendants came up in conversation. So did Dan Fischel. "We're still going to put that little fucker out of business," Lerach was overheard to say, more than once, by more than his own people.

The irony was that, Fischel or no Fischel, thanks to Keating and all those who enabled his shenanigans, business was never better for class action securities lawyers than it was in the early 1990s. The "decade of greed" had given way to . . . another decade of greed. And Lerach was there to, depending on your philosophy, partake of the spoils—or fulfill his obligation to keep the bastards honest.

Stanley Sporkin, the former SEC enforcement officer and later a federal district judge, had certainly done his part. On Thursday, August 24, 1990, Sporkin ruled that Keating and his associates used "a dishonest scheme" to loot Lincoln and defraud investors in American Continental Corporation. Sporkin rejected Keating's appeal to reverse the government's takeover of his financial empire.

---

the corporation to stand for a new trial. A disappointed Coughlin eventually negotiated a $16 million settlement.

In Arizona, Mike Manning, a government attorney, was thrilled. The Resolution Trust representing the FDIC case he headed could go forward with its lawsuit. Bill Lerach was equally elated, and when he called Joe Cotchett, he was even more heartened to learn that the fabled trial lawyer was willing to take the reins of the trial team. Cotchett had gone over the complaint and lauded the Milberg Weiss lawyers for the preparation. He had just one area of doubt: "Why Lexecon? Why Fischel?" Lerach pondered the question, sucked in his breath, and said: "Joe, do you want in on this?" Then it was Cotchett's turn to ponder the issue. Why let Fischel stand in the way of a $30 or $40 million fee? It wasn't his issue, it was a Milberg issue. He was in. They should start taking depositions right away.

There was big money to be made for plaintiffs' lawyers in big cases, obscene amounts. In 1988 Lerach had cleared $2.3 million in salary, while Mel Weiss had taken home $2.6 million. In the following decade each partner averaged $10.3 million in salary annually from 1990 to 1998—a cool hundred million per man per decade.

> • >

ULTIMATELY, LERACH'S GAMBIT WORKED: the most culpable defendants in the Keating case concluded that they didn't want to risk facing Joe Cotchett before a jury. Even as the pretrial wrangling was still taking place, they began clamoring to settle the cases. And Judge Irving proved masterful in mediating these settlements for which Lerach had hired him. They came from some of the biggest-name defendants, accountants, investment banks, other professionals, and even law firms that had represented Keating and his allies. Joining Arthur Andersen were Ernst & Young (which coughed up $63 million) and the prominent law firms of Jones, Day, Reavis & Pogue ($24 million) and Kaye, Scholer, Fierman, Hays & Handler ($41 million). The week before, Offerman & Co., a Minneapolis-based underwriter for some of the bonds, settled (for $1.5 million).

"Any professional who accepted an engagement for Mr. Keating is going to have an exceedingly difficult time before a jury to show that they conducted their professional duties properly," said Popofsky, announcing the settlement of his client Ernst & Young. Such was the mediator's stature that Judge Irving was given a seat near the jury box. Now it was time for the showdown with the defendants who had *not* settled before trial. As he watched Cotchett deliver his opening arguments, Judge Irving was grateful for the privilege he'd earned. And some of the entities that had refused to settle quickly found themselves wishing they had been less truculent.

"Ladies and gentlemen, the evidence will show . . . ," the plaintiffs' advocate began, his voice deep and certain, his timing impeccable, as he instructed an assistant to play for the jury a video introducing his case, a video worth a thousand of his own words. The lights dimmed; up came the presentation, and in it, one by one, the faces of Charles Keating, various American Continental and Lincoln Savings officers, and other wealthy defendants. The images were crisp and came in quick flashes; each person was asked a question and responded by refusing to answer on the grounds of avoiding self-incrimination. What the jury saw was a cascade of faces and voices and the words "self-incrimination."

And Cotchett wasn't through. He offered another video, the American Continental motivational training film. It showed Keating mounting a desktop, reaching into his pocket, shouting, "It's all about the money," and hurling $100 bills into the air. The screen showed bills raining down on his employees, and it showed the employees jostling each other, scrambling to snatch as much money as they could, supplicating themselves before a laughing Charlie Keating. *This is sickening*, Irving thought, as he watched. Glances at the faces of the nearby jurors told him they were reacting similarly.

Later came the parade of witnesses—Rea Luft, Ramona Jacobs, Leah Kane, John Brunner, a sixty-eight-year-old retired puppeteer, and more than two dozen others, including Katherine Bartolone, a seventy-six-year-old retired nurse and widow, who had lost $50,000 that she and her husband had saved for over fifty years at their local Lincoln Savings before it had been taken over, and looted, by Keating.

"I went to roll over this CD," she told the mesmerized jury. "The young man told me that they had another account that was as safe as the Rock of Gibraltar."

John Stoia had courted and prepared each witness prior to their testimony; Joe Cotchett skillfully elicited their tales of victimhood. The trial continued from April through mid-June. As the plaintiffs' case unfurled itself, more defendants opted to negotiate their way out from under the jury's wrath. By now some ninety defendants had settled for nearly $200 million. Those remaining in the dock were Keating himself; his officers; a Phoenix-area businessman named Conley Wolfswinkel; Continental Southern, an Atlanta development firm; Société Brétonneau, a French-owned banking combine; auditors Touche Ross—and of course, Lexecon, the economic consulting firm headed by Daniel Fischel.

Fischel's replacement lawyer Dan K. Webb presented a vigorous defense, calling upon his experience as a former U.S. Attorney for the Northern District of Illinois. Webb had received widespread attention for his courtroom prosecution of retired Admiral John Poindexter, in the Iran-contra scandal, and he was respected as an attorney who knew the boundaries of the law. Nonetheless Webb's motions for a summary judgment to exclude Lexecon and Fischel from the case received no sympathy from Judge Bilby. The precept of attrition, however, would ultimately insinuate a favorable outcome for the consulting firm.

The case was winding down, and certainly the time spent away from their homes and families and practices was having an influence on the attorneys. Webb tried one last gambit. He called Judge Bilby and said his client wanted to present an offer to the plaintiffs' lawyers. Bilby summoned Len Simon to his chambers. The date was June 22, 1989.

There Webb continued to assert his client's innocence, adding that at the very most Lexecon had played only a peripheral role compared to the other defendants. Webb also reminded Judge Bilby and Simon of an assertion he had previously made and was prepared to prove: copies of several bills that Simon had turned up during discovery, bills that American Continental Corporation had paid to Lexecon for services were forgeries. Simon had been dismissive of this assertion, but Judge Bilby had referred the allegation to the FBI, and following its investigation, Mark Sauter, who had left his law firm to become an American Continental vice president, admitted that he had forged the bills, acting out of greed, to defraud Keating and his own company.

Simon, who saw the implications, was in the mood to reconcile. What if Lexecon agreed to forfeit the equivalent of its fee from Keating in service to the plaintiffs? Simon quickly calculated the amount to be just over one million dollars* and then made another private mental calculation of how much money might go out the door to try one of the last plaintiffs in order to . . . get what? Another million, two million, three? They were approaching diminishing returns. Simon said he'd confer with Lerach and get back to Webb. To Simon's surprise, Lerach did not throw a tantrum when the offer was relayed to him. Economics and efficiency were now trumping revenge. Was Cotchett okay with the offer? Lerach wanted to know. Joe didn't care one way or the other about Lexecon, Simon reminded Lerach. "Okay, let's take the deal and get on with our lives," Lerach told his colleague.

Simon and Webb returned to Judge Bilby's chambers. The settlement offer was accepted. But Webb demurred. His client would not sign a "settlement" agreement.

Exasperated, Simon asked, "Well, what will he sign?"

Webb answered, "A disposition," meaning that the judge would resolve the differences between both sides regardless of any conveyance of money or property. It was a subtle, legal nuance but one meant to avoid a stigma for the defendant. Simon understood the difference between settlement and disposition, and he also understood that this resolution would not require "forty pages of boiler-plate crap that come with traditional settlements." So in the interest of a speedy conclusion, he agreed. After being dogged for months by allegations that he was a crook, after being tainted as a potential expert witness, possibly costing his consulting company millions of dollars in fees, Daniel Fischel was in the clear. But one matter was overlooked. Even though the resolution was untraditional, a traditional exercise normally follows. It requires a release, meaning both parties agree not to subsequently sue the other. The concluding documents in the case of the plaintiffs versus Lexecon did not contain a release document.

* Ultimately the amount came to around $700,000.

"Joe overlooked it, Bill overlooked it. But I was there and should have gotten it," Simon lamented sixteen years later. When he belatedly approached Fischel, asking him to sign the release, Fischel refused, telling Simon what he had told Simon's partner Patrick Coughlin in the Apple trial: "I may want to use this against you later."

Eight days after the cease-fire was signed with Lexecon, on Wednesday, July 1, 1992, exactly three months to the day the trial against Keating and the remaining defendants began, Judge Bilby issued his instructions to the jury and bade them to weigh the evidence presented before considering the gravity of the stakes. Although he must have known that the jury was well aware that Charles Keating was now in state prison near Bakersfield, California, the judge dutifully directed them to deliberate in good conscience and refrain from any outside influences that might influence their decision.

On July 10 the jury announced it had reached its conclusion. In his San Diego office Bill Lerach had tried to stay focused on the cases that lay in their accordion files and boxes on the floor before him. But when Kathy Lichnovsky, his secretary, buzzed him and told him Len Simon was on the line, he nearly knocked his own phone off the desk.

"Bill," was all Simon had to say. Lerach could tell from his colleague's tone, they'd hit the jackpot. "Three *billion* three in damages," Simon said, breathlessly. "Another five against the other guys." In actuality, the jury had awarded $600 million in compensatory damages against Keating and another $1.5 billion in punitive damages. Under the federal racketeering laws, the compensatory damages were to be tripled. Even with Keating's bankruptcy, the overall take from the settlements and verdict against the remaining defendants would be worth hundreds of millions. Investors would get a significant portion of their money back. He congratulated and thanked Simon even as Kathy Lichnovsky announced that Joe Cotchett was calling. Lerach congratulated Cotchett and himself for his own good judgment in bringing the famed trial lawyer in on the case. As Lerach told K. L. to ring Mel Weiss, John Stoia asked his assistant to begin contacting Ramona Jacobs and the other victims so he could deliver the news.

> • >

THE SEEDS OF RETRIBUTION had been sown during that April night eight years earlier when, in drunken ruin following the Nucorp defeat, Lerach was heard to announce his intent to put Fischel out of business. It had certainly gained more force with subsequent threats and the attempted branding of the University of Chicago professor and expert witness as a crook. Fischel had felt the effects personally and economically, noting a sudden drop-off in business from even regular clients, not to mention the nearly $4 million he and his firm had spent paying their own legal fees and the $700,000 "nonsettlement" to resolve the Lincoln Savings case. Fischel had also heard from colleagues that Lerach had often disparaged him at securities litigation conferences for giving Keating "a clean bill of health." The final blow came in a letter Milberg Weiss attorney Kevin Roddy wrote to the *National Law Journal*, discrediting Fischel as an expert witness. In his ill-advised missive Roddy repeated that Lexecon had "settled" in the Lincoln case. Even more distressing to Fischel, Roddy had also said that Lexecon had committed "wrongful activities on behalf" of Keating, a convicted felon, and had conduced "fraudulent dealings with regulators."

Fischel took out a yellow legal pad and began drafting ways to explore his remedies. He approached his challenge both as a law professor and as an expert witness in his own behalf. Milberg Weiss was spreading lies against him. Milberg Weiss had sued him as a RICO defendant in the Lincoln case not because they were convinced he had been complicit as a fellow "corrupt racketeer" but to shred his credibility and, with it, his business. The more research he did, the more convinced he was that Milberg Weiss had abused the legal process against him. Would a judge and jury buy his theory? Moreover, was he up to another prolonged war with Milberg Weiss Lerach? If he lost would he put himself out of business? And what about Dan Webb, his lawyer? They had virtually lived together through the Lincoln ordeal. Was he up for more bloody combat? As it turned out, Webb was not.

That was why, in October 1992, the phone rang in the Mayer Brown office of Alan Salpeter, then forty-five, a senior partner and experienced trial lawyer. "I'm Dan Fischel at the Chicago Law School. Could we meet for lunch today?"

Salpeter immediately recognized the name. Fischel and his colleagues at Lexecon had been expert witnesses in Mayer Brown cases.

"I'm considering filing a lawsuit. It's against Milberg Weiss," Fischel told him. "I'd like you to consider taking on the case." Fischel said he'd already drafted a complaint and would fax it. Salpeter and another partner, Michele L. Odorizzi, who'd been on the *University of Chicago Law Review* with Fischel, quickly glanced at the sixty-page complaint when it arrived at the Mayer Brown offices shortly before eleven A.M. They continued to read aloud to each other as they made the fifteen-minute walk to the stately, red-granite Chicago Club and then mounted the ornate stairway to the dining room overlooking Lake Michigan. By the time Fischel arrived with two other Lexecon partners, Dennis Carlton and Andrew Rosenfeld, the Mayer Brown lawyers had finished reading the drafted complaint.

Salpeter, a physically fit former college third baseman, could feel his competitive juices flowing. He loved trial work, loved matching his skills against his opponents' in front of juries. He was familiar enough with Milberg Weiss to know that their bread and butter relied on staying away from juries and settling before trial. From what Fischel had put down on paper, he was more than eager to take this case to a jury.

"First I have a few questions," Salpeter said, as his prospective clients settled at their table in the opulent dining room that had once been the province of Marshall Field, George Pullman, N. K. Fairbank, and Mayor Richard Daley. "Are the facts true?"

Fischel, stonefaced, replied, "Yes."

"A couple of more questions, then," Salpeter said.

Fischel leaned forward as if to invite them.

"How strong is your stomach?" Salpeter asked. "How deep are your pockets?"

Fischel appeared to smile, ever so slightly. "Don't worry about either one of them."

> • > • > • > • >

THE VISIBLE HAND OF GREED

The night the Keating trial ended, or possibly the night before, someone casually approached a relatively understated house in the fashionable Brentwood neighborhood of Los Angeles. The visitor carried an oversize, rectangular cardboard box resembling a pizza container. Instead of ringing the doorbell, the intruder unlocked the front door, strode into the front hallway, and went straight to an alarm, disarming it effortlessly. With equal efficiency the burglar turned back down the hallway, went into the library, and approached a framed twenty-by-twenty-inch painting of a cottage perched on a precipice overlooking the sea. Plucking the object with both hands, he then disengaged the stretched canvas from the frame, carefully sliding it into the container that had been padded for this purpose.

Turning back into the hallway, the prowler climbed a stairway to a bedroom and advanced on another painting, this one about ten inches high and a foot wide. The piece depicted a jumbled female torso before a mirror. With care, the bandit lifted the art and, leaving it in its frame, placed it in the padded cardboard box. The thief sealed the box with packing tape. Once secured, he retraced his steps, rearmed the alarm, and disappeared into the mild summer night.

The following Sunday, July 12, 1992, Bill Lerach received a call at home. It was Steven Cooperman, his newfound serial plaintiff. "We got burglarized," he said, relating that he and Nancy had returned from vacation to find two paintings missing.

"Which ones?" asked Lerach, who had been to the Cooperman home and had admired his collection.

"A Monet and a Picasso," Cooperman replied.

The Monet was *The Customs Officer's Cabin at Pourville*, and the Picasso was *Nude Before a Mirror*. Lerach recognized the name of the latter work of art. Cooperman told Lerach what he had told the Los Angeles police officers. "There was no sign of a break-in. The alarm was still armed."

Lerach asked the obvious question, and Cooperman told him, yes, they were insured. He had taken out the policies a couple of months earlier. How much? Lerach asked.

"About twelve million," Cooperman replied. Sixteen years later, while in federal prison, Lerach would recall this about the phone conversation: "An amber warning light suddenly went off."

> • >

BY THE SUMMER OF 1992 Lerach had fully transformed himself into a case spotter and developer, initiating and managing lawsuits as a hedge fund manager might manage a portfolio. The huge jury awards in Lincoln and Apple had stirred the rival realms of business and the law, and the number of class action securities cases was growing exponentially—up 50 percent from just one year before—as was the indelible fear in boardrooms of being Lerached. The net effect was that 90 percent of all securities cases were now settling out of court; more than one-third of them fell under the jurisdiction of the federal district court governing Northern California. The average settlement rose too, from $6.3 million to $9.8 million. More than $700 million was paid out in 1991 alone, even before the enormous jury awards in Lincoln and Apple.

By 1992 Lerach's firm commanded more than 25 percent of all class action securities cases nationwide. This prodigious market share would keep rising through the decade, as interested parties—industry advocates, entrepreneurs, tort reformers, members of Congress, and would-be competitors—began tracking with mounting alarm the juggernaut named Milberg, Weiss, Bershad & Lerach. With success and money and technology, the firm grew larger and more efficient, turning itself into a virtual lawsuit machine or, as some saw it, a legal raptor.

"He's got quite an operation over there," defense lawyer Chuck Dick told a prominent Bay Area technology writer in 1996. "He has a team of people in his office who do nothing but maintain a database of information about the companies they have under surveillance. They start charting a company with the announcement of an initial public offering . . . It's an impressive operation, but it also means he needs to meet this huge overhead nut every month. He always has to have a large enough volume of cases, regardless of the strength of his documentation or tangible evidence, to keep his business going."

In the eyes of the typical Silicon Valley executive, this was putting things too charitably. Most of them believed William Lerach had become little more than a shakedown artist, albeit an extremely formidable one. Prominent Silicon Valley venture capitalist L. John Doerr, in an edgy *Wired* magazine article, was quoted as saying of Lerach: "He's an exceptionally smart, shrewd, entrepreneurial, economic terrorist."*

Doerr, who was exceptionally smart, shrewd, and entrepreneurial himself, knew what he was talking about. Of the eight prominent high-tech companies that had tapped Doerr to serve on their boards, by the early 1990s, five had experienced the double-whammy of having their stock price dip and then being nailed immediately with a Lerach-generated class action claim. Doerr estimated the cost of fighting the claims, settling the suits, and purchasing the requisite D&O insurance at $120 million—just for those

---

* There was nothing subtle about where the editors of *Wired* stood on class action securities lawsuits: the headline of their Lerach piece was "Bloodsucking Scumbag." Showing perverse pride, Lerach responded by including the article in his packet of press clippings he'd hand to journalists who came to interview him.

five companies. It was a sum, he liked to say, that would pay the salaries of two hundred top-flight engineers or programmers for a decade.

Lerach's success did, however, spawn a growth industry in Silicon Valley: it led to the proliferation, and expansion, of corporate law firms such as Wilson, Sonsini, Goodrich & Rosati, specializing in defending high-tech companies from class action suits. The firm's premier corporate attorneys— Bruce Vanyo, Boris Feldman, and Steve Schatz—found themselves counseling many prospective clients and current clients with this message articulated by Vanyo: "For small and medium-size (emerging firms in volatile markets) the drain could be relatively huge in cost of litigation, the psychic energy expended, the diversion of resources and attention to preparation, let alone the vagaries of juries that might not be favorably disposed toward companies jurors might perceive to have deep pockets."

High-flying high-tech executives ignored this advice at their peril. Even those who followed it faithfully often found it impossible to avoid Bill Lerach's gunsights.

Duane and Theodore Roth, two brothers from Iowa who had moved to San Diego to run a small medical research company, learned this lesson the hard way. Duane, a Republican, was CEO and chairman of the board of Alliance Pharmaceutical Corporation; his younger brother Ted, a Democrat, was a vice president and director of the company, seeking to develop a product called Oxygent, a human blood substitute for hospital use during surgical procedures. In September 1992, after the Federal Drug Administration asked for details in Alliance's testing protocols, the company announced a delay in Oxygent's clinical trials. Predictably, the company's stock dropped at this news, and following the Alliance press release, Milberg Weiss filed a class action suit alleging fraud on the part of the company and its officers.

This swift legal strike would have surprised no Silicon Valley executive. Ironically, it caught Ted Roth off guard—precisely because Roth knew Bill Lerach socially. Both were active in San Diego County Democratic Party circles and had attended fund-raisers together, some hosted by Lerach. In fact, Ted Roth's daughter Kristin attended Torrey Pines High School with

Lerach's daughter Shannon. The girls were friends and had enjoyed sleepovers at the Lerach home.

"I think I can talk to him," Ted told his brother Duane and other Alliance Pharmaceutical officers. "I'll explain to him what we do, why the trials were delayed . . ." Roth believed he had a hole card: except for some stock options he himself had exercised six months earlier because they were about to expire, none of the officers had sold a thing. Thus there was no insider trading; there was only a delay in clinical trials on the part of a relatively small firm—some 150 people were employed by Alliance Pharmaceutical, most of them scientists.

At a political fund-raiser, Ted Roth buttonholed Lerach, who told him to come by the office. "Look, Ted," Lerach said, "this is business, it's nothing personal." It was quite personal to the Roth brothers, however. Ted Roth got on Lerach's calendar for a face-to-face meeting at Milberg Weiss's San Diego office tower. When Roth and his attorney, Julia B. Strickland, arrived, they found an unsmiling Lerach flanked by two other Milberg Weiss lawyers. Strickland and Roth made their pitch: the firm was not guilty of fraud or anything else, they said, and would happily cooperate with Lerach even without a subpoena. They offered to show Milberg Weiss litigators around their office, open their books, even assign a staff researcher to help them decipher the technical stuff.

"Maybe we could save everyone time and bother," Roth offered.

"I don't give a fuck about the merits," Lerach replied coldly. "We've already calculated the damages—and it's $10 million to $15 million. If you want to talk about a *settlement*, we can negotiate."

"Bill, look who you're talking to," Roth tried one last time.

Lerach cut him off. "As I told you," he said, "this is not personal. It's business."

At this point most company directors facing Lerach's scorched-earth tactics would cave. Often their insurance companies would virtually insist on it. What Lerach didn't know was that Alliance Pharmaceutical's D&O insurance carrier was trying to weasel out of covering the cost of litigation on a technicality: because Alliance had no product yet in the market, the insurance carrier was claiming that there was no "product failure" as contemplated in the policy. So Duane Roth, now additionally incensed at how his kid brother had been treated at Milberg Weiss's office, and without any deep pockets inducing him to settle, vowed to fight the case.

The following year Julia Strickland's motion for summary judgment was granted by U.S. District Court Judge Irma E. Gonzalez. Milberg Weiss appealed, and in 1995, when the appeal was assigned to a three-judge panel that Lerach considered unfavorable, he called Strickland with an offer: if Alliance would reimburse Milberg Weiss for its own litigation costs, the suit would be withdrawn. No deal, said the Roth brothers. A couple of days before scheduled oral arguments, Lerach simply dropped the suit.

In the end, Alliance Pharmaceutical's insurance carrier *did* reimburse the company for most of the estimated $2 million in legal fees it incurred. Nonetheless, the litigation took its toll in energy, lost time, and embarrassment from scientific researchers unaccustomed to having sheriff's deputies drop subpoenas on their desks. And Bill Lerach had turned a well-connected friend into a well-motivated adversary.

> • >

ON FRIDAY, AUGUST 7, 1992, Ann Baskins, an in-house attorney for the hallowed firm of Hewlett-Packard, was driving south over the Santa Cruz Mountains to play golf at Pebble Beach. Suddenly she heard the news she'd been bracing for over the car radio. The day before, HP had announced its quarterly earnings were far below expectations—and considerably lower than the two previous quarters. She and her colleagues had been warned to expect the market to react, and it did. HP stock was down twelve points, she heard the reporter say. Immediately, she pulled her car over and called a colleague in the legal department. "Get ready," she said. "We're going to get hit."

In his San Diego office Bill Lerach had already been alerted to HP's earning reports. At first even Lerach was reluctant to take on the legendary Silicon Valley icon that had been launched in a Palo Alto garage and grown into one of technology's global leaders, a $14.5 billion company that was known for conducting itself beyond reproach. Plus, Hewlett-Packard had very deep pockets and a huge legal staff, plenty of ammunition to fight a legal war of attrition. As he mulled these realities, Lerach called Len Simon and told him to track the usual trail—the company's SEC reports, press releases, and sales of shares by insiders. Simon reported back quickly: all the usual signs were there.

On Monday, August 10, John A. Young, HP's president, took a phone call from Ann Baskins. "We're being sued," he heard her say. "The lawyers from Milberg Weiss Lerach filed this morning in federal court in San Jose. We're being accused of hyping forecasts to inflate stock prices and cashing in shares before the announcement of our earnings decline. They want a hundred million dollars."

Young was incredulous. Now sixty, he had joined the company's sales and marketing division in 1958, and while working his way up the ranks of the company, he'd become inculcated with the famed "HP way" that his mentors Bill Hewlett and David Packard had insisted upon. Even as he was receiving the news from Baskins, Young was mystified by the shift in the earnings report. HP was so vast, so diverse, with so many elements, no one could point to one thing, one product, one division to locate where the company had missed the mark. It could be many factors, each small and inconsequential individually, but taken together, the company had been negatively impacted.

Baskins had more grim news. The volume of documents and exhibits that the plaintiffs would seek would be staggering, perhaps a million items. HP would have to spend time preparing a defense and identifying and protecting trade secrets that could be inadvertently exposed during the lawsuit, including products in the works, profit reports, market strategies. Young was beginning to fathom what lay ahead.

Baskins could say nothing to reassure Young, except that she would get back to him before the end of the day. Immediately she placed a call to the law firm of Wilson Sonsini. When she called Young the next time, she told the HP president that she was hiring Steve Schatz, a former federal prosecutor, and Bruce Vanyo, a securities specialist, both Wilson Sonsini partners, to help them prepare a defense.

After HP spent nearly $2 million, used more than one thousand hours of its officers' and managers' time, and, as Baskins had predicted, provided a million documents, Vanyo and Schatz concluded that the specter of a jury trial was very real. "We are vulnerable to the market place," Vanyo told his clients.

Then a momentous thing happened. HP's share price started rising. And it kept rising. Simon and Lerach followed the trajectory. Would the price bounce help the defense argument and influence the jury? The element of doubt worked both ways. A trial could be long and certainly costly—to Milberg Weiss as well as to Hewlett-Packard. Besides, David Packard was not Charles Keating. John Young was not in jail. "How much are we into it?" Lerach asked his colleague. Simon said the firm costs were over half a million dollars. The two attorneys decided to fold their case. Simon went to his office and called Steve Schatz to say the plaintiffs were dropping their lawsuit.

These two cases—Alliance Pharmaceutical and Hewlett-Packard— were the exception, not the rule, and in hindsight they reveal a lesson that was rarely mentioned at the time by either Lerach's defenders or detractors. That lesson was, if you really had done nothing wrong, it made sense to fight these class action security cases in court. If more firms had done that successfully, there likely would have been fewer plaintiffs' lawsuits. Milberg Weiss wasn't bluffing exactly, but there was a rationale behind Bill Lerach's bullying. He *wanted* these companies to settle. What his adversaries didn't comprehend was that their willingness to capitulate so readily convinced Lerach not that he'd perfected a devious and unjust legal instrument of torture but that these executives were almost always hiding something, and that significant fraud was rampant in U.S. boardrooms.

> • >

"I DIDN'T KNOW SHIT about running a business," Lerach would confess years later. Yet by the end of 1992 he was indeed running a business. He was filing nearly 80 percent of the cases and generating 80 percent of the fees driving $46.4 million in profits for the entire law firm. His passion lay in generating cases and writing the initial drafts of all complaints, which he insisted on, often working until midnight, even on weekends, returning his marked-up drafts, stained by food and drink, to Kathy Lichnovsky to decipher his handwriting and clean up his copies. The upside was becoming apparent. By the end of 1992 Lerach would earn $9.3 million, second only to Mel Weiss.

It all came at a price. He and Kelly had built a new home in Fairbanks Ranch, a golf and horse community northeast of San Diego that hosted the equestrian endurance event in the 1984 Olympic Games. Even surrounded by luxury, Kelly grew progressively unsettled, demonstrably unhappy with a work-obsessed husband. The strain grew, but Lerach, while not oblivious to it, was not inclined to alter his own course. "I need someone on the team," he would admit years later. "Whatever my makeup is, I need someone positive around me."

He found it in Star Soltan, an attractive young associate at his law firm. After graduating from the University of California, Davis, School of Law, she joined a New York law firm based in San Diego. When that firm downsized, the newest lawyers were let go. Her old boss, Michael L. Lipman, a former assistant U.S. attorney, knew Lerach and admired his casework. He recommended Soltan to the firm, advising his former colleague to "pay close attention to Bill Lerach," who was then trying an important case called Nucorp. She did and found herself "working longer and harder than I had ever imagined." Soltan remembered being buoyed by recovering money for defrauded investors and by the idealism and zeal of her new boss.

"He had more energy than anyone else in the firm," she recalled. "His commitment was infectious and the complaints and briefs he wrote were impeccable." She and the other attorneys remembered Lerach's insistence that their court materials be error free. "If you made a mistake on a brief, and if a judge called you on it, there would be hell to pay," she remembered. "On the other hand, if a judge complimented someone on a brief, he would be proud."

On her first case working with Lerach, the team won an $18 million judgment. "For me, then, that was a big win," she said. She was grateful for the opportunity Lerach had given her. Lerach was likewise impressed. His already strained marriage to Kelly was about to end. And Star Soltan would soon become his third wife, and bear him a son.

> • >

BY NOW LERACH HAD perfected for his disciples a formula that amalgamated economics with morality. While preparing for a case, he would produce a series of charts showing a timeline, the price of the target company's stock, its corporate earnings, the value of the directors' stock options, and a record of insider stock sales during the period covered by the class action lawsuit. Pointing to a spot on the chart, he would say: "Here is where the declining stock price would have met the option price. That makes the option worthless." Then he would retrace to a point on the timeline before the stock started its decline: "Here is the stock price when the managers began flooding us with reassuring public statements." He'd move his finger to another point indicating profits at the time of the rosy statements: "Here is how depressed earnings were when management began making its fair weather statements." Then he'd move to another point showing an upward trend in stock prices: "And here is where the insiders started unloading their stock." He'd then follow the timeline to a point where management issued devastating news: "Here is where the ordinary investor—you and me and our clients—got stuck holding the bag."

Alarmed CEOs throughout Silicon Valley and Wall Street found Lerach's analysis overly simplistic and his methods highly objectionable. There *were* coincidences in the business world, as the Hewlett-Packard case revealed: unforeseen market competition, unforeseen missteps in an obscure division causing a chain-reaction impact on the bottom line, ruthless tactics by overseas competitors. All of this placed U.S. companies, especially emerging ones in volatile markets, at potential risk. And risk, after all, is what drove much of American capitalism.

"How is a CEO supposed to avoid liability?" Thomas Lavelle, in-house counsel for chip-making giant Intel, complained to a business magazine after being Lerached in early 1993. "Should he just tell investors not to invest in his company because he can't give an ironclad guarantee they won't lose money? If you believe Lerach, then this industry is staffed by people who commit fraud repeatedly."

Lerach paid a news service to track all news coverage of him, and he saw

Lavelle's quote. His reaction: "The fact that you go to church on Sunday doesn't mean you're incapable of securities fraud on Monday."

Going tactical, Lerach would begin pushing the hot buttons. Once his class action gained certification, discovery was granted. It was akin to the opening of fishing season with no limits. Wilson Sonsini attorney Bruce Vanyo, who had defended Hewlett-Packard as well as dozens of other Silicon Valley companies against Lerach, came up with a term for Lerach's tactics. He called it the "break-your-business" method. The alternative, as it was often presented during pretrial negotiations, was to settle. Lerach, while never indicating that he was eager, was always open to reaching a price point and letting his targeted company get on with its business.

His formula worked against Carol Bartz and her company Autodesk, a leading maker of design software for architects and industrial designers. A product flop, a poor quarterly report in the fall of 1992, and a precipitous drop in stock brought a hasty response from Lerach. Wilson Sonsini attorney Boris Feldman was hired to defend the company, and when he sized up the situation, he was not encouraged. Having had no previous experience with class action litigation, Autodesk had no D&O insurance. The veteran attorney knew the risk to Autodesk's bottom line: the company faced a "break-your-business" situation. Still, Feldman spent nearly as much time persuading Bartz, the CEO, to enter into a settlement negotiation as he did preparing to defend the company in a trial. Finally a $5.5 million settlement was agreed upon. The paperwork was complete and the payment scheduled. Then Bartz committed a near deal-breaker.

Early in 1993, shortly after Bill Clinton's victorious campaign, the president-elect invited Bartz and other tech executives to an economic summit in Little Rock. When it came her turn to speak, Bartz related the details of the recent class action lawsuit against her, citing the threat to her business, and called for tort reforms against securities lawyers who were impeding entrepreneurship.

Lerach was paying attention to the Arkansas economic summit. In August 1992, two weeks before the Democratic National Convention, he had made a stunningly large $100,000 "soft money" contribution to the

Democratic Party for use in electing Bill Clinton and other Democrats to federal office. He did not do so with the expectation that the party would suddenly champion tort reform. So Lerach, incensed by Bartz's plea for relief from trial lawyers, called Feldman: "Fuck her, we're not settling. The deal is off!" Feldman reminded Lerach that the settlement had been signed and that, as far as he knew, Autodesk had already authorized the money. "Fuck you, too. You might as well move to South America because you're never going to practice law again," Feldman remembers Lerach saying before adding his own rejoinder. "He knew they couldn't get out of it. But that was full Bill. He could be so unpleasant."

To avoid such unpleasantness, companies were now settling out of court at a rate of eight in ten cases. In 1992 alone, more than 202 shareholder lawsuits had been filed nationwide, 72 of them Milberg Weiss cases.

It took three years and $1.4 million in fees to Wilson Sonsini lawyers before Adaptec chairman John Adler finally threw in the towel. Lerach was not wildly elated. Three years of litigating, deposing witnesses, sorting through the evidence, and filing motions, and no more than $4.3 million to show for it was not within the business model—except for the fact that during those years Adaptec was one of more than 170 lawsuits the firm would file on behalf of plaintiffs, nearly 60 percent of all shareholder lawsuits nationwide. More than $700 million was paid in settlements during that period with about $227 million in fees going to the plaintiffs' firms. Between 1992 and 1993 the profits at Milberg Weiss jumped more than 90 percent. And because of the scale of its business, the firm could afford long fights, for even minor settlements, knowing that it injected fear (not to mention loathing) in boardrooms where tense conference calls between CEOs, even competitors, and lawyers were taking place. The stakes were not just about paying settlements. The stakes involved the diminishing ability to attract top-flight directors, who were becoming wary of risking their reputations as well as their wealth in stock options. CEO recruiting was taking a hit. Tech-savvy people grumbled about fleeing to protect their nest eggs. Venture capitalists held tighter to investment money, worrying about throwing good money at the likes of Bill Lerach. Cypress Semiconductor

CEO T. J. Rodgers, whom Lerach had sued three times, spoke for an entire industry when he posed the big question: "How to get rid of this scourge who's lower than pond scum?"

> • >

IN THE SAN DIEGO offices of Milberg, Weiss, Bershad & Lerach, Pat Coughlin was trying to rid the world of a different sort of scourge: in one word, tobacco. His father had died of lung cancer in 1985, and his mother had recently been diagnosed with emphysema. Both had been lifelong smokers. "I looked at the age which most people start smoking, and I realized that most of them can't make lifelong decisions at that age," he would say, pointing to a recently released *Journal of the American Medical Association* report demonstrating an increase in teen smokers and alleging that tobacco companies were targeting teens through marketing and advertising. His class action lawsuit, filed in San Diego Superior Court, had charged the tobacco companies with "manipulating nicotine to addict smokers and with conspiring not to develop or market safer cigarettes."

Within the firm there was some consternation with Coughlin's lawsuit. Since 1913 more than eight hundred cases had been filed against tobacco companies, and not one had gone the way of the plaintiffs. After maintaining for years that the health hazards related to their products were uncertain, the tobacco industry's argument had evolved into a more elusive line of defense. If a person chose to smoke, the tobacco makers could hardly be blamed. If there was a culprit, it was free will. So Coughlin set out on a different attack, examining whether the industry had hidden damaging evidence about the toxicity and addictive nature of its products. In other words, he was searching for evidence of fraud.

In San Francisco sole practitioner Janet C. Mangini had been reading a newspaper article focusing on R.J. Reynolds Tobacco Company's cigarette advertising. The article quoted three *Journal of the American Medical Association* studies concluding that the popularity of Camel cigarettes had increased markedly within three years after the company introduced a cartoon character to carry its banner in advertising campaigns. The character was named Joe Camel. Children as young as six recognized Joe, the studies stated, as children of a previous generation recognized Mickey Mouse.

Mangini was not a consumer fraud specialist. But she was bothered enough to mention the tobacco company studies to Alan Caplan and Philip Neumark, attorneys at the firm of Bushnell, Caplan & Fielding, from whom she rented an office. What if they could prove that R.J. Reynolds had set out to sell its products with minors in mind? What if they began focusing on Joe Camel promotional advertising and collateral such as caps, jackets, mugs, and other Joe items that presumably appealed to youths?

Then one of them had an even brighter idea. Why not call the most powerful shareholder class action law firm in America? On the receiving end of that phone call, Bill Lerach immediately began to envision the crossover between Pat Coughlin's case and the one Janet Mangini was proposing. "They're putting Joe Camel on lunch boxes and claiming they're targeting blue collar workers, not kids," Alan Caplan told Lerach. Although they had no documents stating that R.J. Reynolds was specifically targeting a youth market, by filing a lawsuit, the plaintiffs might pry open a door to discovery. Lerach understood. He also understood how arduous the battle would be. What's more, the fee amount might not be as large as the San Francisco lawyers anticipated. Why? Because the legal attack would ask for injunctive relief—to force R.J. Reynolds to send Joe Camel into permanent exile without seeking damages. Still, he committed his firm to shoulder 80 percent of the workload. This made the Bushnell lawyers happy. Mangini was also pleased to be the named plaintiff.

Mangini v. R.J. Reynolds Co. was filed in San Francisco Superior Court in December 1991. R.J. Reynolds retained H. Joseph Escher III to defend it. A 1977 University of Chicago Law School graduate, Escher began sketching out a defense, enlisting his colleagues at his San Francisco firm of Howard, Rice, Nemerovski, Canady, Falk & Rabin as sounding boards: "Can you hold an advertiser liable because the advertising might encourage someone to break the law? Is there anyone who thinks that no advertisement for beer is appealing to twenty-year-old men who can't legally purchase beer?" The answers to those questions would break new legal ground.

Filing a motion to dismiss the case, Escher argued that under the Cig-

arette Labeling and Advertising Act, the federal government regulated all tobacco advertising and promotions, therefore any individual or state claim
was preempted by federal law. A San Francisco judge agreed. Lerach and
Coughlin were undeterred. "It just means we appeal under the argument
that R.J. Reynolds is targeting underage kids in the state of California," Lerach told Coughlin. "Let's get the state involved, some cities, too."

Coughlin put in a call to San Francisco city attorney Louise Renne.
Would the city join the case? She did not hesitate. Meanwhile Associate Justice Donald B. King of California's First Court of Appeals sided with the
plaintiffs, ruling that there was enough evidence showing R.J. Reynolds was
targeting San Francisco kids with its Joe Camel ads that the case could go
to trial. The news startled Escher, who appealed to the state Supreme Court.
Coughlin went to notify his law partner, who appeared distracted by the
piles of cases promising big payouts. After a moment Lerach swung his
chair around, appearing to peer out the window to the splendid harbor below. Then he swung it back, grinning. "There's glory for all of us in this. I'll
argue the case myself!"

> • >

SEYMOUR LAZAR HAD PROVED to be a great plaintiff. And Milberg Weiss,
in turn, made good on its end of the bargain. From 1984 through 1993
Lazar's name appeared in more than a dozen successful cases ranging from
Standard Oil, to biotech research company Genentech, to Beverly Hills
Savings and Bear Stearns. Milberg Weiss did well in those cases, earning in
excess of $10 million in fees, and so did Lazar, earning $1.4 million against
less than $10,000 in losses. By comparison, the thousands of class action
plaintiffs the firm represented received an average of sixty-five cents on
every dollar lost.

Lazar had followed up on Mel Weiss's admonition to find himself an intermediary lawyer, choosing a longtime legal adviser and Palm Springs
neighbor Paul T. Selzer. A 1965 Stanford Law School graduate, Selzer was
a managing partner of Best, Best & Krieger, a hundred-year-old Southern
California law firm. With a handsome chiseled face, athletic physique, and

full head of white hair, he had the mannerly bearing of a senator. Selzer preferred to practice land use law in the desert cities in and around Palm Springs, living comfortably with his family while maintaining a status as one of the social pillars of the resort and retirement community. Through the arrangement Lazar made with Milberg Weiss exchequer Dave Bershad, checks would be sent to Best, Best & Krieger to defray Lazar's "legal bills" with the firm. It would take years for one of the young partners to wonder, in what would be an incriminating memo, why the income from Milberg Weiss seemed to exceed the amount owed to the firm by Lazar.

On the East Coast another stalking horse had joined the stable. His name was Howard J. Vogel, a forty-seven-year-old real estate mortgage broker living with his wife, Eugenia, in Englewood, New Jersey. Both were acquaintances of Robert Sugarman, a new partner in the Milberg Weiss New York office. Vogel, a laconic and bookish man who had suffered from polio as a child, told Sugarman that he was intending to retire and, through a retirement fund, began investing. One of his first big plays, a $10,000 investment in Valero Energy Co., a huge Texas refining company, came a cropper. As far as he could tell, there were insider sell-offs. He wanted to lead a lawsuit, and he wanted $1 million for sticking his neck out. Sugarman took the offer to Bershad and Mel Weiss. They agreed to set up a meeting. When they did meet, David Bershad and Steve Schulman countered with 14 percent of their fee, well over the normal 10 percent they'd been sending Lazar (for whom they sometimes made exceptions upward) and Steven Cooperman. They also offered to reimburse Vogel the $10,000, provided they won the case. Then they told him to get an intermediary lawyer, which he did.

The class action lawsuit, *Howard J. Vogel v. Valero Energy*, was filed in San Antonio on August 20, 1991. Vogel recruited Gary Lozow, his fraternity brother at Indiana University, to be his go-between. Lozow was practicing criminal law in Denver. (He would later represent the family of Columbine killer Dylan Klebold.) Like Paul Selzer, Lozow had never represented members of a class action securities claim. Two months from filing the lawsuit, Bershad sent Lozow a retainer agreement, promising to pay him 14 percent of its Valero fee, should it earn a jury award or settlement. Two months later, the case settled for nearly $20 million. Milberg Weiss collected $4.75 million for its work on the lawsuit. Milberg Weiss cut Lozow a check on December 28, 1992, for $637,223, knowing it would be passed to Lazar.

Steven Cooperman too was now deep into the action. By the beginning of 1993, he had collected more than $1.6 million from Milberg Weiss on wins that included American Continental/Lincoln, for which he received separate checks of $440,000 and $250,000 within eight months, with another $330,000 due.

Cooperman had also hired an intermediary—two actually. The first was Richard Purtich, a Los Angeles real estate lawyer, who had represented Cooperman in previous deals. The second was James Tierney, also from Los Angeles. Tierney was an entertainment lawyer, with actor Timothy Hutton and singer Gloria Estefan in his portfolio. Together over nearly a decade Purtich and Tierney would handle more than forty checks, plus cash, totaling $6.5 million. As it turned out, even that would not be enough for Cooperman, whose greed would inadvertently bait the trap for America's most feared and loathed law firm.

> • >

BILL LERACH, WEARING KHAKIS and a polo shirt, remained long after most of his colleagues had left the office. On his desk was a draft of one of the most important projects he'd worked on all year. It was the annual breakdown of his office's income and expenses. It showed Milberg Weiss West now returning more than 80 percent of the firm's income in 1992. The aggravating part was reconciling the inequitable remuneration from the New York office. Lerach had been hearing from his San Diego partners about this for months. For the first time he sensed a possible flight of his own handpicked attorneys, even Alan Schulman, who was becoming his nemesis.

Lerach had made Schulman managing partner of the West Coast office, which meant Schulman was responsible for the books. Knowledge of the firm's financial pipeline was power. The authority Lerach handed Schulman allowed him a peek behind the curtain at how Lerach exercised what he felt were his own financial prerogatives—paying favored cooperating law firms, underpaying others when he felt they hadn't performed up to his standards, and funneling millions to his friend and expert witness John Torkelsen. When Schulman confronted Lerach over the inflated bills, Lerach would explain impatiently that on cases the firm lost or settled for less than anticipated, Torkelsen would also lose. It had to be made up, according to their contingency arrangement; otherwise they might lose their star witness to their competitors. This explanation disturbed Schulman. Lerach was making up the rules as he went, Schulman would complain sotto voce to other attorneys in the firm. In some cases, when Lerach learned from Torkelsen that Schulman had refused to pay certain invoices, an audible confrontation could be heard between the two partners. The noise reached New York through back channels. Schulman was now delivering disquieting reports to Mel Weiss and Dave Bershad.

Still, Lerach felt obliged to include Schulman among the partners who deserved more money, thinking a raise might placate him. But a law partnership is a zero-sum game. Taking money from New York would mean persuading the partners there to forfeit some of their own shares—even as they were raking in unprecedented profits. On the face of it, Lerach let himself think, this should be logical. Deep down he knew better. He had grown to hate the annual executive retreats where these issues would rear up. "Knife fights," he characterized them, admitting to his closest allies and his wife that he'd grow sick to his stomach on the eve of these events. Weiss had recently added fuel to the fire, at least in Lerach's mind. He'd been deferring more and more internally to a tough new partner, who, as far as Lerach could tell, did not give a second thought about mixing it up over perks and her own percentages. When the suggestion arose of redistributing her own take from the firm, Patricia Hynes could be as shrewd and tough an infighter as anyone in the firm, which was saying a lot.

A graduate of Queens College and Fordham Law School and a former executive U.S. attorney for Manhattan, Pat Hynes had joined the firm in 1982 as a complex litigation specialist. Moreover she had handled several big cases for the firm, and she had delivered. Having her name on their letterhead as a name partner, Mel had repeatedly reminded his West Coast protégé, was an asset. Lerach anticipated a fight, and so on the plane from San Diego to Dallas, where an executive retreat was to be held at the exclusive Rosewood Mansion on Turtle Creek, he'd decided to tend to it with a preemptive strike. He launched it during the firm's first evening session.

Asking for the floor, Lerach circulated documents drawn from the drafts he had completed just the day before. As his partners studied the numbers, he began his opening argument, as if he were, once again, facing a jury. "You can see from the figures, there is a big disparity between what our office is delivering and what we are receiving. I'm asking each of you to give up points so that our lawyers who have been working out there can be made whole," he began. Immediately Pat Hynes interrupted. Scattering the papers before her as if throwing down the gauntlet, she looked at Mel Weiss and sneered: "This is nothing but a piece of paper."

In more normal circumstances, this act might have led to a family feud, with the patriarch, Mel Weiss, mediating a mutually agreed-upon outcome. But Lerach reflexively stood, his face red, his fist clenched, and directed a fusillade of profanity at Hynes that even he, in retrospect, thought intemperate. Fueled by indignation and alcohol, he fumed aloud until he could fume no more. Then he slammed the table and walked out.

The next morning, in the tree-shaded courtyard by the pool, Lerach encountered Mel Weiss pacing, coffee cup in hand. To Lerach, he looked to be in a state of mourning. And he was. "Pat Hynes left this morning," Weiss said gravely. "She's gone back to New York."

Lerach surprised even himself with his response to his old mentor. "Well, you guys go fuck yourselves. I tried to make a rational presentation. My guys are earning all the money you guys are pocketing. Something better give, and if it's her, she can go fuck herself, too."

Weiss stared at his protégé long enough to make Lerach feel he wished he'd bitten his tongue. It wasn't as if the two had never laced disagreements with profanity. This was different. In front of the whole firm, Bill Lerach had drawn a battle line. What he now saw in his mentor's wounded eyes was the future of the firm. And it was not rosy.

> • > • > • > • >

REVENGE OF THE REPUBLICANS

Although his legal practice—the business of suing businesses—was booming, the forces arrayed against Bill Lerach by 1993 stretched from California to the East Coast. They were beginning to reach critical mass, especially
among top officials in the political party that Lerach had once belonged to
and now openly disdained.

The signs of a counterattack began in California, where some plaintiffs
(those *not* receiving special considerations from Milberg Weiss) began raising hell about how much money the attorneys in these class action suits
were making, and how small a return was being repatriated to the shareholders who had been defrauded. In August the shouts of one disgruntled
shareholder rang through the halls of the federal courtroom in San Diego.
Magistrate Harry McCue was putting the last touches on a Lerach-
orchestrated settlement of $14.6 million against the directors of a failed
thrift called Great American Bank when seventy-two-year-old Eugene
Novidvor, who had owned 2,000 shares of Great American stock, voiced
displeasure at rumors that the plaintiffs were to receive as little as three cents
per dollar for their shares.

"So far, I've only heard what the attorneys will get!" Novidvor shouted at Lerach. "But we never know what the shareholders will get."

Lerach answered evenly that Novidvor's share of the settlement was unknowable until the court had concluded the process of evaluating and verifying claims from all responding shareholders.

"Give me a hint," Novidvor replied angrily. "Look me in the eye and tell me you have no idea."

The discontent with Lerach, his firm, and its methods spread to Texas, where a federal jurist said aloud what many had been thinking: Milberg Weiss kept presenting the same plaintiffs in lawsuit after lawsuit. That summer U.S. District Court Judge Joe Kendall dismissed a class action against a company called Urcaro with a notation that seemed more wry than ominous: "Plaintiffs seek to represent a class of investors who were allegedly defrauded by the concerted bad acts of this litany of wrong-doers, and have among their ranks one of the unluckiest and most victimized investors in the history of the securities business, Mr. Steven G. Cooperman, who spends a good deal of his time being a plaintiff in class action securities fraud suits," Kendall wrote. "He has been a plaintiff in 38 class action securities fraud cases."

The ill winds of 1993 were blowing in Chicago too, where Fischel's lawsuit made the *American Bar Association Journal*. Melvyn Weiss described the lawsuit as "ludicrous," while Joe Cotchett opined to the bar journal that he found "the whole thing extraordinary." Lerach himself uncustomarily declined comment. So did Fischel, who preferred then as always to do his speaking about Bill Lerach and Mel Weiss in court. Alan Salpeter, Fischel's attorney, confidently told the ABA that he intended "to prove every word" in Fischel's legal complaint.

In New York, Weiss dealt with the brushfire Lerach had started at the Turtle Creek Mansion in Dallas by publicly elevating Pat Hynes to the stature of "name partner," one of the few women so honored by a major American law firm. Thus did Milberg, Weiss, Bershad & Lerach, with its eighty-two attorneys in New York and San Diego, officially become Milberg, Weiss, Bershad, Hynes & Lerach. "She's a superstar as a lawyer," Mel Weiss told *Crain's New York Business*. Lerach toed the public line, telling his colleagues that he was pleased Mel Weiss had elevated such an upstanding attorney for the New York office—and trying to sound sincere when he said it. Privately, he fretted that another name partner meant another big share, money that Lerach could be paying one of his own budding superstars.

The most direct challenge facing the firm and its two principal partners, however, was in Washington, D.C., where Republicans led by Newt Gingrich had formulated an agenda that they hoped would put their party in control of Congress for the first time since the Eisenhower administration. One of their campaign tactics was to target greedy lawyers; and one of their stated goals, if they took power, was to curb class action securities lawsuits and put Bill Lerach out of business.

> • >

TORT REFORM HADN'T BEEN a partisan issue when President Reagan began talking about it regularly during his second term in office. It wasn't even called tort reform. Nor were class action securities suits often mentioned in Washington during Reagan's time in the White House, and never once by the president himself. What animated Reagan, and ultimately the Republican Party, were so-called "frivolous" lawsuits, whose causes of action seemed tortured in their logic, or civil cases in which the verdict sounded comically excessive: $3 million in damages to the New Mexico woman who put her hot McDonald's coffee cup between her legs—and was scalded when she opened the lid by pulling it toward herself; $2.7 million to the West Virginia convenience store clerk who claims she hurt her back opening a pickle jar; another $2 million to a doctor from Alabama who sued when BMW touched up his new car with paint without telling him. The phrase Reagan used to describe such judgments was "absurd results." Gradually, the political positions of the two parties would harden into polarized partisan camps. By 1991 Vice President Dan Quayle sought to burnish his conservative credentials, and prop up his own popularity, by going after lawyers directly at the American Bar Association convention in Atlanta.

"Our system of civil justice is, at times, a self-inflicted competitive disadvantage," said Quayle, who noted that he chaired the President's Council on Competitiveness. "Does America really need seventy percent of the world's lawyers? Is it healthy for our economy to have 18 million new lawsuits coming through the system annually?"

A year later, when he accepted the Republican presidential nomination for the second time, President George H. W. Bush warned of "sharp lawyers running wild" to the point that doctors were "afraid to practice medicine" and some mothers and fathers shied away from coaching Little League for fear of being sued. "I am fighting to reform our legal system, to put an end to crazy lawsuits," Bush said that night. "If that means climbing into the ring with the trial lawyers, well, let me just say, round one starts tonight. After all, my opponent's campaign is being backed by practically every trial lawyer who ever wore a tasseled loafer. He's not in the ring with them; he's in the tank."

The most visible and controversial of those loafer-wearing lawyers helping Bill Clinton was Bill Lerach. And far from ending the debate on the issue of legal reform, Clinton's victory over Bush in 1992 only hardened the battle lines. A showdown was coming on Capitol Hill, where Lerach would not only be the designated stand-in for all the perceived ills of the plaintiffs' bar but the single combat warrior representing class action securities lawyers.

> • >

WHILE GROWING UP IN St. Paul, Christopher Cox's father, a former Californian, would tell his son while they shoveled the Minnesota snow, "You wouldn't have to do this if you lived in Southern California." After high school Chris Cox dutifully set out for the University of Southern California, where he earned a degree in three years, then headed for graduate school at Harvard, earning a joint degree in business and the law. In 1987, while eating in the White House mess hall where he worked in the counsel's office, Cox learned of an open seat in a reliably Republican California congressional district. Impulsively he decided to run for it, a decision that would put him on a direct collision course with Bill Lerach.

In 1994, as House Republicans geared up for the midterm elections,

Newt Gingrich and his lieutenants produced a ten-part platform called the Contract with America. The ideas weren't new—most had been cribbed from various Reagan State of the Union addresses—but packaged together they constituted a quick compendium of conservative thought on how to shrink government or make it less powerful. Item number nine was litigation reform. The Republicans promised, if given control of Congress, to pass a legislative package that they dubbed the Common Sense Legal Reform Act; the catchy name was chosen by an up-and-coming young Republican political pollster and consultant named Frank I. Luntz. When Gingrich and House Republican leader Dick Armey asked for Luntz's help framing the argument, he told them to start by never saying the phrase *tort reform* again.

"Nobody knows what a tort is," Luntz told the Republican leaders and their staffs. "They think it's a French pastry."

In his focus groups, Luntz had learned that although Republicans might detest "trial lawyers," the American public didn't. When voters heard that phrase, they thought of Perry Mason or, if they were younger, of the popular television series *L.A. Law.* "A *trial lawyer*—that's Jimmy Smits," Luntz told Republican congressional leaders. "But a *personal injury lawyer* is an ambulance chaser."

And so the GOP went about the task of trying to make Bill Lerach into an ambulance chaser. Their legislation called for uniform product liability laws, a "loser pays" rule for those who bring lawsuits to court, ending contingency fees for witnesses, and various other measures targeted at "strike suits"—class action securities fraud cases filed against companies that experienced a drop in their stock prices. Milberg Weiss was the number one generator of those suits. There was simply no denying it, and the Republicans didn't try: the proposed legal reforms enumerated in the Contract with America were aimed directly at William S. Lerach.

"Bill Lerach was the guy whose picture had the target on it," Mark Nebergall, a software industry lobbyist recalled after the 1994 political campaign ended. "When you thought of securities litigation reform, you thought of trying to put Bill Lerach out of business. He was—he was the Antichrist, if you will."

The GOP subsequently romped to victory in the '94 midterms, gaining control of both houses of Congress for the first time since 1954. It caught the political commentariat with its collective pants down, but it did not surprise the trial attorneys. They had feared such a result; endeavoring to forestall it, they had donated $49.5 million to congressional candidates in the 1993–94 election cycle, most of it to Democrats.* Now had come payback time, and Lerach knew it. The night of the election he was on the phone with Jonathan Cuneo, the lawyer-lobbyist who looked out for Milberg Weiss's interests in Washington. "Man the barricades, Jon," Lerach said. "Here they come."

> • >

ON JANUARY 19, 1995, the House Subcommittee on Telecommunications and Finance took up H.R. 10, the Common Sense Legal Reform Act.

The leadoff witnesses at the hearing were James V. Kimsey, chairman of America Online, testifying on behalf of the American Electronics Association, a Silicon Valley organization representing three thousand high-tech companies; and Dennis Bakke, founder and president of AES Corp. The second pair of witnesses? None other than Bill Lerach and Dan Fischel. This was not a coincidence. The session began with remarks from Republican congressman Thomas J. Bliley, the new chairman of the full commerce committee, who left no doubt that the hearings were an attempt not to gather evidence but, instead, to marshal public opinion. Bliley's opening statement also revealed that the Republicans had refined their target: it was now mostly about class action securities suits.

"Companies, directors, and auditors are being forced to settle these meritless suits because the costs of defending themselves is prohibitive and

* The American Trial Lawyers Association kicked in $2.5 million, 92 percent of which went to Democrats. Of the individual law firms in the United States, the $587,000 donated to candidates by Milberg Weiss partners ranked second only to Akin Gump, the highly placed Washington lobbying shop. But nearly one-quarter of the Akin Gump money went to Republicans. Not so with Milberg Weiss—every dollar of its partners' contributions went to Democrats.

the money recovered enriches lawyers while it gives pennies on the dollar to the injured investors," Bliley said. "As a result, the goals of the securities laws have been skewed. Fraud is not deterred because these suits are filed regardless of fraud."

Sitting in the audience, Jon Cuneo winced. In the decade since Ronald Reagan put litigation reform on the agenda, conservatives had honed their argument into a sharp sword. Republicans were now on the side of the little guy, at least rhetorically. As Cuneo saw it, the GOP argument had been reduced to two powerful talking points. Bliley had hit on the first: *Pennies for plaintiffs, millions for the lawyers!* Several ensuing members of the subcommittee, including a Democratic member who represented Silicon Valley, would hit on the second: *You are suing the companies that are bringing the riches of the Garden of Eden to America.* Cuneo had warned his fellow lawyers to be prepared for these lines of argumentation, and Lerach had been listening to his friend's advice. Sitting at the witness table as the Republicans began their presentation, Lerach made a mental note to address these criticisms directly when his chance came to speak.

Before he could do so, subcommittee chairman Jack Fields of Texas laid the groundwork for the second GOP point that Cuneo had distilled so succinctly. "Just look at some of the facts," Fields said. "Nineteen of the thirty largest companies in the Silicon Valley have been sued since 1988, with an aggregate settlement value of $500 million . . . This explosion in speculative litigation has led to less disclosure, not more; companies pursuing more expensive capital rather than the public corporation route; companies hesitant to introduce new drugs and new technologies for fear of failure and the resultant filing of a class action lawsuit."

Following House procedures, Fields yielded the microphone to Representative Edward Markey of Massachusetts, the ranking Democrat on the subcommittee, who invoked a different set of horrors—those perpetrated by corporations—and warned that if the legislation was rushed to the floor, as Republicans seemed hell-bent on doing, Congress would be "tilting the scales of justice sharply" away from the little guy and in favor of heartless corporations that sought profit above all else.

When it came his turn to talk, Chris Cox wanted to talk about ill-gotten gains too—but to him that meant trial lawyers' profits. "We are here today to address a national scandal of corruption on a scale Congress hasn't witnessed since the days of Eliot Ness and Al Capone," Cox began. "The only difference between the organized crime of the 1930s and today's extortion racket run by strike-suit lawyers is that today's lawyers' conduct is technically legal."

Seamlessly making the Republicans' recent transition from the McDonald's coffee case to securities class actions, Cox continued: "At the hands of a small band of amoral plaintiffs' lawyers and their allies on the bench and in law schools, America is quickly becoming a nation of victims. No injury, real or imagined, occurs in America today without a lawsuit to compensate the alleged victim—whether it is a cup of hot coffee in a woman's lap in a moving car or a drop in a stock price caused by bad luck in the stock market. Every accident comes with its own lawyer and its own lawsuit."

Unlike Lerach, who had coauthored that 1972 law review article criticizing securities lawsuits while at Pitt, Cox had always felt antipathy for such suits. His own attention to this issue dated to the mid-1970s, when he'd coauthored an article critical of such suits for the *Harvard Law Review*. Unlike Lerach, Cox had not changed his mind—his views about the attorneys who filed them had hardened.

"The lawyers think they should be able to inflict this kind of injury, often destroying many jobs, wasting America's resources without any responsibility," Cox said, looking at Lerach. "This is how Bill Lerach, our distinguished witness today, makes his money. This is how legal extortion works."

> • >

PRIOR TO HIS APPEARANCE, Lerach had submitted prepared testimony running some 13,000 words, including a raft of exhibits. He and Cuneo had rehearsed Lerach's testimony the night before at America Restaurant in Union Station on Capitol Hill. His preparation showed. In his actual testimony, which Lerach delivered without benefit of notes, he rattled off all the major points in his written submission—paying close attention to covering Cuneo's two admonitions—and was conversational and cool, despite the forces arrayed against him.

"I was happy to accept the invitation of the majority to travel from San Diego here today to offer my testimony and views about H.R. 10—although I must say, given the rhetoric I have heard in opening statements, I have some reservations of the wisdom of that," Lerach began with a wan smile.*

"Now, there is no question that lawyers are a popular political target today and it appears that lawyers who have devoted their time to representing fraud [cases] and investors are being singled out for heightened criticism," Lerach added. "I hope . . . as you pursue these important amendments to the 1934 Act you will keep in mind that while you claim to be taking a swing at lawyers, you are going to end up hitting your constituents in the nose. You are going to end up hitting decent, hard-working people who make money, save money and invest money, and all-too-frequently are victimized by fraud artists and dishonest executives."

Cox began his second round of questioning of Lerach by asking him how much money he earned in 1994. This was an ambush, masquerading as a cheeky inquiry, but Lerach was prepared, and he gave the answer he'd tried out on Cuneo the night before. "You know, my mother told me when I was growing up, the most impolite question you could ever ask another person was how much money they make," Lerach replied. "I don't ask other people what they make, and I don't tell other people what I make."

But Cox's intention wasn't merely to be discourteous; it was to make a point about the trial lawyers' partisanship and their monetary generosity toward Democrats—a barb aimed at Ed Markey as much as Lerach. Noting that Federal Elections Commission records revealed that Lerach had do-

---

* Lerach received no such parochial consideration from the San Diego congressional delegation. Although not a member of the subcommittee, Republican congressman Brian Bilbray of San Diego showed up at the hearing—in support of Chris Cox, not his hometown law firm. "These lawsuits amount to legalized blackmail," Bilbray testified. "We must reform this law so we can stop criminalizing innovation."

nated $255,000 in political contributions in 1994, Cox then said, "I guess you made more than that. I won't embarrass you by asking you how much more than a quarter of a million dollars you make."

In his testimony, Dan Fischel made the same point: "In assessing the arguments made by opponents of litigation reform, it is critical to understand that litigation, in general, and private securities litigation, in particular, is a big business," he said. "Plaintiffs' class action counsel file hundreds of lawsuits alleging federal securities violations and earn hundreds of millions of dollars in fees from prosecuting these cases every year.

"The plaintiffs' bar constitute a cohesive, well-financed and powerful interest group," Fischel added. "William Lerach, who appears with me on the panel today, a named partner in one of the country's most successful plaintiffs' firms, is probably one of the biggest contributors."

Several subcommittee Democrats put up a spirited defense of Lerach and the plaintiffs' bar, going after Fischel with gusto. Markey led the attack, noting Lexecon's work for Charles Keating and for David Paul, the owner of CenTrust Savings and Loan, a failed Florida thrift that had also invested heavily in Michael Milken's junk bonds.

Markey began his questioning of Fischel with a dig at Cox: "I'm not going to ask you how much you made as a consultant in that field, but we will just assume it is a fairly lucrative practice, as is Lerach's."

"*Very* lucrative," replied Fischel.

"Very lucrative—I appreciate that," Markey replied. "All sides have done well in this business."

"Extremely well," Fischel agreed.

The witness's candor may have been appreciated by Markey, but it didn't take Fischel off the hook with the Democrats. Markey and, minutes later, Democratic Congressman John Bryant of Texas launched into recitations of controversial Lexecon cases—pointedly mentioning not only its role in the Keating case but the $700,000 that Lexecon had forked over to Lerach's clients to make the lawsuit go away. Neither Democrat, speaking under benefit of congressional immunity, attached any significance to the legal nicety that Lexecon had technically agreed to a "disposition" and not a "settlement." Both congressmen pointedly used the word "settle" themselves, and Markey implied that Fischel's decision to sue Milberg Weiss over the difference was a semantic trick.

"Mr. Fischel, your firm appeared to settle this case for $700,000," Markey said. "But Lexecon apparently objected to characterizing what it called a 'voluntary payment' to the class plaintiffs as a 'settlement.' So what did Lexecon do? Because it didn't like this choice of words, it filed a lawsuit against the plaintiffs' lawyers, which included Mr. Lerach's firm—such a small world—for malicious prosecution."

Fischel begged to differ, replying that Markey had made "serious misrepresentations" of the facts. This retort incensed Congressman Bryant. He went back at Fischel over the Lincoln Savings and CenTrust reports that Lexecon had prepared. "Now, Lincoln and CenTrust together account for $3.5 billion that the taxpayers had to shell out, based upon advice that you gave that things were going to be okay," he said.

Fischel disagreed with this characterization as well, asserting that Bryant was taking quotes from the report out of context.

"Then why did you not go ahead and take your case to the jury when you were sued by Mr. Lerach's firm over here for being a part of the problem at Lincoln?" Bryant asked. "Instead, you decided to settle and pay $700,000 in settlement when you could have taken what you just told me to the jury."

Fischel responded to that barb by reading from the court order: "defendants Bankers Trust, Saudi European Bank, Star Bank, and Lexecon Inc. have been dismissed from the case."

"Now, Mr. Fischel, one thing you should not do in here is mislead a member of Congress, many of whom are lawyers," Bryant snapped. "The fact is, I have read what Judge Bilby said . . . You weren't dismissed until you paid to avoid having your case taken before the jury."

"Congressman, I think one of the important things is [that] congressmen should not mislead the public," Fischel shot back. "We didn't pay a cent at the time we were dismissed from the litigation, not one red cent."

"I don't think that is correct," said Bryant. "Mr. Lerach, would you like to elaborate?"

"Lexecon paid $700,000 in cash to resolve the claims asserted against it by the victims of Charles Keating," Lerach replied evenly.

Irrespective of these fireworks, H.R. 10 passed out of subcommittee, was renamed the Private Securities Litigation Reform Act (PSLRA), and sailed through the House Committee on Commerce in February on a 33–10 vote, with eight Democrats joining the Republican majority. Such a margin suggested that the full House might pass the bill with a veto-proof margin, crowed Chris Cox, which it did on a margin of 325 to 99. By this time, the bill was much changed and, from the standpoint of the securities plaintiffs' bar, much improved. Republicans had agreed to strip out the "loser pays" provision. This was a significant win for the securities trial bar, but for the partners of Milberg Weiss it was bittersweet. Although they were winning important concessions, as the bill took shape, it became clear that Milberg Weiss had earned the dubious distinction of having legislation aimed directly at it—a single law firm—and its star litigator.

At some point Republican staffers in Congress and journalists in the Capitol Hill press galleries started calling the bill the "Get Lerach Act." For his part, Lerach had taken to deriding the bill as the "Crooks and Swindlers Protection Act of 1995," a phrase he borrowed from Frank Greer, the Democratic political consultant assisting the National Association of Shareholder and Consumer Attorneys (NASCAT). But it was going to take more than sarcasm to defeat this legislation. While Republicans were united, the Democrats in Congress were divided. So was the legal community. That summer at the annual convention of the American Bar Association, U.S. District Court Judge Vaughn R. Walker of San Francisco expressed the increasing misgivings of many of those on the federal bench. "Securities litigation is like no other," Walker said. "And the primary feature that distinguishes [such lawsuits] is there's no client. It's the rare case where a real plaintiff takes an interest. Most of the time, the clients are purely nominal and cases are driven entirely by lawyers."

Whether the legislation designed to curb this type of litigation would be enacted into law was up to the U.S. Senate—and the President of the United States.

> • >

LERACH AND CUNEO HAD higher hopes for the Senate, always proud of its reputation as a more deliberative body, but their optimism was short-lived. Ultimately the Senate side of the Capitol proved just as hostile to securities lawyers as the House side. Nearly all the Republicans were arrayed against them, along with about half the Senate Democrats, including Dianne Feinstein, whom Lerach knew well and had supported in all her political campaigns. Only four Republican senators stood with the plaintiffs' attorneys, one of whom was John McCain, Lerach's old dance partner from the Keating Five scandal. (Another was William Cohen of Maine, who would end up serving in Bill Clinton's cabinet before the decade was out.) It clearly wasn't enough. On June 28, 1995, the full Senate passed the PSLRA on a 70–29 vote, a margin suggesting that even if Clinton could be persuaded to veto the bill, it would not necessarily settle things.

As 1995 wound to a close, neither side knew where the president's heart or head was on this bill—or whether they were in the same place. His senior advisers were themselves divided. Treasury Secretary Robert E. Rubin was believed to head a faction favoring the new curbs. Among those who thought Clinton should veto the bill was Bruce R. Lindsey, the intense and wiry attorney whom Clinton had brought with him from Arkansas to Washington, where he served as a personal consigliere to the president, and Clinton political adviser Dick Morris, whose Rasputin-like political machinations concealed a soft spot for effective governance. Morris asked Cuneo to prepare an informational packet on the legislation.

"There's a lawyer I know in New York I want to take a look at this," Morris said. "His name is Eliot Spitzer."

The future New York attorney general and governor—and scourge of Wall Street—counseled against the president signing the bill. But in a conference committee mark-up, where differences in the House and Senate versions of the PSLRA were ironed out, all the impetus was clearly on the other side.

In the end, the conference committee language stated that the PSLRA "seeks to protect investors, issuers, and all who are associated with our capital markets from abusive securities litigation." In its final form the PSLRA had ten major components. For starters—and most importantly—

it heightened the burden by which a lawsuit could claim "fraud." Plaintiffs now would have to cite evidence of fraud before proceeding to the discovery stage. Previously, plaintiffs' counsel would allege fraud in the initial pleadings, confident that the discovery process would provide substantiation of their claims—or, more likely, that the company would settle first. The PSLRA also provided for the staying of discovery until after the defendants' motions for summary judgment could be heard; and it eliminated the triple damages under the RICO statute—unless the defendants were convicted criminally of securities fraud.

In addition, the PSLRA contained provisions for fuller disclosure to all plaintiffs of proposed settlements; set "reasonable" (if undefined) limits on attorneys' fees; limited damages to the "mean trading price" in ninety-day blocks of time, instead of anomalous dips in the stock that made it seem as though investors had lost more than they had; and in a provision that was extremely important to high tech—and the bill's most controversial feature—it provided a "safe harbor" for executives who made optimistic predictions about their own company's anticipated success.

Making the losing side foot the cost of litigation was one area in which the Contract for America language did not survive.* On the other hand, the final version contained a series of provisions aimed directly at Lerach and his firm. These provisions revealed their critics' suspicions about how Milberg Weiss got so many clients: the PSLRA prohibited some types of referral fees, set limits on the number of claims that named plaintiffs could file, barred shareholders from buying stock specifically so they could sue, and forbade members of the class from receiving payments disproportionate to their share of the recovery.

Late in the year, as the legislation headed to the White House, Clinton's political standing was unexpectedly bolstered by brinksmanship with the Republican Congress on the federal budget. The impasse led to two partial government shutdowns, both of which bolstered Clinton's standing in

---

* The bill did contain a face-saving, very watered-down version of "loser pays" that wouldn't kick in unless the plaintiffs' attorneys were guilty of actual misconduct in bringing the claim.

public opinion—and his reelection effort. To be sure, the president had many other issues on his plate besides litigation reform.* A grassroots lobbying effort orchestrated by Cuneo and Lerach aimed at opinion makers in cities, counties, and states across the United States was beginning to pay off. Newspaper editorials and op-eds cropped up questioning the wisdom of fast-tracking such an important piece of legislation. When Clinton went home to Arkansas in December, NASCAT placed an ad in his hometown paper urging a veto of the bill. But was there enough time for the securities lawyers to make their case with Clinton?

Lerach had certainly been supportive of Clinton and his political party. The year before, he'd attended one of Clinton's notorious "White House coffee" fund-raisers, immediately afterward forking over $90,000—half in his name and half in his wife, Star's—to the Democratic National Committee. One had to be careful playing a card like that with a sitting president. The year before, when one of the guests at a White House coffee, a wealthy Asian immigrant, started to ask Clinton in broken English for a specific regulatory favor, Lerach had winced in horror and amusement. The man was quickly shushed by aides and other guests.

With the deadline for the veto looming, Lerach could not contain himself. While in Washington for a White House Christmas party, Lerach found time at a fund-raiser preceding the party to buttonhole his old friend. Under Clinton, the Democratic Party had become a relentless fund-raising machine, and at a December 7, 1995, event at the Hay Adams Hotel across from Lafayette Square Park, the president had been caught on film boasting to the wealthy donors how their "soft money" contributions had been used. (By law, those large chunks of money had to go to party-building

---

* Besides the demands of the budget and the PSLRA, the president was wrestling with the burden of his own libido. On November 15, the second day of the shutdown, the president visited the office of White House chief of staff Leon Panetta. There the forty-nine-year-old chief executive made eye contact with Monica Lewinsky, a twenty-two-year-old unpaid intern from California. Lewinsky lifted her jacket to show Clinton the straps of her thong underwear. By that night, they were having sex in a room adjacent to the Oval Office.

endeavors.) Clinton regaled the donors by relating how it had been funneled into television ads that had helped convince Americans that the government shutdown was the Republicans' fault.

Ten days later Clinton dropped by a similar event at the Hay Adams, the one in which Lerach was in attendance. He'd been warned not to press the point of a veto too directly with Clinton, but as Lerach observed Clinton, he thought to himself, *I've got to get him alone. I've got to talk to him.* As Clinton was getting ready to take his leave, Lerach approached the president, who greeted him by name.

"That securities bill is coming your way," Lerach told Clinton. "You have got to stop it."

"Don't worry," Clinton assured Lerach with a knowing nod.*

But Cuneo, Lerach, and the rest of the securities lawyers were plenty worried. Clinton had issued only six vetoes as president—five of them relating to the budget stalemate of 1995—and Congress had never overridden him. There was always a first time. The opposition was better funded than the securities lawyers were and, in Congress, better organized. Not only were Republicans nearly unanimous in support of the bill, but the Democrats' rank and file remained divided. Moreover, in the Senate, the position of influential Connecticut Democrat Christopher J. Dodd had hardened against them. The compromises added to the bill were enough, Dodd believed. The insurance industry—so influential in his home state—needed relief. Dodd was hardly the only liberal to break with the trial lawyers. So did Feinstein, Maryland's Barbara Mikulski, New Jersey's Bill Bradley, and Tom Harkin of Iowa. A populist, Harkin was emblematic of something else as well: Lerach had made enemies within the Democratic Party. Earlier in the year Harkin's fellow Iowan Ted Roth, the San Diego high-tech executive

---

* Conservative critics of Lerach—and of Clinton—have maintained that Lerach lobbied Clinton at the White House for the veto. Lerach countered that he had never discussed the PSLRA with the president. Apparently, neither version was accurate. Lerach did indeed discuss the legislation with the president, he now concedes, but not at the White House. Lerach revealed the Hay Adams conversation in an interview with Pat Dillon at the Federal Correctional Institution in Safford, Arizona, on October 19, 2008.

befriended—and later sued—by Lerach had visited Harkin. *"I don't give a fuck about the merits,"* Lerach had said when Roth called and tried to settle the thing amicably.

Senator Harkin cared very much about the merits of the PSLRA, and a couple of nights before the Senate vote on whether to override Clinton's veto, the senator called Roth at home. It was about midnight in Washington.

"I just got a call from the White House—the president wants to talk to me in an hour about this legislation," Harkin informed Roth. "You gotta give me some ammunition." Roth obliged. He didn't bore Harkin with facts and figures. He simply related to a fellow Democrat his tale of being sued because Alliance Pharmaceutical's stock had gone down pursuant to a government-mandated delay in clinical trials. White House aides were learning to their dismay that, thanks to Lerach, Dodd's job of rounding up votes was easier than Clinton's.

Bruce Lindsey would call NASCAT's chief lobbyist from the White House. "Okay, Jon, who do we have the president call?" Cuneo would give him a list of lawmakers believed to be on the fence, only to get another call from Lindsey three hours later and report: "The President called these senators—but Dodd had already talked to them."

The denouement of the "Get Lerach Act"—the Private Securities Litigation Reform Act of 1995—was ultimately anticlimactic. On December 19 Clinton vetoed the bill—his sixth veto of the week—while issuing a statement that read more like a law review article than a presidential veto.

Clinton's explication was widely ignored—and derided by both sides. "This is a payoff to a major, fat-cat trial lawyer," said Michael Collins, the spokesman for Tom Bliley. Collins made it clear he was referring to Lerach, whose firm had donated $180,000 to Democrats in the first six months of 1995 alone. Lerach claimed to a Washington reporter who phoned him that he had not discussed the bill with Clinton—that he hadn't needed to take that step. "My opinion is known to everyone in Western civilization," Lerach said. "The legislation is horrible. It will result in incredible fraud against elderly people and pension savings."

It was a Tuesday night, and a light snow was falling in Washington. Normally, a snowfall just before Christmas would have cheered a lifelong

Washingtonian like Jon Cuneo, but inclement weather notoriously snarls things in the capital city, which was also in the midst of a second government shutdown, and as he looked out the window of his Capitol Hill office, Cuneo worried whether the president's veto—issued hours before the PSLRA was to become law—wouldn't physically reach the House of Representatives in time to be official. It did reach the House, but it didn't matter. Newt Gingrich had plenty of Democratic votes for an override, as did Senator Dodd, who was at the time chairman of the Democratic National Committee. The House vote came the next day. The override succeeded with room to spare, on a vote of 319–100. Two days later, on December 22, 1995, Dodd and the Senate followed suit, 68–30.

Eleven months earlier Lerach had been summoned to Washington to testify against this legislation. He had known he was walking into an ambush but had hoped he could help shape the debate. He was unsuccessful in achieving that goal, but that didn't necessarily mean his argument lacked merit. Time would tell, as it does with most legislative reforms. Considering what would happen to the U.S. economy in the next dozen years, perhaps Congress should have paid more attention to Lerach. In his opening statement to the House Subcommittee on Telecommunications and Finance in January, he had cautioned that dire consequences would result if Congress rushed the Private Securities Litigation Reform Act into law.

"The fraudsters and the dishonest people are there, and if the prohibitions against fraud are removed, they will come forward—they will become more active," Lerach had told Congress. "In ten or fifteen years you will be holding another hearing with the debacle in the securities market that will make you remember the S&L mess with fondness."

This warning would prove prescient. In fact, regarding the time frame, his prediction proved too conservative. Another reckoning was coming, and it would arrive sooner than even William S. Lerach expected.

> • > • > • > • >

REVENGE OF THE NERDS

Out in Silicon Valley, they smelled blood. High-tech executives ranging in disposition from the temperate Ted Roth to the animated Al Shugart believed their longtime adversary was wounded and that their chance had come to drive a stake through his heart.

Shugart was still smarting over Milberg Weiss's three lawsuits against Seagate, as well as Lerach's "more is coming" response to his advertisement asking for high-tech executives to send him their business cards if they'd been Lerached. Five years later, flushed in the afterglow of their victory in Washington, Shugart faxed a message to Lerach: "Dear Bill, more is coming."

Precisely what was coming was a series of statewide referendums aimed at Lerach, his law firm, and his imitators designed to curtail, if not end, class action securities lawsuits brought by the "Strike Suit King" and his imitators.

Since 1911, when California governor Hiram Johnson and his Progressive Party enacted laws allowing voters to recall governors and judges and to place initiatives on the ballot for a direct vote of the people, the state had enjoyed, if that is the right word, a form of direct democracy. The Progressives' motivation was to break the griplike control that corporations, particularly Southern Pacific Railroad, held over the legislature. Now Lerach's long-suffering adversaries in the high-tech industry were planning to use direct democracy against him. It wasn't quite like taking on Southern Pacific, although in the minds of certain executives, it was just as vital. Passage of the "Get Lerach Act" warmed the hearts of entrepreneurs and computer geeks up and down the West Coast.

In their visions of a future with a defanged Bill Lerach, no longer would innovators have to couch every expression of optimism about their company's latest invention in dry, lawyerly language. No longer would the prospect of a dip in their company's stock price leave them tossing at night in a cold sweat. No longer, two days after that drop in their company's publicly traded shares, would a cookie-cutter lawsuit arrive at the door under Milberg Weiss letterhead accusing them of fraud. No longer would they or their fellow CEOs be profanely berated by Lerach at high decibels during settlement conferences. No longer would they, founders of profitable companies employing thousands of workers, be identified as perpetrators of "fraud" in court filings and called "evil" or "a crook" by Lerach in public interviews. No longer would they write seven-figure checks to make the threat of a calamitous jury verdict go away. Most of all, never again—after having written those checks—would they be forced to listen, seething silently, to the Lerach lecture or to read about their supposed moral failings in news coverage of a post-mortem Lerach press conference.

The mid-1990s was a time of invention and disruption and success on the West Coast. Tech stocks helped push the Dow Jones Industrial Average over 5000 for the first time in history. *Newsweek* dubbed 1995 "The Year of the Internet." It was a period of untrammeled wealth. The only snake in the modern Garden of Eden was Bill Lerach, his firm, and his legal emulators. In 1996 the American Electronics Association, high tech's Santa Clara County California–based trade association, revealed that fifty-three of its one hundred largest firms had been subject to class action securities suits—some more than once—and most of them had been filed by Lerach.

T. J. Rodgers, the CEO of Cypress Semiconductor in San Jose, compared Lerach in interviews to a carjacker. "He's a greedy guy," added Al Shugart. "Imagine the feeling of powerlessness," Intuit cofounder Tom

Proulx told Gary Rivlin, a knowledgeable Bay Area technology writer. "Someone accuses you of fraud. You know with absolute certainty that it's a lie. You want to fight, but then you find out you really don't have the opportunity. You're a dumb businessman if you fight it. So you settle."

Silicon Valley was united by one thing amid the political election season of 1996: it wanted to make Lerach's business model illegal. The field commander of the anti-Lerach army was Tom Proulx (pronounced "Prew"), a political neophyte who believed he had devised an ingenious and preemptive counterattack against Lerach that would protect high-tech executives from future securities lawsuits.

Proulx helped raise $12 million to put three measures on the March ballot in California. The first was Proposition 200, which called for rewriting the state's auto insurance laws so that California would essentially become a no-fault state. No matter who was at fault in an accident, insurance companies would pay the claims of their own policyholders. Huge punitive damage awards would be curbed. The second, Proposition 201, picked up where Congress had demurred while passing the Private Securities Litigation Reform Act: it called for a "loser pays" provision in California securities litigation. The third, Proposition 202, restricted attorneys' fees to 15 percent of any settlement in civil litigation.

Three separate proposed changes in state law, with one target: lawyers.

The first salvo in the antilawyer ad campaign was a shark-finned Cadillac, presumably driven by an unscrupulous attorney, chasing an ambulance through the streets of San Diego—Lerach's town. Called the "terrible two hundreds" by the lawyers, the initiatives were placed on the ballot on the day of California's March presidential primary in their sponsors' hopes that the 1996 Republican nominating contest would draw conservatives to the polls. Thus did the federal "Get Lerach Act" beget the California "Get Lerach Initiative," conveniently paired with a couple of other measures that his adversaries believed would make it easier to pass.

They were mistaken. For starters, the major insurers wanted no part of a protracted initiative war with the attorneys, and they sat the fight out. The computer guys were also wrong about the image of attorneys. Cadillac ads notwithstanding, millions of voters had a soft spot for trial lawyers too.

Notwithstanding Frank Luntz's adroit massaging of the Republicans' message, Bill Lerach had not supplanted Perry Mason in Californians' imaginations—at least not yet—and on March 26, 1996, all three of the antilawyer "terrible two hundreds," including the "Get Lerach Initiative," went down to defeat.

But the fight was not over.

> • >

EVEN BEFORE HIS VICTORIOUS sweep in the California initiatives, Lerach began laying the groundwork for a counteroffensive. He would use the referendum process himself to make his adopted state permanently safe for class action securities suits. He was counting on support from his friend in the White House as well as other powerful Democrats. One was Bill Carrick, a transplanted South Carolina political consultant who managed Dianne Feinstein's campaigns—and who was advising the Clinton reelection effort in California. Carrick had met Lerach six years earlier during Feinstein's 1990 campaign for governor when Feinstein, then mayor of San Francisco, was in a fight for the Democratic gubernatorial nomination with Attorney General John Van de Kamp. Lerach harbored a covert grudge against Van de Kamp—he thought the attorney general could have been more aggressive on behalf of Charles Keating's victims—and his feelings were about to be secret no more.

"Dianne is in this heated primary with Van de Kamp when Bill calls me," Carrick recalled many years later. "He says, 'I've got all these Keating victims, and they want to be for you. Let me help you set up an event.'"

The Lerach-planned rally took place in a San Fernando Valley school. Carrick made certain the news cameras were there—he had hoped a dozen victims would show up—and when Lerach brought his Lincoln Savings survivors, they numbered three hundred strong. "Bill was a folk hero to those people," said Carrick. "Then he gave this stem-winder of an introduction. They all went wild for Dianne. I was impressed."

Feinstein won the 1990 nomination over Van de Kamp but lost in November to Senator Pete Wilson, who went on to serve two terms in

Sacramento.* Carrick and Lerach stayed in touch after that campaign, frequently sharing their views on candidates and campaigns. "He had damn good political ideas almost all the time," Carrick believed.

The summer of 1996 was not one of those times. Just as Tom Proulx had mistaken his meteoric rise in the cutthroat competition of Silicon Valley for political acumen, Lerach mistook his March victories for voters' validation of his business practices. The defeat of the "terrible two hundreds" could have been the end of it, but Lerach had spent hundreds of thousands of dollars gathering signatures to qualify his pro–securities class action initiative, Proposition 211, for the November ballot. "The Silicon Valley guys had worked him over pretty hard," recalled Carrick. "So Bill went ahead to try and enact 211. He said to me, 'Let's see if we can pass this.'"

The searing nature of his recent experiences in Washington had reminded Lerach of the reasons he'd left the East in the first place—and of why Southern California was where he felt truly at home. By 1996 he had grown disillusioned with Washington politics and all three branches of the federal government: Congress had morphed him into Public Enemy Number One; a president he had supported generously had done little to help him in his hour of need; and worst of all, the U.S. Supreme Court had turned on the plaintiffs' securities bar in a 1994 ruling that seemingly arrived out of the blue.

> • >

THE FACTS IN *Central Bank of Denver v. First Interstate Bank* were not in dispute. In 1986 and 1988 a quasi-public agency called the Colorado Springs–Stetson Hills Public Building Authority raised $26 million in bond sales for a planned residential and commercial development in Colorado Springs. To show potential investors that their money was safe, the Authority named a respected Colorado financial institution, Central Bank of Denver, as the trustee of the bonds.

* Wilson's departure from Washington created a vacancy that was filled after a brief interregnum—by Feinstein—in a 1992 special election.

While the 1988 bond offering was taking place, Central Bank appraisers became concerned. Land values in that part of Colorado had declined significantly since the original 1986 appraisal, yet this drop was not reflected in either the appraisal or the paperwork for the second bond offering. When the senior underwriter for the 1986 bonds alerted Central Bank officials to the discrepancy, Central Bank confronted the developer about it, but was assured that $10 million worth of improvements at the site made the appraisal valid and the bond holders' investments safe. Central Bank agreed to delay an outside appraisal until after the 1988 bond offering was concluded. This proved to be a mistake. The Stetson Hill project went belly-up, and the authority defaulted on the bonds.

First Interstate had purchased $2.1 million worth of the bad bonds and sued Central Bank on the grounds that the delay in getting the outside audit was so feckless as to constitute the aiding and abetting of a fraud. Nothing in the 1934 Securities Exchange Act had expressly authorized private sector securities suits—let alone third-party liability for aiding and abetting fraud—although lower courts had allowed both since the 1940s, without a peep from Congress or the Supreme Court. A careful observer of the court, however, might have detected latent enmity for class action securities lawsuits that went back to the earliest days of Milberg Weiss's success.

In 1975 the Supreme Court agreed to hear an appeal brought by Manor Drug Stores against Blue Chip Stamps. The facts of the case were atypical for a securities lawsuit: Blue Chip, under an antitrust consent decree to divest, was accused of offering unduly *pessimistic* predictions about its financial future, which the drugstore chain claimed had discouraged it and other prospective investors from purchasing shares. A U.S. District Court judge dismissed the suit, saying that Rule 10b-5 of the 1934 Securities Exchange Act was simply not elastic enough to include injuries from entities that had declined to buy stocks. A federal appeals court, finding enough evidence of chicanery, disagreed and reinstated the lawsuit. The Supreme Court surprised many legal observers by taking the case and even more by overruling the appellate judges.

Writing for the majority, Justice William H. Rehnquist noted: "When we deal with private actions under Rule 10b-5, we deal with a judicial oak which has grown from little more than a legislative acorn." Rehnquist also went beyond the facts in the instant case, going so far as to describe securities litigation as being "vexatious" to business. A plaintiff with even "a largely groundless claim," he wrote in the 1975 case, can create an irresistible urge for executives to settle rather than fight.

Apparently because the circumstances of the Blue Chip Stamps case were so singular, neither the 6–3 decision, nor the language of opinion penned by the future chief justice, altered the state of securities law for the next two decades—until the Central Bank case reached the high court in 1994. Rehnquist, it turned out, had himself planted an acorn that grew into an oak.

In a contentious 5–4 decision written by Anthony Kennedy, the court went beyond the facts in the Colorado case and issued a ruling that called into question whether third-party liability securities suits could be brought at all. Kennedy's decision employed two separate arguments. First, it ruled that third parties could not be held liable for either material misstatements or omissions unless they had actively participated in deceiving the public themselves, apparently on the grounds that—as Dan Fischel had maintained many times—it was difficult to demonstrate that the omissions and misstatements of third parties directly resulted in investors purchasing the securities in question.

"A plaintiff must show reliance on the defendant's misstatement or omission to recover under 10b-5," Kennedy wrote. "Were we to allow the aiding and abetting action proposed in this case, the defendant could be liable without any showing that the plaintiff relied upon the aider and abettor's statement or actions." Kennedy was joined in his opinion by Rehnquist, Sandra Day O'Connor, Antonin Scalia, and Clarence Thomas.

In its second rationale, the court's majority pointed out that Rule 10b-5 makes no mention of third-party liability. The question before the court was "not whether imposing private civil liability on aiders and abettors is good policy but whether aiding and abetting is covered by the statute," Kennedy wrote. "Policy considerations cannot override our interpretation of the text and structure of the act."

This assertion, and the court's blithe disregard for established precedent, clearly irked the minority, led by Justice John Paul Stevens, along with the rest of the high court's liberal wing: Harry Blackmun, David Souter, and Ruth Bader Ginsburg.

"In *hundreds* of judicial and administrative proceedings in every circuit in the federal system, the courts and the SEC have concluded that aiders and abettors are subject to liability under 10 (b) and Rule 10b-c," Stevens wrote. "All eleven Courts of Appeals to have considered the question have recognized a private cause of action against aiders and abettors . . . Indeed, in this case, petitioner *assumed* the existence of a right of action against aiders and abettors, and sought review only of the subsidiary questions whether an indenture trustee could be found liable as an aider and abettor based only on a showing of recklessness."

That reasoning did not carry the day. Instead, under the guise of being strictly constructionist, the majority overturned a precedent so well established that the plaintiffs hadn't even asked for the relief they were granted. Moreover, the majority's hair-splitting about whether investors relied on specific omissions or deceptive statements of outside auditors and trusts begged the question of whether victims of securities fraud could be compensated for their losses at all. If the court's ruling in *Central Bank* was taken literally, a fraudulent operator could say he had relied in good faith on a reputable third-party expert—auditors, trustees, or consultants. When the plaintiffs then turned for relief by suing the third parties for aiding and abetting in the fraud, those third parties could say, "The Supreme Court says you can't sue us."

This was circular logic—a classic catch-22—but you couldn't appeal a Supreme Court ruling. The only place for relief was Capitol Hill, except that Congress had turned Republican and declared open season on Lerach and the rest of the securities plaintiffs' bar. To Lerach, California's legal system was looking better all the time.

> • >

WITH HELP FROM Jon Cuneo and Bill Carrick, Lerach was framing Proposition 211 in stark and simple terms: his initiative would make California a haven for retirees and investors—and hell for anyone who would cheat them. Proposition 211 (the number, incidentally, that law enforcement officers in California used over their police scanners to designate a robbery in progress) would have prohibited the California legislature from restricting attorney-client fee arrangements, allowed CEOs or directors to be found personally liable for fraud committed by their business, and shifted the burden of proof for securities violations back to the defendants.

Striking while Charles Keating and the Lincoln Savings and Loan scandal were still fresh in the public conscience, a Lerach-sponsored front group called Citizens for Retirement Protection and Security told California voters: "Congress gutted the law that allowed the victims of Charles Keating's fraud to recover most of their money . . . According to the Federal Trade Commission, Americans are losing one billion dollars a year to investment swindlers." As part of the strategy, Lerach brought out his bilked Lincoln Savings and Loan clients for one last dramatic reprise. At a California Public Employees' Retirement System (CalPERS) hearing in Sacramento, the Keating victims were in full force.

"Bill Lerach looks after the people who need looking after—the little guy," said eighty-four-year-old Sam Epstein, a North Hollywood resident who said he had recovered most of the $65,000 he lost in Keating's S&L scam. "If you're wondering, do I think he makes too much money, hell, no. I think he deserves every penny he gets."

This was Lerach's answer to the ads accusing him and other plaintiffs' lawyers of being ambulance chasers. Inside the legal profession, the phrase then applied to attorneys who took securities cases on contingency was "bounty hunters." In the narrative constructed by Cuneo and Lerach, with help from Carrick and Democratic pollster Paul Maslin, Lerach and his ilk were neither ambulance chasers nor bounty hunters. They were defenders of the working class.

Lerach was convinced he was about to rout the high-tech industry again, but Jon Cuneo had no such confidence. Politics was in Cuneo's DNA, and he could sense a losing hand as instinctively as a professional poker player. He had grown up in Washington, the son of a lawyer-turned-newspaper columnist who had done legal work for journalistic legends Walter Winchell and Drew Pearson. Cuneo attended St. Albans, an exclusive, all-male Washington prep school. From there he'd gone to Columbia University and then Cornell Law School, where the nation's white-shoe law firms would identify by their second year the students they wanted for high-dollar civil work. Although he excelled at his studies, that life wasn't for Cuneo. By the time he graduated from law school, he realized that he found big-firm civil litigation about as exciting, in his words, as reading the back of an airline ticket. So he returned to the city of his youth, landing policy jobs with the Federal Trade Commission and later as counsel to the House Judiciary Committee, where he served under famed New Jersey congressman and Judiciary chairman Peter W. Rodino, Jr., of Watergate fame.

Cuneo had not succeeded in preventing the "Get Lerach Act" from passing Congress, but Lerach certainly did not blame him. The two men had become close, and in September 1995, even before the fight over the PSLRA was over, Lerach had invited Cuneo to a strategy session in San Francisco to discuss the "terrible two hundreds," along with Lerach's own counteroffensive, Proposition 211. Seniors' groups were represented, as was the California Trial Lawyers Association. Although no one was designated as the field general, Lerach knew who he had in mind for the job. Over the Thanksgiving weekend he called Cuneo at home to see if he would consider playing an active role in California.

Lerach had originally petitioned the state to have Proposition 211 titled on the ballot "The Retirement Savings and Consumer Protection Act." Republican Attorney General Dan Lungren wouldn't go for that and gave it a less positive-sounding title: "The Attorney-Client Fee Arrangement Securities Fraud Initiative." Nonetheless, all summer it held a lead in public opinion surveys, although early polling in referendums is not always significant. Sabotage from Republicans such as Lundgren was to be expected. More ominously, Lerach and his allies had received squirrelly responses when they had solicited President Clinton's support. But that summer some unusual political alliances were forming in California and Silicon Valley around Lerach's ballot proposition. For starters, influential venture capitalist L. John Doerr had taken the reins from Tom Proulx as the chief organizer in opposition to the Lerach initiative. For another, Silicon Valley was playing both sides of the street: although Doerr still publicly claimed to be a Republican, he openly admired Al Gore and had attended the Democratic National Convention that summer in Chicago.

Wiry and hyperkinetic, John Doerr was a forty-five-year-old former inventor and design engineer for Monsanto (and later marketing manager for Intel, the giant chipmaker). For sixteen years as a venture capitalist and entrepreneur, he personally helped shape the Silicon Valley, betting on emergent companies such as Intuit, Netscape, Amazon, and Sun Microsystems.

From the outset of the information age, prominent Democrats hoped the moguls of these new industries would gravitate toward their party. The politicians trying to woo the techies called themselves Atari Democrats, after the company that invented Pong, one of the first video games. "We prefer *Apple Democrats*," quipped tech-friendly Colorado congressman Timothy Wirth. "It sounds more American."

Atari was a Japanese word (although a California company), but Apple Computer would indeed have been a better symbol because Apple CEO Steve Jobs was a liberal Democrat who in 1996 gave $100,000 to the Clinton campaign. It wasn't nearly as much as Bill Lerach, but it was a lot, and it was the tip of an industry's iceberg. Doerr enlisted Jobs in the effort to defeat Proposition 211. Doerr's involvement was key, and if Lerach and Mel Weiss had known more about Silicon Valley politics, they might have been more worried.

Like many Silicon Valley movers-and-shakers, Doerr had found it disconcerting, during the fight over the PSLRA, that Lerach enjoyed such easy access to the president. Doerr craved that kind of clout for *his* industry, and several young Democrats arrived on the scene about this time to help Doerr achieve his goal. One was a Californian from a moneyed family named Wade Randlett, who had an Ivy League education, a law degree, and a passion for politics. Randlett believed he could make a name for himself—and do the Democratic Party a lot of good—by making the Atari Democrats' long-standing dream come true. At age thirty-one, Randlett had established himself as one of the top "bundlers" in the Democratic Party. (Bundlers raise large amounts of cash for the party, by getting dozens—or hundreds—of donors with similar interests to write checks that are then given in one large tranche to the party, or to a specific candidate.)

Doerr and Randlett met for the first time on July 2, 1996, at a fundraiser for one of the stars of the centrist, pro-business Democratic Leadership Council, Connecticut senator Joe Lieberman. It was held at the San Francisco home of Sanford "Sandy" Robertson, one of Doerr's fellow high-tech venture capitalists. Doerr had already vowed to his partner Brook Byers that he would "crush" Lerach and his initiative. Now he'd found someone—a Democrat, no less—who could help him do it. With Doerr's blessing, Randlett virtually ran the anti-Lerach campaign out of Kleiner Perkins's headquarters on the Sand Hill Road near Stanford University, which that summer and autumn featured a huge banner reading "NO ON 211."

The air war against Lerach was conducted by Goddard Claussen, the top-drawer Sacramento-based media campaign consultancy responsible for the "Harry and Louise" ads that helped derail then–first lady Hillary Clinton's 1993–94 health care initiative. The firm's first wave of television ads began with a scare tactic: "The wealthy East Coast lawyers are coming," and the picture of some presumed shyster emerging from a Learjet. ("Jon, do you think they are talking about me?" Lerach asked his confidant impishly.) Lerach was so sanguine because demonizing him had failed in the March referendum, and he believed it would fail again.

Doerr had a similar perception. He needed something big, and during a presidential year nothing was bigger than the endorsement of a frontrunning incumbent—unless it came from the president *and* his challenger. First, the anti-Lerach forces set about nailing down Bob Dole's support, which wasn't a hard sell—Dole had little use for trial lawyers—and on August 6 the Republican nominee came out in opposition to Proposition 211. The next day President Clinton arrived in Silicon Valley for a campaign stop that was essentially hosted by Steve Jobs. Immediately prior to his campaign event, Clinton met privately with Jobs, Doerr, and a handful of other top Valley executives and assured them that he was also opposed to 211. White House chief of staff Leon Panetta dutifully passed this information along to the traveling press corps: "He believes securities laws should be done on a national, rather than state-haphazard basis," explained Panetta.

Others suggested baser motives. Just as Silicon Valley had noticed when Lerach could contribute oodles of money to Clinton, and then get a private audience with the president, Steve Jobs's $100,000 contribution did not pass unnoticed in the tech community, and it was hardly the last of its kind. Prop 211 had opened a spigot. In mid-September Clinton attended a fund-raising dinner in Sunnyvale, California, for a dozen well-heeled business leaders—the price tag was $50,000 per plate. This new generosity on the part of high-tech executives toward Democratic candidates suggested a different—or at least, an additional—rationale for the president's change of heart than Panetta's good-government explanation. "Clinton wants to nail down California, and our high-tech community needs his support to defeat Prop 211," George Sollman, chief executive of San Jose's Centigram Corp., told *Time* magazine. "So there you have an equation."

Lerach, after all he'd done for the president, learned of Clinton's betrayal in the newspapers. "Say goodbye to the Lincoln bedroom," he glumly griped to his wife, Star.* Lerach had been hoping that Bill Carrick's job as an adviser to Clinton's California campaign would help keep the president neutral, but the fix had been in all along. Earlier that summer Randlett had squired Doerr around at the Democrats' Chicago convention, Doerr's entrée being assured by Simon Rosenberg and Celia Fischer, two other well-positioned "New Democrats" who had been with Clinton in 1992. If Doerr was cultivating prominent Democrats mainly so he could undermine Proposition 211, the party professionals were using him to advance their own agenda—namely, getting their party, and their president, more in the ballgame when it came to high-tech political contributions, activists, and votes. In John Doerr, Lerach had met his match.

"I've learned in politics that you cling to rich donors, great spokespeople, and people who get shit done," Fischer said later. "Doerr is all three."

Late that summer polls showed the measure tightening, although

---

* Lerach had never spent the night in the Lincoln Bedroom and wouldn't be an overnight guest in the White House for four more years, but the Clinton-Gore fundraising scandal was beginning to break, which Lerach knew. According to Jon Cuneo, Lerach had received a questionnaire from Charles Lewis, founder of the nonpartisan Center for Public Integrity, asking him—as Lewis did other large donors—about favors he may have received from the Clintons, including overnight stays at the White House.

Lerach's side remained ahead. Fund-raising now became an issue. In April and May Cuneo and Carrick had set up focus groups to delve more deeply into citizens' attitudes. What they heard in those sessions had utterly taken the wind out of their sails. "When we brought up 'securities,' half the people thought we were talking about alarm systems for their homes," Cuneo recalled later. "I didn't know whether to laugh or cry."

It was clear to Carrick, after seeing the focus groups, that Californians had grown weary of the whole battle between Lerach and his enemies: "They'd been warned about 'corporate wolves,' then they'd been told, 'No, no, it's the lawyers who are really ripping you off,'" Carrick recalled. "They didn't know who to believe. They just wanted to stop thinking about all this crap." After one such depressing session Cuneo and Carrick walked out into the Los Angeles night together.

"Fuck this," Carrick said. "This is going to be brutal."

"It's going to be very difficult to pass," Cuneo agreed.

The two demoralized Lerach lieutenants also agreed on a temporary solution to their dismay: they adjourned to the bar at Cuneo's hotel and ordered several rounds of drinks. "We got shitfaced," Carrick said.

> • >

MEANWHILE, THE OTHER SIDE was not complacent; far from it.

At seven thirty on a Monday morning in early October, the anti-Lerach brain trust gathered in the boardroom of Kleiner, Perkins, Caufield & Byers. The host was John Doerr. Those gathered in his conference room included Tom Proulx and Bill Campbell of Intuit; Hewlett-Packard's John Young; Cisco Systems' John Chambers; Ed McCracken of Silicon Graphics; and Judy Estrin of Doerr-backed Precept Software; along with various directors on the boards of Sun Microsystems, Federal Express, and Rockwell International. Even John Neese, the head of the Santa Clara County Building and Trades Council, was there. As one of the state's top labor leaders, Neese was normally at odds with union-averse Silicon Valley. Not this time. Those present owed Doerr more than a debt of gratitude, they owed him their very companies and, indeed, whole new industries that their companies helped create. This meeting, Doerr told them, was about jobs and the very future of the region that had created the most jobs and wealth since World War II—the Silicon Valley. Collectively, those around the table employed more than 150,000 people, and their combined market capitalization exceeded $100 billion.

Doerr got right to the point. "We are looking at the loss of nearly 160,000 jobs," he said. "Economists are telling us that the stock market will decline by fifteen percent. That's trillions of dollars. Directors are saying they will resign their seats rather than put themselves at personal risk." Then he laid his hands on the table, as if showing his cards. "I sit on six boards. If this thing passes, I will sit on none."

"This Proposition 211 is the greatest threat to our industry since the Japanese threat of the mid-1980s," added Intel chief Andrew Grove.

With three weeks to go, Lerach and his allies had spent about $8 million and expected to spend another $4 million, Doerr pointed out. He also acknowledged the $11 million hit that Valley executives had taken just seven months earlier, in March, in unsuccessfully backing the ill-conceived "terrible two hundreds." This time the stakes were exponentially higher, he assured them. They had momentum, but Proposition 211 was leading in the polls. To win they would have to spend at least $30 million, Doerr grimly told his colleagues. He also laid out the strategy that this money (which would come pouring in after the meeting) would finance. They were now in phase three of the campaign. Phase one had been softening up their target with personal attacks on Lerach. Phase two was softening up the voters with the Dole-Clinton ads. Although Doerr didn't put it this way, phase three was scaring the bejesus out of people. From now on, it was all about jobs—the jobs that would flee California if 211 passed.

This was to be the message, in both the "free media" and the paid media advertisements. On October 3, 1996, the American Electronics Association (AEA) released a survey of its members purporting to show that 47 percent of its 239 member companies might relocate their operations outside California's borders if Proposition 211 passed. "That would mean the loss of 61,000 jobs in California," Chris Ullman, an AEA spokesman added helpfully. In addition, 98 percent of the companies surveyed said that

Proposition 211's passage would make it harder to recruit top-quality executives and directors.

Judy Estrin, who had founded three successful Silicon Valley companies, threatened in interviews to not take Precept public if Proposition 211 passed, adding that she would quit her other board of directors positions the next day.

"If this passes, the only people who will be willing to be officers and directors of companies will be indigent or stupid or both," Doerr warned. It was a reference to the Lerach initiative's loosely worded language allowing for punitive damages—uninsurable by D&O policies—to be paid personally by corporate officers found to have committed vaguely defined "reckless" behavior. This provision would obviously make it difficult for companies to recruit outside directors.

"I'd expect my entire board to resign the day Prop 211 passed," added Centigram Communications' George Sollman, a CEO who had been sued once by Lerach (settling the case for $1.5 million) and didn't want to go through the experience again. "It'd be like an IQ test for directors. If they'd stay on the board, you'd have to question that person's intelligence."

Doerr and his strategists knew that the average voter didn't care much about the problems of a handful of wealthy entrepreneurs. But those board seats represented companies that had done a lot of recent hiring as California emerged from the recession of 1991–92, and voters wanted those companies to thrive—and remain inside the borders of the Golden State. On cue, tech giants Microsoft, IBM, Compaq, and Dell issued joint press releases opposing the measure. With those heavy hitters in the game, other big companies, their vendors, and various corporate partners followed suit. Wall Street money flowed into the "Get Lerach initiative" coffers as well, along with big contributions from top insurance companies. With two weeks to go, the fund-raising goals had been met. Not coincidentally—they were now seriously outspending Lerach's forces in the air wars—the "Yes on 211" lead was slipping.

Mel Weiss called Lerach for a status report. The news was not encouraging. The poll numbers were hemorrhaging, and the state's major media outlets were aligning against their initiative. The *Los Angeles Times* called it "a measure that would mainly line lawyers' pockets." The state's legislative analyst had come out against it, as had the governor, the attorney general, the president of the California Taxpayers Association, and the president of the state chamber of commerce. Even the supposedly neutral League of Women Voters appeared heavily tipped against the pro-211 forces. And of course, President Clinton had double-crossed them.

"We've gone from Plan A to Plan B and now we're hearing that we may be needing Plan C?" Lerach heard his mentor ask in a low, grave voice. "Are you saying we should be thinking about readjusting our business approach?" Lerach hadn't exactly said that, but his immediate silence signaled that Mel had guessed right.

Cuneo and Carrick had feared the bottom would fall out of their support. Now it was happening. This brought on a dilemma. When Lerach had asked Cuneo to run the campaign, Lerach had said playfully, "I'll be the producer and you be the director." Cuneo took this to mean Lerach would raise the money, and Cuneo would guide the effort. In the waning days of what now seemed a certain loss, their quandary was whether to continue raising money to try to keep the margin respectable or fold their tent. Lerach and Cuneo concluded that they couldn't in good conscience ask their friends and allies to keep backing a losing hand, and they essentially shut down their fund-raising operation. "We came to believe," Cuneo recalled later, "that there was no hope at all."

The fear was well founded. On November 5 California voters buried Proposition 211 by a margin of three to one. John Doerr and the vast business alliance he assembled had outspent Lerach's proponents by nearly the same percentage, $32 million to $11 million, even donating an additional $1.75 million to fight another proposition that would have reinstated a higher tax bracket for wealthy Californians.

Amid the din of celebration at the Holiday Inn in Palo Alto, Tom Proulx could be overheard heralding the vote as a significant milestone in the evolution of the New Age economy. "We took a mortal threat to our industry and turned it into an opportunity to organize ourselves into a political force," he proclaimed. "Thanks to the campaign that was mobilized against Proposition 211, the technology industry is now poised to become as influential a player in state politics as the trial lawyers."

Doerr was slightly more circumspect, saying: "Today voters decided growth is good. It creates opportunity for all of us."

It certainly created opportunity for Doerr. During the 1996 campaign he had become close to Al Gore and four years later served as a key adviser in the Gore presidential campaign. In early 2009, his fiction of being a Republican long since retired, Doerr would be introduced at the White House by President Obama as a member of the president's Economic Recovery Advisory Board. On a bigger canvas, Proposition 211 did more in one fell swoop than all the position papers the Atari Democrats had ever put together. Never again would Silicon Valley be caught off guard in politics— and never again would its denizens be taken for granted by either political party.

"A sleeping giant has been awakened," Doerr's partner Brook Byers said. Bill Lockyer, a California Democratic official with statewide ambitions, used identical imagery, as did influential California Republican Dan Schnur. But Schnur did not employ the passive voice: "*Bill Lerach* has awakened the sleeping giant," he said.

The day after the Prop 211 vote, chipmaker Intel issued an upbeat forecast for the pending fourth quarter, saying it anticipated forthcoming revenues to be "significantly higher" than the $5.14 billion generated in the immediate past quarter. Within months its stock price would break through $120 a share. (To celebrate its extraordinary year, the company would reward each of its employees with a $1,000 bonus.) That was nice, but it didn't really compare to the $98 million reaped in 1996 by Intel CEO Andy Grove—$94.6 million of it coming from cashing in stock options. This dwarfed any previous annual compensation in Silicon Valley, and Grove was not alone. The old record would have been broken by two other high-tech executives that year: Cisco CEO John T. Chambers ($33.2 million) and Cisco vice president Frank J. Marshall ($28.4 million). It had been a good year, politically and financially, in the Valley.

In San Diego on the day of Intel's bonus announcement, Bill Lerach sat at his desk, nursing a hangover, and began drawing up a new business plan. Although dejected, he was trying to see ahead. He and his firm had been made vulnerable by political tectonics that he had misread. If the rules had changed, the goals hadn't: fight the corporate swindlers and make a lot of money doing it. But how could Milberg Weiss become more protean, like the most successful companies, including those he'd sued?

The reality of the past two years, at least the way he saw it, was that the courts and lawmakers had made it easier to get away with fraud. When men like John Doerr uttered phrases such as "growth is good," they meant that innovation, jobs, and profits were good for the U.S. economy. But that wasn't how Lerach interpreted it. *Greed* is good—that was what Lerach heard.

"As long as greed is a growth industry we're in business." Mel Weiss had said that, such a long time ago. Now the skids had been greased. Greed was definitely going to grow.

> • > • > • > • >

MISTAKE BY THE LAKE

He was tall, toothily handsome, self-assured at forty years of age, and an attorney to boot. So it was not difficult to understand why Pamela Davis latched on to J. J. Little upon meeting him at Salmon Dave's, a surf-and-turf restaurant in Rocky River, a Lake Erie enclave about five miles west of Cleveland. It was, fittingly, April Fool's Day 1996. As Bill Lerach was girding for his epic political battle two thousand miles away, Little made an initial foray toward forging a relationship with a good-looking woman. He would succeed, at least for a while, although the subsequent detonation of this pairing would generate a remarkable amount of collateral damage on two coasts.

Little, who had been married to an actress and former *Playboy* model, had recently moved from Los Angeles, where he'd practiced entertainment law. He'd just joined the old-line law firm of Arter & Hadden and had, among his clients, Microsoft and boxing promoter Don King. Would he miss Los Angeles? Of course. He'd even appeared in a couple of "bullets, bombs, and babes" movies.

Pam Davis possessed a résumé, and a past, of her own. She was thirty-seven, a pharmaceutical representative, and had served as party chairwoman of the Kidney Foundation of Ohio annual ball. Her picture had been in the newspaper. She was not eager to tell Little that she was on probation for charging more than $5,000 worth of women's clothing to the American Express account of Cleveland Browns fullback Tommy Vardell. Prosecutors were able to prove that she had accessed the account through records kept by her husband, who was Vardell's accountant.

There was also a part of Little's personal history that he was not anxious to disclose. He had a cocaine habit. Back in Los Angeles, he and his law partner James Tierney had represented Brian Wilson, the founder of the Beach Boys, helping Wilson win a $10 million settlement against his music publisher, only to be sued by Beach Boys lead singer Mike Love. The entertainment press had been all over the story, digging up Little's misconduct. His mother's illness had been a convenient excuse to bolt from California.

Two months after their first encounter Little and Davis entered the U-Store-It facility in nearby Lakewood, Ohio, to retrieve a tennis ball machine. While there, Little began sorting through other contents. He came across two cardboard boxes that were unfamiliar and asked Davis to help him carry them outside to the parking lot so they could open them.

"We found what appeared to be two very significant paintings," he would tell police months later. To Davis, he quickly explained that they belonged to a friend for whom he'd been storing them back in California. In his hasty move he must have mistakenly included them among the articles he brought to Ohio.

Two months later, on August 22, Rocky River Police Sergeant Carl Gulas and Detective Gus Carlson responded to a call on Beachwood Drive, a two-block street near Lake Erie. When the officers arrived, they found an obviously distressed woman identifying herself as Pamela Davis on her front porch. A male, in his forties, was leaning against an SUV in the driveway— J. J. Little. Davis claimed Little had manhandled her. Little, in turn, claimed Davis had attacked *him* after he tried to break off the relationship. The officers returned to the porch, repeated what Little had told them, and were greeted with a nearly incoherent, anguished reply. She was pregnant with Little's child, she claimed, although she was married and living with her husband and five-year-old son. Then she dropped some bombs. "He's a meth addict, a drunk, he's assaulted me before," she murmured. "He's sitting on stolen art worth millions, in a secret location."

The cops weren't sure what to make of that claim. "That comment was hidden between so many other allegations that she was throwing around, and that's all she knew—that the paintings were at some unknown location in Cleveland or California," Gulas would report. "It was like 'Lady, you're talking about a Cadillac in a cornfield somewhere.'" When pressed for more details, she changed the subject. The officers warned the pair and returned to their patrol car, agreeing that what they'd just witnessed had the makings of "a real mess." They had no inkling of the enormity of that understatement.

> • >

THE MORE BILL LERACH thought about the calamities that had befallen him in the previous year—the Supreme Court's illogical and unexpected *Central Bank* decision, congressional passage of the PSLRA, and finally, the landslide defeat of Proposition 211—the more his indignation grew. *We can't pull back, we have to grow*, Lerach thought to himself. *We have to refocus, look for ways around the restrictions.*

Taken together, the "restrictions" eliminated the race to the courthouse, an exercise Milberg Weiss had perfected with its stable of plaintiffs. And now, under the federal rules, the court-certified plaintiffs would be those that suffered the greatest losses. *We've got to find new partners, bigger, more powerful plaintiffs*, he repeated to himself.

Then, before he'd finished the thought, it hit him: big institutional investors, pension funds, labor unions, and public employees. They were a giant class of plaintiffs unto themselves. Looking at the problem, Lerach felt a metamorphosis. He'd have to become a great salesman before he could become a great lawyer again. First, they'd have to restore their good names. They would have to be associated with something other than "strike suits"—God, how he hated that term—or his epic battles with the high sector. They needed to generate some air cover. They needed a dose of positive public relations. Lerach picked up the phone and conferenced in Mel Weiss and David Bershad. He reminded the two partners of the bounce the firm had gotten for giving $100,000 to the Holocaust Museum just a few years earlier. Now the firm name was inscribed on the wall.

"Mel, I've been to the museum," he'd pitched to his partners back then. "You've been to the museum. Clinton wants you to be on the board. But how can we be a good Jewish law firm if we don't have our firm name on the wall?" he had argued.

Although Mel said nothing, Lerach heard a sigh on the other end of the phone and could tell what his mentor must have been thinking: "A good Jew. Haven't I dedicated myself to one mitzvah after the other? I received the annual Gotham Anti-Defamation League Award the same year you joined the firm. Who led the B'nai B'rith delegation to Buenos Aires when the Israeli embassy was bombed by terrorists in 1992? And again two years later, when the Jewish center got bombed? Who raised money for the memorial on the site of the embassy bombing? Whose name is on a plaque now at the memorial? Who's leading the lawsuit against Volkswagen for their slave labor camps during the Holocaust? Speaking of the Holocaust, who's closing in on billions in reparations from those reprehensible Swiss and German banks who kept the deposits of the victims? Who's doing it on a pro bono basis? Who loaned his secretary's temple $50,000 for repairs, with no strings attached? Who's on the board of directors of the Israeli Policy Forum? A good Jew? Who's been tutoring you about the teachings of the Torah? And served you and your family matzos? Who holds seder at his house? You are not even Jewish and you are telling me to be a good Jew?"

It was a blessing and a curse to know a man as well as Lerach knew Weiss (and vice versa), to know what the other man was thinking. Weiss had said nothing, nothing at all, but Lerach couldn't hold his tongue. He was too hyped up. Responding to his mentor's silent censure, he continued: "On my honeymoon with Star, you remember, we visited Treblinka, the Jewish Museum there. And it's me, not you, who's on the board of the Holocaust Museum."

Sensing he'd said too much, Lerach fell silent, waiting for his partner's rebuke. Instead he heard Bershad's voice. "I don't know," the phlegmatic and parsimonious partner responded. "We don't need to be spending that kind of money." He listened for Mel's response, and there was only silence at the other end of the phone. Seconds passed. Then he heard his mentor's voice. "Goddammit, Dave. Do it!" And he knew the check would be cut and on its way to the museum.

Following the rewriting of the rules of civil procedure that Congress had mandated, Mel Weiss had been keeping his own counsel. While it surely created a setback for the plaintiffs' bar, it would hit less endowed law firms hardest. Firms such as Milberg Weiss, with a large infrastructure, experience, and a big bank account, were essentially handed competitive advantages in their own markets. That is, if they could retool.

Indeed, without announcing it, perhaps without immediately realizing it, from the depths of defeat, the firm of Milberg, Weiss, Bershad, Hynes & Lerach was on the threshold of its greatest success. On the horizon corporate America, emboldened by defanged shareholder legal threats and tepid government regulation, was also retooling to create vast, fast-growing, complex businesses sustained by shareholder money, mergers, acquisitions, marketing, and nearly unfathomable accounting and financial tools. The chieftains who ran these companies would eventually swirl themselves once again into the gunsights of Bill Lerach and Mel Weiss—although the two partners would begin to embrace different formulas to keep themselves in clover.

Lerach's shooting star would be the huge pools of money created by the 1947 Taft-Hartley Act, mandating the formation of employee pension funds, particularly by public employees' unions and other large labor organizations. Weiss chose to concentrate on a narrower client base while representing institutional investors as a cocounsel or subordinate counsel.

> • >

AT THE BEGINNING OF 1997 Pam Davis took up with a new acquaintance named Dennis Drabek, a forty-two-year-old deck builder. Over drinks, she lamented her on-again, off-again relationship with Little. Since it was currently off-again, she felt free to confide how abusive her former boyfriend had been. Perhaps because Drabek was attentive and sympathetic, she told him something that truly grabbed his attention. Her former lover and tormenter was trafficking in stolen art. She had seen the pieces and knew they had been in a nearby self-storage place. Drabek asked her if she could identify the art. All she could say was that one was a Monet and one looked like a Picasso.

Drabek did his homework, scanning news clippings and calling friends in California. Within a day he learned that two pieces—a Picasso and a Monet—had indeed been stolen from a Los Angeles area home and were still missing after five years. The insurers offered a reward of $250,000, which was in the offing through the Art Loss Register of the International Foundation for Art Research in New York. Drabek called and reached Anna Kisluk, the director. He asked deliberately obtuse questions to try to determine whether the reward was for the same paintings Pam Davis had told him about. By the time he hung up, he was convinced it was.

He called a friend, a former FBI agent named Bob Friedrick, who suggested he arrange a three-way call between Davis, Drabek, and himself. The two men persuaded Davis to elaborate on what she had seen when she and Little opened the cardboard boxes. After the call, Friedrick called Drabek back and told him to contact his lawyer. Drabek called former Cleveland Municipal Court Judge Edward F. Katalinas and told him what he knew. Katalinas arranged a meeting with Cleveland FBI agents Dick Wren and Scott Brantley.*

The same day agents Wren and Brantley received another call concerning the missing art. It was from Anna Kisluk of the Art Loss Register. She recounted her conversation with Drabek, saying she had grown suspicious at the interest he was showing in the reward. The agents called Special Agent Virginia Curry, their bureau counterpart in the Los Angeles field office. Curry, a native of New Jersey, had joined the FBI in 1979, after having had her fill of teaching high school Spanish and Italian "to a lot of

---

* Two years later Katalinas would be disbarred and fined for diverting more than $300,000 in savings and bonds into his own account from a client whose finances he had been managing.

wise-guy wannabes from Jersey." She was also interested in art, which landed her cases whenever thefts occurred.

She and her partner, Agent Pete Munoz, had paid the initial call on Steven Cooperman at his Brentwood home following the police report of an art theft. While Cooperman had appeared to be cooperative, one thing still stood out in her mind from that meeting. Cooperman had been joined by his attorney Richard Purtich. "Why does a guy bring his attorney along if he's got nothing to feel guilty about?" she had asked her partner. Curry placed a call to Los Angeles police detective Don Hrycyk, then head of the department's special art theft detail.

Hrycyk, it seemed, had been speaking to a woman named Roberta Vasquez, a former Playboy Bunny and J. J. Little's ex-wife. She knew about some paintings he kept and had her own suspicions. But when he left, the paintings had left with him. The FBI agents obtained a search warrant and paid a call to J. J. Little at his apartment, but not before interviewing Davis. She confirmed to them what she had told Drabek. They thanked her and left to talk to Little, who instantly knew he was cornered. He asked to call his lawyer, Gerald Gold. Negotiations commenced. Little had a story and was willing to tell it, provided he received consideration for cooperating.

Wren, a veteran FBI hostage negotiator, arranged the cooperation agreement. And Little told his story. He had been asked by his Los Angeles law partner James Tierney to store a couple of boxes for him, he told investigators, swearing he'd been unmindful of what the boxes contained until he had opened them in the Cleveland-area storage facility. He recounted moving the boxes to a new location in nearby Olmstead Falls, fearing Davis would tell everyone she knew about what she had seen. They were in a locker under the name of the gardener for his mother, JoAnn Remington, a Shaker Heights public relations executive. "I was just trying to get the paintings back to the insurance companies no questions asked," he tried to explain.

On February 2 Little led the agents to the Mill River Indoor Self-Storage on Bagley Road in Olmstead Falls, about a ten-minute drive south of Rocky River. There the missing masterpieces were found, undamaged, in their cardboard boxes. Satisfied that Little was intent on cooperating, the agents sent word to Curry. But the FBI still needed more from him.

Further investigation confirmed that the paintings were those stolen five years earlier from Cooperman. Calls to Anna Kisluk at the Art Loss Register and art dealers helped establish that Cooperman had purchased the pieces— the Monet from the Montgomery Galleries in San Francisco in 1987 and the Picasso from Sotheby's in New York the same year. The Sotheby's catalog showed that the painting had sold for $870,000. Agents were able to learn that the Monet sold for slightly more. Even more telling information was obtained from two insurers the FBI was able to track down. From Lloyd's of London, Cooperman had been able to obtain a $5 million policy on the Picasso. From AXA Nordstern Art Insurance Corp., he purchased a policy insuring the Monet for $7.5 million. Immediately after the theft, Cooperman and his wife, Nancy, filed insurance claims. Both were denied. The Coopermans sued in California Superior Court, and the insurers agreed to settle for $17.5 million in late 1993—with $12.5 million paying off the original claim and another $5 million in punitive damages Cooperman collected, successfully alleging that he had been under emotional duress from both the art theft and the subsequent balking by the insurers on paying his claim.

One more bit of information supplied by Los Angeles police added to FBI agents Wren and Brantley's growing certainty that they were onto a big case. Among the legal clients of James Tierney, whose cardboard boxes had ended up in J. J. Little's self-storage locker, was Dr. Steven Cooperman. The agents met again with Little, persuading him that it would be in his interest to help them set up a sting. He had no choice.

Remarkably, Virginia Curry conducted most of the investigation from a Los Angeles hospital, where her thirty-nine-year-old husband, Herb Curry, Special Agent, U.S. Fish and Wildlife Service, suffering from melanoma, lay near death. Knowing that Tierney had previously been an organized crime prosecutor in New York, she accurately predicted the first thing he would do when J. J. Little came calling.

"I left the hospital and went to the FBI lab. We couldn't wire J. J. the traditional way. The wires we were used to carrying felt like lunch boxes.

Tierney would certainly pat J. J. down and discover the wire," she remembered. As it happened, the bureau was experimenting with a new digital transmitter, small enough to withstand a search from even a practiced hand.*

On Valentine's Day 1997, with agents stationed outside, Tierney met Little at the Marriott Hotel in Marina del Rey. As expected, Tierney refused to talk in a hotel room, thinking it might be bugged. He insisted they walk outside, in traffic. First he patted Little down, not once but three times, even asking him to empty the contents of his cigarette pack. Finding nothing, the two left the hotel and walked along the promenade facing the water. As they talked, agents listened. What they heard convinced them that J. J. Little had not been lying. Tierney was part of an art theft conspiracy.

The next day Curry telephoned Tierney and asked him to come to the U.S. attorney's office in downtown Los Angeles—and to bring his attorney. When Tierney showed up, he was accompanied by Brian Sun, a former assistant U.S. Attorney with whom Curry had worked on numerous cases. On a table in the room Curry had placed a recording device. "Does this sound familiar?" she said, switching on the recorder. She and assistant U.S. attorney Richard Robinson registered the shock on the faces of Sun and Tierney as the incriminating dialogue between Tierney and Little was replayed.

"Will I lose my license to practice law?" Tierney asked, his face revealing panic. That might be the least of his concerns, he was told, considering that he faced twenty years in prison for art theft. As he himself had told suspects countless times as a federal prosecutor, Tierney had a choice: cooperate or go to prison. He did not hesitate. He had taken the art. Cooperman, his client, was $4 million in debt and facing foreclosure on his Brentwood home and had asked him to do it. The story was plausible, but to back it up, Tierney would have to let the FBI listen in and record his telephone conversations with Cooperman about the stolen art.

On June 5, with FBI agents recording the conversation, Tierney and Cooperman referred to Little as "Cleveland Indian" and to the missing paintings as "baseball cards." Tierney said he was worried about Little and his drug

---

* Although she has since retired, Curry remained constrained from disclosing the precise nature of the technology, which is still being utilized by the FBI.

habit, wondering aloud whether the stolen paintings were safe with him. Maybe they should figure out a way to have them returned, he suggested.

"No. Let sleeping dogs lie," Cooperman said tersely, and then suggested, "Drop them in a Dumpster."

Tierney balked, saying into the tapped phone: "But the problem with a Dumpster is that the garbage man comes, and he picks 'em up, and he might say, 'Hey, this looks like a Monet.'"

Cooperman had another idea. "Why not run them through a shredder?"

"A shredder? It'll break a shredder," Tierney protested.

"Well . . ." Cooperman could be heard to pause. Then he got another idea. "We have shears, garden shears, I think."

Tierney said he'd have to think about it and would call back the next day. The following morning, under coaching from the FBI, Tierney again called Cooperman. He tried to act agitated, telling Cooperman that he had just received a phone call from a reporter telling him that *The Cleveland Plain Dealer* was reporting the FBI's recovery of the lost paintings. The paper had identified Cooperman as the owner, Tierney said, explaining that the reporter had contacted him because records showed that he had represented Cooperman as his attorney.

Cooperman asked what Tierney had told the journalist.

"I said: 'That's great news,'" the attorney replied.

"Good," Cooperman said. "They don't know nothin' from nothin'."

Tierney said he was still worried about Little and his drug problem and that his former law partner might implicate them both.

"That's utterly ridiculous," Cooperman was heard to say. "People are very aware of [what] cocaine does to people. They become paranoid, they become crazy. They become not credible."

The next day, June 7, the *New York Times* picked up on *The Cleveland Plain Dealer* story. Quoting FBI special agent Robert Hawk, the paper confirmed that the art had been found earlier in Cleveland. The *Times* added additional information, though, reporting that in 1991, in a complaint filed in federal court in Los Angeles, the Paul Revere Life Insurance Company had accused Dr. Cooperman of insurance fraud, claiming that it had been one of fifteen separate companies paying Cooperman $58,000 a month for eighteen disability-income insurance policies without the good doctor having revealed a previous history of heart disease or the existence of the other policies. Toward the end of the piece, the *Times* noted that Cooperman had been a named plaintiff in at least thirty-eight class action securities fraud cases. What no newspaper reported or even knew about, and what the FBI and the Los Angeles police did not know either, was that by the middle of 1997 Steven Cooperman and his relatives had collected more than $6.5 million in secret payments from the law firm of Milberg, Weiss, Bershad, Hynes & Lerach. The money had come directly from David Bershad's office credenza. Sometimes it came in checks, sometimes in cash. Sometimes it came through his attorney Jim Tierney, who would receive the money in the form of "case referral services," for which he had referred not a single case.

> • >

WITH THE STOLEN ART located, and with audio recordings of phone calls between Tierney and Cooperman, Assistant U.S. Attorney Richard Robinson had evidence to take before a grand jury. Unlike many federal prosecutors, Robinson, lanky and taciturn, with thinning brown hair, a graduate of the University of California's Boalt Hall Law School, harbored no ambitions to collect trial experience and then move on to a more lucrative job at a private law firm. He had already been in private practice, spending nearly seven years representing entertainers. Those unfamiliar with his background were also surprised to learn that he had been something of a musical prodigy as a kid, adept at various instruments ranging from the bass to bass guitar to keyboard. He'd even formed his own rock band, streaked his hair purple, worn fluorescent earrings, and played in clubs in West L.A. That stood in sharp contrast to the now understated and mostly apolitical Democrat who was content to work in the federal bureaucracy. He relished the ideal of fairness and justice and working in law enforcement.

With eighteen million residents, seven counties, and thirty-five cities within its jurisdiction, the Central District of California office was responsible for the most populous and diverse area in the nation. Its 250 assistant U.S. attorneys were second in number only to New York. Like New York, L.A. generated its fair share of white-collar scam artists. Robinson especially loved working in the major frauds division, but this was the first art-theft-turned-insurance-scam he'd encountered. On tape, with Tierney's assistance, Cooperman could not have been a more cooperative, albeit unsuspecting, witness against himself. Wasn't that how these things usually went down? With no honor among thieves, once you flipped one, the stampede was usually on.

Still, Robinson was reluctant to tip his hand, insisting that every piece of evidence be ironclad. Nine years earlier he had gone into a grand jury confident of securing an indictment, only to have the case thrown out. He vowed never to repeat that mistake. On the other hand, he had FBI agents on his team—one in particular—who didn't brook any foot-dragging.

"I wasn't going to let this case die," Curry recalled later. "The clock was running and time for the grand jury to be empanelled was just about up. I called over to the U.S. attorney's office and said, if they didn't get this case going, I would take it to New York."

Robinson presented the case to a Los Angeles grand jury in July 1998. Behind closed doors he furnished witnesses, including Tierney, Little, and Curry. Robinson presented evidence that included photographs of the stolen art and the fax inflating their value to the insurers, and when he walked out, he had a sealed indictment charging Steven Cooperman with eighteen felony counts of crimes ranging from insurance fraud to tax fraud. Even then, the extent of Cooperman's larceny was greatly understated.

> • >

IN CONNECTICUT, COOPERMAN HAD become Steve Schulman's plaintiff. For his part, Bill Lerach was relieved. When Cooperman had called Lerach, telling him about the art theft, the Los Angeles police weren't the only ones putting two and two together. Lerach certainly had his suspicions. How could he not? He'd been dealing with Cooperman for ten years. So when he read in the newspapers that the art had surfaced in Cleveland, when he saw the names J. J. Little, Jim Tierney, and Steven Cooperman, Lerach experienced a sense of gratitude that Cooperman had fled to Connecticut, for all intents and purposes removing himself from Milberg Weiss West.

Which is why, in the early fall of 1998, when he received a phone call from Jim Tierney, Lerach's internal alarm bells again sounded. "Can you meet me for lunch?" Tierney asked. Fearing the phone might be bugged, Lerach did not ask what the invitation was about. They agreed to meet the next day at the Hotel Bel-Air in Beverly Hills. When Lerach hung up, he called Mel Weiss in New York and told him of Tierney's request. Weiss warned him to be careful.

The next day, feeling nervous, Lerach parked at the valet spot and entered the sumptuous pink-terracotta Mediterranean-style spa and resort. Tierney was waiting at a table in the uncrowded dining room. Lerach looked around, noting how quiet their surroundings were, and suggested, "It's a nice day, why don't we eat outside?" even though the tables were closer together and filling with guests. So they adjourned to the terrace, to a table overlooking swans cruising on a small lake. Lerach, dressed casually in a polo shirt, noticed that Tierney wore a coat and tie. "Jim. Please take your coat off," he insisted. Tierney, the former federal prosecutor, looked bewildered and then laughed. "Bill, I'm not wearing a wire. I promise." But he took off his coat.

The two sat, and immediately Tierney let Lerach know why he'd called. "Okay, we have a problem." Lerach felt his stomach tighten. "I didn't get my money, Bill. I'm due one million dollars, and I haven't seen a check. Where is it?"*

Lerach braced himself. "I don't know what you are talking about," he half whispered. Tierney said he'd submitted his invoices months earlier for cases that had been settled. He'd called Steve Schulman, who'd looked into the problem. The invoices had been received, Tierney was assured, and the

* The amount remained in dispute. Former Assistant U.S. Attorney Robert McGahan recalls the amount "being in the lower six figures."

checks had cleared the bank. "But I never cashed those checks because I never got them," Tierney insisted.

Lerach said he would investigate. That afternoon he went to the Los Angeles office of Milberg Weiss and called New York, speaking directly with David Bershad, the firm's managing partner.

Clearly alarmed, Bershad said he would recheck the books, adding: "He'd better not be lying."

Less than a week later Bershad called Lerach. "Tierney's telling the truth," he said gravely. Bershad had retrieved copies of the checks from the bank. They had been endorsed to the account of Steven Cooperman. Tierney's signature appeared on the backs. "It's not Tierney's signature," Bershad said. Then he added a shock: "I gave those checks to Cooperman. He was here and said he'd bring them to Tierney."

Now the firm really did have a problem. Cooperman, their star plaintiff, to whom the firm had paid more than $6 million over the years, had extorted them. And they had no recourse.

"We certainly can't go to the cops," Bershad told Lerach, stating the obvious. "I'll take care of this." He would have another check drafted and forwarded directly to Tierney.

Lerach phoned Tierney and told him what had transpired. Without mentioning the art theft and his part in it, or his subsequent cooperation with the FBI, Tierney then said: "I certainly didn't want to have to take action against Dave Bershad for being negligent. But you guys should not have trusted Steve Cooperman."

> • > • > • > • >

PHOENIX RISING

Even before Proposition 211 crashed and burned—even before Congress passed the "Get Lerach Act"—Lerach was beginning to tire of the eternal chase. There were not only too many enemies, there were too many competitors. The constant "race to the courthouse" was a grind. The surreptitious payoffs to their stable of professional plaintiffs were feeling like extortion payments.

Even if few dared accuse Milberg Weiss directly, the firm's opponents had come to suspect there was some chicanery to their methods. The earliest versions of the GOP anti–"strike suits" legislation contained provisions prohibiting plaintiffs in a class action from receiving extra remuneration. Although Lerach's tangling with Chris Cox during the January 1995 House hearings made headlines, two other exchanges with members of the subcommittee got more to the heart of the matter. When it was his turn to question Lerach, Dan Frisa, a Republican congressman from Long Island, wasted no time:

"Mr. Lerach, if you could, could you explain briefly how clients find you?"

"Well, they find us in a variety of ways," Lerach had replied, explaining that he'd been bringing fraud cases for a number of years, with some success, adding, "so there are a lot of investors throughout the country who know us from their participation in prior successful class actions lawsuits—"

"Excuse me, I just want to clarify," Frisa interjected. "So you have repeat clients?"

When her opportunity arose, California Democrat Anna Eshoo, whose congressional district encompassed most of Silicon Valley, approached this issue more directly, even if she had no inkling of the full picture.

"Mr. Lerach, has there ever been a case where you have gone out and sought a shareholder and tapped them on the shoulder and said, 'We think that there is something that you need to be made aware of'?" she asked. "Is it in every case that you know of . . . that a shareholder—more than one shareholder—came to you wanting you to obviously look into it, represent them?"

It wasn't clear from Eshoo's deferential phrasing that she understood just how dark the suspicions ran in Silicon Valley toward Lerach. Her query certainly did not contemplate the machinations of Seymour Lazar—let alone the crimes of Steven Cooperman—yet Lerach himself knew where such questions could lead, and he chose not to parse, but to deny unequivocally.

"We do not solicit plaintiffs," Lerach replied. "It is not necessary. When people are furious, when these stocks are cut in half in one day and they find out there is insider selling, the phone rings. We do not solicit plaintiffs."

This line of inquiry attracted little attention, but Lerach had noticed and reacted accordingly: an alternative version of the Private Securities Litigation Reform Act, drafted by Lerach and Cuneo and offered by Ed Markey, contained a prohibition against filing class action lawsuits before actually having genuine clients. The Democrats' compromise went nowhere, and Lerach's acquiescence to a reform that would have undermined Milberg Weiss's own business practices was promptly forgotten.

Late one afternoon in the spring of 1996, however, at a Milberg Weiss retreat at the Boulders resort in suburban Phoenix, Bill Lerach, Mel Weiss, and Dave Bershad huddled for drinks at the hotel bar. Noting that the prohibition against paying plaintiffs was now codified into law, Lerach recalls taking each man by the hand as if in a small half circle. "Look, we can't pay plaintiffs anymore—we can't do it," he told them. "*No más.*"

The New York partners agreed, but their assent begged the question of what the firm's new business model would look like. In *Central Bank*, the Supreme Court had made it tougher to go after the bankers and accountants who facilitated corporate fraud. Congress had followed up that decision by enacting PSLRA, which made it difficult to sue those perpetrating the frauds unless the plaintiffs had some kind of whistleblower embedded inside the offending corporation. Nonetheless Lerach exhorted the lawyers in the San Diego office to keep filing cases, which they did.

On January 10, 1997, Lerach and his partners filed suit against Net-Manage, a Silicon Valley firm that made Internet servers and connectivity-related software. The suit alleged NetManage's officers reaped $14 million in insider trading "before the truth regarding NetManage's business and finances was revealed."

A week later they sued the officers of Read-Rite Corp., a maker of recording heads for hard disk drives. "Seven of the individual defendants unloaded 86 percent to 100 percent of their Read-Rite holdings, while the eighth—Read-Rite's chairman and CEO—sold off 69 percent of his holdings," a Milberg Weiss press release stated.

On January 24 Lerach went after Sunglasses Hut on the grounds that its officers concealed evidence of sluggish sales, increasing inventory, and marketing problems—and stock dumping by top executives. On February 24 Milberg Weiss led a consortium of plaintiffs' lawyers who sued America Online in federal court in Alexandria, Virginia, alleging that AOL founder Stephen M. Case and seventeen other AOL officers and directors reaped some $95 million in "insider trading profits."

And so it went, all through 1997 and into 1998. "One thing that is very clear is that plaintiffs have not gone away—the courthouse door is still open," said Stanford Law School professor Joseph A. Grundfest, not altogether approvingly. Grundfest, a former Securities and Exchange Commission member, coauthored a study of the effects of the PSLRA that backed up this impression with hard numbers. According to the study, the number of securities class action suits had held steady, at about 150 per year. There was one significant difference, however. Before the "Get Lerach Act" had passed in 1995, Milberg Weiss had accounted for 30 percent of all such strike suits nationally. By early 1997 Grundfest was reporting that this percentage had doubled—to roughly 60 percent.

"I warned Congress before passage of the act that one very negative consequence would be to chill the assertion of meritorious claims, especially by smaller law firms," Lerach responded. "My firm is larger, better capitalized, and we made a decision that we are not going to withdraw, that we would continue to fight for what we believe in." Although Lerach's observation sounded self-serving, it was literally true. Other plaintiffs' lawyers had simply abandoned the field, while Milberg Weiss had doubled down on its bets.

San Francisco litigator Steve Sidener was one example. Sidener had been filing class action securities cases for eleven years, most of them in concert with class action securities pioneer David Gold. In their salad days Gold and Sidener had unearthed some of the most breathtaking examples of fraud in Silicon Valley, including their case against Miniscribe, the disk drive company that padded its sales by shipping bricks. Gold had died in 1995, the year that the PSLRA had passed, however, and the following year Sidener hung out his own shingle—as a general law practice, not as a security class action firm. "The dance is over," he told friends.

Sidener wasn't alone. The dance hall was cleared of numerous competitors. A law aimed at Lerach was now directly *helping* his law firm: a less crowded sprint to the courthouse meant that Milberg Weiss attorneys could take the time to draw up stronger complaints. In other words, the PSLRA raised the threshold for making a lawsuit stick, but by decimating Milberg Weiss's competitors, the reform law made it easier for Lerach to draw up lawsuits that were more likely to meet this higher standard of proof.

Another factor that served to make Milberg Weiss an even bigger player in the field of class action securities lawsuits was subtle differences of interpretation in the various appellate circuits over the extent to which the Supreme Court's *Central Bank* decision shielded "aiders and abettors" in securities fraud cases. Justice Anthony Kennedy, perhaps to keep his tenuous majority together, had carefully drafted his opinion to ensure that the immunization conferred on ancillary players was not absolute. "The absence of 10(b) aiding and abetting liability does not mean that secondary actors in the securities markets are always free from liability," Kennedy had written for the court's 5–4 majority. "Rather, any person or entity, including a lawyer, accountant, or bank, who employs a manipulative device or makes a material misstatement (or omission) on which a purchaser or seller of securities relies may be liable as a primary violator under Rule 10b-5."

What did this language mean in practice? The answer soon revealed itself: it meant different things in different circuits.

In New York, the Second U.S. Circuit Court of Appeals devised a "bright line" test under which secondary players could be held liable only if they made a publicly attributed misstatement of fact or material omission that was relied upon by the investing public. The test case was *Wright v. Ernst & Young*, brought on behalf of Irene Wright, a named shareholder, by a New York law firm, Wolf, Haldenstein, Adler, Freeman & Herz, in litigation concerning the activities of BT Office Products.

The case against Ernst & Young hinged on a January 30, 1996, press release issued by BT Office Products touting its growth in 1995 and predicting a bang-up 1996. Auditors at the firm soon concluded that an accrual problem noticed by Ernst & Young, but not initially thought to be a problem, was indeed serious. BT Office Products revised its 1995 financial performance, and its stock promptly lost 25 percent of its value. The Irene Wright class action suit alleged that Ernst & Young's "recklessness" was the primary cause of the problem, noting that the accounting firm had "signed off" on the January 30 press release.

Ernst & Young's attorneys argued that because it had made no false statements of its own about BT—had made no public statements at all, actually—the suit was a back-door attempt to resurrect "aiding and abetting" liability. The Second Circuit agreed, noting in its August 6, 1998, decision that the press release in question had not attributed its sunny forecast to Ernst & Young, meaning that the auditor had communicated no misrepresentations to investors, either directly or indirectly.

Meanwhile the appellate district with the most class action securities claims drew a different inference from *Central Bank*. The Ninth Circuit discerned another criterion that came to be known as the "significant role" standard. This was a Milberg Weiss case, filed against a Silicon Valley company named Software Toolworks and its accountant, Deloitte & Touche. In letters to the SEC, Software Toolworks wrote that it "anticipated" revenues for the next quarter of between $21 million and $22 million. Privately, the company provided information to Deloitte raising doubts whether such numbers were attainable. Yet the company had shown those letters to Deloitte and referred the SEC to two Deloitte auditors for further information. This made the accounting firm liable, to the minds of the Ninth Circuit judges, who noted the company's SEC presentation had been "prepared after extensive review and discussion with . . . Deloitte." The appellate court's conclusion: "*Central Bank* does not absolve Deloitte on these issues."

Out of this ambiguity would come the theories of "scheme liability" that Lerach would apply to the huge banks, accounting firms, and other entities that enabled a landmark fraud otherwise known as Enron.

> • >

IN THE WAKE OF THE PSLRA, Lerach had started doing what he hadn't done since his days as a young lawyer in Pittsburgh, scrambling to find clients. He began calling on potential plaintiffs. One of the first was James P. Hoffa, president of the 1.4 million-member International Brotherhood of Teamsters, an organization with $16 billion in assets—and no appetite for losing it, since the money represented the pension funds of its members. Lerach made himself known to the hierarchy and fund managers of numerous other labor organizations. They included the California Steel Workers; the Alaska Electrical Workers Pension Fund; the gigantic California Public Employees' Retirement System (CalPERS), and the California State Teachers' Retirement System, the largest and third-largest pension funds in the country, with more than $300 billion under management; the University of California Retirement System and the retirement system for New

York and New Jersey and Illinois; investment councils for various states from New Mexico to New York; various archdioceses of the Roman Catholic Church, and pension managers for Wisconsin's public employee unions.

Jon Cuneo said that his friend did some of his best work in the years after 1996. Lerach retooled himself, his firm, and how he practiced law, and did it without firing lawyers or missing a beat. Bill Carrick said that Lerach reminded him of an ambitious young presidential candidate, flying all over the country, working fourteen- and sixteen-hour days, making his presentations to pension managers from coast to coast. Even the lawyers in his own firm who were used to his manic pace marveled at his energy. Under the new rules, being first to the courthouse wasn't enough. Judges would determine the counsel of record in class action fraud cases, and they usually picked the law firm with the most juice, the most expertise in the particular case, and—more than anything—the law firm that represented the client or entity that had lost the most money.

And a lot of money was out there to be lost.

Hundreds of billions of dollars were in play. Miles of fiber optics being laid daily, much of it fueling a dot-com boom for which Lerach expressed early and loud skepticism. "Dot-con," he would come to call it. Emerging permutations of the telecom industry and information technology grafted themselves into the much-heralded New Economy. The stock prices of these start-ups floated like snowflakes, and price-earning valuations defied gravity. As Wall Street speculated wildly, new classes of victims with deep pockets would soon emerge—Lerach could just feel it. And so he began to cultivate the fertile fields of a new prospective turf. Once Lerach controlled market share, and once fraud arrived on the backs of new companies but under the same old skins of greed and self-dealing, lawyering would follow as sure as "night follows day." That's what he promised his colleagues in San Diego and New York.

Making good on their end of Lerach's promise, public pension funds acted as lead plaintiffs in fourteen securities lawsuits in 1998 and seventeen in 1999. The number would rise farther and faster in the coming years.

Getting clients was one thing. But even as he was realizing new opportunities, Lerach and his fellow class action securities lawyers would encounter one roadblock after another resulting from the PSLRA. One experience in particular set the tone for a bitter war between plaintiffs' attorneys and district appellate courts that would last well into the coming decade. It was a case that previously would have been a slam dunk—the kind that would have been settled so fast, it probably wouldn't have made the newspapers outside Silicon Valley.

The case involved a company called Silicon Graphics Inc. (SGI). Based in Mountain View, California, SGI produced high-end, commercial workstations featuring 3-D graphics, with uses ranging from health care diagnostics to digital graphics used in the entertainment industry. In the amped-up early 1990s, SGI was a buzz company, and its stock prices reflected its prominence. At its peak the corporation commanded $7 billion in market capitalization. The problem was competition. Personal computers that were far cheaper, with fast, complex computing capabilities, including high-speed video processing, had hit the market. By mid-decade SGI's sales were in a funk. Desperate for fresher products, SGI announced it was on the brink of developing "must have" industry-changing components. Accordingly, its stock zoomed from $20 to $50 per share. But no further product announcements were forthcoming.

In the fourth quarter of 1996 SGI starting losing money. Its stock plummeted. In November 1997, a year after he had helped defeat Lerach's Proposition 211, SGI's chairman Edward R. McCracken resigned; Gary Lauer, head of the company's world trade division, stepped aside as well. The company laid off more than one thousand people—10 percent of SGI's workforce. Prior to the stock collapse, with no new products actually in the pipeline, SGI executives, including McCracken and Lauer, sold 300,000 shares of SGI stock, generating $7.4 million for themselves.

Although Milberg Weiss was not the first to jump on the case, Lerach's quick maneuverings put his firm in the position of lead counsel. In short order Lerach's legal team discovered evidence suggesting that SGI's former and current officers had tried to negotiate an exchange of convertible stock for $200 million worth of outstanding debentures. "To do this, the officers had to artificially inflate the price of its stock," Lerach wrote in the complaint. Once the debt was exchanged, insiders were able to sell their stock, he wrote. He took note of a company announcement that its fourth-quarter fiscal 1997 results showed improvement over the previous five quarters. But it didn't take long to discover the reason: the company had booked orders from future quarters against its fourth-quarter results. Voodoo accounting.

The class action lawsuit against SGI on behalf of stock purchasers was filed in the federal Northern District of California on October 17, 1996, and it drew attention nationwide. This lawsuit would be the first of its type since the 1995 PSLRA. While the evidence mirrored dozens of previous, successful cases, the barriers for introducing evidence had been substantially raised. Lerach and his legal team quickly learned just how high.

Milberg Weiss partner Len Simon argued the case on behalf of the plaintiffs. He was opposed by an old foe, Bruce Vanyo of Wilson Sonsini. The judge was Fern Smith, a Stanford Phi Beta Kappa and Stanford Law graduate, appointed by President George H. W. Bush. Appearing in court to argue against the defense's motion for a summary judgment dismissing the suit, Simon presented a straightforward case. He argued that the lawsuit should proceed because "based upon a review of SGI's SEC filings, securities analysts reports and advisories about the company, press releases issued by the company, media reports about the company, and discussions with consultants," SGI executives had committed fraud for their own enrichment. Vanyo's defense also was relatively direct. There was no conscious intent to misrepresent, he contended. Judge Smith agreed, saying "motive, opportunity, and non-deliberate recklessness may provide some evidence of intentional wrongdoing, but are not alone sufficient scienter (knowledge of wrongdoing) unless the totality of the evidence creates a strong inference of fraud."

Simon was mortified. Previously, you had merely to get inside a company's financial statements and records to prove your case. Now the judge was saying that you had to get inside the defendant's head.

An appeal was filed before the Ninth Circuit. Based in San Francisco, the district's jurisdiction covered nine western states ranging from Alaska to Hawaii to Montana to Arizona, with California at the center, making it the largest district in the nation. Twenty-eight judges sat on its benches. The three-judge panel chosen to hear this appeal was composed of Judge Joseph

T. Sneed, James R. Browning, and a district judge assigned to hear the appeal named John S. Rhoades.

Sneed was considered the strongest voice of the three. In the past he had not shown overt hostility to plaintiffs' class action suits. A 1947 graduate of the University of Texas Law School, he worked summers as a cowboy on his uncle's ranch in the Texas panhandle. A brilliant student, he was offered a teaching job at UT Law School and became an associate professor in 1951, spending ten years on the faculty before moving to Cornell Law School, where he taught until 1962. From Cornell he moved to Stanford Law School, then became dean of the Duke University Law School. In 1973 he moved to Washington, to join the Justice Department, serving as deputy attorney general. Within the year President Richard Nixon appointed him to the federal appellate bench.

The case had been submitted and argued over two days in June 1998, with various interest groups, most prominently the American Electronics Association, representing three thousand high-tech companies, weighing in on behalf of the defendants. It would be more than a year before the court would rule. In the meantime William Lerach had pension fund managers to woo—and an unpleasant date to keep in the city of Chicago.

> • > • > • > • >

VENDETTA

The road to the federal courthouse in Chicago had taken nearly six years and a path through a federal courtroom in Arizona, where the case of *Lexecon v. Milberg Weiss Bershad Hynes and Lerach* for "malicious prosecution, abuse of process, tortious interference (intentionally damaging another's business prospects), commercial disparagement and defamation" was heard and dismissed by U.S. District Court Judge John M. Roll.

Alan Salpeter and his colleagues Michele Odorizzi and Mark Hansen had desperately tried to get their case out of Phoenix—out from under the shadow of Charles Keating and Lincoln Savings. Salpeter had initially filed his lawsuit in Chicago, but Jerold Solovy, the wily chairman of Jenner & Block, whom Milberg Weiss retained as counsel, persuaded the federal court in Arizona to transfer the case to itself, arguing successfully that since Arizona was where "a massive document depository is located," it would be more efficient to hear this case where the documents were easily obtained and where there was no need to bring a new judge up to speed.

That was precisely what worried the Lexecon lawyers and why the legal team appealed the transfer to the Ninth Circuit Court of Appeals, but they didn't prevail. Only appellate court Judge Alex Kozinski dissented, warning that self-transfer constituted "a remarkable power grab by federal judges" and exceeded the authority Congress had granted the courts. Salpeter was no longer on the case. His colleague Mark Hansen, a Harvard Law graduate and former federal prosecutor, petitioned the U.S. Supreme Court for a hearing. On March 3, 1998, in a unanimous opinion written by Justice David Souter, the Supreme Court agreed with Hansen—and Kozinski— ruling that the case could be refiled in Chicago. A University of Chicago alum drew the case. U.S. District Judge James B. Zagel, a fifty-seven-year-old graduate of Harvard Law, had been director of the Illinois State Police before President George H. W. Bush appointed him to the federal bench. Alan Salpeter had tried numerous cases in his court.

"We have a good rapport," Salpeter told Fischel over lunch at the exclusive Standard Club in downtown Chicago.

At first Fischel had been puzzled as to why Salpeter had telephoned him. "I thought you had abandoned me," he told the attorney.

Salpeter said he had only decided not to lead the case in Arizona. Now that it was back in a more favorable venue, he was set to go. Quickly, he presented the game plan. It was simple. "I think we can show that in your case, we had lawyers thinking they could act above the law," Salpeter said. "If we can show this, we'll win."

Although he thought it important to convey confidence to Fischel, later, as he was preparing for trial, Salpeter felt a private sense of dread. *I'm taking on the most powerful class action lawyers in America*, he thought. *If I lose this case, Lerach will be coming after me for the next twenty years.*

Now that the case was headed for a showdown in Chicago, Mel Weiss and Bill Lerach were experiencing their own foreboding. "We do not want to get into a jury trial," Weiss had more or less castigated his junior partner during one of their daily strategy phone sessions. "We cannot afford to lose this. Get us out."

But there was no way.

> • >

JUST WEEKS EARLIER, on January 15, 1998, with Janet Mangini standing beside him, Representative Henry Waxman, a California Democrat, held a press conference in Washington. Holding sheaves of documents before television cameras, Waxman said, "Our worst fears about what the tobacco companies might be doing to get kids to smoke were justified."

Mangini, Pat Coughlin, Bill Lerach, and the legal team from tiny Bushnell, Caplan & Fielding had imposed their demands on giant R.J. Reynolds. As a trial date had approached during the summer of the preceding year, R.J. Reynolds CEO Steve Goldstone (the same lawyer who had been sent packing from the Nucorp case) caved under mounting pressure. But if the company wanted to settle, it would have to do much more than make Joe Camel go away. It would have to release to the public its previously secret documents detailing studies about youth smoking and its campaign to target youth smoking. This it consented to do. The company also agreed to spend $10 million in California to educate young people on the health hazards of smoking.

That sounded like a lot of money, but by way of comparison, when the accounts were finally settled, Milberg Weiss would end up expending more than 75,000 attorney hours and nearly $30 million on the case. Henry Waxman, noting that he didn't use the term lightly, had publicly called Pat Coughlin—along with Mangini, Jon Cuneo, and Louise Renne—a "hero."

Coughlin had committed six years, obsessed night and day, and turned a lawsuit into a landmark cause. Yes, there was glory, as Lerach had predicted. Still, Coughlin knew, as did his colleagues in the firm, that glory was something you had to be able to afford to pursue. At times like these the tension was palpable between the Milberg Weiss partners' idealism—using the law for justice—and their desire to use torts as a means to obtain enormous wealth. Still, Coughlin had brought honor to the firm at a time when that was exactly what it needed. How could anybody accuse Milberg Weiss of being money-grubbing scumbags, as some were fond of labeling them, when he and his team had performed such a huge community service?

If they were to take a hit from the New York partners for spending so much time for a relatively small reward, so be it, Lerach told Coughlin. If it meant breaking up the firm, Lerach ruminated to himself, maybe the path was revealing itself.

> • >

IRRESPECTIVE OF JOE CAMEL, Alan Schulman was still receiving outsize bills from John Torkelsen, and Lerach was still justifying them. The coup de grâce, at least as far as Schulman was concerned, had occurred at the end of 1997. The firm's partners, Lerach and Schulman among them, had been hearing Torkelsen complain that he owed $6 million to the IRS, despite the millions he had been receiving from Milberg Weiss. What's more, PNC, Torkelsen's New Jersey bank, had contacted Milberg Weiss to report that Torkelsen was arrears to the tune of $5 million in bank loans—and had pledged as collateral $10 million in receivables from at least fifty Milberg cases that had not yet been decided. The bank had one question: was Milberg Weiss standing behind the money? Mel Weiss and Dave Bershad were stunned. They were about to receive an even bigger shock. The bank was in possession of sign-offs from Milberg Weiss indicating that when Torkelsen offered a Milberg receivable as collateral, he was able to furnish bills the firm confirmed it had received. Over his repeated objections, Schulman told Mel Weiss, Lerach had personally approved Torkelsen's invoices.

The subsequent phone conversation between Weiss and Lerach was predictably taut. "Dave [Bershad] and I have decided to cut him [Torkelsen] off. You are not to hire him on any future cases," Weiss demanded, barely audible, trying to control his rage.

Lerach tried to defend his friend.

Weiss wouldn't hear of it. Then his voice turned even more ominous. "There are people at the firm who want you out," he told his protégé. "They think you are drawing too much attention to yourself and therefore to us. They think you are destroying everything we've built. How can I defend this?"

"Because I bring this firm more money than all the others combined," Lerach replied. "Because you cannot afford to lose me."

Months later Lerach's challenge was put to the test. "Either he goes or I go," Schulman said, giving Weiss a simple ultimatum.

Over the next several weeks Mel Weiss seemed to turn noticeably inward, his appearance even more sullen, and his eyes more downcast than usual. Some blamed the upcoming Lexecon lawsuit. Others knew the squeeze that his two warring San Diego partners had put him in.

Just days before the firm's annual executive committee meeting, Weiss called Bershad into his office. "Dave, I can't do this," he sighed, knowing his decision would cost him an able litigator in Schulman's exit.

> • >

ELEVEN YEARS NEARLY TO the day had passed since Bill Lerach last faced a jury. Now, late in the morning of March 18, 1999, in a Chicago federal courtroom before four women and five men, he was being asked questions like "Do you consider yourself a vengeful man?" and "Is 'little fucker' a term you use?" Even: "How much money did you earn in 1992?" A deal had been proffered at the last minute to avoid such questioning. It was his idea. Milberg Weiss would contribute $10 million to the University of Chicago's School of Law in Fischel's name if he would drop the lawsuit. Fischel flatly refused.

Thirteen days earlier the case of *Lexecon v. Milberg Weiss Bershad Hynes and Lerach* had begun in Judge Zagel's courtroom, with opening arguments signaling that the jury was in for a fierce and nasty show. Alan Salpeter, representing Daniel Fischel and Lexecon, started by telling the jury he would present evidence that Bill Lerach and Mel Weiss had not only sued Fischel and Lexecon under false pretenses in the Lincoln case but had threatened Fischel both personally and professionally. Citing the Nucorp case, Salpeter related that Lerach had been gloating, only hours prior to the jury verdict against the plaintiffs. "Milberg couldn't defeat Dan Fischel in a fair debate in the courtroom," Salpeter told the jury, "so they plotted to put him and his firm out of business."

In short, Salpeter said, this case "is about a vendetta. It's about revenge; it's about greed, it's about lawyers who abused the legal system to line their own pockets, it's about lawyers acting above the law to destroy my client."

His colleague, Mark C. Hansen, went even further, accusing Lerach and Weiss of lying and destroying and concealing evidence.

In his defense of Lerach and Weiss, Jerold Solovy rephrased a firm memo calling Fischel a "money-hungry, reprehensible slob," saying instead: "I would call him a very neat, slick, greedy, avaricious person who ought to attend to his duties at the University of Chicago and not intrude upon this courtroom." While conceding that the Milberg Weiss lawyers had used coarse language in conjunction with Fischel's name, Solovy contended that in the rough-and-tumble world of litigation, epithets were not uncommon. Precluded by the judge's pretrial ruling from showing evidence connecting Lexecon to Charles Keating—"the greatest perversion of justice," Solovy would complain aloud he could only tell the jury that he would prove that at one time Milberg Weiss lawyers had good reason to include Lexecon among the defendants.

Fischel appeared first, taking the stand shortly after ten A.M. on March 9. Displaying a series of charts, he traced a sudden and then steady decline in Lexecon earnings from the time of its inclusion in the Lincoln lawsuit and beyond. Profits dropped from $17 million in 1990 to approximately $10 million in 1991, when Lexecon was first named as a defendant, he testified. Then profits continued to drop with fewer referrals and less business. As a result, he calculated a deflated price of $63 million that Lexecon finally sold for on December 31, 1998. He did not tell the jury that the purchaser was his old friend and convicted felon Michael Milken or that he had authored an apologia for Milken in 1995 entitled *Payback: The Conspiracy to Destroy Michael Milken and His Financial Revolution.*

Salpeter directed Fischel to recall Milberg Weiss attorney Pat Coughlin's attempt to discredit him with the trial judge. "After the Apple trial in 1991, California law firms weren't interested in hiring us anymore," Fischel told the jury. "They stopped us in our tracks, they prevented us from growing in terms of profits as well as revenues, but they profited tremendously during that same period."

In two days on the witness stand, Fischel wove a compelling narrative that withstood withering (and mostly overturned) objections from Solovy, as well as aggressive cross-examination from Ronald L. Marmer, Solovy's partner in the Jenner & Block law firm.

Lerach had seen this movie before. To him, it was like a recurring anxiety dream, a nightmare in which you're in a swimming pool and you can't move, or you are being chased and your legs are too sluggish to respond. In this case, it was Lerach's tongue that couldn't function. He was trapped at the defendant's table, forced to watch silently as Fischel gave answers that Lerach knew were coming, answers that in his mind distorted reality, the sort of answers that Fischel had given to cover the tracks of bandits such as Charlie Keating and Michael Milken.

Would the jury see through it? Here he was in Chicago, Dan Fischel's town, in front of a judge known well to Fischel's lawyer, before a jury of stolid midwesterners. He could only fear the worst. To Lerach, it was all a reprise of Fischel's inscrutable performance under his own questioning during the Nucorp trial. "Dan Fischel could look at a rainstorm and tell you how bright and sunny the day was and do it with a straight face," Lerach told Mel Weiss, who was less than delighted to have already suffered a grilling of his own on the witness stand.

Now came Lerach's turn in the witness box, his first challenge being to keep his rage and indignation in check as he faced the most humiliating experience of his legal career.

Mark Hansen, Salpeter's aggressive law partner, asked the opening question: "You admit, do you not, Mr. Lerach, that you have in the past threatened to drive companies into bankruptcy in the course of your work?"

"Yes," he admitted.

Not missing a beat, Hansen then asked: "Mr. Lerach, have you said publicly, sir, that you believe a class action lawyer on the plaintiffs' side should have a certain element of 'irrationality' in his makeup?"

Lerach equivocated: "I don't know if I said it publicly, but I think I've said it."

Hansen asked him to define *irrationality*.

Lerach appeared to think about his answer before saying: "Unpredictability as to whether or not you will or will not go to trial or you will or will not do something else . . ."

"A tactic to induce fear in the people you sue?" Hansen asked, keeping up the attack.

"Lawyers representing clients are required to zealously advance their interests," Lerach tried to explain. "You do that in a whole myriad of ways: factually, legally, dealing with your adversaries, and by the way, I mean lawyers on the other side. Litigation has a psychological aspect to it, Mr. Hansen." He was being painted as a brute, a monster, he thought to himself. Hell, Charlie Keating was a brute. Joe Camel was a monster.

"Were you trying to induce fear in a man by the name of Al Shugart in the 1980s, Mr. Lerach?" Hansen asked.

Lerach could not contain a chuckle, recalling the one CEO he personally despised, the one who mounted a media campaign against him and whom he had sued numerous times.

"Is there something amusing in your memory with respect to Mr. Shugart?" Hansen wanted to know.

Of course there was. There was the business card he'd sent the Seagate chief, after he'd sued him and won millions, telling him he could expect more lawsuits. But Lerach couldn't say that.

"It's a serious matter, isn't it, Mr. Lerach, to be sued for substantial damages?" Hansen asked.

Lerach, now a defendant, feigned amusement at the irony: "You telling me?"

Hansen, knowing he had Lerach on the ropes, moved back in. "Mr. Lerach, you wouldn't say to me or to anybody in this courtroom that the prospect of being sued for millions of dollars is a laughing matter, would you?"

Lerach glanced at the plaintiffs' table and thought he detected a tight smile emerging from Fischel. "It's not a laughing matter," he conceded.

After spending another twenty minutes reviewing Lerach's legal pursuits against Shugart, Hansen asked Lerach to explain himself for having told a reporter, "I have the greatest practice in the world, I have no clients." Before Lerach could formulate an answer, Hansen asked if he had been misquoted.

"I spoke the words, not in the context that they were published . . . ," Lerach tried to explain.

"Well, you spoke the words," Hansen insisted. Lerach repeated his previous answer. Again, Hansen asked him if he'd been misquoted.

"I was not misquoted—I mean I said that in substance. I don't know if every single word is right, but I said that in substance, but not in the context in which it was quoted."

Hansen looked confused, but only for effect. Judging from the looks on the faces of the jurors, he had succeeded.

This whole trial was out of context, Lerach thought. *Fischel should be answering for the wave of frauds sweeping through this economy. I should not be answering for a few curse words. Of course I wanted to put him out of business. The entire intellectually bankrupt University of Chicago "economic theory of law" should be exposed.*

Suddenly, Hansen asked Lerach: "Do you have any hostility with a lawyer by the name of Stuart Kadison?"

Lerach blanched. "I wouldn't say hostility."

Turning to the jury, Hansen then repeated the infamous elevator incident during the Nucorp trial. "Well, how about this as an example. Did you follow him into an elevator one day and say: 'This is going to be an ignominious end to your mediocre career'?"

Lerach straightened in his chair. "I don't think I was quite that colorful."

"Did you say that or did you not say that, Mr. Lerach?" snapped Hansen, pivoting back on the witness.

"I said something to him about if he lost the case it might be the end of his career," Lerach replied.

"I'm asking you very specifically, very specific words. Did you say to Mr. Kadison: 'I'm going to put an ignominious end to your mediocre career'?"

Solovy objected and was overruled.

"I don't think I said those exact words," Lerach said, barely audible.

"Did you refuse to shake Mr. Kadison's hand at the conclusion of the trial?" Hansen then asked.

"Refuse? No." Lerach answered.

"Did you shake his hand?" Hansen continued.

"That's true, I did not," Lerach conceded. (Earlier, Kadison had testified that in all his fifty years of practicing law, this had been the first time an opposing counsel had declined to shake hands.)

Elsewhere in the courtroom some lawyers took delight in witnessing Lerach's flogging. Others at the firm, Mel Weiss foremost among them, sorely wished that they had been able to avoid this humiliation.

Hansen sustained his attack: "Mr. Lerach, were you angry when the jury came back for the defendants in Nucorp?"

Lerach glared at him. "No."

"Was your face red?" the defense lawyer needled.

"I think my face is always red. Probably got a little redder," Lerach answered.

"It got a little redder during your examination here?" Hansen asked, once again mocking Lerach before the jury.

"Look, I'm taking my blood pressure medicine," Lerach mumbled. "I don't know what I can tell you."

Substantive questions followed. Lerach was compelled to admit that follow-up questions with jurors in the Nucorp trial indicated that they had been influenced by Fischel's testimony.

Hansen then turned to the infamous memo Lerach had authored, construed by many who'd read it to be an attack on jurors. "Mr. Lerach, I'm asking you if someone's sense of class is the most—single most important factor—in deciding a person's attitude toward a case?" Hansen insisted.

Lerach started to explain haltingly: "It says, in other words, and then explains, I thought that—"

Hansen interrupted: "Mr. Lerach, can you answer my question, sir? Do you think class determines people's reaction to cases?"

Lerach stammered: "I thought it was as I said there, an important factor, single most important factor."

Reading from an exhibit, Hansen continued: "Second, you write: 'In other words, conservative, sixty-year-old Republicans are probably so devoted to the system and so wedded to the idea that each person is responsible for what happens to him in his own life that this bias cannot be overcome even though there may be other factors which they have in com-

mon with the claimants in a given case, i.e., they are savers and investors.'"
Hansen put down the exhibit. "Was that your considered view?"

Lerach answered that it was extrapolated from interviewing jurors.

"Mr. Lerach, are you telling us you're simply parroting what a juror told
you? Did a juror tell you that?" And he repeated what he'd just read and
asked again: "Was that something a juror told you?"

"Absolutely not," Lerach replied. "This is a conclusion I reached pro-
cessing and synthesizing the juror interviews that I had done. So that was a
conclusion I reached based on that."

Hansen was satisfied with the path his questions had provided for the
jury. But he had one more line of questioning: "Mr. Lerach, isn't it true you
were just upset about losing the case, and therefore, you were lashing out at
people who you thought had ruled against you?"

Lerach answered "No," but by that time jurors were beginning to find
his answers defensive and predictable. And as Hansen continued to hammer at Lerach's state of mind following the stinging Nucorp defeat, it became apparent to all in the room that no matter how the subsequent
answers were parsed, the same anger Bill Lerach had directed at jurors who
had ruled against him was also aimed at Daniel Fischel, the expert witness
who had turned those jurors in favor of the Nucorp defendants.

The next day the battering continued. And this time the defendant and
his firm would be embarrassed financially. The discovery process that
lawyers for Milberg Weiss, Lerach in particular, had used so ruthlessly and
effectively in forcing corporate defendants to settle rather than risk public
exposure was now being turned against them.

"Didn't you tell *Buzz* magazine, Mr. Lerach, quote: 'I make a shit load
of money'?" Lerach denied making the comment, although Hansen quickly
established that the comment had been made, not to *Buzz* magazine but to
Upside magazine. Fischel's lawyer was laying a foundation for asking Lerach
about his personal income and the income of Milberg Weiss, information
that Mel Weiss had always jealously guarded. Prompted by a chart Hansen
had erected near him, Lerach conceded that his pretax income for 1988, the
year of the Nucorp case, was $2.3 million. Was he worried that his share

would diminish if he kept losing cases? Lerach refuted this inference, saying that the following year he earned around $6.5 million.

"Now," Hansen continued, "the firm profit was approximately thirty-five million, four-hundred-sixty-nine thousand, three-hundred-ninety-nine dollars?" Lerach confirmed the number. Looking on, Mel Weiss was seething.

Following the numbers on the exhibit, which Lerach thought looked eerily similar to the charts he himself often used as evidence, Hansen covered a timeline from 1990 through 1997, showing the firm profit rising to $46 million and Lerach's share rising by 33 percent to $9,399,630 in 1992. Jumping to 1993, the chart showed Lerach earning $13,647,630, with his 1994 pretax income rising to $16,070,091 the following year, nearly matching that of Mel Weiss; the firm's profits exceeded $100 million.

"So, over this period after 1990 when the racketeering lawsuit [against Fischel] was tendered to the court, you increased your percentage ownership in the Milberg firm to the point where you reached the same level as Mr. Weiss, correct?"

There was no denying the numbers on the charts. They had come from Milberg Weiss's own financials, which the firm had been compelled by court order to furnish the plaintiffs. Still, trying a whole case over the disparity of relative incomes was tenuous, Lerach thought. But Hansen and Salpeter were about to take other avenues.

"Do you recall prior to March 26, 1990, Mr. Lerach, whether anybody from your law firm prepared a memorandum evaluating whether there was a valid basis for pursuing a racketeering lawsuit or any other kind of lawsuit against Lexecon or Dan Fischel?" Hansen asked.

Lerach hesitated before answering: "We prepared a fifth amended complaint. I think that is responsive."

Hansen moved to strike the answer. "Can you answer my question, Mr. Lerach?"

Again Lerach hesitated, couching his answer: "Is there a freestanding memo . . . ?"

"Mr. Lerach!" Hansen cut him off.

"Repeat the question then," Lerach requested.

This drew Hansen's ire: "If you don't understand my question, please tell me. Please don't rephrase my question. I understand you're a trial lawyer, sir. I understand that you're used to doing the questioning. I would appreciate if you would simply answer my question or tell me you don't understand it."

Solovy intervened, objecting to Hansen's badgering. The judge sustained but admonished the witness: "Mr. Lerach, one of the problems when you are a lawyer and you get on the witness stand is you think like a lawyer, not like a witness. Mr. Solovy is a very fine lawyer. He will do the lawyering. You do the witnessing."

Lerach asked for the question to be repeated, knowing full well what Hansen was attempting to compel him to disclose. Was there a single memorandum evaluating a basis for suing Fischel?

"No single memorandum," said the witness.

Already knowing the answer, Hansen then asked: "Can you point us to any handwritten notes taken by you or any of your attorneys prior to March 26, 1990, analyzing the basis for your claim against Dan Fischel or Lexecon?"

Lerach appeared to probe his own memory, finally saying: "There were such notes, no doubt, but I do not believe they exist any longer."

"You can't show these notes to the jury, can you?" Hansen said, barely able to contain his relish.

"Of course not," Lerach fairly snapped. "They're gone."

Sensing he was firmly perched on high ground, Hansen asked for and was granted a lunch break. When they resumed, Hansen asked Lerach if he or his attorneys had talked to any federal regulators whom the plaintiffs' lawyers alleged had been defrauded by Fischel and Lexecon through reports they wrote that were favorable to Lincoln and Charles Keating. Lerach admitted none had been interviewed.

Hansen then produced an analysis of Lincoln's operations and the financial performance report that Lexecon had prepared for Lincoln that was submitted to the Federal Home Loan Bank Board.

"My question, Mr. Lerach, is did you—before filing your racketeering lawsuit on March 26, 1990—determine what individuals, what human beings had written this report?"

Lerach answered haltingly: "The people at Lexecon, the human beings that worked at Lexecon had clearly written the report, unless it was forged by someone else."

"Which human beings at Lexecon, Mr. Lerach?"

"Certainly, Mr. Fischel," the witness replied.

"Mr. Lerach, show us where in that report there is any indication that Mr. Fischel wrote that report."

Lerach didn't waste time; he knew what he must say: "His name is not on the report. It's just submitted by Lexecon Inc."

Later Hansen would put his attack into context, asking Lerach: "Have you ever stated publicly: 'Nobody has evidence when they file a lawsuit'? Have you stated those words publicly?"

Lerach turned red again. "I made that statement."

The time had arrived to further impeach Lerach with his own words. "Have you ever used the term 'little fucker' in connection with Dan Fischel?"

"I may have," Lerach answered, explaining that at one point profanity was used in describing most if not all the defendants in the Lincoln case. Asked if he referred to Fischel directly and specifically, if he had said, "I want to put that little fucker out of business," Lerach denied doing so with an emphatic "No."

Lerach had spent enough time in court to know how this was playing with the jury. His personality was on trial, rather than Dan Fischel's cold-hearted theories of "economic law"—and yes, it was clear even to himself that his personality had some rough edges. He had meant what he said in the witness stand. You had to be tough sometimes in the law. When did that become a crime—when did throwing the f-word around become a tort?

Later that night, after dejectedly walking the few blocks from the federal district courthouse on Dearborn Street to the Intercontinental Hotel on Michigan Avenue in a cold rain, and after a few drinks in the bar, he went to his room and called his wife.

"Star, we are getting killed," he said, adding that "the old-boy Chicago Law School network has the fix in. I'm being humiliated." Then he said something out of character, with a crack in his voice. "It's really depressing."

I can't stand this alone. I'm in a state of collapse. I need you to come." She'd come as soon as she could, she assured him. Lerach soon wished he had not made the call. Although he didn't know it, the worst part of the Lexecon trial was still ahead.

> • >

ON WEDNESDAY AFTERNOON, March 31, Hansen resumed his offensive. He held a powerful weapon. It was a document that Lexecon had submitted to the law firm of Sidley & Austin, which had worked as counsel to Charles Keating in his sparring with the Federal Home Loan Bank Board. Again, Lerach was the object of Hansen's attack.

"Mr. Lerach, you didn't tell this jury, did you, that among the documents in your document depository was a letter that was submitted as a cover letter to this report to the same federal regulators who you allege were misled by Lexecon in which the letter disclosed fully that Lexecon was writing the report and submitting it on behalf of Lincoln Savings and Loan? Exhibit 100 is before you, Mr. Lerach. Take a moment to look at it."

While he did so, Hansen stood back and watched the witness redden once again. That morning Lerach had testified that Lexecon had hidden from the federal regulators the fact that it was working for Lincoln when it submitted its report. Here was a cover letter from Lexecon disclosing that it was submitting the report as an advocate for Lincoln.

"This is the letter that accompanied the report to the FHLBB, correct?" Hansen asked the witness.

"I don't know," Lerach answered. "I haven't seen the memo until today."

Hansen was not deterred. "It's a document that was produced at your depository, wasn't it, Mr. Lerach?"

"I don't know that," Lerach replied. "I haven't seen it."

Hansen directed him to look at production code numbers at the bottom of the document and identify whether the document was, in fact, stamped with a Milberg Weiss depository code.

"Those are numbers that are down there" was all Lerach could muster in his reply.

"So it was just an honest mistake on your part in making that allegation?" Hansen asked.

Solovy tried to object, accusing Hansen of being argumentative. But Lerach answered anyway: "All I can tell you is I did not have this letter at the time the fifth amended complaint was prepared."

"But the allegation is clearly a mistake, isn't it?" challenged Hansen.

"If I had had this letter, I would have alleged it differently," Lerach sputtered. "I did not have this letter at the time we prepared the fifth amended complaint."

Hansen asked Lerach if he was aware that then–economic consultant Alan Greenspan had given three separate opinions hailing Lincoln's solvency to the FHLBB. "Were you aware, Mr. Lerach, that Mr. Greenspan had represented to the Federal Home Loan Bank Board that in his opinion Lincoln had, through skill and expertise, transformed itself into a financially strong institution that presents no foreseeable risk to the Federal Savings and Loan Insurance Corporation?"

"I don't know whether I knew he had said that at the time," Lerach answered.

"Were you aware of that opinion at the time you sued Lexecon and Daniel Fischel as racketeers for a billion dollars in the Lincoln case?" Hansen asked.

"I don't know whether I was or not," Lerach answered.

Finally, Hansen shut the door, "You didn't sue Mr. Greenspan, did you?"

"No, we did not sue Alan Greenspan," Lerach's answer faded with the end of the day. He returned to the defense table, slumped into his chair, turned to Solovy, and said: "I was up there for target practice."

> • >

ON SUNDAY, APRIL 4, Alan Salpeter was home composing his closing arguments when his phone rang. On the other end was Mike Cypers, an attorney with the Los Angeles firm of Alschuler, Grossman, Stein & Kahan. He and Salpeter had worked as cocounsel on several cases, becoming friends. Cypers had been following the Lexecon case and had a question: "Would it help if a witness came forward and said he'd attended that Apple Computer party when the Milberg guys were high-fiving and bragging about putting Fischel out of business?"

"Peel me off the ceiling," Salpeter told his friend.

Cypers told Salpeter that Mike Sherman, one of the Alschuler lawyers, had previously worked in the San Diego office of Barrack, Rodos & Bacine, a firm assisting Milberg Weiss on the Lincoln lawsuit. As Cypers explained, the most recent issue of the *National Law Journal* carried an account of the Lexecon trial, noting how contentious and even coarse it had been. The allegations against Lerach and his motivations for suing Dan Fischel in the Lincoln case, along with Lerach's strong denials of stating publicly that he wanted to put Fischel out of business, had caught Sherman's attention.

He had attended the Milberg Weiss victory party at the Omni Hotel. More than once he had heard Dan Fischel's name raised in reference to Apple's defense. And more than once, he'd heard "that little fucker" and "he's dead as a witness . . . he's out of business," raised by more than one Milberg partner, including Lerach. What he had read of Lerach's quotes in the *National Law Journal* did not square with what he knew.

Sherman's account had reached Cypers, who was appalled. Maybe Salpeter would like to hear more from Sherman. Salpeter called him immediately, asked Sherman to relate what he had overheard at the Milberg Weiss party, and inquired if he would be willing to repeat it for the judge and jury.

"No. I've got to work with these guys," the San Diego lawyer replied.

"Would you duck a subpoena?" Salpeter persisted.

Realizing that he could be compelled to testify, Sherman said he would sit still for a deposition, but that it must stipulate that he was an unwilling witness. Salpeter said he'd have an attorney in San Diego within a day or so. He then called Hansen and told his trial colleague: "We're going to turn Lerach into Pinocchio."

Salpeter contacted Judge Zagel and told him he and Hansen wanted to introduce new evidence. On April 8, with the jury seated, Salpeter rose and said: "Your honor, we would like to call a rebuttal witness . . . Can we douse the lights?" Video monitors were placed before the jury but stationed in position for all in the courtroom to see. The lights went down, and the jury saw Michael Sherman, under deposition, repeating the words "that little fucker is dead." And telling the jury he had heard it more than once from several Milberg Weiss attorneys but specifically from Lerach.

When the lights came up, Salpeter faced the audience and announced: "That's all we have, your honor. We are ready for closing arguments." At the defense table Jerold Solovy was speechless, and Bill Lerach boiling.

> • >

CLOSING ARGUMENTS COMMENCED ON April 9. Alan Salpeter led off by telling the jury that he believed he and Hansen had delivered on the promise they had made when the trial began twenty-one days earlier. They had demonstrated that Milberg Weiss had an ulterior motive in suing Lexecon, which was to drive Dan Fischel out of business, and that they acted on this plan and had done actual financial harm to him and Lexecon.

He reminded the jurors of the testimony of those who participated in the Nucorp case, including David Gold and Stuart Kadison, ardent opponents who agreed that following the Nucorp loss Lerach had been "livid, furious, and out of control." Digressing momentarily, Salpeter said that if the Lexecon case were a chapter in a book, he might entitle it "Lawyers Above the Law." Then he deferred to Kadison, "Elder gentleman, lawyer for fifty years, from Los Angeles. I think I like his title better. 'Shabby Business.'

"These are people who have no respect for the very legal system that pays them millions and millions of dollars," he added. "They don't respect judges, they don't respect juries, they don't respect their clients. All they respect is money."

Pointing to Lerach, Salpeter continued his diatribe: "One of his favorite sayings is: 'Revenge is a dish best served cold.' He compares himself to a bounty hunter. Can you imagine that, a lawyer who compares himself to somebody who hunts people down for money? He likened himself to a snake. No wonder lawyers have a bad name in our society.'"

Once more, Salpeter guided the jury through Lexecon's yearly drop in revenues, attributing this harm to Lerach's lawsuit against his client and referring to the charts they had seen previously. "Lexecon was sold for $63 million. It should have been sold for $152 million," he said, giving the jury not-so-subtle hints on calculating damages.

Solovy followed, trying his best to placate the jury by telling them that Lerach, his client, had admitted that the scalding memo he wrote castigating jurors was "dumb." The thrust of his closing argument was this: "Milberg Weiss had a duty to their clients. And their primary purpose was not to hurt Fischel and Lexecon. Their primary purpose was to help the 23,000 people they represented." In a rambling discourse lasting forty minutes, he reconnected Lexecon to Lincoln Savings and Loan, trying to justify the Milberg lawsuit naming Fischel's firm as a defendant. "This institution was in the tank. And that's why the government wanted to shut them down. And that's why Lincoln was paying Mr. Fischel and Lexecon $1.1 million to stop that from happening.

"And if this were a case about vendetta and revenge, look over there [at the plaintiffs' table], ladies and gentlemen of the jury. There is the vendetta and revenge . . . They cannot let go of what happened nine years ago. Milberg defendants are sitting here in the courtroom, their income being discussed publicly, et cetera. So where is the vendetta coming from? You decide that."

Hansen was invited to make final arguments. Since Salpeter had basically covered the burden that the plaintiffs' lawyers were under to make their case, he reverted to what he had already employed—an attack on Lerach. Once again he cited Fischel's testimony in the Nucorp case and Lerach's presumed emotional extrapolation of the jury's reaction. "This is the same Mr. Lerach who comes into this court and says 'I was calm as a cucumber after Nucorp . . . As for the memo I wrote, a calm memo saying all the awful things about women and teachers.' We are not saying Mr. Lerach really believes those things. I don't think the evidence shows that he does.

We're saying Mr. Lerach was hot-headed, and impetuous, and very unhappy about Nucorp."

Hansen continued: "And you should read that memo, because he gives an explanation for it that shows you just how untruthful he was on this witness stand, among lots of other things. He said 'I was writing that memo as an exercise in self-criticism.' Try and read that memo as an exercise in self-criticism. 'Gee, what a mistake I made in not realizing jurors are idiots. Gee, what a mistake I made in not realizing that fat people aren't happy-go-lucky. How wrong of me not to understand that women can't be persuaded. How foolish of me not to realize that jurors forget up to eighty-five percent of what they hear.' That's not self-criticism. That shows you what kind of story Mr. Lerach tells on the witness stand."

At the defense table both Lerach and Solovy tensed. Objections were not allowed in final arguments. By now Star had returned home and Lerach was glad she was gone.

Banging the drum one last time, Hansen said: "Ladies and gentlemen, you will see the evidence is before you to prove that the only motive that Milberg had in suing Lexecon and Fischel was to hurt them and put them out of business and make more money. They acted more like mobsters than like lawyers. They effectively put out a contract on Dan Fischel."

By three P.M. Judge Zagel had completed jury instructions, and the panel filed out to choose a foreman and begin deliberations. Within hours came a request. Could the jury review the reports Lexecon had done on behalf of Keating and Lincoln? Lerach was elated to hear this, as was Solovy. Did it mean they were accepting the defense argument and making the link between Lexecon and Lincoln? "Oh shit," Salpeter remembered saying. Neither side knew at the moment that the jury had only one question. Did Daniel Fischel's name appear on the Lexecon reports that went to the FHLBB on behalf of Lincoln? The answer was as testified to—no, it did not.

At three P.M. Monday, April 12, the jury returned to the courtroom. Lerach smiled confidently while the two plaintiff's attorneys sat stone-faced, as did their client. Then came the announcement. The jury had found for the plaintiff and determined that $45 million in compensatory damages should be awarded the consulting firm. For the second time in a decade Lerach shook his head in horror and disbelief at a jury verdict against him. Nor was this to be the jury's final word. They would continue to deliberate punitive damages. Judge Zagel ordered a hearing to begin the following morning.

This set off a frenzy that lasted well into the night. Although Salpeter told the judge he planned on calling only three witnesses—Mel Weiss, Bill Lerach, and Len Simon, whose initial oversight in failing to secure a release had put the firm at risk in the first place—he and Hansen returned to their offices and began drafting their arguments for punitive damages. In this phase, they could expose the net worth of the defendants, not just what had been exposed during the trial examination but the value of their homes, their personal property such as art, and their investments. It could also be revealed that Weiss, an inveterate gambler, had taken home considerable winnings from casinos in the Bahamas over the years. Salpeter decided to go for another $45 million.

About two A.M. the lawyers received a call from one of their colleagues. Settlement talks were in the works. Robert A. Helman, the recently retired chairman of Mayer Brown, whom Salpeter had suggested oversee any negotiations, was meeting with Milberg partners Pat Hynes and Dave Bershad. No matter; settlement talks were one thing, preparing for a hearing was another. Hansen and Salpeter continued working throughout the night. When the two Mayer Brown attorneys walked into court at eight thirty the following morning, Fischel was already at the plaintiffs' table. Salpeter noticed Pat Hynes at the door to the courtroom. Like them, she looked like she had been working through the night. Hynes asked to speak with Hansen, while Salpeter took his seat next to Fischel.

Within minutes Hansen joined them. "They want to settle the whole thing for $50 million," Hansen reported. Fischel balked. Hansen leaned into Salpeter, saying quietly but firmly, "Talk to him."

Salpeter asked Fischel to join him in the hall. "Dan, get real. You've already got $45 million out of the jury. Now you've got another $5 million out of these guys."

Fischel cracked a smile. "Are you telling me I should do it?" he asked. Salpeter shook his head yes.

"All right, but I want the money today, in cash, all of it," Fischel said. Salpeter gulped and Fischel said: "Otherwise we get on with the hearing."

When Judge Zagel entered, Salpeter rose and announced a settlement had been reached. He conveyed the terms, watching the reactions of Lerach and Hynes, as they found themselves on the losing end of the biggest abuse-of-power verdict and settlement in history. And now Salpeter was telling them the money had to be wired to a Lexecon account by five P.M. He saw what he expected to see—utter shock on their faces. Adding to it, Judge Zagel said he would send the jury home, adding, as if Fischel's demand were the most reasonable thing in the world, that if the money had not been transferred by five P.M., and if he had to preside over a punitive damages hearing, he would triple the penalty.

As they adjourned, testy words were exchanged among the Milberg Weiss lawyers. They hadn't protected themselves from a lawsuit that never should have been filed. They had upped the settlement offer to $20 million, but Fischel had refused because Milberg Weiss refused to admit misconduct. Now they needed $50 million quick, and the firm had only $5 million in liability insurance. The rest would have to come from the partners themselves.

Lerach called home. Unable to disguise his dismay, he told Star: "We got whacked for $50 million," and directed her to sell bonds and other securities—empty the portfolio. How much? He didn't know exactly, "just sell." Within hours, she had $18 million ready to wire to Chicago. Mel Weiss had already contacted Dave Bershad. How much could the firm muster? Not enough to meet the obligation. He directed Bershad to get on the phone to the banks and any lenders he could think of for short-term borrowing.

Just past noon the wire transfers began flowing to Chicago, from San Diego, from Milberg Weiss accounts in New York, and from several New York banks. Before four P.M. Eastern Time, $50 million was settled in a bank account set up on behalf of Lexecon and Daniel Fischel.

By the end of that day Mel Weiss had scheduled a crisis meeting with his partners. Lerach could return to San Diego; what had to be done could be done by teleconference. But he wanted Lerach available, as well as Len Simon. And in New York he wanted Pat Hynes, David Bershad, and Steve Schulman present at the meeting. Everyone on the list knew the agenda— a letting of blood and money.

> • > • • > • >

FRAUD BY HINDSIGHT

Two and a half months after the *Lexecon* verdict, a three-judge panel in the Ninth Circuit issued a 2–1 decision in the Silicon Graphics case. The July 2, 1999, opinion, written by Judge Sneed, was a hammer blow that threatened to cost Milberg Weiss a lot more than the $50 million it had forked over to Fischel and Lexecon.

Sneed, with the concurrence of a federal district judge who had been assigned to the panel temporarily, rejected the plaintiffs' appeal—and put the West Coast circuit at odds with the Second Circuit Court of Appeals, which had reached a decidedly different conclusion in a New York case. Upholding Judge Fern Smith's interpretation of the 1995 Private Securities Litigation Reform Act, Sneed wrote: "Congress intended to elevate the pleading requirements above the [Second Circuit] standard requiring plaintiffs merely to provide facts showing simple recklessness or a motive to commit fraud and an opportunity to do so . . . Accordingly, we hold that a heightened form of recklessness, *i.e.*, deliberate or conscious recklessness, at a minimum, is required to establish a strong inference of intent."

In Sneed's telling, the "Get Lerach Act" had indeed gotten Lerach—as well as taken care of the Milberg Weiss class action model, and any other plaintiffs' attorney who emulated it. Sneed's prose was wordy and at times dense, and his logic was not always easy to follow. But his conclusion was unmistakable: Congress had simply outlawed Milberg Weiss's bread-and-butter style of litigation.

"[Plaintiff's] assertions in the complaint differ very little from the conjectures of many concerned and interested investors," Sneed wrote.

> At one time, an immensely successful company and its officers state publicly that the company will continue to succeed. The officers then sell a noticeable quantity of shares at a considerable profit. Shortly thereafter, the company takes a turn for the worse and suddenly, suspicion abounds . . . In the absence of greater particularity and more incriminating facts, we have no way of distinguishing [these] allegations from the countless "fishing expeditions" which the PSLRA was designed to deter. Congress enacted the PSLRA to put an end to the practice of pleading "fraud by hindsight."

Bill Lerach believed that there was plenty of evidence of fraud right in front of the judges' noses. He had alleged in the complaint that every bit of the negative news that Silicon Graphics had made public on January 17, 1996, had been known to its officers much earlier, meaning that SGI had been making public representations it knew to be false. The support for that contention was a standard Milberg Weiss paragraph—formulated *after* passage of the PSLRA—stating that this assertion was "based upon the investigation of their [plaintiffs'] counsel, which included a review of SGI's SEC filings, securities analysts reports and advisories about the company, press releases issued by the company, media reports about the company and discussions with consultants."

Sneed was dismissive of that assertion. Echoing the language of the trial judge, he referred to it as the "boilerplate section" of the Lerach-drafted complaint and maintained that it was an insufficient basis for a fraud allegation because it failed to aver "with particularity all facts on which [the plaintiff's] belief is formed."

Sneed's reading of the new law, he continued, meant that Lerach's main named plaintiff, Deanna Brody, had not met the threshold required of the 1995 securities law:

> *a plaintiff must provide, in great detail, all the relevant facts forming the basis of her belief. It is not sufficient for a plaintiff's pleadings to set forth a belief that certain unspecified sources will reveal, after appropriate discovery, facts that will validate her claim. In this case, Brody does not include adequate corroborating details. She does not mention, for instance, the sources of her information with respect to the reports, how she learned of the reports, who drafted them, or which officers received them. Nor does she include an adequate description of their contents.*

Of course, as Judge James Browning pointed out in dissent, there was a reason Lerach's complaint lacked the specificity Sneed was demanding: the plaintiffs hadn't been allowed to do any discovery. If Sneed's decision was taken to its logical conclusion, no corporate fraud case would ever be made unless the corporation voluntarily availed plaintiffs' attorneys of incriminating evidence.

"Congress plainly intended the Reform Act to raise the pleading standard . . . but did not intend to restrict the evidentiary bases from which the inference of scienter might be drawn," Judge Browning wrote. "By holding to the contrary, the majority raises the pleading bar higher than that envisioned by Congress, and places the Ninth Circuit at odds with both the Second and Third Circuits."

As far as the technology companies were concerned, this discrepancy worked in their favor—more securities class action suits were filed in the Ninth Circuit than anywhere else. "It's a blockbuster decision," gushed Shirli Weiss, a San Diego litigator who had often represented defendants sued by Lerach. Repeating Sneed's rationale, she added, "The decision requires that plaintiffs state the underlying facts, documents, and sources of information . . . it prevents plaintiffs from alleging fraud by hindsight."

Hindsight, my ass, thought Lerach. This decision all but shut the door to anyone on the outside looking in. The law, as interpreted by Sneed, required plaintiffs to state exactly what they were looking for and why before they could take the crucial next step in discovery. Further, according to Sneed's ruling, the plaintiffs would have to reveal confidential sources, something not specifically called for in the 1995 act. Sneed had turned the 1995 PSLRA into a corporate protective order. Lerach found the opinion so broad, almost punitive, that he wondered whether Judge Sneed had an ulterior motive.

Before long he learned something that only increased his suspicions. On July 20, eighteen days after his devastating defeat, Lerach read in *The Wall Street Journal* an earthshaking announcement by a Silicon Valley giant. A group president from Lucent Technologies, Carly Fiorina, had been named CEO of Hewlett-Packard, making her the highest-ranking—and highest-paid—female executive in the world. It was reported that her compensation package (salary and stock) approached $90 million. Lerach also read with interest about the CEO's previous tenure as an executive at Lucent, a spin-off of AT&T and a company Milberg Weiss had sued successfully for $500 million. There were varying reviews of her performance, including some suggesting that she had been forced out. More to the point, these news reports indicated that her compensation package began in April 1999, four months before she had taken the HP job.

Standing alone, this information would have aroused Lerach only to file it away for a time when HP's financials started to slip. Then he noticed something in her biography that leaped out at him. She was one of three children of Judge Joseph T. Sneed III, a member of the U.S. Court of Appeals for the Ninth Circuit.

Lerach took in a deep breath, contemplating the implications. Here was a person negotiating a landmark payday as head of an industry giant—a company that had filed an amicus brief as an American Electronics client against his plaintiffs in the SGI case—a case her father was hearing. Tracing back, it appeared that Fiorina and HP had been negotiating while her father was deciding the SGI case. "Guess which law firm negotiated her deal—Wilson Sonsini—the same guys who were defending Silicon Graphics," he said aloud. "The law is supposed to protect people from this. Judicial proceedings are supposed to be fair. The law requires a judge to disqualify himself from hearing a case if his impartiality might reasonably be questioned." He could feel his blood pressure rising. "No disclosure was made. Come on! This guy had no business deciding this case."

He shouted for a clerk. Get him the rules on civil procedure governing recusal. It didn't take long. He read it out loud. "The law requires him to disqualify himself . . ." By now a small crowd was gathering inside and outside his office. "And, get this: even an adult child living outside of the judge's home . . . if that child has an interest that could be substantially affected by the outcome of the proceedings . . . This is mandatory. He should have recused himself!"

One of the young attorneys wondered, was this grounds for appeal? Lerach was incredulous that such a foolish question would come from one of his own team. "Of course!" He ordered his troops out and shut the door. Then he called Mel Weiss.

"Here's how we got screwed," he told Weiss. "If I were an appellate court judge hearing arguments in a case where lawyers arguing for the company that had gotten my daughter an $80 million to $90 million package from one of the highest-profile public companies in America, I would be prone to decide the case the way the lawyers wanted me to, my daughter wanted me to, and the company she led wanted me to. That's human nature, right? That's also why we have recusal rules. This is a tainted precedent."

"Are you saying we should go after a judge who has actually been one of the more favorable to us on that bench?" Weiss said. "Or are you practicing some sort of editorial that will have people accusing us of sour grapes?"

"But this is so corrupt," Lerach tried to argue. "The legal system is intrinsically corrupt. Financial interests are so pervasive. They impact everyone, even the judges . . ." He wanted to appeal.

"If we do, we'll trigger a firestorm of resentment from judges," Weiss said firmly. "We can't afford this. We've already brought so much attention on ourselves." Weiss then got quiet. Lerach knew the message implicit in that silence. "Hold your fire."

> • >

THE NEXT MORNING, JULY 21, 1999, more distressing news arrived on Lerach's front stoop. He was reading the *Los Angeles Times* when he saw this headline: "Former Doctor Is Convicted in Art Fraud." Quickly, his eyes advanced through the story:

> A former Beverly Hills ophthalmologist was convicted Tuesday of federal charges that he orchestrated the theft of two paintings from his home to collect an insurance windfall in a case that shocked the nation's art circuit . . . Steven G. Cooperman, 57, who has become notorious as a plaintiff in dozens of insurance and securities lawsuits, sat stone-faced as a judge read the verdicts.

Lerach swallowed hard and read on. "He was free on a $1 million bond late Tuesday, but prosecutors were seeking to increase his bail to $10 million. He faces up to 138 years in prison when he is sentenced October 18."

Lerach didn't have to read any further. The implications were obvious. If ever there was a scoundrel ripe for flipping into a government witness, it was Steven Cooperman. He called New York and delivered the news to Mel Weiss. "When was the last time we paid him?" Lerach asked. Weiss didn't know. He soon found out. The last check—one for $145,305 in the Community Psychiatric Case in California—went out on February 2 of the current year. Too close for comfort, Lerach thought, grateful that he was no longer Cooperman's handler. Then another thought crept into his mind: this was one more wake-up call to revisit separating himself from the firm of Milberg, Weiss, Bershad, Hynes & Lerach.

> • >

STEVEN COOPERMAN, MEANWHILE, had posted a $10 million bond and returned to his Connecticut estate, now frozen with his other assets as Richard Robinson had announced that the government would seek more than $12 million in restitution. Still seething over his fines and conviction, Cooperman added to his legal team Russell Gioiella, a criminal defense lawyer from New York.

Looking at the number of years Cooperman appeared to be facing and the short time until his sentencing, Gioiella asked the legal equivalent of a Hail Mary pass: "Is there anything, anything you might be able to tell the government to help your case?"

There was indeed, Cooperman told him without hesitation.

"It better be good," Gioiella replied. "Because they won't accept peanuts."

Cooperman said it would be good. Could they meet the following day in person? What he had to say, he didn't want to say over the telephone.

> • >

TWO WEEKS LATER, in federal district court in San Jose, California, John Torkelsen stated under penalty of perjury that he had appeared as an expert witness in an earlier securities case, *Provenz et al. v. Miller et al.*, a lawsuit whereby plaintiffs alleged that the defendants had exaggerated sales in order to inflate earnings and influence higher stock prices while selling off their shares. Ironically, the defense had prevailed and Torkelsen had not earned his fee. Nonetheless, he stated under oath that he had appeared for the plaintiffs' attorneys, Milberg Weiss, in the case pursuant to a "non-contingent engagement by the plaintiffs' counsel."

In fact, the opposite agreement was in effect.

Torkelsen by now had become inured to duplicity. Beginning in 1993, when he had gotten into the "independent"-expert-witness-for-hire business, he had submitted more than $60 million in bills to plaintiffs' class action law firms, inflating them by nearly $8 million. Now he was attempting another audacious scam. His investment firm Acorn Technology Fund was raking in millions from the SBA to help start small businesses. In fact, the businesses it was helping were other Torkelsen ventures—SemiSystems and TyreLynx. Still another Torkelsen business, Princeton Technology, was inflating bills to SemiSystems. John Torkelsen's circle of greed was indeed a self-contained loop that curved back into his own bank account. Before his chicanery was discovered, he and his wife and their son Leif Torkelsen fraudulently obtained $32 million in government funds for companies they controlled, funneling at least $5 million to themselves. Torkelsen, his wife, and their son were engaging in the very crimes of self-dealing that he had testified about in court concerning the level of harm caused by securities fraud.

It would take years for the government to catch on. When it did, Torkelsen would be caught in the vise grips of the law—and would pay dearly for his sins. Having already been convicted of driving under the influence three times, divorced by his wife (who turned witness against him), bankrupt and still owing huge back taxes, and facing tax fraud charges, he would become a subject of intense interest for the federal investigators who held his fate in their hands.

Torkelsen didn't hold many cards, but he did hold one: in his possession was a damaging document prosecutors were seeking, the final settlement agreement between Milberg Weiss and Princeton Venture Research, Torkelsen's consulting firm. It codified, at least in the minds of the law firm's partners, their remaining obligations under its contingency agreement with the celebrated expert witness. The document insulated Milberg Weiss from certain monetary demands made by Torkelsen at the same time that it compromised Torkelsen: he had denied, under oath, the main point of the memo—that he was, indeed, paid on a contingency basis for his testimony.* Soon Torkelsen would be confronted by a conflict. Either he would cooperate in a complex probe of fraud on the part of well-known securities lawyers—or spend a long time in prison.

By 1999 the traditional tools of the Milberg Weiss trade—the plaintiffs whom the firm could unleash at a moment's notice, and their referring, intermediary attorneys—were concentrated under the supervision of the New York office, tended to by Dave Bershad, Steve Schulman, and Robert Sugarman. Three plaintiffs had established themselves as the firm's premier

---

* The agreement stated: "No fees or expenses are payable to PVR unless and until and only to the extent or in the amount the court overseeing the firm of Milberg Weiss Bershad Hynes and Lerach in which PVR rendered services to the firm approves and authorizes payment of PVR's fees and expenses, and such order has become final, is not subject to any pending appeal and has not been modified; and the PVR fees and expenses awarded and approved by the court are actually paid to and received by Milberg Weiss Bershad Hynes Lerach."

claimants: Seymour Lazar, through his attorney Paul Selzer of Palm Springs; Howard Vogel, who resided in New Jersey and Florida, through his attorney Gary Lozow of Denver; and Cooperman, now living in Connecticut, through his attorneys James Tierney and Richard Purtich of Los Angeles.

The big three received nearly $12 million over the years, sometimes in large lump-sum payments. A secondary group of premier plaintiffs included Bruce Bjork, Cooperman's brother-in-law; his friends Mel Kinder and Ronald Fischman (Lerach referred to Cooperman, Kinder, and Hirschman as "the Beverly Hills coven"); and Paul Tullman, a former Milberg Weiss partner turned stockbroker, who was supervised and paid by Sugarman. All this was transpiring notwithstanding the fact that the PSLRA had explicitly made such payments illegal. The New York partners had agreed to Bill Lerach's warning delivered in 1996 at the Boulders, but that was an easier admonition to make than to follow. Steven Cooperman, for one, was not someone who would stand idly by while someone shut off the spigot.

There was no civil lawsuit such as Silicon Graphics to adjudicate these payments, no Judge Sneed who could employ legal language to suspend these referral fees simply because they were not part of the public record—not yet, anyway. Out in Los Angeles, however, a painstakingly meticulous federal prosecutor would soon know more about Milberg Weiss's complicated and long-standing system of kickbacks to named plaintiffs than all but a handful of the firm's senior partners.

> • > • • > • >

LET'S MAKE A DEAL

The first signal arrived with what federal prosecutors refer to as a "soft call." It reached assistant U.S. attorney Richard Robinson in Los Angeles in early August of 1999. The caller identified himself as Russell Gioiella, a New York attorney with a client who had recently been convicted of fraud. Robinson didn't recognize the attorney's name, but he knew the drill.

"Would the government be interested in information my client might be willing to offer?" the lawyer wanted to know. The prosecutor played along, steering the conversation in a direction that would compel Gioiella to identify his client. Eventually he disclosed the name. He was representing Steven Cooperman. Robinson winced, even though he'd been half-expecting this call. Cooperman, who was scheduled for sentencing after being convicted of art fraud, was facing ten years in prison. The prosecutor's first thought was that Cooperman was an odious scam artist, hardly credible. Still, he invited Gioiella to continue. And the attorney obliged. If his client was willing to disclose information about another fraud involving millions of dollars, would the government be interested?

Without committing, Robinson asked: "Would you and your client be willing to come to Los Angeles for a meeting?"

Gioiella hesitated, and Robinson guessed he was conferring with Cooperman. Then he heard, "Yes."

> • >

BILL LERACH WEIGHED his options. Contacting Cooperman was out of the question. Besides, the money from the firm had gone to Jim Tierney in the form of attorney referral fees. Nothing illegal about that, at least on the surface. Besides, Dave Bershad had been in charge of the payments. Steve Schulman had been in charge of Cooperman. *Just keep your mouth shut,* Lerach reminded himself. He would do what came easily to him—submerge himself in his work, scouting new cases, and managing them to the brink of trial or settlement. And at the end of each day, he looked forward to filling his Dixie cup with Scotch and driving north to the Tuscan-style villa that he and Star and their son, Dillon, now occupied among equestrian spreads and orange groves in gentrified Rancho Santa Fe. Lerach made a point of arriving in time to patrol the terraced grounds with his dogs, stopping to nip a blossom here and there and making mental notes where to add new citrus or flowering plants, what to remove and where to transfer other vegetation. He loved the lapping sound of the huge Italianate fountain that graced the veranda, and he loved the smell of the blossoms in season. He loved the smooth, shiny black and dark green soapstone Shona art figures, some as high as six feet, imported from Zimbabwe. They lent a fantastic aura to his property.

Just the year before, when Bill Clinton arrived for a fund-raising lunch, the president had been visibly taken with one piece of the African art, a life-size statue of a woman on her knees leaning backward. Without warning, the president strode over to the figure and placed both hands on the object's chest. To the dismay of the agents in his Secret Service detail, not to mention the astonishment of his hosts and their guests—the Monica Lewinsky scandal had broken only weeks earlier—Clinton kept his hand on the statue's breasts, gushing in that famous Arkansas drawl: "This is really, really nice."

For all of that, only one other encounter (until he learned of Cooperman's conviction) had actually unsettled Lerach here in his arboreal enclave.

That was the ubiquitous presence of his neighbor Gerald Parsky. Also an attorney, Parsky had made a fortune as chairman of a Los Angeles–based investment company. He was a prominent California Republican and had served four Republican administrations. Parsky was rumored to be organizing the California effort for the 2000 presidential campaign of Texas governor George W. Bush. Lerach had been peeved, not amused, when on a previous Clinton visit Parsky's wife had puckishly posted a "Dole for President" sign on the couple's front lawn in view of the motorcade.

More to the point, Parsky had campaigned for Pete Wilson, and when Wilson won the governorship, he'd appointed Lerach's neighbor to a twelve-year term as a Regent of the University of California. Currently Parsky was chairman, holding considerable clout over the largest public education system in the world, including its multibillion-dollar employee pension plan. More than once Parsky had signaled his disdain for Lerach's politics and his law practice. As neighbors, Lerach was grateful that ample acreage separated them, but with the Regents of the University of California as a potential client, Lerach couldn't look across his own orange grove toward his neighbor without feeling anxious that Parsky might be an obstacle.

Such thoughts would haunt him in the coming months as pressure began to mount internally and his law firm felt like a rubber band stretching to the breaking point. As he waited for it to snap, he also felt a tension inside his own gut: specifically, he wondered with trepidation what new developments were unfolding beyond his control regarding his onetime client—and now convicted felon—Dr. Steven G. Cooperman. For now his best move, his only move, was to continue to grow the firm, or at least his West Coast division of the firm, and keep it moving toward independence from New York. At the close of 1999, he managed two strategic personnel acquisitions for the San Diego office of Milberg, Weiss, Bershad, Hynes & Lerach.

The first was Paul Howes, a U.S. Marine Corps veteran who had served in Vietnam, later enrolling at the University of New Mexico, where he graduated Phi Beta Kappa. While in school, he also played tympani for the New Mexico Symphony Orchestra. He then attended the University of Virginia Law School in Charlottesville, where he simultaneously earned a master's in public administration. He signed on as a special assistant to William Webster, then director of the FBI, and later clerked for a federal appeals judge in the District of Columbia. Suddenly—precipitously, his friends said—he jumped into television broadcasting, working as a correspondent for ABC News' Washington bureau. Then, just as abruptly, Howes returned to the law and law enforcement as an assistant U.S. attorney for the District of Columbia—"for dirty bathrooms, the lure of cops, junkies, whores and homicides," he quipped.

Perhaps owing to his time in front of a camera, Howes developed a strong reputation for his clear, coherent delivery before judges and juries. He remained in Washington for eleven years, prosecuting felonies ranging from drug rings to high-profile homicides. Eventually he became restless again. When a colleague mentioned an opening for an experienced trial attorney at an aggressive plaintiffs' law firm in San Diego, a city he'd enjoyed while stationed there as a Marine, he interviewed for it. The firm was Milberg Weiss; the partner conducting the interview was Bill Lerach. Suitably impressed, Lerach quickly settled on Howes as his prized new hire. In short order, Howes would be headed for federal court in Houston to help lead the case of a generation.

The other key acquisition, Byron Georgiou, had an equally eclectic résumé. A 1970 Stanford honors graduate with a degree in social thought and institutions, he seemed headed for a think tank, or perhaps field social work in some bucolic hamlet in rural California. For a while he combined both of those instincts. Georgiou had attended Stanford on an academic scholarship, and in an effort to extend a hand to those who grew up in circumstances even more modest than his own, he co-founded Mariposa School, an alternative elementary and middle school in remote Mendocino County, where he also taught seventh and eighth graders, many of them sons and daughters of farmworkers. After a year he enrolled at Harvard Law School, graduating with honors in 1974.

After clerking for a federal judge in San Francisco, Georgiou served four years for the California Agricultural Labor Relations Board, prosecuting unfair labor practices and enforcing the collective bargaining rights of farmworkers. Later, he went to work on the staff of Governor Edmund G.

"Jerry" Brown, Jr., as legal affairs secretary. Georgiou was responsible for advising Brown on issues relating to the state's public employee unions. It was this experience that piqued Bill Lerach's interest. Lerach was not only beefing up his stable of litigators, he was in need of a lawyer with credibility who could act as liaison with what he saw as the future of his law firm—institutional investors, particularly public pension plans and labor unions.

Together these two attorneys would play major roles in the biggest, most prestigious, complex, and richest securities lawsuit ever litigated. Charles Keating and Lincoln Savings, with all its codefendants, had presented a formidable onion to peel. By comparison, Enron would be an eight-hundred-pound bulb.

> • >

TWO WEEKS AFTER HIS CALL, Russell Gioiella delivered Steven Cooperman to the U.S. attorney's offices on the eleventh floor of the federal courthouse in Los Angeles. The interaction between the taciturn prosecutor, Richard Robinson, and the flamboyant defendant who had come to cut a deal was, as could be expected, chilly and awkward. Cooperman opened by letting Robinson know how difficult the trip had been because of his heart condition and all the pressure he was feeling. Robinson, who was disinclined to believe much of what Cooperman said, was less unsympathetic than wary that Cooperman was dissembling even about his health.

Then Cooperman gave him cause to be even more wary. "For more than ten years, I have been a paid class action plaintiff for the firm of Milberg Weiss Bershad Hynes and Lerach," Cooperman blurted out. Robinson was unmoved. He only vaguely recognized the name of the firm. He did know that name plaintiffs were required to swear under oath that they were not receiving kickback payments nor expected to receive any. So was Cooperman admitting that he had committed perjury? That wouldn't necessarily help his cause.

Then Cooperman detailed the extent of his plaintiff-for-hire arrangement, hoping to impress Robinson with the amount of money he'd received (more than $6 million) and the number of cases in which he was a named plaintiff (more than seventy). By Cooperman's estimates, Milberg Weiss had collected more than $250 million in fees from cases he'd participated in. The kickback scheme Cooperman identified involved lawyers who circumvented the law by acting as fronts by receiving so-called "referral fees" from the firm. One of Cooperman's attorneys, Richard Purtich, who had represented him in his claims against the insurance companies in the art thefts, had received at least $3.5 million in three dozen checks over the years, he said. David Bershad, the Milberg Weiss managing partner in New York, signed the checks, he related. He'd been to Bershad's office and seen where he kept the checks, in a locked credenza. He kept money there too, sometimes handing out cash. Another attorney received more than $2 million in referral fees that he then passed along, Cooperman continued. Robinson asked the name of the attorney. Cooperman hesitated and then said, "Jim Tierney."

Robinson was only half-surprised to hear the name of Cooperman's art theft accomplice—the lawyer-turned-government-witness against his client. Was Cooperman now trying to drag his former partner in crime down with him? No, Cooperman assured Robinson, he was just trying to demonstrate how the conspiracy worked. Cooperman's own brother-in-law, also an attorney, acted as a conduit. Milberg Weiss had paid him nearly $300,000 for consulting work, Cooperman explained, adding: "He never did any work for them."

Thinking ahead, the cautious Robinson contemplated the difficulty of making such allegations stick. Sitting at the table was a twisted, manipulative felon, not a good person to put in front of a jury. Besides, he'd have to demonstrate that the money paid to Cooperman rightfully belonged to other plaintiffs as part of their overall share in the class action. Then again, that was precisely the point. By siphoning off some of the share, Cooperman and his alleged coconspirators were committing fraud against the shareholders and the legal system.

Sensing Robinson's hesitation, Gioiella urged Cooperman to bolster his story. "I'm somewhat of a packrat," he offered. He had kept every correspondence, bank record, invoice, canceled check, and memo of understanding—and would make them available. One piece of correspondence, he said, detailed a direct payment from Mel Weiss. It involved an option to buy a painting. Weiss had given him a check for $175,000 for the option on that piece of art.

His career as a paid plaintiff for Milberg Weiss had come to an end because of the art theft, Cooperman conceded. It had all begun with Bill Lerach, he explained, describing their first dinner at a West Los Angeles restaurant, and the terms of the deal they had struck. Lerach too had paid him directly, Cooperman asserted.* Robinson certainly knew that name. Bill Lerach was a big-fish plaintiffs' lawyer, with a knack for publicity. Not wanting to transmit what he was thinking—that a case against William Lerach could be, a very big one—Robinson struck the beginning of a bargain: Cooperman would have to surrender the evidence he claimed he possessed. He would also have to persuade others, including Tierney, to cooperate. He would have to make phone calls and let government investigators listen in and record the conversations. Finally, he would have to wear a wire and initiate face-to-face meetings with members of the law firm.

Cooperman agreed, already knowing he was persona non grata at Milberg Weiss. In return, Robinson said, he would ask the judge to postpone Cooperman's sentencing. If he did assist the government, and the prosecutors found his contributions credible and helpful, then there could be a discussion about reducing his sentence. But first Cooperman would have to demonstrate his worthiness. Cooperman turned to Gioiella, who appeared eager to close the deal. Then he reached out to shake the hand of Richard Robinson, the man who weeks before had presented enough evidence to put him in prison for the rest of his life.

Returning to his office, Robinson began writing a memo to his boss, recounting the meeting. He'd need some backup before taking the case upstairs to George Cardona, chief of the criminal division, who might have to take it further, to John Gordon, the acting U.S. attorney, maybe all the way to Janet Reno, Clinton's attorney general. A case such as this, if there were a widespread conspiracy, could put a considerable drain on the resources of

---

* Lerach has denied paying Cooperman. However, prosecutors located evidence in Lerach's handwriting, convincing them the attorney did pay Cooperman.

the L.A. office. Also, Robinson had no inkling of which way the political winds might blow. He knew this much, however. He'd have to hit the databases searching for every Milberg Weiss class action lawsuit he could find, looking for serial plaintiffs. It would require a painstaking search, but if Cooperman was telling the truth, a pattern should reveal itself among the hundreds, maybe thousands, of plaintiffs. The government had the right man for the job. Robinson was known among his colleagues for being risk averse and methodical, sometimes to a fault.

> • >

AT HIS FIVE-ACRE ESTATE at Oyster Bay, Long Island, Mel Weiss had no inkling what Cooperman was up to, but he had reasons to worry. Yes, the firm had earned a 30 percent profit increase over the three preceding years, immediately following the congressional passage of the bill meant to put him out of business. Yes, he still owned a vacation home in Boca Raton. Yes, he had earned more than $13 million the previous year—everyone in the world knew that now, because of the disclosures he had been forced to make in the Lexecon trial. Following the disclosures, the *National Law Journal* reported that Milberg Weiss had earned more then $650 million over the previous ten years. Yet Weiss felt that the seams at Milberg Weiss, the firm he had helped found, were fraying and widening. One of the secrets he and the others in the executive committee had kept so well—the payments to plaintiffs and reimbursement to themselves—was slowly revealing itself.

There had been that scene during one of the executive retreats. When the customary business was settled—new partners named, profits split, big pending cases identified—it had come time to discuss the plaintiff payouts and partner reimbursement. He had politely excused Pat Hynes, Len Simon, and Alan Schulman, the newest member of the executive committee. But Schulman hadn't gotten it. He demanded to be in on all decisions and hadn't understood why this was an exception. Bill Lerach had had to take him out into the hall.

"Listen, shit-for-brains," Lerach said in words overheard by others. "You do *not* want to be part of this discussion."

Later, Schulman called Bershad to let him know what he suspected had transpired back in the room between Weiss, Bershad, Steve Schulman, and Lerach—and to register his displeasure. Bershad denied any impropriety and apologized, telling Schulman that leaving him out had been a mistake. Then he called Lerach, relating the distressing conversation. Lerach was vexed, telling Bershad he had mishandled the situation. Bershad had reported this to his boss, who saw the situation as another rift the firm did not need.

There was also the matter of the plaintiffs themselves. For the most part Bershad had done a yeoman's job keeping track, signing, and distributing the checks. But the Cooperman check-forging escapade had been a disaster, and it showed how vulnerable the firm was to being extorted. Not only that, Weiss himself had often had to help stock Bershad's credenza with cash. To do so, he'd played to his strength, spending a weekend at Caesar's in Atlantic City, purchasing $200,000 markers to use at the gaming tables—sometimes winning, sometimes losing—but always managing to skim enough off the top from himself so that he could launder $50,000 or $75,000 for the plaintiff funds.

Still, things had gotten sloppy. A couple checks meant for Lazar had ended up in Cooperman's account. Lazar, his first plaintiff, had pushed too hard at times. He had called Bershad, telling him his son Job needed $250,000 in emergency home repairs. Since Job's stepbrother had been a plaintiff in a case against United Airlines, could they send him the money? Bershad had balked, saying that was not the routine. All money should go through Lazar's intermediary attorney. It was all right, Lazar assured him; his son was also an attorney. Bershad sent the check, not knowing that Job Lazar was no longer practicing law.

In different times, these might have been construed as small mistakes. But Cooperman was now in the clutches of federal prosecutors, which meant that the firm was at the mercy of Cooperman's resolve. The only solace that Bill Lerach and Mel Weiss could take was in Cooperman's own disrepute: he was hardly a credible witness and would have to be corroborated by others. Maybe it had been smart to appease Lazar by sending his son the money. On the other hand, where could the firm draw the line? As

1999 turned into 2000, the most feared law firm in America was experiencing internal dread even as Milberg, Weiss, Bershad, Hynes & Lerach was marching toward its greatest victory. At the dawn of a new millennium, the firm's fortunes were hurtling into the future as if on the train tracks of two parallel universes: one of them involved a spectacular civil litigation in Texas, a case that few firms in the United States could even have attempted to pull off—none as skillfully as Milberg Weiss. The other was unfolding in the gritty criminal division of the Los Angeles federal court system.

> • >

FOLLOWING THEIR INITIAL MEETING at the Los Angeles U.S. attorney's office, Russell Gioiella and Steven Cooperman paid eight more visits to Richard Robinson. Cooperman carried documents to add to the dozens of boxes of evidence he had forwarded. They contained bank statements, telephone records, copies of faxes, canceled checks, and names of other witnesses, including his neighbors Ronald Fischman and Mel Kinder, whom he had persuaded to also become plaintiffs. Cooperman produced a litany of some fifty cases he had participated in as a paid plaintiff and furnished another list of two hundred target companies that he said the Milberg Weiss lawyers had considered ripe for suing.

By this time Robinson had asked for help. He received it in the person of Michael Emmick, a thirty-eight-year-old graduate of UCLA Law School. Emmick had run the office's thirty-member Public Corruption and Governmental Fraud unit. His latest assignment had been in Washington, D.C., as the principal deputy to independent counsel Kenneth W. Starr in the probe that had started as an investigation into Hillary and Bill Clinton's actions as investors in a belly-up Arkansas development known as Whitewater. However, it ended up as a detailed investigation into the president's sex life, particularly as it pertained to a White House intern named Monica Lewinsky. Although Ken Starr's reputation suffered when a consensus developed that impeachment was a bridge too far, Emmick had been the prosecutor who actually dealt with Lewinsky personally. Now, back in Los Angeles, Emmick helped Robinson pore over the information Cooperman

fed them. This time Emmick had a stronger set of facts, and a better witness to work with than he had in Washington. Like Robinson, he sensed
that Cooperman's story had the ring of truth.

By the end of July 2000, Robinson and Emmick had persuaded their su-
periors that they were building the foundation of a potentially large case.
Another investigator was assigned to the investigation. Her name was
Catherine Budig, a former mail carrier. She had attended UCLA Law School
at nights and after earning her degree became a postal inspector. "I just loved
working with the Postal Service," she explained. Budig began combing the
evidence Cooperman provided, looking for signs of wire fraud and illegal interstate transfers of funds. What she found encouraged her two colleagues.

With some trepidation, they filed motions to delay Cooperman's sentencing while preparing separate papers petitioning the court for a reduced
sentence—provided Cooperman continued cooperating. Adding to their
growing confidence were fifteen storage boxes, now filled with contents including code names, handwriting samples, and abbreviations that Cooperman had decoded for them, including initials he could identify. The
investigators contacted Purtich, his attorney, who not only verified that he
had helped Cooperman secure the huge payout from the insurance companies for the "stolen" art but also that he had acted as an intermediary attorney for referral money forwarded to him from Milberg Weiss. Tierney too
was cooperating fully, wanting to ensure he was not indicted in the kickback scheme.

The pieces were falling into place. Still, Emmick and Robinson needed
more witnesses. Both attorneys continued the tedious checking and cross-
checking of Milberg Weiss cases, and as they did names kept repeating
themselves. But at this point there was no way to be certain whose plaintiffs belonged to which firms—or just how wide the circle of culpability
might be.

> • >

IN HIS ANALYST REPORT on January 22, 2001, top Enron executive Jeffrey
K. Skilling led off by announcing, "We had a strong quarter . . . Enron had

just an outstanding year." Skilling then detailed nothing short of excellent numbers, hitting all the benchmarks predetermined during rehearsal meetings. His report yielded the equivalent of applause from the analysts. "Strong buy," said Credit Suisse First Boston, which increased its forecast for earnings per share for the next year. "Long-term buy," added Merrill Lynch; and "buy" from JPMorgan, which told investors it expected the company to "maintain its sweet spot" of growth, predicting 15 to 20 percent increases over the next year.

On Wall Street that spring, a trader at Alliance Capital Management placed a big bet on behalf of the state of Florida pension fund. With a series of keyboard clicks that would continue throughout the spring and summer of 2001, he committed the fund to 7.7 million shares of Enron stock (a transaction that would lose $325 million within the year). Another trader, this one at Amalgamated Bank, the nation's largest union-owned savings institution, made a series of purchases for 115,000 shares. In Oakland, California, a financial manager in the office of the treasurer of the 180,000-member University of California Retirement Fund electronically purchased 200,000 shares of Enron stock through an index fund at an average price of $73 per share. This was just months after a portfolio manager in the same office, alerted by Enron's ebullient reports that were echoed by the analysts, had clicked on ENE, the Enron ticker symbol, and electronically purchased 1.5 million shares of Enron stock at $70 per share. These transactions, and others like it, would ultimately cost the fund nearly $150 million.

Other public employee pension funds would join the Enron financial parade. The state workers of Georgia invested enough to lose $127 million. Within a year, so did those in Ohio ($114.5 million), New York City ($110 million), and Washington State ($103 million). CalSTRS, the pension fund for California schoolteachers, would lose $49 million. CalPERS, the pension fund for California state employees, would lose $40 million on a bogus Enron energy project. John Zegarski, a manager of construction facilities for Enron Broadband, would be one of more than 10,000 Enron employees whose 401(k) retirement accounts were inextricably linked to Enron's fortunes. During the first quarter of 2001, using the company's human resources accounting, his 401(k) manager would purchase 500 shares at $84.50 per share.

Enron's stock rose by nearly $15 per share, matching its last great peak at $84 a share, on January 2, 2001. Between that date and the end of the month, Enron insiders unloaded 1.36 million option-shares for $82 million worth of profits. Then the company began its rocket ride into bankruptcy.

Four months later, on August 15, and less than one month after Enron was named the seventh-ranked company among the Fortune 500, the company issued a press release. Jeffrey Skilling, who had been named CEO in February, would be leaving the company "for family reasons." The announcement escaped no one's notice. Earlier reports had estimated that Skilling's take-home for the year would exceed $136 million with a combination of stock sales, salaries, and bonuses. Ken Lay would earn more than $184 million through the same stock sell-off and salary and bonuses. Andrew Fastow, the Enron CFO, would earn $33 million through stock sales, another $30 million through internal partnerships, and $3 million in bonuses, before announcing that he too would be resigning.

"These guys don't quit for family reasons," Bill Lerach told his colleagues at a meeting in his San Diego office. "Let's start digging."

Within weeks the stock had taken a predictable tumble and was still falling when Ron Luraschi, a senior vice president at Amalgamated Bank in New York, received a phone call from Lerach. The California lawyer revealed that he had done his homework, noting to Luraschi that Amalgamated had been founded by garment workers in the 1920s and that, after being hit hard by the Depression, its succeeding generations of officers had carefully monitored its portfolio. Then he got to the point of his phone call: "Do you have a position in Enron?" Luraschi replied in the affirmative, noting ruefully that as of that day Amalgamated's Enron holdings were down $20 million.

Lerach asked whether the bank would be interested in taking the lead in a securities class action against Enron and its enablers. Luraschi was certainly inclined, although he'd need to run it up the flagpole at Amalgamated. Lerach understood that but informed Luraschi that time was of the essence. He left the banker with one final thought. "This case will dwarf Lincoln Savings," Lerach said.

Within a short time Luraschi returned Lerach's call. Amalgamated was on board. Lerach reached for his bullhorn, stepped into the hallway, and announced an all-hands meeting. When enough of his colleagues had assembled, he told them what had just transpired and announced what he intended to do. "We're going to take on just about every Wall Street bank and some of the biggest law firms in the country," he said, his face glowing with glee.

Already Kathy Lichnovsky had commandeered a conference room where the team would set up operations. Within days it would be endearingly dubbed the "war room," as a palpable current of energy coursed through it and out into the hallways and offices of the firm. To Lerach, these times were always the best, these dizzying, almost giddy moments, when the mission was understood by all and the battle flags were struck, when the adrenalin and the camaraderie were running high, no blood yet shed over a crucial and costly mistake.

For the moment, the new big client model appeared to be working—the "Get Lerach Act" would only make Milberg Weiss even richer. Because of the scale of the Enron case and because of the competition that he knew he would face handling this litigation, Lerach would be spending twelve hours a day hunkered down in the firm's war room. He demanded that his staff keep pace as he reconstructed Enron's malfeasance with his patented multicolored timeline, the visual aid that had impressed so many judges and juries—and defense lawyers who urged their clients to settle when they saw it. He cajoled his staff into unearthing vast numbers of duplicitous Enron public declarations and glowing analyst statements. He demanded well-researched legal citations that would sharpen his points of attack in the legal complaint, whose preamble started with a quote from a December 2001 *Fortune* magazine article: "Start with arrogance. Add greed, deceit, and financial chicanery. What do you get? A company that wasn't what it was cracked up to be."

Nearly eighteen months later, when Lerach had finished writing the complaint and filed it on May 14, 2003, the document would run to a length of 653 pages. Kenneth Lay, Jeffrey Skilling, Andrew Fastow, and other officers and directors would have already been indicted on a combined 124 counts, with multiple charges ranging from securities fraud, to money laundering, to insider trading, by a federal grand jury in Houston, and separate trials, criminal and civil, were scheduled in the same city where Enron had ruled, and where 20,000 Enron employees were out of work.

In the meantime the attorneys working with Lerach dared not complain about the hours and the pace, or his nonstop demands—nor even that Enron and Bill Lerach were ruling their lives. They knew, as did their boss, that for a plaintiffs' lawyer, this was a case for the ages.

Eventually Milberg Weiss would accrue costs totaling $130 million in the Enron litigation. That staggering sum came in the form of equivalent billable hours, payments to outside counsel and outside experts, and out-of-pocket expenses associated with essentially setting up a satellite law firm in Houston. Their fee stood to be many times that amount, of which the partners and associates working feverishly on the Enron case were keenly aware. What none of them knew, however, what none of them could have known—including Bill Lerach himself—was exactly what the senior San Diego partner would have to do to make sure that the firm realized this windfall. If anyone had an idea about that, it was Richard Robinson, an honest, if sometimes timorous federal prosecutor who had come to realize that Steven Cooperman represented the tip of an iceberg—an iceberg that now lay in the path of the good ship Milberg Weiss.

> • > • > • > • >

THE HUNTERS
AND THE HUNTED

.

On Tuesday morning, January 22, 2002, a white van parked in front of the Bob Casey Federal Building on the northeast side of Tranquility Park in downtown Houston. Three men and one woman wearing dark business suits emerged. One was Bill Lerach. The others were his law partners Paul Howes, Patrick Daniels, and Michelle Ciccarelli.

They were met by a scrum of reporters, photographers, television camera crews, and onlookers. After introducing themselves to the media, Lerach reached inside the van and retrieved a large open cardboard box. Raising it over his head and then lowering it for the cameras, he announced that the contents were shredded documents—Enron documents.

"It's a smoking howitzer! It doesn't get any worse than this," he called out hoarsely. "Call the cops. Something has to be done here." This Lerachian display became one of the mighty metaphors for the Enron debacle. Lerach announced that his firm was filing a lawsuit on behalf of thousands—including Enron employees—against the fallen energy giant and its officers and directors, along with the banks, accountants, analysts, and law firms that had helped them commit one of the greatest frauds of our time. Then he and Howes and the others entered the courthouse to attend a hearing on behalf of plaintiffs whose attorneys had also filed their own complaints. Some sixty separate lawsuits were filed before a federal judge who was consolidating the complaints. At the top of the list of plaintiffs were the Regents of the 155,000-employee University of California, the nation's largest public education institution. They, along with twenty subordinate plaintiffs and thousands of individuals, were represented in the class action lawsuit by Milberg Weiss. Just two months earlier Howes and a team of lawyers and accountants handpicked by Lerach had descended on Houston. Armed with employee names and addresses, the Milberg Weiss investigators had gone door to door seeking witnesses and evidence they might possess. The team rented suites at the Four Seasons Hotel, eight blocks from the courthouse, and set up a Houston version of the San Diego war room. One day the Milberg Weiss lawyers encountered in the hotel lobby a gathering of out-of-work Enron employees attending a job fair the company had set up.

Recognizing a serendipitous opportunity, Howes handed out business cards to disillusioned ex-Enronites. One person led to another, and finally he was introduced to Maureen Castaneda, a laid off exchange-rate analyst in Enron's foreign investments division.

"They've been shredding documents," she confided to Howes.

He encouraged her to elaborate, which she did. The shredding began just after Thanksgiving, she told him. It continued through the 2001 Christmas and New Year's holidays, and it was still taking place when she walked out the door in mid-January.

Howes asked Castaneda if she'd managed to get a look at the documents. Yes. Ignoring company directives, she had collected boxes of shredded documents and taken them home. With no job, she explained, she had planned to leave Houston—and needed packing material. Once she began examining the contents, she noticed that some of the shreddings were decipherable. She offered to show them to Howes. They arranged a meeting in an out-of-the-way parking lot.

On January 18 Howes inspected the material. By now he'd done enough research on Enron's chicanery to do his own deciphering. He saw references to Jedi II and Chewco and knew these were the off-the-books partnerships set up by CFO Andrew Fastow and facilitated by the banks from which conspirators reaped millions. Castaneda handed the material to Howes and, observing his euphoric reaction, offered to appear as a witness. With the partially shredded incriminating papers in hand, Howes phoned the San Diego war room to tell Lerach, who listened intently. "Paul, I really don't care what happens to you in the next forty-eight hours," he said, "but whatever you do don't lose those goddamn documents."

Three days later, on January 21, Lerach arrived in Houston and got his own view of their bombshell. Since the 1995 PSLRA had raised the barriers of pretrial discovery for plaintiffs, requiring them to show specific allegations when petitioning the court for certification, having actual evidence of malfeasance in hand was a rare bonanza. Lerach was so elated, he called Christopher Patti, the counsel for the University of California Regents, telling him of the discovery—and of his own confidence in the case he was about to make.

> • >

A MONTH AND A HALF EARLIER Lerach and newly recruited partner Byron Georgiou had attended a forum for institutional investors at the Stanford University Faculty Club. Lerach's interest in attending the Stanford conference was threefold: size up potential business, check out the competition, and pitch his own firm. After recounting his firm's greatest hits, Lerach mentioned that he and his colleagues were representing a New York bank that had lost tens of millions of dollars in the Enron collapse.

In his talk Lerach described putting the concepts of secondary liability to the test in securing billions in settlements from the accountants and banks that had helped Charles Keating. This made an impression. David Russ, the treasurer for the Regents of the University of California, approached Lerach and Georgiou after their presentation. The university's losses in Enron continued to mount, he told them. "Why don't you come up and talk to our people about getting involved in your case?"

The following week Lerach, Georgiou, and Paul Howes visited the eighth-floor offices in downtown Oakland housing more than three dozen University of California attorneys. James Holst, the university's general counsel, and Patti, who specialized in complex litigation, joined David Russ. Patti was familiar with Lerach, having served on the losing side as a defense attorney for Apple Computer while in private practice. "They really managed their arguments well," Patti told his colleagues before the meeting. "They are very effective lawyers."

Lerach was highly motivated to impress them. His initial complaint, filed in federal district court in Houston, listed Amalgamated Bank as its lead plaintiff. Although the bank had purchased 115,000 shares of Enron stock and millions in debentures, its $20 million in losses was nowhere near that of several other named plaintiffs in separate and potentially competing lawsuits. The pension funds of New York and Florida had joined to file their own suit, claiming combined losses of $440 million. Although strict adherence to the PSLRA dictated that the plaintiffs with the largest losses should lead the case, the law left room for judicial discretion, based on the quality and experience of the respective plaintiffs' legal teams. Another lawsuit filed by firms in Atlanta and Wilmington, Delaware, claimed combined losses of $300 million for their clients, pension funds in Alabama, Georgia, Ohio, and Washington State. In order to go forward, Lerach would have to land a plaintiff of sufficient size and stature to sway the judge in his favor. UC would certainly fit the bill. Presiding over the nine-campus, 183,000-student, 155,000-employee network with a portfolio of $54 billion, the twenty-three-member board of regents had not taken the estimated $150 million hit from Enron lightly.*

Lerach outlined the case to be made, reiterating his theories of scheme and secondary liability, as he had done at Stanford. There was a chance that with UC joining the lawsuit, he could line up other plaintiffs in addition to Amalgamated in a consolidated attack. In legal briefs—and press conferences—Lerach and his partners would hit on this analogy: Enron and the banks jointly planned the bank robbery—and the banks not only provided

---

* Those were the figures as of 2002. A tenth campus, in Merced, was added in 2005. As of this writing, the UC family included 220,000 students, 170,000 faculty and staff, and some 37,000 retirees.

the getaway car, they drove it. To impress upon his potential clients his grasp of the case, Lerach unfurled his patented graphic, a multicolored taxonomy of Enron's collapse during the class period, beginning in August 1998 and peaking in December 2000 when the stock reached $96 a share, to its crash just twelve months later. The university, he vowed, had a chance not only to recoup its losses but also to realize billions more. Sweetening the presentation, Lerach reminded the UC treasurer and attorneys that his firm, as it did in all cases, would litigate on contingency, a significant factor given the length of time involved and the furious opposition the plaintiffs were certain to face.

After the Milberg Weiss lawyers thanked their hosts and left, the UC colleagues recapped the presentation. The firm had the resources and was probably the best equipped to meet the challenges of a long legal battle. But would it be a proper partner? Would it accept university oversight? The next day Lerach sweetened the pot for the university lawyers—and laid any doubts about his firm to rest. In a conference call with Patti and Holst he offered to discount the firm's fees—8 percent on the first billion dollars in damages, 9 percent on the second, and 10 percent on the remainder. "I am confident we can get more than three billion dollars for you," he added. Lerach also stressed to his potential clients that the clock was ticking in Houston. The decision on which law firm or plaintiffs would lead the case would be made soon.

On Friday, December 21, the university announced it was joining the class action lawsuit against twenty-nine senior executives and board members of Enron, the international accounting firm of Arthur Andersen, and major Wall Street banks. So when Lerach reported to Patti on January 22 that he and Howes had highly incriminating evidence in their hands—the shredded documents—and that he believed the judge would name them lead plaintiff, Patti was greatly relieved. It helped ameliorate a nagging issue regarding the retaining of Lerach and his firm: throughout the preceding autumn, rumors circulated that a criminal grand jury was convening in Los Angeles. The *Los Angeles Daily Journal*, a legal newspaper, reported that the target of their inquiry was the law firm of Milberg, Weiss, Bershad, Hynes & Lerach.

> • >

ON THE THIRD FLOOR of the federal building in Los Angeles, still another war room was under construction. Far more spartan than its counterparts in San Diego and Houston, this space squared by 120-foot walls, under a dimly lit, low ceiling was designated to house the evidence Steven Cooperman had been providing, along with many other boxes of records and memos and court cases involving Milberg Weiss and possibly other serial plaintiffs. Cooperman had been making frequent trips from a federal prison hospital on the grounds of the former Fort Devens Army Base outside Ayer, Massachusetts, where he had begun serving his time following his sentencing on July 2, 2001. Facing the possibility of ten years or more behind bars, Cooperman had received a relatively lenient sentence of thirty-seven months. Terms of the sentence rendered by U.S. District Court Judge Edward Rafeedie were kept under seal so as not to tip potential defendants in the ongoing investigation of the extent of Cooperman's allegations.

Lerach could certainly interpret what a sentence reduced by two-thirds most likely meant. What Lerach didn't know was how extensively Cooperman had been cooperating with assistant U.S. attorneys Robinson and Emmick.

During one of these meetings Cooperman elaborated on the sham art option that he and Mel Weiss had concocted as a means for repaying Cooperman in the Newhall case. On January 29, 1989, Mel Weiss had given him a check drawn on his personal account for $175,000. Not long after the transaction Weiss apparently got cold feet, but by that time Cooperman had already cashed the check. A new arrangement was struck. The firm would send separate checks to Cooperman's brother-in-law, Bruce Bjork, an attorney whom Cooperman had helped land a job as counsel at Milberg Weiss in New York. The money was then forwarded to a company controlled by Cooperman. In turn, Cooperman began repaying Weiss. Cooperman also furnished a cover letter to Weiss, saying: "I think we're almost there." Robinson and Emmick were impressed with Cooperman's recall and even more so with the canceled checks and copies of this correspondence to the law firm. Still, they needed more evidence independent of Cooperman.

On January 2, 2002, just weeks before Bill Lerach and Paul Howes made their dramatic entrance into the courthouse in Houston, a federal grand jury met in Los Angeles. Robinson requested a subpoena to be served on Milberg Weiss specifically calling for production of a November 15, 1990, fax to Bershad. The subpoena arrived at the New York offices of Milberg Weiss on January 8. Upon receiving it, Bershad searched through files secured in his desk and credenza and found the letter detailing the phony art option, plus faxes Cooperman had sent outlining the arrangement to funnel the money back to Weiss. Legally, he was required to turn the documents over to Milberg Weiss's records custodian or to an outside lawyer. Instead, he called Mel Weiss and asked him to stop by. Weiss appeared ashen as he reviewed the documents Bershad handed him.

"David, you had nothing to do with the art option," he said gravely. Then he turned around and, holding the documents, walked out. Returning to his own office, Weiss put the documents in his safe.

Officially, the firm informed the U.S. attorney's office that it was unable to locate the material requested—and that it deemed any other documents to be the personal property of Melvyn Weiss and David Bershad. Although the prosecutors believed Cooperman's criminal record made him a thin reed on which to indict Milberg Weiss, their witnesses' obsessive record-keeping had provided the blueprint for a fraud case. And the brazenly defiant response to the subpoena on the part of Milberg Weiss made it clear to prosecutors that the firm's partners feared as much.

Methodically, Robinson extracted the names of Milberg Weiss's serial plaintiffs and cross-checked them against the referral fees paid to the attorneys in those cases. He even checked the congressional hearing transcripts looking for lawyers testifying in opposition to the PSLRA, seeking to link them to Milberg Weiss and their plaintiffs. He issued ever more subpoenas. The results began to take shape in case-building taxonomies taped together along the wall in the kind of accessible timelines Lerach used when assembling his own cases. One was headed "Seymour Lazar." Soon Lazar's attorney Paul Selzer would be added. Within months the name Howard Vogel would generate its own timeline, with flags tethered to it signifying plaintiff-for-hire transactions. Other names and separate timelines would follow. Eventually these chronologies would travel on parallel paths around nearly the circumference of the prosecutors' war room.

> • >

AS CRIMINAL AUTHORITIES TURNED up the heat on Enron, speculation intensified over who would steer the massive class action lawsuit. From his Houston war room, Lerach employed colorful press conferences to level charges of document destruction and conspiracy against the bankers and accountants who had helped to scheme Enron and its investors' money into oblivion.

"Mr. Lerach is getting desperate," sniffed James M. Finberg, a partner in the San Francisco office of Lieff, Cabraser, Heimann & Bernstein, representing the combined pensions of New York and Florida state employees. "We're not out for a frolic, posing for TV cameras." At the time Finberg's plaintiffs' losses outmatched the Milberg Weiss plaintiffs by $440 million to $150 million. Like Milberg Weiss, Lieff Cabraser carried an impressive pedigree into the competition, having racked up numerous wins in big cases, including a record $3 billion settlement for accounting irregularities with the Cendant Corporation in 2000, and it had helped secure settlements—working alongside Milberg Weiss—from European banks for the families of Holocaust victims.

Lerach was unfazed, announcing at still another news conference: "The only way this story gets out is if there is publicity. If we didn't [go public], they would still be shredding documents over at Enron today, and the FBI wouldn't be on the nineteenth and twentieth floors [of the Enron Tower]."

The choice of plaintiffs would come down to the preference of trial judge Melinda Harmon, who presided in room 9C on the ninth floor of Houston's federal district courthouse. In her mid-fifties, she had served on the federal bench for a dozen years, having been appointed by President George H.W. Bush in 1989. Judge Harmon was born in Port Arthur, Texas, the Gulf Coast oil refining town that had spawned rock legend Janis Joplin and Dallas Cowboys coach Jimmy Johnson. She attended Radcliffe College, graduating in 1969, before heading to the University of Texas Law School in Austin. After clerking for a Houston judge, she worked from 1975 to 1987 as an attorney for Exxon, leaving a year before the *Exxon Valdez* ran aground in Alaska, dumping ten million gallons of crude oil into Prince William Sound.

After the initial judge recused herself as the Enron trial attorney because she had once owned Enron stock, the case had fallen into Harmon's lap. She was aware of the leaks regarding the Los Angeles investigation of Milberg Weiss and was determined, for the time being, to set them aside in order to focus on determining the best organized, most coherent representative for the plaintiffs. Her challenge became less complicated when it was disclosed that one of the class plaintiffs for Lieff Cabraser had obtained its Enron stock with questionable financial transactions of its own. This undermined the only other powerhouse law firm in the competition. Lieff Cabraser's loss proved to be Milberg Weiss's gain. Flexing his firm's muscles, Lerach confidently argued to Harmon that his was the only legal team with the experience and might to carry on such a complex and important case on behalf of such heavyweight plaintiffs led by the University of California. His arguments carried the day. On February 15 Judge Harmon released an eighty-four-page opinion naming the UC Regents as the lead plaintiff.

"Regents presents itself as a single, organized, coordinated organization represented by a competent and resourceful law firm," Harmon declared. "The court has found that the submissions of [Milberg Weiss] stand out in breadth and depth of its research and insight." Then she provided Lerach with a veritable valentine. "Mr. Lerach has justifiably 'beat his own drum' in demonstrating the role his firm has played thus far in zealously prosecuting this litigation on plaintiffs' behalf."

Word reached Lerach while he was skiing at Steamboat Springs, Colorado. Nevertheless he ordered up a celebration in San Diego and also directed Kathy Lichnovsky to book rooms at a resort for an "all hands retreat." Within the week virtually the entire firm moved temporarily into the luxurious Ritz Carlton Hotel on the bluffs overlooking the Pacific Ocean in Laguna Niguel, about halfway between Los Angeles and San Diego. Looking at his colleagues and staff, Lerach began gleefully deputizing them on the spot. Ultimately thirty partners, led by Paul Howes and supported by

Helen Hodges, a former accountant, along with thirty-nine associates and seven attorneys of counsel, plus clerks and paralegals, would play a role in the litigation.

"All right. Let's go," Lerach commanded. "Get ready to say goodbye to your wives, husbands, girlfriends, boyfriends, family. This is going to be a long and wild ride." Adding to the sense of a forced march was this: they had only thirty days in which to file the complaint.

"Enron could not have happened without the direct participation of the banks in these crazy deals—deals that were totally meaningless," Lerach would intone while Alexandra Berney, a new associate, scrambled at his command to find evidence and points of law to back his assertion. This was more than a rallying cry. It was the basic underpinning of a legal theory that, if proven by Lerach's team, would mean untold billions to their clients and millions more to the firm: the banks and accountants were equal partners in the fraud that was Enron. *It could not have happened without the banks*. It was a mantra that Berney would hear ringing in her ears. "I'd get home late at night and still hear Bill saying this over and over," she recalled later. "It was like a war chant."

Days and nights merged into a blur as Lerach would sit, a maestro in the middle of the war room. "Get me Citibank's 10K!" he would holler without looking up. The young associates at his beck and call observed no seniority protocol—whoever was closest to the document would grab it. If it was down the hall in the firm's document center, whoever was closest to the door would jump up and run down the hallway. "Get me that public statement, that one in September '99 with Skilling saying they expected a breakout quarter!" Lerach would order almost as soon as he'd completed his previous demand. In the midst of this seeming chaos, something highly organized began taking shape. Armed with his yellow legal pads, Sharpie pens, scissors, and Scotch tape, Bill Lerach began assembling what would become a 653-page legal complaint.

Bankrupt, not to mention facing possible prosecution, Enron executives would not go quietly. The firm hired Washington *über*-lawyer Robert Bennett, who had defended the Keating Five before the Senate, former defense secretary Caspar Weinberger in the Iran-Contra hearings, and President Clinton in the Paula Jones scandal. Bennett came to Houston full of advice. Among his first was for the defendants in Lerach's emerging civil suit to prepare motions to petition Judge Harmon for summary judgment, dismissing them from trial. This well-worn strategy would slow down the plaintiffs' efforts to gather evidence and force them to counter the motion— meaning they would have to defend their own complaint and do it for every single defendant as parties to the motion. In addition, Judge Harmon's decision on the motions would help the lawyers on both sides gauge the judge's respect for the plaintiffs' arguments.

One of the attorneys keen on securing a summary judgment was Alan Salpeter, the Chicago lawyer who had helped embarrass Bill Lerach while winning a $50 million award in the Lexecon trial. Salpeter was now representing the Canadian Imperial Bank of Commerce, a defendant, in the UC Regents' lawsuit against Enron. If there was a question of whether Lerach was girding for a rematch against Salpeter, he would eventually answer: "I'm a human being, and human beings can never possibly forget all of what's happened to them in the past." If it was vindication, as well as victory, that he wanted, he would ultimately get it. When the case was over, an image of Lerach, dressed in a toga looking like Julius Caesar, would appear in an article about the Enron case in *American Lawyer* magazine. The image would depict him holding Salpeter's head on a platter. The headline would say: "A Dish Best Served Cold."

> • >

IN THE LOS ANGELES war room, Richard Robinson and Michael Emmick had full plates of their own. A flurry of subpoenas had gone forth to various plaintiffs in Milberg Weiss lawsuits as well as to attorneys at firms listed as cocounsel. Among the first to receive notices was Richard Purtich, Cooperman's attorney, whom Cooperman had identified as receiving more than $1 million from Milberg Weiss in referral fees, some of which were then passed along to Cooperman. Seymour Lazar would receive a subpoena at home in Palm Springs. Paul Selzer would receive his at his Palm Springs office. The subpoenas would demand tax records and other documents pertaining to their separate transactions with Milberg Weiss. Selzer's former colleagues at Best, Best & Krieger, the law firm that had represented Lazar and where Selzer had been a partner, also received subpoenas. While no one at Best, Best & Krieger would have thought to link Selzer, its decorous one-time managing partner, to any money-laundering scheme, more than one attorney in the firm recalled being puzzled by the imbalance between the referral fees the firm had received from Milberg Weiss checks and the legal bills Lazar owed. "It made us nervous," one partner later recalled. The prosecutors would ultimately learn why, but nothing was yet coming easy for the government in this investigation.

Moreover, there was a top leadership void in the prosecutor's office, and a morale problem left over from the pardons (including one to a politically connected drug dealer prosecuted by the Los Angeles office) that Bill Clinton had issued on his way out of the White House. Rumors were circulating that a former assistant U.S. attorney, Debra Yang, now a Superior Court judge in Los Angeles, was a contender for U.S. attorney. The daughter of Chinese immigrants, she had been a respected prosecutor during her seven years in the U.S. attorney's office before Pete Wilson appointed her to the municipal bench in 1997. In 2000 Wilson's successor, Governor Gray Davis, a Democrat, elevated her to Superior Court. If President Bush were to appoint her, she would be the first Asian-American to serve as U.S. attorney. Her strongest advocate was Gerald Parsky, the Republican powerhouse who had chaired the Bush-Cheney California campaign in 2000.

Another Parsky-Bush-Enron connection had not been made public. In 2002 Parsky was still chairman of the University of California Board of Regents. In 1999 and 2000, in a series of secret meetings, he spearheaded a reorganizing of the university's investment office, transferring control of the funds to a Los Angeles investment firm, Wilshire Associates. Records showed that Wilshire contributed tens of thousands of dollars to George Bush's California presidential campaign. Records also showed that the rate of return on UC investments dropped dramatically after the shift. Adding to the plunge, of course, was a securities sinkhole named Enron.

Parsky had not been present when the board approved Milberg Weiss to represent it in the lawsuit against Enron. But he'd gone along with the decision—to a point. Not long after Lerach and his law firm and UC were named lead attorneys and plaintiffs, Parsky and Lerach crossed paths at a social gathering. According to Lerach, Parsky pulled him aside and said: "I still have the power to put up a red light and stop your representation. If you take this lawsuit into the White House, I will see to it that you are removed from the case. Do I have your assurances that you will not?"

Lerach was accustomed to being threatened and had done his share of it himself. But he had to consider this warning seriously. He knew the Enron case was supercharged politically as well as economically. He weighed the consequences soberly. And then Lerach assured Parsky that he would not turn Enron into a referendum against Ken Lay's friend, George W. Bush.

> • >

EVENTS WERE BREAKING Lerach's way. In front of a congressional committee, Arthur Andersen all but admitted its part in the Enron scheme. Two weeks later, on March 14, assistant attorney general Michael Chertoff charged Arthur Andersen with obstruction of justice. A criminal trial date was set for May. Within a month, David Duncan, Andersen's lead partner for Enron, pleaded guilty to obstructing justice and agreed to cooperate with the government. On May 6, at the beginning of the criminal trial against Arthur Andersen, defense lawyer Rusty Hardin laid out the stakes for the jury. The venerable firm's "very existence is in jeopardy," Hardin said. No matter: on June 15, a Houston jury convicted Andersen of obstructing justice.

The spectacular failings of Enron, WorldCom, and Arthur Andersen, all companies Lerach was now suing, had exposed huge conflicts of interest between auditors and companies that retained them. Other conflicts came to light as information was traded between congressional investigators and Lerach's team. Half a decade later the litany would be repeated in the biggest financial meltdown since 1929.

The revelations, borrowed verbatim from the Lerach hymnal were incorporated into legislation sponsored by Senator Paul Sarbanes, a Maryland

Democrat, and Representative Michael Oxley, an Ohio Republican. Known as the Sarbanes-Oxley Act, the legislation called for stricter standards of behavior—on penalty of criminal sanctions—for managers, directors, and accountants. It also called for greater transparency, including auditor independence, by prohibiting auditors from engaging in consulting agreements while verifying the books of companies they audited, and for beefing up the SEC to better carry out its enforcement responsibilities. Pointing directly at CEOs and CFOs, the legislation required that they take full responsibility for each and every financial statement issued to the public. President Bush signaled that he would support the measure, and on June 18, 2002, it passed the Senate Banking Committee on a 17–4 vote.

One week later Bernard Ebbers stunned analysts by informing them that WorldCom had overstated its earnings by more than $3.8 billion during the past five quarters. Just five years earlier Ebbers had been hailed as the "Telecom Cowboy" on the cover of *Business Week* after his company, WorldCom, which began as a small chain of eight local Mississippi motels, swallowed MCI, a communications giant two-and-a-half times the size of WorldCom, for $36.5 billion in cash and stock in the largest merger in U.S. history. Now, as that comapny began evaporating, Mel Weiss and his legal team rejoiced over the news, since Milberg Weiss had already joined with other firms in a consolidated class action lawsuit against WorldCom in Manhattan. In San Diego, Bill Lerach reacted differently. "There's billions in this case," he told his colleagues. "Mel's being too timid. There is no reason for us to stand by while someone else tries it and divides the spoils." Seeing the huge potential payoff, Lerach was already mapping a strategy to opt out of the very lawsuit his partner Mel Weiss had committed the firm to help litigate. Milberg Weiss West, Lerach told his San Diego colleagues, would represent a huge pension fund and fight the bankers and executives in a labor-friendly state court on his own.

On April 25 the House of Representatives voted 334 to 90 to pass Oxley's bill. Less than three months later the Senate passed its own version, sponsored by Senator Sarbanes. The vote was 97–0. Members of both houses cited Enron and WorldCom for hastening their votes. In a July 30 White House ceremony, President Bush, declaring the legislation "the most far-reaching reforms of American business practices since the time of Franklin D. Roosevelt," signed into law the Sarbanes-Oxley Act of 2002.

The SEC's Harvey Pitt was quoted in the *New York Times* as saying: "We are determined to give real teeth and meaning to the protections of the new law." This was hard for Lerach to stomach. Lerach remembered Pitt as the SEC lawyer who had lobbied hard for the passage of the 1995 "Get Lerach Act." The same corporate leaders and their lawyers who had proclaimed victory for American business by aligning against Lerach with the passage of the PSLRA in 1995 were now crowing that they had clamped down on potential fraud, never mentioning their own long war of attrition against the attorneys who had already been fighting it. As Lerach saw it, there were many other culprits, including the sainted Alan Greenspan—and a Democratic president to whom Lerach had contributed so generously.

Beginning in the late 1990s, when Republicans controlled Congress and Bill Clinton was in the White House, the government began dismantling the oversight functions that had been performed by the federal agencies and departments since the Great Depression. One key milestone was Clinton's signing of the Financial Modernization Act of 1999, known as Gramm-Leach-Bliley after its sponsors. This deregulating measure essentially repealed Glass-Steagall, allowing investment banks and commercial banks to perform the same functions.

"Glass-Steagall law is no longer appropriate to the economy in which we live," President Clinton had said at the November 12, 1999, signing ceremony. "It worked pretty well for the industrial economy, which was highly organized, much more centralized, and much more nationalized than the one in which we operate today. But the world is very different."

That theory would be sorely tested in the decade to come. Even at the time, despite his staunch support of Clinton, Lerach was more simpatico with the most liberal wing of the Democratic Party than with the pro-business centrists. The liberal view was ably expressed by North Dakota Democrat Byron Dorgan, one of only eight senators to vote against the final version of the Glass-Steagall repeal. "I think we will look back in ten years' time and say we should not have done this," Dorgan proclaimed.

In 2002, as the evidence of financial misdeeds and malfeasances began to pile up, Lerach—despite his massive caseload—managed to appear more frequently at forums and before the media, casting himself and his firm as, essentially, an extra arm of the SEC.

"Even in those halcyon days, there were a few of us—viewed as cranks at the time—who warned that underneath this veneer of prosperity and profit actually lay widespread accounting rot, falsified profits, inflated asset values, and executive chicanery which would collapse the system," he said in an address at Stanford Law School. "What happened did not happen by accident, and a full accounting is owed to the people who were fleeced."

If Lerach was declaring himself to be the champion of ordinary investors, he wasn't alone. "Is This America's Top Corporate Crime Fighter?" an article in *The Nation* asked. Other laudatory stories appeared about him in *California Lawyer* and *The New Yorker*. Lerach also found time to pen his own version of an I-told-you-so, a twenty-eight-page screed called "The Chickens Have Come Home to Roost: How Wall Street, the Big Accounting Firms and Corporate Interests Chloroformed Congress and Cost America's Investors Trillions."

In this paper Lerach denounced the barricades that government had helped business erect to protect itself from regulation, oversight, and class action lawsuits. "It wasn't as if Congress wasn't warned," he wrote. "After these powerful interests achieved their longed-for goal of curtailing the ability of investors to sue and hold them accountable for securities fraud, there has been a massive upsurge in securities fraud."

Those who knew Lerach personally could read his populist stream-of-consciousness prose and hear his gravelly Pittsburgh-accented voice in their ears. It read just as he talked, an array of damning facts, laced with high-octane adjectives, delivered staccato-style. To those who disagreed, Lerach could come across as a bit unhinged, a cross between William Jennings Bryan and Karl Marx, a man whose real complaint was against human nature—or capitalism itself—although Lerach would counter by saying that, no, capitalism wasn't the problem, the problem was unchecked avarice.

"Let's learn this," he wrote. "Wall Street is dishonest, and . . . it took only a few years after Glass-Steagall was repealed for commercial and investment banks to morph into the huge financial colossi they are today—and to do what they did with Enron. Is Enron an isolated incident resulting from the misconduct of a few bad apples? Or is it evidence of rot across the system? Watch for others that are coming."

> • >

IN NEW YORK, Mel Weiss grew increasingly uncomfortable with his California partner's constant self-promotion, particularly while the winds of scandal were blowing from the U.S. attorney's office in Los Angeles. At home in Rancho Santa Fe, Star Lerach had grown uneasy too. Her husband had buried himself in Enron—and was building another giant case, this one against WorldCom. She recognized the obsessive rhythms he fell into while litigating big cases, but there was more going on now, and she knew it. For one thing, Milberg Weiss was under the cloud of a criminal investigation, and she was smart enough to know that her husband, with his name on the door, must be part of it. Star Lerach had come reluctantly to another revelation: she no longer wanted to play a supporting role in Bill Lerach's movie.

Newly arrived attorney Michelle Ciccarelli had captured Lerach's attention nearly as much as the Enron lawsuit he had assigned her to research. She was in her midthirties, ash blond, self-assured, and possessed of a singing voice worthy of a Nashville recording studio—she worked her way through a small college in Texas belting out country music and torch songs at local venues. Lerach might have appointed his new associate as his personal factotum—he was unabashed about signaling his attraction to her. But almost immediately after she joined Lerach's firm, her credentials—law clerk for the chief judge of the Kentucky Court of Appeals, representing immigrants housed at the federal penitentiary in Kentucky and training other lawyers in the intricacies of deportation hearings, while also assisting Haitian refugees seeking asylum status—earned her a substantive assignment overseas. "Someone said loud and clear, 'we need a labor lawyer . . . anyone here a labor lawyer?' I had done some labor work, so I raised my hand," she recalled. "The next thing, I'm on a plane to the Marianas."

She spent months on Saipan, part of the U.S. commonwealth in the South Pacific, along with partners Al Meyerhoff and Patrick Daniels, investigating claims by garment workers that they were being abused as "indentured servants" by U.S. companies—including Liz Claiborne, Ann Taylor, The Gap, and Ralph Lauren—that subcontracted production to Chinese-owned factories. The workers, most of them women imported from rural China and the Philippines, worked twenty-hour days at sewing machines to earn back their "recruitment fees" and pay for food and housing. Their products were technically "made in America," and yet the Marianas were removed from U.S. labor laws. They were, in the eyes of many, home to some of the worst sweatshops in the world. But not in the eyes of then House majority whip Tom DeLay, who praised the Marianas as "a Petri dish of capitalism." DeLay, with help from his Capitol Hill crony, lobbyist Jack Abramoff, had succeeded time and again in keeping labor reform bills aimed at the Marianas from reaching the House floor.

Ciccarelli and her colleagues had major litigation hurdles to overcome. Most notably, none of the potential plaintiffs would allow themselves to be identified, fearing reprisals from their employers. A motion was filed in federal court to allow anonymous plaintiffs. After strong opposition, the Ninth Circuit Court of Appeals sided with the plaintiffs, citing *Roe v. Wade*, with its anonymous plaintiff, as a precedent. The plaintiffs' team could proceed, but to ensure the safety of their clients, the team would clandestinely rendezvous with their plaintiffs and transport them in the trunks of their cars to a hotel for depositions and return them exhausted for work the next morning.

Through dogged litigation, Ciccarelli and her teammates helped secure a $20 million settlement and a precedent-setting monitoring program to oversee labor and human rights practices in the garment factories in the Marianas. That DeLay and Abramoff would both experience their own legal comeuppances only added to her stature in the Lerach firm.

She soon found herself assisting Lerach closely, logging more than one thousand hours as she helped him, often working well into the night amending the Enron complaint, drafting motions and countermotions and otherwise turning the screws on the suit itself. Meanwhile Paul Howes, Helen Hodges, and their team fanned out across America and Europe taking depositions that would number more than 420 before they were finished.* In professional parlance, the Milberg Weiss lawyers on the Enron case were *living with one another*. In the case of Lerach, soon to be divorced for the third time, by the spring of 2002, the expression was no longer a colloquialism. He and Michelle Ciccarelli were sharing a home on a golf course near Rancho Santa Fe.

In the meantime Lerach kept alert for relevant news from Los Angeles. He had seen the press release from the U.S. attorney's office dated May 17: "In a private ceremony this afternoon, Debra W. Yang was sworn in as the United States Attorney for the Central District of California." The release quoted the new U.S. attorney as being grateful to President Bush for her appointment, which Lerach took as an omen against his law firm. As if he needed any more on his agenda, Lerach couldn't help but notice that another giant well-connected Houston corporation had run into trouble. Months earlier, on January 4, the stock of Halliburton, a multinational oilfield services corporation, had tanked at $8.60 a share—a fifteen-year low—and down from $55 a share only four months earlier. Tracing the stock history, Lerach saw that the company had experienced an indelible pattern of jagged peaks and valleys going back to 1998. The patterns were vivid and recurring. Words such as "strong restructuring" sent the stock up. Insider selling usually followed quickly, not at the very peaks but heavily on the intermediate increases, perhaps so as not to attract attention. When the stock hit lows around the thirties, the company's public relations department and investor relations offices would fire a volley of positive announcements. The stock would shoot past fifty. Inside sell-offs would follow. The SEC had issued a couple of warnings about accounting irregularities.

The pattern of rising and falling stock prices was neither as compact nor as sharp as he had seen with the abrupt rise and fall of WorldCom. In fact, it more resembled that of Enron's longer, slower corporate agony. But what Lerach saw in his analysis was something far more dramatic.

---

* Howes would perform the equivalent of 14,000 billable hours; Hodges, more than 11,000. Years later, when the totals were added, the firm's attorneys would have accumulated 248,803 hours on the Enron case. In billable hours, that would be the equivalent of $113.2 million—on contingency.

It appeared that during the four-year period under review, from January 1998 to January 2002, as company stock fell from near $60 a share to just over $8 a share, Halliburton insiders had unloaded nearly two million shares and collected about $66 million. It was not much compared to the looting of Enron, Lerach pointed out, but one fact intrigued him: the largest beneficiary of the insider selling was Dick Cheney, Halliburton's CEO until he resigned in 2000 to become George Bush's running mate.

Perhaps there was nothing more to Cheney's windfall than fortuitous timing: required by federal ethics laws to divest his stock to reenter politics, he had simply been lucky. That was one possibility. Lerach suspected something more sinister. What about all the other Halliburton insiders who had unloaded their stock—how was that a coincidence? These were the questions Lerach intended to probe. "I think it will be fair for us to ask: If Cheney didn't know about this, why didn't he know?" Lerach exclaimed as he set the documents into order. "What was his salary for?"

Milberg Weiss had filed class action securities claims on a lot less evidence than the circumstantial case against Halliburton's officers. And Lerach certainly wasn't deterred by the prospect of tangling with Dick Cheney. Quite the contrary. On June 3, 2002, Milberg Weiss announced that it had filed suit against Halliburton on behalf of shareholders who had purchased stock in the company between July 22, 1999, and May 28, 2002. The thirty-page initial complaint accused Halliburton of numerous violations of the Securities Exchange Act by "issuing a series of false and misleading statements to the market." The Milberg Weiss partner listed on the press release was Steven G. Schulman. Lerach's name was not mentioned. Even more conspicuously absent from the complaint was the name Richard Cheney.

"We'll get him in time," Lerach told curious colleagues as reams of Halliburton documents now joined the Enron documents littering his desk and the floor of his San Diego office. "For now, let's do our due diligence. Depose the obvious suspects. Once we get our feet in the door, then we'll depose him—the goddamn vice president of the United States."

Irrespective of what he had told Gerald Parsky, Lerach also admonished those attorneys in San Diego working on Enron to keep their eyes on the immediate prize. "After we get Kenny Boy, we'll go after Cheney."

> • > • > • >

"NOBODY CAN STOP ME"

Ritually, William Lerach rose before seven A.M. to catch the morning financial news on television, keeping abreast of the market's gyrations as any day trader would. Then he scanned the headlines of the national and local newspapers: the *New York Times*, *The Wall Street Journal*, the *Financial Times*, the *Los Angeles Times*, and the *Los Angeles Daily Journal*, the Southern California legal newspaper, to follow the cases of his competitors and colleagues in the plaintiffs' bar—and look for early signs of corporate misdeeds. Occasionally, he came across articles signaling what he feared was taking place in the federal building in Los Angeles. First came the headline in the January 24, 2002, issue of the *Los Angeles Daily Journal*, "Milberg Weiss Faces Probe Into Conduct," just a month after the firm announced its lawsuit against Enron.

"It's about Milberg Weiss buying plaintiffs," one source was quoted as saying.

Follow-up stories appeared the next day in the *Los Angeles Times*, the *San Diego Union-Tribune*, and *The Wall Street Journal*. It was a minor bombshell in the legal community, surprising even some of Lerach's most venerable foes. "It doesn't jibe with the Milberg Weiss I know," Lerach's

Nucorp nemesis Chuck Dick told the *Union-Tribune*. On February 13 the *San Francisco Chronicle* picked up the story, reporting: "Milberg Weiss Bershad Hynes & Lerach, the nation's top law firm specializing in shareholder lawsuits, is under a federal grand jury investigation to determine whether it employed improper tactics to recruit plaintiffs, including whether it paid kickbacks to lawyers and brokers for referrals, informed sources say."

Other stories appeared throughout the winter and into early spring, invariably quoting anonymous sources. Lerach complained privately that the Bush administration was using the press to try to blunt his assault on Enron. He was also assuring Mel Weiss and the other top partners about the same thing that the prosecutors in Los Angeles were telling each other: that Steven Cooperman would eventually self-destruct as a government witness. Seymour Lazar? He was a tough old bird and well insulated by a respectable intermediary attorney. Besides, ever since he received the government subpoena in January, Lazar had voluntarily backed off his plaintiff relationship with the firm. Lerach assumed (incorrectly) that Howard Vogel had done the same. Even so, Lerach knew that his counterpunching about government interference in the Enron case was beginning to ring hollow among a growing chorus of doubters, including some of his own clients.

Gerald Parsky's apprehensions were so acute that he was developing buyer's remorse. He began questioning the wisdom of the University of California's decision to hire Lerach's firm in the first place. James E. Holst, the chief counsel, got the message. After conferring with Chris Patti, they decided to hire a consultant, someone who could act both as an overseer and as a go-between for the university and Lerach. This mediator could assist in facilitating settlements they were seeking with the numerous defendants and, if need be, help vet and hire a new firm should Milberg Weiss's legal issues make further litigation on behalf of the university untenable.

In mid-April 2002 they sought out the very man Bill Lerach himself had turned to for help in mediating settlements in the Lincoln Savings case. "We're looking for an independent consultant in our litigation against Enron," retired federal district Judge J. Lawrence Irving heard Holst say when he answered the phone call in his San Diego office. Irving had previously conducted important mediations with the University of California's legal team, and of course he knew Lerach well from the Nucorp case. After hearing Holst explain his predicament, Irving said: "If you are looking for a Bill Lerach detractor, you won't find one in me. I know Bill professionally, and I have nothing but the highest regard for him."

Holst said he was grateful to hear the endorsement and explained why, with the stakes so high and the politics so sticky, they needed an independent consultant.

"Do you mind if I call Bill?" Irving inquired. Holst did not mind.

"Aha," Lerach responded with a laugh, when the judge called. "So they want adult supervision." It was not a hard pill for Lerach to swallow. Irving had represented the plaintiffs magnificently in Lincoln, negotiating huge settlements from big, tough defendants. Lerach felt relieved to have Irving watching his back as well as the university's and told him so.

Judge Irving called the UC counsel's office the next day to accept their offer. He also told them he needed them to hire a team that included a bankruptcy expert, a securities lawyer, and a lawyer who happened to be an accountant. They agreed. Thus began the process of insulating the lead plaintiffs in the landmark Enron lawsuit from the very attorney who was suing on their behalf. Within the week Irving began assembling his team. Gerry Parsky in particular was pleased with Judge Irving's choice of a securities expert, a lawyer named Robert H. Fairbank, who was considered one of the best business attorneys in the nation. Fairbank, while a partner at Gibson, Dunn & Crutcher—the old-line, Republican-heavy Los Angeles firm where Parsky had also been a partner—had specialized in "bet the company" cases. He had also been on the defense side in several Milberg Weiss lawsuits.

Within a week Fairbank and Irving identified their bankruptcy expert, Kenneth Klee, a Harvard Law School graduate who had served on several legislative panels including the House Judiciary Committee from 1974 to 1977, where he helped draft the nation's bankruptcy code. For their accounting specialist, the team chose R. N. "Rock" Hankin, a former Price Waterhouse general partner and professor of accounting at UCLA's school of management who was then the chief executive of a management-consulting firm that bore his name. Fairbank was well acquainted with Hankin, having used him as an expert witness *against* Milberg Weiss.

From the outset, Irving made it clear that the team would review, but not write, the Milberg Weiss cases against the defendants. They would also look at similar large cases—Cendant, WorldCom, for instance—and try to find valuable lessons from successes and mistakes in pleadings, legal doctrine citations, anything that would make the job of Lerach's legal team easier and comfort their mutual clients at the University of California.

> • >

"I DON'T WANT TO use the term, but 'penis envy,' that's almost what it is," Bill Lerach was explaining to veteran journalist William Greider, national affairs correspondent for *The Nation* magazine. "It's like, 'Gee, when the CEO of that company over there is making $20 million, I ought to make $24 million.' Then the other guy says, 'Well if he makes $24 million, then I've got to make $30 million.'"

The subject of the interview was corporate greed. In the summer of 2002—with a consolidated lawsuit under way against dozens of defendants connected to Enron, with others against AT&T, Global Crossing, Qwest, and AOL Time Warner, with still another lawsuit in the final draft taking aim at Martha Stewart, and with an eye on Halliburton and WorldCom—Lerach had proudly positioned himself as America's greatest fighter of corporate corruption, even as the U.S. attorney's office in Los Angeles was investigating him for similarly motivated conduct.

"The CEO ultimately gets brought down by the very personality characteristics that made him successful in the first place," Lerach explained. "How did these guys get to the point where they control a big public company? It's not because they take 'no' for an answer. Their whole life has been fighting and overcoming people who say 'No, you can't do it, don't do it, it's illegal.' These guys say, 'To hell with you, we're doing it, we're getting it done, nobody can stop me.'"

Those who knew Milberg Weiss's business practices intimately thought

Bill Lerach was talking about himself when he critiqued his adversaries in this way. He emphasized to Greider, for instance, that companies such as Enron, Global Crossing, WorldCom, and Halliburton had paid millions in campaign contributions. Chief among their beneficiaries were George W. Bush and John McCain. Lerach was a major political donor himself and had been for years. Yet he made a point of outlining the daisy chain of contributions linked to policy decisions—the interlocking circles of greed that entwined the White House and offices on Capitol Hill.

Another point stressed by Lerach was more straightforward: in 2000 court awards to plaintiffs in private securities lawsuits amounted to $4.9 billion, compared to $488 million recovered by the SEC. The following year $1.9 billion was recovered by private plaintiffs' attorneys versus $522 million by the SEC. As 2002 was shaping up, he estimated that private attorneys would win nearly $3 billion for their clients, at least twice as much as their governmental counterparts. His own firm had recovered $1 billion from Drexel Burnham compared to $650 million by the SEC. From the Washington Public Power settlement, Milberg Weiss had returned $750 million to shareholders—the SEC zero. Clients recovered $630 million from Lucent, while the SEC settled for $25 million. The message: when it came to enforcing securities laws, private attorneys delivered the goods.

If anyone needed further proof, he could now display his first scalp in the Enron litigation. On August 26, 2002, Andersen Worldwide, a Swiss-umbrella company separate from the Chicago-based firm that had audited Enron and earned $50 million a year for "consulting services," announced it was settling with plaintiffs in Lerach's lawsuit for $40 million. Noting that this amount was small compared to the $20 billion in estimated losses to Enron creditors and shareholders, University of California lawyer Jim Holst announced: "We regard this settlement only as a first step in obtaining recovery for the class and will continue to pursue damages from the remaining defendants."

From Lerach's perspective, time now favored them, as did the playing field. The "Get Lerach Act" provided that when a case went to trial, the jury could find the degree of liability of the defendants and extract awards to the plaintiffs proportionately. However, if a defendant settled early, any subsequent judgment would be discounted by the previous settlement. The incentives to settle early were now greater than before the PSLRA. As in criminal cases where sentencing guidelines punished holdouts, those who settled first now usually settled for less.

> • >

AS SHE ASSUMED HER DUTIES as the new U.S. attorney in Los Angeles, Debra Yang inherited a case that had divided her office. It was one thing to allege ethical violations against a prominent and powerful law firm. It was quite another to bring criminal charges. Where were the victims? Who was really damaged? Milberg Weiss cases had been certified by sitting federal judges. Most had settled by virtue of agreements with defendant companies outside of court or with the court's supervision. Some awards had been returned by juries. So where was the fraud?

Explicit guidelines had been set three years earlier by then-deputy attorney general Eric Holder, outlining what could and should be considered criminal conduct by a business or corporation. In the autumn of 2002 prosecutors in the Los Angeles office of the U.S. attorney's office were uncertain whether their budding case against Milberg, Weiss, Bershad, Hynes & Lerach or its individual partners met the Holder guidelines. One skeptic was Jeffrey Isaacs, deputy chief of the major fraud division. Isaacs was not timid. He had successfully prosecuted Credit Lyonnais for using shell companies as fronts to acquire Executive Life Insurance, for which the French-owned institution forfeited $775 million. In 1997, along with Michael Emmick, he'd prosecuted Arizona governor Fife Symington for fabricating information enabling him to fraudulently secure millions in bank loans.

Aware of the doubt about their case felt on the twelfth floor where Yang and her top deputies presided, Emmick and Richard Robinson had cast a net for more witnesses and evidence, but it was so wide they were having trouble hauling anything in. In the process, they would uncover what appeared to be similar abuses in other firms as well. "Do we want massive litigation that would be more like a government reform or do we want a sharp and efficient prosecution?" they asked each other. For economy's sake, the government lawyers would choose the latter, going after the firm with the greatest market share, thus sparing dozens of other firms.

So far, other than Steven Cooperman (a convicted art thief), James Tierney (Cooperman's accomplice), and Richard Purtich (who'd helped Cooperman scam the insurance companies), the prosecutors lacked key and credible witnesses. Robinson knew that to have a winning case, the feds could not simply parade a cast of witnesses who had been granted immunity or been promised reduced sentences as incentives to testify. At some point he believed he would have to produce witnesses who had no other motive but to tell the truth. He was determined to bring the case, and equally determined to make it tight, even at the risk of being accused of overstrategizing and micromanaging, a rap leveled at him in the previous regime. He had a new boss now but lacked any feel for her patience or even her politics.

Robinson, a Democrat, knew that Lerach's very public lawsuit against Enron and his routine denouncements of Bush and Cheney probably made the famous trial lawyer persona non grata in the White House—and, therefore, with the new leadership in the Justice Department. So any premature and unfounded prosecution would certainly bring allegations of a political vendetta. Perhaps that was the notion Lerach was already trying to plant with constant criticism of the president and vice president. Robinson wanted no part of such a debate. His best course was a careful one. Caution lent him comfort because he could easily rebut any challenge by saying that the cases he tried were complex and required meticulous assembly. No one could accuse him of rushing to judgment. He was a responsible government servant, and his integrity and therefore his self-esteem rested on the thoroughness of his preparation.

Still, three years had passed since Cooperman's attorney had first called, offering to flip his client. Cooperman was now nearly finished serving his prison sentence. Fortunately for Robinson, however, Cooperman's shenanigans—even while in prison—would buy the prosecution more time. Chronically ill with heart disease, Cooperman had been forging his doctor's signature on documents required to receive disability payments—some $40,000 a month—that were routed to his wife. When the insurers began calling, Nancy Cooperman told federal prosecutors. Worse, Cooperman soon confessed, he had at times used the prosecutors as couriers to forward his fraudulent forms to the insurance companies. Robinson and Emmick were furious. The credibility of the star witness had taken another felonious dip, and their sketchy case took a step backward.

News of Cooperman's latest antics did nothing to boost the twelfth floor's confidence in the thirty-six-month investigation against Milberg Weiss. What's more, Robinson and Emmick were experiencing trouble getting approval from the Department of Justice in Washington for the subpoenas they wanted issued to all the law firms that had done business with Milberg Weiss. Since this was a RICO investigation, under the Holder guidelines, "main Justice," as the DOJ headquarters was called, had to approve all such subpoenas. "They won't even return our phone calls," Robinson complained to Emmick. Robinson had discovered from mining legal databases that at least two plaintiffs—Seymour Lazar and Howard Vogel— had lent their names to Milberg Weiss lawsuits many dozens of times. But court documents did not indicate whether Lazar and Vogel had been exclusively Milberg Weiss plaintiffs. The prosecutors had also unearthed a pattern of large "referral fees" to lawyers representing the two plaintiffs. Were those kickbacks? That was literally the million-dollar question. Or perhaps a better question, one that Yang and her top deputies were starting to ask, was: When to pull the plug?

Isaacs thought the questions fair. He also had an idea. For all Robinson's strengths as a strategist and meticulous prosecutor, he sometimes was inclined to investigate to all eternity. Isaacs decided they needed some fresh legs. Emmick would soon be reassigned to the high-profile espionage-related prosecution of Katrina Leung, an accused double agent who worked for both the FBI and the People's Republic of China. To fill the vacancy, Isaacs selected a recent addition to the office.

Thirty-nine-year-old Bob McGahan had quickly established himself trying drug, gang, and immigration cases, the assortment routinely assigned to newly hired assistant U.S. attorneys. After graduating from Georgetown Law School with honors in 1993, he'd joined a boutique Washington law firm and found himself, with growing dissatisfaction, defending wise-guy criminals, the same types he was now prosecuting for the U.S. government in Los Angeles. He yearned to work on white-collar crime, and so when Isaacs offered him a chance to fill the vacancy on Richard Robinson's team investigating possible plaintiff kickbacks by a high-flying law firm, he eagerly accepted.

Once inside the windowless war room across from the courthouse, McGahan was quickly brought up to speed. The investigation had one eager witness (Cooperman) and two not so eager (Tierney and Purtich), none of whom would be any prize in front of a jury. Subpoenas had been issued but had yielded little. "A third-year associate in a rinky-dink law firm could destroy Cooperman on the stand," Isaacs told McGahan. The key would be to prove the existence of kickbacks between the firm and other plaintiffs it hired. So far the only kickbacks, it seemed, had arguably been Cooperman's to himself. Finally, however, McGahan was told something compelling. There were other suspects. Their names were mounted on the timelines taped along the wall. While relating what they had learned about them, Robinson and Emmick paused at Seymour Lazar. His name had appeared more than sixty times as a plaintiff in Milberg Weiss cases. His penchant for dodgy deals made him a candidate for the type of fraud Cooperman described. McGahan was delighted with the challenge Robinson assigned him. His mission would be to sharpen the government's focus on Lazar.

> • >

IF THE APPOINTMENT OF Irving to look over Lerach's shoulder brought relief to Judge Harmon, she would not reveal it, at least for the record. For the moment she was preoccupied with the defendants' motions for a summary judgment to be dismissed from the Enron case. The plea had been delivered jointly and separately by the defendants in forty-one separate motions, most of them one hundred pages or more, each requiring responses from Lerach and his team, many of which he drafted himself.

Adding to the pressure on Lerach was the firm's annual retreat—attendance mandatory—this time at the Barton Creek Lodge and Spa in Texas's Hill Country outside Austin. There was certain to be more tension than normal between the West Coast and East Coast offices because of a dispute over securing Enron plaintiffs. Steve Schulman and others in the New York office had made a preliminary run at gaining a lead plaintiff for themselves, but Lerach had preempted his own partners by securing the UC Regents. Dutifully, Lerach and his Enron team showed up, but in what seemed an in-your-face gesture, instead of packing golf clubs, the Milberg West lawyers brought their binders, fax machines, word processors, and legal pads.

"Bill was like a dog at a hot stove, standing over the fax machine," recalled Alexandra Bernay, who worked with Lerach to construct the motions countering the defense call for summary judgment. "The other members of the firm were out playing golf, jogging, playing tennis, water-skiing. We just sat around this big, windowless, business center and worked and worked and worked, never seeing the sunlight."

By the third day, the tension and fatigue and outdoor deprivation began to take their toll. Breaking into tears, Bernay asked her boss: "Please, can I just go get a pedicure?" Lerach looked at her as if she had wounded him. "Okay Xan," he conceded. "But how long will it take?"

Even with a critical deadline looming, Lerach steadfastly observed his own ritual, however. When the clock struck five, out came the Johnnie Walker Blue Label. Work would continue, and no matter how many drinks he'd tossed back and no matter the time of night, Lerach's focus remained acute, at least in the eyes of those working with him.

They were literally writing their way around the hurdles that the PSLRA had attempted to impose on plaintiffs' pleading standards as well as the immunity the Supreme Court seemed to confer by virtue of its *Central Bank* decision on those who "knowingly aided and abetted" securities. It was as if the court had seen Enron coming, Lerach complained. But he would soon see about that. His argument was this: Even secondary actors could commit primary violations, and therefore they were just as guilty and liable as the primary actors when they lie and mislead. The banks and accountants had concocted side bets to keep billions of dollars in debt off the balance sheet for Andy Fastow and others at Enron based on phony valuations of Enron stock. When the fraudulent deals were inserted on the books, Enron, with the help of the underwriters, would pump out phony earnings reports, and the market would react, and as it did, share prices would rise. Once it began, this cycle of deception between the banks and underwriters and Enron, vouched for by Andersen, would continue until the fraud finally fell in on itself. To this end, Lerach would argue, the banks, underwriters, and accountants did more than help disguise Enron's true worth from shareholders, while insiders became rich. They helped finance and promote these schemes and were as culpable as the company itself. The argument had been made, in one form or another, in various circuits, but not in a case with this kind of scope—or in one that seemed surely destined for the Supreme Court.

For all his reputation as a pest and a bully or as a relentless "strike suit" extortionist, Lerach thrived in this rarefied arena of legal scholarship—and intellectual brinksmanship. One of the signs of his nervous delight was his compulsive licking of the lenses of his oversize glasses, a source of amusement and reassurance for his acolytes. It meant that the master was feeling his groove. He'd need it in this case. In Enron he was attempting to do nothing less than circumvent a Supreme Court decision aimed at his own business model and an act of Congress aimed at him personally. Before filing the massive legal motions to counter the defendants' move for dismissal, he had an associate do a computer search of the document making sure that "aiding and abetting," terms that were antithetical to the Supreme Court's *Central Bank* decision, appeared nowhere in it. He substituted "schemed" or "scheming" instead. From here on out, the defendants weren't the only ones on trial. So was the doctrine of "scheme liability."

Having survived still another firm retreat, Lerach and Mel Weiss returned to doing what had helped them attract so much attention in the first place—finding fraudsters and getting on their tails. On August 20, in New York, the firm filed a class action lawsuit on behalf of purchasers of securities of Martha Stewart Living Omnimedia. The complaint essentially rode the government's investigation of insider trading between Stewart and her friend Sam Waksal, who helped her dump shares of ImClone one day before the biopharmaceutical company issued a devastating quarterly report sending its share prices plummeting. The lawsuit launched against Martha Stewart was tonic for Mel Weiss, who gleefully announced that he would try the case himself. Privately, he expressed satisfaction when an opposing attorney, Howard Sirota, told *Forbes* magazine: "Mel Weiss is manipulative, deceptive and ruthless . . . he works twenty-five hours a day at getting more—more money, more power."

> • >

IN HOUSTON, JUDGE HARMON was doing her best to compartmentalize the looming collision of a government investigation of Milberg Weiss and the firm's full-ahead litigation against big-name defendants. She had her own big-name defendants to deal with, and now Bill Lerach had upped the stakes by filing a motion asking the judge to rule that all Enron-related documents obtained from the defendants remain unsealed and available to the public. The plaintiffs' lawyers had so far been stymied in retrieving any documents from the defendants, who were protected by the PSLRA from having to furnish subpoenaed documents to Lerach's team until Judge Harmon had resolved all defense motions asking for dismissal from litigation. The defendants did, however, have to turn the material over to government investigators, and Lerach was seeking a back-door way to get a look at it.

On June 15 a criminal court in Houston, just down the hall from Judge Harmon, handed Lerach the keys to the kingdom. A jury convicted Arthur Andersen of obstructing justice, stemming from its massive document shredding. Now the evidence Andersen had not destroyed was publicly available—and it would provide, from an accounting perspective, a blueprint to the money-shuffling and phony transactions between Enron and the banks. On October 31 the plaintiffs were handed another victory. The federal grand jury sifting through the mass of criminal evidence indicted Andrew Fastow on seventy-eight charges of conspiracy, fraud, money laundering, and numerous other counts. Money laundering alone carried a possible sentence of twenty years in prison, and securities fraud could result in a ten-year term, the *Houston Chronicle* noted the following morning. The paper also mentioned the possibility that his wife, Lea, who had received some of his ill-gotten money, might be prosecuted as well, which the newspaper suggested gave the government leverage toward securing Fastow's cooperation.

Defense attorneys in the civil case against their Enron clients took notice. Andy Fastow's testimony could ruin their cases. Lerach also took notice of the presence of Fastow's attorney, John Keker, thinking that if Fastow had hired one of the shrewdest criminal defense lawyers in the nation, the former Enron CFO must be in deep trouble. He made a mental note to invite Keker to make his client available as a witness for the plaintiffs in the civil case.

Joe Grundfest, the former SEC commissioner and Stanford Law School professor who had hosted the event where Lerach had made contact with his future Enron clients, had been following the litigation closely. In September, as Grundfest read about the case, one article caught his attention. It was a piece in *California Lawyer* that began by recounting the legal maneuvers that the Enron plaintiffs and defendants had waged over the summer. Then Grundfest got to this passage:

> *Many of Lerach's opponents are praying for grand jury action. "If the allegations have substance," says one white collar defense lawyer, "it would indicate that certain firms have been soliciting plaintiffs to bring class action suits. If true, the allegations would contribute to the belief that most of these lawsuits are manufactured."*

Grundfest was taken aback. It was as if the writer had been reading his mind. All along, Grundfest had been distrustful of the nation's most feared plaintiffs' lawyer. "He uses fraud to fight fraud," he had told colleagues privately. From what he was reading, it appeared that others shared his suspicion.

In the nearby Palo Alto offices of Wilson Sonsini, Boris Feldman had also been following the events in Houston and the press leaks out of Los

Angeles. His reaction to the investigation against Milberg Weiss differed from Grundfest's. Feldman was surprised at what he'd been reading. In his mind, Milberg Weiss was—as Mel Weiss had professed—the Rolls Royce of plaintiffs' law firms. For all their adversarial encounters in and out of courtrooms, Feldman held Lerach and his firm in high professional regard, commending them on the elegance and originality of their complaints and the clarity of their briefs—and even on their conduct during negotiations. "This sounds like something some chop shop in New Jersey or Brooklyn would do," Feldman told colleagues. "Not Milberg Weiss."

So far the trickle of dark news had not dissuaded Judge Harmon from continuing to view Milberg Weiss as viable representatives of the Enron plaintiffs. On December 18, in a 306-page ruling, she denied the motions of JPMorgan Chase, Citigroup, Credit Suisse First Boston, Canadian Imperial Bank of Commerce, Barclays Bank, the accounting firm Arthur Andersen, and Vinson & Elkins, Enron's corporate legal counsel, to be dismissed from the case. Fraud claims against Bank of America and Lehman Brothers were dismissed, but the claims of liability against the two banks remained. In announcing her decision, Judge Harmon also upheld the plaintiffs' motion for unsealing and making available to the public documents provided by the defendants during discovery. "This decision confirms the validity of our legal claims against the major defendants," Lerach said in a written statement, "and leaves in the case defendants with resources to pay substantial compensation to the class. It should also open the way for discovery, which has been stayed pending the decision to commence."

While the words were measured, the reaction in the San Diego offices of Milberg Weiss was not. Amid the euphoria, Melinda Harmon's ruling had opened hunting season for the plaintiffs' lawyers. "The lids are off the missile silos," Lerach declared—and some five dozen Milberg Weiss lawyers took to the field.

> • >

IN LOS ANGELES THE net cast by the prosecutors had begun turning up more names of interest. Beginning in 1992 and continuing until the subpoena was sent to Seymour Lazar in January 2002, his wife had been a plaintiff in numerous Milberg Weiss lawsuits. So had his mother-in-law. His daughter's name appeared in several others—and his son's as well. A check of relatives of Howard Vogel uncovered a similar pattern. Robinson knew what needed to happen next. They would ask for subpoena power to find tax records, bank records, or any other means of following a paper trail—tying the plaintiffs to kickbacks from the firm. That effort would produce, from the files of the Southern California offices of the law firm Best, Best & Krieger, a little time bomb. It came in the form of an eight-year-old internal memo written by a land use lawyer named Daniel Olivier. In 1994, when he authored the memo, Olivier had been at the firm eleven years. His mentor had been another land use attorney, Paul Selzer, the patrician senior partner, whose clients included Seymour Lazar, the polymath risk taker whose ventures included land speculation. Selzer was about to leave the firm and start his own, and he wanted the arrangements with his clients, Lazar among them, put into writing to ensure a smooth transition.

Olivier, preparing to inherit some of Selzer's clients, found the instructions from his former boss contradictory and decided to recount them in a memo. "Seymour Lazar has requested that Best Best & Krieger treat monies received from Seymour's class action law firm in New York as current income of Best Best & Krieger, not as Seymour's funds held in trust," a perplexed Olivier wrote, noting that Best, Best & Krieger had done nothing with the New York firm that would have merited referral fees. Yet the fees were designated by Selzer to help pay Lazar's legal bills at Best, Best & Krieger. Even more incongruous, the fees were far in excess of those bills. Writing further, he related: "Mr. Lazar does not wish to have this relationship documented. He points out that this relationship has been going on for years."

He circulated the memo selectively and did not include Selzer. The reason was explicitly declared: "We have indicated to him (Lazar) on several occasions our concern over participating in some type of conspiracy to defraud the Internal Revenue Service or to otherwise violate the laws prohibiting plaintiffs in class actions from receiving fee splits." Finally, Olivier concluded: "This just smells bad and probably would to an investigator."

The memo was tucked into desks and cabinets; more than a decade would pass between the time it was authored and the moment prosecutors got their hands on it. It smelled bad all right. It was just what Robinson and McGahan had been searching for. They finally had something tangible against Milberg Weiss that had nothing to do with Steven Cooperman. Now they would pick up the pace.

24

> • > • > • > • >

THE PATIENCE OF JOB

Little in the way of personal exchanges now entered the preamble of the regular business conversations between Bill Lerach and Mel Weiss. Once there had been rambling, reciprocal check-ins about their families, or (usually from Mel to Bill) the latest stock market tips. A few years back Mel had even bragged about his inclusion in an exclusive investment fund run by a friend by the name of Bernie Madoff. Told it was a sure thing, Lerach flinched. "Sure things" touted by Mel often did not pan out.*

On this day Weiss was furious with his protégé and let him know it. "I just got a call from Max Berger," Weiss said stonily.

Lerach knew Max A. Berger as a star partner of the big plaintiffs' firm Bernstein, Litowitz, Berger & Grossman. The firm was representing the New York State Common Retirement Fund, the lead plaintiff in the World-Com case. Bernstein Litowitz was a frequent "friendly" competitor for big cases and cocounsel on others, especially in the Southern District of New

---

* Among the many victims of Bernie Madoff's Ponzi scheme was Mel Weiss. Although the amount of his loss was not disclosed publicly, Bill Lerach estimated it to be between $20 million and $30 million.

York, Mel Weiss's home turf. In the familiar low-pitched growl that sounded as if it were coming from the lair of a crouched beast, Weiss told Lerach: "He says you are undermining this case."

Lerach was not surprised. Ever since he and Byron Georgiou had approached the huge California Public Employees' Retirement System, the largest pension fund in the United States, about suing WorldCom for misleading investors in a May 2001 bond offering, he had expected pushback from Weiss. His partner and his New York friends did not appreciate Lerach's poaching. In Lerach's mind, however, even though most of the litigation—criminal and civil—was destined for New York courts, Milberg Weiss West had as much right to the case as any firm in New York, even Milberg Weiss East.

> • >

WORLDCOM CHIEF BERNIE EBBERS practically boasted of his own ignorance. "The thing that has helped me personally," he said to *Time* magazine in 1997, "is that I don't understand a lot of what goes on in this industry." Five years later that didn't sound so smart. WorldCom had consistently paid far too much for the many telecom companies it had acquired, it did a poor job of integrating those companies into its own business model, and it failed to discern that available new technologies meant long distance rates were going down, and fast.* In any event, the Justice Department's blocking of a merger with Sprint caused trauma at both Sprint and WorldCom headquarters. In the case of WorldCom, the damage was permanent.

WorldCom's stock price began a steady decline from its $60-per-share range in 1997 to $30-something per share by the summer of 2000. In

---

* "I know what I don't know," Ebbers would later testify at his own trial. "I don't know technology and engineering. I don't know accounting." The charges against him hinged on the last of those three claims, and the jurors and a federal judge chose not to believe him. But if Ebbers *had* been more conversant in the technology and engineering components of his business, WorldCom might not have resorted to fraudulent accounting practices—and Ebbers wouldn't have been hauled into criminal court in the first place.

September of that year Ebbers borrowed $50 million from the company to cover his own margin calls on debts he owed to purchase shares of his company's now-depressed stock. On October 26, 2000, WorldCom announced that it was writing off $685 million, sending its stock plummeting below $8 per share. That $685 million, it turns out, was the least of the company's problems. Under pressure from Ebbers to "hit the numbers," WorldCom CFO Scott Sullivan directed three midlevel accounting managers to cover up a projected first-quarter 2001 shortfall of $771 million by shifting operating expenses to capital expenditure accounts. This continued for a year. In all, some $3.8 billion in fraudulent accounting practices had taken place. By then, the spring of 2002, the three accountants were spilling the beans to the FBI, the SEC, and the U.S. attorney's office.

Naturally, Ebbers and Sullivan had outside help. As the feds focused their firepower on criminal wrongdoing in WorldCom's Mississippi boardroom, Bill Lerach and other plaintiffs' lawyers began focusing on the fraud's enablers. Lerach spent three weeks constructing his patented chart with its jagged timeline showing the rise and collapse of WorldCom stock from $15 on October 1, 1996, to nearly $70 in June 1999, to less than $10 in March 2002. His chart noted key dates and the major events—the booking of uncollectible bills as revenue, capitalizing operating costs to inflate apparent cash flow, failing to write down overvalued goodwill, inflating assets and net worth, taking excessive "merger" charges to inflate apparent earnings—that comprised the fraud and set the stage for WorldCom's fall.

When he and Byron Georgiou flew to Sacramento and met with CalPERS officials, they had little difficulty persuading the pension fund managers to join the legal battle to reclaim their investment in WorldCom from the banks and underwriters—CitiGroup, Bank of America, Deutsche Bank, JPMorgan, Lehman Brothers, Credit Suisse First Boston, and UBS Warburg—that had pushed the fraud onto the market.

"Forget class action, we're going to call this mass action," Lerach told CalPERS officials, including Mark Anson, CalPERS's chief investment officer, and Kayla Gillan, its chief counsel. He invited the nation's largest, richest institutional investor to take the lead in a litigation involving as many as fifteen other plaintiffs. He posted his chart, pointing out where and how CalPERS lost its hundreds of millions, and watched the eyes of his prospective clients bulge with indignation. "We have beautiful claims against these banks," Lerach told his small, attentive audience. "All you have to do is sit back and enjoy the ride while we get your money back."

One of the subordinate members of the CalPERS group identified himself as an investment officer and raised a mild objection. "What about suing Citibank and JPMorgan? We have to do business with these people."

Anson, his boss and a man reputed to be almost priestly in his demeanor, pounded the table and said, "Fuck them! All that matters on Wall Street is a basis point [a means for calculating interest rates]. They'll be back selling us something else in a week."

Lerach and Georgiou exchanged looks, trying to keep their glee in check. They stood, shook hands with their hosts, and left their business cards on the table. Then Lerach did something else. Since it appeared that his chart had helped incite the indignation he had hoped for, he gave it to Anson as a souvenir.

Anson accepted the gift and immediately turned to the bond buyer who had balked at suing the banks. "Here," he said, handing him the chart. "You put it in your goddamn office so you can look at it every day."

In the elevator, as they were giving each other high-fives, Lerach said to Georgiou, "I like their spirit."

The next day Kayla Gillan, the CalPERS in-house lawyer, called Lerach. "Let's go," she said.

When Lerach had initially called Weiss to convey the news, he was startled to hear Weiss's negative reaction. Just as he had unilaterally drummed up the CalPERS business without telling Weiss, so had his mentor been doing his own business development, working his own political contacts, beginning with H. Carl McCall, comptroller for the State of New York. "I just talked to Carl McCall," Weiss told his partner. "The state portfolio suffered a huge loss in WorldCom's collapse. We're going to be retained by the State of New York. This will be great for us."

Now it was Lerach's turn to signal his lack of enthusiasm. "Mel, quit it," he barked into the phone. "You can't do this, we already have a client and it's huge."

Lerach then recited the comparative attributes of the respective clients. As for the California public employees, there was nothing like them in the country. CalPERS had 1.6 million members, had double the assets of the New York client, and claimed more than $400 million in WorldCom losses. Furthermore, those losses were directly tied to now-worthless bonds that Citigroup, JPMorgan Chase, Bank of America, and Deutsche Bank had underwritten. Strictly interpreting the PSLRA, Lerach tried explaining, Lerach's clients had superior standing for controlling the case.

Weiss wasn't satisfied. "This is humiliating," he said angrily. "The State of New York . . . You mean to come in here with a California client and take over a case in New York?" Lerach wouldn't back down.

The conversation ended, but not in a stalemate, as far as Lerach was concerned. He would push on, preparing a complaint that would win the day in any courtroom. Actually, Mel Weiss intuited something that his West Coast–based partner did not: like Bernie Ebbers, whose criminal case would also be wrested from outsiders by a New York court, Lerach was heading into hostile territory. Lerach had discovered in Chicago during the Lexecon trial how huge a factor home field advantage could loom—and he was about to learn this lesson all over again.

> • >

IN ADDITION TO Max Berger and Mel Weiss, three other New York legal fixtures would set the course for the WorldCom litigation—and the respective fates of Bernard Ebbers and Bill Lerach. The first two were female federal judges who had been appointed to the bench by Bill Clinton. The women were friends and former prosecutors in the U.S. Attorney's Office for the Southern District of New York. The third was a former officer in the U.S. Navy. The three worked together as federal prosecutors, and even after they left that life, they tended to see bright lines in the law—and to stay on their side of it.

Barbara S. Jones was born in Southern California and majored in political science at Mount St. Mary's College in Los Angeles. After graduating, she moved to Boston and worked as a school administrator while studying social psychology at Boston University. She decided to attend Temple University's law school and, after earning her law degree, went to work for a Justice Department task force investigating and prosecuting organized crime in New York. By 1977 Jones was working as an assistant U.S. attorney in the prestigious Southern District of New York. She was joined that year by Denise L. Cote, a midwesterner with a Catholic education of her own. "Dee" Cote, one year older than Barbara Jones, attended St. Mary's College in Indiana when it was the sister college to Notre Dame. From there Cote moved to New York, earning a master's degree in history at Columbia University and teaching for a year at a Catholic girls' school in Manhattan. She too abruptly switched gears, leaving the field of education to study law. She graduated from Columbia Law School in 1975, then clerked for a federal judge in Brooklyn.

By 1977, both women were working as federal prosecutors in the prestigious Southern District of New York under a succession of U.S. attorneys, including Robert B. Fiske, the first special prosecutor who probed Bill Clinton's involvement in the Whitewater case; Rudolph Giuliani, who would go on to become mayor of New York and a Republican presidential candidate; and Clinton appointee Mary Jo White, the first woman to hold the office. Cote, after a six-year hiatus in private practice in the New York firm of Kaye Scholer, returned under White to become the first female chief of the criminal division. In 1994 Cote left the office when President Clinton appointed her to the federal bench. The following year Clinton appointed Barbara Jones to the bench as well. Although they enjoyed good reputations in the New York bar, neither judge had ever presided over anything like the circus WorldCom would become. Cote was assigned the massive WorldCom civil litigation. Soon afterward Jones would be assigned the criminal cases against Ebbers and five WorldCom subordinates.

Until WorldCom, Cote had not presided over a shareholder grievance alleging scheme liability. And as Lerach was to find out, she also possessed little tolerance for law firms competing for the same case, especially when it promised huge returns and huge fees. Clinton had appointed Cote and Jones, in part for reasons of diversity and also to send a signal that under his leadership Democrats took crime-fighting seriously. As the litigation unfolded over the next three years, both judges revealed that they retained the mind-set of prosecutors. This would particularly accrue to the detriment of the "Telecom Cowboy," as Judge Jones gave Ebbers what amounted to a life sentence, while sentencing Scott Sullivan, the accountant she herself identified as the "architect" of the fraud, to only five years.* Meanwhile Dee Cote's clear sense of right and wrong would create hurdles for the legal cowboy from California.

The third musketeer in the WorldCom case was yet another former prosecutor from the Southern District of New York, and he would prove a formidable adversary for Bill Lerach. John P. Coffey, whom everyone called Sean, was a former colleague of Cote's and a rising star at Max Berger's firm, Bernstein Litowitz. So besides fighting a rearguard action against his own mentor and facing a skeptical New York judge, Lerach was about to undergo the out-of-body experience of squaring off against his heir apparent for primacy in the class action securities bar.

> • >

LIKE BARBARA JONES and Dee Cote, Sean Coffey, a Bronx native and the oldest of seven children of Irish immigrants, was the product of a Catholic education, attending Chaminade High School, an all-boys institution in Mineola, New York, where he excelled enough academically to receive an appointment to the U.S. Naval Academy. He graduated from Annapolis in 1978, accepting his assignment as a spotter on a Navy P3-C Orion, a plane used to track Soviet submarines. He would also serve as a junior officer

---

* Ebbers did not plead guilty, took his case to trial, lost, and was sentenced to twenty-five years in prison. He was sixty-three at the time and suffering from heart problems. Under federal sentencing rules, Ebbers is ineligible for release until he turns eighty-five. The severity of the sentence appalled his lawyer, Reid Weingarten, and stunned Ebbers, who wept quietly at the defense table as Jones delivered her sentence.

assigned to the Joint Chiefs of Staff and as a White House military aide assigned to Vice President George H. W. Bush.* A lifelong and highly partisan Democrat whose politics differed utterly from Bush's, Coffey respected the man who had deferred college for four years to become a decorated Navy combat pilot in World War II. Also, like most of those who worked for the elder Bush over the years, Coffey found Bush Forty-One to be a warm and decent man. While assigned to the White House, Coffey attended Georgetown Law School at night. Given the frequent travel associated with his day job, his professors weren't sticklers about his class attendance, but Coffey studied diligently—it's not every law student who could say he'd read his con-law texts while sitting in the Kremlin.

After retiring from active duty, Coffey took a job as a prosecutor in the U.S. attorney's office in Manhattan in 1991. For nearly two years he prosecuted complex corporate fraud cases supervised by Dee Cote. A year after she left for the federal bench, Coffey left too, doing a three-year stint as a litigation partner with Latham & Watkins. In 1998 he accepted Max Berger's offer to join Bernstein, Litowitz, Berger & Grossman.

The PSLRA may have stopped the unseemly "rush to the courthouse" in securities class action cases, but the system that replaced it had unseemly attributes as well. Securities cases became an insider's game. Bill Lerach and Mel Weiss had made the transition: their firm had been the most prolific under the old system and was under the new one as well. It helped to be flush with money and fast on your feet—and politically well connected. But Milberg Weiss wasn't the only firm that fit that description. Max Berger and his partners figured they could play the new game as well as anyone. Bernstein Litowitz intended to challenge Milberg Weiss's supremacy. Hiring Sean Coffey was a step in this direction. The rules of the road, post-PSLRA,

---

* Many years after Bush left the White House—during the WorldCom litigation—Coffey's photograph ran in the newspapers in Houston. By the time he got out of court that day, there were three messages from Bush. Coffey called him back and the former president gushed about Coffey's success so much that Coffey reminded the tort reform–minded Bush, "You know, Mr. President, I'm a *plaintiff's* lawyer." Bush laughed off the caveat: "I don't give a shit—you're great. You're our guy."

meant courting big clients and their patrons. In New York the state employees' pension fund was headed by the state comptroller, and Comptroller McCall was a Democrat with gubernatorial ambitions. Accordingly, trial lawyers who coveted the New York State Common Retirement Fund as a client tended to never miss a McCall fund-raiser. Between 1998 and 2002 Bernstein Litowitz, and Philadelphia-based Barrack, Rodos & Bacine, donated some $140,000 to McCall's political coffers. McCall directed the general counsel of the New York pension fund to invite Bernstein Litowitz and Barrack Rodos to take the lead in the state's class action against WorldCom and its banks and auditors. That autumn McCall lost in a landslide to Republican Governor George Pataki, but his successor as comptroller, Alan G. Hevesi, had also been courted by Bernstein and by Barrack, and their status as lead counsel for the New York pension fund was unchanged. But would New York be ousted by California? This was the issue raised by Lerach at an August 12, 2002, hearing before Denise Cote.

The judge's courtroom was packed with some seventy-five lawyers wanting a piece of the action. Bernstein Litowitz was concerned only with one other firm, Milberg Weiss, and as he listened to Sean Coffey's presentation, Lerach realized that Coffey was trying to undermine him with Judge Cote. "He might as well be sitting with her," Lerach whispered scornfully to Weiss, as Coffey addressed the court. "They haven't even figured out scheme liability."

At this point Lerach was asserting that Milberg Weiss's claim to the case was greater because their clients had cumulatively suffered more harm. That was a compelling argument, Coffey knew, although the premise was debatable. But in seeking out CalPERS and other institutional investors and in focusing primarily on the banks and underwriters of bonds, Coffey was arguing that Lerach was actually impairing the class action against WorldCom and the subordinate defendants. Coffey also accused Lerach of attempting to cherry-pick the best claims, an action that was "denigrating" the judge's class action, in order to seek a competitive advantage to himself.

Three days later, on Tuesday, August 15, 2002, Cote delivered her ruling. It was no surprise. "The New York State Common Retirement Fund is appointed Lead Plaintiff," she ruled matter-of-factly. "Bernstein, Litowitz,

Berger & Grossman LLP and Barrack, Rodos & Bacine shall serve as Co-Lead Counsel for all plaintiffs in the consolidation actions." Neither Lerach nor his firm merited a mention in the judge's seven-page order.

From the bench Cote looked at Lerach, who still had numerous clients in the WorldCom case, and told him that although he was not the attorney of record in the class action that she was in the process of certifying, he could certainly tag along with lawyers from the lead counsel firms while they conducted depositions. Lerach felt a familiar flush come over his face and knew that Cote and everyone in the courtroom were watching his reaction to this humiliation. He shook his head but bit his lip. "I'm appealing," he whispered bluntly to Mel Weiss.

The appeal would be filed before the Second Circuit Court in Manhattan and ask the court's permission to remove certain plaintiffs—both current and future clients of Lerach's—from the federal class action. This "opt out" tactic had seldom been tried. It was an audacious end run, and Judge Cote did not take kindly to it.

While Weiss contemplated whether he wanted the firm to follow their California cowpoke on his wild ride, Lerach went back home and reassured the CalPERS officials that their lawsuit would be heard even if it meant going to state courts. Lerach also spent a good part of the winter of 2002 and spring of 2003 drafting letters to prospective clients—institutional investors with significant losses in the WorldCom bankruptcy, including those that had already signed on to be part of the class action lawsuit in New York, warning them that the defendants were mounting counterattacks to dismiss all bond claims. "We wish to pursue a series of cases in a coordinated litigation throughout the United States and achieve a very significant recovery for them, apart from whatever happens in the class action on behalf of all purchasers of all securities in WorldCom in New York," he wrote. By the spring of 2003, he had assembled an array of pension funds that would eventually grow to more than forty, and he began filing a flurry of complaints in state courts around the country. Coffey saw this as a cavalier provocation. By staging his revolt, which included continuing to solicit plaintiffs, Lerach was unilaterally engaging in "a de facto class action" when—as a Milberg Weiss partner—he was already part of one. This is certainly how Sean Coffey viewed it, and, more importantly, how Judge Cote saw things. On May 20, 2003, she issued an order that even in the dry language of a federal court order, conveyed her frustration with Lerach. "This opinion addresses a third attempt by Milberg Weiss Bershad Hynes & Lerach to return to state court," she began. "For reasons discussed below the motion for remand is again denied." The reasons she cited were, essentially, that under procedures established nationwide by the federal judiciary, an independent panel called the Judicial Panel on Multi-District Litigation had concluded that the class action suits had to be consolidated into one case and assigned to one judge and that judge was her. Lerach had an answer to the criticism that he was horning his way into a lawsuit that had been assigned to two other firms: he had written letters to pension funds as disparate as the Asbestos Workers Local 12 Annuity Fund and the Anchorage Police and Retirement Fund, which were harmed by the bond losses, warning that they were in danger of being cut out of the lawsuit because Berger's clients, the New York state pension fund, had held no bonds.

On May 30, 2003, in his rage at Cote's ruling ten days earlier, Lerach fired off two copies of a threatening letter, overnighting them via UPS to Jeffrey W. Golan of Barrack, Rodos & Bacine and to Sean Coffey, with whom he had actually never spoken. Under Milberg Weiss letterhead, Lerach stated that he was writing on behalf of forty-one pension fund clients who had opted out of the class action and were throwing their lot in with his firm.

"Our clients have asked us to request that you notify your firms' malpractice carriers of these obligations which have been placed on your firms by the district court's Order. Under the terms of the Order you will be responsible for taking significant action which will impact the economic value of our clients' litigation claims, which, if mishandled, could lead to significant damage to our clients for which your firms may be liable. This is especially troubling to our clients in light of the fact that we believe your client, the New York Common Fund, has interests which conflict with the interests, rights and claims of our clients."

When he opened his mail, Sean Coffey stared at the letter, flabbergasted. "He's telling us not to screw up this case or he'll sue us!" he fumed to Max Berger. "This guy is off his meds!"

Berger assumed correctly that Mel Weiss had no inkling Lerach was going to issue such an unusually uncollegial—and empty—threat, and he called Weiss to register his resentment. Weiss, in turn, vented his indignation to Lerach. In his phone call to California, Weiss repeated what Berger had apparently told him: "'Has Bill Lerach lost his mind? He's completely off the reservation.'" Then Weiss told Lerach he would be writing a letter to Berger requesting that, on behalf of the firm, the letter Lerach had sent be withdrawn from the files.

Lerach listened, his teeth clenched. After hanging up, he complained to his San Diego partners: "All Mel cares about is respectability. He craves it. Well, this is it. We *are* off the reservation."

The phrase spoken in anger was prophetic. Lerach was forging ahead with his "opt out" clients to pursue their own litigation against WorldCom defendants—a move that panicked the banks, which were fearful of having to fight a conflagration of lawsuits in numerous venues. Lerach's tactic was unprecedented for its boldness and scale—as well as its potential disruption to the litigation under way in New York. In effect, Lerach was forswearing the very methods he and Mel Weiss had spent twenty years perfecting into a practice in which they were preeminent. And on June 4, 2003, Weiss followed through on his vow to Lerach, sending a fax to Sean Coffey and Jeffrey Golan, apologizing for his partner's intemperance and "any inconvenience it may have caused you or the New York State Common Retirement Fund" and asking the recipients to withdraw Lerach's letter.

Actually, Lerach's threat caused neither Bernstein Litowitz nor their clients any inconvenience at all, as Coffey had simply ignored the letter's demands. Lerach's missive did, however, seal the inevitability of a process started a decade earlier at Turtle Creek. The letter essentially broke Milberg, Weiss, Bershad, Hynes & Lerach LLP apart.

When Sean Coffey and Bill Lerach finally met in person, the setting was a courtroom in Birmingham, Alabama, in a mediation session in the class action case against HealthSouth, the once-high-flying firm headed by Richard M. Scrushy, who would later be indicted on fraud charges, convicted in federal court, and sentenced to eighty-two months in prison.

As in the WorldCom litigation, both Bernstein Litowitz and Milberg Weiss were attempting to take control of the class action. The Birmingham judge gave them each a role—a forced marriage—and on this day in September 2003, Coffey watched Lerach at work. It was an image he never forgot. Lerach sat at his table feverishly going through brief after brief, consulting an impressive array of legal sources—and simply tossing papers on the floor when he was finished with them. Although the teams were working under time pressure without the presence of a jury or the prying eyes of the public, the courtroom was decorous, and Coffey found himself simultaneously admiring Lerach's industry and appalled at his messiness. *His corner of the room looks like a pig sty,* Coffey thought to himself. At one point, while the judge was speaking and the lawyers stopped their work, Lerach actually began clipping his fingernails. Worried that the sound would annoy the judge, Max Berger hissed at him, "Bill, will you cut that out?"

Lerach was unfazed, for he was a man in a hurry. Also, he knew something the New Yorkers didn't: in this courtroom, promptly at five P.M., a liquor cabinet was rolled out, and Lerach wanted to be ready to imbibe. Coffey and Berger noticed as Lerach poured himself a drink of an amber liquid—Scotch whiskey, they presumed—and then another. Coffey allowed himself a beer and, as he savored its taste, looked up from his seat to see Lerach standing over him.

"I think you're a terrific lawyer," Lerach told him, extending his hand.

Coffey had perfunctorily shaken Lerach's hand at the beginning of the day, but this was different. Coffey did not yet consider himself Lerach's peer in securities law. He had admired the San Diego lawyer from afar when he began practicing securities litigation, and now Lerach was paying homage to his skill as a lawyer. Yet the memory of that threatening letter in late spring had not gone away.

"Bill, that's great," Coffey replied. "But please: stop sending me those fucking letters."

"I had to do it," Lerach replied, unruffled. "I had to do it for the clients."

"Well, it wasn't the highlight of my day," Coffey answered. "I can tell you that."

"Mine either," Lerach said in a tone that sounded wistful to Coffey. "It broke up my firm. It would have happened anyway, but that was the last straw."

> • >

ON NOVEMBER 10, 2003, within minutes after arriving at One Penn Plaza, Gary Lozow, the Denver attorney representing his college friend Howard Vogel, set about addressing unfinished business left behind by former Milberg East partner Bob Sugarman. Beginning in 1992, Sugarman recruited Vogel as one of Milberg Weiss's serial plaintiffs. Sugarman was designated to manage Vogel and see that he was paid through Lozow, and it was Sugarman who certified him as a named plaintiff in dozens of cases, vouching that Vogel had "the same interests in the outcome of the case as the other members of the class," which was, of course, patently false.

On October 14, 1992, Sugarman had sent Lozow a retainer agreement offering to pay Vogel 14 percent of fees awarded plus $10,000 for expenses, on a single lawsuit against energy company Valero Natural Gas. The $10,000 itself was significantly more than the amount Vogel had paid for the stock. The case settled for $4.75 million and soon after Vogel's intermediary attorney received a referral fee for $637,223, plus an additional $10,000, most of which was passed to Vogel. This tidy arrangement netted Vogel more than $2 million over the next dozen years. But one transaction hadn't been so tidy, which provoked the November 10 meeting between Weiss and Lozow.

In early October 1997 Vogel had read a research report containing a negative financial analysis of Oxford Health Plan, a huge HMO. Within days he'd set up a trust named the Howard Vogel Retirement Plan, of which he was the sole trustee. On October 8, the trust purchased fifty shares of Oxford stock for $3,918. As he later told Sugarman, his intent was to position the trust as a named plaintiff in a securities fraud class action. On October 31, following instructions from Sugarman, Vogel signed under penalty of perjury a court certification stating that the trust had not purchased Oxford Health "in order to participate in any private action arising out of federal securities laws" and would "not accept any payment for serving as a representative party on behalf of a class beyond plaintiff's pro rata share of any recovery"—a standard and mandatory declaration in the wake of the PSLRA.

In 1999, with the Oxford Health suit still under way, Sugarman called Vogel to tell him he was leaving Milberg Weiss and that a Milberg Weiss partner named Steve Schulman would take over managing Vogel's relationship with the firm. On June 27, 2003, Milberg Weiss was awarded a $40 million fee in the settlement with Oxford Health. Vogel received a subsequent phone call from Schulman instructing him to direct his attorney to call Mel Weiss to arrange for Vogel's share of the settlement. A few days later, Vogel received a phone call from Schulman. Weiss was uncomfortable with discussing the proposal over the telephone. Could Vogel's attorney meet Weiss in New York?

"We are under investigation," an apologetic Weiss told Lozow, when the two met on November 20. But when they concluded their meeting, Lozow was assured his client would receive a payment. Because the fees were so large, and Milberg Weiss had other payment obligations, it was to be considerably less than 14 percent, but Vogel's share would still be in excess of a million dollars. Less than a month later Lozow received a check for $1.1 million. With it came a cover letter dated December 18, 2003, and signed by Schulman confirming the payment "reflecting your share of court ordered attorneys' fees in consideration of our clients in connection with Oxford Health." Another check for $120,000 arrived days later, with another note repeating the first. Both bore the signature of the person who signed the checks, David Bershad. On January 8, 2004, following Vogel's instructions, Lozow wired $1,205,932.37 to a bank account controlled by Vogel. The circle was complete.

> • >

THROUGHOUT THE AUTUMN OF 2003, Sean Coffey noticed with increasing exasperation as Lerach continued poaching clients in the WorldCom case. On October 29 he sent Judge Cote a letter asking her to issue a cease and desist order. This incited a flurry of replies and motions. Cote, like a referee who feared losing control of the players on the football field, summoned both parties to a hearing on November 13 to hash things out in person. Each side made its case: Coffey said that Lerach, having lost lead plaintiff status, was undermining the class for his own benefit. As of October 3 he had signed up forty-seven clients (although some had since defected), and had done so by urging them that time was of the essence. This was ironic, Coffey maintained, because by urging them to opt out of the class, Lerach was actually putting his own clients in danger: the federal statute of limitations provisions protected plaintiffs in a class action from having the clock run out on them, but it wouldn't necessarily protect Lerach and his renegade pension funds—in fact, the defendants had already been arguing for dismissal on those very grounds.

Lerach offered what defense he could. The letters were not solicitations, he said. The firm had been merely responding to requests from concerned clients. Rather than try to steal plaintiffs, he had rendered a legal opinion, sought by some of the plaintiffs, on the state of the litigation—and why those who bought bonds might be disadvantaged by being with a class of those who bought stock. He even tried to persuade Judge Cote that the letters were covered under the First Amendment. Under prodding by Cote, the underlying source of the friction between plaintiffs' counsel also emerged at that hearing. Originally Mel Weiss had been in discussions to represent the New York State Common Retirement Fund—only to be waved off by Lerach. Milberg Weiss was a house divided. The hearing adjourned, to await Cote's ruling.

It came four days later, on Monday, November 17, 2003, in the form of a stern nineteen-page ruling that kept the WorldCom case on its current course—and altered the very pecking order in America's plaintiffs' bar.

First, the judge set forth the background of the case as she saw it. She then parsed four letters that Lerach and those working with him had subsequently written to various pension funds—and ticked off the reasons she found them deliberately misleading. For instance, in a May 23, 2003, letter to an attorney representing an asbestos fund, Lerach maintained that defendant banks were already moving to dismiss bondholder claims from the class action. "The May 23 letter did not mention that just days before, on May 19, the Court had largely denied the motions to dismiss the class action complaint," the judge wrote in plain, but obviously peeved, prose. And so her decision went, page after page. In her findings section, the judge wrote that it was important to enunciate some "bedrock truths." One of them, she said, was that "Milberg Weiss has engaged in an active campaign to encourage pension funds not to participate in the class action and instead file individual actions with Milberg Weiss as their counsel."

A second bedrock truth, she said, was that "at this stage, Milberg Weiss is running the coordinated individual actions as a *de facto* class action." Another: "The communications with Milberg Weiss have resulted in some confusion and misunderstanding of the options available to class members." She then listed nine examples of Lerach's muddying the waters of litigation. In the end, Cote stopped short of giving Coffey everything he asked for, which was an order essentially handcuffing Lerach's ability to prosecute the civil case the way he saw fit, for the first "bedrock truth" the judge had mentioned was that "every investor who has suffered a loss" had a right to seek redress.

But if the judge denied Coffey's request to rid the New Yorkers of Lerach altogether, she also put the kibosh on Lerach's gambit to answer to no court at all. In the last part of her order, Cote took forceful steps to regain control over the information flow in her case. She did this by instructing Coffey to draft a "curative," an order that would communicate to all parties—and potential parties—where things stood, not in Lerach's mind, but in hers, advising them of their available options.

What Dee Cote had done in November 2003 was reestablish her own priority, which essentially boiled down to another "bedrock" value cherished by Milberg Weiss attorneys, East and West, and by those with Bernstein Litowitz and with Barrack, Rodos & Bacine: the banks and other WorldCom defendants would have to answer for their fraud. Moreover, the curative order left Coffey's firm as co–lead counsel—and Coffey himself as the first among equals among the cocounsels—while freeing Lerach to keep the clients he already had. (He would hold on to forty-one of the forty-seven.) Judge Cote could not, however, repair what was broken between Bill Lerach and Mel Weiss. Quite the contrary, after what had transpired in that hearing, and after Judge Cote's order laid it bare to the world, the only thing left to do was what Lerach had predicted to Coffey in that Birmingham courthouse.

Mel Weiss viewed the whole WorldCom imbroglio as a professional embarrassment, and he told Lerach so. As in a marriage gone bad, words were spoken that could not be taken back. Some of them concerned the federal investigation. Mel Weiss was convinced that the prosecutors were after Lerach. Even if it *was* a government vendetta, as Lerach insisted, it didn't matter. William S. Lerach was a liability to Milberg Weiss and therefore to Melvyn I. Weiss. The firm had announced its plans to eventually split in two the previous June. Following the New York hearings, neither saw any reason to wait any longer: Both men returned to their offices to begin drafting the terms of separating the two-hundred-twenty-attorney firm—the largest of the plaintiffs' securities bar.

They would divide the firm's capital, cases, and clients. Secretly, but not insignificantly, they concurred that the partners in the separate offices would have a say in how the firm responded to the criminal investigation. In other words, even if the feds' main focus was on Lerach, Weiss and colleagues such as Dave Bershad and Steve Schulman would offer counsel and extract from Lerach a promise to protect them in return. As for the clients? Weiss and his lawyers would retain a huge lawsuit they had initiated against every major Wall Street bank for their hands in inflating and manipulating numerous IPOs, and several other cases, including their suit against Martha Stewart. Lerach and his colleagues would keep their Enron case and whatever they could salvage out of the WorldCom mess. One more point in the agreement, which was announced on May 2, 2004: both firms would share fees from cases that had been started and conjointly litigated prior to and after the breakup. At the time, the arrangement appeared logical and mutually beneficial. Eventually, this stipulation would also benefit the prosecutors.

> • >

JOB LAZAR, SEYMOUR'S SON and a lawyer himself, also got a piece of the Milberg Weiss action. In March 1995, after the firm received a $969,000 fee in a United Airlines class action (Job's half-brother Adam had served as plaintiff), the firm sent a $250,000 check dated March 10, 1995, to Job, identifying the money as "your participation in our fee" from the United suit. Bob McGahan had found this peculiar. In his experience as a private attorney and now an assistant U.S. attorney, he'd never come across a referral reward that had consumed such a great percentage of the overall fee. McGahan's curiosity was aroused further when he learned that the Oregon State bar had suspended Job Lazar's license to practice law earlier in 1995. Although the younger Lazar had applied for reinstatement, he'd been working in real estate, not the law.

Tracing the flow of money, government investigators discovered that three days after the check was sent to Job Lazar, it was deposited in his wife's personal account. And they found other Milberg Weiss checks that had been sent to Job Lazar. Although smaller than the United Airlines fee, they were not insignificant amounts. One was for $125,000, another for $50,000, and still another for $75,000—a pattern of referral fees to an attorney who was no longer an attorney.

Investigators traced other cashed checks sent from Milberg Weiss to a Palm Springs law firm and specifically to Paul Selzer, a partner. The checks bore the signature of David Bershad, usually accompanied by a notation, "participation in the most recent fee." Some were even more specific: "In recognition of your contribution to the legal effort in the Denny's litigation."

At this point in the investigation, neither Lazar (who referred all entreaties to his lawyer, former assistant U.S. attorney Thomas H. Bienert, Jr.) nor Selzer had cooperated directly or answered subpoenas specifically. Cooperation had come, however, from another source. The subpoena to Best, Best & Krieger that had yielded Daniel Olivier's "smelled fishy" memo had convinced the Los Angeles prosecutors to keep applying the pressure.

After reviewing the accumulated evidence with his colleagues Richard Robinson and George S. Cardona, as well as postal inspectors Jim Harbin and Catherine Budig, McGahan raised the possibility that the prosecution had finally found a weak link in what was obviously a coordinated and nearly impenetrable circle composed primarily of lawyers or people who had acted on the advice of their attorneys. That link might be Job Lazar— and possibly his ex-wife, Audrey.

On May 6, 2003, Harbin flew to Portland, Oregon, and interviewed Audrey Lazar. Evidently, her divorce from Seymour Lazar's son had not been amicable. Audrey was eager to cooperate with authorities. What did she know about the $250,000 fee in the United Airlines case? She knew plenty. In fact, she had initiated the transaction, she told the investigators. In 1995, while still married, she and Job had gotten in over their heads on a home remodeling project in the Portland suburb where they lived. Job Lazar was estranged from his father and didn't want to ask for help. But Audrey told the investigators that she and her father-in-law had retained a strong relationship. It was she who asked for the money. Within days a check for $250,000 from Milberg Weiss arrived. Like other checks, this one bore the signature of David Bershad. She even recalled the cover letter noting; "your participation in our fee in the United Airlines litigation in accordance with our agreement."

Harbin spent nearly two weeks trying to locate Job Lazar before finally obtaining a cell phone number. On May 17 he reached Lazar, who said he was not pleased to be contacted and not inclined to cooperate. Harbin had managed to deliver a message, however: after the phone call, the younger Lazar retained an attorney.

In early July, McGahan and Harbin flew to Portland to meet with that attorney, Michael Greenlick in the old federal building, while Lazar remained in an adjacent office. The prosecutor and postal inspector laid out their evidence, pointing to the kickbacks from Milberg Weiss and even displaying IRS statements that they said had been dummied up by Lazar. McGahan signaled that he would seek authority to be designated a special assistant in the Oregon U.S. attorney's office, granting him power to pursue an indictment against Job Lazar. "What am I going to do with your guy?" McGahan wondered aloud for effect.

"Thank you very much, that was helpful," Greenlick replied. "We'll get back to you." The meeting lasted less than twenty minutes.

When McGahan returned to his office the following day, a voice mail awaited him. Job Lazar was willing to meet and discuss what he knew. On July 28, in Los Angeles, Lazar and his attorney met with McGahan, Harbin, and Catherine Budig at the federal building. "I do not want to go to jail for my father," Job Lazar said quietly.

The prosecutors weren't after Job Lazar, but they had been waiting for five years for someone on the inside to walk them through the maze. Now they had that person. Seymour Lazar was a serial plaintiff for Milberg Weiss, and he had made millions over the years, his son told the investigators. And he had recently learned that his father's wife had received close to half a million dollars in fees. Afterward McGahan reviewed the testimony and retraced the paper trail, appraising Job Lazar's place in the criminal narrative that he and his colleagues were piecing together along the walls of the government war room. The prosecutors were now in possession of strong circumstantial evidence showing that over his twenty years as a Milberg plaintiff, Seymour Lazar had repeatedly denied under oath that he was getting paid. Now the search turned to reaching someone inside the actual conspiracy itself, a witness who could paint an indelible picture for a jury, so that they could not only indict but convict Mel Weiss, David Bershad, Bob Sugarman, Steve Schulman, or even more tenuously, but possibly, Bill Lerach.

> • >

IN WASHINGTON, D.C., criminal investigators for the Enron task force had put together their own narrative, and it was so compelling that Bill Lerach, leading the civil action against the Enron defendants, called it a Christmas gift.

Months of probing documents and hours of depositions yielded a clear picture of how Canadian Imperial Bank of Commerce had fit into the Enron scheme. As the U.S.-based savings and loans had done in the mid-1980s, CIBC had transformed itself from a conservative lender and safe repository for savings into a reckless investment juggernaut. Starting in 1998, CIBC had participated in complex financial transactions with Enron, earning millions of dollars in fees from the rogue company. Only one thing eluded the proud and newly ambitious financial institution. It had not been designated a "Tier One" bank by Enron, meaning that it was not on the company's list of "favored" lending institutions. To curry favor, bank officials got creative. CIBC began helping Enron move assets off its books by financing "special purpose entities" created by Andrew Fastow. These allowed Enron to book positive earnings and cash flow at the end of each quarter. CIBC, in turn, received its reward in the form of "Tier One" status. This upgraded distinction gave CIBC entry into Enron's circle of greed.

In ensuing years, CIBC became an equity holder in many off-the-books transactions intended to create the appearance of greater cash flow and earnings for Enron. When confronted with what the Justice Department had unearthed, the Canadian bank agreed to accept responsibility and cooperate in the criminal investigation of Enron.

"We've seen recently that corporate corruption extends far beyond cooking one's own books," Deputy Attorney General James B. Comey, Jr., announced on December 22, 2003. "Third-party facilitators have played a critical role in allowing corporate misconduct to happen, whether it be outside counsel, accountants, advisors, or as we see in this case, a bank whose financing schemes fueled Enron's misdeeds and damaged the integrity of the financial marketplace."

In San Diego and Houston, where Lerach's Enron team was about to take a few days off, Comey's pronouncement was greeted with unrestrained glee. The Justice Department had made the scheme liability case against the Canadian bank. What's more, looking at the civil lawsuit from the perspective of proportionate liability, CIBC had been a major offender and therefore had put themselves at greater risk than other Enron defendants. It meant, Lerach estimated aloud in a team meeting conducted via conference call, that they could be looking at a disposition in excess of a billion dollars.

Enron defendants began contacting the attorneys for Enron plaintiffs. The honeyed word *settlement* suddenly hung in the air. The consulting and mediating team of Judge Irving, Bob Fairbank, Ken Klee, and Rock Hankin was literally beginning to pay off. Through Judge Daniel Weinstein, a federal mediator in San Francisco, the Bank of America settled on Saturday, July 3, 2004, for $69 million. "We anticipate this settlement will be the precursor of much larger ones in the future, especially with the banks that face liability for participating in the scheme to defraud Enron's common stockholders," Lerach said publicly.

True to the prediction, Lehman Brothers settled for $222.5 million on October 29. Again, Lerach's press release was as much a warning to the remaining defendants as a declaration of victory. "We expect that we will achieve even larger settlements or judgments from those defendants whose potential liability is much greater."

The message resonated sharply with Alan Salpeter. "We had a gun to our heads," Lerach's public tormentor before a jury in the Lexecon case would recall later. Although Salpeter had not been the bank's attorney when it committed fraud, or when it coughed up the damning evidence against itself to avoid criminal prosecution, he was now stuck with the massive mess it had created for itself. CIBC had admitted its liability. Now it would pay the price. In the late fall of 2004 Alan Salpeter decided to call Bill Lerach before the once-humbled and now-high-flying plaintiffs' attorney called him.

Lerach relished the redemptive moment when he and University of California attorney Chris Patti greeted Alan Salpeter in the conference room of the Houston office of the firm now known as Lerach, Coughlin, Stoia & Robbins. Not wanting to linger longer than necessary in Lerach's moment of absolution, Salpeter got quickly to the point. "My clients have authorized me to offer a settlement on their behalf," he told the two attorneys, his voice all business but downbeat. "We propose two hundred fifty million dollars."

Lerach met the offer with silence. When he finally responded, his voice dripped with incredulity turning to disdain.

"It's a joke, right?" he asked. "This is a fucking joke?"

Salpeter told him it was not. CIBC would pay no more than what it had just offered.

"Then leave," Lerach commanded. He stood. Salpeter stood. Lerach walked out. Salpeter, who never even got to unsnap his briefcase, left the building, climbed into his town car, and went to the airport.

Lerach went to work preparing a summary judgment asking for a massive recovery from CIBC based on the bank's disclosures to avoid criminal prosecution. Before filing the motion with Judge Harmon, Lerach would make certain that Alan Salpeter got a look at it. The gun that had been pointed at his client's head was now cocked. Salpeter knew what he had to do. He called Toronto and reached Michael G. Capatides, CIBC's general counsel and chief administrative officer, and recounted Lerach's response.

"It wasn't unexpected," he would recall. Nor was the bank's next move unanticipated. They would have to ante up—way up.

> • >

IN THE WAR ROOM on the third floor of the federal building in downtown Los Angeles, names were being added to the event-filled timelines growing along the walls. As they gazed at the evidence arrayed before them, and contemplated the vast trove of supporting evidence contained in a growing number of storage boxes, the investigators concluded that although they now knew what had occurred, to get convictions—or guilty pleas—they would still need an insider to walk a jury through it. And no insider was going to come knocking on their doors without an incentive.

Such was the state of the investigation when the team added another member, Douglas Axel, thirty-five, a graduate of the University of California's Hastings College of Law in San Francisco, a man blessed with both a love of law and a scientific mind. He had earned an undergraduate degree in aerospace engineering from UCLA in 1991. After law school, Axel clerked for a U.S. district court judge and then for the Ninth Circuit in San Francisco, before joining a private firm where he spent four years defending tort claims.

When Axel first arrived in the prosecutor's office, he had been assigned to work with Richard Robinson and Michael Emmick on the Milberg Weiss case, but Jeff Isaacs had needed him for another complex fraud prosecution and borrowed him for a time. In the fall of 2004 Axel came back to his former case, which from his fresh perspective, appeared to have grown legs in his absence. Cooperman had provided corroborating physical evidence, the facts McGahan was amassing against Lazar and Selzer seemed solid, and Robinson had compiled a paper trail leading from Vogel to Bob Sugarman and then Steve Schulman. There was direct as well as hearsay evidence against Bershad. It became obvious to Axel that the time had come to spring the trap on an insider—or someone now on the outside who'd once been on the inside. Someone, perhaps, with an ax to grind. There was such a person, and the prosecutors knew who he was. He had once been the second most powerful person in Milberg Weiss West. He'd once been Bill Lerach's friend, best man, and confidant. Now Alan Schulman was a competitor and an antagonist.

Then fifty-five, Schulman (no relation to Steve Schulman) had resigned from Milberg Weiss in 1999 and opened the West Coast office of Bernstein, Litowitz, Berger & Grossman. As the onetime managing partner of Milberg Weiss's West Coast office, Schulman had handled the firm's finances, which included authorizing expenditures and signing checks. His public battles with Lerach over expenses were well known. His accusations that Lerach had acted recklessly, vindictively, and dangerously had been published by *Fortune* magazine. His complaints to Mel Weiss about Lerach's profligate leadership and his ethics were less well known—until Schulman was subpoenaed to appear before a grand jury impaneled in October 2004.

Schulman sought and was granted immunity from prosecution. With that protection, he spoke freely as a witness and, under the rules of secrecy, without fear that his testimony would become public. Thus he was able, in a lawyerly way and by sticking to the facts, to vent his disdain for Bill Lerach. Schulman detailed Lerach's early relationship with Cooperman and other Los Angeles plaintiffs. He told of the annual partner meetings when he and others were excluded from the sessions dealing with plaintiff kickbacks. He recounted his battles with Lerach over the excessive compensation paid to John Torkelsen, their star expert witness, and Torkelsen's contingency arrangement with the firm. When asked to finger a Milberg Weiss executive with intimate knowledge of the kickback scheme, Schulman gave up the name prosecutors had already zeroed in on: David Bershad, his counterpart in the East Coast office.

A second insider, Robert Sugarman, revealed what he knew as well. His testimony remains secret, but he apparently gave the U.S. attorney's office what it needed as it tightened the noose around the senior partners of Milberg Weiss.

The spokes of evidence depicted on the walls of the government's war room were now leading toward the hub of the circle of deception. The prosecutors, consulting with the postal inspectors and IRS agents, assembled their cases into a consolidated narrative. When it was completed, the draft was circulated through the offices of the twelfth floor, where it eventually reached George Cardona, the head of the criminal division.

Cardona was impressed. He was certainly mindful of the implications of indicting a law firm, one that had become a political lightning rod, along with its top lawyers individually. As he scrutinized the evidence and reviewed witnesses' testimony, as he plotted the course of the conspiracy, noting that it still did not lead directly (at least in any preponderance) to either Bill Lerach or Mel Weiss, he felt a prosecutor's professional misgivings, even in the face of some sentiment around the office that a case could and should, by now, be made. Cardona needed another opinion. So he called Jeff Isaacs.

Isaacs had already read the draft and was also impressed. Before he gave his opinion, he called Bob McGahan, saying: "Let's go to lunch."

The tree-shaded patio of the Cathedral of Our Lady of Angels and its outdoor café provided an inviting oasis for those who worked in the otherwise stark blocks surrounding the federal buildings in downtown Los Angeles, particularly in the late autumn, when the city could swelter during one of its Santa Ana heat waves. McGahan and Isaacs found shelter at a canopied table and studied their menus. Before the waiter arrived, McGahan told Isaacs he felt he'd gone as far as he could in assembling a case against Seymour Lazar, the man they hoped would prove the tip of the Milberg Weiss iceberg. Isaacs replied that he'd seen the draft and, in his opinion, the whole investigation had reached a critical point of whether to keep investigating, discontinue, or push forward and out into the open.

Did he have an opinion? McGahan was anxious to know.

Yes, Isaacs told his younger colleague, previewing what he would recommend to Cardona. "Let's indict."

> • > • > • > • >

THE NOT-SO-PERFECT CIRCLE

Richard Robinson slipped into courtroom number 1030 unnoticed and took his place at the prosecutors' table. Within minutes, on November 12, 2004, he would attain a milestone in the prosecution of America's most feared lawyers. On that morning, in the federal courthouse with views overlooking the Great South Bay on southern Long Island, Judge Joanna Seybert would accept the guilty plea of Paul L. Tullman. Five months earlier, prosecutors had charged him with a single felony count of falsifying his tax returns. Among other phony expenses, the federal complaint said, he had deducted payments to a secretary and support staff that did not exist.

Tullman, then sixty-nine, and in declining health, had not fought the allegations. On the contrary, he had been extremely cooperative. How it had come to pass that Robinson, an assistant U.S. attorney based in Los Angeles, oversaw the investigation all the way to its conclusion with Tullman entering his plea in a Long Island federal courthouse was owing to an entirely different scam—a concentric circle within the circle of greed, this one relating to a government loan designed to help small business.

After graduating from law school, Tullman had joined a fledgling New York law firm where he practiced as an associate and subordinate partner until 1981. The law was not his calling, however, and he left the firm to become a stockbroker. In time he became financially well off. Curiously, his wealth wasn't earned through his market prowess. For more than twenty years, Tullman had supplied the partners in his old firm with plaintiffs for whom the firm would pay. It seemed a perfect circle. When their investments turned sour, particularly if a suggestion of corporate fraud might be worth pursuing, those clients had what amounted to an in-house law firm where they sought redress. When Tullman or an attorney in his old firm spotted a potential corporate target, Tullman would encourage a client to purchase a small number of shares to be strategically situated for a potential lawsuit. If the lawsuit ensued and if the firm earned fees, a percentage of those fees would be returned to Tullman, who would reward his clients as well. The circle, in other words, was warped—and illegal.

All told, some seventy cases netting more than $100 million in fees were brought by the firm using Tullman-supplied plaintiffs. For his part, Paul Tullman earned more than $9 million from this arrangement over the years. These were the facts he had surrendered while bartering with prosecutors for leniency.

Richard Robinson had gotten himself deputized as a special assistant U.S. attorney for the Southern District of New York in order to monitor the seemingly unrelated tax case. But it wasn't unconnected at all. Tullman's old firm was Milberg Weiss. His presence in the Long Island courtroom that morning in late 2004 was to ensure two important elements of the five-year investigation. The first was to make certain that Tullman's plea went off without any hitch. Second, he wanted to ensure that the conditions of Tullman's plea—what he had told prosecutors—would be sealed and kept secret.

Another aspect of the circle was also coming into focus. Just as Tullman had provided plaintiffs to bring the cases, John Torkelsen, the expert witness for Milberg Weiss, would be conveniently on hand to testify that the damages being sought were fair. Also, he would help the jurors or judges calculate the amounts favorable to the plaintiffs. His incentive to do so was purely economic—he was paid on contingency—and this too was illegal. The more persuasive he was on the stand or in depositions, the greater chances he'd earn a multimillion-dollar payback. That was the theory federal prosecutors in Los Angeles had been pursuing for several years. They'd come hard after Torkelsen. They'd subpoenaed him. They'd questioned him. They'd not been able to shake him.

Torkelsen had weathered a federal probe of a $50,000 campaign contribution witnesses said had been solicited from the White House by President Clinton. He'd given generously to New Jersey senators Bill Bradley and Robert Torricelli, who were among the recipients of more than $400,000 he had donated to federal elections, along with another $225,000 to support Bill Lerach's California ballot referendums. He had been a significant player in New Jersey Democratic politics, and beyond. It wasn't so much that he was well connected as it was that he was frustratingly recalcitrant. The more he dragged his feet, the less enthusiastic prosecutors in Robinson's office had become in pursuing him. Moreover, he'd stalled them so long that by 2004 Torkelsen hadn't appeared as an expert witness in a Milberg case for seven years, which made him close to being obsolete as a prosection witness.

But the game had recently changed. The U.S. attorney's office in Philadelphia sued Torkelsen, his wife, Pam, his son Leif, and a business associate for scheming to fraudulently obtain more than $30 million in government-backed loans through the Small Business Administration that would be matched—two for one—by investors to help emergent businesses. Among the investors were prominent securities lawyers for whom Torkelsen had been an expert witness. Most prominent among those lawyers were partners at Milberg, Weiss, Bershad, Hynes & Lerach—including Mel Weiss and Bill Lerach. Had they invested in Torkelsen's company, Acorn Technology, to launder their contingency paybacks? It seemed a logical question.

The FBI was following up. The Bureau was less interested in Acorn's investors or the Milberg Weiss connection than in evidence that Torkelsen, his wife, son, and colleague, had engaged in self-dealing, literally stealing the SBA money. Torkelsen was now on the ropes. Besides racking up his second and third drunk-driving convictions within months of each other, his wife was seeking a divorce. The 6,000-square-foot Victorian they'd renovated in Princeton, with a recently added million-dollar marble patio, was on the auction block. On top of those comedowns, Torkelsen knew he could be facing ten years or more for defrauding the government. The man had lived on incentives, Robinson thought. Now the government was moving into position to offer him another. Even if Torkelsen still refused to cooperate, the government might find his wife, who could be facing multiple years of her own, a willing witness.

With the Tullman plea entered and the terms—ongoing cooperation— sealed in secrecy, with federal prosecutors from another jurisdiction preparing to squeeze Torkelsen and his wife, Robinson headed back to Los Angeles armed with a small, but confident smile about the progress of this case that he had not permitted himself in more than five years.

> • >

IN SAN DIEGO, Bill Lerach was riding his own wave of resiliency. A federal district court in Dallas had all but handed him the platform for going after Dick Cheney pursuant to allegations that Halliburton employed accounting practices that improperly inflated revenues and earnings from May 18, 1998 (when Cheney was the company's CEO) through May 28, 2002.

On June 7, 2004, U.S. District Court Judge David C. Godbey gave initial approval to a $6 million settlement agreement between Halliburton and Private Asset Management, a one-thousand-client financial advisory firm based in Southern California. The agreement was forged between Halliburton's attorneys and Richard Schiffrin, a partner in a Philadelphia-based law firm specializing in securities suits. Private Asset Management was one of the lead plaintiffs in the case. Another lead plaintiff was the Archdiocese of Milwaukee Supporting Fund, which was represented by Neil Rothstein of Scott & Scott.

Rothstein opposed the settlement, which he said was forged without his knowledge or that of the other shareholders who had lost money on Halliburton. Rothstein also maintained that this settlement set a bad precedent that was likely to adversely affect the claims of his clients and some 800,000 other defrauded shareholders. Although Rothstein was in the process of appealing the judge's ruling to the Second Circuit Court of Appeals, realistically there was little he could do to stop it. Then providence intervened. In

an August 3 letter to counsel for all the parties in the lawsuit, Judge Godbey stated that he had learned a day earlier that his parents had at some
point purchased Halliburton stock for their grandchildren—his children.
The shares had passed to Godbey, and he had sold them—he couldn't remember when—and put the money in a mutual fund trust for his children
precisely to avoid conflicts of this nature.

Although the matter was trivial—the judge offered in his letter to opt
his children out of any Halliburton class action—Rothstein saw his opportunity, and leaped at it. He sent a letter to the court stating that federal rules
require a judge to step aside, "however small" his or her financial interest in
the case. Godbey recused himself. Fatefully, the case was transferred to U.S.
District Court Judge Barbara M. G. Lynn. On September 10, pulling no
punches, the Clinton appointee called the $6 million agreement inade-
quate. "What made your case so bad so fast?" the judge asked Schiffrin.
"That's what I don't understand . . . I find this proceeding peculiar because . . . all of a sudden the great case becomes positively rank."

When Rothstein called San Diego to relay the news, Lerach was already
at work on an amended complaint, while publicly licking his chops at the
prospect of deposing Cheney—of grilling the sitting vice president under
oath. What's more, all evidence gathering, including the transcripts of the
deposition, would be made public, Lerach had insisted. The prospects
reached beyond reclaiming some $3.1 billion in estimated losses. Lerach
was in position to wage a public opinion campaign against the Bush White
House. He would, he announced, proceed vigorously.

Instead, Lerach would find himself attempting to douse flames much
closer to home, beginning with the panic induced by the indictment of one
Seymour Lazar and his attorney. Richard Robinson had come back from
New York and was ready, at last, to light the fire he had taken nearly five
years to set.

> • > • > • > • >

ALL FALL DOWN

Criminal complaints against Seymour M. Lazar and Paul T. Selzer were leveled formally by a grand jury in Los Angeles, which on Thursday, June 23, 2005, handed down a seventeen-count indictment against them on an array of charges including mail fraud, money laundering, and conspiracy to obstruct justice—all relating to Lazar's receipt over the years of "secret and illegal payments" for work as a professional plaintiff.

The five-and-a-half-year investigation revealed itself in the painstaking text of the initial indictment, which ran sixty-seven pages in length. It did not name Lerach or Weiss or even identify their old law firm. Within the legal profession, however, it was widely assumed that this might be the first of several indictments. That revelation also unlocked old memories of those who had worked with—or against—Lerach in the past.

In San Diego, Colin Wied, his cocounsel on the Pacific Homes case, couldn't help but recall how Lerach had denied years earlier—without being asked—that he paid clients to find lawsuits. Jon Cuneo remembered his friend's blanket denial of wrongdoing when the Los Angeles criminal investigation became common knowledge in 2002. Some of the lawyers who'd lost the race to the courthouse—and some whom Milberg Weiss had sued over the years—couldn't help but ruminate over Lerach's flat denial the year before to *Forbes*: "I never paid a plaintiff."

Government prosecutors had amassed a body of evidence that said quite another thing. According to the indictment, the $2.4 million in illegal kickbacks that Lazar had received came in fifty class action lawsuits against publicly held U.S. corporations. The unnamed firm in the indictment—the government identified it as "the New York firm," but everyone in the trial bar knew it was Milberg Weiss—realized $44 million in fees in those cases, the government said.

Debra W. Yang, the U.S. attorney in charge of the L.A. office, preferred to let her office speak through the indictment against Lazar and Selzer—for now—but others in the nation's long-standing debate over tort reform were not so shy.

"The government is fifteen years too late," groused Al Shugart, one of Lerach's favorite targets.

In the Silicon Valley, talk even turned to suing Lerach and his firm to recover the money they'd paid out to his clients over the years. "Maybe [a previously sued company] could try to come up with a malicious-prosecution theory, or some kind of abuse of process," Wilson Sonsini partner Bruce Vanyo mused aloud. "There's going to be some very angry people out there."

Mel Weiss issued an obligatory statement saying that he was "outraged" about the "baseless" allegations. A few days later William W. Taylor III, a defense lawyer retained by Milberg Weiss, issued a more specific denial: "Neither Milberg Weiss, nor any of its attorneys, had any knowledge of a secret arrangement between Mr. Lazar and his law firm, if one existed."

Chris Mather, a spokesman for the Trial Lawyers of America, went further, saying: "This sounds like another example of the Bush administration attacking someone who opposes their political agenda."

An unbowed Lazar echoed this theme. He picked up the phone himself when a reporter from his local newspaper called for a comment. "I thought I was doing a lot of good, actually," Lazar told *The Riverside Press Enterprise.*

Lerach was uncharacteristically reticent, and Pat Coughlin declined comment, but others spoke on their behalf. John Keker, the defense lawyer whom Lerach had come to admire in the Enron case—he represented Fastow—had quietly been retained by Lerach himself. In the wake of the Lazar indictment, Keker was not quiet at all. He alluded to both the Halliburton and Enron cases and said darkly that Lerach had made "powerful enemies" while aggressively going after corporate fraud.

For their part, the government attorneys leading the criminal investigation had already left clues that when it came to Milberg Weiss and Lerach Coughlin—Milberg East and Milberg West—prosecution was not necessarily a zero-sum game. "Once you go out and indict someone, you've gone out and crossed the Rubicon," warned Columbia University law professor John Coffee. "Once you indict someone, you have put events irrevocably in motion."

> • >

LERACH'S OFFICE HAD SAID he was in Europe when the Lazar indictment was announced. It didn't announce that he'd been celebrating the scalps he had taken that very month. On June 14, 2005, nine days before Lazar was indicted, JPMorgan had settled its Enron liabilities for $2.2 billion. Four days before that Citigroup had come in at $2 billion. It was starting to become clear that the Enron settlements would eclipse the record $6.13 billion that Wall Street firms paid to settle the WorldCom litigation.

Bill Lerach's life seemed to be moving in opposite directions at once. On August 8, 2005, *The Wall Street Journal* reported that prosecutors had granted immunity to Alan Schulman and that he had testified before the Los Angeles grand jury. The next day Lerach announced his $2.4 billion settlement for his Enron clients with the Canadian Imperial Bank of Commerce—nearly ten times Alan Salpeter's initial offer. And so it went for the better part of a year. The federal investigation was hardly slowing him down, although one question that arose, as Robinson and company proceeded at a Chinese water torture pace, was how the burgeoning criminal case would impact Lerach's lawsuit against Halliburton.

The first inkling came courtesy of Neil Rothstein, Lerach's ally on the Halliburton lawsuit. Rothstein's firm, Scott & Scott, had initially been listed as cocounsel with Milberg Weiss on the case. Rothstein had taken a leave of absence from the firm before quitting and becoming "of counsel" to the Archdiocese of Milwaukee Supporting Fund to ensure he kept a piece of the action. Now the tables were turned, and Rothstein was relaying concerns of the clients: "The Justice Department is investigating both Halliburton and you." Lerach responded that he had not been named in any criminal indictment, adding that he had every confidence he would not be.

Nonetheless, Rothstein was worried, and on May 18, 2006, a federal grand jury in Los Angeles validated his concerns. Another set of indictments was handed down. This time they were against the Milberg Weiss firm itself. That morning Rothstein reported the unpleasant news to Paula N. John, the president of the archdiocese fund. She berated Rothstein for failing to alert them of Lerach's impending plight. It was clear to Rothstein that his own standing on the case was in jeopardy because of his association with the San Diego lawyers who had once been part of Milberg Weiss. He delivered a message to Lerach: There was a good chance Lerach's firm would get kicked off the Halliburton case. Lerach's response was quick and sharp: he would fight to keep this case. Privately, he was choking back feelings of self-doubt—a rare emotion for him—and trying to ignore a sense of foreboding.

> • >

THE LONG-ANTICIPATED INDICTMENT of Milberg Weiss was 102 pages long and charged the firm and two of its name partners, David J. Bershad and Steven G. Schulman, with multiple felonies, including obstruction of justice, perjury, bribery, and fraud. No law firm in the United States as prominent as Milberg Weiss had ever been indicted, and this time Debra Yang was front and center.

"This case is about protecting the integrity of the justice system in America," the U.S. attorney declared. "Class-action attorneys and named plaintiffs occupy positions of trust in which they assume responsibility to tell the truth and to disclose relevant information to the court. This indictment alleges a wholesale violation of this responsibility." The indictment covered activity spanning the years 1981–2004, included new charges against Lazar and Selzer, and named as coconspirators Steven Cooperman and Howard Vogel. Yang stated publicly that Cooperman, previously convicted in the art fraud case, was cooperating with the government. She also noted that Vogel had signed an agreement to plead guilty and forfeit $2 million and that he too was assisting in the prosecution. Although Bill Lerach and Mel Weiss were not named in the indictment, they were plainly referenced in the complaint, appearing ominously as "Plaintiff A" and "Plaintiff B."

The circle was closing.

All Lerach would say publicly was that neither he nor members of his San Diego firm were named in the indictment. He expressed sympathy for his former partners—along with his confidence that they would be exonerated. Those who knew him from a distance were struck by the mildness of the response. Those who were privy to what was on his mind knew that Lerach was starting to quake—and that he had his reasons. To at least one person he trusted, Lerach confided: "I did a lot of stuff."

Among plaintiffs' firms and their allies across the country, considerations of self-preservation started to come into play. What about the other firms that had split fees with Milberg Weiss? What about all those politicians who had taken their money and done their bidding? Sean Coffey, now managing partner of Bernstein Litowitz, quietly began going though his firm's records looking for payoffs to plaintiffs—he found none—while also scouring the firm's payments to plaintiffs' witnesses such as John Torkelsen for evidence of impropriety.

Elected officials were not allowed to undergo this process in private. On May 24, 2006, six days after the indictment, New York attorney general Eliot Spitzer, a Democratic candidate for governor, made a show of announcing that he was returning $124,000 in political contributions from the tainted firm. Other beneficiaries of Milberg Weiss took the opposite tack. On June 9, 2006, four Democratic members of Congress leaped to the firm's defense. A half-page ad appeared in the *New York Times*. At the top appeared the letterhead of the Congress of the United States. Beneath was the headline: "Statement on the federal indictment of Milberg Weiss." And below that came the following message:

> The Justice Department's crusade against trial lawyers, the first line
> in the average citizen's protection against corporate greed, has taken
> a new low in the indictment of an entire leading law firm in the
> plaintiffs' bar.

Three House members from New York—Charles Rangel, Carolyn McCarthy, and Gary Ackerman—signed the statement, as well as Robert Wexler from Florida. All but Wexler had received significant political donations from Mel Weiss and his partners.

Such bravura did little to hearten Pat Hynes. At a lawn party in the Hamptons in June, the star Milberg Weiss litigator huddled with a former colleague from the U.S. attorney's office in Manhattan named Pamela Rogers Chepiga. Hynes's friend was now a partner in the New York office of Allen & Overy, one of the five so-called "magic circle" of London law firms with international reach. Pam Chepiga told Hynes that her firm wanted to upgrade its U.S. practice. While the remainder of the conversation was private, what resulted became known within days.

Hynes asked for a meeting with Mel Weiss, and when the two convened, she told him she would be leaving the firm for one in the McGraw-Hill Building, a few blocks north. Weiss was not surprised, but he was taken aback by her demand that her severance package include her full partner's share several years into the future, which meant she'd be cashing in on cases that were still pending. She had Weiss over a barrel and he knew it. The last thing he or the firm could afford was to have an embittered Pat Hynes telling inside stories—particularly to prosecutors. "And believe me," Lerach would observe. "She knew a lot."

By this time the exodus was in full swing, notwithstanding Mel Weiss's best efforts to prevent it. In the evening of July 28 he rented a 160-foot party yacht, the *Duchess*, disembarked from the Chelsea Piers at 41st Street, and carried Milberg Weiss partners and guests down the Hudson on a sunset cruise that would take them past Ellis Island and the Statue of Liberty.

The celebration seemed to more than one guest to be contrived—a heroic effort by Mel Weiss to show grace under pressure. Two dozen attorneys had left the firm, and competitors all over Manhattan were fielding calls from remaining Milberg Weiss attorneys. "It's heartbreaking," Weiss confided wistfully to a reporter for the *New York Observer*. "Because people worked so well together, and we serviced our clients in the most remarkable way— and we still do." Then he added: "How can it be the same? It's impossible."

Out in California, months earlier, Lerach had performed a nautical display of his own, albeit unwittingly. Michelle Ciccarelli, with help from Kathy Lichnovsky, Lerach's daughter Shannon, and a few others, conspired to celebrate Bill's sixtieth birthday by commandeering the USS *Midway*, a decommissioned aircraft carrier at anchor in San Diego Harbor. The party was a surprise for Lerach, who was told he was going to give a speech to insurance underwriters, and he showed up with a PowerPoint presentation under his arm. Unbeknownst to the honoree, his brother, Richard, had flown west to emcee the party. The Pittsburgh contingent also included Gene Carney, with whom Bill had last shared a birthday celebration fifty years earlier, and various Pennsylvania cousins and family friends. Although the government investigation was dogging the firm, those not associated with the law firm detected no pall over the event. Quite the contrary: when Lerach found out he wouldn't be needing his PowerPoint to speak to this audience of 350, he turned the tables on Michelle with a surprise announcement of his own.

"In a triumph," he announced, "of optimism over experience," he was going to marry for the fourth time. Then he impulsively informed everyone aboard the *Midway* that they were invited to the wedding.

> • >

KEN FEINBERG WAS CHEERED that his clients, the banks that had not yet settled in the Enron litigation, expressed in their initial joint meetings a willingness to negotiate. Lerach's concept of scheme liability had given them pause, as had the billions of dollars in settlements already disgorged. Only one attorney, Stuart Baskin, representing Merrill Lynch, seemed to be looking to take the fight to a higher court. Baskin certainly had encouragement from his client. Lawyers representing four Merrill executives convicted criminally in a bogus transaction involving Nigerian barges, had pressed for and won an opportunity to present oral arguments asking the U.S. Court of Appeals for the Fifth Circuit to strike down their federal court conviction. To Baskin, who'd been editor of the *Stanford Law Review* and a clerk for Supreme Court Justice Brennan, the idea that his client could be held accountable for primary liability by buying and selling back Enron property in a structured business deal was objectionable on its face. He was itching to challenge Judge Harmon's ruling.

In Lerach's mind, the scenario most likely to play out called for the banks to feign that they were planning to appeal, as a way of increasing their leverage, while negotiating with Feinberg to settle. Yet they would simultaneously appear to be preparing to battle Pat Coughlin and Paul Howes in Harmon's court, even knowing it to be inhospitable territory. To his dismay, as well as Feinberg's, the defendants weren't bluffing. On July 17, 2006, defendants Credit Suisse First Boston, Barclays, Merrill Lynch, and the law firm of Vinson & Elkins filed petitions in the Fifth Circuit challenging Harmon's granting of class certification of the plaintiffs in the Enron class action.

Credit Suisse argued in its appeal that the appellate court should resolve an unsettled matter over whether secondary actors could be held for primary liability—directly attacking Lerach's pioneering theory. Credit Suisse's attorneys also sought to defy Judge Harmon's position on presumption of reliance, saying the plaintiffs could not argue they had acted directly on Credit Suisse's misrepresentation or omission of essential information. In essence, the petitioners were reprising the 1994 *Central Bank* precedent that Lerach had managed to circumvent in Judge Harmon's court. Barclays and Merrill more or less proffered the same argument.

The seventeen-judge Fifth Circuit was broken into three-judge panels hearing cases in Louisiana, Mississippi, and Texas. Its headquarters was in New Orleans, where the courthouse was named for John Minor Wisdom, one of the "Fifth Circuit Four"—the southern appellate judges who had valiantly faced the reality of implementing the Supreme Court's *Brown v.*

Board of Education decision in the Deep South. Lerach, a history buff, considered New Orleans a fitting venue for shareholder plaintiffs who would not have possessed their standing as a class without the equal protection that the Fifth Circuit judges had implemented forty years earlier.

Times had changed, however. The Fifth Circuit bench of 2006 was an altered body. More than half of its judges had been appointed by Presidents George H.W. Bush and his son George W. Bush. Five others were Ronald Reagan appointees; only the remaining three had been appointed by Bill Clinton. All of those Republican presidents had run for office vowing to appoint judges who "interpreted" the law rather than made it. Not coincidentally, underlying its strict constructionist bent was a reflexive adherence to free market principles.

> • >

THE CRIMINAL CASE AGAINST Milberg Weiss and its two named partners acquired an indelible face on the morning of July 19, 2006. In federal court in Los Angeles, U.S. District Court Judge John F. Walter, a sixty-one-year-old George W. Bush appointee, was cleared to preside over the trial. Douglas Axel, who represented the U.S. attorney's office, addressed him: "There's certainly a significant possibility of new indictments, but we're not in position to know what the contours are." This was a clear signal that a grand jury was still hearing evidence. Axel requested a trial date in July 2007. The judge demurred but did issue an order authorizing prosecutors to seek defense documents and depose witnesses outside the grand jury—a more efficient process for the prosecution. The case was now seven years old, the judge noted pointedly, urging the government lawyers to pick up the pace.

Before the status conference, attorneys for the firm and for Bershad and Schulman appeared with their clients in front of a federal magistrate. David Bershad, looking wan, was flanked by his attorneys Robert Luskin (who had defended presidential adviser Karl Rove in the Valerie Plame mess) and San Francisco Bay Area criminal defense attorney Cristina Arguedas (who had been part of O. J. Simpson's murder defense team). Steve Schulman had added two additional lawyers to his defense—Gordon A.

Greenberg, a former federal prosecutor from Los Angeles, and Herbert J. Stern, a sixty-year-old former federal judge from New Jersey. The obligatory bombast emanated from the several defense lawyers, who told the judge they were looking forward to the fight before a jury. Perhaps they were simply doing the equivalent of painting their faces before a battle, but with full-on discovery about to begin and with each of the defendants knowing what was about to be disclosed, the tough talk would soon devolve into discussing how to exchange information for reduced prison time.

> • >

ON AUGUST 1 a Fifth Circuit panel dealt an indirect blow to the plaintiffs. In a unanimous decision that encouraged Merrill Lynch attorney Stuart Baskin, the court tossed out the government's criminal convictions of four ex–Merrill Lynch executives on conspiracy and wire fraud. This was the case Bill Lerach had considered an early break for his clients in the class action against the Enron defendants. It focused on the 1999 transaction between Enron and Merrill for the electricity-generating Nigerian barges, which Enron allegedly had sold to Merrill, with the understanding that Enron would buy the barges back. The government had insisted it was a sham, no more than an attempt to veil a loan from Merrill to Enron.

The appellate court ruled that the government had failed to prove the Merrill executives had acted solely for personal gain. The decision was written by Judge E. Grady Jolly, a sixty-nine-year-old Mississippian and Reagan appointee, who'd been on the bench since 1982 and was considered one of its staunchest constructionists. "The only personal benefit or incentive originated with Enron itself—not from a third party as in the case of bribery or kickbacks," Jolly wrote.

Not only did the decision potentially remove Merrill from the Enron scheme in the civil case by designating the underwriters as secondary actors, it cleaved closely to the detested 1994 *Central Bank* decision that Lerach had been attempting to steer around. "Let's hope we don't draw Judge Jolly or the other two," Lerach told his colleagues. Actually, the chances of drawing Judge Jolly in December were better than anyone could have foreseen.

A few weeks later, and for a few taut moments, the plaintiffs' attorneys experienced another reason to rein in their optimism. On Monday, October 23, in federal court in Houston a few doors down from Melinda Harmon's chambers, Jeffrey Skilling, arguably the most vilified of the Enron criminal defendants, was sentenced to twenty-four years and four months in prison. The duty to inform Andy Fastow, the plaintiffs' newfound cooperating witness, fell to Paul Howes.

Following an agreement struck by Bill Lerach and John Keker, Fastow's lawyer, Howes and Fastow had met every day for three weeks, with Fastow reciting everything he knew about the Byzantine scheme between Enron and the banks and auditors. The U.S. marshals had complied, delivering Fastow from the federal detention center to the Lerach Coughlin war room in Houston every day. There the attorney and his witness spoke for up to eight hours a day, as Fastow filled in the gaps in Lerach's lawsuit against the remaining banks.

On schedule Fastow was escorted to the plaintiffs' attorneys' offices the day of Skilling's sentencing to resume their depositions. While it was true that Skilling, then forty-two years old, had first faced more than a hundred years of confinement, Howes was nervous about informing Fastow of the sentence, fearing its severity might unsettle their potential star witness or perhaps cause him to break off his cooperation. Fastow was famous for flying off the handle and was growing edgy as his own sentencing approached. Howes felt tight in the stomach. Fastow greeted him cordially. Howes tried not to project his own anxiety as he delivered the news. The two sat, facing each other. "Jeff got twenty-four years," Howes said evenly.

Fastow looked at Howes as if Howes himself had rendered the judgment. Then he exploded. "Every moment I spend with you is a moment I spend away from my family," he railed. "Look at me—I could still get ten years!" He turned away, trying to right himself. Then, as if mentioning his family had provided a source of inner strength, he turned back to Howes. "All right. I gave you my word," Fastow said softly. "I'll keep my word to you."

> • >

IN THE MONTHS LEADING up to the decision by the Fifth Circuit on whether to hear the Enron banks' appeal to be discharged from the civil lawsuits, Lerach's powers of concentration were put to the test by a litany of distractions that would have filled a decade with angst for most people.

In August, John Torkelsen, his friend and expert witness, entered federal prison in Morgantown, West Virginia. Flat broke but still proud, he had asked for no help from his friends in finding a private defense attorney, relying on a court-appointed public defender instead. Now that he was doing five years in prison, the prosecutors were letting him know that as their investigation continued and as they turned over more evidence from his billing records, he could stay longer if they decided to bring perjury charges against him for lying about his fees as an expert witness for Bill Lerach. Lerach soon learned through the grapevine that Torkelsen was being transferred intermittently to Los Angeles, where investigators were reviewing his handwriting and financial records.

The calls with Mel Weiss were now only occasional, but both men made a point of staying cordial. Much as they wanted to, they also tried not to talk openly about the criminal investigation, in case someone was eavesdropping. Knowing also that they were now competitors, Lerach was also circumspect about discussing new or potential civil cases. Sometimes he would inquire about Dave Bershad or Steve Schulman. Adding to Lerach's worries, Weiss was now reporting only sporadic conversations with his two former partners fighting federal charges. Both Lerach and Weiss fretted about the possibility of the two turning on them.

Finally, of mutual concern were the messy matters of Alan Schulman, Lerach's onetime nemesis in San Diego, and Robert Sugarman, the so-called "Partner E" in the indictments. Both men had been obviously cooperating with the federal prosecutors. Even more disquieting, having heard of Pat Hynes's generous severance, they were claiming in court that both firms, Milberg Weiss and Lerach Coughlin, owed them money from legal fees earned while the two partners were at the firm but not received until after they had left. Millions of dollars were at stake. So was principle. In Lerach's mind, not only had the two partners left on their own before the split, but they were now betraying Weiss and Lerach. How greedy was that?

Even so, Enron in all its permutations still occupied the forefront of Lerach's attention. Several members of the University of California Board of Regents had become jittery. Chris Patti, the University of California lawyer, remained a Lerach ally. He assured any doubters that he had spoken to their now-tainted litigator and reported back that Lerach was "saddened, determined to move forward with respect to his own situation and do his work." It was as much a message to the remaining Enron defendants as it was to the UC Regents, who found themselves in a quandary. Lerach had fashioned settlements that would return more than $7 billion to them. As much as $10 billion or more was still out there. Should they jettison Lerach and risk losing a bigger prize? Patti and Judge Irving steadfastly reminded queasy members of the UC board that Lerach had not been charged with any crime. So far at least, after numerous phone conversations with board members, including an agitated Gerald Parsky, they seemed to be prevailing. So far, serious money trumped serious misgivings.

But on November 1, 2006, something happened that Irving and the Regents of the University of California were powerless to prevent. The announcement from the Fifth U.S. Circuit Court of Appeals had the effect of sounding an air raid siren in the Houston and San Diego war rooms of the law firm of Lerach, Coughlin, Stoia & Robbins. The panel determined that the remaining Enron defendants could appeal. A thirty-day window was also allowed for those defendants, Credit Suisse, Barclays, Merrill Lynch, and the law firm of Vinson & Elkins, to file their briefs buttressing their appeals, while plaintiffs' attorneys Lerach Coughlin were given the same opportunity to rebut the defense. Oral arguments were now scheduled for February 7, 2007.

> • >

STILL ANOTHER MATTER WAS now competing for Bill Lerach's attention, and in this he took solace and great joy.

By three o'clock on the afternoon of November 11, 2006, Armistice

Day, more than three hundred guests, many of the same people who'd feted him on his sixtieth birthday nine months before, passed through the tall, wide security gates and descended one hundred yards upon gray cobblestones worn by age and imported from Brooklyn. The stone walkway curved through lush camellias and citrus trees and ferns in sloping gardens adorned with eight-foot-tall, two-ton terracotta Spanish and Italian olive oil casks as well as anthropomorphic African stone sculptures, some twice the size of humans, standing sentry to the 16,000-square-foot, caramel-colored Italianate villa below. This was the house on the hill that Bill Lerach had espied curiously from the La Jolla beach nearly thirty years earlier. In September, the year before, this estate, perched on a six-acre, arrowhead-shaped peninsula above the Pacific Ocean, with unblocked views seventy-five miles north to Orange County, south to the promontory town of La Jolla, west to near eternity, and occupying top-tier status on *Forbes*'s list of most expensive houses in America, became his.

He had sued two of the previous owners, and another had lost a bundle in the savings and loan meltdown. The three-story house was constructed from French limestone and featured six bedrooms and eleven bathrooms. From the circular driveway steps led downward to a large courtyard featuring an ancient Italian fountain and more African statuary. Visitors entered a great hall filled with enough art treasures—oils, tapestries, African and Polynesian masks and figures, oriental rugs, antique European furniture, and sculptures—to outfit a medium-sized museum. A wide stairway led to the living quarters above. A hallway led to another room of nearly equal size also filled with art treasures and antique rugs that the six dogs of the house—an aging greyhound, a Papillon, two boxers, a whippet, and a Chihuahua—used as runways for gaining traction when launching themselves into play or to answer an alarm. In front, a two-tiered, partly covered and colonnaded portico big enough to accommodate at least a hundred guests, overlooked a swimming pool, and beyond that and a few steps down lay a great lawn flanked by immaculate, cantilevered, microclimate-appropriate botanical gardens, and fruit orchards and palms. Beyond, a fenced walkway skirted the far edge of the sea cliff with a wrought-iron gazebo at the apex of the overlook.

These grounds provided Lerach's favorite paths for patrolling with his garden shears, timing his sojourn so he could attend the day's climactic event when the descending sun combined with marine air to leave behind a parfait-laminated sky. Often, as he had made his rounds at dusk, he thought of his deceased mother who had not beheld this glorious estate. She had been the strong one, the deserving one—not his father—his mother. She could have run a corporation, and no one would have sued her, not because they didn't have the guts but because she was tough-minded and scrupulous and thus would have been lawsuit-proof. He liked to tell people that he hoped some of his mother might have rubbed off on her two sons.

Flanking the villa on its north side was a tennis court, now tented in an extravagant Arabian-nights flair that only someone sporty—Jay Gatsby in that time, or Malcolm Forbes in his day, and now Bill Lerach in his—would have insisted on. On this day of their marriage, her first and his fourth, with an aplomb that would have made Mel Weiss's target Martha Stewart envious, Michelle Ciccarelli had arranged and would oversee the entire pageant, marshaling the caterers, florists, valets, musicians—three bands would play—and of course, the wedding party itself.

While her greatest achievement as a Milberg Weiss attorney had been as part of the team that had caused American clothing manufacturers to settle with garment workers in the Marianas, her added contributions in Enron and WorldCom had allayed most of the tongue-wagging about her relationship with Lerach; many of the wedding guests had come as much out of respect for Michelle as they had for the name partner of the law firm where they both worked—but where, because of nepotism rules, she was soon to be *of counsel.* Sara Walter Combs, the widow of Kentucky governor Bert Combs, would officiate at the ceremony staged on the lawn overlooking the ocean. A former schoolteacher, she was the first woman elected to Kentucky's Supreme Court. After narrowly losing reelection, she was appointed to the Kentucky appellate court, where she became its chief. One of her star clerks had been Michelle.

Among the guests were a Pittsburgh contingent, colleagues inside and outside the firm, judges he'd tried cases before, politicians he'd supported—and foundation and museum administrators he'd also supported. The ring bearer looked Fred Astaire suave in his hand-sewn black tuxedo and pulled off his obligation without a hitch, registering a performance that impressed all who witnessed it—especially considering that it was executed by Tommy, Bill's beloved Chihuahua. At one point in the ceremony a small squall, not uncommon this time of the year, formed far out at sea. Through the marine mist a perfect rainbow formed, and someone in the awestruck crowd was heard to say: "Wonder how much they paid for that?"

All praised the day as being close to perfect, and only some remarked sotto voce that conspicuously absent were Mel Weiss, Bill's longtime partner and mentor, and Mel's wife, Bobbi. Even so, the guests, especially the attorneys and staff who had been toiling on Enron and Halliburton, and those lawyers trying other cases or developing new ones, and nearly all those who knew that Bill Lerach was now under a darkening cloud, appreciated the moment for what it was: a respite before the storm.

> • >

BILL LERACH HAD SEEDED the clouds, and just weeks after the wedding, legal thunderclaps could be heard. Nearly a year earlier, impatient with the pace and management of the Halliburton litigation, he had added three plaintiffs to join the Archdiocese of Milwaukee Supporting Fund: the Plumbers and Pipefitters National Pension Fund, the city of Dearborn Heights (Michigan) Police and Fire Retirement System Fund, and the Laborers National Pension Fund. Taken together, the new plaintiffs surpassed the original plaintiff in membership, wealth, and investments. By showing new muscle, which he hoped to elevate to lead status over the Milwaukee diocese fund, Lerach intended to gain control of the lawsuit—and provide impetus for Halliburton to settle.

This plan seemed workable, at least until the *Chicago Tribune* reported on June 22 that William K. Cavanagh, a legal adviser for Plumbers and Pipefitters and other union pension funds, had received $750,000 in referral fees and legal work from Milberg Weiss. An unidentified attorney at Lerach Coughlin nuanced the revelation, telling the *Tribune* reporter that the payments mirrored long-standing practices throughout the legal profession.

The unidentified attorney also accused the *Tribune* of retaliating because Lerach Coughlin was suing its parent company in a class action lawsuit.

The story not only caught the eyes of prosecutors in Los Angeles, it alarmed the original plaintiff. When an already-wary Paula John, president of the Archdiocese of Milwaukee Supporting Fund, read two weeks later in *The Nation* magazine that Lerach was looking forward to grilling Vice President Cheney under oath, she got a sinking feeling that Lerach was pursuing a personal agenda on the back of her fund—his client.

The last straw was provided by Peter Elkind, the reputable editor-at-large for *Fortune* magazine. In a 9,200-word cover story entitled "Fall of America's Meanest Law Firm," Elkind reprised nearly the government's entire case against Milberg Weiss and its partners and pointed a well-informed finger at Mel Weiss and Bill Lerach.* Paula John called Neil Rothstein, who had started a think tank focusing on legal ethics. When she asked Rothstein what to do about Lerach, he suggested removing him from the case. The most delicate way, he advised her, might be to persuade Lerach's cocounsel, and Rothstein's former firm, Scott & Scott, to discreetly wield the knife.

"Due to the strong manner, tone, and factual information stated in Elkind's article, I feel that I am left with no choice but to direct you to remove Lerach and his firm from the Halliburton case," John promptly wrote to David Scott, a name partner at his firm. Scott, the forty-two-year-old son of the founder of his law firm, had worked with Lerach on cases prior to Halliburton, and he had agreed with Lerach's strategy of bringing big-foot plaintiffs into Halliburton. But the directive was unmistakable. If he wanted to keep his firm on the case, he would have to dissociate Lerach.

Scott called Lerach, predicting his cocounsel's response before he heard his voice on the phone. He knew there would be profanity, uttered at high volume. Sure enough, as he gingerly broached the subject of his ally

---

* Elkind also coauthored, along with *Fortune* reporter Bethany McLean, *Enron: The Smartest Guys in the Room*, a best-selling 2003 book documenting the Enron scandal. A 2005 documentary film based on the book won the Independent Spirit Award for Best Documentary Feature and was nominated for Best Documentary Feature at the 78th Academy Awards. Bill Lerach provided commentary throughout the film.

stepping away from the case, Lerach's voice rose to battle-stations decibels. When his friend's tirade was finished, Scott assured Lerach he would remain steadfast with him.

Meanwhile, working through Dallas attorney E. Lawrence Vincent and with the help of Rothstein, the archdiocese fund had nearly completed its brief urging the court to permit it to dump Lerach. Just as Lerach had added union muscle to his own lineup of plaintiffs, the archdiocese fund solicited a worthy stand-in. It was the firm of Boies, Schiller & Flexner, more specifically David Boies. The fifty-five-year-old Yale Law School graduate and founder of his firm possessed a stellar résumé. He had represented IBM in an antitrust case that the government had unsuccessfully tried. Turning around, he had represented the government in its antitrust lawsuit against Microsoft. He had represented New York Yankees owner George Steinbrenner in a lawsuit against Major League Baseball and defended CBS in the libel suit filed by former Army General William Westmoreland. He helped American Express win $4 billion in a suit against Visa. He'd had a key role in defending Bill Clinton during impeachment, and he'd played a leading part on the legal team battling for Al Gore in the infamous 2000 Florida recount. In 2003 Boies had even represented Andrew Fastow in the first round of depositions in the Enron case.

Understanding the exquisite delicacy of the Halliburton disorder, Boies signaled his willingness to take on the role of lead counsel, but only after the unfinished business of removing Lerach had been accomplished.

And so, by the second week of November, attorneys for the archdiocese fund informed Lerach that they planned to file a motion in federal court in Dallas with Judge Barbara Lynn, to remove Lerach Coughlin and Neil Rothstein's former firm, Scott & Scott, as lead counsel in the lawsuit against Halliburton. They cited the criminal investigation of Lerach and claimed a lack of responsiveness to requests for all documents between the two law firms as the main reasons. Rothstein was to remain a "special counsel." Although the choice of Boies as a replacement camouflaged it, another rationale for jettisoning Lerach—perhaps the more incandescent reason— involved politics. The plaintiffs decried what they described as Lerach's public posturing in trying the Enron case and, more particular to their own case, his stated intention of pursuing Vice President Cheney. The petition was filed on November 22. Lerach didn't know who to be angriest at, and there was no shortage of possible culprits.

His frustration came to a head in the San Diego office conference room in early December, as lawyers from Lerach Coughlin frantically prepared a countermotion to try to hang on to the case. One young attorney, Ramzi Abadou, a relative newcomer to the firm, was troubled by the developments. After graduating from Boston College Law School in 2002, he found himself under Lerach's wing. The bond had been forged earlier when Abadou, as a college undergraduate, worked summers as a document clerk.

When Abadou—whip-fit, personable, but intense—joined the firm as an attorney, Lerach set him to work developing new clients. Abadou knew he was being groomed and was grateful for the opportunity. He also had been taken with Lerach's professional comportment, particularly the way he prepared for battle. "When you take a guy like that who already knows almost everything and prepares with the zeal of a new convert to the law, he's just unstoppable," he had told colleagues.

But during the summer and fall of 2006, Abadou was drilling into dry holes in search of new clients. And he could point to the reason—the criminal investigation. He too was encountering a backlash about Lerach's public pronouncements of going after Cheney. To Abadou, this had become counterproductive. When the crisis over being dismissed from the Halliburton case arose, Abadou counted himself among a nonvocal group of Lerach Coughlin lawyers who thought the best thing to do would be to bow out gracefully.

At the strategy meeting, Abadou voiced his concerns, urging Lerach to consider withdrawing. He even suggested the firm issue a press release saying that while the firm regretted the client's decision, in the best interests of the class, the firm would offer to help Boies, Schiller & Flexner get up to speed as quickly as possible. While Abadou idolized his boss, he hadn't accurately analyzed him.

Lerach went ballistic. "I will not be told what to do!" he screamed. "This is my firm. This is my case. This is personal."

No one knew whether he meant because Rothstein had betrayed him or if he was referring to his visceral antipathy for Dick Cheney, a man whom he'd never actually met—and no one had the courage to ask.

Later, Abadou reflected: "He shouldn't have told anyone. He should have just taken Cheney's deposition and then said something about him later."

> • > • > • > • >

A NARROW DEFINITION
OF DECEIT

On November 1, 2006, Geralyn Maher, a calendar clerk for the Fifth Circuit Court of Appeals in New Orleans, drew three judges' names from a
wheel in a high-stakes courthouse version of Bingo. For the case of the *University of California Regents v. Credit Suisse First Boston, Merrill Lynch, and
Barclays*, the names that emerged from the wheel were Jerry Edwin Smith,
James W. Dennis, and Rhesa Hawkins Barksdale. In their hands would lie
the future of scheme liability. From what Bill Lerach knew about the three
men, he was not encouraged.

Jerry Smith was a Reagan appointee from the Texas border town of Del
Rio known primarily for writing the majority opinion striking down affirmative action at the University of Texas Law School, a decision that would
be superseded seven years later by the U.S. Supreme Court's 5–4 decision
upholding affirmative action at the University of Michigan Law School.
The next jurist, James Dennis of New Orleans, was appointed by President
Clinton in 1995. Although he had figured in few noteworthy decisions,
Lerach considered him sympathetic toward victims of corporate fraud. He
was happy with Judge Dennis. The remaining member of the panel was
Rhesa Barksdale of Mississippi. Appointed by President George H.W. Bush

in 1989, Barksdale was a 1966 graduate of the U.S. Military Academy. In his book *The Long Gray Line*, Pulitzer Prize–winning journalist Rick Atkinson traced the experiences of Barksdale's West Point class in Vietnam and quoted the then-young cadet as saying: "I look forward to going to Vietnam. Every American has a commitment to go to Vietnam to do his part."

Following his combat tours, Barksdale left the Army and graduated from the University of Mississippi Law School, clerked for Justice Byron White on the Supreme Court, entered private practice, and was teaching at Ole Miss Law School when Bush tapped him for the Fifth Circuit. A conservative, business-friendly Republican, Barksdale was rumored to be short-listed for Supreme Court when Bush's son came into office.*

The three judges' names were disclosed in January 2007, less than two weeks before the panel was to hear oral arguments. Looking to try to change the equation, University of California attorney Chris Patti noticed something about Barksdale. That distinctive last name was the same as that of Jim Barksdale, the flamboyant founder of Netscape, the once-dominant Internet browser. Patti checked and learned that the two Barksdales were brothers. Was it something they could use to get Judge Barksdale off the case? He called Lerach to confer.

Lerach told him that Milberg Weiss had sued Jim Barksdale and that he was a defendant in a current Lerach Coughlin lawsuit against AOL/Time Warner—Barksdale served on its board. After he hung up the phone, Lerach directed an associate, Eric Isaacson, to draft a motion calling for Barksdale's recusal. Speed was essential, and Isaacson finished in two days. The motion reached the clerk's office in New Orleans with little time to spare—but enough for Judge Barksdale to recognize that he had no choice but to step aside. When they heard the news, the plaintiffs' attorneys rejoiced, then held their collective breath waiting for the next selection. But their luck had actually taken a turn for the worse. The final judge hearing the banks' appeal would be E. Grady Jolly.

Meanwhile, in a courthouse in St. Louis, in a case with no Enron or

---

* Apparently he wasn't conservative enough, or perhaps not young enough: When a vacancy arose in September 2005, Bush selected Samuel Alito for the court instead.

Lerach Coughlin lawyers involved, the fates of Lerach's plaintiffs took another hit. The case was *Stoneridge Investment Partners v. Scientific-Atlanta and Motorola Inc.* It began in August 2000 when top officers of Charter Communications, a St. Louis cable company, realized they were not going to make their numbers. Their solution was to cook their books by entering into "wash" transactions with two of their suppliers, Motorola and Scientific-Atlanta. Charter asked those companies to charge $20 more than market price for the digital boxes that customers were required to have in their homes. In turn, Charter directed their vendors to return the extra money in the form of advertising revenue that Motorola and Scientific-Atlanta neither wanted nor needed—at five times the going rate. This allowed Charter to make it appear to analysts and investors that they were reaping millions more in advertising dollars than was really the case.

Charter ran this shady arrangement by its accountant, Arthur Andersen, which said it could not recognize the "advertising" payments as revenue if they were, in fact, tied to the purchases of the boxes. In late September, Charter ginned up misleading written agreements with Motorola and Scientific-Atlanta setting the price of the boxes at the higher amount and including contracts to purchase advertising—as separate agreements, even though they really weren't—and then backdated the agreements to August. When the accounting tricks came to light, four of Charter's top financial officers pled guilty to felony conspiracy charges, two of whom went to prison.

In the ensuing civil litigation, Charter agreed to pay $144 million to settle with its major outside shareholder, Stoneridge Investment Partners of Malvern, Pennsylvania. But Stoneridge attorney Stanley Grossman also sued Motorola and Scientific-Atlanta (which, significantly as it would turn out, later became a unit of Cisco Systems). This was a classic example of scheme liability, Grossman argued: Charter simply could not have pulled off the fraud without being joined in the ruse by the two vendors.

Citing the Supreme Court's *Central Bank* decision, however, a federal district judge in St. Louis determined that the defendants, at worst, had aided and abetted the cable company and could not be sued. Grossman appealed, but in April 2006 an appellate panel in St. Louis upheld the dismissal.

Months later in Pasadena, California, a three-judge panel of the Ninth

Circuit—one member a Reagan appointee, one a George H.W. Bush appointee, and the third a Clinton appointee—heard a case called *Simpson v. AOL Time Warner*, which had a set of facts similar to those of *Stoneridge*. The plaintiffs, the California State Teachers Retirement System, were represented by Joe Cotchett, Lerach's *Lincoln Savings* colleague. Cotchett argued that a sell-and-buy-back scheme between the media giant and an Internet real estate company constituted a deception concocted for one purpose—to defraud investors. Lerach bolstered Cotchett's argument in an amicus brief, emphatically identifying the alleged chicanery as "scheme liability," not aiding and abetting. The SEC, now headed by Lerach's old adversary Christopher Cox, surprised many by allowing SEC senior counsel Michael L. Post to also submit a friend-of-the-court brief in support of the plaintiffs. The Ninth Circuit agreed that a trial should go forward.

With dueling appellate court decisions, the Eighth Circuit's ruling on *Stoneridge* would not necessarily be binding in the UC Regents' Enron case pending in the Fifth Circuit and, indeed, might be overturned. Lerach phoned Stanley Grossman to discuss how they might rebound from an adverse ruling by the Eighth Circuit. This wasn't an academic conversation: the Supreme Court had accepted Grossman's appeal. A hearing was set for April 2007. In agreeing to hear the *Stoneridge* case the high court was agreeing to define just how far it had intended the tentacles of its *Central Bank* decision to stretch.

> • >

ON WEDNESDAY, DECEMBER 6, 2006, Steve Schulman asked Mel Weiss to meet him for breakfast the next day. There he delivered the news that his criminal trial date had been set for January 2008. Schulman's attorneys were advising him that he faced an uphill battle with the prosecutors in Los Angeles and to devote all his energy to fighting the charges. Therefore he was resigning from the firm.

On Friday, December 8, Weiss dutifully issued a written statement praising Schulman as a "brilliant lawyer," and giving no hint of the stress Schulman was under. "This was his decision," Weiss said blandly, "and doesn't imply anything other than he wants to do his own thing." Schulman reiterated his earlier pledge to "vigorously fight the indictments, while Sam Singer, his designated spokesman, added that his client had been planning to leave Milberg Weiss for some time. Singer flatly denied the speculation that Schulman might be cooperating with the prosecutors.

What Schulman did not admit was that he was terrified of going to the penitentiary. As far as the Los Angeles prosecutors were concerned, however, he wasn't yet doing anything that would keep him out of a prison cell. That would soon change, even if it meant others would have to do time behind bars instead, including the man he had invited to breakfast on this December day—and also his famous protégé—Bill Lerach.

> • >

ON MONDAY AFTERNOON, February 5, 2007, Patrick Coughlin entered the three-story granite John Minor Wisdom U.S. Court of Appeals Building on Camp Street in New Orleans, to take his place at the respondents' table. Under his arm he carried a copy of the 182-page response to the banks' petition for what amounted to immunity from liability. With him to show support was his mother, who took her place in the visitor gallery. Joining her was Bill Lerach, his wife, Michelle, Judge Irving, University of California attorney Chris Patti, and Lerach Coughlin partner Byron Georgiou and his wife, Therese. Appearing for the petitioners were Stuart J. Baskin on behalf of Merrill Lynch, David H. Braff (the Sullivan & Cromwell attorney representing Barclays), and Richard W. Clary (of Cravath, Swaine & Moore, representing Credit Suisse First Boston). The three judges, Smith, Jolly, and Dennis, strode solemnly to their chairs at the head of the bench.

Judge Smith opened by praising both sides for their clear and compelling briefs. Then the questions began. They were courteous but rigidly focused on precedent and the evolution of the cases cited by counsel back to *Central Bank*. The questions, Coughlin thought to himself, especially those from Jolly and Smith, had a federalist bent, which seemed to reinforce the attorneys for the banks. This alarmed him. Judge Dennis remained mostly silent.

Coughlin and Lerach considered Judge Dennis their best hope. If previous decisions were any indication, Judge Jolly was going to be a tough sell. So the plan was to focus their arguments for Judge Smith and hope if they were able to persuade him, Jolly might go along. Even if he didn't, a 2–1 vote would carry the case. Smith, therefore, was considered the key. It was Smith who seemed to be challenging Coughlin to convince him that it was the deceptive conduct of the banks and the reliance on their conduct by the plaintiffs that had caused the plaintiffs harm. Coughlin applied Lerach's scheme liability reasoning, arguing that the conspiracies entered by Merrill Lynch, Credit Suisse, and Barclays with Enron were so integral to Enron's frauds that, when it came to liability, Enron and the banks were indistinguishable.

As the plaintiffs' attorneys and their families departed the courthouse two hours later, they could not say they had won or lost, although to Coughlin, it felt as though the judges were trying to save the banks. Coughlin and his mother split off, and the Lerachs and their party continued past Canal Street into the French Quarter where they encountered evidence of Mardi Gras, the second annual celebration since Hurricane Katrina had devastated the city. They arrived at their destination, Nola, a happening new restaurant with a decor of light wood and exposed brick operated by celebrity chef Emeril Lagasse. Their party was seated, and as they scanned their menus, Judge Jolly walked in accompanied by two men.

The trio strode past Lerach and his friends without acknowledgment or eye contact. During their meal, however, Jolly surprised Lerach by rising from his seat and walking over to the table where the Californians were seated. Displaying gentlemanly decorum, he made brief small talk before mentioning, as all New Orleans residents did in those days, the ongoing suffering that Hurricane Katrina had left in its wake. As he took his leave, Jolly intoned in his Mississippi drawl, "We want to thank y'all for comin' and helpin' our economy." With that, he turned and returned to his table.

The exchange struck Lerach as patronizing, as if they were in New Orleans by choice, and he felt a flash of his famous temper. As the judge and his party rose to leave, Lerach rose too and positioned himself near the doorway. Seeing the obstacle, the judge altered his stride, stepping around

Lerach without speaking or making eye contact. Lerach returned to the table and let out a deep sigh. "I suspect we've lost," he said.

On March 19, his premonition was proven true. In a 2–1 decision, with Judge Jolly writing the majority opinion and Judge Dennis dissenting, the Fifth Circuit sided with the banks. The panel couched its ruling in conciliatory language, conceding that their decision "may not coincide . . . with notions of justice and fair play." But the judges clung fiercely to the crimped reasoning of *Central Bank* and, taking a narrow definition of deception, upheld the petitioners and decertified the shareholder class action against the banks.

"Presuming plaintiffs' allegations to be true, Enron committed fraud by misstating its accounts, but the banks only aided and abetted that fraud by engaging in transactions to make it more plausible; they owed no duty to Enron's shareholders," Judge Jolly wrote for the court.

Lerach and his colleagues were incensed. Al Meyerhoff, a Lerach Coughlin partner who had led the fight against the Marianas sweatshops, analyzed the ruling this way: "The effect of the opinion is to allow investment banks to both charge fees and escape liability for constructing and carrying out transactions that they understand have no other purpose than to falsify financial results reported to investors."

He wasn't alone in this assessment. Peter Lattman, the estimable writer for *Fortune Law Blog* and no enemy of business, found the court's logic so restrictive as to constitute a perversion of fair play: "Executives owe honest services to those shareholders, and one of the most basic is to report finances accurately," he wrote. "This time I'm with Lerach."

Regardless, the upshot was that Paul Howes and his huge team of lawyers, experts, and assistants had been shut down. They had put in thousands of hours preparing for a trial that was scheduled to start in two weeks, which had a hundred witnesses, including Andy Fastow, lined up to testify, along with hundreds of depositions and millions of documents and exhibits to throw at the defendants in support of the arguments Pat Coughlin was ready to present to a jury. Judge Melinda Harmon had no choice but to postpone the trial. To Howes, the former U.S. Marine and Vietnam combat veteran, the decision by the Fifth Circuit was "a gut shot."

Richard Clary felt a letdown even though his side had won. As the lead defense attorney for Credit Suisse, he had prepared for five years for a trial that now wouldn't happen. Poolside in Florida on the afternoon of March 19 when his BlackBerry sounded, one minute he was jubilant, he told *The American Lawyer*, the next he was disappointed. "But," he added, "I'm probably less disappointed than Lerach."

Lerach was more than disappointed. "What this pretty much means is that the courthouse door was slammed in the face of the Enron victims," he told reporters angrily. "We think the decision is wrong under the law, and we think it's unfair to the victims of the worst securities fraud in recent memory to be denied the chance to even prove their case against the banks."

But it had not ended the possibility that class plaintiffs would get their day in court, to pursue crooked bankers, he added. The most recent setback by the Fifth Circuit simply ratcheted up the disagreement over the scope of primary liability. Two other appellate courts were already in conflict, and now this one had joined the fray. A remedy was at hand, and Lerach announced it: "We are going to seek review in the U.S. Supreme Court as quick as we can."

> • >

DURING THE WEEKEND OF February 24, Lerach tried to take his mind off the news expected out of U.S. District Court Judge Barbara Lynn's Dallas court on Monday. For weeks, the Clinton appointee had deliberated on who should stay and who should go as plaintiffs' counsel in the Halliburton case—and who should serve as designated lead counsel suing the company once run by Dick Cheney. On Sunday, Lerach and his wife went to a colleague's home for a buffet dinner and viewing of the Academy Awards. The Oscar for best picture went to *The Departed*. Lerach tried not to project too much into that, except that Martin Scorsese's movie evoked dark implications about a brash young man who'd crossed the line and the sinister father figure who had led him there.

The next morning Judge Lynn announced that while she was not asserting that Lerach's firm had done "anything unethical, immoral, or otherwise improper," she was ruling in the best interests of the Archdiocese of Milwaukee Supporting Fund in finding that its relationship with Lerach Coughlin "was no longer productive."

Halliburton—and anything the vice president may have done—would now be David Boies's challenge, as Judge Lynn also approved the archdiocese fund's request to replace them with the firm of Boies, Schiller & Flexner. Attempting to be philosophical, Lerach found himself wondering whether, seven years earlier, if David Boies had been successful in his representation of Al Gore and Joseph Lieberman in their challenge to the election of George W. Bush and Richard B. Cheney, he would have even sued Halliburton in the first place. The standard Lerach answer would have been: *This wasn't personal. It was strictly business.* In this instance, he admitted long after the fact, that claim would have been disingenuous.

> • >

THE LIGHT, AIRY, but intimate decor of L'Atelier restaurant in the Four Seasons Hotel at East 57th Street and Park Avenue helped offset the mood at the table where Bill Lerach and Mel Weiss met for dinner. It was Sunday, May 27, 2007, the day before Memorial Day. The two legal leviathans were sitting across from each other at a time when the divide between the high-rise offices overlooking San Diego Harbor and those at One Penn Plaza was the greatest in their history together. This division went unmentioned. The talk began with shared consolation for mutual defeats in different federal courts. For a moment it was like old times, especially when Lerach regaled his former partner by telling him how close he'd come to deposing Dick Cheney. That prompted harmonic vitriol from both men toward the Bush administration and its dark princes. The conversation turned to family, mutual friends, reminiscences of past cases, victories on behalf of their clients and themselves—triumphs, they said, on behalf of *society.* As the conversation began to sound like an epilogue of their many years together, what was on both Bill Lerach's and Mel Weiss's mind eventually insinuated itself.

The government had made overtures to both of them to settle the score. Lerach repeated what the prosecutors had been conveying: work out a negotiated disposition, one that might require a hefty but doable fine, an acknowledgment that mistakes had been made, accept some oversight and get on with business. His mentor looked at him sharply. "You're a higher profile than me," he said raspily, almost sounding sympathetic to his younger colleague.

Lerach felt himself tightening and knew his face was beginning to turn red. "Mel, the statute of limitations on Cooperman has all but run out on me," he said. To which Weiss retorted tersely, "Congratulations."

Lerach turned the conversation. How was Mel getting along without Dave or Steve? Weiss's reply startled him. Some of the other partners, the younger ones, were pestering him to resolve the government's beef with the firm. "But without Dave and Steve, I have no one to veto my decisions. I'm not settling."

"Have you heard from Dave?" Lerach asked.

"No. I haven't called him," Weiss replied, dabbing at his mouth with his napkin. "And he hasn't called me."

With the meal over, the men stood and walked slowly to the restaurant entrance where Weiss's town car was waiting. They shook hands, each placing their free hand on the other's shoulder. As the limo turned the corner and drove out of sight, Lerach lingered outdoors in the warm evening, running an equation through his mind: *Dave won't give Mel up. But he would give me up. But to give me up he would* have *to give Mel up.* Bill Lerach was rarely confused about anything, but he was now: he felt neither consoled nor free from harm. And something else had been nagging at him, something he hadn't shared with his longtime friend and former partner.

Three months earlier, on Wednesday, February 7, 2007, at an evening event at the Sheraton Hotel in Birmingham, Pat Coughlin, whose name appeared second to Lerach's in the lineup of the firm's name partners, had taken him aside. The reason both men were in Alabama was to attend Coughlin's engagement party. Coughlin asked Lerach to step away from the celebration with him. As they walked into the lobby, Lerach noticed his friend and colleague was looking hesitant, and he started to needle him about the pending nuptials. That wasn't what was bothering Coughlin, and it wasn't what he wanted to discuss. Uneasily, he suggested to Lerach that he should consider taking a leave of absence until the criminal investigation had run its course. From his partner and confidant, Lerach heard words he hadn't ever thought possible: "Bill, you could be hurting our firm."

The morning after the dinner with Mel Weiss in New York, Bill and Michelle were sitting over coffee in the terminal at Newark International Airport awaiting their flight home when his cell phone rang. He recognized the number of the caller. It was Mel Weiss. Lerach excused himself and walked into the concourse area.

"I just got off the phone with Ben Brafman," he heard Weiss say. "Dave's going to cut a deal. Our friend has been cooperating."

When Lerach returned, he could tell that Michelle was reading his face, which he figured was flushed with worry. "That was Mel," he told his wife. "I didn't like what he said."

Later—in the emotion of the moment they couldn't remember if it was before or after they entered the first-class cabin of the aircraft—Lerach turned to his new wife and said, "We're done."

Later, both would recall the transcontinental plane ride, always long flying east to west anyway, being extenuated to an excruciating degree by Weiss's message. They would remember the fits and starts of their talks that would carry into the night once they reached their villa on the hill. Together the husband and wife, both lawyers, hashed out the imbroglio that had finally and fully become part of their lives.

"I thought I was safe," Lerach said late one afternoon as the couple left the house, walking toward their outlook over the Pacific. "I was wrong."

Dave Bershad, Lerach explained carefully to his spouse, had been meticulous, keeping legal pads with all the transactions—the payments and credit due. He and Mel had set up the firm's secret coffers to pay plaintiffs for their services and repay the partners for their contributions.

To some degree, the firm's secrets had been revealed earlier to Michelle, through both the indictments and her husband's persuasive explanations of why the indictments would not touch him. Smart enough to draw her own conclusions, she had known what she was getting herself into when she became Lerach's fourth wife.

But she was not about to relinquish her standing as an attorney, not in her own home, not with her husband under fire. She recited the facts. Cooperman was a bad witness. The statute of limitations might have lapsed. Lazar had not been prompted by the firm to sue targeted companies.

"We can fight this," she insisted. "We both know you can win. What they have is . . . what? Torkelsen? Another felon who could also be impeached. Then what?"

"Lazar," he told her. "He got paid. He stood in front of a judge and swore he was not being paid."

Besides, Lazar was ailing. He was vulnerable. If he got beaten down and finally shaken, he might cooperate. And Vogel? Lerach hadn't known much about him, had never met him, but Lerach had willingly taken a piece of the Oxford Health settlement that Vogel had helped them get, even though he had no idea whether Mel's firm was still paying him to be a plaintiff. "I could kill Dave for doing this," he said. "I could be wanted for murder instead of fraud."

Their intense discussions continued. The specter of prison rarely came up, but when it did, Lerach became more, not less, resolute about what he must do. Suddenly he was the CEO he had made a career of suing. He now felt, as those CEOs must have, that he was essentially being extorted.

"I can fight this," he told his wife, "and even if I have a 90 percent chance of winning, what happens if I lose?" He was not being rhetorical. He'd already been holding out, and under the federal sentencing guidelines the longer a suspect repudiated the government's charges, the more the potential for a heftier penalty. In essence, it was not so different from the formula Lerach had used to secure big settlements from those he sued. Mel Weiss would be called to testify against him, he reminded his wife, so would Dave Bershad and Steve Schulman. In fact, they could likely lessen the sentences they were facing if they agreed to testify against him.

Recalling Pat Coughlin's exhortation, Bill told Michelle: "The longer I fight this the more it hurts the firm. They could get indicted." There was also the question of the Enron settlement—no small matter. As much as $700 million could be coming to the firm from the settlements already hammered out. Lerach's own take could be as high as $70 million. He did not want to put that money at risk. With a win in the Supreme Court against the nonsettling banks, the Enron payout could double.

Finally, addressing the 10 percent chance he would lose if, as Bernie Ebbers did, he insisted on going to trial—and those odds might be higher—Lerach looked at his wife of all of six months and said solemnly: "I could be gone for twenty years instead of one or two."

On the Wednesday after Memorial Day, Jon Cuneo answered a cell phone call in Hawaii. Immediately he recognized Lerach's voice. "Jon, we found out over the weekend that Dave has flipped. This is bad news," Cuneo heard Lerach say. "I may have to work out a negotiated disposition."

Cuneo thanked his friend for the heads-up and put down the phone, stunned. He knew immediately the implications of the alert: disbarment, disgrace, the end of Bill's run as lead lawyer in Enron and any other securities cases, probably prison. That day Lerach also directed Kathy Lichnovsky to call John Keker, his defense attorney in San Francisco, and make an appointment, "the sooner the better."

In Los Angeles the prosecutors remained less than certain about the strength of their case against Lerach. They too were aware that Cooperman's credibility was shaky—Keker had pointed it out to them in an earlier meeting, when he told the government lawyers: "I have a black heart. I will eviscerate Steven Cooperman on the stand." The government had no real evidence that Lerach had paid a single plaintiff following passage of the PSLRA a dozen years earlier. John Torkelsen was not cooperating, and his wife, Pam, could only furnish hearsay testimony.

The key, then, was Bershad. So in the early weeks of June they were pleased to see Cristina C. Arguedas, his attorney, with Bershad in tow. Uniformly they would later praise Arguedas for guiding Bershad through his testimony, which prosecutor Douglas Axel characterized as "direct and very helpful."

One week after Memorial Day, in Keker's stylishly understated three-story office tucked into a brick courtyard located in San Francisco's Barbary Coast neighborhood, Lerach paced, refusing to sit. He was blunt. He was willing to cop a plea. But he would cooperate with the government against no one but himself; not against Mel Weiss, not Milberg Weiss, and certainly not Lerach Coughlin or any attorneys connected to the firm. Prosecutors would have to promise to pursue neither his old firm nor his current one and not to try and freeze the Enron fees or enjoin his firm from pursuing their appeal against the remaining banks with the Supreme Court.

Then he turned slightly conciliatory, asking Keker: "How much time do you think I have to serve?" Keker, who had managed to get four years shaved off Andy Fastow's sentence (partly because he persuaded Fastow to cooperate in both the criminal and civil Enron cases), said he would try to negotiate what is known as a section 11(c)1(c) plea agreement under the federal rules of criminal procedure. That would mean trying to predetermine a cap on how long he could serve.

"I'll do three years if necessary," Lerach told his attorney.

Still, it would involve some judicial discretion, Keker replied. It would also mean paying a big fine. Lerach balked.

Keker held firm. "That's what they'll want, Bill," he said, underscoring his client's demands by reminding him that walking into the U.S. attorney's office with both guns blazing wasn't the way to begin negotiating.

"What if Mel comes with you?" Keker asked.

Lerach was taken aback, but not for long. Within a week Lerach and his lawyer flew to New York. The afternoon meeting took place at the Ritz, at a table beneath a window overlooking Central Park. Lerach and Keker sat on one side, Weiss and his attorney Ben Brafman on the other.

Lerach got right to the point. "John thinks we can do only about a year if we go in together," he offered. "We can negotiate to keep our firms intact, but we'll have to admit some wrongdoing and pay a fine. I'll even volunteer to do more time than you."

The words had barely left Lerach's mouth when Weiss replied, "No. They want you, not me."

Brafman, whom Lerach had assumed favored a negotiated plea, amplified Weiss's answer. "My client is a great humanitarian. He has led a generous and philanthropic life. He is a pillar of the community. He will not humiliate himself." To which Weiss added: "If we go to trial in this town and get a couple of Jews on the jury, we'll win."

On their way to the airport to fly home, Keker told his client that Weiss and Brafman had a few surprises coming. "Fat chance of getting a change of venue to New York," he told Lerach. "When Bershad opens, the dam will burst." The pointed message was really aimed at his own client.

Keker's next trip would be to Los Angeles to begin negotiating with acting U.S. attorney George Cardona and Richard Robinson and his team. Immediately, Keker sensed the government lawyers were in the mood to make a deal. What he did not know was that the prosecutors had been seriously debating only weeks earlier whether they had a strong case against Lerach—or one good enough to take to a jury at all. But as Keker had foreseen, Bershad was indeed the watershed witness.

Bill Lerach, his client, was willing to admit guilt, pay a fine, and even do time, Keker told the prosecutors. He would not cooperate in any prosecution against his former partners in either New York or San Diego, and he wanted a binding agreement. "If my client makes a public statement or his plea becomes public and then backfires, we will not go forward," Keker announced. Then he suggested a prison sentence—one year.

Cardona was in no mood to make a deal and have it publicly fall apart, either. But prosecutors were contemplating a prison term of between thirty months and three years, Keker was told to tell his client.

> • >

IF *STONERIDGE V. SCIENTIFIC-ATLANTA* had been a medieval battlefield, the view of the field would have been dominated by a vast array of opposing forces, their war flags at full staff and flying colors, horizon to horizon.

Influential Democratic committee chairmen on Capitol Hill who had always been supportive of Lerach—and vice versa—weighed in on the plaintiffs' side. With a quiet assist from Jon Cuneo, Barney Frank, chairman of the House Financial Services Committee, and John Conyers, Jr., chairman of the House Judiciary Committee, filed an amicus brief in the Stoneridge case, saying that "if the Supreme Court decides against investors in this case, third parties will effectively be immune from suit no matter how reprehensible their conduct."

Scientific-Atlanta and Motorola had retained Mayer Brown, the Chicago-based law firm Lerach had faced in Nucorp, Lexecon, and earlier Enron cases. This time the Mayer Brown attorney would be Stephen Shapiro, who had appeared before the Supreme Court more than a dozen times. Offering support was Joe Grundfest, the former SEC commissioner, Stanford professor, and frequent Lerach critic, who told *The Wall Street Journal* that supporters of the plaintiffs have "been running this more like a political campaign than a Supreme Court brief."

So was the other side. Virtually every Wall Street bank, and many of the nation's most prominent Fortune 500 companies, along with brigades of free market economists, lawyers, and pundits had lined up on the side of Charter Communications' vendors. Just as an earlier generation of Republicans had caricatured the infamous McDonald's spilled coffee case, conservatives now singled out *Stoneridge* as a poster child for litigation run amok. It was easier to play this card in an obscure business dispute like *Stoneridge* than it would have been in the Enron case. Securities litigation, Secretary of the Treasury Henry M. Paulson, Jr., had proclaimed the previous November—without mentioning Enron—is the "Achilles' heel of our economy."

John Engler, former Republican governor of Michigan and president of the National Manufacturers Association, put it this way: "For America's global economic strength, Washington's biggest decision in 2007 will not be made in Congress or the White House but in the Supreme Court." Echoing this sentiment, the editorial page editors of *The Wall Street Journal* called *Stoneridge* "the business case of the year." *The Economist* went further, terming the case "by general consent the most important securities-litigation clash for a generation."

The Bush administration was of two minds, apparently because the president was conflicted. He was no fan of the plaintiffs' bar, but George W. Bush had been burned by his perceived closeness to Ken Lay and the spate of corporate fraud cases unfolding on his watch. In his first term, Bush had given a major speech about corporate responsibility that surprised many people, which he followed up by signing Sarbanes-Oxley. Bush's ambivalence filtered out from the White House to other executive branch agencies and offices, including the SEC chairman's suite occupied by Christopher Cox and the solicitor general's post manned by Paul D. Clement.

One of the youngest solicitor generals in U.S. history, Clement was establishing himself as among the finest legal minds in the country. He was conservative—of that there was no question—but the former star student at Harvard Law performed skillfully in a challenging political environment for a lawyer with intellectual independence. Among other things, Clement had cautioned the Bush administration officials that their plans to water down Environmental Protection Agency rules governing ozone protection contradicted the agency's previous submissions to the Supreme Court and had warned White House lawyers of the adverse implications of the administration's policy regarding indefinite detention of Guantánamo prisoners—even while arguing the government's position before the Supreme Court.

Historically and statutorily the solicitor general and the SEC commissioner, although appointed by the president, are insulated somewhat from the political pressures emanating from the White House. Chris Cox had inherited a staff that believed private class action securities lawsuits were one of the most effective weapons in policing corporate larceny, and he had allowed the SEC to file an amicus brief in favor of the plaintiffs before the Ninth Circuit. His staff was inclined to do likewise in *Stoneridge*. This time his board was split, with two Democratic members of the SEC favoring the plaintiffs and the two Republicans being against. Cox, the former California congressman who had played a lead role in passage of the PSLRA and who had singled out Lerach for personal condemnation, surprised the legal community by siding with the Democrats.

By statute, the rules governing whether the SEC files amicus briefs are different before the Supreme Court; the 3–2 vote was really to ask the solicitor general to convey the commission's view to the high court. This, Clement was ultimately unwilling to do because it did not reflect the view of the administration or, as became clear, of President Bush himself. Treasury Secretary Paulson was on record as favoring curbs on securities lawsuits, and after the SEC vote was taken, White House economic adviser Al Hubbard, a close friend of the president, told the Associated Press that Bush believed federal securities regulators, not shareholders, were the proper watchdogs over bad corporate actors. "We think the SEC is the right entity to bring those lawsuits and make sure investors are protected," Hubbard said. "We are a society that is overly litigious."

Clement believed that if two parts of the executive branch hold divergent policy perspectives while holding "equally legally viable" positions, the solicitor general was obligated to ask the White House for guidance. When Clement did this in the *Stoneridge* case, he was informed by William K. Kelley, a lawyer in the White House counsel's office, that the president believed the most important public policy consideration at play was reducing the number of "unnecessary lawsuits."

The upshot was a nuanced thirty-six-page brief from the solicitor general arguing against the plaintiffs. In it, Clement acknowledged the value to shareholders of investor lawsuits, but he laid down a subtle marker: although the SEC supported such litigation, Clement essentially responded that the SEC shouldn't be foisting off its own responsibilities for ensuring honest conduct in the nation's boardrooms solely onto private sector lawyers. Using the logic of the *Central Bank* case, Clement also pointed out that nowhere in their pleadings did Stoneridge Securities allege that it had been duped by public statements made by Scientific-Atlanta or Motorola. Finally, Clement noted that Congress had had ample time to amend the *Central Bank* case but had not done so. "Congress considered, then rejected, a proposal to create an express right of action for aiding and abetting," he wrote.

To those who knew Clement, this was the nut of his argument: whether or not the *Central Bank* case was bad law, only Congress could fix it now. The same month longtime Lerach nemesis Joe Grundfest published a paper with the same conclusion. The title said it all: "Scheme Liability: A Question for Congress, Not for the Court."

To Lerach and the plaintiffs' bar, relying on the reasoning of the *Central Bank* case took securities law into an Alice-in-Wonderland world where words no longer had any objective meaning. The Eighth Circuit and now the solicitor general, they believed, were employing circular logic. Yes, it was true that shareholders didn't rely on Scientific-Atlanta and Motorola's deceptive conduct when they purchased stock in Charter Communications, and that it was Charter's public statements they relied upon. Yet Charter simply could not have made those public assertions without the collusion of its vendors. It was all well and good to essentially call for tighter SEC enforcement, but how could the shareholders recover their losses?

By the summer of 2007 it was out of the hands of politicians, government lawyers, and plaintiffs' attorneys. The case was now in the arms of the justices of the Supreme Court—at least those who hadn't recused themselves, or who had recused themselves and then vacated their recusal, and those who didn't recuse themselves but perhaps should have.

> • >

IN EARLY SUMMER *The Wall Street Journal* and various online outlets reported that David Bershad was talking to prosecutors. One headline on a respected Web site referred to Bershad, a Cornell graduate, as the Ivy League Joe Valachi—the first Mafia member to publicly disclose not only the existence of the mob in America but its inner workings.

This news confirmed Lerach's worst fears. In Los Angeles, Bershad, sixty-seven years old and facing the real possibility of a prison sentence of twenty years or more, was detailing for prosecutors Mel Weiss's trips to Florida carrying cash for plaintiffs as a way of avoiding paper trails. He described the slush fund paying the plaintiffs, set up in New York with Lerach's participation, and how the partners were repaid by income from the firm—money withheld from unknowing partners. He disclosed the deal Weiss had struck with Howard Vogel's attorney to pay his plaintiff-client, well after the PSLRA forbade such payments. He detailed the payments to Seymour Lazar, who would now face charges of perjury, and to his attorney, Paul Selzer.

Three weeks later, on July 9, 2007, Bershad entered a guilty plea in the Los Angeles courtroom of U.S. District Court Judge John F. Walter. Once entered, the plea was made public. In its most telling section, paragraph eighteen, Bershad was said to "cooperate fully with the USAO, the Internal Revenue Service and the United States Postal Service." Robert Luskin, one of Bershad's defense lawyers, proclaimed: "David Bershad is committed to making amends for what he has done."

Separately, Bill Lerach, Mel Weiss, and Steve Schulman took notice and began making plans. Heeding Pat Coughlin's counsel, Lerach began writing letters to his clients, and those letters, sent in secret, contained words he would use in his retirement announcement before the end of the summer. He also began planning what he would say to his former wife Star and to his three children, Gretchen, Shannon, and Dillon. And what he would say in court, when he pled guilty.

Steve Schulman began rethinking his own holdout. He called his own lawyers, dropping his indignant and defiant tone. Now his concerns centered on how he could salvage a minimum prison sentence. He knew the price would be high. He'd have to tell prosecutors everything. But with Bershad in ahead of him, he might not be able to improve on what his former partner probably had already told the prosecutors or was about to tell them; Schulman sensed the window for his own opportunity shutting. He too was authorizing his representatives to initiate negotiations for a plea.

Mel Weiss called Ben Brafman, his attorney, and told him he was redoubling his defense. As far as he was concerned, he was still "Partner A" in the indictment. They should continue to prepare for a criminal trial.

In the war room in Los Angeles, assistant U.S. attorneys Richard Robinson, Doug Axel, and Bob McGahan were working on a new indictment. It would supersede the previous citation against the law firm of Milberg, Weiss, Bershad & Schulman. New allegations would be made and a new name added: that of Melvyn I. Weiss.

> • >

ANOTHER WEDDING BROUGHT Bill Lerach and Mel Weiss together during the summer of 2007. This event took place in a villa outside Bologna, Italy, where Tara Lazar, the Italian-trained culinary artist and daughter of Seymour Lazar, was married.

At first Weiss had balked at attending, telling Lerach that any overt gesture toward their indicted friend and coconspirator would draw undue attention to them. "For Christ's sake, Mel," Lerach had responded, "he's been a loyal friend for over twenty years. He loves you. We owe him support. Besides, we're honoring his family. The prosecutors aren't going to care. Michelle and I are going. You and Bobbi should too."

Lerach knew the pathway to Weiss's vulnerabilities—appeal to his pride and sense of honor. Weiss said he'd talk it over with his wife.

Which is why, on the afternoon before the wedding, Bill and Michelle Lerach found themselves sitting at the bar of their hotel near the grand Piazza Maggiore in the heart of old Bologna with Bobbi Weiss, Mel Weiss's wife of more than forty years. Showing his appreciation that Mel and Bobbi had decided to join the celebration, Lerach asked her how she was faring under the pressure of the investigation. She seemed startled by the question but kept her composure. "I just don't understand why they don't understand all those good deeds he's been doing all his life," she replied. "Bill, why won't they excuse this?"

Neither Lerach nor Michelle had an answer.

Late the next afternoon, the wedding party assembled in the ancient piazza. From there they would travel by bus to the historic Villa Dolfi Ratta in the city of San Lazzaro di Savena, about six kilometers from Bologna. As they waited, Lerach and Weiss encountered each other, and the younger man suggested they take a walk through the giant square.

The two strolled on Etruscan cobblestones burnished by millions of feet over half a millennium to the piazza's statues of high order—Neptune, Pope Gregory XIII, and a Madonna. The heat of the day had passed, and the soft light that enveloped everything, filtered by old growth above and around them, took on a gauzy, languid disposition that provided momentary asylum.

Gently but imploringly, Lerach tried one last time. "Mel, I'm going in. You've got to come with me. It's the only way."

Weiss took a step backward and looked benignly at his protégé. "I've already told you. They want you more than me."

"I'm going, Mel," Lerach repeated, trying to dislodge Weiss.

"Godspeed," Weiss replied.

The wedding commenced at sunset, with Tara Lazar's cousin Rabbi

David Lazar marrying the couple under the *chuppa*, the traditional Jewish matrimonial canopy. Afterward, as they were about to sit down to the wedding supper at a huge horseshoe table seating 150 guests, Lerach spied a roaming photographer. He grabbed Lazar by one tuxedoed arm and Weiss by the other and proposed loudly, "Let's get a photograph of the three conspirators!" Weiss shrieked in horror and bolted.

Seymour Lazar's newly married daughter Tara witnessed the scene, which some guests found amusing. Tara didn't. "It broke my heart," she recalled.

> • > • > • > • >

A BROAD DEFINITION
OF DECEIT

For months, rumors had been rampant, not about whether he would step aside but when. Since early June the Lerach Coughlin Web site had broadcast this message: "As has been speculated on Internet blogs and in newspaper articles, after thirty-five years of successfully practicing law, Bill Lerach is considering retirement. The investigation into allegedly improper activity at Milberg Weiss has continued for almost seven years, and Mr. Lerach is cognizant of the fact that although our firm has never been a target of this or any other investigation, the investigation should not become a distraction to our firm and its ongoing work."

In his office high above the city of San Diego and its harbor stretching all the way to the Pacific, from where he'd personally reordered wealth in America—wrenching it from corporations, along with their banks, auditors, and insurance companies, and redistributing the money (minus his own cut) to private and institutional investors—Lerach composed to friends and colleagues his final memo, his farewell. The phone rang. Calling was Dillon, his eleven-year-old son. A Boy Scout who had attained the rank of Star—two levels shy of Eagle Scout—Dillon had every reason to be proud. That wasn't why he was calling on this summer's day. At camp some other boys had called him "a cheat—just like your father." Dillon was upset.

Months earlier, in school, as news accounts began speculating about his father's possible indictment, Dillon's teachers had taken him aside, consoled him, and tried to persuade him that his classmates didn't read newspapers. Obviously, that wasn't true. Now he was being ridiculed, and he wanted to know why. Before calling his dad, the boy confronted Star, his mother, demanding to see the articles written about his father. She reluctantly turned over clippings she'd been keeping, and Dillon had read every one.

"Dad, I need to know," he told his father when he called. "Did you do the things that they accused you of in the paper?"

Nervously, Star eavesdropped, hoping her former husband would neither deflect that question nor stick to the party line about the system being against him because of what he had accomplished.

"Yes, Dillon, I did the things they said," Lerach softly told his youngest child. "I did something wrong and I have to pay a price . . . You will have to make decisions later in your life that will be hard." Lerach held his breath, listening to the silence on the other end of the phone.

"I'm glad you didn't lie to me," he heard his son say. "I still love you."

A week later, on the last day of August, following a brief ceremony akin to striking the colors, Lerach's name was deleted from the rolls of the firm. From now on the only attorney Lerach would be working with was John Keker, his defense lawyer.

> • >

CONTRARY TO WHAT HE had initially told Keker, the prospect of serving three years in prison unsettled Lerach. At his bidding, Keker countered with eighteen months. The prosecutors held firm. After frustrating exchanges, one of the attorneys on Keker's team suggested judicial mediation. The concept called for a judge other than the trial judge to review the evidence and arguments and arrive at a resolution that not only would satisfy both the prosecution and defense but would be likely to withstand the scrutiny of the judge who would ultimately pass sentence on Lerach.

Keker floated the idea to George Cardona, the practical-minded prosecutor, whom he respected. The acting U.S. attorney agreed, provided the mediator would be U.S. District Court Judge A. Howard Matz, a Harvard Law graduate and former criminal defense lawyer. Matz had overseen the grand jury hearing evidence in the case and, with the exception of the trial judge, was the jurist most familiar with the facts.* What's more, with Matz, a sixty-four-year-old Clinton appointee, little time would be wasted. His chambers were next door to those of Judge John Walter, who was overseeing all the Milberg Weiss criminal court cases. Matz and Walter were not only neighbors in the federal courthouse but friends as well.

Judge Matz believed Judge Walter would never accept an eighteen-month sentence. Matz ultimately advised both sides that twenty-four months might be the magic number to reach a deal—along with a fine of several million dollars.

Speaking for the government, Cardona agreed with the terms: there would be no separate indictment of Lerach, nor one against anyone in his firm or the firm itself. Lerach would not be compelled to testify against anyone. There would be no freezing of assets. This time there would be little resistance from Bill Lerach. And with the agreement would come vindication for Richard Robinson and the rest of the government lawyers. With Lerach's guilty plea, the complaints about a political vendetta would have to go away—or so they assumed.

> • >

THOM MROZEK, SPOKESPERSON FOR the U.S. attorney's office for the Central District of California, spent most of Monday, September 17, preparing the press release that his office would issue the following morning. When he finished, it said: "William S. Lerach, formerly a name partner in the law firm now known as Milberg Weiss, has agreed to plead guilty to a federal conspiracy charge and acknowledge that he and others agreed

---

* Judge Matz also presided over the first legal challenge to the U.S. government's treatment of detainees at Guantánamo Bay.

to conceal from judges in federal courts Milberg Weiss' secret payment arrangements with named plaintiffs in class-action lawsuits."

Gleeful voices from Wall Street to Silicon Valley shouted out their predictable hosannas when called upon for reaction by the financial press. In certain quarters within the nonbusiness media, however, it sounded almost as if a kind of buyer's remorse had already kicked in.

The *San Jose Mercury News*, the closest thing to a paper of record for the high-tech industry, was emblematic of that ambiguity. It published an epitaph that gave Lerach his due without demonizing him: "For the past two decades, the dreams of Silicon Valley executives have been plagued by two great foes. To the north, there lies Microsoft. And to the south, there is Bill Lerach, whose San Diego law firm filed numerous securities class-action lawsuits against valley companies. But Lerach's crusade is over."

"He's obviously had a profound impact," Steve Schatz, an attorney at Wilson, Sonsini, Goodrich & Rosati, was quoted as saying. "He was clearly one of the most significant lawyers in the country. And this is accordingly a significant event."

Another significant event was unfolding in Los Angeles, although it would take months to resolve. In mid-July, shortly after Dave Bershad entered his guilty plea and as Lerach and Keker were nearing their agreement with the prosecutors, Ben Brafman, Mel Weiss's attorney, called Lerach with a question. "Bill, are any of those two-year sentences still available?"

Lerach did not think so, but he replied that the only way to find out was to ask the prosecutors. Brafman subsequently did just that, although what he heard were terms that his client could not yet abide. Because Weiss had been holding out for so long, any deal would also have to include a guilty plea on the part of Weiss's law firm and would require a hefty fine. Even then, prosecutors informed Brafman, Weiss would likely be facing several years, not just one or two in prison. It was too much. Even with Bershad in the fold and Lerach about to come in and Schulman likely to follow, Weiss dismissed the idea of a plea bargain before Brafman had begun to negotiate in earnest.

During the weeks leading up to Lerach's plea, Steve Schulman's attorneys were concluding negotiations with Robinson, McGahan, and Axel. As part of the agreement, Schulman agreed to testify that he and Weiss had conspired to conceal secret payments from judges. The plea was entered on September 20 and averted a possible twenty-year sentence. Schulman had given them every reason to be confident. The same day he entered his plea, a seventy-five-page, twenty-count superseding indictment was issued against the firm of Milberg Weiss and against its founder, Mel Weiss. The charges were breathtaking in their accuracy and scope, beginning with detailed payments to Seymour Lazar and his attorney Paul Selzer, and ending with conspiracy to pay kickbacks to Howard Vogel. In all, the complaint outlined fraudulent acts that netted the firm at least $250 million in attorneys' fees.

> • >

FOR THE REGENTS OF the University of California, the news of Lerach's plea and subsequent indictment of his former firm gave all the more credence to the roles of Judge Irving and his team as intermediaries handling the Enron case. Urgent phone calls between Pat Coughlin (speaking for the Coughlin Stoia attorneys), Judge Irving, and Chris Patti (speaking for the university) brought reassurance that the entreaty to restore the plaintiffs' certification for lawsuits against the remaining banks would still be made in the Supreme Court. In fact, a motion was being prepared to consolidate the Enron case with the petition by the *Stoneridge* plaintiffs. As it stood, the high court had agreed to hear *Stoneridge*, and by conjoining in that case, Chris Patti, Judge Irving, and the Coughlin Stoia attorneys believed they would have a better chance of being heard.

Meanwhile, under Judge Harmon's direction, the lead attorneys prepared a motion to distribute $7.2 billion to the plaintiffs in the Enron settlements. An accompanying motion for attorneys' fees was due in federal court around the first of the year. The indictments and guilty pleas did not wipe out the settlements, although lawsuits demanding that the fees be nullified were certain to follow.

> • >

ON THE MAIN FLOOR of Bill Lerach's La Jolla villa, his home office featured a deep, four-foot-wide fireplace, a twelve-foot ceiling, a view through French doors to the garden, the size and scale of which sometimes made puttering more of an engineering conundrum than a landscaping issue. Nearly replicating his San Diego office, documents competed with documents and news clippings for space on his desk, where only one area was sacrosanct, that holding the wicker basket containing Tommy, his companionable Chihuahua. Above the fireplace on the forty-eight-inch flat panel screen, the CNBC financial channel was on anytime he occupied the room, and even when he wasn't, and on this day, Tuesday, January 15, 2008, the screen held his attention. The subprime meltdown continued to rage. Citigroup, the largest U.S. bank, reported losses of nearly $10 billion for the fourth quarter and announced it would cut dividends to investors by 41 percent. Banks, investors, mortgage brokers, and accountants were blaming each other for the losses now heading into the trillions of dollars.

Hadn't he predicted all this?

On this morning, a legal case before the Supreme Court shared the top of the news with the subprime mess. The heart of the case that the Supreme Court would rule on this morning was whether Charter Communications' vendors—Scientific-Atlanta and Motorola—could be seen as schemers who were themselves culpable in helping lead Charter's investors astray. His own law firm was asking for as much as $30 billion in recoveries in a similar case against the remaining Enron defendants. His colleagues had tried but failed to persuade the high court to link the two cases. Although not directly involved, Lerach had shaped the strategy for how the Stoneridge plaintiffs were going after third parties, just as he had led the way in the Enron case. Lerach's firm had joined thirty state attorneys general in lobbying for the plaintiffs, even filing their own briefs with the high court. Lerach's firm had even covered the Stoneridge plaintiffs' costs. Lerach also had dispatched Dan Newman, a seasoned communications and political operative, to Capitol Hill. There Newman enlisted Pennsylvania Republican Senator Arlen Specter and Connecticut Democratic Senator Christopher Dodd, chairman of the banking committee, to write letters to the court supporting the plaintiffs' arguments.

With his own clients maneuvered out of the case directly, *Stoneridge* was now the proxy for his former firm's lawsuit against Enron's third-party schemers. As the drama built toward a climactic landmark, some curious developments unfolded.

After the high court agreed in March 2007 to hear *Stoneridge*, Chief Justice John G. Roberts, Jr., and Justice Stephen G. Breyer recused themselves. Neither gave any explanation, but a review of their 2006 financial disclosure forms revealed that both justices owned somewhere between $50,000 and $100,000 of stock in Cisco Systems, which had acquired Scientific-Atlanta in 2005. Rumors were rife among the lawyers involved in the case that one or both judges might sell their stock and rejoin the case.

That is ultimately what occurred. But, on September 20, 2007, the Supreme Court put out an official announcement without elaboration stating that Roberts had reentered the case. Court watchers, extrapolating from *Central Bank* and other business law cases, believed that the lineup was now stacked against plaintiffs' lawyers. Six of the nine justices on the court in 2007 sat in 1994. Three of them—John Paul Stevens, Ruth Bader Ginsburg, and David Souter—had dissented in the *Central Bank* case. Justices Antonin Scalia and Clarence Thomas had joined Anthony Kennedy's majority opinion. Among the three new judges were Roberts and Samuel A. Alito, Jr., both staunch judicial conservatives. The third new justice, Stephen Breyer, was a Democratic-appointed liberal who essentially seemed uninterested in business law. Besides, he held to his recusal in *Stoneridge*. Pat Coughlin, waiting in the wings with his Enron case, was hoping for a 4–4 tie. Such a result would have left the Eighth Circuit's decision intact and thus wouldn't have helped Stanley Grossman or his Stoneridge investors— but it would have definitely put the Enron case, which was next in the queue, front and center. And siding with Enron's banks wouldn't have been easy—even for justices with lifetime appointments.

Shortly before 8:30 A.M. Pacific Time, the news arrived. The high court ruled 5–3 against the *Stoneridge* petitioners. Writing for the majority, as he had in *Central Bank*, Justice Kennedy ruled that investors were not entitled to damages because they did not rely on the statements of the two accused companies when they chose to buy and hold the Charter stock.*

"Absolutely ridiculous," Lerach hissed, when Darren Robbins, a young partner at the firm where Lerach's name had recently been removed, called to get his take on the decision. "Of course they didn't rely on their statements; there were no statements. They relied on Charter's fraud!" Lerach was now screaming into his cell phone and at his television screen simultaneously. "And how did Charter commit the fraud? It got help from third parties. What's Charter going to do, tell shareholders to ask Scientific-Atlanta and Motorola if they had cooked the numbers to help Charter cook its books? Blow the whistle on the liars who helped it lie?"

Lerach was furious, not surprised. Unfinished business remained with the remaining Enron defendants, but the Supreme Court seemed intent on denying him and his former firm that business. By turning back the Stoneridge plaintiffs, the justices had said that third parties—such as the Enron banks, accountants, and lawyers—even though they colluded in the fraud, could not be sued if investors did not rely on them directly.

"God damn Kennedy!" Lerach continued to shout at the television. "He should have recused himself! His goddamn son is a director of Credit Suisse First Boston! His own blood relative has a vested interest in how the *Stoneridge* case comes out. Now he's set the table. Our case is dead."

Then he made a quick calculation. If the remaining Enron defendants had been forced to settle—or even better, if Paul Howes and Pat Coughlin had managed to get them into trial in Houston—and the ultimate payout would have even approached $20 billion to $25 billion, then his own take would have been $100 million, before taxes. Now, with this precedent, it would probably be nothing at all.

---

* "The decision to extend the cause of action is thus for the Congress, not for this Court," Kennedy wrote, echoing Joe Grundfest's and Paul Clement's line of reasoning. Kennedy added: "This restraint is appropriate in light of the PSLRA, in which Congress ratified the implied right of action after the Court moved away from a broad willingness to imply such private rights."

Lerach was reaching, but not by much. Had his plaintiffs, the Regents of the University of California, been able to argue along with the Stoneridge plaintiffs, they would have petitioned to have Kennedy removed from the case because his son Gregory, as an executive of one of the defendants, had a vested interest in the outcome of the case.

Officially, Bill Lerach was retired, but no visitor would have sensed it. His house, his garden, and his view of the Pacific were to be his Elba, where he was supposed to work in exile. But the emphasis was still on work, not retreat. Adjacent to the fireplace and opposite the windows to the garden rose five wide, eleven-foot bookcases, filled with videos but mostly books. Together with two similar-size bookcases along a wall separating his home office from a smaller communications center containing computers, telephones, and his faxes, the shelves held more than two thousand volumes—biography, politics, philosophy, literature, World War II history, history of religion, history of civil rights, history of our markets, and the world economy. This impressed his friends who guessed he had read every one. He demurred a bit, saying, "Most of them," then added, "but I do remember just about everything of what I've read."

This sagacity had covered up his own admitted insecurities and served him in preparing for legal battles with the top CEOs in America as well as those Olympian lawyers educated at Harvard, Yale, and Stanford who had been favored with judicial clerkships and connections through their preordained networks to the so-called top-tier law firms—Sullivan & Cromwell, Mayer Brown, Ropes & Gray, Cravath & Swaine, Davis Polk, Milbank Tweed, Vinson & Elkins, Gibson, Dunn & Crutcher, and even Reed Smith, his own former firm. He had prepared better, worked harder, framed and presented his cases more clearly. He had won over judges, juries, and journalists—some journalists, anyway. He had made plenty of enemies in business and the bar, some of whom didn't mind admitting that they were jealous of all the money Bill Lerach had made for himself and his partners. And yes, he'd made many friends along the way, too, and soon he was going to draw on those friendships to help him in his biggest fight yet—the one for his freedom.

And so, even with the sound of the talking heads blazing away on television analyzing the dark financial news and the infuriating Supreme Court decision, William S. Lerach plunged back into what he'd been working on frantically for weeks. With his trusty black felt-tip Sharpie pen, he began scribbling edits onto a ninety-page document. This was the tenth version of what would ultimately be his memo to U.S. District Court John Walter, who was scheduled to sentence him on February 11, 2008. The memo was essentially a plea for leniency from the federal guidelines stipulating that he serve twenty-seven to thirty-three months at the discretion of the judge.

The legal brief Lerach was editing and re-editing, adding statutes on sentencing and citing previous cases whose outcomes could be interpreted in his own favor, was one of two final salvos he would fire in his withering self-defense. The second was a bundle of more than 150 reference letters from a wide array of allies, opponents, friends, and family members, including his former wife Star, and former clients. Federal and state judges who had heard his cases were among the petitioners for lenience, as were public officials such as U.S. Senator Carl Levin of Michigan and political activist Ralph Nader.

University presidents and law professors submitted letters, including one by Mary Crossley, dean of the University of Pittsburgh Law School, Lerach's alma mater. Citing previous lectures Lerach had delivered to Pitt law students, she had made the judge an offer: "Given Mr. Lerach's extensive experience as a litigator, he would be able to offer students valuable real world illustrations of how major litigations are conceived and the interplay of substantive law with procedural rules," she wrote on December 21, 2007. Intending no irony, she also proposed that Lerach deliver lectures on legal ethics and professional responsibilities—who more than he knew the perils and pitfalls of legal ethics? What's more, Crossley was proposing that Lerach's teaching commitment begin in January 2009, a date only seven months after he was to enter prison.

Not only did the audacious prospect of reducing his prison time by more than two-thirds animate him, the very idea that he could become an educator, *post partum*, to the pugnacious practice of the law, and the bloody business of it, inspired his imagination. Lerach could envision himself lecturing, not necessarily confined to law, but teaching a new generation about the history of our markets, our financial systems, capital ideology, regulation, and what his friend Robert Monks (author, investor, activist, and a founding trustee of the Federal Employees' Retirement System) called the "competing interests of corporations and society."

The phone rang again, interrupting his reverie. Ed Iwata, a reporter for *USA Today*, was seeking his response to the Supreme Court decision. No, he had nothing to say on *Stoneridge*. That wasn't his case, and because of his predicament, he wasn't allowed to comment. Did he have opinions? When did he not?

"One thing I might suggest, Ed," Lerach said. "Find out whether Justice Kennedy might have recused himself from that case. Find out what his son, I think his name is Gregory, does for a living. You might start by calling Credit Suisse First Boston." He waited, letting the reporter process the connection. "That's right. CS First Boston, one of our Enron defendants. Good luck."

Lerach hung up. Then gazed out the window at the garden, thinking, conjuring. What was that Shakespeare line near the end of *Julius Caesar*? He waited, as if standing before a jury, timing his delivery: "'Mischief, thou art afoot. Take thou what course thou wilt.'" Then he added a line of his own. "Now go do thy work."

> • >

"DOES LIABILITY EXIST UNDER rule 10b of the Securities Exchange Act of 1934 and Securities and Exchange Commission Rule 10b-5, where an actor knowingly uses or employs deceptive devices and contrivances, as part of a scheme to defraud investors in another public company, but itself makes no affirmative misrepresentations to the market?" The question was posed by the petitioners seeking to gain certification from the Supreme Court in order to resume their lawsuit against the remaining Enron defendants.

One week after the *Stoneridge* verdict, Justice Kennedy recused himself when it came time to answer. Justice Breyer did rejoin his colleagues, and together they voted unanimously *not* to hear the petition. What's more, the justices did so without comment. Their silence was universally understood to mean that with the *Stoneridge* decision, scheme liability making secondary parties as culpable as primary perpetrators of fraud was essentially dead. *Stoneridge* was now the law of the land.

If these machinations by the high court not to hear the petition of the Regents of the University of California seem Kafkaesque in hindsight, especially considering what happened subsequently to the economy, they seemed that way at the time to Bill Lerach and his dwindling circle of allies and beleaguered band of San Diego–based partners. By the time *Stoneridge* and, by proxy, the remaining Enron cases were decided, Lerach and those associated with him had been neutralized as critics of capitalism's excesses. Considering what was just around the corner—a deep global recession exacerbated at every turn by unbridled corporate greed, along with fraud and incompetence on an unimaginable scale in the executive suites and boardrooms of the nation's top financial institutions—the failures to heed his warnings about corporate capitalism's impending implosion did not really come at Lerach's expense. They came at the expense of every person in this country who owned stocks and bonds and who'd been planning on using them to buy a home, send a kid to college, or to retire.

> • >

THE FOURTEENTH-FLOOR SUITE of the Beverly Wilshire Hotel presented a sweeping, westerly overlook of a vast urban carpet coming aglow in the fading light on the evening of February 10, 2008. Taking in the vista, an informed viewer might appreciate the allure this urban American landscape held for the aircraft makers and the movie makers and the deal makers who had gravitated to it. Had the city fathers named their metropolis for the spirit that actually animated Los Angeles, they might have named it Los Aspiraciónes, instead of the City of Angels. On this evening Bill Lerach stood silently, his arms outstretched and his hands on the rail of the balcony, taking in the panorama, searching for landmarks and following the flight of jetliners ascending northward and skyward from LAX, unseen and over the hill to the southwest. At that moment he brought to mind a modern Icarus.

His aspirations had taken wing, had flown him higher than he could have imagined as a boy in Pittsburgh. Friends joined him on the balcony, and invariably the conversation turned to the outrageous *Stoneridge* decision and then to Justice Kennedy; the reverie of the moment morphed into the equivalent of locker room banter. It was easier to discuss than tomorrow's reckoning.

Inside the suite other friends, colleagues, and family—his daughter Shannon, his wife, Michelle, and her parents—occupied the sofas and chairs. Some clustered around the buffet table, others stood visiting. The talk was subdued, befitting the occasion; it was a far cry from the surprise party held in the basement ballroom of a downtown San Diego hotel a month before. A clever video had been shown then with Lerach making Forrest Gump–like cameos alongside Spencer Tracy and Fredric March in scenes from *Inherit the Wind*, Al Pacino in *And Justice for All*, and Julia Roberts in *Erin Brockovich*, among a dozen "lawyerly" movies. The tribute ended with a banging chorus of Tom Petty's defiant rock 'n' roll hymn "I Won't Back Down."

Lerach's good-bye speech after the video ended had been upbeat, gracious, and filled with gratitude for his colleagues and the opportunities they'd shared as he recounted the victories, beginning with Pacific Homes, moving to Lincoln Savings and Loan, the sweatshop litigation his wife had worked on in the Marianas, Stringfellow, Big Tobacco, *Exxon Valdez*, and WorldCom, climaxing in Enron, and almost bagging Dick Cheney's Halliburton. There was resilience in his voice, and a recognizable defiance as well. Tears were shed, and the guests recalled his generosity in times of need and his championing of victims he had never met in person.

That party had run late. This one would not. As the hour approached nine P.M., guests began taking their leave, and an awkward spell visited others. No one wanted to tarry. Finally, as if aware of an unwritten protocol, Lerach's oldest friends and longest-acquainted colleagues thanked their hosts and headed for the door. Within half an hour the guests were gone. Lerach was not inclined to linger either. He had a breakfast meeting at seven thirty the next morning, when he and John Keker would go over final details of their appearance at nine before Judge Walter, who would pronounce the sentence.

Lerach and his wife arose at five thirty A.M. on Monday, February 11, 2008, even as limos were returning guests who had attended and appeared in the fiftieth Grammy Awards ceremony and parties the previous night.

Lerach, wearing a dark gray suit, white shirt, and blue tie, and Michelle, clad in a dark pinstripe business suit, appeared shortly before seven. The couple traveled mostly in silence during the thirty-minute trip down Wilshire Boulevard to meet Keker and two of his partners, Elliot R. Peters and Wendy J. Thurm, at the Omni Los Angeles Hotel, a few blocks from the federal courthouse. Over coffee and a light breakfast Keker previewed how he thought the judge would conduct the hearing. "You should probably be ready for a puritanical lecture," Peters interjected.

"What are you going to say, Bill?" Keker asked.

Lerach shuffled in his seat and summoned a mischievous grin. "I hadn't thought about it. I guess I'll make it up as I go?"

Keker was not amused, and he braced his client. "The judge will take this deal. Do not snatch defeat from victory," he admonished. "We had good-faith negotiations. Do not get on a high horse."

Then Keker told Lerach what to say. He told him to acknowledge the professionalism and courtesy the prosecutors had shown. He instructed him to reprise his telephone conversation with Dillon, his son, confirming his errors. He even urged Lerach to recount his horror upon learning that David Bershad and Mel Weiss had continued to pay Howard Vogel.

"Also remember, you're going to be seen as sticking it to Mel Weiss," Keker added. "Just make certain you stick to the facts as you know them. Do not step into a trap. If things seem to be going poorly, do not open the door to . . . perjury."

Gravely, Lerach mounted the steps from the hallway to Judge Walter's second-floor courtroom, acknowledging the clutch of reporters but not answering their questions. Carrying their files, Richard Robinson, Doug Axel, Robert McGahan, the prosecutors, and Catherine Budig and Jim Harbin, the postal inspectors, filed into court and took their seats at the prosecutors' table below and to the right of the judge. In the gallery, seats were filled mostly by those who'd attended the buffet at the Beverly Wilshire the previous night, along with a few others. One was Judge Irving, who'd worked so closely with Lerach on so many big cases. Another was Patrick Frega, Lerach's longtime friend, whom he called "Assassin," noticeably disabled from a war wound and from a recent bicycle accident that had nearly cost him a leg, wincing in pain despite medication.

Judge Walter took the bench at 9:10 A.M. and reviewed aloud the probation officer's report with regard to various sentencing guidelines. Addressing Keker first, the judge noted that Lerach had been the beneficiary to the tune of 13 percent of the $40 million the firm had received in the Oxford Health case in June 2003, in which Howard Vogel had been a paid plaintiff, even while stories about a government investigation of Milberg Weiss were flowing in newspapers.

Keker was quick to respond: "Whatever ridiculous moves people in New York made after that were not pursuant to any conspiracy that Mr. Lerach joined in."

Judge Walter rebuked him: "Well, it depends how you define the conspiracy." Walter detailed his own understanding of the arrangements the firm had made with its paid plaintiffs—Cooperman, recruited by Lerach; Lazar, first brought in by Mel Weiss; Vogel, who was handled by at least two Milberg Weiss attorneys. "Everybody had the same goal in this conspiracy, and that was to secure the paid plaintiffs to act on behalf of Milberg Weiss."

If Lerach had wanted to withdraw from the conspiracy, Walter reasoned, "it would seem to me the prudent thing to do would be to go to the accounting department and say 'We've got these cases, and let's separate or isolate the income that's being derived or generated from these cases, because now that the government's onto this investigation, I don't want any part of this money.'"

To some in the courtroom, the judge's demeanor suggested he was trying a case against Lerach in the absence of a jury that had been preempted by the plea agreement. Lerach himself had another thought, an ironic one: the judge's reasoning mirrored his own explanation of scheme liability against secondary players in securities frauds. In any event, before pronouncing sentence, Judge Walter was handing out bitter medicine. And it was not reserved for Lerach alone.

Because he had announced his intention to move into private practice following Lerach's sentencing, Bob McGahan was given the honor of voicing the government's position. He stood, ready to address the bench, when Judge Walter took the cue to begin a barrage—against the government for its apparent lenience: "Why should I accept this plea?"

McGahan started to explain that it was a compromise reached between the respective parties. "But what are the facts of this case that—indicate that I should accept a plea agreement?" the judge insisted.

"Mr. Lerach caused his counsel, at a time before the government had advised Lerach that he was going to be indicted—before, in fact, the government had decided whether or not to even bring charges against Mr. Lerach, and there was a timely initiation of disposition discussions by his counsel which, from the outset, conceded that Mr. Lerach would plead guilty to a felony," McGahan stammered.

"Mr. Lerach would serve a period of incarceration, that Mr. Lerach would pay a substantial penalty that would consume a substantial part of his liquid net worth," McGahan added. "I'm not aware in the years of my practice where a defendant has caused his attorney to call the government, prior to the time of being told that charges were forthcoming, and offered to plead guilty and go to jail. In several respects, Mr. Lerach was a volunteer."

"The government has been investigating this case for seven years," Judge Walter reminded everyone present, recalling that in the original indictment Lerach was referred to as Partner B. "So it's not like Mr. Lerach just one day knocked on the government's door and said: 'By the way, you probably don't have everybody who's responsible in this case, I want to tell you that I have some responsibility, so I want to own up to that responsibility and let's work out a disposition'. . . Being a former prosecutor, I know that didn't happen."

McGahan shifted his stance, signaling his frustration. "Your Honor, all I can say is that at the time that Mr. Keker called the government and initiated plea discussions, we had not yet made a decision to bring charges against Mr. Lerach," the prosecutor said. "I agree, Mr. Lerach was not on the road to Damascus when he had a sudden conversion and decided, 'Come to think of it, why don't I plead guilty?' He saw the writing on the wall. But what the government is conceding here is essentially what we're asking the court to do, is to sentence the defendant to twenty-four months which, from the applicable guidelines range, that the government thinks is appropriate, we believe is a modest concession."

"Wait a minute," Walter snapped. "Let's assume that Mr. Lerach is included in the second superseding indictment, which includes all of the substantive charges that are in the indictment (with Mel Weiss named as a defendant). What's Mr. Lerach's exposure in terms of a maximum sentence in that case?"

Referring to a cheat sheet, McGahan told the judge: "I think anywhere between eight to ten years, your honor, or it could be higher."

Walter kept boring in. "On the RICO charge? What's the maximum sentence under the RICO statute?"

"The maximum statutory sentence is twenty years," McGahan said. At the defense table Lerach flushed.

Doing his own calculation, the judge then said: "If Mr. Lerach had been indicted in the second superseding indictment, the government would have gone to trial and presumably prevailed, and Mr. Lerach then would have been subject to—totaling up all the sentences—probably somewhere in excess of fifty years if the court ran the sentences consecutive; but even under the advisory guideline range, you're talking about a ten-year sentence . . . So, what it boils down to is that Mr. Lerach, because he knocked on the government's door before the government had any inclination or inkling that they were going to indict him, he gets the benefit of a two-year cap."

The ominous implications of Judge Walter's sermon reached beyond McGahan and the prosecutors, and its impact was twofold. First, it was now obvious to everyone that John Keker had earned his fee—and then some. Second, the message was clearly aimed also at Mel Weiss, who at this point was defiantly challenging the charges outlined against him in the September indictment. Weiss would now realize just how much his intransigence could cost him if and when he found himself standing before this judge at his sentencing.

McGahan conceded the forum to Keker, who recited the other mitigating facts of the plea deal, including the size of the fine Lerach was willing to pay, the humiliation of being disbarred at the height of his career, his stipulation of his own guilt (which removed all element of risk for the government), the testimonials from 150 letter writers on his behalf, his long crusade against fraud on behalf of shareholders.

Judge Walter said he could not dispute Keker's assertions but made a few of his own. "There were lies to the federal district judges. If any of these judges knew what I know now about the misrepresentations, the lies that were told to them, there wouldn't be any of those fees, and they wouldn't have been in their lead counsel status. The whole conspiracy corrupted the law firm, and it corrupted it in the most evil way; and this is, coming into court and having these paid plaintiffs, who were getting kickbacks, make misrepresentations to the court."

Finally, the judge called upon Lerach to speak in his own defense. The sullied lawyer stood erect, repeating the words protocol required: "May it please your honor . . . however much we may have disagreed with the prosecutors as to their view of what went on and how they exercised their discretion, I want to say that we were treated with courtesy and civility throughout. And, I especially want to thank the court for extending us the courtesies it did."

He thanked government employees who assisted in the pretrial paperwork and probation report, then continued:

"I pled guilty in this case because I was guilty," he said firmly. "I knew what I was doing when I did it was wrong. It was, as they say, 'felony stupid.' I just did not have the strength of character or the strength of will not to join in what was going on in our bar.* And so I joined in and I did it. I

* Lerach's words would catch the attention of Senator John Cornyn, a Texas Republican, who would sponsor a bill requiring greater accountability and transparency for securities lawyers.

thought it stopped long ago, as you've heard from the argument. But I did what I did, and it was wrong; I accept that it was wrong, and I know that I'm going to be punished for doing it. The conduct is completely and absolutely unacceptable from anyone, let alone a lawyer, and I know that. I guess all I can hope is that you won't find it completely unforgivable."

Lerach concluded by saying: "I feel very, very sorry to my family, who I've embarrassed, to my partners in my firm I've very much let down, and to the legal system I abused."

Head down, he returned to the defense table.

Judge Walter ordered a ten-minute recess, after which he would pronounce sentence. Few left the room. At 11:06 A.M. he returned to the bench.

"In the court's view, Mr. Lerach's criminal conduct is by far one of the most serious crimes that comes before this court," Walter said. "The scope and duration of this conspiracy was breathtaking. It was a nationwide conspiracy that began in the early seventies and continued for decades . . . The scheme to conceal these secret payments also extended to the many judges who presided over these class actions and the fraud perpetrated on those judges is, in my view, what makes this crime so very serious and deserving of a substantial prison sentence.

"What Mr. Lerach and others did goes to the core of our judicial system. The most egregious wrong that a lawyer can commit is to first commit a fraud on his clients; the second is to commit a fraud on the court."

The judge also made a point of refuting an earlier argument by Keker that few were actually harmed and that many benefited from the suits Lerach led. "First, it fails to take into consideration that this scheme effectively deprived many qualified law firms who played by the rules from becoming involved in earning fees in these cases," the judge said. "Secondly, given the fraudulent and corrupt nature of this scheme and the steps the parties took to conceal this scheme from the courts, it's painfully evident that the paid plaintiffs were motivated to abandon their fiduciary duties to the absent class members and take actions or make decisions in these cases in order to maximize the award of attorneys' fees, all at the expense of the absent class."

Next, the judge acknowledged the letters he had received on Lerach's behalf.

"I've also learned a lot about Mr. Lerach from his colleagues, adversaries, and friends, and they all agree that Mr. Lerach's word or handshake is far better than any promise on a written contract. They uniformly describe him as one of the most honest individuals that they have ever met," he said. "However, with all of his intelligence, this perceived honesty and sense of justice and fairness, I cannot imagine how Mr. Lerach could have lost his moral compass and totally abandoned those qualities, as well as his oath of office as an attorney and become a member, a key player in this conspiracy.

"Without the plea agreement, I would have been considering a sentence substantially in excess of the agreed-upon two-year maximum sentence," the judge said, glancing at the prosecution table and acknowledging that the agreement was "negotiated by three very experienced prosecutors . . . and by Mr. Keker, who is a very experienced and skillful attorney.

"However, there's simply no way that I can fashion a sentence that reflects the seriousness of the offense and which would promote respect for the law and provide just punishment without imposing the maximum sentence agreed in the plea agreement. Accordingly, the court imposes the following sentence."

On cue, Lerach and Keker rose, as did the prosecutors across the well of the court.

First came the fines—$250,000 paid in full within ten days. The forfeiture of $7.5 million. And finally: "It's the judgment of the court that the defendant is hereby committed on the single count information to the custody of the Bureau of Prisons to be imprisoned for a term of twenty-four months." Following prison, Lerach would be supervised by probation officers for two years and perform one thousand hours of community service.

The judge and Keker conferred openly about when and where Lerach would surrender, and the date April 21 was tentatively arrived at, as was the low-security facility in the federal correctional complex at Lompoc, about 175 miles northwest of Los Angeles.

With the business of the court finished, the prosecutors and the defendant converged and exchanged handshakes. Lerach, as he had at his arraignment, congratulated each of the men and the woman who had pursued the case against his law firm and him for seven years. As he had done moments earlier, in front of the judge, he praised each for their diligence and professionalism, and the exchange revealed mutual respect.

Then the opposing parties filed out; the prosecutors marched to the elevator and rode it to their offices on the twelfth floor. After gathering several more colleagues, the government's team strode to a nearby brew restaurant and feted McGahan on his last day. The celebration was subdued, with little gloating at finally putting Bill Lerach out of business. The remaining members of the team were also mindful of the unfinished business at hand—bringing in Mel Weiss.

Bill Lerach collected his wife, daughter, and in-laws and, followed by friends and colleagues, nodded to the press but ignored their questions, even refusing the bait from one television reporter who shouted: "Mr. Lerach, what do you have to say to America?"

He could not avoid the photographers, however, and beginning the following morning, the photo of a low-spirited Lerach leaving the federal courthouse, his blue tie akimbo, papers stuffed under his left arm, with his beautiful but crestfallen wife by his side—a portrait that had by now become a template for perpetrators of white-collar crime—would appear in newspapers and magazines throughout the world. This would be the last time the man *Fortune* magazine once called "The King of Pain," and whom others knew as the most feared lawyer in America, would be seen in battle dress leaving behind him an American court of law.

EPILOGUE

To those who loved William Shannon Lerach, as well as those who detested him, it came as no surprise that he did not go quietly into the dark night known as the U.S. Bureau of Prisons. Certainly Lerach's remorse, insofar as the example he'd shown his young son, was genuine, and his expressions of contrition to Judge Walter were not feigned. But that was not the whole story.

In late spring 2008 online readers of *Portfolio* magazine were treated to Lerach's ruminations about the process he had undergone—musings that infuriated Lerach's brethren in the bar. "You are about to read the words of a convicted felon," the magazine's editors prefaced their piece. "Bill Lerach waged a one-man war on business—he was the most feared class action lawyer in America."

It was never a "one-man" war, of course, but when the incarcerated Lerach began communicating, it reopened recently stitched wounds. He began his piece by asserting that prior to 1995 it wasn't illegal to pay plaintiffs, a statement that wasn't really accurate. (Obviously, plaintiffs were never allowed to commit perjury, as Seymour Lazar and the others had done many times. Nor was it legal to hide the payments from other plaintiffs and the

IRS, as Steven Cooperman had done.) Lerach critiqued a legal system that gives such vast discretionary power to federal prosecutors, and called into question the fairness of plea bargaining itself, pointing out that it coerces Americans to waive their right to a trial in the face of "draconian" prison terms that await those who roll the dice and lose. "The prosecutors hold all the cards," Lerach proclaimed. "The judge holds the gavel, and from the defendant's perspective, it might as well be a bazooka." Lerach had seen what happened to Bernie Ebbers, and he did not want to spend the rest of his own life behind bars. This point was well taken by his fellow lawyers, but Lerach didn't leave it there. He went on to say that whether he really had committed a crime was a gray area, that kickbacks to plaintiffs were "industry practice," and that what he had done was not only a victimless crime but a necessary component in ferreting out corruption in the nation's boardrooms. He punctuated this contention by asserting that the strategy used by NAACP lawyers in *Brown v. Board of Education* would now be illegal.

Finally, Lerach played the partisan card, mentioning that he had been about to move on Dick Cheney when his own case came to fruition, that he was a big Democratic Party supporter, and that the Justice Department was in Republican hands when the investigation against his firm resulted in all those indictments.

Few of Lerach's fellow plaintiffs' lawyers took kindly to this salvo. Sean Coffey, along with his senior partner Max Berger, the new "Kings of Class Actions," according to *Business Week*—particularly resented Lerach's assertions. "It is bad enough that this confessed criminal cheated for years to get an unfair advantage over his rival firms," Coffey told Joe Nocera of the *New York Times*. "But for this guy, on his way to prison, to say that everyone does it is just beyond the pale."

Lerach was impervious to this kind of criticism. He was thick-skinned even before his guilty plea, and sitting in Lompoc in his prison jumpsuit, he seemed grateful simply to still be part of the national debate over tort law and corporate governance. Besides, Lerach was just warming up: he had more to say. The February–March 2009 edition of *Executive Council* magazine carried a two-page bylined piece by Lerach in which he maintained that the financial meltdown wracking the United States had been partially caused by the PSLRA and other acts of government, including insufficient vigilance by the SEC and "hostile" actions by the high court. "The risk-reward ratio shifted and the door for fraud was opened," he said.

In this assertion, Lerach was on much more solid ground. The "collections of imbeciles" in the banking industry described by California senator William Gibbs McAdoo at the outset of the Great Depression were back in full force seventy years later—with predictable consequences. Even as the case against Milberg Weiss and its top partners worked toward its conclusion, the appalling incompetence and corruption inside the nation's investment banks and lending institutions led directly to a housing bubble, a Wall Street collapse, and the Great Recession of 2007–9. These events gave Bill Lerach—even from a prison cell—a soapbox to remind the nation that he had forewarned Congress, the courts, the SEC, and the White House what would happen. The chickens that he had cautioned lawmakers and judges about had indeed come home to roost.

Lerach had long maintained that the dot.com crash and the Enron scandal were not anomalies but rather the inevitable result of the *Central Bank* case, the PSLRA, the repeal of Glass-Stegall, and all the rest. "Simply put, the behavior of man—not just a few corporate executives—has been abominable," he had written in 2002. "There is no excuse for their greedy and dishonest behavior while so many honest people work so hard for so little."

Six years later, when it became evident that rampant fraud was complicit in the stalling of the entire economy, Lerach's worldview started getting a second look. In October 2008 the *New York Times* published a first draft of revisionist history regarding Lerach and his confederates. "Nothing makes lawyers more popular than bad times," its page-one story began. "It seems like just a few months ago—because it was—that trial lawyers, those advocates who take on companies on behalf of investors, customers, or even other businesses, had a wretched reputation. Three of the best-known of those lawyers, William S. Lerach, Melvyn I. Weiss, and Richard Scruggs, had all pleaded guilty to crimes . . . But the pendulum has swung again."

The *Times* singled out other factors and culprits, including Phil Gramm, holding up to the light a few of his past quotes—sentiments that didn't sound so shiny and smart in the wake of the economic crisis. "Some people look at sub-prime lending and see evil," Gramm had said in 2001. "I look at sub-prime lending and I see the American Dream in action." This remark might have been forgotten had not Gramm signed on as economic adviser to the campaign of John McCain, the Republicans' 2008 presidential nominee. Meanwhile McCain, Lerach's unlikely partner in fighting tort "reform" a decade earlier, took the unusual step of calling for Chris Cox's replacement as SEC chairman. That agency had clearly lost its oomph. In the sixty years after the Boston office of the SEC had been the impetus in expanding the commission's reach under the 1933–34 securities acts, that same regional office professed not to see anything wrong with Bernard Madoff's transparent, multibillion-dollar Ponzi scheme—even after it was brought to their attention by a Boston-based trader named Harry Markopolos.

As Madoff appeared to be heading to prison, FBI officials told Congress that despite a huge redeployment of its agents to financial fraud, it would never have the resourses to police the financial markets on the threat of criminal prosecution alone. The sheer volume of greed was so vast that the FBI could only bring its forces to bear on companies or individuals "systematically trying to defraud the system," FBI Deputy Director John Pistole informed the Senate Judiciary Committee in early February. Taking that point to its logical conclusion, a few voices began to question the PSLRA and the wisdom of prosecuting Bill Lerach at all.

Writing for the online version of *The Atlantic*, former Clinton White House aide Matt Miller proposed—only half tongue-in-cheek—"the perfect answer" to dealing with greedy financial industry execs who want to keep their million-dollar bonuses after running the economy into the ditch was: "The feds need to hire Bill Lerach to bring their cases," he wrote. "Whatever else you may think of Lerach, the guy scares corporate America, and he knows how to use that fear to get big settlements for his clients . . . Let Lerach reduce his time by bringing the cases that are tailor-made for his particular brand of hardball." (After Kathy Lichnovsky relayed Miller's item to her boss, Lerach fired back a six-hundred-word response to Miller advising him that a way currently exists to go after "these Wall Street pigs"—convincing the pension funds to sue the boards of directors of the mismanaged financial institutions.)

The following month veteran Democratic consultant John Russonello weighed in on his blog, calling for the Obama administration to pardon the jailed lawyer. "Every day Lerach was on the prowl evened the odds a little bit for the rest of us," wrote Russonello. A pardon, he added, "would send Wall Street a message louder than the day's opening bell—the junk yard dog may soon be back at the gate, so watch your step."

> • >

TO MEL WEISS AND his lawyer, such sentiments were all in the land of make-believe. The real world was much harsher.

"I'm on my knees begging you . . ."

So began the plea from Ben Brafman, standing in the well of the federal district court in Los Angeles, his voice quavering, before Judge John Walter on June 2, 2008. Brafman recounted the nearly five decades of championing victims of fraud, working pro bono for Holocaust victims, giving generously to charity. "I'm asking you to give him back just some months for all that he has given," Weiss's lawyer intoned.

Two and a half months earlier Weiss, now seventy-three, had appeared in the same courtroom before the same judge and pleaded guilty to a racketeering conspiracy stemming from his stable of plaintiffs who had received kickbacks for so long. Now, on the morning of June 4, even Doug Axel, who along with Richard Robinson had engineered the government's case and plea bargain, conceded: "Certainly nobody can dispute that there's a lot of good in this defendant, Mr. Weiss, and that he is deserving of recognition and deserving of being taken into account here today."

Judge Walter invited the defendant to address the court. Weiss rose and moved slowly to a podium set midway between the prosecution and defense tables and directly in front of the judge. He placed a sheaf of papers before him and began in a soft but firm voice: "Your honor, I stand before you very humbly . . . As I have written to your honor, my remorse and contrition for my violations of my oath as a lawyer are beyond my ability to adequately express. I promise you that my contrition is profound and genuine. In judging me and the way I have spent my life, I can only ask that you look at me not only as a confessed wrongdoer that brought me here, but also through the eyes of the hundreds of people who have written to you on my behalf. My punishment has already been great. Being unable to practice law again has ended both my life's passion and my ability to earn a living as a professional. My fall from grace has greatly impaired my ability to work as a public servant and humanitarian, which has always been a part of my life."

When he finished, Mel Weiss returned to the table and bent his head.

Judge Walter cited the need for deterrence "to those that are considering committing similar crimes, that if they get caught, they will face prison," then imposed a fine of $250,000 dollars, an additional forfeiture of $9,750,000—and thirty months in prison. After some back-and-forth with Brafman, August 28 was set as the date Weiss would surrender himself to the federal minimum-security prison camp in Morgantown, West Virginia—the same facility where John Torkelsen was serving his sentence.

Two weeks later the U.S. attorney's office in Los Angeles announced that the government had settled with the law firm of Milberg Weiss. The firm, soon to be known as only Milberg, agreed to pay $75 million dispersed over five years and accept government oversight in return for the removal of charges against it.

In December, four months after Mel Weiss began serving his prison sentence, he learned that his friend Bernie Madoff had fleeced him, along with hundreds of other "exclusive" investors, in the largest private investment fraud in history. Estimates of the amount Madoff bilked ran as high as $50 billion. Mel Weiss alone was believed to have lost upward of $20 million. Weiss was not the only victim in the Milberg Weiss circle. While serving his six-month sentence in the Federal Correctional Institution at Otisville, New York, David Bershad learned that his investments with Madoff had vanished. Pat Hynes, the former partner who was elected president of the New York City Bar Association in June 2008, also lost money with Madoff. Likewise Howard Vogel, the paid plaintiff who helped make the government's case, also got word while serving a three-month sentence at a federal facility in Miami that he too was among Madoff's pigeons.

Spared Madoff's scheme because he claimed he couldn't afford to invest was Steve Schulman, who served his six-month sentence in a federal detention center in Minersville, Pennsylvania. Schulman was, however, required to forfeit $2 million to the government. Paul L. Tullman, the one-time Milberg Weiss partner turned stockbroker, who earned more than $8 million from Milberg's largesse, pleaded guilty to a single count of tax evasion. Because he cooperated and because of his declining health, Tullman was spared prison. Robert Sugarman, known as "Partner E" in the indictments against his former firm, was absolved from prosecution and continued to practice law in New York.

As for the other defendants, John Torkelsen, whom *Fortune* called "the damages expert of choice for the entire plaintiffs side of the securities bar" and who would not give up his friend Bill Lerach, continued to serve his five-year sentence for perjury in Morgantown. He was scheduled for release on July 20, 2011. His wife, Pam, who testified against her husband as well as the firm of Milberg Weiss, was sentenced to three months and was released from prison on December 12, 2008.

Noting Seymour Lazar's age of eighty and his declining health, and also considering the stress of undergoing a seven-year investigation, Judge Walter sentenced him to two years' home confinement and ordered him to pay a $600,000 fine and forfeit $1.5 million more. The judge seemed to take pity on Paul Selzer, sentencing the weeping sixty-eight-year-old attorney to two years' probation, fining him $250,000, and ordering him to perform one thousand hours of community service, for his role in funneling money to Lazar.

Even though he cooperated with prosecutors, Steven Cooperman, who had already served twenty-one months for art theft, was returned to prison following the disclosure that he had committed fraud while in custody. In his role as an illicit plaintiff, Cooperman received some $6 million. For those crimes he was sentenced to four additional months, which he served at a federal prison hospital facility at Devens, Massachusetts, before his release in May 2009. He also paid a $40,000 fine. Richard Purtich was confined for two months and paid $50,000 for his role in funneling money to Cooperman. Purtich also lost his license to practice law. James P. Tierney, the faux cat burglar who sauntered into Cooperman's house to remove masterpieces of art from the walls, was released from custody in 2002 and, as part of his sentence, resigned his license to practice law.

Eleven individuals fell to the prosecution. Counting the fines paid personally by Lerach and Weiss, along with the $75 million forfeited by the firm of Milberg Weiss itself,* the government collected more than $100 million, which was 42 percent of what the firm earned during the two and a half decades prosecutors could trace its fees to cases involving paid plaintiffs.

Those numbers provided more than a hint to the cosmic question that Lerach himself had posed aloud in court during the Pacific Homes litigation so many years ago. In his statement to the jury, Lerach had made a point of stressing the many good works of the Methodists, even acknowledging their noble intentions when launching the ill-fated retirement homes. One question raised by the case, Lerach told the jurors, was this: "How could something that should have been so good end up so bad?" As America's most powerful law firm broke apart, and its top partners headed for prison, this was a question asked *about* Bill Lerach as well.

"We may not be perfect," Lerach had told William Greider of *The Nation* in 2002 when discussing trial lawyers, "but we are not corruptible." Six years later *Mother Jones*, another liberal magazine, reprised that quote, with a different twist. "It's no small irony that Lerach will soon be joining some of those corrupt CEOs in federal prison," *Mother Jones* said, adding that his "scheme had very little to do with combating corporate fraud and a lot to do with making money."

Love of money is not a new sin—it's identified in the Bible as a root cause of evil—but what happened to Bill Lerach and Mel Weiss was nearly existential. "He who does battle with monsters needs to watch out,"

---

* The firm renamed itself Milberg LLP, its original title, after founder Lawrence Milberg, who passed away in 1989 at the age of seventy-six. Despite the stigma of the guilty plea and the enormous fine it paid the government, Milberg enjoyed an incongruous resurgence in early 2009, becoming the counsel of record for more former Bernie Madoff clients than any other law firm.

Friedrich Nietzsche warned in *Beyond Good and Evil*, "lest he become a monster himself."

Bill Lerach was no monster, but he had indeed gone after fraud by using fraud. And he had seen the corrupting power of wealth, somehow not imagining that the love of money could corrupt him as well.

> • >

ON SATURDAY, JULY 5, Shannon Lerach entered the visitor center of the medium-security U.S. penitentiary at Lompoc, California, and signed the form declaring her intent to see prisoner number 46683–112, her father, Bill Lerach. She never made it past the metal detector. A week earlier, following a minor dustup with authorities, Lerach had been transferred from the minimum-security penitentiary he'd entered on May 19 into the more secure facility across the street. Both Shannon and Michelle, his wife, had looked in on him in the visitors' room of his new surroundings and listened to his complaints: slow mail, no-show on his medical prescriptions, confiscated newspapers, an edgier, less hospitable atmosphere, but tolerable.

On this day, however, Shannon was turned away altogether and forced to return to San Diego, a drive of more than four hours' duration, without explanation. Eventually the story would seep out. Bill Lerach had engaged a guard in conversation about San Diego and their mutual interest in the San Diego Chargers NFL team. Lerach, intimating that white-collar crime does pay, allowed that he had been a longtime season ticket holder of very good seats. This got the guard's attention and perhaps ignited his envy.

The conversation went something like this. "Too bad I can't use my tickets," Lerach had said. The guard agreed, bummer, especially since the 2008 Chargers expected a mighty year. "Well," Lerach apparently told his newfound friend, "if you ever want to see a game, let me know."

Little time passed before Lerach was summoned to a supervisor's station and charged with "making a material offer to an officer of the United States Bureau of Prisons." He was then moved to administrative confinement for a period, he was told, of thirty days. There would be no visitors, no exchange of mail, no newspapers, no outdoor exercise except for one hour a week. He would be confined to a small cell with a thick metal door and one tiny window. There he was flanked by opposing, riot-prone Latino gang members, who hurled insults and threats at each other nonstop. He was given a towel matching the size of a washcloth and no washcloth at all. His first change of underwear came at nearly the two-week mark, "when I smelled like a farm animal," he would finally report in a letter, many days after his solitary confinement was long past due. His only consolation, he wrote: "I don't have CNBC so I can't watch my investments go to shit."

His "thirty-day" segregation lasted two months, until September 5, when he was loaded onto a bus and transferred to the low-security prison camp, a complex of short buildings surrounded by three rows of razor wire, crouched beneath desert mountains at Safford, Arizona, eighty-five miles northeast of Tucson. There he would contemplate and discuss America's economic crisis, receive visitors, get several newspapers a day, give lawyerly advice, and pick up new acquaintances, ranging from white-collar criminals to drug smugglers, to a young man who had hacked Wal-Mart's internal computers and was able to change the codes (reducing a $33.95 price to $3.30, for example) for online shopping. Among the more colorful inmates was a huge man covered head to toe with tattoos who passed his time crocheting blankets for other inmates and a Russian sea captain who said he believed he'd been transporting "coconuts" from Colombia to North America. The captain borrowed Lerach's *Wall Street Journal* regularly to check the prices of foreign currency. "Some of those 'coconuts' must have gotten through," Lerach mused. Another favorite was "Mr. Clark," a highly respected octogenarian and formal postal worker who had gone on a murderous rampage, helping to give rise to the term "going postal." In the macabre and utilitarian world behind bars, he was of course assigned to work in the prison post office, Lerach reported in letters to friends.

In his new environment Lerach discovered a like-minded crew who shared his enmity for Wall Street bankers, at whom they would jeer when they appeared on CNBC defending their obscene pay packages. Likewise, he shared with most of the rest of the prison population satisfaction at the November election of Barack Obama, for whom, had he not been barred from voting, would have cast a vote.

Lerach took particular pleasure in Obama's victory over the Clintons, whom he'd helped financially and who'd turned on him, and then over John McCain, the candidate Lerach had once brought to his knees. On a personal note, Lerach managed to lose twenty pounds and, due to a lack of a barber, began slicking back his always unruly mop of hair, transforming him into what one of his visitors described as "the second coming of Gordon Gekko," the character based on Ivan Boesky played by Michael Douglas in the movie *Wall Street.*

> • >

DEBRA W. YANG RESIGNED as U.S. attorney for the Central District of California on November 11, 2006, lured to Gibson, Dunn & Crutcher by a hefty salary and a $1.5 million signing bonus. Yang's move came less than one month before seven other U.S. attorneys were dismissed—and in the wake of White House counsel Harriet Miers raising the possibility to one pliant Justice Department political appointee of replacing Yang. Suspicion arose that White House political aides wanted to quash the investigation of corruption allegations into the activities of Representative Jerry Lewis, the fifteen-term Republican congressman from Southern California, who was being represented by Gibson Dunn. According to a 392-page 2008 Justice Department report into the firings, Miers's motivations were less sinister— and more petty: Yang had declined a White House invitation to apply for an appointment to the Ninth Circuit.

Her successor, George Cardona, left the post in the spring of 2008 following the sentencing of Bill Lerach. He teaches at UCLA Law School. Douglas Axel was promoted to head the major frauds section of the U.S. attorney's office. Michael Emmick divides his time teaching at Loyola Law School in Los Angeles and Pepperdine Law School in Malibu. Jeffrey Isaacs is the chief assistant city attorney for Los Angeles and head of the three-hundred-attorney criminal branch. A week after Lerach's sentencing Robert McGahan resigned as a government prosecutor to join the Los Angeles office of Goodwin Procter, to specialize in white-collar crime and government investigations. Postal inspector Jim Harbin announced his retirement, while his colleague Catherine Budig continued her work. Through mid-2009 she was on special assignment in Washington, D.C. Richard Robinson, who prosecuted the Milberg Weiss case from beginning to end, continued to prosecute white-collar crimes for the government.

Virginia Curry, the FBI agent who helped crack the Cooperman art theft, thus launching the case against the lawyers of Milberg Weiss and their pay-to-play plaintiffs, retired from the FBI and went back to college, where she is studying to earn a master's degree in art history at Southern Methodist University in Dallas.

Sean Coffey, the litigator anointed as the next Bill Lerach, resigned from Bernstein Litowitz on October 16, 2009, to run for attorney general of New York.

J. J. Little, who led authorities to the stolen Picasso and Monet, is again practicing law in Los Angeles. Pamela Davis, his former girlfriend, shown smiling and holding an empty picture frame on the cover of the February 1998 *Cleveland* magazine, alongside the headline "Raider of the Lost Art"—detailing how she helped authorities recover the stolen art treasures and stood to receive the $250,000 reward—married a Cleveland tax attorney. In December 2007 she was sentenced to 180 days in jail for intimidating a witness in a trial, during which she was accused of stalking and harassing neighbors and causing havoc in the neighborhood near the Cleveland Yacht Club. James Tierney, the Los Angeles attorney who stole the art and implicated his former client Steven Cooperman is living in Ireland on disability compensation.

As for the art itself, underwriters Lloyds and Axa Nordstern sued Steven Cooperman and his wife, Nancy, in California for $22 million, seeking to regain not only the $17 million they paid Cooperman for his fraudulent claim but also punitive damages, just as he had done to them. The court ruled against the plaintiffs, finding that the Coopermans lacked the means to repay the underwriters. The two art treasures themselves, once the subject of a conversation about shredding, were sold in 2002 at private auction. The identity of their purchasers and exact terms of the sales remain confidential, although the authors learned that the two pieces fetched a combined $6 million. No reward for their recovery was ever posted.

> • >

ONCE A WEEK IN PRISON Bill Lerach would open an envelope or package, postmarked Los Angeles, with the name and address of his Coughlin Stoia partner Al Meyerhoff on the outside. The actual origin of the intellectual CARE package was Cedars-Sinai Medical Center, where "Big Al" lay dying. In the fall of 2007 Meyerhoff learned he had a rare blood disorder. In the fall of 2008 it turned into leukemia. His condition was terminal and he knew it, yet he continued to write Lerach, challenging, cajoling, and recommending new writers or works or political arguments to his law partner. Lerach looked forward to Meyerhoff's incoming mail, which he always answered, scrawling equally challenging messages on his yellow legal pad. The two had become codependent.

On December 21 Al Meyerhoff passed away at the age of sixty-one, leaving a daughter and his wife and prompting a large wake. The *Times* of both Los Angeles and New York eulogized him as a leading labor, civil rights, and environmental lawyer, citing his victories over garment retailers for their sweatshops in Saipan, for his challenge to a California law preventing illegal immigrant children from attending public school, and for his ongoing war against cancer-causing pesticides in the fields of America.

A memorial was held in San Francisco on February 28, 2009, in the Town Hall of the Delancey Street Foundation the world-famous residential self-help organization for former substance abusers, ex-convicts, and homeless. Actor Mike Farrell emceed. Influential California congressman George Miller, Frances Beinecke, president of the Natural Resources Defense Council, and Carl Pope, executive director of the Sierra Club, all spoke. Bill Moyers offered a televised tribute. Bill Lerach wrote from prison to say, "It broke my heart that Al died when I was in jail—unable to be with him . . . We fought the good fight together trying to advance the progressive causes we both held dear. We traveled the world together—lots of Scotch and steaks—and endless hours of political talk—the very best of times. I loved him then. I love him now."

Perhaps the most moving tribute was provided by Patrick Coughlin, who spoke for all 190 of Meyerhoff's law firm colleagues when he joked that often he, as managing partner, would be the last to know that Big Al had filed a costly case, almost always to right a social wrong, sometimes committing the firm to perform pro bono. In his short speech Coughlin focused this day on the high line of Meyerhoff's accomplishments and the firm's great cases—Lincoln, Enron, WorldCom, the Holocaust reparations, Big Tobacco—as well as those that were ongoing. The firm's lawyers, Coughlin said at Meyerhoff's memorial service, had dedicated themselves to fighting fraud, with, and now, without Bill Lerach, and remained very much in the fray.

Left unsaid was a fascinating footnote. The partners missed Lerach; they also missed John Torkelsen. The firm had never quite found a suitable star witness to replace him, and such an expert was still needed. As a matter of practicality, they had found someone new, however. He was none other than Bill Lerach's old nemesis, Daniel R. Fischel.

On September 10, 2009, Bill Lerach was released from federal prison and began serving his remaining six-month sentence in a halfway house in a low-income, crime-ridden, predominantly Latino neighborhood in southeast San Diego known as Barrio Logan. Weekdays, he worked in a dry cleaning business, earning $10 an hour. Weekends, he was able to return to his La Jolla villa overlooking the ocean. Throughout the fall and winter, he watched America's financial markets struggle to regain their lost value, continued to curse at unworldly compensation paid to banking executives while the nation's unemployment rate headed to 10 percent, and entertained offers to teach at various universities. He also heard from commercial insurers eager for him to consult on their directors and owners coverage policies—to protect, in other words, the corporate moguls he once feasted upon.

Notes

PROLOGUE

1 **a ten-mile route:** Details of Lerach's travel from the Beverly Wilshire Hotel to the federal building and courthouse in Los Angeles are from PD's personal observation, October 29, 2007.

1 **the knee-capper of corporate America:** Peter Elkind and Doris Burke, "The King of Pain Is Hurting," *Fortune*, September 4, 2000.

2 **the most aggressive legal strategist:** See the Coughlin Stoia website, http://www .csgrr.com/.

3 **He often compared his firm:** William S. Lerach, interviews by PD, October 15, 29, 2007; January 9–16, 2008.

4 **"bloodsucking scumbag":** Karen Donovan, "Bloodsucking Scumbag," *Wired*, November 4, 1996.

5 **"Now we're going after Dick Cheney":** *The Archdiocese of Milwaukee Supporting Fund v. Halliburton Company et al.*, U.S. District Court, Northern District of Texas, April 4, 2006.

6 **a 16,000-square-foot Tuscan-style mansion:** Details on Lerach homes are from PD, personal observations.

6 **"Goddamn loser CEOs":** William S. Lerach, "Loser CEOs Raking It In," *Washington Post*, November 11, 2007.

8 **"We'd fire a shot":** William S. Lerach, interview by PD, February 23–29, 2008.

8 **he had called John Keker:** John Keker, interview by PD, March 6, 2009.

9 **For all Keker's bona fides:** Karen Donovan, "The Man Who Will Prosecute Oliver North," *Washington Post*, November 4, 1996.

9 **They wore jail jumpsuits:** Details of appearance at arraignment come from PD, personal observation, October 29, 2007.

10 **greeted by four assistant U.S. attorneys:** PD, personal observation, October 29, 2007.

10 **"Do you understand":** Arraignment and plea hearings of William S. Lerach, U.S. District Court, Central District of California, October 29, 2007, reporter's transcript.

11 **"I can't vote":** PD, personal observations, October 29, 2007.

CHAPTER 1. DRAGON SLAYER

14 **reforming Illinois's antiquated constitution:** "Father of State Constitution Witwer Dies," *Chicago Daily Law Bulletin*, September 14, 1998.

14 **"He was the only man I ever saw":** William S. Lerach, interview by CMC, March 18, 2008.

14 **"We're going to take down the Methodist Church!":** Samuel W. Witwer, Jr., interview by CMC, July 3, 2008.

16 **partners took an immediate liking:** Colin Wied, interview by CMC, April 29, 2008.

16 **Melvyn I. Weiss:** James Granby, interview by CMC, March 19, 2008.

16–17 **"Have you lost your mind?":** Bill Lerach, interview by CMC, March 19, 2008.

17 **the Californians were struck:** James Granby, communication to CMC, June 9, 2008.

17 **"It's a dynamite case":** Colin Wied, interview by CMC, April 29, 2008.

17 **an agreement on the terms:** James Granby, interview by CMC, March 19, 2008.

18 **"The Annual Conference said the residents":** Phyllis Berman, "The Methodists and Mammon," *Forbes*, December 25, 1978.

18 **"upright Christian socialist":** Christopher Caldwell, "Nixon Rising," *National Review*, October 11, 1999.

19 **"The fat was really in the fire":** Quoted in Tim Tanton, "United Methodists Pacific Homes Saga Ends on an Up Note," *United Methodists News Service*, September 10, 1999.

19 **"We started to have them":** Quoted in Berman, "Methodists and Mammon."

20 **"is not the alter ego":** Quoted in Jack Jones, "Church Denies Liability in Pacific Homes' Failure," *Los Angeles Times*, August 15, 1980.

20 **"fiercely independent":** Ibid.

20 **"It would violate":** Betman, "Methodists and Mammon."

21 **"Those 7.5 billion":** Ibid.

21 **he found the young lawyer:** Tharp expressed these sentiments in chambers to CMC.

22 **"enormous" damages:** Carl M. Cannon, "Church's Council to Appeal," *San Diego Union-Tribune*, April 3, 1978.

22 **"To hold otherwise":** *Barr v. United Methodist Church*, 90 Cal. App.3d 259, 153 Cal. Rptr. 322 (1979).

25 **"To default would threaten":** Morton Mintz, "Methodists Ask Court to Remove Them from Suit," *Washington Post*, November 24, 1979.

25 **"would unconstitutionally abridge":** Ibid.

25 **"A trial is like putting on":** William S. Lerach, interview by CMC, March 19, 2008.

27 **"The money was misused":** Mitch Himaka, "Pacific Homes Retirement Case Outlined to Jury," *San Diego Union-Tribune*, August 14, 1980.

27 **"I rise to speak":** Herbert Lockwood, "Pacific Homes' Seniors Early as Suit Begins," *San Diego Daily Transcript*, August 14, 1980.

27 **"After my husband died":** Lee Havins, "Pacific Homes Trial Is Slowed by Objections," *San Diego Evening Tribune*, August 19, 1980.

28 **weary of the ill will:** Ibid.

28 **"The only glue":** Quoted in Jones, "Church Denies Liability in Pacific Homes Failure."

28 **"This gave us full protection":** Quoted in Lee Havins, "2nd Church Witness Linked Church to Pacific Homes," *San Diego Union-Tribune*, August 21, 1980.

28 **"It was our strongest point":** Quoted in "Pacific Homes Promotion Told," *San Diego Union-Tribune*, August 28, 1980.

29 **The presiding judge then read the terms:** *Frank T. Barr et al. v. The United Methodist Church et al.*, San Diego Superior Court, Wednesday, December 10, 1980, Reporter's Daily Transcript, vol. 47.

30 **"I would like to think":** Quoted in ibid.

30 **John McCain would meet Charles H. Keating, Jr.:** Dan Nowicki and Bill Muller, "McCain Profile: Keating Five," *Arizona Republic*, March 1, 2007.

30 **Twenty years later CEOs would make:** Jennifer Gill, "We're Back to Serfs and Royalty," *Business Week*, April 9, 2001.

31 **Photographs taken after the settlement:** Bruce V. Bigelow, "Class Action Gunslinger; It's Always High Noon for William Shannon Lerach, and That's the Way He Likes It," *San Diego Union-Tribune*, April 9, 2000.

32 **"His work ethic":** Samuel W. Witwer, Jr., interview by CMC, July 3, 2008.

32 **"nothing personal":** Samuel W. Witwer, Jr., e-mail to CMC, March 29, 2009.

32 **"Bill was an absolutely brilliant lawyer":** Colin Wied, interview by CMC, April 29, 2008.

33 "Yeah, he'd been here": Ibid.

33 "I thought it was all the money": William S. Lerach, interview by CMC, January 19, 2008.

33 "We took a case": William S. Lerach, interview by CMC, March 19, 2008.

34 "Bill quickly volunteered": Colin Wied, interview by CMC, April 29, 2008.

CHAPTER 2: THE YOUNG MAN FROM PITTSBURGH

35 Son of the Great Crash: Reynolds Holding and William Carlsen, "Phantom Riches," *San Francisco Chronicle*, November 15, 1999.

36 "They treated him": Ibid.

36 "I think what influenced me": Quoted in Jonathan Potts, "Lead Attorney," *Pitt*, March 2002.

36 Harry Truman: President's News Conference, March 14, 1946, *Public Papers of the Presidents*.

37 a middleman: Richard Lerach, Jr., interview by CMC, January 19, 2008.

37 voted against Franklin D. Roosevelt: Ibid.

37 they married in 1938: Ibid.

37 whom the family called Dick: Ibid.

38 Their favorite playground: Gene Carney, interview by CMC, March 9, 2009.

38 "the bloodiest mess": Quoted in Gary Land, ed., *Growing Up with Baseball: How We Loved and Played the Game* (Lincoln: University of Nebraska Press, 2004), pp. 105–13.

38 playing wintertime hockey: Jim Kerr, interview by CMC, March 22, 2009.

38 the coveted male lead: Tricia Sutton, interview by CMC, March 22, 2009.

38 "a great guy" and "BFF": Ibid.

39 "Miss Roberts": William S. Lerach, interview by PD, April 14, 2008.

39 a scholarship was endowed: "Student Awards and Honors," press release, Department of Sociology and Anthropology, University of West Virginia, 2006.

39 after-school and summer jobs: Richard F. and William S. Lerach, interview by CMC, January 18–20, 2008.

39 "Can you pay the tuition?": Ibid.

40 "He never got out of the starting blocks": William S. Lerach, interview by PD, October 19, 2008.

40 a career in engineering: William S. Lerach, interview by CMC, January 20, 2008.

41 an experience that was so galvanizing: Gene Carney, interview by CMC, March 9, 2009.

41 His natural bent for acting: Jim Kerr, interview by CMC, March 22, 2009.

41 he lay down and died: Richard Lerach, Jr., interview by CMC, January 19, 2008.

42 "the best of both worlds": Richard A. Morgan, e-mail to CMC, March 8, 2008.

42 **drifted away from the fraternity scene:** Rev. Erl G. "Puck" Purnell, letter to CMC, March 27, 2009.

42 **"It is a shame my mother":** William S. Lerach, interview by PD, January 10, 2008.

42 **she wanted great things for him:** William S. Lerach, interview by CMC, January 19, 2008.

43 **"I finally found something":** Ibid.

CHAPTER 3: THE YOUNG LAWYER FROM PITTSBURGH

44 **"Our take on the antiwar protests":** Richard A. Morgan, e-mail to CMC, March 8, 2008.

45 **"The plaintiff in such an action":** William T. McGough and William S. Lerach, "Termination of Class Actions: The Judicial Role," *University of Pittsburgh Law Review* 33 (1972), p. 466.

45 **might have to drop out of law school:** William S. Lerach, interview by CMC, January 18, 2008.

45 **this "brilliant" law student:** Dennis Unkovic, interview (by telephone) by CMC, July 27, 2008.

46 **"You know what I think of plaintiffs' attorneys?":** William S. Lerach, interview by CMC, January 20, 2008.

46 **These were the tricks:** Ibid.

47 **Stalling was more profitable:** Ibid.

48 **"I saw myself destined":** William S. Lerach, interview by PD, April 14, 2008.

48 **a San Diego institution known as U.S. Financial:** Don Bauder, "Those Big Fish Are Gonna Get You," *San Diego Reader*, January 25, 2005.

49 **J. Tomlinson Fort IV:** William S. Lerach, interview by CMC, January 20, 2008.

49 **tense relations:** Ibid.

50 **venerable Brown Palace Hotel:** William S. Lerach, interview by PD, January 7–8, 2008.

50 **one of the earliest voices warning:** "Fraud Charges Add to UDC Woes," *Business Week*, April 7, 1975.

50 **"For over 30 years":** Quoted in Caroline E. Mayer, "Accountants: Cleaning Up America's Mystery Profession," *U.S. News & World Report*, December 19, 1977.

51 **His father was an auditor:** Stephen Weiss, memo on history of Milberg Weiss firm, to members of Seeger & Weiss, September 20, 2007.

51 **"taking a knife":** William S. Lerach, interview by PD, January 7, 2008.

52 **"We must go after them":** William S. Lerach, interview by PD, January 7–8, 2008.

52 **he would be in charge:** Ibid.

53 "I thought to myself": Quoted in Timothy L. O'Brien, "Behind the Breakup of the Kings of Tort," *New York Times*, July 11, 2004.

53 "As for Melvyn Weiss": William S. Lerach, interview by PD, January 20, 2008.

53 "Doesn't everybody want to be": Ibid.

CHAPTER 4: GOLDEN STATE

54 as the airliner descended into San Diego: William S. Lerach, interviews by PD, October 15–29, 2007.

55 C. Arnholt Smith: "Mr. San Diego in Dutch," *Time*, June 11, 1973.

55 Smith literally presided: Carl M. Cannon, "Stage Is Set: The State vs. C.A. Smith," *San Diego Union-Tribune*, August 16, 1978.

55 "perhaps the swindler of the century": "Crime in the Suites," *Forbes*, August 15, 1975.

56 "total fraud": "Westgate Scandal," *Time*, October 29, 1973.

56 "does credit to a collection": Otto Friedrich, "F.D.R.'s Disputed Legacy," *Time*, February 1, 1982.

56 Glass-Steagall: Joe Asher, "Glass-Steagall: A Fresh Look," *ABA Banking Journal*, February 1981.

56–7 Truth in Securities Act of 1933: Cabell B. H. Phillips and Herbert Mitgang, *From the Crash to the Blitz: 1929–1939*, p. 139.

57 "problem in a Holyoke": Mayer U. Newfield to Milton V. Freeman, February 8, 1996, SEC archives.

58 "Why don't we just take Section Seventeen": Ibid.

58 in a session that took less than ten minutes: Securities and Exchange Commission, minutes of meeting, May 16, 1942, SEC archives.

58 "Well, gentlemen": Mayer U. Newfield to Milton V. Freeman, February 8, 1996, SEC archives.

58 "No one dreamed at that time": Ibid.

58 "The civil liabilities imposed": William O. Douglas and George E. Bates, "The Federal Securities Act of 1933," *Yale Law Journal*, December 1933.

59 if other parties contributed to this fraud: David M. Brodsky and Jeff G. Hammel, "The Fraud on the Market Theory and Securities Fraud Claims," *New York Law Journal*, October 24, 2003.

59 There were hurdles: Timothy L. O'Brien, "Behind the Breakup of the Kings of Tort," *New York Times*, July 11, 2004.

60 another lawsuit in California: *William Blackie et al. v. Leonard Barrack et al.*, U.S. Court of Appeals for the Ninth Circuit, September 25, 1975.

61 have his legal theory affirmed: Ibid.

61 **where he wanted to live forever:** William S. Lerach, interviews by PD, October 15–29, 2007.

61 **biggest civil case in San Diego history:** Ibid.

62 **Turrentine was the type of jurist:** Howard B. Turrentine, interview by CMC, April 7, 2009.

62 **"Good morning":** quoted by William S. Lerach, interview by PD, January 8, 2008.

62 **schoolboy being sent to the principal's office:** Howard B. Turrentine, interview by CMC, April 7, 2009.

62 **"Young man":** Ibid.

63 **"Is this what you are looking for?":** William S. Lerach, interviews by PD, October 15–29, 2007.

63 **"Here's hoping it's a growth industry":** Ibid.

64 **Weiss invited Lerach to join his firm:** Ibid.

65 **Lerach persuaded Weiss to allow him to remain in San Diego:** Ibid.

66 **alter the pronunciation of the family name:** William S. Lerach, interviews by CMC, January 18–20, 2008.

66 **the conversation in the car:** Observations of Carl Cannon, who accompanied the Lerach brothers in the car from Pittsburgh to Morgantown on January 19, 2008.

67 **" 'Isn't it a shame we lost the Fatherland?' ":** Ibid.

CHAPTER 5: A HOUSE ON THE HILL

68 **an enormous mansion:** William S. Lerach, interview by PD, October 17, 2007.

68 **son of an Armenian immigrant:** "Earl Gagosian Is Dead: Hotel Founder Was 61," *New York Times*, February 14, 1990.

69 **Its succession of owners:** Seth Lubove, "San Diego's Most Expensive Homes," *Forbes.com*, October 10, 2002.

69 **Kerkorian had come a long way:** K. J. Evans, "The Quiet Lion," *Las Vegas Review-Journal*, September 12, 1999.

69 **"keep a back door open":** Ibid.

69 **"embark on a significant":** Robert D. McCracken, *Las Vegas: The Great American Playground* (Reno: University of Nevada Press, 1997), p. 95.

70 **The cost to build:** Ibid.

70 **"The field was not level":** William S. Lerach, interview by PD, October 29, 2007.

71 **"He's in hock up to his eyeballs":** Ibid.

71 **"Your interest gets paid":** Ibid.

72 **"I was right up":** Ibid.

74 **They wanted no more depositions:** Ibid.

CHAPTER 6: OGRE OF THE VALLEY

76 **"Seymour Lazar"**: *U.S. v. Milberg Weiss Bershad & Schulman LLP, David Bershad, Steven G. Schulman, Seymour Lazar, and Paul T. Selzer*, United States District Court for the Central District of California, May 18, 2006, testimony of Seymour Lazar.

76 **"You do remember me, then?"**: Ibid.

77 **a litany of legal dustups**: Rhonda Rundle, "A Career in Courts Leads to Trouble for Seymour Lazar," *Wall Street Journal*, January 19, 2006.

77 **"I was very shapely"**: Ibid.

77 **predicting mergers and acquisitions**: Ibid.

77 **an easy way to make money**: Timothy L. O'Brien and Jonathan D. Glater, "Robin Hoods or Legal Hoods?" *New York Times*, July 17, 2005.

78 **"If I read *The Wall Street Journal*"**: Ibid.

78 **the Ampex case**: *Blackie v. Barrack: William Blackie v. Leonard Barrack et al.*, U.S. Court of Appeals for the Ninth Circuit, September 25, 1975, 524F. 2nd 891.

78 **"You are too busy"**: *U.S. v. Milberg Weiss et al.*, U.S. District Court for the Central District of California, May 18, 2006, testimony of Seymour Lazar.

79 **Why not designate**: Ibid.

79 **put themselves at risk**: Ibid.

79 **picking off targets**: Ibid.

80 **"Wait a minute!"**: William S. Lerach, interview by PD, January 11, 2008.

81 **"We sued them again"**: Ibid.

81 **"extremely aggressive"**: Nancy Rutter, "Getting Mugged on the Courthouse Steps," *Upside*, April 1990.

81 **former Disney CEO Ronald W. Miller:** David McClintick, "Tales from the Fable Factory," *New York Times*, May 10, 1987.

81 **"of blackmail euphemistically called greenmail"**: Al Delugach, "Disney Raider to Pay Investors for 'Greenmail.' $45 Million Settlement Seen as First of Its Kind," *Los Angeles Times*, July 13, 1989.

82 **"Did you go to the office?"**: William S. Lerach, interview by PD, January 11, 2008.

83 **Lerach was perfecting his skill**: Robert Lenzner and Emily Lambert, "Mr. Class Action," *Forbes*, February 2, 2004.

83 **a knack for boring in on witnesses**: Lyle Crowley and Karen Dillon, "One Man Bull Market in Shareholder Suits," *American Lawyer*, March 1998.

83 **Mattel was launched in 1945**: *Business Week*, March 29, 1976.

83 **Sales took off**: Ruth Handler Papers, Radcliffe Institute for Advanced Study, Harvard University, 2003.

84 **Five class action securities suits**: Ibid.

84 **Richard H. Borow:** William S. Lerach, interview by PD, January 12, 2008.

84 **Borow's characterization:** Richard H. Borow, interview by and subsequent e-mail exchanges with CMC, March 30–31, 2009.

85 **"This isn't Burger King":** William S. Lerach, interview by PD, January 12, 2008.

85 **"I'm not taking this crap":** Ibid.

86 **he vowed that after it was over:** Ibid.

86 **Borow was having different thoughts:** Richard H. Borow, interview by and subsequent e-mail exchanges with CMC, March 30–31, 2009.

86 **a figure of $3.9 million:** The settlement amount comes from the recollection of William S. Lerach, supplied through his assistant Kathy Lichnovsky, on March 31, 2009.

87 **"I have the greatest law practice":** William P. Barrett, "I Have No Clients: Attorney William Lerach Sues Public Corporations When Their Stock Prices Collapse," *Forbes*, October 11, 1993.

87 **"less than pond scum":** Peter Elkind quoting T. J. Rodgers, chairman of Cypress Semicomputers, in "The King of Pain Is Hurting," *Fortune*, September 4, 2000.

87 **class action security lawsuits:** Robert Lenzner and Emily Lambert, "Mr. Class Action," *Forbes*, February 16, 2004.

88 **"These suits were not clientless":** Rutter, "Getting Mugged on the Courthouse Steps."

88 **"All I had to do was bring the cases":** William S. Lerach, interview by PD, January 11, 2008.

88 **Keith Park:** William S. Lerach, interview by CMC, January 18, 2008.

89 **the day of the handshake:** Ibid.

89 **"if other firms did not come to us":** Lorine Flemons Wright, "The Corporate World's Worst Nightmare: A Man Named Lerach," *Rancho Santa Fe Review*, June 3, 1993. In this question and answer interview he reveals his two favorite movies—*Godfather I* and *II*.

89 **one of his signature achievements:** Jimmy Carter, "The State of the Union Annual Message to the Congress," January 16, 1981, *Public Papers of the Presidents*.

90 **"will make the thrift industry":** Ronald Reagan, "Remarks on Signing the Garn–St. Germain Depository Institutions Act, 1982," *Public Papers of the Presidents*.

90 **a communist hoax:** William S. Lerach, e-mail (through Kathy Lichnovsky) to CMC, April 9, 2009.

90 **joined the other families:** Gene Carney, e-mail to CMC, March 27, 2009.

91 **The boys made parachutes:** Gene Carney, interview by CMC, March 26, 2009.

91 **new IPO zillionaires:** "The Golden Geeks," *Time*, February 19, 1996.

92 **Paul N. "Pete" McCloskey, Jr.:** Carl M. Cannon, "Rocinante Rides Again," *National Journal*, June 3, 2006.

92 "There's something going on": Quoted in Roger Parloff, "Scandals Rock Silicon Valley's Top Legal Ace," *Fortune*, November 17, 2006.

92 at the crossroads of venture capital: Ibid.

92 The strategy was to represent: Gary Rivlin, "A Counselor Pulled from the Shadows," *New York Times*, July 30, 2006.

93 "That was a period of raw greed": Quoted in Parloff, "Scandals Rock Legal Ace."

93 D&O policies: Michael H. Diamond, "D&O Insurance: Pitfalls in a New World," *National Law Journal*, August 26, 2002.

94 average settlement was $8 million: Ibid.

94 "I'd go in and scare the shit": William S. Lerach, interview by PD, January 10, 2008.

94 "As long as I paid": Quoted in Rutter, "Getting Mugged on the Courthouse Steps."

94 "I mean, Mr. William Weinberger": Ibid.

95 "Why are you doing business": William S. Lerach, interview by PD, January 12, 2008.

95 John Torkelsen: Elkind and Burke, "King of Pain Is Hurting."

96 like hand and glove: William S. Lerach, interview by PD, January 12, 2008.

96 Paul L. Tullman: Anthony Lin, "Milberg Agrees to Pay $75 Million to Settle Criminal Charges Against New York Lawyer," *New York Law Journal*, June 17, 2008.

96 these three accomplices: Elkind and Burke, "King of Pain Is Hurting."

98 Valley of the Heart's Delight: "Valley of the Heart's Delight: Santa Clara Valley, California," http://santaclararesearch.net.

CHAPTER 7: THE BIG CON

99 Edwin J. Gray: Ronald Reagan, "Nomination of Edwin J. Gray to Be a Member of the Federal Home Loan Bank Board," February 17, 1983, *Public Papers of the Presidents*.

100 Federal Savings and Loan Insurance Corporation: Kenneth B. Noble, "Political Foot Soldier; Reagan's Friend at the Bank Board," *New York Times*, May 29, 1983.

100 "All in all, I think": Ronald Reagan, "Remarks on Signing the Garn–St. Germain Depository Institutions Act," October 15, 1982, *Public Papers of the Presidents*.

100 an astonishing array of schemers: William K. Black, *The Best Way to Rob a Bank Is to Own One* (Austin: University of Texas Press, 2005), p. xiii.

101 "three-six-three": William Sternberg, "Cooked Books," *Atlantic Monthly*, January 1992.

102 were suddenly obsolete: Stephen P. Pizzo, "The Real Culprits in the Thrift Scam," *New York Times*, April 2, 1990.

102 **nearly 85 percent of the nation's 3,800 S&Ls:** Stephen Rose, "Understanding the Financial Crisis," *Statistical Assessment Service*, September 26, 2008.

102 **"If you were in real estate":** William K. Black, interview by PD, October 6, 2008.

103 **Charles H. Keating, Jr.:** Black, *Best Way to Rob a Bank*, pp. 63–65.

104 **Alan Greenspan:** Stephen Pizzo, Mary Fricker, and Paul Muolo, *Inside Job* (New York: HarperCollins, 1991), p. 539.

104 **Lerach had been radicalized:** William Lerach, interview by CMC, March 18, 2008.

105 **doling out contributions to key congressional members:** Paul M. Clikeman, *Called to Account: Fourteen Financial Frauds That Shaped the American Accounting Profession* (London: Routledge, 2008), p.104.

105 **a stunningly large $850,000 gift:** "Excerpts from Ethics Committee's Session on Five Senators," *New York Times*, Nov. 17, 1990.

105 **John McCain:** Dan Nowicki and Bill Muller, "John McCain Report, The Keating Five," *Arizona Republic*, March 1, 2007.

105 **"McCain's a wimp":** Quoted in Michael Binstein and Charles Bowdon, *Trust Me: Charles Keating and the Missing Billions* (New York: Random House, 1993), p. 281.

106 **more cards to play:** Ibid., p. 282.

106 **no surprises this time:** William K. Black, interviews by and e-mail exchange with PD, October 3, 6, 9, 2008.

107 **presumption of scheme liability:** Ibid.

107 **"They have a client":** Quoted in William Sternberg, "Cooked Books," *Atlantic Monthly*, January 1992.

108 **Ivan Boesky:** Ivan Boesky commencement address, University of California Berkeley, May 18, 1986, transcript.

108 **"Greed is all right":** Ibid.

109 **Milken's operation:** Connie Bruck, *The Predator's Ball: The Inside Story of Drexel Burnham and the Rise of the Junk Bond Raiders* (New York: Penguin, 1989), pp. 78–79, 109, 120, 173–78, 217.

109 **the longer the list of defendants grew:** William S. Lerach, interview by PD, January 11, 2008.

110 **"decade of greed":** Ed Rubenstein, "Decade of Greed?—Nineteen Eighties," *National Review*, December 31, 1990.

110 **"What is wrong with intervention":** Quoted in Walter Goodman, "Critics Notebook; Senators and Their TV Awareness," *New York Times*, November 20, 1990.

110 **"the little lady who didn't get":** Quoted in Richard L. Berke, "Helping Constituents or Themselves?" *New York Times*, November 5, 1989.

CHAPTER 8: INTO THE BREACH

112 **M. Danny Wall:** Michael Binstein and Charles Bowden, *Trust Me: Charles Keating and the Missing Billions* (New York: Random House, 1993), p. 300.

112 **a celebration was in full swing:** Bill Muller, "The Keating Five," *Arizona Republic*, October 3, 1999.

113 **risky bets in raw landholdings:** Norman Strunk and Fred Case, *Where Deregulation Went Wrong: A Look at the Causes Behind the Savings and Loan Failures in the 1980s* (Chicago: U.S. League of Savings Institutions, 1988).

113 **"Lincoln, with assets of $4.9 billion":** "Savings Unit Gets New Chief," *New York Times*, December 3, 1987.

113 **"Always remember," the memo stated:** *Sarah B. Shields et al. v. Charles H. Keating Jr. et al., Consolidated with Ronald Fishman et al. v. Lincoln Savings & Loan et al.*, U.S. District Court, District of Arizona, June 1992.

113 **Wall could not sit:** Nathaniel C. Nash and Philip Shenon, "A Man of Influence: Political Cash and Regulation: A Special Report: In Savings Debacle, Many Fingers Point Here," *New York Times*, November 9, 1989.

113 **American Continental filed:** "American Continental Files for Chapter 11 Bankruptcy," *New York Times*, August 5, 1991.

113 **Immediately, it stopped making payments:** Leah Kane, interview by PD, May 12, 2008.

113 **the FHLBB seized Lincoln:** Nathaniel C. Nash, "Collapse of Lincoln Savings Leaves Scars for Rich, Poor, and the Faithful," *New York Times*, November 30, 1989.

114 **a man of habits:** Kathy Lichnovsky, interview by PD, October 10, 2008.

115 **the huge corner office:** by PD, personal observation.

115 **he had earned $2.3 million:** William S. Lerach, interview by PD, January 14, 2008.

115 **in excess of $10 billion:** Robert Lenzner and Emily Lambert, "Mr. Class Action," *Forbes*, February 2, 2004.

115 **Priam Corp.:** Nancy Rutter, "Getting Mugged on the Courthouse Steps," *Upside*, April 1990.

116 **"so non-productive":** Paul M. Wythes, testimony before the Senate Committee on Commerce, Banking, and Urban Affairs, November 3, 1991.

117 **Born with a clubfoot:** Jill Wolfson and Bruce Phebus, "Q & A with Al Shugart," Tech Museum of Innovation, San Jose, Calif., May 4, 1997.

117 **left the staid "Big Blue" for Memorex:** Patricia Sullivan, "Al Shugart, 76; Was Silicon Valley Pioneer," *Washington Post,* December 15, 2006.

117 **Shugart Associates:** Mary Anne Ostrom, "Pebble Beach, Calif., Technology Executive Short on Cash," *San Jose Mercury News*, June 30, 2002.

117 **"I had a tough time"**: Quoted in Peter Burrows, "Al Shugart Is in the Disk Drivers' Seat," *Business Week*, March 18, 1996.

117 **Finis Conner**: Peter Brennan, "Al Shugart's Orange County Namesake," *Orange County Business Journal*, October 16, 2000.

117 **"Find a parade"**: quoted in Chris Mellor, "RIP Al Shugart," *Techworld*, December 14, 2006.

117 **Shugart's parade needed a little rain**: William S. Lerach, interview by CMC, January 17, 2008.

118 **Lerach "and his kind"**: quoted in David A. Kaplan and Andrew Murr, "The Lawyer CEO's Love to Hate," *Newsweek*, February 26, 1996.

118 **"Al Shugart hated lawyers"**: Quoted in Reynolds Holding and William Carlsen, "Phantom Riches: Beneath the Glitter of Booming Silicon Valley, Executives Have Been Accused of Lying About Their Products and Doctoring Their Books, Leaving Devastated Investors in Their Wake," *San Francisco Chronicle*, November 15, 1999.

118 **"mind share"**: Ibid.

118 **"Dear Al: There's more coming"**: Quoted in Joseph Nocera, "The Lawyer Companies Love to Hate," *New York Times*, July 2, 2005.

119 **"I have his picture"**: Quoted in Lawrence M. Fisher, "Profile: William S. Lerach; The Pit Bull of Silicon Valley," *New York Times*, September 19, 1993.

120 **"I probably would have become"**: Quoted by William S. Lerach, interview by PD, January 17, 2008.

120 **"In no other profession"**: Patrick Frega, interview by PD, January 12, 2008.

120 **"There's no stopping him"**: William S. Lerach, interview by PD, January 15, 2008.

120 **"He took Ron Perelman's deposition"**: Ibid.

120 **"He was aggressive"**: Ibid.

120 **A twenty-one-count indictment**: Tony Perry, "Two Former San Diego Judges, Lawyer Get Prison Terms," *Los Angeles Times*, June 13, 2000.

121 **Lerach paid for Frega's four children**: Patrick Frega, letter to federal district judge on behalf of William S. Lerach prior to Mr. Lerach's sentencing, November 16, 2007.

122 **"Thank God I hadn't"**: William S. Lerach, interview by PD, January 17, 2008.

CHAPTER 9: MAKING A CASE

123 **Nucorp Energy**: Details of Milberg Weiss's San Diego offices are based on PD's numerous personal observations from May 1996 to May 2008.

124 **"I'll be living in his house"**: *Nucorp Securities Litigation*, U.S. District Court, Southern District of California, October 19, 1987, to April 22, 1988.

124 **others he deemed responsible**: Ibid.

124 **The only negative:** William S. Lerach, interviews by PD, January 8–15, 2008.

124 **the worst one-day percentage decline:** Nicholas F. Brady, *Brady Report; Presidential Task Force on Market Mechanisms* (U.S. Government Printing Office, 1988).

124 **more than a dozen defense lawyers:** *Nucorp Securities Litigation*, U.S. District Court, Southern District of California.

125 **"What if it turns out":** Ibid., reporter's transcript.

125 **a jury consisting of a retired navy electrician:** Voire dire, October 14, 15, 1987, Ibid.

125 **"evidence of a true life story":** Ibid.

126 **"I was surely impressed":** Juror Russell Colson, interview by PD, July 23, 2008.

126 **"I have to tell the court":** *Nucorp Securities Litigation*, U.S. District Court, Southern District of California, reporter's transcript.

126 **Judge Irving, too, obviously:** J. Lawrence Irving, interview by PD, January 11, 2008.

127 **a court order compelling Goldstone:** *Nucorp Securities Litigation*, U.S. District Court, Southern District of California, reporter's transcript.

127 **"No, your honor":** William S. Lerach, interviews by PD, January 8–15, 2008.

127 **Goldstone received the news:** James Goldman, interview by PD, September 6, 2008.

128 **Goldstone was risking:** Ibid.

128 **equally shocked:** Ibid.

129 **the giant tobacco company:** Milo Geyelin, "Forty-Six States Agree to Accept $206 Billion Tobacco Settlement," *Wall Street Journal*, November 23, 1998.

129 **John Torkelsen:** *Nucorp Securities Litigation*, U.S. District Court, Southern District of California, reporter's transcript.

129 **a unique and secret agreement:** Walter Olson, "Milberg Expert Torkelsen Pleads Guilty to Perjury," *Overlawyered*, March 3, 2008.

130 **"I don't think the defense":** William S. Lerach, interviews by PD, January 8–15, 2008.

130 **barrage from James Goldman:** *Nucorp Securities Litigation*, U.S. District Court, Southern District of California, reporter's transcript.

133 **"Kadison, this case":** Reynolds Holding and William Carlsen, "Phantom Riches: Beneath the Glitter of Booming Silicon Valley, Executives Have Been Accused of Lying About Their Products and Doctoring Their Books, Leaving Devastated Investors in Their Wake" *San Francisco Chronicle*, November 15, 1999.

134 **just not how much:** *Lexecon v. Milberg Weiss Bershad Specthrie & Lerach*, U.S. District Court, Northern District of Illinois Eastern Division, March 1, 1998, to April 14, 1999.

134 **Fred Hervey:** For the history of Circle K, see http://www.circlek.com/Circle K/AboutUs/History.htm.

134 **"And it was a surprise":** *Nucorp Securities Litigation*, U.S. District Court, Southern District of California, reporter's transcript.

137 **something was happening in the jury box:** Nucorp jurors Richard Bunch and Richard Colson, interviews by PD, July 28, 2008.

138 **"I was impressed":** Patrick Coughlin, interview by PD, February 26, 2008.

138 **Daniel R. Fischel:** *Nucorp Securities Litigation*, U.S. District Court, Southern District of California, reporter's transcript.

139 **"economic analysis of the law":** Richard Posner, "The Problematics of Moral and Legal Theory," 111 *Harvard Law Review* (1998): 1637–717.

139 **"law and economics movement":** Richard Posner, "The Best Offense," *New Republic*, September 2, 2002.

139 **It was irrelevant:** *Nucorp Securities Litigation*, U.S. District Court, Southern District of California, reporter's transcript.

139 **"Someday I'm going to wipe":** William S. Lerach, interview by PD, January 13, 2008.

140 **"He is here to testify":** *Nucorp Securities Litigation*, U.S. District Court, Southern District of California, reporter's transcript.

140 **"Frankly, Mr. Goldman":** Ibid.

141 **"the death zone":** "Everest: the Death Zone," *Nova*, PBS, February 24, 1998.

CHAPTER 10: MAKING ENEMIES

142 **Fischel delivered a haymaker:** *Nucorp Securities Litigation*, U.S. District Court, Southern District of California, October 19, 1987, to April 22, 1988, reporter's transcript.

142 **Lerach comforted himself:** William S. Lerach, interview by PD, January 14, 2008.

142 **"put all its eggs":** Ronald Reagan, Executive Order 12287, Decontrol of Crude Oil and Refined Petroleum Products, January 28, 1981, *Public Papers of the Presidents*.

142 **Reagan had decontrolled the price of oil:** Ibid.

143 **The jurors seemed attentive:** Nucorp jury foreman Richard Bunch, interview by PD, July 28, 2008.

144 **"These two really went at it":** Lawrence J. Irving, interview by PD, January 11, 2008.

146 *Blackie v. Barrack*: *Blackie v. Barrack*, U.S. Court of Appeals for the Ninth Circuit, September 25, 1975.

146 **like a cheap wristwatch:** Gary Rivlin, "The Man High Tech Would Love to Lynch," *Upside*, November 1996.

147 **sounded like common sense:** Richard Bunch, interview by PD, July 28, 2008.

148 **"Well, chumming is when"**: Richard Keyes, M.D., "Modern Bank Fishing, Chum and Chuming," Carp Anglers' Group, 1992, online at http://www.carpangleres group.com/chumming.html.

149 **Lerach felt a hard-earned exhilaration**: William S. Lerach, interview by PD. January 14, 2008.

151 **"In addition to the usual reasons"**: *Nucorp Securities Litigation*, U.S. District Court, Southern District of California, reporter's transcript.

151 *"That's a pretty logical"*: Russell Colson, interview by PD, July 28, 2008.

153 **Dick was born in Manhattan, Kansas:** Michael Kinsman, "A Standout Litigator," *San Diego Union-Tribune*, March 8, 2005.

153 **an elderly victim:** *Nucorp Securities Litigation,* U.S. District Court, Southern District of California, reporter's transcript.

155 **the personalities of the attorneys:** Magistrate Judge Edward C. Voss, United States District Court, Arizona, "Trail Conduct and Decorum," a memorandum.

155 **"Lerach treated us like school kids"**: Richard Bunch, interview by PD, July 28, 2008.

158 **"We find against the plaintiffs"**: *Nucorp Securities Litigation*, U.S. District Court, Southern District of California, reporter's transcript.

158 **"One hundred forty-five million!"**: William S. Lerach, interview by PD, January 14, 2008.

CHAPTER 11: THE WITNESS FROM HELL

159 **the drive northward:** City of Del Mar Web site: http://www.delmar.ca.us/.

159 **Lerach was not going home:** William S. Lerach, interview by PD, January 15, 2008.

159 **"heavyset jurors"**: Ibid.

160 **the confidential internal memo:** Ibid.

161 **Coughlin would join Milberg, Weiss:** Patrick Coughlin, interview by PD, February 26, 2008.

161 **"I began to get cynical"**: William S. Lerach, interview by PD, February 24, 2008.

161 **chance of being sued by shareholders:** Wyatt Company, http://www.watson wyatt.com/.

162 **an even more contentious battle:** Robert Lewis, interview by PD, February 28, 2008.

162 **"You like Scotch, I hear."**: Ibid.

163 **"We settled for around"**: William S. Lerach, interview by PD, February 28, 2008.

164 **the largest commercial litigation:** *Sarah B. Shields et al., v. Charles H. Keating Jr. et al.*, U.S. District Court, District of Arizona. No. 88-md-0551.

164 **"I know who you are":** *Lexecon v. Milberg Weiss Bershad Hynes & Lerach*, U.S. District Court, Northern District of Illinois Eastern Division, March 1 to April 14, 1999.

164 **"referral fund.":** William S. Lerach, interview by PD, October 29, 2007.

165 **annual bonuses:** *United States v. William S. Lerach*, sentencing hearing, February 11, 2008, reporter's transcript.

165 **"furtherance of arrangements":** *United States v. Milberg Weiss Bershad & Schulman LLP, David Bershad, Steven G. Schulman, Seymour Lazar, and Paul T. Selzer*, U.S. District Court for the Central District of California, May 18, 2006, testimony of Seymour Lazar.

165 **Steven G. Cooperman:** Myron Levin and Molly Selvin, "Divorce Sheds Light on Probe," *Los Angeles Times*, August 7, 2005.

166 **"Everything was totally":** Ibid.

166 **"unprofessional conduct":** Carol Vogel, "The Art Market," *New York Times*, August 7, 1992.

166 **"You are like a cold, wet blanket":** Myron Levin and Molly Selvin, "Divorce Sheds Light on Probe."

167 **IPM Technology:** William S. Lerach, interview by PD, February 29, 2008.

168 **"I want to do business":** Ibid.

169 **Newhall Land and Farming Company:** Ibid.

170 **Weiss flew to Los Angeles:** Ibid.

171 **a bonanza to prosecutors:** *U.S. v. Milberg Weiss Bershad & Schulman LLP*, U.S. District Court for the Central District of California, May 18, 2006, testimony of Steven Cooperman.

171 **their case against Lincoln Savings and Keating:** *Shields et al. v. Keating et al.*, U.S. District Court, Central District of California, June 1992.

171 **a prize among the hundreds:** Kevin P. Roddy, interview by PD, August 26, 2008.

172 **That was Lerach's hope:** William S. Lerach, interview by PD, February 29, 2008.

172 **tripling the award:** On RICO laws, see U.S. Code, Title 18, *Crimes and Criminal Procedure*.

CHAPTER 12: A GIFT HORSE NAMED KEATING

174 **"Well, you're not going to be able":** William S. Lerach, interview by PD, October 15, 2008.

174 **"We will not be blackmailed"**: Ibid.

174 **These were fortuitous developments**: Michael Manning, interview by PD, October 16, 2008.

175 **the potential whack-up**: Ibid.

176 **"We had them right"**: Kevin Roddy to PD, August 26, 2008.

176 **"They're trying to taint you"**: M. Laurence Popofsky, interview by PD, April 9, 2009.

176 **"I just received a call"**: Stephen Neal, interview by PD, October 22, 2008.

176 **"Okay Dan"**: Ibid.

177 **"I'm not interested"**: William S. Lerach, interview by PD, February 24, 2008.

177 **"Nearly fifty deep-pockets"**: Ibid.

178 **Richard Mansfield Bilby:** Wolfgang Saxon, "Richard Mansfield Bilby, 67, Judge in Charles Keating Case," *New York Times*, August 14, 2008.

178 **a lopsided somersault:** William S. Lerach, interview by PD, February 24, 2008.

178 **Arizona senator John McCain's wife:** Jerry Kamer and Andy Hall, "Kin's Deals, Trips Reveal Close McCain-Keating Tie," *Arizona Republic*, October 8, 1989.

179 **Henry B. Gonzalez:** Michael Barone, *Almanac of American Politics, 1992* (Washington, D.C.: National Journal Group, 1991), pp. 1223–25.

179 **"Up against the likes"**: Hearing of the House Committee on Banking, Finance, and Urban Affairs, November 14, 1989, Federal Transcript Service.

180 **"Mr. Keating and his coconspirators"**: Ramona Jacobs, interview by PD, May 12, 2008.

180 **"Are you ready to answer"**: Dennis Cauchon, "Key Target Is Silent in S&L Probe," *USA Today*, November 22, 1989.

180 **"On the advice of counsel"**: Jeff Weir, "Keating Takes the Fifth," *Orange County Register*, November 22, 1989.

180 **a three-page press release:** Nathaniel C. Nash, "Savings Executive Won't Testify and Blames Regulators for Woes," *New York Times*, November 22, 1989.

181 **"scapegoat"**: Martin Crutsinger, "Wall Resigns Amid Controversy over Role in S&L Bailout," *Associated Press*, December 4, 1989.

181 **"One question, among the many"**: Jonathan Lansner, "Keating Connections Kept Regulators at Bay," *Orange County Register*, April 25, 1989.

181 **"We're going to get them"**: William S. Lerach, interview by PD, February 24, 2008.

181 **"How would you like"**: Jon Cuneo, interview by PD, September 15, 2008.

182 **Rea Luft:** Ramona Jacobs, interview by PD, May 12, 2008.

183 **"The man is a coward"**: Quoted in Sam Stanton, "Snubbed S&L Victims," *Arizona Republic*, January 31, 1990.

183 **Alan Cranston:** Ramona Jacobs, interview by PD, May 12, 2008.

184 **"I have betrayed my family"**: William S. Lerach, interview by PD, February 24, 2008.

184 **"He looked very embarrassed"**: Ramona Jacobs, interview by PD, May 12, 2008.

CHAPTER 13: A TROJAN HORSE NAMED KEATING

185 **forthright in his testimony:** Excerpts of McCain statement to Senate Ethics Panel, *New York Times*, February 28, 1991.

185 **"I guess we're going to ruin":** Kevin Roddy, interviews by PD, August 28, September 4, 26, 2008.

186 **more than 100,000 Lisas:** For sales history of the Apple Lisa, see http://old computers.net/lisa.html.

186 **Popofsky was prepaid to argue:** M. Laurence Popofsky, interview by PD, April 9, 2009.

187 **"He's named as a defendant":** *Lexecon v. Milberg Weiss Bershad Hynes & Lerach*, U.S. District Court, Northern District of Illinois Eastern Division, November 10, 1997, to March 3, 1998.

187 **"I heard you called me a crook":** Patrick Coughlin, interview by PD, April 17, 2008.

187 **"Ladies and gentlemen":** Ibid.

188 **A new, hostile sentiment:** Joseph C. Goulden, *The Money Lawyers* (New York: St. Martin's Press, 2006), p. 249.

188 **"We're still going to put":** *Lexecon v. Milberg Weiss Bershad Specthrie & Lerach*, U.S. District Court, Northern District of Illinois Eastern Division.

188 **"a dishonest scheme":** William Sternberg, "Cooked Books," *Atlantic*, January 1992.

189 **"Why Lexecon?":** Ibid.

189 **Why let Fischel stand:** *Lexecon v. Milberg Weiss Bershad Specthrie & Lerach*, U.S. District Court, Northern District of Illinois Eastern Division.

189 **a cool hundred million:** Goulden, *Money Lawyers*, p. 266.

190 **"Ladies and gentlemen, the evidence":** *In re: American Continental Corporation/Lincoln Savings and Loan Securities Litigation*, March 1, 1992, reporter's transcript.

190 *This is sickening*: J. Lawrence Irving, interview by PD, October 29, 2008.

190 **"I went to roll over":** *In re: American Continental Corporation/Lincoln Savings and Loan Securities Litigation*, June 1992.

191 **more defendants opted to negotiate:** Elliott Blair Smith, "Settlement Gives Lincoln Patrons $87 Million More," *Orange Country Register*, March 31, 1999.

191 **By now some ninety defendants:** *In re: American Continental Corporation/Lincoln Savings and Loan Securities Litigation,* June 1992.

191 **Mark Sauter:** "Lincoln Officer Pleads Guilty," *New York Times*, March 26, 1991.

192 **Economics and efficiency:** William S. Lerach, interview by PD, February 26, 2008.

192 **"forty pages of boiler-plate crap":** Leonard Simon, interview by PD, November 10, 2008.

193 **"Joe overlooked it":** Ibid.

193 **"Three *billion* three":** William S. Lerach, interview by PD, February 26, 2008.

194 **Kevin Roddy wrote to the *National Law Journal*:** See http://altlaw.org/v1/cases/1064857.

194 **"I'm Dan Fischel":** Alan Salpeter, interview by PD, January 5, 2009.

195 **"First I have a few questions":** Ibid.

CHAPTER 14: THE VISIBLE HAND OF GREED

196 **disengaged the stretched canvas:** Los Angeles Police Detective Donald Hrycyk, interview by PD, December 3, 2008.

197 **"Which ones?":** William S. Lerach, interview by PD, October 15, 2008.

197 **the number of class action securities cases:** Trial Lawyers Inc. California, *A Report on the Lawsuit Industry in California* (New York: Manhattan Institute, 2005); Michael A. Perino, ed., *Securities Litigation: Fifth Annual Capital Matters: Managing Labor's Capital Conference* (Pensions and Capital Stewardship Project, Harvard Law School), May 2–4, 2007.

198 **"He's got quite an operation":** Gary Rivlin, "The Man High Tech Would Love to Lynch," *Upside*, November 1996.

198 **"He's an exceptionally smart":** Karen Donovan, "Bloodsucking Scumbag," *Wired*, November 4, 1996.

198 **Doerr estimated the cost:** Ibid.

199 **"For small and medium-size":** see http://www.wsgr.com/.

199 **Duane and Theodore Roth:** Theodore Roth, interview by CMC, December 29, 2008.

200 **"I think I can talk to him":** Ibid.

200 **"Maybe we could save everyone":** Ibid.

201 **Lerach simply dropped the suit:** "Alliance Pharmaceutical Corp. Announces Dismissal of Shareholder Suit," *Business Wire*, June 3, 1996.

201 **insurance carrier *did* reimburse:** Theodore Roth, interview by CMC, December 29, 2008.

201 **Ann Baskins:** Pat Dillon, "Shareholder Lawsuits: A Double-edged Sword?" *San Jose Mercury News*, October 27, 1996.

201 **"Get ready":** Ibid.

202 **"We're being sued":** Ibid.

202 **Baskins could say nothing:** Ibid.

203 **"We are vulnerable":** Ibid.

203 **decided to fold their case:** Ibid.

203 **He *wanted* these companies to settle:** Katrina M. Dewey, "Lerach & Co," *California Law Business*, April 18, 1994.

203 **"I didn't know shit":** William S. Lerach, interview by PD, October 15, 2008.

204 **"I need someone on the team":** William S. Lerach, interview by PD, April 15, 2008.

204 **and bear him a son:** Star Lerach, interview by PD, October 28, 2008.

205 **"How is a CEO supposed to avoid liability?":** Quoted in Lawrence M. Fisher, "William S. Lerach; The Pit Bull of Silicon Valley," *New York Times*, September 19, 1993.

206 **"The fact that you go to church":** William S. Lerach, "Plundering America: How American Investors Got Taken for Trillions by Corporate Insiders and Their Assistors," *Stanford Journal of Law, Business and Finance* 8, no. 1 (Autumn 2002).

207 **"Fuck her, we're not settling":** Boris Feldman, interview by PD, October 6, 2008.

207 **companies were now settling:** Larry L. DuCharme, Paul H. Malatesta, and Stephan E. Sefcik, "Earnings Management, Stock Issues, and Shareholder Lawsuits," University of Washington School of Business, March 10, 1999.

207 **More than $700 million:** Donovan, "Bloodsucking Scumbag."

208 **"How to get rid of this scourge":** Quoted in Peter Elkind and Doris Burke, "The King of Pain Is Hurting," *Fortune*, September 4, 2000.

208 **"I looked at the age":** Patrick Coughlin, interview by PD, April 16, 2008.

208 **Janet C. Mangini:** Nina Siegal, "The Last Days of Joe Camel: How a Team of Lawyers Defeated Big Tobacco," *California Lawyer*, November 1998.

209 **What if they could prove:** Janet Mangini, interview by PD, November 25, 2008.

209 **envision the crossover:** William S. Lerach, interview by PD, January 22, 2009.

209 **"They're putting Joe Camel":** Ibid.

209 **"Can you hold an advertiser liable":** Siegal, "Last Days of Joe Camel."

210 **"It just means we appeal":** William S. Lerach, interview by PD, January 22, 2009.

211 **Lazar's "legal bills":** *In re: United States of America v. Milberg Weiss et al.*, U.S. District Court, Central District of California, May 18, 2006.

212 **deep into the action:** Ibid.

212 **Alan Schulman:** William S. Lerach, interview by PD, April 15, 2008.

213 **Lerach would explain impatiently:** Elkind and Burke, "King of Pain Is Hurting."

214 **"You can see from the figures":** William S. Lerach, interview by PD, April 15, 2008.

CHAPTER 15: REVENGE OF THE REPUBLICANS

215 **Eugene Novidvor:** Mike Allen, "Judge Approves Great American Case Settlement," *San Diego Daily Transcript*, August 12, 1993.

216 **"Give me a hint":** Ibid.

216 **"Plaintiffs seek to represent":** James P. McDonald, "Milberg's Monopoly: Restoring Honesty and Competition to the Plaintiffs' Bar," *Duke Law Journal*, December 1, 2008.

216 **"to prove every word":** Mark Hansen, "Expert Sues Three Law Firms," *American Bar Association Journal*, March 1993.

216 **"She's a superstar":** Judy Temes, "Trailblazer Lawyer Now Name Partner," *Crain's New York Business*, July 19–25, 1993.

217 **comically excessive:** David G. Savage, "GOP Targeting Huge Punitive Damage Awards," *Los Angeles Times*, November 25, 1994.

218 **"You wouldn't have to do this":** Dena Bunis, "Low Key Cox Thrust into Limelight," *Orange County Register*, July 17, 2005.

219 **never saying the phrase** *tort reform*: Frank I. Luntz, interview by CMC, January 10, 2009.

219 **"A** *trial lawyer*—**that's Jimmy":** Ibid.

219 **"Bill Lerach was the guy":** Hedrick Smith, "Bigger Than Enron," *Frontline*, PBS, June 20, 2002.

220 **they had donated $49.5 million:** Figures compiled by the nonpartisan Center for Responsive Politics, available on their website at http://www.opensecrets.org.

220 **"Man the barricades":** Jonathan W. Cuneo, interview by CMC, January 6, 2009.

220 **"Companies, directors, and auditors":** Common Sense Legal Reform Act, hearings before the Subcommittee on Telecommunications and Finance of the House Committee on Commerce, January 19, 1995.

221 **the GOP argument had been reduced:** Jonathan W. Cuneo, interview by CMC, January 6, 2009.

222 **Cox had always felt antipathy:** Jeff Gerth, "Overhaul of Securities Laws: A Fast Track to Change or a Hasty Decision?" *New York Times*, May 26, 1995.

222 **Prior to his appearance:** Jonathan W. Cuneo, interview by CMC, March 19, 2009.

226 **the Private Securities Litigation Reform Act:** David Henry, "On the Defensive; New Congress' Securities Litigation Reform Aims to Limit Barrage of Lawsuits against Corporations," *Newsday*, February 27, 1995.

226 **the "Get Lerach Act":** Bruce V. Bigelow, "'Get Lerach Act' Falls Short of Expectation," *San Diego Union-Tribune*, April 10, 2000.

226 **"Crooks and Swindlers Protection Act":** Jonathan W. Cuneo, interview by CMC, January 9, 2009.

226 **"Securities litigation"**: Lynne Bolduc, "A Case Without a Client, The Private Securities Litigation Reform Act of 1995," *Federal Lawyer*, May 1996.

227 **"There's a lawyer I know in New York"**: Ibid.

227 **the PSLRA had ten major components**: Lynne Bolduc, "A Case Without a Client.

229 **careful playing a card**: William S. Lerach, conversation with both authors, summer 1997.

230 **the Democrats' rank and file remained**: Editorial, "First Veto-Override; Securities-Fraud Bill: Clinton Reversed by Democrats Angry at His Flip-Flop," *Baltimore Sun*, December 26, 1995.

231 **"You gotta give me"**: Theodore D. Roth, interview by CMC, December 29, 2008.

231 **a statement that read more**: "Message to the House of Representatives Returning Without Approval the Private Securities Litigation Reform Act of 1995," December 19, 1995, *Public Papers of the Presidents*.

231 **"My opinion is known"**: Quoted in John F. Harris and Sharon Walsh, "Clinton Vetoes Measure to Limit Securities Suits," *Washington Post*, December 20, 1995.

232 **"The fraudsters and the dishonest people"**: Common Sense Legal Reform Act, hearings before the Subcommittee on Telecommunications and Finance of the House Committee on Commerce, January 19, 1995.

CHAPTER 16: REVENGE OF THE NERDS

233 **"Dear Bill, more is coming"**: Ed Mendel, "Tort-Reform Fight Is Backed with Personal Bad Blood," *San Diego Union-Tribune*, March 13, 1996.

233 **a series of statewide referendums**: Tim W. Ferguson, "Tort Retort," *Forbes*, February 12, 1996.

234 **visions of a future**: Gary Rivlin, "The Man High Tech Would Love to Lynch," *Upside*, November 1996.

234 **The mid-1990s**: "Year of the Internet," *Newsweek*, December 25, 1995.

234 **a carjacker**: Lawrence M. Fisher, "William S. Lerach; The Pit Bull of Silicon Valley," *New York Times*, September 19, 1993.

234 **"He's a greedy guy"**: Dan Morain, "The Lawyer Prop. 201 Backers Love to Hate," *Los Angeles Times*, March 21, 1996.

234 **"Imagine the feeling"**: Rivlin, "The Man High Tech Would Love to Lynch."

235 **Proulx helped raise $12 million**: Karen Donovan, "Bloodsucking Scumbag," *Wired*, November 4, 1996.

235 **Proposition 201**: Ibid.

235 **a shark-finned Cadillac**: Ed Mendel, "Battle Over Tort Reform Hitting Streets, Air: Foes' TV Ads to Counter Backers' Shark Car Gag," *San Diego Union-Tribune*, February 13, 1996.

235 **the major insurers:** Marc Lifsher, "Three Measures, One Target: Lawyers," *Orange County Register*, January 14, 1996.

236 **Bill Carrick:** Bill Carrick, interview by CMC, February 11, 2009.

236 **"Dianne is in this":** Ibid.

237 **"The Silicon Valley guys":** Ibid.

237 **The facts in *Central Bank*:** *Central Bank of Denver v. First Interstate Bank*, U.S. Court of Appeals for the Tenth Circuit, November 30, 1993, to April 19, 1994.

238 **In 1975 the Supreme Court agreed to hear an appeal:** *Blue Chip Stamps v. Manor Drug Stores*, U.S. Supreme Court, March 24, 1975, to June 9, 1975.

238 **"When we deal with private actions":** Ibid.

240 **"In *hundreds* of judicial and administrative proceedings":** Ibid.

241 **"Congress gutted the law":** "Rebuttal to Argument Against Proposition 211," California Secretary of State's Office, 1996.

241 **"Bill Lerach looks after":** Julie Pitta, "Fighting Prop. 211 Becomes Crusade for High-Tech Execs," *Los Angeles Times*, September 23, 1996.

241 **Politics was in Cuneo's DNA:** Jonathan W. Cuneo, interview by CMC, January 9, 2009.

242 **Over the Thanksgiving weekend:** Jonathan W. Cuneo, interview by CMC, March 20, 2009.

242 **all summer it held a lead:** Ed Mendel, "Proposition 211 Registers a 14 Point Lead," *San Diego Union-Tribune*, September 18, 1996.

242 **some unusual political alliances:** Jonathan W. Cuneo, interview by CMC, January 9, 2009.

242 **playing both sides of the street:** Sara Miles, *How to Hack a Party Line: The Democrats and Silicon Valley* (New York: Farrar, Straus & Giroux, 2001), pp. 32–33.

243 **"We prefer *Apple Democrats*":** Evan Thomas, John F. Stacks, and James Kelly, "Basking in Reagan's Troubles," *Time*, June 12, 1982.

243 **gave $100,000 to the Clinton campaign:** Jeffrey Birnbaum and Viveca Novak, "The Corporate Dole," *Time*, September 23, 1996.

243 **Wade Randlett:** Miles, *Hack a Party Line*, pp. 4–6.

244 **"The wealthy East Coast lawyers":** Quoted in Howard Fine, "Tort Wars II: Dollars Flow in, Negative Ads Roll," *Orange County Business Journal*, August 12, 1996.

244 **"Jon, do you think":** Jonathan W. Cuneo, interview by CMC, January 9, 2009.

244 **"He believes securities laws":** Quoted in Alison Mitchell, "Clinton Touts Technology on California Visit," *New York Times*, August 8, 1995.

245 **a fund-raising dinner in Sunnyvale:** Alison Mitchell, "Building a Bulging War Chest: How Clinton Financed His Run," *New York Times*, December 27, 1996.

245 **"Clinton wants to nail down":** Quoted in Birnbaum and Novak, "Corporate Dole."

245 "I've learned in politics": Quoted in Miles, *Hack a Party Line*, p. 34.

246 "When we brought up 'securities'": Jonathan W. Cuneo, interview by CMC, January 9, 2009.

246 "They'd been warned about": Bill Carrick, interview by CMC, February 11, 2009.

246 the anti-Lerach brain trust gathered: John Markoff, "A Political Fight Marks a Coming of Age for a Silicon Valley Titan," *New York Times*, October 21, 1996.

247 "We are looking at the loss": Ibid.

247 a survey of its members: "Forty-Seven Percent of High-Tech Public Member Companies Would Consider Leaving California if Prop 211 Passes, American Electronics Association Survey Shows; 61,000 Jobs, Continued Economic Growth at Risk," *Business Wire*, October 3, 1996.

248 Judy Estrin: Donovan, "Bloodsucking Scumbag."

248 "If this passes": Quoted in Philip J. Trounstine, "California Business Frets over Securities Fraud Measure: Proposition Would Help Shareholder Lawsuits," *San Jose Mercury News*, July 29, 1996.

248 "I'd expect my entire board": Quoted in Gary Rivlin, "The Man High Tech Would Love to Lynch," *Upside*, November 1996.

249 "We've gone from Plan A": William S. Lerach, interview by PD, June 24, 1997.

249 "We came to believe": Jonathan W. Cuneo, interview by CMC, March 20, 2009.

249 California voters buried: Dawn Kawamoto and Christine MacDonald, "Voters Reject Prop. 211," *CNET News,* November 6, 1996.

249 "We took a mortal threat": Quoted in ibid.

250 "A sleeping giant": Quoted in Miles, *Hack a Party Line*, p. 30.

250 Bill Lockyer: Mary Anne Ostrom and Hallye Jordan, "Execs Flex Muscle in Sacramento Access," *San Jose Mercury News*, November 2, 1996.

250 "*Bill Lerach* has awakened": Donovan, "Bloodsucking Scumbag."

250 To celebrate its extraordinary year: Janet Rae-Dupree, "Intel Caps Super Year with Bonuses for Workers," *San Jose Mercury News*, January 15, 1997.

250 Intel CEO Andy Grove: Scott Herhold, "Intel's CEO Andy Grove Raked in $98 Million for '96," *San Jose Mercury News*, April 9, 1997.

251 nursing a hangover: William S. Lerach, interview by PD, October 4, 1995.

CHAPTER 17: MISTAKE BY THE LAKE

252 He was tall: This account of Pam Little's meeting J. J. Little is from interviews by PD with Cleveland FBI agent Richard Wren, November 17; Rocky River Police Sergeant Carl Gulas, November 21, 2008; Los Angeles Police Detective Don Hrycyk, December 3, 2008; and Los Angeles FBI agent Virginia Curry, December 8, 2008.

252 **Pam Davis possessed a résumé:** Ibid.

253 **"We found what appeared":** Rocky River Police Sergeant Carl Gulas, interview by PD, November 21, 2008.

254 **"He's sitting on stolen art":** Ibid.

254 *We can't pull back*: William S. Lerach, interview by PD, October 28, 2007.

255 **"Mel, I've been to the museum":** Ibid.

255 **"A good Jew":** The history of the Milberg Weiss firm is detailed in a memo from Stephen Weiss to members of his firm Seeger & Weiss, September 30, 2008.

255 **"On my honeymoon with Star":** William S. Lerach, interview by PD, October 15, 2008.

255 **"I don't know":** Ibid.

256 **Following the rewriting of the rules:** William S. Lerach, interview by PD, February 24, 2008.

256 **employee pension funds:** Steven E. Abraham, "The Impact of the Taft-Hartley Act on the Balance of Power in Industrial Relations," *American Business Journal* 33, no. 3 (1996).

256 **institutional investors:** William S. Lerach, interview by PD, January 22, 2009.

256 **Dennis Drabek:** Rocky River Police Sergeant Carl Gulas, interview by PD, November 21, 2008.

257 **International Foundation for Art Research:** For tracking lost art, see http://www.artloss.com/.

257 **Cleveland FBI agents Dick Wren and Scott Brantley:** Cleveland FBI agent Richard Wren, interview by PD, November 17, 2008.

257–58 **"to a lot of wise-guy wannabes":** Los Angeles FBI agent Virginia Curry, interview by PD, December 8, 2008.

258 **paid a call to J. J. Little:** Richard Wren, interview by PD, November 17, 2008.

258 **Negotiations commenced:** Virginia Curry, interview by PD, December 8, 2008.

258 **"I was just trying":** Richard Wren, interview by PD, November 17, 2008.

259 **From Lloyd's of London:** Virginia Curry, interview by PD, December 8, 2008.

259 **set up a sting:** Ibid.

260 **a new digital transmitter:** Ibid.

260 **"Does this sound familiar?":** Virginia Curry, interview by PD, March 7, 2009.

261 **Quoting FBI special agent:** Carol Vogel, "A Picasso and a Monet Turn Up in Storage," *New York Times*, June 7, 1997.

262 **lanky and taciturn:** Richard Robinson, interview by PD, February 26, 2009.

263 **no honor among thieves:** Richard Robinson, interview by PD, December 10, 2008.

263 **"I wasn't going to let this case die":** Virginia Curry, interview by PD, December 8, 2008.

263 **Los Angeles grand jury:** Richard Robinson, interview by PD, December 10, 2008.

264 **a sense of gratitude:** William S. Lerach, interview by PD, March 24, 2008.

265 **"He'd better not be lying":** Ibid.

CHAPTER 18: PHOENIX RISING

266 **Lerach's tangling with Chris Cox:** Diana B. Henriques, "Parties Clash at Hearing on Securities Litigation," *New York Times*, January 20, 1995.

267 **"We do not solicit plaintiffs":** Common Sense Legal Reform Act, hearings before the Subcommittee on Telecommunications and Finance, House Committee on Commerce, January 19, 1995.

267 **an alternative version:** text of the Private Securities Litigation Reform Act of 1995, see http://www.law.cornell.edu/uscode/15/usc_sec_15_00000078===u004=.html.

268 **"Look, we can't pay plaintiffs":** William S. Lerach, interview by PD, January 22, 2009.

268 **The New York partners:** Ibid.

268 **"before the truth regarding":** "Class Action Suit Filed Against NetManage, Inc. and Its Officers and Directors Alleging Misrepresentations, False Financial Statements and Insider Trading," *Business Wire*, January 10, 1997.

268 **"Seven of the individual":** "Class Action Suit Filed Against Read-Right Corporation and Its Officers," *Business Wire,* January 17, 1997.

268 **"insider trading profits":** "Class Action Suit Filed Against America Online Inc. and Its Officers, Directors and Accountants," *Business Wire*, February 24, 1997.

268 **"One thing that is very clear":** Quoted in Leslie Eaton, "Class Action Lawsuits Are Not Turning Out Exactly as Congress Planned," *New York Times*, February 27, 1997.

269 **this percentage had doubled:** A Statistical and Legal Analysis of Class Action Securities Fraud Litigation Under the Private Securities Litigation Reform Act of 1995," working paper, Stanford Law School, February 1997.

269 **"I warned Congress":** Quoted in Eaton, "Class Action Lawsuits."

269 **"The dance is over":** Quoted in Herb Greenberg, "Why One Prominent Class Action Attorney Calls It Quits," *San Francisco Chronicle*, February 29, 1996.

270 *Wright v. Ernst & Young*: Nicholas F. Schanbaum, "Scheme Liability: Rule 10b-5(a) and Secondary Actor Liability After *Central Bank,"* *Review of Litigation*, Winter 2007.

270 **The Second Circuit agreed:** Ibid.

271 **filed against a Silicon Valley company:** *Dannenberg et al. v. Software Toolworks, Inc., Deloitte & Touche, et al.*, U.S. Court of Appeals for the Ninth Circuit, February 18, 1994.

271 **"prepared after extensive review":** Ibid.

271 **calling on potential plaintiffs:** William S. Lerach, interview by PD, April 16, 2008.

272 **did some of his best work:** Jonathan W. Cuneo, interview by CMC, January 6, 2009.

272 **"Dot-con":** William S. Lerach, "The Chickens Have Come Home to Roost," Milberg Weiss, Hynes & Lerach internal document, 2002.

272 **public pension funds acted as lead plaintiffs:** Randall Thomas, "Pension Funds as Shareholder Activists," *En Banc: Vanderbilt Law Review* 61 (October 2008).

273 **Edward R. McCracken:** Cynthia Bournellis, "SGI's CEO McCracken Tumbles," *Electronic News*, November 3, 1997.

273 **negotiate an exchange of convertible stock:** "Class Action Suit Filed Against Silicon Graphics, Inc. and Its Officers and Directors," *Business Wire*, June 23, 1998.

273 **"To do this":** *Edmund J. Janas v. Edward R. McCracken et al.*, U.S. District Court, Northern District of California, October 17, 1996. See http://securities.stanford.edu/1011/SGI96/068.html.

274 **"based upon a review":** Floyd Norris, "Stage Set for Appellate Ruling on Class Action Suits vs. Companies," *New York Times*, May 30, 1997.

274 **"motive, opportunity":** Dan Goodin, "SGI Stock Suit Could Set Precedent," *CNET News*, June 10, 1988.

CHAPTER 19: VENDETTA

276 **"a massive document depository":** Jerold S. Solovy, interview by PD, December 16, 2008.

277 **"a remarkable power grab":** *Lexecon v. Milberg Weiss Bershad Hynes & Lerach*, http://supreme.justia.com/us/523/26/index.html.

277 **"We have a good rapport":** Alan Salpeter, interview by PD, December 4, 2008.

277 *I'm taking on the most powerful:* Ibid.

277 **"We do not want to get":** William S. Lerach, interview by PD, January 22, 2009.

278 **"Our worst fears":** Lauran Neergaard, "Secret Memo Shows R.J. Reynolds Targeted Teenagers," *Associated Press*, January 15, 1998.

278 **R.J. Reynolds CEO Steve Goldstone:** Janet Mangini, interview by PD, November 24, 2008.

278 **when the accounts were finally settled:** Patrick Coughlin, interview by PD, April 16, 2008.

278 **"hero":** Representative Henry A. Waxman, statement, January 18, 1998.

278 **If they were to take a hit:** William S. Lerach, interview by PD, January 22, 2009.

279 **outsize bills from John Torkelsen:** Peter Elkind and Doris Burke, "The King of Pain Is Hurting," *Fortune*, September 4, 2000.

279 **"Dave [Bershad] and I have decided":** William S. Lerach, interview by PD, April 15, 2008.

279 **"There are people at the firm":** Ibid.

280 **"Dave, I can't do this":** Quoted in Elkind and Burke, "King of Pain Is Hurting."

280 **"Do you consider yourself":** *Lexecon v. Milberg Weiss Bershad Hynes & Lerach*, U.S. District Court, Northern District of Illinois Eastern Division, March 1 to April 14, 1999.

281 **"the greatest perversion of justice":** Ibid.

282 **Would the jury see through it?:** William S. Lerach, interview by PD, April 15, 2008.

282 **"Dan Fischel could look at a rainstorm":** William S. Lerach, interview by PD, January 22, 2009.

282 **"You admit, do you not":** *Lexecon v. Milberg Weiss Bershad Hynes & Lerach*, U.S. District Court, Northern District of Illinois Eastern Division.

284 **Judging from the looks:** William S. Lerach, interview by PD, April 15, 2008.

287 **Mel Weiss was seething:** Ibid.

287 **"So, over this period after 1990":** *Lexecon v. Milberg Weiss Bershad Hynes & Lerach*, U.S. District Court, Northern District of Illinois Eastern Division.

288 **"There were such notes":** Ibid.

289 **"Star, we are getting killed":** William S. Lerach, interview by PD, October 15, 2008.

290 **She'd come as soon:** Star Lerach, interview by PD, October 28, 2008.

290 **"Mr. Lerach, you didn't tell this jury":** *Lexecon v. Milberg Weiss Bershad Hynes & Lerach*, U.S. District Court, Northern District of Illinois Eastern Division.

292 **"Would it help":** Alan Salpeter, interview by PD, November 25, 2008.

292 **"We're going to turn Lerach":** Ibid.

292 **Salpeter contacted Judge Zagel:** *Lexecon v. Milberg Weiss Bershad Hynes & Lerach*, U.S. District Court, Northern District of Illinois Eastern Division.

296 **Salpeter decided to go for:** Alan Salpeter, interview by PD, December 4, 2008.

296 **Hansen and Salpeter continued working:** Ibid.

296 **"Dan, get real,":** Ibid.

297 **"We got whacked":** William S. Lerach, interview by PD, April 15, 2008.

CHAPTER 20: FRAUD BY HINDSIGHT

299 **written by Judge Sneed:** *Janas v. McCracken et al.*, Ninth Circuit Court of Appeals, Northern District of California, No. 97-16204, San Francisco, July 2, 1999.

299 **"Congress intended":** Ibid.

300 "[Plaintiff's] assertions": Ibid.

300 "based upon the investigation": *Janas v. McCracken et al.*, U.S. District Court for Northern California, June 7, 1997.

300 "with particularity": For Judge Sneed's decision in Silicon Graphics, see *Janas v. McCracken et al.*, Ninth Circuit Court of Appeals, Northern District of California, No. 97-16204, San Francisco, July 2, 1999.

301 "Congress plainly intended": For Judge Browning's dissent in Silicon Graphics, see ibid.

301 "It's a blockbuster": Quoted in Dan Goodin, "Securities Fraud Ruling Protects Tech Firms," *CNET News*, July 6, 1999.

302 Lerach found the opinion: William S. Lerach, "A Tainted Decision," internal memo, 2004.

302 Carly Fiorina: Peter Burrows, *Backfire: Carly Fiorina's High Stakes Battle for the Soul of Hewlett-Packard* (New York: John Wiley, 2003), p. 229.

302 She was one of three children: Bob Egelko, "Judge Joseph Sneed Dies— Longtime 9th Circuit Judge," *San Francisco Chronicle*, February 14, 2008.

302 "Guess which law firm": William S. Lerach, interview by PD, April 16, 2008.

303 "Here's how we got": Ibid.

304 "A former Beverly Hills ophthalmologist": Jeff Leeds, "Former Doctor Is Convicted in Art Fraud Case," *Los Angeles Times*, July 21, 1999.

305 John Torkelsen stated under penalty: Amanda Bronstad, "Former Milberg Expert Pleads Guilty to Perjury," *National Law Journal*, May 2, 2008.

306 the very crimes of self-dealing: "U.S. Files Suit Against John Torkelsen, Richard Propper, Daniel Beharry, & Sovereign Bank Alleging Fraud of $32 Million Against the Small Business Administration," press release, U.S. Attorney's Office, Philadelphia, December 29, 2006.

306 Either he would cooperate: Elkind and Burke, "King of Pain Is Hurting."

307 The big three received: *United States v. Milberg Weiss Bershad & Schulman LLP, David Bershad, Steven G. Schulman, Seymour Lazar, and Paul T. Selzer*, U.S. District Court, Central District of California, May 18, 2006.

CHAPTER 21: LET'S MAKE A DEAL

308 The first signal: Richard Robinson, interviews by PD, June 2, 11, September 10, 30, October 31, December 10, 2008; January 21, February 2, 2009.

309 the Tuscan-style villa: William S. Lerach, interview with and personal observations by PD, April 14, 1997.

309 "This is really, really nice": William S. Lerach, interview by PD, February 26, 2008.

310 his neighbor Gerald Parsky: Cullen Couch, "Gerald Parsky, '68, Blends Poli-

tics and Principle to Achieve Reform," *University of Virginia Law Review*, Spring 2007.

310 **Lerach had been peeved:** William S. Lerach, interview by PD, February 26, 2008.

310 **Such thoughts would haunt him:** Ibid.

310 **what new developments:** Ibid.

310 **two strategic personnel acquisitions:** For biographies of Paul Howes and Byron Georgiou see Coughlin Stoia Web site, http://www.csgrr.com/.

311 **"for dirty bathrooms":** Paul Howes, interview by PD, January 15; 2009.

311 **clear, coherent delivery:** Robert McGahan, interview by PD, May 22, 2008.

312 **"For more than ten years":** Richard Robinson, interview by PD, September 10, 2008.

312 **Robinson was unmoved:** *United States. v. Milberg Weiss Bershad & Schulman LLP et al.*, U.S. District Court, Central District of California, May 18, 2006.

313 **"He never did any work":** Richard Robinson, interview by PD, September 10, 2008.

314 **Weiss had given him a check:** *United States v. Milberg Weiss Bershad & Schulman LLP et al.*, U.S. District Court, Central District of California, May 18, 2006.

314 **then there could be a discussion:** Richard Robinson, interview by PD, September 10, 2008.

315 **a pattern should reveal itself:** Ibid.

315 **fraying and widening:** Peter Elkind, "The Fall of America's Meanest Law Firm," *Fortune*, November 13, 2006.

315 **that scene during:** William S. Lerach, interview by PD, January 22, 2009.

315 **"Listen, shit-for-brains,":** Robert McGahan, interview by PD, January 6, 2009.

316 **Lerach was vexed:** William S. Lerach, interview by PD, October 15, 2008.

316 **stock Bershad's credenza:** Walter Olson, "Inside Milberg's Credenza," *Wall Street Journal*, May 22, 2006.

316 **skim enough off the top:** Douglas Axel, interview by PD, January 13, 2009.

316 **his son Job needed $250,000:** Robert McGahan, interview by PD, December 12, 2008.

317 **eight more visits:** Richard Robinson, interviews by PD, June 2, 11, September 10, 30, October 31, December 10, 2008; January 21, February 2, 2009.

317 **Michael Emmick:** For Michael Emmick biography, see http://www.lls.edu/academics/faculty/emmick.html.

317 **dealt with Lewinsky personally:** Monica Lewinsky interrogation, January 16, 1998, Transcription, Office of the Independent Counsel.

318 **the ring of truth:** Michael Emmick, interview by PD, February 25, 2009.

318 **"I just loved":** Catherine Budig, interview by PD, February 15, 2009.

318 **names kept repeating themselves:** Richard Robinson, interview by PD, December 10, 2008.

319 **Amalgamated Bank:** *In re: Enron Corporation Securities Litigation, The Regents of the University of California, et al., Individually and on Behalf of All Others Similarly Situated v. Kenneth L. Lay et al.,* U.S. District Court, Southern District of Texas, Houston Division, First Amended Complaint, May 14, 2003.

319 **nearly $150 million:** Christopher Patti, interview by PD, December 17, 2008.

319 **John Zegarski:** *In re: Enron Litigation,* U.S. District Court, Southern District of Texas, Houston Division, First Amended Complaint, May 14, 2003.

320 **Enron insiders unloaded:** Information regarding Enron's impending collapse comes from four sources: *United States v. Jeffrey K. Skilling,* U.S. District Court, Southern District of Texas, Houston Division, Case no. 06-208885; Department of Justice, Government Exhibit no. 004469: "Schedules: Enron Earnings Release External Format and Forecast, January 25, 2001"; Enron Annual Report from 2000; and finally the unheeded warning sounded by business reporter Bethany McLean in her insightful piece "Is Enron Overpriced?" *Fortune,* March 5, 2001.

320 **"These guys don't quit":** William S. Lerach, interview by PD, February 26, 2008.

320 **"Do you have a position in Enron?":** William S. Lerach, interview by PD, October 15, 2008.

321 **"We're going to take on":** Rebecca Clarren, "Paradise Lost, Greed, Sex Slavery, Forced Abortions, and Right Wing Moralists," *Ms. Magazine,* Spring 2006.

321 **"Start with arrogance":** Bethany McLean, "Why Enron Went Bust," *Fortune,* December 24, 2001.

322 **Milberg Weiss would accrue costs:** Helen Hodges, *Declaration in Support of Lead Counsel's Motion for Attorney's Fees, in re: Enron Litigation,* U.S. District Court, Southern District of Texas, Houston Division, January 2, 2008.

CHAPTER 22: THE HUNTERS AND THE HUNTED

323 **"It's a smoking howitzer!":** Documentary, *The Smartest Guys in the Room,* Magnolia Pictures, April 23, 2005.

324 **University of California:** *In re: Enron Litigation,* U.S. District Court, Southern District of Texas, Houston Division, First Amended Complaint, May 14, 2003.

324 **"They've been shredding documents":** Carrie Johnson, "Enron Auditor Admits Crime; Andersen's Duncan Ordered Shredding," *Washington Post,* May 14, 2002.

324 **references to Jedi II:** Paul Howes, interview by PD, January 15, 2009.

325 **"Paul, I really don't care":** William S. Lerach, interview by PD, February 15, 2009.

325 **he called Christopher Patti:** Paul Howes, interview by PD, January 15, 2009.

325 **"Why don't you come up":** William S. Lerach, interview by PD, February 27, 2008.

326 **"They really managed":** Christopher Patti, interview by PD, December 18, 2008.

326 **line up other plaintiffs:** Ibid.

326 **bank robbery:** Tom Fowler, "Cooperation Could Pay Off for Fastow," *Houston Chronicle*, September 26, 2006.

327 **multicolored taxonomy:** Christopher Patti, interview by PD, December 18, 2008.

327 **"I am confident":** Ibid.

327 **a criminal grand jury:** "Milberg Weiss Face Inquiry, Report Says," *New York Times*, January 26, 2002.

328 **still another war room:** Richard Robinson, interview by PD, June 11, September 10 and 30, 2008.

328 **a relatively lenient sentence:** Timothy L. O'Brien and Jonathan D. Glater, "Robin Hoods or Legal Hoods," *New York Times*, July 17, 2005.

328 **how extensively Cooperman:** Richard Robinson, interviews by PD, June 11, September 10 and 30, 2008.

328 **"I think we're almost":** Michael Emmick, interview by PD, February 25, 2009.

329 **"David, you had nothing":** *In re: United States v. Milberg Weiss, Bershad, Schulman, LLP et al.*, U.S. District Court, Central District of California, Bershad testimony.

329 **put the documents in his safe:** Ibid., Weiss guilty plea, March 20, 2008.

329 **blueprint for a fraud case:** Richard Robinson, interview by PD, June 11, September 10 and 30, 2008.

329 **looking for lawyers testifying:** Richard Robinson, interview by PD, February 29, 2009.

330 **these chronologies:** Robert McGahan, interview by PD, June 6, 2008.

330 **"Mr. Lerach is getting":** Edward Iwata, "Law Firms Tussle over Enron Case," *USA Today*, February 11, 2002.

330 **Finberg's plaintiffs' losses:** Flynn Roberts, "Lawyers Fight for Big Prize: Enron Lead Attorney," *Chicago Tribune*, February 11, 2002.

330 **"The only way this story":** Iwata, "Law Firms Tussle over Enron Case."

331 **"Regents presents itself":** Rosanna Ruiz, "Judge Names University as Lead Plaintiff in Enron Case," *Houston Chronicle*, February 17, 2002.

331 **"all hands retreat":** William S. Lerach, interview by PD, January 17, 2008.

332 **"I'd get home late":** Alexandra Bernay, interview by PD, April 16, 2008.

333 **"I'm a human being"**: Andrew Longstreth, "A Dish Best Served Cold," *American Lawyer*, October 1, 2005.

333 **The image would depict him**: Ibid.

334 **"It made us nervous"**: Peter Elkind, "The Fall of America's Meanest Law Firm," *Fortune*, November 3, 2006.

334 **Parsky-Bush-Enron connection**: Chris Thompson, "Parsky's Party," *East Bay Express*, May 9, 2007.

335 **"I still have the power"**: William S. Lerach, interview by PD, April 18, 2008.

335 **Arthur Andersen all but admitted**: Senator Joe Lieberman, "Enron Insecurity and Social Security," United States Senate, February 13, 2002.

336 **"There's billions in this case"**: William S. Lerach, interview by PD, April 16, 2008.

336 **"the most far-reaching reforms"**: Elisabeth Bumiller, "Bush Signs Bill Aimed at Fraud in Corporations," *New York Times*, July 31, 2002.

337 **"Glass-Steagall law is no longer"**: William J. Clinton, "Remarks on Signing Legislation to Reform the Financial System," November 12, 1999, *Public Papers of the Presidents.*

337 **"I think we will look back"**: Stephen Labaton, "Congress Passes Wide Ranging Law Easing Bank Laws," *New York Times*, November 5, 1999.

338 **"Even in those halcyon days"**: William S. Lerach, guest lecture in course number 429, Stanford Law School, spring 2002.

338 **he wasn't alone**: William Greider, "Is This America's Top Corporate Crime Fighter?" *Nation*, August 22, 2002.

338 **Other laudatory stories**: Jeffrey Toobin, "The Man Chasing Enron," *New Yorker*, September 9, 2002.

338 **"It wasn't as if"**: William S. Lerach, "The Chickens Have Come Home to Roost," internal document, 2002.

339 **"Someone said loud and clear"**: Michelle Ciccarelli, interview by PD, January 15, 2008.

340 **anonymous plaintiffs**: Ibid.

341 **the stock of Halliburton**: S. C. Gwynne, "Did Cheney Sink Halliburton? (And Will It Sink Him?)," *Texas Monthly*, October 2002.

342 **"I think it will be fair"**: William Greider, "Cheney and HAL," *Nation*, June 22, 2006.

342 **"issuing a series of false"**: *Richard Moore et al. v. The Halliburton Co.*, complaint, June 3, 2002.

342 **"For now, let's do"**: William S. Lerach, interview by PD, February 26, 2008.

CHAPTER 23: "NOBODY CAN STOP ME"

343 "It's about Milberg Weiss": John Ryan, "Milberg Weiss Faces Probe into Conduct: Grand Jury Investigates Whether Law Firm Solicited Stock Investors for Class Actions," *Los Angeles Daily Journal*, January 24, 2002.

343 "It doesn't jibe": Michael Kinsman, "Newspaper Says Milberg Weiss Is Grand Jury Target," *San Diego Union-Tribune*, January 25, 2002.

344 "Milberg Weiss Bershad": Christian Berthelsen, "Law Firm Being Investigated: Federal Grand Jury Looking into Dealings with Plaintiffs," *San Francisco Chronicle*, February 13, 2002.

344 beginning to ring hollow: Ibid.

344 they decided to hire a consultant: Christopher Patti, interview by PD, December 17, 2008.

344 "We're looking for an independent": J. Lawrence Irving, interview by PD, December 12, 2008.

345 "So they want adult supervision": William S. Lerach, interview by PD, January 22, 2009.

345 one of the best business attorneys: Robert Fairbank, interview by PD, January 6, 2009.

346 the team would review: J. Lawrence Irving, interview by PD, December 12, 2008.

346 "I don't want to use the term": William Greider, "Is This the Nation's Top Corporate Crime Fighter?" *Nation*, August 22, 2002.

346 "The CEO ultimately": Larry Mackinson and Larry Noble, "Returning the Favor: Bush Huddles with Big Campaign Donors," Center for Responsive Politics, January 2, 2001.

347 private attorneys delivered: William S. Lerach, "Proposal re: Auditor Independence," comments to the SEC, September 25, 2000.

347 "We regard this settlement": Quoted in Trey Davis, "UC Settles with Arthur Andersen's International Firms in Enron Lawsuit," University of California News Release, August 27, 2002.

348 Explicit guidelines: For Private Securities Litigation Reform Act of 1995 text; see http://www.law.cornell.edu/uscode_sec_15_00000078—u004-.html.

348 Jeffrey Isaacs: Larry D. Thompson, Deputy Attorney General, "Principles of Federal Prosecution of Business Organizations," memo superseding that of Deputy Attorney General Eric Holder, January 20, 2003.

348 "Do we want massive litigation": Jeff Isaacs, interview by PD, January 7, 2009.

349 For economy's sake: Michael Emmick, interview by PD, February 25, 2009.

349 a cast of witnesses: Ibid.

350 **Nancy Cooperman told:** Richard Robinson, interview by PD, January 21, 2009.

350 **credibility of the star witness:** Myron Levin and Molly Selvin, "Divorce Sheds Light on Probe," *Los Angeles Times*, August 7, 2005.

350 **Were those kickbacks?:** Richard Robinson, interview by PD, January 21, 2009.

351 **could destroy Cooperman:** Jeff Isaacs, interview by PD, January 7, 2009.

351 **So far the only kickbacks:** Ibid.

351 **mission would be to:** Robert McGahan, interview by PD, January 15, 2009.

352 **"Bill was like a dog":** Alexandra Bernay, interview by PD, April 16, 2008.

352 **"Please, can I just go":** Ibid.

353 **the banks, underwriters, and accountants:** *In re: Enron*, First Amended Complaint, May 14, 2003.

353 **"schemed" or "scheming":** William S. Lerach, interview by PD, October 15, 2008.

354 **"Mel Weiss is manipulative":** Robert Lenzner and Emily Lambert, "Mr. Class Action," *Forbes*, February 2, 2004.

354 **indicted Andrew Fastow:** Michael Hedges and Mary Flood, "Fastow Faces 78 Counts: Indictment Includes Obstruction of Justice Charge," *Houston Chronicle*, November 1, 2002.

355 **one of the shrewdest criminal defense:** William S. Lerach, interview by PD, October 15, 2008.

355 **one article caught his attention:** Michael A. Drummond, "Lerach Strikes Back," *California Lawyer*, September 4, 2002.

355 **"He uses fraud to fight fraud":** Joseph A. Grundfest, interview by PD, November 11, 2007.

356 **"This sounds like something":** Boris Feldman, interview by PD, October 6, 2008.

356 **"This decision confirms":** Quoted in Trey Davis, "Federal Court Rules to Keep Most Defendants in Enron Shareholders' Lawsuit," University of California Press Release, December 20, 2002.

356 **"The lids are off":** William S. Lerach, interview by PD, February 26, 2008.

357 **an eight-year-old internal memo:** Robert McGahan, interview by PD, December 12, 2008.

357 **"This just smells bad":** Justin Scheck, "Indicted Lawyer's Firm Smelled Trouble," *Recorder*, January 3, 2006.

CHAPTER 24: THE PATIENCE OF JOB

359 **"Sure things":** William S. Lerach, interview by PD, January 22, 2009.

359 **"I just got a call":** William S. Lerach, interview by PD, April 18, 2008.

360 "The thing that has helped me": Quoted in Tim Padgett and Alice Jackson Baughn, "The Rise and Fall of Bernie Ebbers," *Time*, May 13, 2002.

361 spilling the beans: Walter Hamilton, "Ebbers Pushed Others to 'Hit Numbers,' CFO Says," *Los Angeles Times*, February 9, 2005.

361 patented chart with its jagged timeline: WorldCom stock prices from October 1, 1996, to September 30, 2002, a timeline, exhibit filed with the court in World-Com litigation, http://www.worldcomlitigation.com/html/kdm.html.

361 "Forget class action": William S. Lerach, interview by PD, April 18, 2008.

362 "What about suing Citibank": Ibid.

362 "I just talked to Carl McCall": Ibid.

362 "Mel, quit it": Ibid.

363 home field advantage: Ibid.

363 female federal judges: For biographies of Federal District Judges Denise Cote and Barbara Lynn, see Federal Judicial Center, http://www.fjc.gov/public/home.

364 Barbara S. Jones: Gretchen Morgenson and Ken Belson, "The Sisterhood Judging WorldCom," *New York Times*, January 30, 2005.

364 Denise L. Cote: Ibid.

365 they retained the mind-set: William S. Lerach, interview by PD, April 18, 2008.

365 Sean Coffey: John P. "Sean" Coffey, interview by CMC, February 24, 2009.

366 studied diligently: John P. "Sean" Coffey, interview by CMC, February 20, 2009.

367 never miss a McCall fund-raiser: Shaila K. Dewan, "Accountants Gave to McCall After Getting State Contract," *New York Times*, August 23, 2002.

367 would New York be ousted: William S. Lerach, interview by PD, April 18, 2008.

367 "He might as well": Ibid.

367 "The New York State Common": *In re: WorldCom Litigation*, U.S. District Court Judge Denise Cote, order regarding August 12 pretrial conference, August 15, 2002.

368 "I'm appealing": William S. Lerach, interview by PD, April 18, 2008.

368 "We wish to pursue": Anthony Lin, "Milberg Weiss Taken to Task for Conduct in WorldCom Case," *New York Law Journal*, November 19, 2003.

368 a flurry of complaints: For key events in WorldCom litigation, see http://www.worldcomlitigation.com.

368 "a de facto class action": William S. Lerach, interview by PD, April 18, 2008.

369 clients who had opted out: Copies of both letters obtained by the authors.

369 "He's telling us not": John P. "Sean" Coffey interview with CMC, February 20, 2009.

370 "Has Bill Lerach lost": William S. Lerach, interview by PD, April 18, 2008.

370 "All Mel cares about": Ibid.

371 **"Bill, will you cut"**: John P. "Sean" Coffey, interview by CMC, February 24, 2009.

371 **"I think you're a terrific lawyer"**: Ibid.

372 **The case settled for $4.75 million**: *United States v. Milberg Weiss Bershad & Schulman LLP et al.*, U.S. District Court, Central District of California, May 18, 2006.

372 **"in order to participate"**: Ibid.

373 **Each side made its case**: Stephen Taub, "Class Action and 'Opt Out' Lawyers Duke It Out," *Compliance Week*, November 8, 2005.

374 **a stern nineteen-page ruling**: Lin, "Milberg Weiss Taken to Task."

375 **Lerach's gambit**: On key events in WorldCom litigation, see http://www.world comlitigation.com.

376 **Mel Weiss viewed the whole**: William S. Lerach, interview by PD, April 18, 2008.

376 **split in two**: Renée Beasley Jones, "Milberg Weiss Makes Its Case for Splitting in Two," *San Diego Business Journal*, June 30, 2003.

376 **to begin drafting the terms**: William S. Lerach, interview by PD, April 18, 2008.

376 **They would divide**: Patrick Coughlin, interview by PD, December 12, 2008.

376 **the agreement**: *United States v. Milberg Weiss Bershad & Schulman LLP et al.*, U.S. District Court, Central District of California, May 18, 2006.

376 **Job Lazar**, Robert McGahan, interview by PD, December 12, 2008.

377 **Tracing the flow of money**: *United States v. Milberg Weiss Bershad & Schulman LLP et al.*, U.S. District Court, Central District of California, May 18, 2006.

377 **referred all entreaties**: Thomas Bienert, interview by PD, February 18, 2009.

377 **nearly impenetrable circle**: Robert McGahan, interview by PD, December 12, 2008.

378 **"your participation in our fee"**: James Harbin, interview by PD, January 16, 2009.

378 **"What am I going to do"**: Robert McGahan, interview by PD, December 12, 2008.

378 **"I do not want to go"**: James Harbin, interview by PD, January 16, 2009.

379 **Seymour Lazar was a serial plaintiff**: *United States v. Milberg Weiss Bershad & Schulman LLP et al.*, U.S. District Court, Central District of California, May 18, 2006.

379 **strong circumstantial evidence**: Richard Robinson, interview by PD, February 26, 2009.

379 **Canadian Imperial Bank of Commerce**: *In re: United States v. Richard A. Causey, Jeffrey K. Skilling, Kenneth L. Lay, et al.*, U.S. District Court for the Southern District of Texas, July 7, 2004.

380 **"We've seen recently"**: "Canadian Imperial Bank of Commerce Agrees to Co-operate with Enron Investigation, Exit Structured Finance Business, Implement Reforms, with Oversight by Monitor," U.S. Justice Department, press release, December 22, 2003.

380 **proportionate liability:** William S. Lerach, interview by PD, October 15, 2008.

380 **The consulting and mediating team:** Hon. J. Lawrence Irving, interview by PD, November 18, 2008.

380 **"We anticipate this settlement"**: Simon Bowers, "Bank of America Settles Enron Lawsuit for $69 million," *Guardian*, July 3, 2004.

380–81 **"We expect that we will achieve"**: Trey Davis, "UC Reaches $222.5 Million Settlement with Lehman Brothers in Enron Securities Case," UC Newsroom press release, October 29, 2004.

381 **"We had a gun"**: Alan Salpeter, interview by PD, October 26, 2008.

381 **"My clients have authorized me"**: Ibid.

381 **"It's a joke, right?"**: William S. Lerach, interview by PD, October 15, 2008.

382 **"It wasn't unexpected"**: Alan Salpeter, interview by PD, March 23, 2009.

382 **Douglas Axel:** Douglas Axel, interview by PD, January 13, 2009.

382 **spring the trap on an insider:** Michael Thomas, blog, *Daily Caveat*, May 22, 2006; Peter Elkind, "The Fall of America's Meanest Law Firm," *Fortune*, November 3, 2006.

384 **"Let's go to lunch"**: Jeffrey Isaacs, interview by PD, January 7, 2009.

384 **"Let's indict"**: Robert McGahan, interview by PD, December 12, 2008.

CHAPTER 25: THE NOT-SO-PERFECT CIRCLE

385 **guilty plea of Paul L. Tullman:** Richard Robinson, interview by PD, January 21, 2009.

386 **some seventy cases:** Anthony Lin, "Milberg Agrees to Pay $75 Million in Settlement over Kickback Scheme," *New York Law Journal*, June 17, 2008.

386 **more than $9 million:** Ibid.

386 **deputized as a special assistant:** Richard Robinson, interview by PD, January 21, 2009.

386 **Torkelsen, the expert witness:** Peter Elkind with Doris Burke, "The King of Pain Is Hurting," *Fortune*, September 4, 2000.

387 **They'd subpoenaed him:** Richard Robinson, interview by PD, January 21, 2009.

387 **campaign contribution:** Don Van Natta, Jr., "Memorandum Suggests That Clinton Made $50,000 Call from the White House," *New York Times*, September 23, 1997.

387 **a significant player:** Richard Robinson, interview by PD, January 21, 2009.

387 **The more he dragged his feet:** "U.S. Files Suit Against John Torkelsen, Richard Propper, Daniel Beharry & Sovereign Bank Alleging Fraud of $32 Million Against Small Business Administration," press release, U.S. Attorney's Office, Philadelphia, December 29, 2006.

387 **for scheming to fraudulently obtain:** "John Torkelsen, Liar, Thief, Drunk," *New Jersey Justice*, June 9, 2006.

387 **on the ropes:** Justin Scheck, "Federal Prosecutors Put Pressure on Milberg Weiss' Star Expert," *Recorder*, June 9, 2006.

389 **purchased Halliburton stock for their grandchildren:** Lisa Sanders, "Halliburton Judge Recuses Himself," *Market Watch*, August 10, 2004.

389 **"What made your case":** Ibid.

389 **proceed vigorously:** Ibid.

CHAPTER 26: ALL FALL DOWN

390 **"secret and illegal payments":** *United States v. Seymour Lazar and Paul Selzer*, U.S. District Court for Central District of California, June 24, 2005.

391 **"I never paid a plaintiff":** Robert Lenzner and Emily Lambert, "Mr. Class Action," *Forbes*, February 16, 2004.

391 **"The government is fifteen years":** Peter Burrows, "Payback Time for Bill Lerach," *Business Week*, June 30, 2005.

391 **"a malicious-prosecution theory":** Ibid.

391 **"baseless":** Ibid.

391 **"Neither Milberg Weiss":** Timothy O'Brien and Jonathan D. Glater, "Robin Hoods or Legal Hoods," *New York Times*, July 17, 2005.

391 **"This sounds like another example":** Ibid.

391 **"I thought I was doing":** Quoted in David Olson, "Attorney Facing Federal Charges," *Press Enterprise*, June 24, 2005.

392 **"powerful enemies":** Quoted in Joseph Nocera, "The Lawyer Companies Love to Hate," *New York Times*, July 2, 2005.

392 **"Once you go out":** Quoted in Molly Selvin and Myron Levin, "Indictment Heats Up Probe of Law Firm," *Los Angeles Times*, July 8, 2005.

392 **the Enron settlements:** For Bernstein Litowitz and WorldCom settlement, see http://www.blbglaw.com/cases/00108.

392 **immunity to Alan Schulman:** John R. Wilke and Scott J. Paltrow, "Wide Net Cast in Milberg Case," *Wall Street Journal*, June 8, 2005.

393 **"The Justice Department is investigating":** Quoted in Roger Parloff, "Lerach Firm Will Fight Client to Stay in Halliburton Case," *Fortune Legal Pad*, December 13, 2006.

393 **had not been named:** Ibid.

393 **a federal grand jury in Los Angeles:** "Truth in Corporate Justice LLC Attorney Denied Access to Annual Halliburton Meeting," Rothstein's account to shareholders and clients, published at PRWEB.com, May 22, 2006.

393 **Another set of indictments:** Roger Parloff, "Firm Ejected as Lead Counsel in Fallout from Milberg Weiss Indictment," *Fortune Legal Pad*, February 26, 2007.

393 **he would fight:** Ibid.

393 **"This case is about":** John R. Wilke, Nathan Koppel, and Peter Sanders, "Milberg Indicted on Charges Firm Paid Kickbacks," *New York Times*, May 19, 2006.

394 **The indictment covered activity:** *United States v. Milberg Weiss Bershad & Schulman LLP et al.*, U.S. District Court, Central District of California, May 18, 2006.

394 **"I did a lot of stuff":** William S. Lerach, interview by PD, January 17, 2008.

394 **considerations of self-preservation:** John P. "Sean" Coffey, interview by CMC, October 9, 2008.

394 **Eliot Spitzer:** Peter Lattman, "Why Wasn't Spitzer Involved in the Milberg Weiss Investigation?" *Wall Street Journal Law Blog*, May 24, 2006.

395 **Such bravura did little:** Julie Creswell, "Another Prominent Lawyer Departs from Milberg Weiss," *New York Times*, August 25, 2006.

395 **Pamela Rogers Chepiga:** "Lawyer Global 100," *American Lawyer*, November 2006.

395 **upgrade its U.S. practice:** Creswell, "Another Prominent Lawyer Departs."

395 **her full partner's share:** William S. Lerach, interview by PD, October 15, 2008.

395 **"She knew a lot":** Ibid.

396 **"It's heartbreaking":** Anna Schneider-Mayerson, "Save This Firm! Milberg Weiss Is Nearing Iceberg," *New York Observer*, August 25, 2006.

396 **Bill's sixtieth birthday:** Michelle Ciccarelli, interview by PD, March 3, 2009.

396 **Ken Feinberg was cheered:** Bob Van Voris and Jeff Feeley, "Firms Request Enron Class Status Be Voided," *Bloomberg News*, February 5, 2007.

397 **In Lerach's mind, the scenario:** Ibid.

397 **petitions in the Fifth Circuit:** "Banks Appeal Ruling Allowing Enron Investors to Sue as Class," *New York Times*, February 6, 2007.

397 **Its headquarters was in New Orleans:** Jack Bass, *Unlikely Heroes* (New York: Simon & Schuster, 1981), pp. 46–51.

398 **fitting venue for shareholder plaintiffs:** William S. Lerach, interview by PD, January 22, 2009.

398 **The Fifth Circuit bench of 2006:** U.S. Court of Appeals for the Fifth Circuit, Federal Judicial Center, http://www.fjc.gov/history/home/.

398 **Judge John F. Walter:** Ibid.

398 "There's certainly a significant": *United States v. Milberg Weiss Bershad & Schulman LLP et al.*, U.S. District Court, Central District of California, status conference, September 21, 2007.

399 four ex–Merrill Lynch executives: Alexei Barrionuevo and Vikas Bajaj, "Fastow Testifies Lay Knew of Enron's Problems," *New York Times*, March 9, 2006.

399 "The only personal benefit": "U.S. Court Overturns Convictions in Enron Case," *Reuters*, August 2, 2006.

399 "Let's hope we don't draw": William S. Lerach, interview by PD, January 22, 2009.

400 The duty to inform Andy Fastow: Paul Howes, interview by PD, January 15, 2009.

400 "Jeff got twenty-four years": Ibid.

401 Now that he was doing five years: Douglas Axel, interview by PD, January 13, 2009.

401 Lerach was also circumspect: William S. Lerach, interview by PD, October 15, 2008.

401 Alan Schulman . . . Robert Sugarman: Ibid.

402 "saddened": Molly Selvin, "Unsettling Days for the King of Class Action," *Los Angeles Times*, July 23, 2006.

402 Patti and Judge Irving: Hon. J. Lawrence Irving, interview by PD, April 15, 2008.

402 Still another matter: Michelle Ciccarelli, interview by PD, March 12, 2009.

403 The stone walkway: PD, personal observations.

403 house on the hill: Seth Lubove, "San Diego's Most Expensive Homes," *Forbes.com*, October 10, 2002, http://www.forbes.com/2002/11/08/cz_sl_1108feat.html.

403 previous owners: William S. Lerach, interview by PD, October 28, 2007.

404 as he made his rounds: PD, personal observations.

404 Flanking the villa: William S. Lerach, interview by PD, October 15, 2008.

404 Among the guests: Michelle Ciccarelli, interview by PD, March 12, 2009.

405 Chihuahua: Kathy Lichnovsky, interview by PD, February 18, 2009.

405 "Wonder how much they paid": Michelle Ciccarelli, interview by PD, March 12, 2009.

405 added three plaintiffs: William Greider, "Cheney and HAL," *Nation*, June 22, 2006.

406 already-wary Paula John: Ibid.

406 "Due to the strong manner": Roger Parloff, "Lerach Firm Ejected."

406 Scott called Lerach: William S. Lerach, interview by PD, January 22, 2009.

407 Boies signaled his willingness: Daniel Fisher, "Battle of the Class-Action Titans," *Forbes.com*, November 28, 2006.

407 **The plaintiffs decried:** Parloff, "Lerach Firm Ejected."

408 **The petition was filed:** Roger Parloff, "Client Yearning to Fire Attorney Lerach Says Fortune Story Was Last Straw," *Fortune online,* CNNMoney.com, December 13, 2006.

408 **"When you take a guy":** Ramzi Abadou, interview by PD, January 16, 2008.

409 **"He shouldn't have told":** Ibid.

CHAPTER 27: A NARROW DEFINITION OF DECEIT

410 **drew three judges' names:** Charles R. Fulbruge III, interview by PD, January 29, 2009.

410 **Jerry Smith:** For Judge Jerry Edwin Smith biography, see http://www.1b5 .uscourts.gov/judgebio/FifthCircuit/.

410 **James Dennis:** For Judge James W. Dennis biography, see http://www.1b5 .uscourts.gov/judgebio/FifthCircuit/.

410 **He was happy:** William S. Lerach, interview by PD, January 22, 2009.

410 **Rhesa Barksdale:** For Judge Rhesa H. Barksdale biography, see http://www.1b5 .uscourts.gov/judgebio/FifthCircuit/.

411 **"I look forward to going":** Quoted in Rick Atkinson, *The Long Gray Line* (New York: Henry Holt and Company, 1989), p. 144.

411 **Bush tapped him:** Tony Mauro, "The Right Stuff," *American Lawyer,* November 3, 2008.

411 **the two Barksdales:** Christopher Patti, interview by PD, February 19, 2009.

411 **Jim Barksdale:** William S. Lerach, interview by PD, January 22, 2009.

411 **Speed was essential:** Eric Isaacson, interview by PD, February 28, 2009.

411 **E. Grady Jolly:** Paul Howes, interview by PD, February 15, 2009.

412 **Their solution was to cook:** Gregory A. Markel and Gregory G. Ballard, "In re: Charter Communications (Stoneridge)," *Securities Regulation Law Review* 33 (2006), p. 246.

412 **Charter ran this shady arrangement:** Stephen Taub, "Former Charter CFO Pleads Guilty," CFO.com, January 28, 2005.

412 **a classic example of scheme liability:** Markel and Ballard, "In re: Charter Communications (Stoneridge)."

413 **a similar set of facts:** Gregory A. Markel and Gregory G. Ballard, "In re Charter Communications, Inc. Securities Litigation and Simpson v. AOL Time Warner Inc.: Circuits Split Over the Validity of 'Scheme' Liability Under Section 10(b)," *Securities Regulation Law Journal,* Winter 2006, p. 246.

413 **identifying the alleged chicanery:** Vaughn Marshall, "Simpson v. AOL Time Warner: The SEC and the Definition of Primary Liability under Rule 10b-5," The RacetotheBottom.org, June 6, 2007.

413 **how they might rebound:** Jaclyn Jaeger, "'Secondary Actor' Lawsuit Hits Fever Pitch," *Compliance Week*, June 26, 2007.

413 **Steve Schulman asked:** Ashby Jones, "Steve Schulman Resigns from Milberg Weiss," *Wall Street Journal Law Blog*, December 8, 2006.

413 **"This was his decision":** quoted in Julie Creswell, "Partner at Law Firm Resigns to Focus on Criminal Charges Against Him," *New York Times*, December 9, 2006.

414 **"vigorously fight the indictments":** Elizabeth Goldberg and Justin Scheck, "Name Partner Exits Milberg Weiss," Law.com, December 11, 2006.

414 **Under his arm he carried:** Patrick Coughlin, interview by PD, January 16, 2009.

414 **strode solemnly to their chairs:** William S. Lerach, interview by PD, January 22, 2009.

414 **This alarmed him:** Patrick Coughlin, interview by PD, January 16, 2009.

415 **So the plan was:** Ibid.

415 **it felt as though the judges:** Ibid.

415 **evidence of Mardi Gras:** Byron Georgiou, interview by PD, February 28, 2009.

415 **Nola, a happening new restaurant:** Ibid.

415 **"We want to thank y'all":** Michelle Ciccarelli, interview by PD, March 9, 2009.

416 **"I suspect we've lost":** William S. Lerach, correspondence to PD, February 24, 2009.

416 **"Presuming plaintiffs' allegations":** Julie Creswell, "Court Rejects Suit Against Enron Banks," *New York Times*, March 20, 2007.

416 **"The effect of the opinion":** Isaiah J. Poole, quoting Al Meyerhoff, "A License to Commit Fraud," TomPaine.com, March 28, 2007.

416 **"Executives owe honest services":** Peter Lattman, "Fifth Circuit: No Class Action in Enron Shareholders' Suit," *Wall Street Journal Law Blog*, March 19, 2007.

416 **"a gut shot":** Paul Howes, interview by PD, January 15, 2009.

417 **"I'm probably less disappointed":** Ben Hallman, "Oh, The Hours They Would Have Billed," *American Lawyer*, May 2007.

417 **"What this pretty much means":** Julie Creswell, "Court Rejects Suit."

417 **"We are going to seek review":** William S. Lerach, interview by PD, January 22, 2009.

417 **Lerach tried not to project:** Ibid.

417 **"anything unethical, immoral":** Roger Parloff, "Lerach Firm Ejected as Lead Counsel in Fallout from Milberg Weiss Indictment," *Fortune*, February 26, 2007.

418 **that claim would have been:** William S. Lerach, interview by PD, January 22, 2009.

419 **"You're a higher profile":** Ibid.

419 **"But without Dave":** Ibid.

419 *"Dave won't give Mel up"*: Ibid.

419 **Coughlin's engagement party:** Patrick J. Coughlin, interview by PD, January 16, 2009.

420 **"Bill, you could be hurting":** Ibid.

420 **"I just got off the phone":** William S. Lerach, interview by PD, January 22, 2009.

420 **"That was Mel":** Ibid.

420 **"We're done":** Michelle Ciccarelli, interview by PD, March 4, 2009.

420 **"I thought I was safe":** William S. Lerach, interview by PD, January 22, 2009.

420 **keeping legal pads:** Ibid.

421 **She recited the facts:** Michelle Ciccarelli, interview by PD, March 6, 2009.

421 **"We can fight this":** Ibid.

421 **"He got paid":** William S. Lerach, interview by PD, January 22, 2009.

421 **"I could kill Dave":** Ibid.

421 **"I can fight this":** Ibid.

422 **"I could be gone for twenty":** Ibid.

422 **"Jon, we found out":** Jonathan W. Cuneo, interview by PD and CMC, February 12, 2009.

422 **"I have a black heart":** *In re: United States of America v. William S. Lerach*, U.S. Federal Court, Central District of California, February 12, 2008, sentencing memo.

422 **no real evidence:** Richard Robinson, interview by PD, January 19, 2009.

422 **"direct and very helpful":** Douglas Axel, interview by PD, January 13, 2009.

422 **Lerach paced:** John Keker, interview by PD, March 6, 2002.

423 **"How much time":** Section 11c1c of the Federal Sentencing Guidelines, http://www.ussc.gov/guidelin.htm.

423 **"I'll do three years":** John Keker, interview by PD, March 6, 2002.

423 **"That's what they'll want":** Ibid.

423 **"We can negotiate":** William S. Lerach, interview by PD, October 29, 2007.

423 **"No. They want you":** William S. Lerach, interview by PD, January 22, 2009.

423 **"My client":** Ibid.

424 **"Fat chance of getting a change":** John Keker, interview by PD, March 6, 2009.

424 **the prosecutors had been seriously debating:** Richard Robinson, interview by PD, January 19, 2009.

424 **"If my client makes":** Ibid.

424 **Cardona was in no mood:** John M. Broder and Nick Madigan, "Charges Are Dropped in Spy Case Involving Woman and FBI Agent," *International Herald Tribune*, June 8, 2005.

424 **prosecutors were contemplating:** Richard Robinson, interview by PD, January 19, 2009.

424 "if the Supreme Court": "Frank and Conyers File Amicus Brief in Stoneridge Case," Lerach, Coughlin, Stoia press release, June 30, 2007.

425 "been running this more": Kara Scannell, "Big-Money Battle Pits Business vs. Trial Bar," *Wall Street Journal*, October 9, 2007.

425 "Achilles' heel": Stephen Labaton, "Treasury Chief Urges 'Balance' in Regulation of U.S. Companies," *New York Times*, November 21, 2006.

425 "For America's global": John Engler, "Washington's Biggest Decision," *Washington Post*, July 2, 2007.

425 "by general consent": Kevin LaCroix, "Why Stoneridge Matters," *D&O Diary*, October 8, 2007.

427 "We think the SEC": Marcy Gordon, "President Weighed In on Case; Outcome Will Impact Enron Investors," *Associated Press*, June 13, 2007.

427 "equally legally viable": Paul D. Clement, interview by CMC, March 15, 2009.

427 "unnecessary lawsuits": Ibid.

427 thirty-six-page brief: *In re: Stoneridge Investment Partners v. Scientific-Atlanta, Inc., et al.*, "Brief for the United States as Amicus Curiae Supporting Affirmance," Paul D. Clement, Thomas G. Hungar, and Kannon K. Shanmugam, August 2007.

427 "Congress considered": Ibid.

427 Grundfest published a paper: Joseph A. Grundfest, "Scheme Liability: A Question for Congress, Not for the Court," working paper, Stanford Law School, September 9, 2007.

428 the Ivy League Joe Valachi: "U.S. v. Milberg Weiss . . . David Bershad Is the New Joe Valachi," Sirota & Sirota website, http://blog.sirotalaw.com, January 14, 2007.

428 detailing for prosecutors: Richard Robinson, interview by PD, January 19, 2009.

428 "cooperate fully": *In re: U.S. v. David J. Bershad*, U.S. District Court, District of Central California, Exhibit A: Statement of Facts in Support of David J. Bershad Plea Agreement, July 10, 2007.

429 began making plans: William S. Lerach, interview by PD, January 22, 2009.

429 he was redoubling his defense: Roger Parloff, "Only Mel Weiss Can Save Milberg Weiss Now," *Fortune Legal Pad*, July 10, 2007.

429 In the war room: Richard Robinson, interview by PD, January 19, 2009.

430 "For Christ's sake, Mel": William S. Lerach, interview by PD, January 22, 2009.

430 "I just don't understand": Ibid.

430 As they waited: Tara Lazar, interview by PD, March 11, 2009.

430 "Mel, I'm going in": William S. Lerach, interview by PD, January 22, 2009.

430 **The wedding commenced:** Tara Lazar, interview by PD, March 11, 2009.

431 **"Let's get a photograph":** William S. Lerach, interview by PD, January 22, 2009.

CHAPTER 28: A BROAD DEFINITION OF DECEIT

433 **"a cheat":** Star Soltan Lerach, "Letter to the Sentencing Judge," November 28, 2007.

433 **"Dad, I need to know":** William S. Lerach, interview by PD, January 22, 2009.

433 **judicial mediation:** John Keker, interview by PD, March 6, 2009.

434 **A. Howard Matz:** Ibid.

434 **the magic number:** Ibid.

434 **Cardona agreed:** Richard Robinson, interview by PD, January 19, 2009.

434 **"William S. Lerach, formerly a name partner":** U.S. Attorney's Office Press Release No. 07–114, September 18, 2007.

435 **Gleeful voices:** Jeff Nash and Carleen Hawn, "Legal Eagle Grounded by His Own Kickback Schemes," *Financial Week*, September 24, 2007.

435 **"For the past two decades":** Chris O'Brien, "Pioneering Class-Action Suits Leave Lasting Impact on Silicon Valley," *San Jose Mercury News*, September 19, 2007.

435 **"He's obviously had":** Ibid.

435 **"Bill, are any":** William S. Lerach, interview by PD, April 16, 2008.

435 **prosecutors informed Brafman:** Peter Elkind, "Mel Weiss Is Sinking His Firm," *Fortune Legal Pad*, September 24, 2007.

436 **Schulman agreed to testify:** Douglas Axel, interview by PD, January 13, 2009.

436 **the complaint outlined:** "Top Class Action Lawyer Indicted: Melvyn Weiss Charged in Long-Running Federal Probe Against Law Firm That Sued Companies," *CNN/Money*, September 20, 2007.

436 **Urgent phone calls:** Patrick Coughlin, interview by PD, February 2, 2009.

436 **motion to distribute $7.2 billion:** *In re: Enron Litigation*, U.S. District Court, Southern District of Texas, Houston Division, Helen Hodges, Declaration in Support of Lead Counsel's Motion for Attorney's Fees.

437 **On the main floor:** Details of Lerach's home office and his reaction to *Stoneridge* decision observed by PD, January 15, 2008.

438 **some curious developments:** Kara Scannell, "Big Money Battle Pits Business vs. Trial Bar," *Wall Street Journal*, October 9, 2008.

438 **both justices owned somewhere:** Tony Mauro, "Issue of 'Strategic Recusals' Arises in Key Supreme Court Case," *Legal Times*, August 20, 2007.

438 **Roberts had reentered:** Tony Mauro, "Chief Justice Back in the Stoneridge Case," Law.com, September 21, 2007.

439 **"Absolutely ridiculous":** PD, observations, January 15, 2008.

439 **the ultimate payout:** William S. Lerach, interview by PD, January 15, 2008.

440 **petitioned to have Kennedy removed:** SCR Code of Judicial Conduct Chapter 60.01, governing recusals: "Member of the judge's family" means the judge's spouse, child, grandchild, parent, grandparent and any other relative or person with whom the judge maintains a close familial relationship.

440 **"Most of them":** William S. Lerach, interview by PD, January 12, 2008.

441 **more than 150 reference letters:** Letters to the Court, Sentencing Memo to U.S. District Court Judge John Walter, Central District of California, case no. CR 07-00964-JFW.

442 **"competing interests":** Robert Monks and Nell Minow, *Watching the Watchers* (New York: John Wiley, 1996), p. 36.

442 **"One thing I might suggest":** PD, observations, January 15, 2008.

444 **Friends joined him:** PD, observation of details of gathering at the Beverly Wilshire Hotel, February 10, 2008.

444 **There was resilience in his voice:** PD, observation of details of gathering at Ivy Hotel in San Diego, November 16, 2008.

445 **even as limos were dropping off guests:** Frank Cucinotta, interview by PD, February 11, 2008.

445 **"You should probably":** PD, observation of Lerach meeting with defense lawyers in Los Angeles, February 11, 2008.

445 **"The judge will take this deal":** Ibid.

445 **Gravely, Lerach mounted the steps:** PD, observation of sentencing hearing for William S. Lerach, February 11, 2008.

446 **Judge Walter took the bench:** *United States v. William S. Lerach,* reporter's transcript of sentencing hearing, February 11, 2008.

451 **"It's the judgment of the court":** PD, observation of sentencing hearing for William S. Lerach, February 11, 2008.

452 **The celebration was subdued:** Robert McGahan, interview by PD, February 22, 2009.

EPILOGUE

453 **"You are about to read":** Bill Lerach, "I Am Guilty," *Portfolio,* July 2008.

454 **Sean Coffey, along with his senior partner:** Brian Grow, "The Kings of Class Actions," *Business Week,* May 16, 2005.

454 **"It is bad enough":** Joe Nocera, "Serving Time, But Lacking Remorse," *New York Times,* June 7, 2008.

455 **"The risk-reward ratio":** William S. Lerach, "How Tort Reform Paved the Way for the Financial Meltdown," *Executive Council,* February/March 2009.

455 "Simply put, the behavior": William S. Lerach, "The Chickens Have Come Home to Roost," Milberg Weiss, Hynes & Lerach internal document, 2002.

455 "Nothing makes lawyers": Quoted in Jonathan D. Glater, "Financial Crisis Provides Fertile Ground for Boom in Lawsuits," *New York Times*, October 17, 2008.

456 "Some people look at sub-prime lending": Quoted in Eric Lipton and Stephen Labaton, "The Reckoning: Deregulator Looks Back, Unswayed," *New York Times*, November 16, 2008.

456 "systematically trying": Josh Meyer, "FBI Can Focus Only on Biggest Cases of Financial Bailout Fraud, Official Tells Senate Panel," *Los Angeles Times*, February 12, 2009.

460 "We may not be perfect": William Greider, "Is This America's Top Corporate Crime Fighter?" *Nation*, July 18, 2002.

460 "It's no small irony": Stephanie Mencimer, "The Fall of a Corporate Crime Fighter," *Mother Jones*, February 14, 2008.

Index

429–31, 435, 448–49, 457–58; Dolly
Madison Industries, 59–60; earnings,
115, 204, 315; on Federal Civil Rule
23, 58–59; Fischel lawsuit and, 277–
78, 315; fraud on the market theory,
45, 59, 60–61, 60n, 93, 139, 143–44;
government's investigation of, 379,
394, 401, 413–14, 436; greed as a
growth industry, 63, 93, 250; Holocaust Museum and, 255–56; Kerkorian case and, 70; Lazar and, 76–79,
96, 210–11; Lerach break with, 359–
71, 375–76, 405; Lerach first meeting, 49, 49n; Lerach joins firm,
64–65; Lerach mentorship, 49, 49n,
52–53, 70, 76, 115, 156–57, 160–61,
170, 214, 249, 255–56, 357, 362,
365, 405, 419; Lerach's Nucorp loss
and, 160–61; Lerach's percent of firm's
income, 212–14, 216–17, 279–80;
Lerach's self-promotion and, 339;
lifestyle, 61, 296, 315, 316; Lozow
and, 372–73; Madoff and, 359, 359n,
458–59; Martha Stewart case, 353–
54, 376; money laundering, 316; Nucorp Energy case, 156, 157, 158;
Pacific Homes case, 16–17, 29;
Proposition 211 and, 248–49; secondary defendants and, 60, 60n, 63, 74;
securities lawsuits, 59–61, 76, 96–97,
111, 455; Sneed decision in SGI and,
303; Torkelsen and, 96; Tullman and,
96; U.S. Financial case, 49–53, 49n;
Vogel and, 445; Washington Public
Power case, 164; WorldCom case,
359–60, 362–63, 374
Weiss, Shirli, 301
Westerman, Jeff, 119–20
Wexler, Robert, 395
White, Byron, 411
White, Mary Jo, 364
Wied, Colin. W., 15–16, 32–33, 34, 390

Wied & Granby attorneys at law, 15–16
Wiener, Howard B., 22–23
Williams & Co., 37
Wilshire Associates, 334
Wilson, Pete, 236–37, 237n, 334
Wilson, Sonsini, Goodrich & Rosati, 188,
199, 202, 206, 302, 355–56, 391,
435
Witwer, Samuel W., Jr., 14, 27, 29, 32
Witwer, Samuel W., Sr., 13–14, 14n, 18,
20, 21, 28, 31
Wolf, Haldenstein, Adler, Freeman &
Herz, 270
Wolfswinkel, Conley, 191
WorldCom, 2, 97, 104, 335, 336, 341,
346, 347, 359–76, 392, 404, 466
Wren, Dick, 257, 259
W. R. Grace, 79
Wright, Irene, 270
Wright v. *Ernst & Young,* 270
Wyman, Bautzer, Rothman & Kuchel, 72
Wythes, Paul M., 116

Xerox, 79

Yang, Debra W., 334, 341, 348, 391, 393–
94, 463
Yardley, David J., 16, 19, 24
Yates, Alfred G., Jr., 95, 175
Young, Arthur, 174
Young, John A., 202, 203, 246

Zagel, James B., 277, 280, 292–93, 295,
296, 297
Zegarski, John, 319